Road to Number One

Road to Number One

A Personal Chronicle
of Penn State Football

BY RIDGE RILEY

With a Foreword by Head Coach JOSEPH V. PATERNO

DOUBLEDAY & COMPANY, INC.
Garden City, New York
1977

"... I shall be telling this with a sigh
Somewhere ages and ages hence:
Two roads diverged in a wood, and I—
I took the one less traveled by,
And that has made all the difference."

ISBN: 0-385-11397-8
Library of Congress Catalog Card Number 75-40740

TO
Margaret Tschan Riley
WIFE AND EDITOR
FOR ALL SEASONS

Contents

Foreword

This book manifests Ridge Riley's life of devotion to Penn State. More than any single individual I have ever known or known about, Ridge wanted Penn State to be Number One; Number One in its commitment to our commonwealth as the state university; Number One in the quality of life it offered our academic community. As student, administrator, and trustee, he did everything in his power to develop the pride a great institution must command from its own people and from the people of the fellow institutions it serves.

Ridge had a half century love affair with our university and our athletic teams. Not just football, but all athletics fell within his ardor and—perhaps in this area—he brought his most unselfish, self-sacrificing commitment. How could he make athletics better, and how could he make football Number One? He and I spent hours discussing Penn State football, sometimes in the ecstatic moments after a great win, sometimes in the anxious and uncertain hours before a game, and sometimes in the fitful, stomachaching grief of a bitter defeat. I have sat and listened to him talk of Penn State's history, her glory, her problems, and her future, always woven within the ever-present dream "to be Number One." This book then is a beautiful man's effort to put into writing his pride and his love for the wonderful people who together created great moments, noble traditions, and exciting challenges. There are no villains in this drama; some may appear as less than heroes, but there is no effort to create them. Ridge labored hard and long to make this an accurate history. His love of these people and their efforts calls to mind the opening line of Virgil's *Aeneid:* "Of arms and the man I sing." Truly, this is a story of men and battles, big and small, a long story of many battles and many men.

I was the last person to talk to Ridge. He died in my house talking about this book. His last words were, "Joe, where do we stand? Where are we right now?"

This is the story of Penn State football to this era, where we are, how we arrived here, and of one man's lifelong involvement in that story.

What the future holds for Penn State football will in a great way be influenced by what has been written in this book and by the warm, wonderful, beloved man whose act of love we share as we read.

JOSEPH V. PATERNO
Head Football Coach
The Pennsylvania State University

Preface for the Author

After he finished the 1976 Sugar Bowl *Football Letter* to Penn State alumni on January 6, 1976, Ridge's list of "Things to Do" began with "Write chapter on 1975 season and closing commentary." That evening he died of a coronary occlusion while visiting Joe and Sue Paterno for a note-taking session with the coach about the shape of things to come for Penn State football.

Ridge planned *Road to Number One* (and chose the title carefully) to show how intimately Penn State figured in the rise of football as an American intercollegiate sport after its origin in the northeastern United States. Along the way, he would place the Nittany Lions in their scenic central Pennsylvania campus setting, and say a little about the parallel rise of public higher education as shown by the development of Penn State, oldest and largest land-grant university on the Eastern Seaboard.

Students made athletics, music, debate, dramatics, and publications part of college life; only when programs got beyond undergraduate managerial capabilities did the faculty exert some control for the general welfare. Alumni influence next was felt, sometimes too much, as happened with varsity football in the early 1920s. College officers everywhere had to curtail such overemphasis. But common goals were not everywhere sustained in good faith by common action. As spectator interest spread, football moved westward and southward, with the East's stars as coaches.

A personal chronicle, this historical account is less about games (many but not all are described) than about people involved in them —the unpadded, unhelmeted early teams; the trainer-coach-players in charge before full-time coaches came; the emergence under Bill Hollenback, Dick Harlow '12, and Bezdek; the "purity period" frustrations surmounted by Bob Higgins '18; and the Nittany Lions rampant under Rip Engle and Joe Paterno. The road to recognition for the isolated "mountain lions" meandered, but gradually Penn State became an eastern power, then a perennial eastern leader, and for ten years has been well up among the top teams nationally.

Striving for accuracy, setting up no idols or devils, Ridge worked from official records, printed sources, reminiscences, correspondence, interviews, and, since the late 1920s, personal association and observation. Writing about the 1975 season fell to his successor as *Football Letter* correspondent—John W. Black '62, associate executive director for administration in the Penn State Alumni Association office. Publication now would have been impossible without the interest of Samuel S. Vaughan '51, the book's editor and president of Doubleday Publishing Company.

Ridge regretted the impossibility of mentioning by name everyone who has been part of Penn State football—at times we feared he'd try to. In some measure, he meant to dedicate the book to all who participated in front of Saturday crowds or "backstage" through the long seasons of hard and often unrewarded drudgery.

Roadblocks notwithstanding, "true believers" regard the *Road to Number One* about which Ridge wrote as a highway to excellence in much more than football for Penn State and its people.

MARGARET TSCHAN RILEY '32

Part I

THE EARLY YEARS

1881 and 1887

1

"Wish, Wack—Pink, Black!"

For one clearly discernible reason, the teammates of George H. Linsz elected him captain of Penn State's first two teams. He owned the only available football.

No one "father of football" is acclaimed at Penn State, because the game was established officially in the fall of 1887. The two undergraduates most responsible were Linsz (later changed to Lins) and Charles C. Hildebrand, both in the Class of '92, Philadelphians who had been inspired by the earlier development at the University of Pennsylvania.

Penn played some of its first games on the site of what was to be known as the Triangle. Later, important opponents were faced on the grounds of the Germantown Cricket Club. Linsz, son of a minister, had learned some of the finer points as an Episcopal Academy student. His familiarity with the rapidly developing, truly American game, plus possession of a scarred, sometimes partly deflated ex-Episcopal football, gave him a certain distinction as a "leader." He also tried to popularize cricket, but with less success.

For nearly thirty years, students enrolled at Penn State had tolerated the rustic austerities of the small experimental college struggling for identity. Many had a farm background, but more than a few came from urban areas, some because they hadn't adapted to traditional learning establishments. Their parents hoped the hard work and discipline of the school "near Bellefonte" might produce a miraculous change.

To the early students who first saw it unfinished, surrounded by open farmland, in the dead of winter (February 1859), the building called Old Main must have seemed a grim and lonely fortress in which to live and learn. Their long day included several hours of manual labor to help operate the physical plant (for part of which, eventually, lab practicum could be substituted) as well as military drill, required when the so-called Farmers High School became the Agricultural College of Pennsylvania, and, soon after, the Commonwealth's Land Grant institution (1862–63). Literary society meetings and compulsory chapel filled most waking "idle hours" except for rebels who risked and generally received severe penalties.

In the seventies the YMCA was added, women students were admitted, and the broad scope of the institution was emphasized by its new name, the Pennsylvania State College (1874). An era of sweeping innovation came in the late eighties when a few undergraduates decided that Penn State students could and should have everything other collegians had.[1]

Igniting this spirit were leaders like George R. Meek and James C. Mock of the Class of 1890; Linsz, Hildebrand, J. Franklin Shields, and Charles E. Aull, of the Class of 1892. They persuaded the Board of Trustees to permit installation of the first Greek-letter fraternity (1888), organization of the Athletic Association (1886–87), and publication of *Free Lance* (1887)—a monthly newspaper soon prone to pointed criticism of "the administration." This was more than seventy-five years before the student journalists of the 1960s and '70s who believed they were innovators when, shaking off the traditional fetters, they shook the tree of knowledge.

As juniors in 1889, the Class of 1890 printed *LaVie,* the college yearbook, and a year later the Philharmonic Trio, earliest student musical group, gave its first concert. Even greater cultural heights were attained when President George W. Atherton, acceding to their desires, convinced the trustees that it was time to lift the ban on mixed dances. This triumph of campus integration was largely symbolic: Only eight coeds were in residence.

The president had perceived unruly tendencies developing among the students. Rivalries were reaching a peak of ferocity and reckless

[1] Some were enrolled as "Preps" in 1886 and 1887.

ingenuity in scraps and rushes as a physical release from monotonous isolation. In addition, although Penn State had been coeducational since 1871, it afforded inadequate social activities for the predominantly male enrollment. Resentful of the few who were welcome at the "socials" held by the girls in the Ladies' Cottage, the men formed their own "State College 400" to sponsor a Bal Masque. Elaborate costumes were contrived by the all-male masked dancers, who competed unscrupulously for prizes.

Ending the ban on mixed dances broadened the social calendar, but the masked ball continued as *the* event of the winter season. Since profits from the first function had saved the bankrupt baseball team, it became an annual benefit for struggling athletic squads. The isolated coeds had a long wait for equal rights, for most of the men invited "imports" to the two major dances—Senior Ball in April and Junior Assembly at June commencement week.

During the first early autumn of football in '87, play was strictly informal. When Linsz appeared with his ball in front of Old Main, students—never more than fifteen or twenty—would pick sides and play. Only a handful knew the rules, but most thought they did. What resulted was a weird mixture of the American game spiced with a little rugby. American football was emerging from the chaos of yearly rule changes. Since they had no official coach, George Meek, who usually could be relied on to do the sensible thing, sent for a rulebook.

Bucknell University, playing a formal schedule, followed a game with Lafayette in 1883 by challenging its State College neighbors about sixty miles away for a game on November 12, 1887, at Lewisburg. The inexperienced Penn Staters, who wanted to "do things right," sensed the historic importance of the occasion and accepted Bucknell's challenge zealously. (Vague, unsubstantiated rumors that a State College team once had played an official football game were dismissed as fantasy.)

Hildebrand, firmly entrenched on the team as a guard and one of the "rushers" up front, later joked that "at first our coach was a rulebook." The Bucknell trip, however, was unthinkable without a coach and a manager. Clarence Grant Cleaver '89 was prevailed on to assume the honors when he could spare the time from his preparation for Dickinson Law School. John Fletcher Morris '89, another prelaw student, was enlisted as manager. In the photograph of the

1887 squad, Coach Cleaver and Manager Morris flank the top row, resplendent in stiff white collars and jaunty high silk hats. A formidable group of young men is shown, solemn representatives of their alma mater on the field of play. Captain Linsz is clutching his Episcopal Academy football.

Assembling personnel was easier than equipping the players. Determined not to appear in Lewisburg with scrubby-looking outfits, a committee from the group ordered twelve pairs of pants and twelve jerseys from the local tailor, Schaffer and Sons, who also made the students' military uniforms. The squad was limited to twelve because that was the number of pants they could afford. The jerseys were to be made of canvas, with lacing up the front; the trousers, knee-length, would be Canton flannel. What colors? At a hasty conference in Mr. Schaffer's stock room, Penn State's colors were designated: pink and black! Later, some insisted that they were meant to be cerise and black. Having settled the major purchases, the committee splurged and with outrageous recklessness bought twelve ski caps with tassels. Each player was to wear black stockings and tennis shoes of his own choice.

Spirit and camaraderie developed easily among the team members in the close confinement of Old Main, where all students lived and acquired a family unity. The Class of '92 even had a secret society in a basement room allotted to them by President Atherton after a committee had asked for space to indulge in "physical activity and recreation." Serious plans were made here for the general good, but quite possibly some skulduggery was fomented as well.

While the squad practiced faithfully for two weeks prior to the game, another "first" was in preparation. A college cheer somehow had to be composed and whipped into shape. After several had been rejected, one was finally evolved for the use of the little band of students who accompanied the twelve-man squad:

> Yah! Yah! (Pause) Yah! Yah! Yah!
> Wish, Wack—Pink, Black!
> P! S! C!

Both the colors and the yell had a mercifully short life. Skeptics who doubt that students would voluntarily select pink and black for college colors need only examine an early *LaVie* with its unmistakably pink-and-black cover. Sweat and a few washings faded the bright new pink uniforms to plain white, and not long after this helpful tragedy, dark blue and white were adopted officially as the college colors.

The traveling squad's twelve members, with an equal number of fans, boarded two of the available stage hacks—*The Mountain Echo* and *The Mail Coach*—in front of the hotel on Friday before game day. The trip to Lemont took half an hour, and from there to Lewisburg was a few hours by train. The boys paid their own expenses. Bucknell had agreed to play in State College the following week on the same terms.

Possibly the Bucknellians were overconfident. Possibly they were dazzled by the sparkling pink-and-black Canton flannel pants. Whatever it was, the Bisons were slaughtered, 54–0. About all Bucknell got out of the game were the ski-cap tassels, which disappeared after the first play from scrimmage.

Few other details of the game were recorded. According to one source, "the two teams were well matched in size and strength" and "neither side could gain anything by what is called rough playing." All points, said Penn State's student newspaper, "were made by the skillful playing of 'tricks.' "

At State College a week later the Lewisburg eleven battled the local collegians to a near standstill in the first half. The contemporary student press consistently presented the home team in the most favorable light possible. The *University Mirror* (Bucknell) of December 1887 covered the game in this manner:

> Our boys met the opposing team, exulting in their former victory on Bucknell's campus, and succeeded in reducing last week's score more than a half. The first half of the game gave a score of 4 to 0 in favor of State College, and the closing half, when the goals were changed, the home team (PS) took advantage of an inequality of the ground which the Bucknell boys had not noticed when they might have used it, and the score was run up to 24 to 0.

This contest, played on November 19, 1887, in front of Old Main, was the first intercollegiate football game at State College. Halfback John Price Jackson (later to become dean of the School of Engineering), Captain Linsz, at quarterback, and George Barclay, a slashing end, were the home stars. Jackson made the only touchdown in the first half, while Linsz scored three times in the second. John Mitchell, the town postmaster's son, kicked two points-after-touchdown.

Elated by the two victories, Manager Morris diligently sought a game with Dickinson College, tentatively arranged for Tuesday, November 22, at Carlisle. It was canceled because Dickinson could not meet Penn State's request for a forty-dollar guarantee and would not accept a fifty-dollar guarantee to play at State College. This was the first of many disputes marking their early rivalry.

By starting its uninterrupted seasons of intercollegiate football in 1887, Penn State became one of the nation's leaders, at least among the "public" institutions, as distinct from the private colleges on the Eastern Seaboard. Only Michigan, Minnesota, and California claim prior founding dates. In the East, where the American sport was born with the famous Princeton-Rutgers game in 1869, Columbia, Yale, Harvard, Pennsylvania, and Brown also list the beginnings of their football before 1880. Dartmouth, Lafayette, Navy, Bucknell, Wesleyan, Fordham, Lehigh, and Dickinson follow between 1880 and 1885. Cornell, Purdue, and Notre Dame joined Penn State with inaugural games in 1887.

Early football historians took scant notice of those two games between Penn State and Bucknell. Parke H. Davis, most prolific and authoritative football writer of his time, pointedly ignored them. "Only one event occurred in 1887 to signalize that year in the annals of football, but that event was naught else than the appearance of Cornell in its first gridiron battle, a game with Union at Ithaca, November 12, 1887."[2]

Nevertheless, Captain Linsz and his teammates could tell future generations of Penn Staters that the 1887 team played pure American football, or as "pure" as it could be in those days of rapid change. It certainly wasn't the Association game (soccer) used by the renowned Princeton and Rutgers squads of 1869, nor was it the Rugby Union variety displayed by Harvard, Yale, Princeton, and Columbia after the mid-seventies.

By the late eighties American college football was a distinctive game, with mere vestiges of rugby remaining. The scrummage or "scrum" was but a memory, and the scrimmage, with the quarterback putting the ball in play after a snap from center, had emerged. The other major change from the British influence—the establishment of the "downs system"—was effected in 1882.

The transformation from British rugby to American football

2 Parke H. Davis, *Football: The American Intercollegiate Game* (New York: Charles Scribner's Sons, 1911).

derived its principal impetus from the revered Walter Camp of Yale and was nurtured at frequent rules committee conclaves of officials from Yale, Princeton, Harvard, Columbia, and Pennsylvania.

Penn State and Bucknell presumably played on a field that had been reduced to 110 yards long and 53 yards wide, with 11 men on a side (the linemen were still called forwards or "rushers"); the ball had changed from a round, rubber, Association variety to an "oblate spheroid," less pointed than the one in use today, but almost 9 inches wider. Signal-calling with words, phrases, or sentences was a tactic introduced by Camp. The scoring system showed the strong influence of soccer and rugby by the valuation of kicking points over touchdowns. A field goal scored 5 points; a touchdown, 4; a goal-after-touchdown, 2; and a safety, 2.

Proving their awareness of the latest in football, Penn State and Bucknell used both a referee and an umpire in their first games, although the umpire had been officially added only during the 1887 season. His particular assignment was to have jurisdiction over the players; the referee was to follow the ball. The rules also suggested having a linesman to keep track of the distance and downs, but this was not mandatory.

In 1887 Yale was embarking on the first football dynasty, thanks to the coaching skill, knowledge, and leadership of Camp. In 1888 he put together what has often been classified as the first of the really great teams. It included such famous football names as Amos Alonzo Stagg, W. W. (Pudge) Heffelfinger, and George Woodruff, Penn's inventive coach of the nineties. Yale's team of '88 won 13 games and was not scored upon, while rolling up 698 points.

Princeton was undefeated in 1889 (10–0) and Harvard in 1890 (11–0), but in 1891 Yale returned to the front ranks with a team sometimes rated even better than the '88 eleven. Along with Heffelfinger, whom many critics consider the greatest lineman of all time, Yale had a phenomenal end, Frank Hinkey, referred to as "The Disembodied Spirit." This team went 13–0, and Yale added another 13–0 record the following year when quarterbacked by Vance McCormick of Harrisburg (a trustee of Penn State from 1908 to 1946).

Into this rarefied football world Penn State bravely ventured with relatively inexperienced players, no professional coaching until beyond the turn of the century, and squads seldom of more than 20 players from a male student body of less than 200. These spirited young men, seeking identification with the rapidly growing excitement and glamor of football, were ready to schedule anyone, anywhere, for as long as their own pocketbooks could stand the pressure.

The highly ambitious and sometimes cocky Penn Staters were even willing to take on football's giants—Yale, Princeton, Pennsylvania, and Cornell. They went West to Ohio and South to Virginia in the very early days. They argued over rules, fought over and with officials, were sometimes cheated, sometimes attacked by spectators, roughed by opponents, and accused of the same crimes. They once played nearly a full half of a regular game with nine men and lost by the horrendous score of 106–0 to Lehigh in 1889. With their high times and some triumphs, these pioneers established the reputation for rugged play and indomitable spirit that still symbolizes Penn State football.

2

"Not Up to All Their Dodges"

Thirty-five years after the two historic games between Penn State and Bucknell, ten members of the 1887 team assembled for a reunion in New York City. It was Friday, October 27, 1922, the day before the first Penn State-Syracuse game, at the Polo Grounds. The New York Alumni Club, entertaining the former players at the Hotel Commodore, found them enthusiastic about the next day's game, but also abounding in memories and anecdotes, proud of having originated a tradition of winning football.

Coach Hugo Bezdek, at the pinnacle of his success and popularity, presented each of the "founders" with a gold football charm on which was engraved: "1887, The First Penn State Team."[1] The next day Bezdek's eleven battled Syracuse to a scoreless tie, extending Penn State's non-losing streak to thirty. December 1922 was an exciting month for students and alumni because Penn State had been chosen to meet Southern California in the Rose Bowl on New Year's Day. At the same time the pioneers of '87 had a battle of their own in

[1] The honored guests had much to say as they received their awards on that long but memorable evening. Present were James R. Rose '88, John Price Jackson '89, Watson L. Barclay '89, John S. Weller '89, Manager John F. L. Morris '89, Charles M. Kessler '89, James C. Mock '90, Harvey B. McLean '90, Harry R. Leyden '90, Charles C. Hildebrand '92, and Captain George H. Lins '92. The only deceased member of the team was John G. Mitchell '88.

which their prestige—and some believed even their honor—was at stake.

Others were claiming their title.

Following the first publicity given the New York reunion, Alumni Secretary E. N. (Mike) Sullivan received a number of aggrieved protests from an earlier crop of players. Irvin P. McCreary '82, most vociferous of the letter writers, claimed that Penn State had played a football game in 1881, six years before the "official" beginning in 1887.

By the fall of 1880, McCreary wrote, Penn State students had caught the football fever prevalent throughout the East and organized an informal club, with a captain and a book of rules. The movement continued with vigor in the fall of '81. Through a friend of McCreary's at Bucknell[2] a game was scheduled at Lewisburg, Pennsylvania, on November 12. Billy Hoover, a tailor who lived in Shingletown Gap, made the "togs." The players left State College for Spring Mills in livery rigs on Friday afternoon and from there finished the trip by train.

The next afternoon, on a muddy field in a drizzling, sleetlike rain, Penn State won the game, 9–0. Immediately afterward, McCreary went to the telegraph office and wired John W. Stuart, postmaster at Bellefonte: "We have met the enemy and they are ours; nine to nothing." McCreary had arranged to have the message picked up in Bellefonte because there was no telegraph office in State College. After he had delivered the telegram, Mr. Stuart further broadcast the news, copying it on a large sheet of pasteboard, which he hung above the post office delivery window.

Although the Penn Staters stopped on their way home Saturday for a victory dinner at the Myers Hotel in Old Fort, when they arrived on campus at midnight, enthusiastic students were waiting to greet the warriors with a college yell written for the occasion. The football used in the game was presented to Professor William A. Buckhout, secretary of the faculty and also secretary of the Alumni Association. Neither the yell nor the football have survived the ages.

McCreary reported that he had not played in the game, but was the team's manager and also the umpire, with James G. White '82 as the referee. White wrote that they had "no paid coach, no special training table," and made "none of the present-day elaborate prepara-

2 Called University at Lewisburg until 1886.

tions." He remembered that George S. Chadman '82 was the star, but had no recollection of the score. "It was a pleasant outing," he recalled, "and a cordial and friendly spirit prevailed."

The 1887 veterans reacted to this news with some skepticism and soon had rebuttal letters on Secretary Sullivan's desk. Some of their chagrin came from the '81 eleven's claim to having first established blue and white as Penn State's colors.

George Lins wrote that *if* a game was contested in 1881, it certainly was not played under American college football rules, but must have been the English rugby game (a fact the challengers hotly denied). Others said it was obviously a pickup game. Most of the '87 letter writers insisted that the earlier game was "unofficial" because competitive football was not on record from 1881 to 1887.

Charlie Hildebrand, who played on the first five teams at least, was the most disturbed of the '87 group. He flatly rejected evidence that a real game was played in 1881. For ten years the normally affable Hildebrand bristled when anyone mentioned the subject. In the fall of 1932, still unconvinced, he wrote to Bucknell's registrar, who consulted the publicity director and reported that no evidence of a game with Penn State in 1881 existed—just rumors. Charlie accepted this as a repudiation of the claim. His complacency was soon shaken when the alumni secretary produced a letter dating back to October 9, 1923, from Dr. Milton G. Evans, president of Crozer Theological Seminary, stating that he participated with the Bucknell team against Penn State in 1881. Dr. Evans had been unable to recall details or whether the game was American or the rugby type. "I simply know that we had a good time," he wrote.

Researchers in the early twenties were handicapped, because in 1881 State College had no local papers, no student paper, and no college yearbook, but the '81ers gained their first breakthrough when George Meek, editor of the Bellefonte *Democratic Watchman,* reported that his newspaper could settle the squabble. From the *Watchman* issue of November 25, 1881, he noted that "a game" had been played at Lewisburg "two weeks hence."

The clincher came when McCreary produced the actual rulebook used to govern the game. Preserved in good condition in the files of the Penn State Collection, the book was published by Peck and Snyder, New York, in 1870, covered the playing rules of several sports, but was actually titled *The Latest Rules of Lacrosse.* The football section is no more prominent than those for ten pins and shuffleboard. The claim of some members of the early team that "American football" was played seems vulnerable, since only Rugby Union rules and the Association game (soccer) were included.

On the flyleaf McCreary wrote: "In accordance with these rules, Penn State College played a match with Bucknell at Lewisburg Nov., 1881. Game played on a wet field in a drizzling rain in A.M. Score, 9–0, in favor of Penn State."[3]

On this team were some of the best athletes then enrolled. Six played varsity baseball, which had taken firm hold in the seventies. Marcus Elmore Baldwin, a pitcher who became Penn State's first professional baseball player, dropped out for a few years, but returned to get a degree in 1887 and went on for an M.D. During his academic recess and also after 1887 he played with the Chicago National League team, and with both New York and Pittsburgh of the National League.[4]

That the '81 game was no myth was proved with the discovery of an account in the University at Lewisburg (Bucknell) *Mirror* of January 1882. It read, in part:

> The first football match which had been played for some time, on our campus, came off near the close of last term, between the University team and the State College boys. The University team were defeated; but were willing to accept the defeat with the lesson. The State College team was well uniformed and disciplined, whereas our boys, although having considerable practice, were not up to all their dodges. It was apparent in this game that our team was a match for if not superior to their antagonists, in all but practice and knowledge of their arts. These can be acquired. Having met them once, and having gained experience they may reasonably expect victory in the coming game. We do not despair of winning back our laurels, and new

[3] He then listed these names: William W. Bruner '82, George S. Chadman '82, John M. Dale '82, Captain Robert Tait '82, Joseph H. Hollis '83, Cummings C. Chesney '85, Robert F. Whitmer '82, Philip D. Foster '84, W. Ross Foster '84, James D. McKee '85, and Marcus E. Baldwin '87. The names of James G. White '82 and Irvin P. McCreary '82 appear as the game officials. McCreary added this note: "Two ex-students of State College, Adolph Spotford and Gary Wood, played with the Bucknell team."

[4] Baldwin compiled a remarkable endurance record even for the days of the iron-arm hurlers. During his first season with Chicago his record was 18–17. Returning to Chicago after a stint with Columbus, he had a 34–24 win–loss mark, and ended his playing career in 1893 with the Pirates, having a seven-year record of 156–165 and an earned-run average of 3.36.

ones in addition. The contest certainly exerted a beneficial influence upon our zest for athletic sports. . . . Since the organization of the Athletic Association our first team has procured new, strong, beautiful uniforms and are employing all available time in practice, and will yield no future game without a struggle.

With fine diplomacy, Alumni Secretary Sullivan mediated the great dispute by awarding concessions to the real pioneers of '81 for playing Penn State's first intercollegiate contest, however informal, and for selecting the blue and white worn ever since by Lion teams except for one season; and to the 1887 eleven as the first "official" team, beginning an unbroken series of varsity intercollegiate schedules.

The 1881 football team, official or not, provided one of the few bright spots that year for the struggling young college. Only 45 full-time students and 85 "preps" rattled around in Old Main, and state legislative investigations were under way. Joseph Shortlidge, the sixth president, resigned on April 8, 1881, after nine chaotic months, leaving Vice President James Y. McKee to preside over a faculty of 15 and a student body of only 145.

Statewide criticism and hostility, along with internal unrest, hampered Acting President McKee and General James S. Beaver, president of the Board of Trustees, while the search for a new president proceeded. Football was not all that had to be neglected for the next six years.

Students continued to "kick the ball around" on front campus, but without any organized athletic association and with no visible support from the faculty. Penn State made no contribution to the rapid transition of the American game from the English rugby. Students living in Old Main in the 1870s enjoyed informal football somewhere between the building and the country road that later became College Avenue, as is evident from a notation in faculty minutes for May 1878 forbidding the playing of football nearer the main building than "the other side of the ellipse."

Arthur B. Cram '70, of Royal Oak, Michigan (first alumnus known to have lived more than one hundred years), reported to the Alumni Office when he was over ninety that prior to 1870 there was no athletic team activity of any kind. Gymnasium equipment was set up outdoors in a grove of trees back of old Main. Baseball and football games among students gradually evolved, he wrote, but only for the sake of play and exercise.

> The games played were thoroughly in earnest and were "gentleman" games without rigid rules, and were played solely for amusement, but with éclat to the performer who made an extraordinary play. Baseball was the first sport widely played, but the baseball itself was the only thing professional about it. The ball was handled without gloves—these things being considered effeminate. The football was only kicked from goal to goal, but the game was much in vogue.

By 1881, the relatively few eastern colleges experimenting with football had made major strides toward the development of the American game, but evidence that the first Penn State-Bucknell contest leaned toward rugby is substantial. Kicking was still the name of the game; there was no system of "downs," and the ball could be retained indefinitely by one side unless given up voluntarily by kicking or through fumbling. Nevertheless, the '81 game probably was contested by 11 players to a side on a field reduced from rugby's 140/70 yards to 110/53 yards The two teams are likely to have conformed to the new trend abolishing the "scrum" to favor the American scrimmage. Thus, instead of the ludicrous (to American eyes) method of putting the almost round ball in play through mass effort, the quarterback could handle it after a hand snapback from center, or receive a difficult flip from the foot of a lineman. The quarterback, however, was forbidden to run with the ball.

The positions on the American eleven-man football team (reduced from fifteen in 1880) had been stabilized by 1881—ends, shortened from end men; tackles, formerly called next-to-ends, but renamed because they made the most tackles; guards, formerly called next-to-center, but renamed guards because they guarded the center. When fifteen players had constituted a team, there were nine on the "rushline," a quarterback, two halfbacks, a three-quarter back, and two fullbacks.

The first important move toward the American adaptation of rugby came in 1873 when representatives from Columbia, Princeton, Yale, and Rutgers adopted the first American code of rules. Harvard, still playing under the rugby code, staged a historic game with McGill University at Cambridge under mixed Canadian and rugby regulations. Trying to bring about some kind of mutual understanding, Harvard and Yale, the two early powers, fought it out in

1875 under a code referred to as "concessionary rules." Harvard won, 4–0. The following year (1876), meeting at Massasoit House (Springfield, Massachusetts), Princeton, Columbia, Harvard, and Yale adopted the Rugby Union code, formed the first American Intercollegiate Football Association, and agreed to play a round-robin series of games.

The Massasoit meeting made few concessions to the "American way." Official recognition was given the touchdown, at first equal to only one fourth of a goal, and forty-five-minute halves were adopted, with a ten-minute intermission. Until 1880 the only important changes reduced players to fifteen on a side and eliminated "tights" as the uniform of the day, substituting canvas pants and jackets. The most significant development came in 1880—out went the "scrum." For the first time the quarterback could receive the ball directly from center.

This was the status of football in 1881 when Penn State made its brief but happy appearance. During the next six years, while President Atherton strove for academic revival, football returned to its former intramural status as a front-campus diversion from the otherwise rigorous daily schedule of the students. By the time it reappeared the sport at last had become recognizable as American football, played nowhere else in the world.

During those six years of drastic changes, the rulemakers made a new ball game and unwittingly almost consigned it to oblivion as well. The system of "downs" saved it from becoming an excruciatingly dull exhibition, but it also became dangerous (and exciting) when the solons failed to legislate promptly against the V trick or flying wedge and other perilous mass plays.

In 1882 for the first time teams were required to make five yards in three downs, a simple enough procedure by today's standards, but not so easy in the early eighties, when nearly everything favored the defense. The system of downs was established to combat a tendency toward dullness, reaching its ultimate at the famous Princeton-Yale game of 1881. Princeton, holding the ball (but not trying to advance it), made effective use of the "block game" for all but 4½ minutes of the first half. In cricket terminology, Princeton "stonewalled" it. Yale retaliated by holding possession for the entire second half. In the overtime the farce continued until darkness ended it in a scoreless tie. Affected by the mutinous mood of the few spectators who remained and by derisive press reaction, the Rules Committee hurriedly did some repair work. The resulting "downs system" became the very heart of the modern game and gave football a "new look," even changing the appearance of the field. By the addition of parallel white lines, the "field" or "grounds" became the "gridiron" forever more.

Princeton often is awarded the doubtful distinction of introducing the V trick or wedge, forerunner of the other dangerous mass plays that nearly shelved the game during the early twentieth century. Some football historians credit Lehigh equally for this innovation in 1884. The wedge in its many variations and some simpler methods of "interference" evolved about the same time to counteract the distinct advantage given to the defense. Interference started with the practice of "guarding" or running a player on either side of the ball carrier to make tackling difficult from the side.

The touchdown as the primary object of the game also emerged in the eighties. When the 1884 season began, the touchdown had a two-point value and the goal-after-touchdown four points. By the end of the season these were reversed, but a goal from the field still had top value, at five points.

Visiting college football teams in the eighties often were justifiably uneasy about getting fair play. Many early games ended in disputes or forfeits, after free-swinging brawls. The traveling team could bring its own "partisan judge," who had equal standing with the home judge, while the referee, supposedly neutral, settled all judges' disputes. Because a verbal fracas among the three officials would seriously delay the game, the judges were abolished in 1885 and the referee took all the punishment alone for two years until an umpire was added in 1887.

And so when the ambitious Penn Staters in '87 fielded what they assumed was the first team to represent their college, the game of American football had almost completed its metamorphosis from English rugby, and was inescapably dominated by its three principal founders, Yale, Harvard, and Princeton.

The 1887 Penn State team, at its New York reunion thirty-five years later, basked in the acclaim and pride of the other alumni present. The Lions of '22 were near the top of the football world, but the old-timers on hand never let it be forgotten that the sport had made an auspicious start with that pair of Bucknell victories long ago.

Actually, the '87ers caused the recognition of the '81ers, belated as it was. Publicity ensuing from the 1922 reunion drew the protests from the real pioneers of '81, whose exploits otherwise might have remained undiscovered. As it was, Penn State's official athletic family did not acknowledge the earlier team for fourteen years. Finally, on October 6, 1936, gold footballs and varsity "S" letters—earned fifty-five years before—were awarded to the four survivors from '81: Captain Robert Tait, Manager I. P. McCreary, C. C. Chesney, and James G. White, umpire.

Part II

STRUGGLE FOR RECOGNITION

1888–1905

3

"What Happened at Lehigh, Charlie?"

In Penn State's annual football brochure one particular line—Highest Opponent Score—is a shocker:

Lehigh 106; Penn State 0 (1889)

The 1891 *LaVie* listed the game within a black-bordered rectangle. The 1889 players always were loath to discuss that haunting holocaust at Bethlehem, but piece by piece the story has emerged and survives in fully garnished detail.

When the agony ended—Lehigh had generously agreed to shortening the second half by five minutes—the thirteen-member Penn State squad, stunned and wanting to hide, reluctantly boarded the train for Lemont. The fearful prospect of a "reception" at Lemont Station prompted a successful maneuver wherein they got off the wrong side of the train and circled around the building to the horse-drawn rig waiting to take them to State College. A few of the more timid disembarked some distance from the hotel, the traditional gathering place for a welcoming committee.

Among the deserters was Captain Jim Mock, who realized he would have to be the spokesman for the woebegone warriors at their unwelcome party. The waiting students weren't cheering—they had not yet heard the outcome of the game.

Charlie Aull, the apologist because he was nearest the rear exit, was among the team's most popular members. Charlie paused head down, doubly embarrassed by having been one of the two who had strayed from the official party and missed most of the first half.

"Who won the game, Chutz?" was the first question.

"Lehigh," was the unembellished answer.

"What was the score, Chutz?" Now the news had to break.

"Hunert and six to nothing," Charlie almost whispered. There was a period of silence.

"What happened?"

Aull's reply was succinct and totally relevant: "We couldn't get at the son-of-a-bitch with the ball."

The despondency of the battered players, who were mute about their mortification, could have caused a lapse in the chronicle of Penn State football like that between 1881 and 1887, but *Free Lance* did report a few bewildering details and the remarkable avowal that "our team played stubbornly and *excelled Lehigh in tackling.*" Much later it was learned that Penn State had played almost the entire first half with nine men.

The Lehigh game, on Monday, November 11, followed a Saturday encounter with Lafayette on a trip preceded by a home victory over Swarthmore (20–6), played in front of Old Main and costly in injuries. The axiom that you can't scrimmage a football team into shape hadn't been learned. Aull had twisted a knee, Hildebrand's badly sprained ankle had kept him out of both games, and Harvey McLean, another of the "walking wounded," was in for only part of the Lafayette contest.

The official party of a dozen or so spent Friday night in Harrisburg and started off at Easton with some much needed aid from the sidelines. Clarence Cleaver—unofficial coach of the 1887 team and a graduate law student at Dickinson—was discovered among the spectators and recruited on the spot. He played the entire game, won by Lafayette, 26–0. Under the circumstances, the Penn Staters felt they hadn't done too badly.

Hildebrand left immediately for home, having received a telegram telling him of his young sister's death. Two other players accompanied him to Philadelphia, expecting to be at Bethlehem by game time Monday, but only nine players were present when Lehigh insisted on a prompt start—or no expense money. The Staters risked mayhem for that twenty-five-dollar guarantee, and this decision was a disastrous gamble.

Being shorthanded was bad enough, but the defenders had trouble with the Lehigh ball carriers for another reason. Four or five years earlier, Lehigh's coach, J. S. Robeson, had introduced the V trick, a form of mass interference commonly regarded as a Princeton invention. That the Engineers had mastered the frightening wedge and utilized it with terrible persistence is obvious from Charlie Aull's apt explanation of Penn State's dilemma.

The *Free Lance* reported that at 4:05 P.M., when the first half ended, Lehigh was in front, 58–0. Four minutes before the intermission the prodigals returned and Penn State fielded eleven men, but their presence was of little consequence. Captain Mock's team struggled on toward that guarantee. As Lehigh approached an even hundred, the referee made the merciful, game-shortening concession.

To survive adversity, a team needs strong leadership, as all good coaches know. Mock, Hildebrand, Linsz, and McLean—all veterans of the pioneer 1887 team—were such leaders, inspiring and unifying their team with a rallying cry to be heard many times in the next decade: "Beat Bucknell."

The neighborhood rivalry had been heightened the year before (1888) at Lewisburg, when the Penn Staters had stalked off the field to end a rhubarb. Acrimony was fanned by the two student newspapers, the Bucknell *Mirror* opening with taunts over Penn State's defeat by the Lewisburg baseball team the previous spring:

> We were giving them the same dose and at the moment when our fellows were going to make a touchdown, Cleaver, their referee, gave a rank decision. Our boys objected to the injustice and State College was only too glad to find a chance to escape, so they quit playing. They were perfectly willing to sneak off without demanding any money for expenses.

Free Lance lengthily replied that Bucknell, unable to produce a rulebook and refusing the referee's suggestion to settle the argument in favor of the home team, played the game under protest, but agreed to accept a later decision by a proper authority.

"As to sneaking off without our guarantee, this is a lie," snorted *Free Lance*. "We asked for our guarantee of $20 and the Bucknell manager said he didn't have any money." What's more, the newspaper claimed Bucknell had not paid up for the last two games—now owing the Penn State management a total of $65.50.

The scarcity of well-qualified officials—at that time, at least, in central Pennsylvania—contributed to many squabbles, forfeits, and canceled games. Charlie Hildebrand later recalled that the dispute concerned the snapback. Since the scrimmage line was supposed to go *through* the center of the ball, his team was trying for an advantage by using the whole ball. Whether there was a forfeit, and if so, to whom, is unknown. Penn State's records omit the game entirely.

For more than a week following the humiliation at Bethlehem, the disheartened players quit training and practice, but as the Thanksgiving Day game with Bucknell approached, they rallied for a "revenge" battle. Just as the Lewisburgers had been part of the pioneer games in both '87 and '81, now their very presence on the campus would strengthen football by the solidarity of the forces against them. Presumably Bucknell had paid up the $65.50.

Penn State continued its championship of mid-Pennsylvania with a 12–0 victory and "to some extent," said *Free Lance,* "redeemed its season." Much of the old sore was healed, it continued, and the game "was one of the pleasantest and most friendly that has yet been played between the two institutions."

In reviewing the season, the newspaper pointed out that the defeat by Lehigh "forcibly reminds us . . . that we need better organization. But we did win from two colleges of our own rank and lost to two of a higher standing." There is nothing like a victory to heal the wounds and restore confidence in the future.

4

First Champions of Pennsylvania League

Penn State set its sights high for the 1891 season, although most veterans of the earlier years had departed. The starting team of the larger than usual squad was built around Charlie Hildebrand, playing his fifth season as guard, and Chutz Aull, captain and fullback. A new backfield star and focus of campus enthusiasm was one of the reasons for an optimistic outlook. Charles M. H. Atherton, son of President George W. Atherton, made his letter in 1890, and was to follow Hildebrand as the second five-letter winner of the nineties.

Considerable impetus came when representatives from Bucknell, Dickinson, Franklin and Marshall, Haverford, Swarthmore, and Penn State organized the Pennsylvania Intercollegiate Football League in Harrisburg on September 26, 1891. State's delegate was Manager J. Franklin Shields, who later was on the Board of Trustees for many years and was its president from 1929 to 1946. Lafayette and Lehigh, considered slightly above the others in general ability and experience, weren't included, and Pennsylvania, of course, was far too exalted as a member of the illustrious "Big Four."

Shields, first chairman and then president of the new league, needed all his charm and tact to get a consensus from the six colleges, represented by undergraduates. First things came first on the agenda, and item one was how to dispose of the game receipts. The decision to divide the net receipts "equally between the contesting teams in all championship games" led to a heated argument on the meaning of "net receipts."

All delegates fought for games on the home grounds, but Penn State's opponents unanimously resisted traveling to "isolated" State College. That Manager Shields was bested in this exchange is evident from the Penn State league schedule:

> Oct. 17   Swarthmore at Swarthmore
> Oct. 24   Franklin and Marshall at State College
> (later changed to Lancaster)
> Nov. 4   Haverford at Haverford
> (date changed to Dec. 5)
> Nov. 7   Bucknell at Lewisburg
> Nov. 26   Dickinson at Altoona

Penn State played all its games in 1891, including nonleague games with Lehigh, Lafayette, and Gettysburg, away from its home fans. The problem was that football had come to mean big money. League regulations called for the referee and the umpire, both chosen from neutral colleges, to receive five dollars per game, plus travel and local expenses. Each college was assessed ten dollars for membership and two dollars for the secretary's expenses. A silk pennant would be awarded to the championship team.

The most significant league action, after hours of discussion and compromise, was the first agreement on an eligibility code. "A man may play only six years, and no professionals are allowed; a player must be a bona fide member of the college community with at least fifteen hours of classroom work assigned."

Penn State warmed up for the league schedule by meeting Lafayette and Lehigh, determined not to let this trip become the debacle it had been two years back. Lafayette was downed, 14–4, but Lehigh proved too strong and won the game at Bethlehem, 24–2.

Three victories in a row over Swarthmore, Franklin and Marshall, and Gettysburg made *Free Lance* confident about the championship: "We do not wish to crow prematurely, yet we feel that we have a good chance to congratulate ourselves that we have the championship of the State League." When the ax fell at Bucknell, the *Lance* had the temerity to criticize the players for being overconfident. After Franklin and Marshall whipped Bucknell, hope returned that a victory over Dickinson might still bring the pennant to Old Main. It wasn't easy to accomplish.

The Altoona field scheduled for the Dickinson game inadvertently had been cut up into building lots. Dickinson refused to come to State College but offered to play in Altoona, Carlisle, or Harrisburg. The home team then secured the Cricket Club Field in Altoona, only to have differences over expenses. Manager Shields sent telegrams, few of which were answered. Finally, Dickinson officials demanded guaranteed full expenses. Already assured of a sellout crowd, Shields wired agreement, but received no reply. On the day before the game a telegram arrived: "Men scattered. Telegram came too late. Sorry."

Penn State, claiming a forfeit, expected at least a tie for the championship with Bucknell, each with a 3–1 record, and even hoped for an edge, because a postponed game with Haverford was still pending. Played at Haverford on December 5 in miserable weather, it was won by Penn State, 58–0, and local reports heaped praise on Haverford for agreeing to play the game, so important in the title race. "Spectators," said one account, "were made up of a few pretty girls, a half hundred Haverfordians, a few U of P and Swarthmore players, and a poor, frightened rabbit that occasionally darted across the field of play."

Officials who met in Harrisburg on January 9, 1892, awarded the championship to Penn State and expelled Dickinson from the league.[1]

The 1891 championship season fittingly closed the "official" playing career of Charles Conrad Hildebrand, for whom a chemistry degree received in June 1892 was a minor miracle. Philadelphia-born, on Buttermilk Street, in 1866, he went from eighth grade to work five years with the Baldwin Locomotive Works. To appease a voracity for learning, he attended a business school at night, studied drawing and the violin, and in summer learned to swim at Asher's Natatorium, which had the only pool in Philadelphia. Training for the catering and ice cream business, his later occupation, was acquired at Baldwin in the employees' food service, one of the many divisions in which he worked there.

---

[1] The Dickinson version of the incident differs somewhat from Penn State's account. The *Dickinsonian,* reporting that the league was not a howling success, said the game contract with Penn State was only verbal and that the exchange of telegrams was a problem because of the time factor. "But," said the newspaper, "if the league can live without Dickinson, Dickinson will not weep at the separation." The league lived for one season without Dickinson. And Penn State's pennant apparently never materialized.

The opportunity to enter Penn State's "Prep" Department in 1886–88 came by default. His mischief-prone brother Bill (W. R. Hildebrand, ex-'92) had been shipped off to State College "for corrective purposes" because a friend and former Penn Stater had given their father the impression that this was a sort of reform school in central Pennsylvania. When President Atherton terminated the relationship, the younger and more stable Hildy was permitted a try. The city boy took to the rural life and the family closeness of Old Main. With his best friend, Charlie Aull, he joined Phi Gamma Delta, Penn State's first authorized chapter of a national social fraternity. Once in college, however, Hildy's desire for knowledge turned from the academic to the extracurricular, especially football. Dr. George G. (Swampy) Pond, his chemistry professor and later dean, threatened to withhold his degree because he had gone to Swarthmore with the team instead of making up a lab experiment.

Stability and loyalty compensated for Hildebrand's unspectacular playing skills, as he later wrote to a friend:

> I was always ready to shake hands after a slug in the face, feeling that my opponent might regret having done same. All through life this has worked and I learned it in football.

This was no way to inspire a following in those days of derring-do, and he never captained any of the five squads on which he played.

Charlie always was acutely embarrassed when friends kidded him about being thrown out of the 1891 Bucknell game at Lewisburg— a crucial Pennsylvania League defeat. The penalty then for "roughness," as Hildy often explained, was unreasonable because a culprit couldn't possibly be singled out. He pleaded for understanding:

> Honestly, there was nothing to the charge—nobody was carried off the field and no one needed medical attention. Our team even had to intimidate a policeman to keep him from throwing me off the sideline.

His first job after graduation ended with the closing of Pottstown Steel Company in the 1893 depression. He then began an ice cream business at Twentieth and Christian streets in Philadelphia, where the patronage of athletes led to his second (or third) football career. In Pottstown he had played with the Pennsylvania Railroad YMCA team under Princeton's three-time All-America guard (1892–94), A. (Beef) Wheeler. Steel mill superintendent Jake Robeson, one of the wedge-play originators at Lehigh, taught him some techniques to counteract the wedge, which he used successfully in a game against the Hill School. "This was when I found out," said Hildy, "that the rougher and tougher you played, the less chance there was of getting hurt."

Between jobs, he revisited Penn State to assist with coaching and playing in 1893, and in 1898 he helped prepare for the Bucknell game at Williamsport, won by Penn State, 16–0. Bucknell was captained that year by the great Christy Mathewson of baseball fame. Hildebrand was last officially connected with football between 1898 and 1902 when he worked in Ridgway, where he coached, officiated, and is credited with organizing one of the first high school football leagues in the state, with Ridgway, Kane, St. Marys, Punxsutawney, and others.

Resuming business in 1903, he became one of Philadelphia's leaders and a president of the Businessmen's Association of Germantown. Any visitor with a Penn State connection had entree to Hildy's heart. He was a founder of its first club in Philadelphia, attended all Penn State athletic contests there, and came to many on campus, including nearly every Homecoming game, until the end of his life at 84 on February 24, 1950.

5

The Part-Time Coaches

Penn State's official athletic records list a head football coach for every season beginning in 1892, but actually the first to serve full-time—William H. Hollenback, a graduate of Penn in 1909—was employed as "advisory coach" in 1909 and 1911, as was his brother, Dr. Jack Hollenback, in 1910, when Big Bill took a leave of absence to coach Missouri. He did not acquire the title of "head coach" until 1912.

Three of the first coaches of record—George W. Hoskins, Dr. Silvanus B. Newton, and William N. (Pop) Golden—were appointed "directors of physical training," with little or no football coaching experience. Coming as trainers for the athletic teams, they gradually took on coaching duties, often with the help of alumni assistants hired on a short-term basis. Most prominent of these were Leroy (Henny) Scholl '01, Edwin K. Wood '04, Andrew L. Moscript '05, Henry (Irish) McIlveen '07, and Edward H. (Bull) McCleary '10. McIlveen (1909) and McCleary (1911) had the title of "head coach," to indicate the Athletic Board's "wholly Penn State system," under full-time "advisory coach" Bill Hollenback.

GEORGE W. HOSKINS, 1892–95

George (The General) Hoskins became Penn State's first director of physical training through his friendship with Dr. Jaccb K Shell, coach of the Swarthmore football team and a prominent physician, with whom he rowed in the same eight of the "Schuylkill Navy." Hoskins accompanied Shell when Swarthmore played at Penn State in the fall of '89, and an introduction to President Atherton led to his eventual hiring in January 1892.

Hoskins, an excellent athlete, had no experience as a football coach, but had played the game at Burlington (Vermont) Military Academy, where he graduated in 1882. Participating as an amateur in wrestling, track, lacrosse, and rowing, he also took a four-year course in physical training and anatomy under Dr. Shell in Philadelphia, and then went to the University of Vermont as athletic trainer. On December 20, 1890, he won the middleweight AAU wrestling championship in New York City.

"General" Hoskins was exceedingly popular with the student athletes, possibly because they were unaccustomed to such skillful attention. He took a personal interest in getting the football players into shape, often coming into their rooms in Old Main to rub them down with a mysterious "milky substance." His solicitude kept them from objecting to a prebreakfast run from the main gate on front campus to Centre Furnace—a distance of about two miles.

Hoskins had another avenue coaches today might envy. During a scrimmage he became so frustrated trying to correct a lineman's mistakes that he took his place, and then decided to start himself in Saturday's game. No protests from opponents are recorded about this procedure, which was commonplace in the nineties. The General won three letters, 1892–94.

Unfortunately, Hoskins ended his Penn State career under a cloud —by students' standards. He left at the end of the 1895 season to take a similar job at the Western University of Pennsylvania, and compounded this treachery by playing on the 1896 Pitt team. Although Penn State won 10–4, the embittered *Free Lance* claimed that Hoskins, both captain and trainer of the Pitt team, made the game "disinteresting" by his style of play "He gave such an exhibition of the unmanly defiance of all fair rules which degrades the game as to make it a lasting example for the 'anti's' to hold up to public opinion." Then the student newspaper apologized to all Penn State's opponents "if such were the means of success of our former coach."

DR. SILVANUS B. NEWTON, 1896–98

The second director of physical training and probably least known of the early coaches, apparently was considered an asset to the faculty. President Atherton describes Newton in the 1896 Annual Report as a thoroughly trained physician, intimately associated with athletics. "Under his direction this important branch of training will be raised to its proper standard as a means of promoting the development of a complete physical manhood."

Born in Yarmouth, Maine, Newton was educated in the Eton School, Maine Wesleyan Seminary, Williams College (1891), and the University of Pennsylvania Medical School. Football was his consuming hobby. In the fall of 1894, while an assistant gynecologist at the Methodist Hospital, Philadelphia, he was an assistant coach at Penn under the famous George Woodruff, but left both positions to spend a month coaching football at Trinity College, North Carolina.

Newton couldn't resist the Penn State opening that could lead to the football coaching job. After two mediocre seasons, a championship year was predicted in 1898, but he was never really accepted by the students, who weren't accustomed to the discipline he demanded, often with sarcastic wit.

Victories on the gridiron eluded him, although he worked hard to develop his forte: the art of place-kicking. One triumph that did affect his career was the 1898 defeat of Lafayette, 5–0. Without a full-time coach that season, Lafayette had lost every game and had two to go when its authorities invited him to be one of a team of experts to "advise." This formidable group of coaches, including former Penn stars By Dickson, George Brooke, and Lewis Vail, enabled Lafayette to defeat strong Bucknell and end its season in glory by beating archrival Lehigh, 11–5. Newton left Penn State in 1899 to become head coach of Lafayette for more money and a position considered more eminent.[1]

Dr. Francis A. March, Jr., Lafayette football historian, called

[1] Francis A. March, Jr., *Athletics at Lafayette* (Easton, Pa.: Lafayette College, 1926).

Newton "the cleverest coach Lafayette ever had . . . a splendid scholar, a Phi Beta Kappa, a prize winner . . . a high-class physician, a gentleman of birth and breeding . . . a great student of the theoretical side of the game."

Alas, Dr. Newton continued to impress his opponents. After three successful years he moved on to Bethlehem as Lehigh's coach, at a higher salary. His last Lafayette team had beaten Lehigh, 41–0; his first team at Lehigh bested an even stronger squad at Lafayette, 6–0. Newton's coaching career is not known to have continued beyond the Lehigh experience, and it's assumed that he finally took his medical practice seriously.

SAMUEL A. BOYLE, JR., 1899

As an end on Penn's superteam of 1897, Boyle made Camp's second All-America team. His only notable accomplishment was to preside over the defeat of Army, 6–0. It was not to happen again for sixty years. In 1900 Boyle coached at Dickinson, and defeated Penn State, 18–0.

WILLIAM NELSON (POP) GOLDEN
1900–2

Foremost among early developers of Penn State intercollegiate athletics, the director of physical training in 1900 also was head coach of all teams, trainer, and confidant of the players. The student-managed Athletic Association eventually gave Pop Golden the title of director of athletics, the first person at Penn State to hold such overall responsibilities. Football coaching probably was his weakest competence, but he usually had the aid of "graduate assistants" for the last few weeks of the season.

The intercollegiate athletic program can trace its firm foundation in the early 1900s to Golden's standing with the faculty, whose respect he had, and with the students, who sensed that he understood them. A buoyant and dynamic personality, he was most revered as the "friend of students" for his kind and patient vigilance in caring for them. Golden liked to become involved in their extracurricular activities, sometimes appearing in theatricals. He'd perform as interlocutor (end man) in the Pharsonian minstrels, and often put on boxing exhibitions against the best campus athletes.

Schooled in Chicago under the old German system of physical education, Golden became athletic trainer at Purdue University, and was in charge of physical education at YMCAs in Syracuse, Johnstown, and Williamsport before coming to Penn State. To obtain new and improved athletic facilities, he made a personal and successful appearance before a state legislative committee for funds to construct New Beaver Field.

Pop relinquished football coaching when Bill Hollenback came in 1909, but because of his recognized affinity for young people, he was used to contact high school athletes, thus becoming Penn State's first unofficial "recruiter." When Golden left to enter the insurance business in Pittsburgh at the close of the 1911–12 academic year, the students sponsored a reunion of all Penn State athletes from 1900 to 1912 who had worked under the popular director. Richard C. Harlow '12, representing the student body, presented him with a "valuable signet ring." Golden was a successful insurance man, but lost most of his money in the Depression of the early thirties. Pittsburgh alumni, including George Deike, Sr., B. C. (Casey) Jones, and John T. Ryan, Sr., along with J. L. (Pete) Mauthe and Ed Yeckley, raised a substantial fund for his assistance until he died at the age of 81 on August 30, 1949.

DAN A. REED, 1903

Students were delighted when Director of Athletics Golden announced that Dan Reed would coach the football team during the last month of the 1903 season. Penn State had lost decisively to Penn and Yale on successive Saturdays, but new spirit infused the squad with the coming of the famous guard who made Walter Camp's All-America third team as a member of Cornell's strong 1898 eleven under Pop Warner. Reed started auspiciously, with a 59–0 triumph over Pitt and a 17–0 victory over Navy, but Penn State then unaccountably lost its big game in Williamsport to Dickinson, 6–0. After a victory over Washington and Jefferson, ending the season with a 5–3 mark, Reed returned to his home in Buffalo. He became assistant coach at Cornell under Dr. Albert Sharpe, and later entered politics, representing his home district in Congress.

TOM FENNELL, 1904–8

Again looking toward Cornell for help, Penn State luckily secured the services of Tom Fennell, an ex-football player and member of the Big Red crew in the mid-nineties. Fennell was a practicing attorney in Elmira, New York, and later became a judge. He might be classed as the first "professional" coach hired exclusively for football, even though his tours of duty at State College varied from two to eight weeks each season, with Golden in charge during his absence.

Fennell coached Penn State's first really major teams. Of 11 games in the 1905 season, the only losses were to the Carlisle Indians, Yale, and Navy. The following season nine opponents went scoreless, and only powerful Yale inflicted defeat, 10–0. An indication of the wide respect he enjoyed for his coaching ability came in November 1906, when the Canton Bulldogs, a leading professional team of the time, spent nearly two weeks in Bellefonte to visit the campus daily for practice sessions under Fennell's expert guidance.

An excellent speaker, Fennell gave the football squad its first taste of real dressing-room oratory. Edwin Erle Sparks, who became president in 1908, heard about Coach Fennell's eloquence and invited him on several occasions to give the Sunday chapel address. The appearance of a Catholic at the strictly Protestant service astonished some of the faculty, but the students were enthusiastic. To the regret of the entire community, he departed after the 1908 season to give his full attention to law.

6

Mayhem and Robbery in the South

With a legitimate "championship" under their canvas jackets following the 1891 season, the aspiring Penn State football players—abetted by the local newspapers—claimed another title in 1892 on a 5–1
record. Typically, students disregarded the expected defeat in the
opener with a Pennsylvania team that won fifteen of sixteen games,
and based their claims on five victories over "teams in our class."
Free Lance held it "fair to assume that only five or seven teams in the
country could at present win from us—Yale, Harvard, Princeton,
and Cornell; but neither Wesleyan nor Michigan gives us the opportunity for a comparison of eastern play."

Sanguine predictions about the 1893 season were reasonable.
George Hoskins was beginning his second year as coach-trainer-
player, and among his many progressive moves was the establishment in 1892 of spring practice; Charlie Atherton, in his fourth
season, had developed into an exciting competitor; officials had arranged the first schedule with an intersectional flavor to gain more
prestige for their high-reaching players; and dedication of the new
grandstand was planned for the opening game with Dickinson on October 7. Finally, word got around that a southern "giant," weighing
220 pounds, had enrolled as a football potential. Beers by name, he

would join the veterans, Captain Ed Haley, Hoskins, Atherton, Ben Fisher, and a few more established stars.

Hopes evaporated quickly. Beers didn't live up to expectations, failed to make the '93 squad, and was listed only as a substitute in 1895 and 1896; the grandstand dedication had to be postponed because of "some trouble at the Carlisle institution"; the Dickinson cancellation was only the first of several scheduling breakdowns involving Johns Hopkins, F&M, and Rutgers; and the 1893 team had to open with an unprecedented two-game trip to the unfamiliar South. A semipro team in Washington, D.C., the Columbia Athletic Club, would be played on Friday, October 12, and the University of Virginia the following day at Charlottesville.

Everybody got a lift early in the last week of preseason practice when one of the "old boys" turned up on the field. Charlie Hildebrand, who had been playing semipro ball, was persuaded by Coach Hoskins to help the team get ready, and he was soon in the lineup at his old guard position. With Hoskins at center, the middle of the line was almost impregnable—or so the boys thought. Despite almost nonexistent eligibility rules, Hildy was uneasy about Hoskins' plan to use him in the weekend games, fearing someone might question a six-season veteran. But evidence that he played in both games under the name "Wolfe" is indisputable.

When the Penn Staters arrived in Washington on Friday morning in a downpour, both sides decided to postpone the game until Monday. Proceeding to Charlottesville and their rooming house near the railroad station, the Pennsylvanians found no southern hospitality on the playing fields of Virginia. The malevolent crowd hurled insults and other things at the visitors, and cast aspersions on their northern lineage. Captain Haley and the Virginia captain opposite him in the line both came up with bloody faces after the first play. To avoid ejecting the two captains, the harassed officials announced that no penalties would be assessed for a "first offense." Every serious infraction thereafter was announced as a first offense.

The game became rougher and the crowd more unruly when Atherton scored after a Virginia fumble and kicked the goal, giving Penn State a half-time lead, 6–0. The Virginia coach, Johnny Poe of Princeton fame, decided to substitute himself in the second half, and Virginia began to take control of the game.

Chiefly through Poe's efforts, the southern team had reached State's 30-yard line with 12 minutes remaining when Atherton, apparently retaliating for some unrevealed insult, punched a Virginia player in the nose. The officials ejected Atherton for this too-flagrant bit of slugging, the enraged Poe walked over to the sideline and threw a wild punch at him, and a spectator came through the ropes to bash the Penn State player from behind, knocking him cold.

At this point in the ominous situation, Captain Haley led his men off the field. Years later, Hildebrand wrote that the Virginia players begged them "not to leave the field of honor," and recalled that some of the spectators and Virginia players mounted their horses to depart for their homes. The visitors withdrew to their rented rooms, few venturing out until the next day, when their train left for Washington. It was learned later that the officials had awarded the game to Penn State, 6–0.

Captain Haley's men—a rugged bunch able to handle themselves on a give-and-take basis—received little better treatment in the capital. Against the more mature Columbia AC eleven, comprised of some local gentry of doubtful background and a few ex-college players, their chief adversaries were the officials, especially the referee, who established himself as a "homer" beyond compare. One report called the game "a miserable burlesque on fair and honest sport."

Penn State's new star, listed as "Wolfe," scored early after recovering a fumbled punt, but from then on the frustrated and irritated visiting eleven constantly had to battle the referee for its rights. Apparently unable to keep track of the downs, this official allowed the home team all it needed to make the required 5 yards.

Although thirty-minute halves had been agreed to, the Penn Staters claimed the second half lasted at least an hour to allow the home team to score twice. As darkness approached, some CAC substitutes helped the first eleven to push the ball across the goal line. The referee ignored the visitors' protest and announced that thirty seconds remained. He'd call out "twenty seconds to play," "fifteen seconds to play," etc., while spectators joined the Columbia players as they pushed for the winning touchdown. When the referee announced "five seconds to play," Captain Haley took his team off the field for the second time in two games. CAC scored while the Penn Staters were walking in the dark to their dressing room. Penn State's athletic officials handled the matter by making it a nongame, never recording the score at all.

Cancellation of the opening game with Dickinson postponed dedication of the grandstand at Beaver Field.[1] The event was rescheduled for the November 6 game with Western University of Pennsylvania, the first in what became the long and bitter Pitt rivalry.

This time atrocious weather caused a delay until Monday, as *Free Lance* reported: "When the boys from Allegheny [Pittsburgh's North Side was once called Allegheny City] arrived, they found the vilest kind of weather and agreed to the postponement." The Pittsburghers, quartered in the several fraternities, may have been too well entertained over the weekend, for they seemed sluggish Monday afternoon, when Penn State won the game, 32–0.

General and Mrs. James A. Beaver of Bellefonte were among those attending the informal dedication of the new five-hundred-capacity grandstand, with its overhanging roof and three flagpoles. The students had gratefully named their athletic field for Beaver, a Civil War veteran, judge, former governor, a trustee, and president of the Board at intervals from 1874 to 1914. His awareness of the state's obligation to support Pennsylvania's land-grant college had expedited the first appropriation for buildings and maintenance, including athletic facilities (1887).

The student yearbook, *LaVie,* based its description of 1893 as a championship season on the results among "colleges of our class." Its reasoning: Penn State *scored on* Pennsylvania (while losing, 18–6), defeated Virginia (the Southern League champions who had beaten Navy, North Carolina, Georgetown, and Virginia Military Institute), and won from both Western University of Pennsylvania (which became the University of Pittsburgh in 1908) and the Pittsburgh Athletic Club.

[1] Then located in the area between today's Osmond and Frear laboratories.

7

Atherton's Historic Kick

Charlie Atherton's prodigious contributions to Penn State football during his five years as a regular, 1890–94, and his achievements as a place-kicker are generally overlooked in present-day record books. In the 1894 opening game—a 60–0 victory over Gettysburg—Atherton scored three touchdowns and had ten chances for points-after-touchdowns, all of which he made. It is a Penn State record that is still unmatched.

The kicking rule in vogue at the time makes the ten-for-ten record unusually impressive. After a touchdown the ball was brought on the field for the extra points (a successful try counted two, a touchdown four) from a point in line with the spot where the scorer had been tackled or had run beyond the goal line, with the result that many tries were made from difficult angles. The scoring team did have the option of a free kick (a puntout), with the receiver standing where his team hoped to try the placement. The receiver, making a fair catch, was allowed only two steps before catching the ball. Since an accurate puntout was difficult, teams often took the option of an angled place-kick attempt. The puntout rule was not abolished until 1920.

Against Oberlin in 1894, Atherton's 25-yard placement kick from scrimmage won the game, but the historic accomplishment was hardly noticed in the eastern press and is ignored by football historians, except for Christy Walsh, who lists this field goal as a "first" in his book *College Football,* published in 1950. Football authorities, both before and after Christy's revelation, have assumed that the placement from scrimmage was originated by an Ivy League kicker because the Ivies so completely dominated the game during its formative years.[1]

Realistically, the 1894 team should not have been especially strong, but as usual the local press predicted a "championship," and for once the prophecy was warranted. Benjamin Franklin (Big) Fisher was captain, and Coach Hoskins held down the center of the line like a rock. Atherton, W. M. Suter, Fred Robison, and Walter McCaskey were the backfield stars. McCaskey went to West Point after he finished at Penn State, but returned in the 1930s as head of the Department of Military Science and Tactics.

Robison made ten touchdowns that season, four against Lafayette, including one after a 75-yard run. He won the Bucknell game (12–6) in the last few minutes of play, scoring a touchdown after runs of 30 and 10 yards. After 1894, when he left to enter dental school at Pittsburgh, he played with a professional team in Greensburg, and with the Pittsburgh AC. In 1898 and 1899 he captained and coached the Pitt (WUP) team while earning his dental degree, and later became a prominent State College dentist.

Manager George Spence, in the clutch of preseason enthusiasm, successfully brought about the first training table for the football team, and then arranged an unprecedented schedule, including Penn, Princeton, Virginia, Navy, Bucknell, Lafayette, and W&J, among others. After the team rolled over Gettysburg (60–0) and Lafayette (72–0) in its first two games, the schedule began to crumble. The cancellations from Penn, Princeton, and Virginia following such an early display of power may have been a coincidence, but *Free Lance* was indignant, especially with Penn and Princeton—the big-timers. The Philadelphia *Press* excused the Red and Blue because "the Penn team was overtrained and could only indulge in signal practice." The

[1] Edward R. Bushnell wrote in the *Franklin Field Illustrated* in 1939 that John Minds of Pennsylvania kicked the first placement from scrimmage against Harvard in 1897. Others claimed the honors for Princeton, while Amos Alonzo Stagg of Chicago—getting in a word for the Midwest—credited his own great kicker, Clarence Herschberger, who booted three against Michigan in 1897, but also admitted that a Princeton player had performed the feat earlier in the season. The unheralded Atherton was three years ahead of them all.

Lance asked, "Is it possible that Penn was afraid of *not* running up a score? Or even being defeated by 'little State College'?"

Princeton canceled by telegram the day before the scheduled game, stating that the team was badly crippled and "in no condition to meet with such a strong team as State would line up against them." "Such is the penalty of greatness," said *Free Lance,* adding that no college of any standing in the football world had as much trouble securing games as Penn State had because of "an isolated position up here in the mountains." "Write to the big schools first," exhorted the student press, listing Cornell, Virginia, VMI, W&J, Oberlin, Navy, Michigan, Princeton, Yale, and Lehigh as suitable opponents. Penn State had outgrown Dickinson, the newspaper said, and WUP wasn't quite up to the necessary level. The Dickinson series was resumed in 1896.

Other reasons made 1894 renowned. Not counting the brief two-game campaign of '87, it was Penn State's first undefeated season (6–0–1). The 6–6 tie with Navy, understandably considered a moral victory by the students, was the first game with either of the service academies. Frankly, the Middies, while not yet in the Yale-Harvard class, could hardly be blamed for viewing it as a practice skirmish. Navy had already started its series with Army (1890) and was flirting with the football élite. Prior to the Penn State game in 1894, the Midshipmen had beaten Georgetown, the Carlisle Indians, and Lehigh, and lost only to Penn by a close score.

The Bellefonte *Democratic Watchman* was caustic whenever the editor felt that criticism was justified. After the tie with Navy and in spite of the general local jubilation, the *Watchman* reported:

> Though our team did not accomplish their intention of defeating the U.S. Naval Cadets at Annapolis, Md. last Saturday it was not because the thing was an impossibility, but rather because of the "horse play" the boys indulged in in the first half when they had a chance to win.

Bill Suter circled the Navy end in the first quarter for a 90-yard touchdown run—still standing as the longest run from scrimmage in Penn State football history. Atherton kicked the goal, and State led at half time, 6–0. Navy's D. R. Merritt scored a safety and a touchdown on a 40-yard run in the second half, but missed the try-for-points.

Friday and Saturday games of a western trip were scheduled with

W&J and Oberlin College (a replacement for one of the canceled games). The team was shorthanded because Robison and Dunsmore, a guard, were having scholastic difficulties but defeated W&J in Washington, Pennsylvania, 6–0, and proceeded to Oberlin, Ohio, to meet a team coached by the eminent John Heisman.

In this memorable November 24 contest—the only one between the two colleges—Oberlin controlled the first half, missing a touchdown because of a penalty, but making another and kicking the goal for a 6–0 lead. The visiting Pennsylvanians took charge in the second half, with Atherton scoring. Charlie was chagrined when he missed the goal, because the home team kept its 6–4 lead until near the end of the battle. With ten minutes remaining, Oberlin was forced to punt from within its own 10-yard line against the wind. Charlie Thomas, right halfback, made a free catch near the Oberlin 20.

How the unheard-of idea of a placement field goal came about is not reported. Placements were used for the points-after-touchdowns, but a dropkick was the orthodox play from the field. It was probably Atherton's own idea—he was a daring and resourceful player. Dropping back, with Thomas holding near the sideline on the 25, he kicked the nearly round ball over the crossbar.

Consternation, excitement, and bewilderment erupted on the field. The Penn Staters were ecstatic, but Coach Heisman claimed the kick was illegal, and Referee Fred White of Oberlin, who had never seen the play, so ruled. Strangely enough, no animosity among the players, coaches, and officials marred the discussion, perhaps because the Penn Staters themselves were vague about the play's legality. The game was completed with the visitors claiming they had won, 9–6, and the home team insisting the score was 6–4 in their favor. Coaches Hoskins and Heisman agreed to leave the final decision to Walter Camp of Yale, the unofficial "czar" of college football.

Other Oberlin officials pointed out that when Thomas made a fair catch, Penn State was entitled to a free kick, but that Atherton's "field kick" could not be considered a free kick. They admitted that the rulebook did not define a field kick. Penn State's one ally, the sports editor of the Cleveland *Leader,* maintained that since no rule prohibited such a field goal, this should be accepted as a legal five-point play.

The rough and bitter conflicts characterizing this period of college football, especially the intersectional games, add significance to this statement, part of an editorial in the Oberlin *Review* of November 27, 1894:

> The Pennsylvania State team made a most favorable impression. There was a total absence of slugging during the game. The same good feeling was manifested during all the discussion that followed. And they left Oberlin in perfect good humor even though a very critical decision, about which the highest football authorities differ, had gone against them. We most earnestly hope that athletic contests with teams from Pennsylvania State may be included in our future schedules.

Although the game is recorded as a 9–6 victory, no trace has been found of Camp's official ruling—in writing. That his reply favored Penn State's claim is assumed, and apparently Oberlin was finally convinced. The Oberlin annual, *Hi-O-Hi,* 1895, page 121, lists the score: Penn State 9; Oberlin 6 (by decision of Walter Camp).

While the successes of the football team from 1891 through 1894 often were overplayed by zealous students and their supporting press, during these years Penn State did make its first headway toward eastern recognition with an overall record of 22–4–1. Veteran stalwarts like Aull and Hildebrand started the winning tradition in '91, and others carried it on, among them Atherton, Haley, Hoskins, McCaskey, Fisher, Robison, Suter, Henry Dowler (another five-letter winner), Gus Read, John L. Harris, and the three Dunsmore boys—James A., James G., and William D.

Atherton's achievement against Oberlin was the conspicuous event of his five-year gridiron career (1890–94). In his final game, on Thanksgiving Day, Penn State defeated a good Pittsburgh Athletic Club team, 14–0.

Despite being "the president's son," Charles M. H. Atherton successfully made his way among the high-spirited, rugged football and baseball squads of the nineties. When some football players spotted his unusual athletic ability during his sophomore year (1889), Jim (Jeffy) Mock, team captain, braved an interview with the president. Atherton, Sr., wasn't afraid that Charlie, not yet 16 at the time, would get hurt, but was concerned that on trips "he might be influenced by evil companions." Assured that Mock personally would separate Charlie from bad company, the president granted permission. Young Atherton won his first letter the following year at the age of 16.

Charlie's many interests and talents were apparent when he was a schoolboy in New Brunswick, New Jersey, while his father was a professor of political science at Rutgers University. An accomplished musician and eventually a choir director, Charlie wanted to try other fields before making music his career. He enrolled in chemistry at Penn State and took graduate work after receiving the B.S. degree in 1892, continuing to play on the football team for three more years. As a chemist with the Cambria Iron Company, he started a professional baseball career in 1894 with Johnstown's Atlantic League team, later becoming the manager. Moving to Wilkes-Barre, he was considered the best second baseman in the league, and Hugh Jennings tried to sign him with the Brooklyn Dodgers (then called the Bridgegrooms), but the Wilkes-Barre management refused his release. He finally had a year (1899) in the major leagues with the Washington Senators, where he played third base in 63 games and the outfield in 1 game, hit .248 and batted in 23 runs. He also hit 5 doubles and 6 triples with the Senators.

Atherton returned to Penn State for more graduate study and helped with the football team before turning to music. From 1906 to 1931 he was choir director for the Jan Hus Presbyterian Church in New York City, but during World War I he worked in Russia with the YMCA and spent a brief period with the Czecho-Slovakian army. Back in New York he resumed charge of the church programs for young people in music and athletics. He once directed a group singing an original operetta, "Peggy's Dream," produced in Carnegie Hall with Mrs. Andrew Carnegie present. In 1931 Atherton went to Vienna as a choir director and music teacher, and died in Austria on December 19, 1934.

8

Facing the Eastern "Giants"

With a few exceptions, Yale, Harvard, and Princeton continued to dominate eastern football throughout the nineties; in fact, the entire national picture belonged to the oldest Ivies despite the game's rapid development in the South, Southwest, and Midwest. Pennsylvania was the first to intrude on the Big Three, fielding some of its greatest teams from 1894 through 1898. Lafayette entered the race briefly in 1896 after an undefeated season, including a scoreless tie with Princeton and victories over Penn and Navy. If the press had named a "national champion" in 1899, it might have selected little Sewanee University in Tennessee. The southerners, a squad of only twenty-one players coached by Herman Suter of Princeton, were undefeated in twelve games and scored upon only by Auburn. Chicago, under Stagg, won the Western Conference that year, but was tied by Pennsylvania and Iowa. Although 1899 was an "off" year for the traditional eastern powerhouses, Walter Camp named ten players from the newly expanded Big Four to his All-America team. The eleventh was a Carlisle Indian halfback named Seneca.

Development of the wedge and other mass-formation plays nearly brought dissolution of the game in the 1890s, starting with a breakup of the Intercollegiate Football Association. Harvard and Pennsylvania withdrew from the league in 1894, largely because they opposed curtailment of what other members saw as a menacing trend. In 1895 two sets of rules were proposed when Princeton, Navy, and Yale favored a check on the brutal and sometimes fatal momentum wedges introduced by Loren F. Deland at Harvard in 1892. Deland was really the "father" of the flying wedge and an interesting variation called the "turtleback." Cornell, Harvard, and Pennsylvania were the balky "renegades" opposing a ban on formations inherently detrimental to life and limb—and football.

Early Penn State teams, lacking the manpower and speed for effective mass-formation plays, often were victims of the new offensive strategy in their unequal clashes with Penn, Yale, Princeton, and Cornell. In December 1893, a surprisingly constructive and prescient editorial in *Free Lance* pointed out that the popularity of football was not yet endangered by professionalism and raised questions about the game's future. The publication predicted that mass plays would probably be forced out by public pressure, because they were dull as well as brutal. The newspaper accurately forecast a more open game, with "quickness and activity" becoming the most important factors:

> We cannot deny that it is the most dangerous sport in which one can engage, and we of course forgive the opposition it is meeting from parents and older, conservative people; but we see no good excuse for such action as that taken by the Chief of Police of Pittsburgh. That gentleman has issued an edict to the effect that this season marks the end of all football playing within the limits of his jurisdiction. Whether this order so bravely delivered will be carried out remains to be seen. It certainly is unjust and insulting as well, for it puts football on a plane with pugilism.
>
> For that matter, however, we might as well grin and bear it. Everybody is jumping on football now. It is becoming quite the fad. The comic papers have taken it up, and the unfortunate devotees of the game are being dragged across the coals of their satire. But the game is here to stay. It has fastened its hold on the minds of the younger generation, and it is bound to thrive.

Penn State's student management made strenuous efforts to schedule the Big Four with some success, and the students stoically measured performance either by the closeness of the scores or merely by ability to score on the giants. This willingness to tackle the best—and always on the opponent's home field—brought the team into contact with some of the great players of the period. Penn's Truxton Hare,

Charlie Gelbert, and George Brooke, and Yale's Ned Glass and Tom Shevlin have all been selected by experts for all-time All-America teams. Playing Pennsylvania thirteen times between 1890 and 1905, Penn State had to contend with such other All-Americas as Harry Thayer, John Minds, John Outland, and Andy Smith. Among Princeton's greats were Addison Kelly, Doc Hillebrand, Lew Palmer, and Arthur Poe. Harvard did not schedule Penn State in this period; Cornell, regarded on a more equal plane, was an opponent only twice in the nineties.

The first game at Ithaca, in 1895, ended in a scoreless tie, hailed naturally as a great achievement. George Hoskins, still the Penn State coach but apparently no longer a participant, was one of the umpires "frequently hissed" for being "grossly partisan," according to Cornell accounts. *Free Lance* thought the Philadelphia papers had "again attempted to belittle the playing of our football team" and wondered how one official and seventeen players (the Penn State squad) could "bulldoze" three other officials, seventy Cornell players in uniform, plus thousands of spectators on their own home grounds. The team had to face Cornell's famous Bucky Starbuck, who was at the beginning of his career. He did not have a good game, fumbling once on the Penn State one-yard line.

Two years later Cornell vengefully smothered Penn State, 45–0, in a game notable because it was the initial appearance of Pop Warner's incredible "hidden ball" play. Before the rulemakers got around to calling it "unsportsmanlike conduct," some coaches went to great lengths to confuse their opponents and the officials—and the great Warner was no exception. The Carlisle Indians, later known as the principal advocates of Warner's ingenious invention, scored against Harvard in 1903 with the ball concealed under a player's jersey, reputed to be the first time such a maneuver was attempted. Actually, it wasn't the first time, as Warner admitted to Allison Danzig.[1] The famous coach said he used it late in "a practice game with Penn State in 1897, just as an amusing stunt for getting a little fun out of a scrimmage practice." Scrimmage practice, indeed.

Cornell was ahead, 39–0, with a few minutes left to play. The Big Red players surrounded their kickoff receiver, who slipped the ball under Mike Whiting's jersey. Why Penn State kicked off, trailing 39–0, is unexplained. While the visitors tried to get at the original

[1] Allison Danzig, *The History of American Football* (Englewood Cliffs, N.J.: Prentice-Hall, 1956).

receiver, Whiting ran the length of the field for a touchdown. The referee (Dr. Newton, Penn State's coach) is supposed to have remarked after declaring a touchdown, "I'll be darned if I know how the ball got there."

Penn State played Princeton five successive years, from 1896 to 1900, and unquestionably took the games more seriously than its adversary, which was undefeated in 1896 and held every team scoreless except the Carlisle Indians. In 1898 the Tigers had another great team (11–0–1) and anticipated no problem with Penn State, which had been slaughtered by Penn and defeated by Navy. Such tenuous prospects seemingly had no effect on the enthusiasm and optimism of the players or the dauntless students. The local State College *Times,* commenting on the Navy defeat (16–11), said:

> The score was a surprise to the admirers of State here as it was confidently expected that she would win this game, but owing to the fact that there was a game scheduled with Princeton on Wednesday, Dr. Newton did not care about taking any chances of having any of his men injured as it was considered that holding the Princeton score down would be more of a victory than winning the game against the Naval Cadets.

Princeton's skimpy 5–0 victory, based on one touchdown after twenty minutes of play, confounded the football world. Penn State's Dave Cure missed a field goal by inches, one that might have tied the score. The Tiger lineup read like a Who's Who in Princeton football, with Arthur Poe—hero of two victories over Yale—and Lew Palmer as ends, and Captain Doc Hillebrand and Big Bill Edwards at tackle. In 1899, virtually the same Princeton team again took the game lightly, and was glad to win by 12–0. Two of Penn State's backfield —Earl Hewitt and Cure—didn't play because they had been injured the week before against Army.

The one-sided rivalry with Pennsylvania for many years made the Philadelphia game one frustration after another for the upstart upstaters, who suspected that they were looked upon as "country cousins" by their city rivals. After Penn won the first meeting, 20–0, in 1890, *Free Lance* said:

> The Penn game reflected great credit on our players—when you think we must pick 11 men from 300 and the University has a choice of 1500—and also pays salaries to professionals (in an indirect way). Also, we played them on *their* grounds and had to battle 12 men instead of 11. If the referee could be

considered a man. Decisions lacked good judgment or were devoid of that quality of justice which should characterize a referee.

In 1903 *Free Lance* wryly commented that the Philadelphia press "called us farmers, but Penn was fortunate in securing one of those farmers." The reference was to Andy Smith, who later made All-America at Penn, but had played at Penn State for nearly two seasons (1901–2) before transferring abruptly. He was Penn's leading ground-gainer—as he had been against Pennsylvania the year before.

One of the moral victories over the Red and Blue occurred in 1900, when the team held Penn to seventeen points and scored five points. Not so much the touchdown as how it was scored tickled Penn State backers. Their team did it on a "quarterback kick" (forerunner of the quick kick) invented by George Woodruff, Penn's famous coach until 1901 (when he departed for a successful career in law and government service). In other words, the country boys became city slickers in using one of Coach Woodruff's patented plays against him.

So named because the quarterback took the snap from center and stepped back a yard or two to execute a short punt, Woodruff's play often was used to counteract what later would be called "blitzing." According to the rules of the day, the kick could be recovered by any back "onside," meaning in back of the kicker, and sometimes was even caught in the air. Penn State's quarterback in the 1900 Penn game was Earl Hewitt, a very accurate punter. Down near the Penn 30-yard line he called the play and kicked toward the left side of the field. The ball hit on the 10-yard line and rolled into the end zone, where it was recovered for a touchdown by halfback Arthur Gill.

In the decade, Penn State won only once against Pennsylvania, and that was a practice scrimmage in 1898. Coach Newton, a Penn alumnus, had been disturbed because a rigorous trip arranged by the student manager included games with Navy, Princeton, and a good club team from Pittsburgh mysteriously listed as DC and AC (posterity discovered this meant the Duquesne Athletic Club). En route to Annapolis, Coach Newton paused in Philadelphia to have the boys meet George Woodruff.

While visiting along the sidelines at Franklin Field—then only three years old—Woodruff proposed a practice scrimmage. The State College boys were more than willing. Penn used its regulars, who had scored a 40–0 victory over the guests earlier that season. John Outland, Penn's All-America halfback that year,[2] made the first touchdown, but then the visitors displayed an astonishing aggressiveness and scored from the Penn 25-yard line. According to the State College *Times,* "Woodruff went wild. He asked the Penn State team to take the ball on the 25-yard line and repeat the trick—which they did to score again, and later kicked a field goal. This was too much for Woodruff, who sent his team to the training quarters after a good lecture."

Coach Newton, to interrupt the tough schedule of three games in five days, took a day's layoff before meeting Princeton after Navy, then stopped at Franklin Field for another scrimmage with Penn before the trip to Pittsburgh.

The season of 1898 had a buildup like none other in Penn State's ten-year football history, and despite the brave front, including big talk about the "victory over Penn," the three-defeat road trip was a bitter disappointment. Penn State had lost to Navy, 16–11; Princeton, 5–0; and Duquesne AC, 18–5.

A preseason practice period at Hecla Park, about 15 miles from the campus, had held promise, but Dr. Newton's medical duties in Philadelphia unfortunately delayed his arrival until after the first game with Gettysburg. Penn State won the opener, 47–0, with three former players in charge—Mac Curtin, J. A. Dunsmore, and Amby Diehl—increasing the excitement for a banner year. Newton appeared just in time to accompany his team to Philadelphia for the deflating game with Pennsylvania (40–0). These circumstances caused the first "fire the coach" campaign by the local papers, with muttering by some students and alumni. "What is lacking is a first-class coach." said the *Times,* urging the college to recall George Hoskins. The Bellefonte *Watchman* decided that "all State needs is the proper coaching to make the team one of the strongest in the country." *Free Lance,* the most blunt, stated that "the trouble wasn't poor coaching, there just wasn't any coaching at all."

Such unusual criticism from the home press embarrassed the director of physical training, who wanted recognition as a coach of professional stature. A crowning blow was losing both his watch and his pocketbook on the Pittsburgh trip. External pressure, however, didn't force Newton's departure after the season—a brighter future

[2] The trophy for the nation's outstanding interior lineman was named for Outland, who made Camp's 1897 All-America team as a tackle.

appeared to await him at Lafayette with a team his Penn Staters had beaten, 5–0.

As a climax to the season's dismal side, Hewitt missed the train out of Pittsburgh and had to "hoof" it to the Tyrone connection.

Victories over six traditional opponents within the state, including three on the road against Bucknell, W&J, and Dickinson, made the '98 campaign successful by ordinary standards. The optimistic outlook had been due partly to the presence of three backfield standouts —Hewitt, Cure, and Fred Heckel, who divided the quarterback duties with Hewitt and also played halfback. (Heckel was the first Penn Stater to enter the coaching ranks at another college, becoming head coach at Allegheny College in 1900.) Two linemen ranked among the best of the early years—Leroy (Henny) Scholl, left tackle, and Carlton A. (Brute) Randolph, left guard.

Scholl, the only Penn State player to win six varsity football letters, continued without a break from 1896 to 1901, and then spent several seasons as an assistant coach. Randolph, captain of the team in 1899, had what might be termed an "interrupted career." From Lewisberry, Pennsylvania, he was several years older than most of his teammates before entering in 1895 for a year. He played at Drexel and also for the Camden Athletic Club, returning in 1897. Randolph was the first Penn State player to be recognized by Walter Camp, who named him to the third team as a guard in 1898.

Success against all small-college opponents, and the team's fine showing in its practice game with Penn, again led to "championship" claims. The *Times* devoted its entire front page of December 15, 1898, to a review of the season, featuring an unusual squad picture etched from a photograph and headed "State's Championship Football Team."

Of all the élite eastern teams played by Penn State through its first two decades of football, the players and other students were most enthusiastic over their performance against the seven Yale teams they faced. Considering the vast difference in manpower, experience, and reputation, the Pennsylvanians made a creditable showing and gained respect in eastern football.

The first game, in 1899, was typical. New coach Sam Boyle—a former Penn player—attempted to introduce the "guards back" formation learned at Penn under Woodruff, its originator. In this mass play the guards were brought into the backfield to precede the ball carrier. They weren't big enough to handle this assignment, while Yale's defense could have demoralized any team that season.

With oddly high hopes for the Yale game, students waited at the telegraph office for word from Manager Rolland (Kid) Diller. "Yale 42. Penn State 0. The team played well" was the message read to the gathering, an unforgettable commentary on Penn State's early struggles for identity in the football world.

The Elis won with a bewildering attack, as did Coach Woodruff's team at Penn (47–0) the following week.

Two years later, the New Haven *Register* headlined "State Holds Yale to 22 Points" over its account of "one of the most remarkable games ever played at Yale field." Remarkable, perhaps, because the Penn Staters hadn't been expected to do more than show up. Yale had some of its greatest names—Tom Shevlin, Chuck Rafferty, Jim Hogan, Ralph Kinney, Ned Glass, and Henry Holt. All made All-America during their careers. The *Register* reported that "no eleven has torn up the Yale line so persistently, and broken her interference." The 22–0 score might have been even closer if Penn State hadn't fumbled three times near the Yale fifteen. Led by Andy Smith, its backs gained more ground than all other Yale opponents put together. Another newspaper account said, "Penn State was hard as rocks and full of sand," and Captain Hewitt declared that "we showed we weren't afraid of the *Y* on the Yale sweaters."

Here are the headlines the next year in the State College *Times* of October 24, 1902:

CELEBRATION AT STATE
STUDENT BODY REJOICES OVER
GAME WITH YALE
Welcomed Home Amid Cheers and College Yells
Old Brass Cannon Peals Forth the Score

Hardly a victory, since the score was Yale 11, Penn State 0. But it was against a Yale team that scored 286 points to 22 by opponents, and won 11 games (tied by Army). "Seldom, if ever, in the history of the college," said the *Times*, "did the enthusiasm run higher than it did at the announcement of the glorious victory—for nothing short of victory can it be called at Yale."

Yale was without the service of Captain George Chadwick, twice an All-America halfback, but the Elis had six other players also named on Camp's 1902 team. Writing about the Penn State-Yale game of that year, Camp said:

> Those Penn State players who had been beaten by the University of Pennsylvania, 17–0, went up to New Haven and met the hitherto unbroken stone wall line of Yale and not only held them to two scores, one in each half, but made things so particularly interesting that Yale was not in a position to make replacements by changing players, but was looking for the very best to put the game out of danger.

Some important football personalities of the period played brilliantly in their New Haven debut—Ed Yeckley, Henry (Irish) McIlveen, and Carl Forkum—but Andy Smith again was the running star. He had one run of 35 yards against the supposedly almost impregnable Bulldog defense.

Three hundred students met the players on the outskirts of State College Monday morning, unhitched the horses from the hack, and hauled the team to the campus for a mass meeting. Captain Ralph Cummings, borrowing a line from the previous year's captain (Hewitt), said that the team had been able to take a strong grip "with both hands" on the ends of those *Y*'s. Coach Pop Golden said student spirit had helped. Many observers gave much credit to E. K. Wood, a former player who had spent two or three weeks with the squad as a part-time coach. He was paid $45.83 for his services. The rest of the economics were big-time, too. The Yale guarantee was $450, and the Penn State management spent $376.57 on the trip.

Things didn't go so well at New Haven in 1903 and 1904, but in 1905 the *State Collegian* (successor to the *Free Lance*) could crow: "For the first time in Old Penn State sports history we have turned out an eleven able to cope with Yale." (Penn State 0; Yale 12). The team outgained Yale by rushing, 203 yards to 110. Yeckley was captain this year, and other prominent players were Bill Wray, W. T. (Mother) Dunn, Bayard Kunkle, John Gotwals, Cal Moorhead, and V. L. (Hi) Henry. Both of Yale's touchdowns were scored by P. L. Veeder, who made All-America fullback in 1906 and became one of the first adept forward passers later in his career. The pass was brand new in 1906 when he threw one for 30 yards that was instrumental in beating Harvard.

No changes in college rules during the period 1890–1905 were comparable to the establishment in the eighties of the "downs system," and the exit of the "scrum" to be replaced by the "scrimmage." In 1893–95, when opposition to mass plays developed rapidly, a few colleges wanted to legislate against them, but the majority continued their use to good advantage. Because an inordinate number of deaths and injuries resulted in 1905, President Theodore Roosevelt (a Harvard graduate) called representatives of Yale, Harvard, and Princeton for a conference at the White House and told them in no uncertain terms to do something constructive with the football rules or else face drastic consequences, such as elimination of the game. This led to the reforms of 1906 and thereafter.

Rule changes prior to the presidential conference included:

1892: Following a try-for-goal after touchdown, ball brought to center of field and given to defending team. Previously the defensive team had put it into play on the 25-yard line.

1896: Five players required to be on offensive line when ball was snapped. ("Guards back" and "tackles back" plays still retained their legality.)

1897: Scoring system changed, with a touchdown counting 6 points; try-for-point, 1 point; field goal, 5 points; safety, 2 points. (A touchdown had been 4, an extra point, 2.) Substitutions, previously allowed only with consent of the referee, permitted any time at discretion of captains.

1900: Coaching prohibited from sidelines by coaches or substitutes.

1902: Teams required to change goals after a try-for-point following a touchdown; also after a field goal.

1903: Option of kicking off or receiving given to team scored upon; quarterback allowed to run with ball between the two 25-yard lines, providing he crossed scrimmage line 5 yards from point where he received ball.

1904: Six men required on offensive line; value of field goal reduced from 5 to 4 points.

9

Small-College Rivalries

Head coaches like to talk about the fun of playing college football; players generally concede that Saturdays are fun, especially winning Saturdays. Only the most cynical deny that the roar of the crowd is exhilarating.

When football began at Penn State, participants often paid their own expenses on trips and bought their own equipment to cope with skimpy budgets. Passing the hat at games brought in a little revenue, but not until the late 1890s was a modest student fee assessed, which produced $800 in 1902, for example. Guarantees from opponents played on the road barely covered expenses, and a season seldom broke even financially.

These pioneers would have marveled at such amenities as jet air travel and deluxe hotels, expensive equipment, artistically marked artificial-turf fields, and carpeted dressing rooms. Fans survived and even multiplied through the years minus television, elaborate electric scoreboards, PA announcers telling them what's going on, two-hundred-piece bands, and baton-twirling beauties. The public even got along without bowls and weekly polls. But players and their ardent followers in the dear dead days did have the kind of fun coaches now talk about wistfully.

One luxury, acquired in 1901 after the Football Committee deliberated lengthily, was a tackling dummy. The committee's minority held that this new-fangled gadget, in use elsewhere for several years, had little practical value for learning the art of tackling—an opinion later proved correct.

The wholehearted support of Penn State students during the trying struggle for recognition made the game fun even when the team was losing; mythical "championships" were created from so-so seasons; ordinary players were hailed as All-Americas, and the undergraduates took pride in everyone on the field because the team truly belonged to the students. Rallies, mass meetings, and welcome-back parties accompanied nearly every game as demonstrations of loyalty, even in defeat. Students watched practice daily whether the varsity was on hand or away, as it frequently was. The "scrubs" working out or playing a scheduled game got attention and respect. A *Free Lance* editorial urged students to refrain from calling the substitutes "scrubs"—it had an uncomplimentary connotation—and suggested that the "scrub" team be designated the college team. From then on writers adopted this dignified practice.

Playing football became general among the students, the less skilled participating on class or pickup teams. For a decade, beginning in 1895, the football season ended not with the varsity's Thanksgiving Day game but with the exceedingly popular "Tumbler-Toothpick" encounter between squads selected from the fattest and the thinnest members of the student body.

Football trips ranked as glorious adventures, especially for the many who came from small towns and farms and had never previously traveled beyond the county fair. Countless stories are told of high jinks—pranks and gags played on the public and on each other. Once the squad checked into a small hotel in Sunbury posing as a minstrel troupe and asked for a "quiet" front room. The other occupants of the hotel asked for quiet before the night was over. Colorful nicknames, generally bestowed for some specific reason, were plentiful—Indian Ruble, Quaker Penrose, Bottle Miller, Silent Man or Princess Hewitt, Cranberry Merchant Harding, and, inevitably for an early physician-coach, Sawbones Newton.

Meetings with the Big Four were serious excursions, but the most competitive rivalries developed with small Pennsylvania college opponents. Since Penn State frequently had the upper hand, students assumed an important role in the ventures. Although Bucknell was the earliest of these rivals, for some reason the Dickinson encounter became "the game," the season's finale on Thanksgiving Day at Seminary Field in Williamsport. Nearly half the Bucknell and Dickinson games were played there, partly because larger crowds could be accommodated and were available in a metropolitan area, but especially because these teams resisted coming to State College, a place they considered inaccessible and rabidly partisan. As a visiting team, the Penn Staters were no less suspicious, and the fact is that until the move to New Beaver Field in 1909, home fans suffered through only one setback on "Old Beaver." Nevertheless, it was getting the books out of the red that prompted Penn State and its opponents to schedule so many early games on well-populated neutral grounds— Williamsport, Wilkes-Barre, Harrisburg, or Altoona.

Of the thirteen Bucknell encounters from 1887 through 1900, when the series was terminated for eight years, Penn State won ten to Bucknell's three. A few ended in violent disputes occasioned by accusations of roughness, or differences in interpretations of rules. The 1892 game, in the mud and snow on Old Beaver Field, actually was an 18–0 victory, but it ended with four minutes to play when a Bucknell player was seriously injured and carried from the field. "It is beyond our dignity," *Free Lance* stated, "to reply to the claims of the Lewisburg *Mirror* that our players were brutal and that we were a slugging, padded team." They had previously reported that "the visitors played a fair and gentlemanly game, but were clearly outclassed."

Betting was an established and well-publicized custom, especially among undergraduates of Penn State, Bucknell, and Dickinson. Reported to have had hard work coaxing any money out of the Bucknell visitors in 1892, most of it going begging at five to three odds, students were in a belligerent mood, since they had lost their shirts at Lewisburg the year before (Bucknell 12, Penn State 10).

The eighty students who accompanied the team to Lewisburg in 1893 had another lean weekend financially, although Penn State won, 36–18. With odds of four to one, the gamblers could find few takers. It was noted that "the Bucknell men showed us every attention, in marked contrast to the manner in which the townspeople acted towards us . . . a crowd of probably 2,000 had gathered, brilliant with Bucknell colors and armed with everything from fish-horns to pick-handles and baseball bats."

A Bucknell victory—10–0 in 1896 at Williamsport—drew ungracious comments in the State College area newspapers. One reported:

"Many remarks were made by non-partisans upon the aged appearance of the Bucknell players—one looked to be at least thirty-five, and there was a decided contrast when the lithe, vigorous State team came on the field. Between age and beauty, age took precedent." Another admitted that the glory of the victorious Lewisburgers had been diminished by State's pregame disclaimer of a possible win.

In 1897, again at Williamsport, Penn State prevailed, 27–4. Attracted by a special ticket rate of $1.00 between Bellefonte and Williamsport, its backers and the "State College and Consolidated Bands" journeyed to the game site, where they formed a parade "three squares long" and marched to the Park Hotel for lunch.

The 1899 loss in Williamsport was laid to the terrible condition of the field. Penn State was behind 5–0 when Billy Burns, in the clear, "slipped in one of the ditches used to make the five-yard lines, and fell." *Free Lance* allowed that "Bucknell played a fast game when she played, but her dilatory tactics in giving signals and her playing for time was not a display of that highest kind of sportsmanship which is dear to every lover of sport."

With eleven minutes to play in the 1900 game, Bucknell, ahead 12–4, disputed a referee's decision and walked off the field. The game was awarded to Penn State on a forfeit, 6–0. At this point the series wisely was terminated for a cooling-off period, which lasted until 1908. Because the three games in 1908–10 were almost embarrassingly one-sided, the series was broken off again for five years. Students had a special "song" to welcome the visitors from Lewisburg. It began with the following verse:

> Penn State was Penn State
> When Bucknell was a pup
> Penn State will be Penn State
> When Bucknell grows up

This generation of students had conveniently forgotten that the old rivals had been "pups" together.

Dickinson, Penn State's second earliest opponent, played home-and-home games in 1888, with a 6–6 tie resulting at State College and Penn State the loser at Carlisle, 16–0. Resuming the series was difficult. In 1891 Dickinson failed to show up at Altoona for a controversial league match, and in 1893 it canceled a meeting scheduled at State College.

Penn State and Dickinson arranged an 1892 Thanksgiving Day

feature at Island Park, near Harrisburg, but a dispute ended the game when Dickinson players left the field.

With Penn State leading 10–0, S. H. Brown punted to Ben Caswell of Dickinson. According to a State College report, Caswell failed to cover the kick, and George Hoskins picked up the ball to run half the length of the field for a touchdown. Dickinson reports claimed that Caswell (who became the first captain of the Carlisle Indian team the following season) called "down," presumably killing the play, and that Hoskins had then "stolen" the ball. Dickinson players left in a huff when the referee awarded their opponents another touchdown.

Dickinson's proud "Golden Years" from 1896 through 1899 yielded only one 6–0 victory (at Sunbury in 1897) in four meetings with its rival, which won 8–0 in 1896, 34–0 in 1898, and 15–0 in 1899. The high point came in the Thanksgiving Day game of 1902 when Penn State had lost only to Yale and Penn, while Dickinson had scored notable victories over Navy and Lehigh. Big plans of students for a crusade to Carlisle were slowed down by the cost of the train fare, but the organized effort of all student leaders induced 167 to sign up for the trip—nearly half the student body. Confident Dickinson backers reputedly offered two to one and even three to one odds and arranged a victory celebration, hired two bands, and bought up all the horns and loose wood around town.

The crusaders assembled in front of Meek's drug store on College Avenue early on the morning of the game, with "Paddy" Godard's band, to begin their march to the Lemont railroad station, three miles away. Any conveyance would have been difficult if not impossible to locate, and not half as much fun. When the train arrived at Lemont, big "State" banners were hanging from each side of every car.

A short layover in Harrisburg, reached at 11:30 A.M., brought a wild rush for refreshments at the station, for no one had thought to pack a lunch. Pulling into Carlisle, as the train flashed by Irving College—a girls' school—the Penn Staters were all set for the waving young ladies, who had somehow found out about the *State Special,* and about when it would pass.

At Carlisle the group expanded to over 300, joined by the junior class fresh from its banquet in Harrisburg the night before. Penn State's large contingent received a special welcome from Dickinson students and Carlisle citizens before reaching the hotel, where it was found that such a crowd could not be accommodated for "dinner." Having to go without a midday meal didn't seem to bother most of the visitors. *Free Lance* reports:

> There were pretty girls, good-looking girls, stylish girls, and almost every kind. In fact, not a few were on the State side of the gridiron.
> The field was a pretty sight. On the one side was a solid mass of red and white, while the other side was almost as solid a bank of blue and white. The Indian band was stationed at the head of the field and discoursed music throughout the game.
> While waiting for the teams to come on, the sides employed the time yelling at each other. Dickinson had more concerted action, but State made up for that with the quantity of the noise they put forth.

When the team came out, the band's attempt to play the college song was drowned out by cheering. Captain Ralph Cummings led the way, but three others seemed to dominate the squad because of their size—the two guards, Fred Dodge and Jim Junk, and right end Bill Miles.

Penn State won the unexpectedly one-sided game, 23–0, with three touchdowns scored by Ed Whitworth and one by Carl Forkum, who kicked three extra points. The victory celebration began at once. Students paraded through the streets of Carlisle, stopping at every cross street to count out the score. Their train left at 6:45, but the demonstration continued during the Harrisburg stopover with a march to the homes of the governor and the mayor, both of whom luckily were out of town.

Arriving in Lemont at one o'clock on Sunday morning, they began their hike to State College. This part of the journey was less fun than had been anticipated—buoyant spirits were dulled by empty stomachs and the cold mountain air. Still, it had been a satisfying "crusade" for Penn State. "On this day," said *Free Lance,* "her ancient rival had been trailed in the dust, and the greatest exhibition of college spirit shown that has ever been known at State."

Dickinson students, ready for a turnabout in 1903, held nightly mass meetings to generate spirit before the game at Williamsport—called the "Queen City." Authorities brought in several outside coaches as advisers for the team's preparation. The charged-up atmosphere preceding the game drove a group of enterprising students to a slightly macabre stunt involving their former mascot, a dog. They collected a fund to reclaim the body from a taxidermist who had obligingly mounted it for a trophy, but had never been paid for his work. If "Dick's" pregame appearance in front of the parading Dickinsonians affected the outcome, as some claimed, the 6–0 Dickinson victory may be the only one in football annals attributable to a deceased mascot. Halfback S. Brittain Seeley, who had formerly played for Penn State, made the winning touchdown in a tough contest with just 40 seconds to play.

Penn Staters continued their excellent support of the team throughout the trailblazing days of football. In 1905—again on Thanksgiving Day—a good 500 or more backers from State College, joined by 200 from Bellefonte, boarded a special train for the Dickinson game in Williamsport, where the event had become a "classic." Two engines hauled 12 jammed cars. Spectators numbered 8,000, the largest football crowd thus far in central Pennsylvania. The keyed-up, optimistic Penn State adherents were rewarded with a 6–0 victory when "Mother" Dunn's blocked kick very late in the game led to the lone touchdown by John Gotwals. Powering his way into a mass of players on the goal line, Gottie would have been thrown back past the goal posts without a score on fourth down had he not, to quote *Free Lance,* "reached out and clasped the upright, pulling himself across the line with a magnificent effort."

10

Stars over the Service Academies

During the Army game of 1957, an elderly gentleman moved restlessly along the sidelines near the Penn State bench on New Beaver Field. He was a familiar figure, by no means looking his 85 years. Coach Rip Engle (and Bob Higgins before him) had made futile efforts to keep him in the stands, Bob once urging the business manager to tempt him with a handful of 50-yard-line tickets for every home game. Earl Hewitt, Sr., would have none of it. The retired state legislator, coal dealer, Number One citizen of Indiana, Pennsylvania, and oldest surviving football letterman, reproached Coach Higgins tearfully: "No, Bob, you can't do that to me, I couldn't stand it up there. I belong down here."

The Army game always had special significance for him. In the exciting first half of that 1957 game, he wandered away from the security of the bench while Coach Engle and his players were exhorting the Lions to stop an Army threat. The Cadets, trailing by seven points in the second quarter, were driving hard for a score near the Penn State 30. Army halfback Harry Walters piled up with two interferers and a couple of Penn State defenders about two yards off the side mark. Fans and some of his relatives were horrified to see the old man go down under the pile of youthful brawn, but Earl, Jr., remained calm. "They can't hurt Pop," said he.

Pop was almost the first one on his feet, shaking both fists at the baffled Cadets. Without even an interval to catch his breath, he screamed: "You couldn't get me in 1899, and you can't get me now." To the somewhat embarrassed Cadets, Earl's challenge was unintelligible, but his statement was accurate. He had beaten them exactly 58 years before, returning a punt 65 yards for the only touchdown in the first game of the Army series, and giving Penn State its initial football victory over a major eastern team. Soon after his run, Hewitt was severely injured tackling a Cadet, who was apparently on his way to an Army score.

The only other successes of the 1899 team, coached by Sam Boyle, were over Mansfield, Gettysburg, and Dickinson, while Army numbered Dartmouth, Syracuse, and Navy among its victims, and was anchored by one of its most famous players, Paul Bunker, playing as a plebe.[1]

Captain Randolph, Cummings, Scholl, and E. K. Wood led a strong defense that held Army scoreless, staving off a threat in the final few tense minutes when the husky Bunker, put into the backfield on fourth down and only a yard to go, was stopped without gaining an inch.

The newest thing in football in 1899 was the "tackle-back" formation devised by Dr. Harry Williams, as coach at Penn Charter School in Philadelphia. It brought one tackle to the backfield directly behind the other tackle on the line. Dr. Williams was no stranger at West Point, having coached there in 1891 (part-time and even by correspondence) when he was located at Newburgh, about ten miles away. Whether the innovation, which he offered to Army coach H. J. Koehler, was used against Penn State, isn't known, but Bunker was moved from his tackle position to the backfield in crucial situations. The Cadets employed it effectively in winning their last two games, against Syracuse and Navy.

Among Penn State's offensive stars that day was Billy Burns, who played both halfback and fullback.[2] Burns kicked the extra point

[1] Bunker made Camp's All-America in 1901 as a tackle and again as a halfback in 1902, duplicating the feat of John Outland at Penn, who first accomplished the lineman-back "double" on Camp's teams of 1897 and 1898; and Walter Eckersall of Chicago on the 1904 and 1905 teams as end and quarterback.

[2] Burns, a Frank Merriwell type, was popular with the local kids for his prowess on the diamond as well as on the gridiron. One of the best college pitchers

after Hewitt's touchdown, and had the longest run from scrimmage. *Free Lance* reported that "Burns made a masterful effort, but fell short of the goal line by 5 yards, exhausted after running the whole length of the field, but for 10 yards." Since the field in those days was 110 yards, the run may have been 100 yards and possibly one of Penn State's longest.

Earl Edward Hewitt was older than most of his classmates when he enrolled in mining engineering with the Class of 1902. As captain of the 1901 football team he was listed as 26, and only late in life did he reveal that he was born July 22, 1872. He was 30, therefore, when he joined Connie Mack's Philadelphia professional team in the fall of 1902 as a quarterback during Mack's brief venture into football with his long-time diamond partner, John Shibe.[3] Hewitt enjoyed talking about football, relating every detail of the 1899 Army game, especially his winning score, and always crediting Eddie Wood, who erased West Point's last defender and captain, W. D. Smith.

In 1900 Hewitt was the only member of the 1899 backfield still around, but most of the defensive stars were available, and West Point was held to a scoreless tie. The teams were not to play again until 1939. Hewitt was also proud of scoring the deciding touchdown against W&J in 1898 (11–6) at a time when the quarterback, according to the rules, was limited in his scoring possibilities.

After his pro football career and a short try at professional baseball, Hewitt became a coal dealer and had a security business in Indiana, Pennsylvania; he soon was involved in local politics, winning election to the state legislature (1938–54). As a devoted alumnus and vociferous champion of all athletic teams, he was hard on those who dared to disagree. He could be a severe critic with insiders, but as years passed, he restrained his belligerence toward outsiders. With

---

at the turn of the century, he won his most important game in June 1899 but didn't realize its significance at the time. His opponent on the mound for Bucknell was Christy Mathewson. Bucknell had 10 hits to State's 7; Mathewson struck out 8 to Burns' 11; walked 4 to Burns' 0. The Penn Stater batted cleanup and had 3 hits; Mathewson made 1, batting seventh. Bucknell's 5 errors contributed to the downfall of "Big Six," loser by a score of 4–3.

[3] Other former Penn Staters signing with Mack were Scholl, Wood, Randolph, and Lynn Sweet, the 1901 center who was a typical "migrating" athlete playing at Bucknell (1900) and W&J before joining the Philadelphia A's. This team closed the season against a Pittsburgh challenger in a game publicized as the "Pennsylvania championship." Hearing no complaints, the promoters quickly changed the billing to "World title game." The A's won, 12–6.

the mien of a royal personage, Hewitt insisted on giving pep talks to the team and advice to the coaches. He had beaten Army and couldn't understand the successes of post-World War II Army teams. The Penn State Club of Indiana County honored Earl on his one hundredth birthday, and gave him a Lion statuette with an engraved tribute: "For his 75 years of devoted service to Penn State." He died in 1972 shortly after the celebration.

Of the two service academies, Navy was the more frequent opponent in the early days, Penn State journeying to Annapolis ten times through 1905, winning 3, losing 6, and tying 1. The only unequal contest was won by Navy in 1900, 44–0. The next season the Middies—coached by Doc Hillebrand of Princeton fame—took the game lightly, and lost to the eleven captained by Hewitt, 11–6. The ever-present Scholl, in his sixth varsity season, scored first with a field goal, and then tallied the winning touchdown in the closing minutes after Andy Smith blocked a kick recovered by Jim Junk on Navy's 5. *Free Lance* describes the final 45 seconds after Captain Neil Nichols of Navy had attempted a fake kick:

> The ball was passed from center to fullback and the fullback passed it to the quarterback, who had run around behind the fullback to receive the ball. The quarterback tried to run with it, but State was on the alert and as the cry "Look out for a trick play" went around, Smith dove through the line and knocked the quarterback off his feet. As the quarterback was struggling to regain his feet, Art Biesecker fell on the quarterback's neck and held him fast. The whistle ended the game.

Leroy (Henny) Scholl, a Williamsport native who arrived on campus in the fall of 1896, was considered a "tough guy" by the other students, who were a little afraid of him. At the first practice Coach Newton questioned him about rumors that he had a blackjack in the back pocket of his football pants. Surrendering the weapon, Henny explained that in his "league" at home such safeguards were necessary for survival.

The next year (1897) Scholl's "surprise" was a homemade helmet —the first any member of the squad had seen. It was made from an old derby hat with the brim cut off, the padding stuffed inside. Three or four other players with derby-helmet ideas had Calvin Kline, local shoemaker, sew some leather protectors on the hat tops and also straps to tie under their chins. Historians claim that the first football helmets were used in 1896—if so, Penn State players weren't far behind.

Among dominant players in the early 1900s was Ed Yeckley, an end and halfback through four seasons and captain in 1905. In his first game (1902), with only three minutes to play, Ed's recovery of a fumble led to the winning touchdown, scored by Smith, with Carl Forkum adding the extra point. A forceful personality, Yeckley was a successful businessman in later life and maintained a close interest in Penn State football until a violent disagreement with Coach Hugo Bezdek in the late 1920s. Partly for this reason he opposed having his son enroll at his alma mater. William H. Yeckley captained the Princeton football team in 1931.

To the huge satisfaction of the students, Penn State made it three in a row over Navy by defeating the Middies at Annapolis in 1903, 17–0. This wasn't one of Navy's better teams, but the victory margin was surprising, and the home team was able to make only two first downs, one in each half. Captain Ed Whitworth ran 50 yards for the first touchdown, and kicked a 25-yard field goal for a half-time lead of 11–0. In the second half Forkum scored after a short gain, and later Whitworth barely missed a 45-yard field goal attempt. The points were already on the scoreboard—22–0—when the referee made a delayed negative decision. In this game, Navy used a fullback named Halsey, who would later rise to admiral and fame. Students receiving the news back in State College broke up their old grandstands at Beaver Field and consigned them to a victory bonfire.

A 6–6 tie in the first Navy game (1894) caused the players to complain that had the officials at Annapolis allowed them to use their "trick" play, it would have been a victory. Some of the more ingenious gridders had sewn "handlebars" on the seat of the pants of two halfbacks in order to hoist the ball carriers over the heads of the opposition—a sort of human shotput.

A famous threesome emerged in 1901 when veterans Hewitt and Scholl were joined by Andrew Latham Smith of Dubois, Pennsylvania. Hewitt, who had known Smith as a promising high school athlete, persuaded him to enter Penn State, where he enrolled in electrical engineering, joined Sigma Alpha Epsilon fraternity, and roomed with Hewitt. Smith promptly won a place on the football team as fullback to begin his career as a nationally known star and later a celebrated coach.

Smith's playing in the 1901 season and the first eight games of

1902 against the stronger opponents—Penn, Yale, and Navy—was outstanding. His departure after the 1902 Gettysburg game to enroll immediately at Penn brewed a storm of controversy and recriminations between the two institutions. In 1903 his eligibility was seriously questioned by Harvard and some other Ivy schools.

Earl Hewitt stoutly defended his protégé and resented implications that there was anything sinister or unusual about his transfer. "It was just a question of money," said Hewitt, many years later. "Andy Smith was a poor boy, and he could get financial aid at Penn. He couldn't make ends meet at Penn State, and we had no way to help him." To Hewitt, Smith was always a Penn Stater and could do no wrong, not even by contributing to Penn's 1903 and 1904 victories, which must have been fratricide by Earl's own standards.

A fullback at Penn for three years (1903–5), Smith made Walter Camp's first All-America team in 1904. He was Penn's freshman and varsity backfield coach for four seasons, and head coach in 1909. Ironically, Penn State had its first successes against the Red and Blue (1909, 1911, and 1912) while Smith was coach. In 1913 Andy moved on to Purdue and in 1916 to the University of California at Berkeley.

Smith is justly recognized as the father of West Coast football, focusing national attention on the area for the first time in the California "golden years" with his "Wonder Teams" of 1920–24 and a 44–0–4 record. The ties were with W&J in the 1922 Rose Bowl, Nevada in 1923, and Washington and Stanford in 1924. California's record under Smith in 1920 and 1922 was 18–0, including the defeat of Ohio State in the 1921 Rose Bowl, 28–0.

Overwork contributed to Andy Smith's death of pneumonia in Philadelphia on January 8, 1926, and at his request his ashes were dropped by air over the California Memorial Stadium. On the California side of the field an Andy Smith Memorial Bench bears this inscription:

> We do not want men who will lie down bravely to die, but men who will fight valiantly to live . . . winning is not everything. And it is far better to play the game squarely and lose than to win at the sacrifice of an ideal.

Penn State played surprisingly well in 1902 despite the departure during the season of Hewitt, Smith, and Brit Seeley, a regular tackle who had transferred from Dickinson and went back there promising to return to Penn State in 1903 when he was "further prepared in his work." The 1903 campaign, presided over by Coach Dan Reed of Cornell, included a loss to Dickinson (6–0), with Seeley making the winning touchdown. There is no record that he ever returned.

Penn State alumni first gave more than vocal support to the team in 1903 when they were asked to contribute for a building to house athletes, principally football players. The result was the Track House, ready in 1904 with living and dining quarters, a club room, locker rooms for both home and visiting teams, and training facilities. This was the home of major athletes for twenty years.

In 1904 a prosperous era began with the coming from Cornell of the popular and able Tommy Fennell. A 6–4 season in 1904 was followed by one of the best campaigns in history (8–3), with Penn State losing only to the Carlisle Indians (11–0), Yale (12–0), and Navy (11–5). The performance at New Haven was properly applauded by the eastern newspapers, since Yale had one of its greatest elevens (10–0), and was scored upon only by Princeton. Fennell's five-year record (1904–8) was 33–17–1. The 1905 team, captained by Yeckley, included some memorable names—Bill Wray, Bayard Kunkle, Mother Dunn, Irish McIlveen, John Gotwals, Cal Moorhead, and Hi Henry.

From the first official team in 1887 to the close of the "building years" in 1905, Penn State football rosters listed many lettermen who were later outstanding in their professions and in the service of their alma mater. Among them were:

John Price Jackson '89, personnel director, Consolidated Edison Company, New York; dean of the College of Engineering, Penn State; and member of the Board of Trustees.

James C. Mock '90, president, Railway Signal Association, 1904–5; signal engineer, Michigan Central Railroad; chairman, Committee on Standard Designs, Railway Signal Association.

George R. Meek '90, editor and publisher, *Democratic Watchman,* Bellefonte; first graduate manager of athletics at Penn State.

J. Franklin Shields '92, attorney; president of the Board of Trustees, 1929–46.

Charles W. Heppenstall '93, president, Heppenstall Steel Company, Pittsburgh.

Colonel Walter B. McCaskey '96, graduate, U. S. Military Academy; commandant of Penn State's Department of Military Science and Tactics in the early 1930s.

Charles A. Mechesney '98, electrical engineer with the Equitable Gas Company, Pittsburgh.

Ambrose N. Diehl '98, president, Columbia Steel Company, San Francisco; chairman, Penn State Athletic Board of Control.

Arthur S. Shoffstall '00, general manager of Huntington Works, International Nickel Company; named Distinguished Alumnus, 1954.

Fred P. Dodge '03, general manager, Texas Company plant at Port Arthur, Texas; named Distinguished Alumnus in 1959.

William R. Miles '03, electrical engineer with American Smelting and Refining Company, East Helena, Montana.

Andrew L. Smith '05, famed football coach at Penn, Purdue and the University of California.

Colonel John C. Gotwals '06, Army Engineer Corps; Distinguished Service Medal World War I; Army Engineers' commissioner of District of Columbia.

William T. Dunn '07, physician and surgeon, Maui, Hawaii.

V. L. Henry '07, mining engineer for Pittsburgh Plate Glass, Creighton, Pennsylvania; burgess of Tarentum, Pennsylvania, for thirty-two years.

Bayard D. Kunkle '07, General Motors vice president in charge of overseas and Canadian operations, Operations Policy Committee, and member, Board of Directors; established Penn State's Bayard D. Kunkle Loan Fund; named Distinguished Alumnus in 1951.

William Wray '07, district sales manager, Allis-Chalmers Corporation, Pittsburgh; chairman, Penn State Board of Athletic Control.

Penn State's players of 1900–5, continuing to face some of the East's better teams, took the field regularly and eagerly against such all-time greats as Truxton Hare, Frank Piekarski, Vince Stevenson, and Andy Smith of Penn; Yale's "Irish" contingent, with the great Tom Shevlin leading fifteen other All-Americas from there in the six-year period; and Army's Paul Bunker.

Football in the early twentieth century—before drastic rule changes in 1906 altered its direction—was dominated by one of the last vestiges of the mass-formation plays, the "tackles-back tandem," probably originated by Stagg at Chicago in 1894 and refined by Walter Camp. The play was prominent in eastern football, especially in 1900, 1902, and 1905, when the Elis won all of their games except a tie with Army in 1902.

The strength of Yale, Harvard (12–0, 1904), Cornell (12–0, 1901), Princeton (10–0, 1903), and Penn (12–0, 1904) so enthralled eastern experts that they overlooked signs of football resurgence in the Midwest. About the time Harry Williams was putting life into the game at Minnesota, Fielding H. (Hurry Up) Yost started his long reign at Michigan. His famous point-a-minute teams, 1901–5, compiled a super record of 55–1–1, scoring 2,821 points to 42 by opponents, an average of 51.2 points per game. Under Williams, Minnesota tied the Wolverines 6–6 in 1903, deadlocking the Western Conference; Chicago, under Stagg, shockingly upset Yost's team, 2–0, in the final game of 1905. The brilliant Walter Eckersall quarterbacked the victorious eleven. Points for the winning safety were the only ones scored against Michigan that season, and in the Rose Bowl on January 1, 1902, the Wolverines manhandled Stanford, 49–0.

Eastern sportswriters nevertheless continued to be unimpressed. On the all-time All-America team, published by the New York *Evening World* in 1904, every selection was from either Yale, Harvard, or Princeton, except Charley Daly of Army, noticed perhaps because he had once played at Harvard. Walter Camp recognized Willie Heston—Michigan halfback who scored 93 touchdowns in his career—in 1903 and 1904, and Eckersall in 1904 and 1905, but that was all. When Michigan had its greatest team in 1901, Heston qualified for Camp's third eleven, and made it again in 1902. Camp caught up with Adolph (Germany) Schultz in 1907, although he had played on Yost's eleven as center in 1904. Unmentioned anywhere were such Michigan greats as Captain Hugh White (1901), Neil Snow, Dan McGugin, George (Dad) Gregory, and Harrison (Boss) Weeks. In 1920 Grantland Rice selected Heston for his all-time All-America backfield (along with Jim Thorpe, Ted Coy of Yale, and Eddie Mahan of Harvard), and also had Schultz at center.

Part III

ACCEPTANCE AS AN EASTERN POWER

1906–17

11

"Mother" Dunn and "Wrong Way" Cyphers

The "small college" football era came to a close with several meaningful events after 1905, but Penn State ascendancy continued to be a gradual process. The ancient Bucknell rivalry virtually ended after 1910 for sixteen years; the historic and exhilarating Dickinson series closed after Penn State's 1907 victory, 52–0, at Williamsport—the Dickinsonians had had enough. Small Pennsylvania colleges predominated as opponents, but in those days warming up in the early season with "breathers" and scheduling weak teams before the big ones were common practice. No eyebrows were lifted when scores went to 80, 90, even over 100.

The team continued to play Penn annually and Cornell now and then, while Harvard, Dartmouth, and Notre Dame appeared on the schedule for the first time after 1912. With these games growing more competitive, the student press seldom mentioned the moral virtues of close defeats. Initial victories were registered over the Carlisle Indians, in the heyday of their power (1906); Cornell, the alma mater of part-time coach Tommy Fennell (1907); and Penn (first in eighteen games), alma mater of Coach Bill Hollenback (1911).

A Penn Stater first appeared on Walter Camp's All-America team in 1906 with the selection of "Mother" Dunn, center and captain. No others were named until 1919, but a few turned up with some regularity on Camp's second and third elevens: Dexter Very, second-team end in both 1911 and 1912; Eugene E. (Shorty) Miller, third-team quarterback, 1913; Bob Higgins, second-team end, 1915; R. N. (Punk) Berryman, third-team fullback, 1915; and Stan Czarnecki, second-team guard, 1917.

Pete Mauthe, captain and fullback in 1912, later was elected to the National Football Foundation's Hall of Fame (1957). Shorty Miller was posthumously named in 1974, and Dex Very received the honor in 1976. Dick Harlow, tackle in 1910–12, was selected as a coach in 1954, and Higgins, also as coach, in 1954.

Four seasons of unprecedented success, beginning with 1906 (8–1–1), marked this "era of transition." The next three followed the arrival of Coach Bill Hollenback—1909 (5–0–2), 1911 (8–0–1), and 1912 (8–0). Traditionalists like to link the rise in football fortunes with the emergence of Penn State's Nittany Mountain Lion mascot. The suggestion was made in 1907 by H. D. (Joe) Mason '07 in the March 17, 1907, issue of *The Lemon,* a small sub rosa campus publication of which he was the anonymous editor. It caught on almost immediately, but not without some confusion in distinguishing between the Pennsylvania mountain lion species and the maned African king of beasts. By the 1930s the mountain cat won the battle, and the symbol became official in 1942 when the Board of Trustees accepted a sculpture of the Nittany Lion by Heinz Warneke, a gift of the Class of 1940.

Penn State's slow rise in the football world had paralleled its gains as an educational force during President Atherton's administration, the longest in its history (1882–1906). This uninterrupted leadership by a determined president, able faculty, and increasingly enlightened Board of Trustees enhanced its stature as Pennsylvania's representative in the national system of land-grant colleges and universities, then showing the first signs of their great significance.

Identification problems confronting Penn State in intercollegiate athletics were less serious than the difficulty of securing the recognition to which this new kind of public higher education was entitled through the commonwealth's acceptance of the Morrill Land-Grant Act of 1862 and related congressional actions that followed.

The Pennsylvania legislature only slowly yielded assistance as enrollment rose from 150 at the beginning of Atherton's administration to about 800 in 1906, with faculty increasing accordingly. Buildings for engineering and mining, chemistry and the natural sciences, and eventually agriculture began to surround Old Main, but were soon outgrown. Courses of study were grouped into schools with their own deans (1896), and the Preparatory Department waned in importance and passed out of existence after 1906. The liberal arts awaited equality except for their two "laboratories," Penn State's only buildings given by individuals. Charles M. Schwab, the steel magnate and a trustee, presented an auditorium (1903), while Andrew Carnegie, also a trustee, provided a library building after the legislature had agreed to maintain it (1904). Academic excellence received encouragement through scholarships and awards funded by the Carnegies and by James G. White '82.

Because Old Main no longer sufficed as a dormitory, students had the option of living in the town's growing number of rooming- and boardinghouses, often operated by enterprising families to finance the education of their own children. Fraternities evolving from eating clubs built houses to help alleviate room shortages. At this time, some additional campus housing appeared, including the Track House, home of the athletes.

The semiweekly *State Collegian* (1904) superseded *Free Lance,* offering broader and more timely coverage of campus activities along with the town's first newspaper, the weekly State College *Times* (1898). Also in 1898 Penn State Thespians began its unbroken series of annual productions, usually musicals with all-male performers, and the battalion's drum and bugle corps expanded to a cadet band, which became Penn State's famous marching Blue Band. The alma mater—"For the Glory of Old State" by Professor Fred Lewis Pattee—was officially adopted in 1901. In the semicentennial year the Penn State seal was changed to carry the 1855 charter year, instead of the previously used 1859, the opening date.

When President Atherton died in July 1906, worn out by his mushrooming responsibilities, a two-year period of readjustment began, with General Beaver, president of the Board of Trustees and a resident of nearby Bellefonte, performing the duties of acting president. Since he could not supervise the day-to-day operations, a new administrator was appointed as vice president. Dr. Judson P. Welsh, whose title was changed to Dean of the College before he left in 1910, was efficient, but he lacked rapport with the faculty. The students chose this chaotic period to press for privileges of self-government. It began in 1905 when they had walked out of classes in a "great strike" as a protest against rules about class cutting at vacation periods.

This was the framework of unrest when the football team in the fall of 1906 unexpectedly accomplished its finest season to date. Concerned observers feared that the loss of such four-year veterans as Ed Yeckley, Irish McIlveen, Andy Moscript, and other stalwarts could not be overcome, and they had another worry: Could Penn State's players cope with the drastic rule changes of 1906? The addition of the forward pass and enforcement of restrictions against mass formations were expected to give football a completely new look. These resulted from President Theodore Roosevelt's not so gentle prodding of the Rules Committee, which solemnly conferred in New York City on January 12, 1906, to reduce the game's brutality for players and make it more interesting for spectators.

Adopted to "open up" the strategic possibilities of the game, the forward pass was so restricted as to almost neutralize its beneficial effects. For instance, the receiver could not complete a pass thrown more than 20 yards (repealed in 1911); an incompleted pass constituted a foul with a 5-yard penalty (repealed in 1917); a forward pass could not be thrown until the passer ran at least 5 yards to the right or left of the center (repealed in 1910, but the passer had to be at least 5 yards back of the scrimmage line before releasing the ball). In connection with this rule, the field was to be marked every 5 yards *lengthwise,* but the resulting checkerboard gridiron fortunately went out with the repeal of the rule. Finally, if the ball was touched but not caught after a forward pass it could be recovered by either side.

The Rules Committee persisted in discounting the salutary influence of the pass and tried to limit its effectiveness. In 1914, a forward pass going out of bounds after being touched by an eligible player of either side would be awarded to the opponent. The committee also mistrusted the screen pass, apparently associating it with the discredited flying wedge. The screen was developed first by Bob Zuppke (Illinois) at Oak Park High School in 1910, but Bob Folwell (W&J), Dick Harlow, and Hugo Bezdek of Penn State have been credited with perfecting it. This effective pass weapon was counteracted in 1924 by requiring ineligible receivers to keep out of the way of defensive players.

In 1926 a penalty of 5 yards was imposed for all incompleted passes after the first one in a series of downs (repealed in 1934). Until 1938 all passes incompleted in the end zone were considered touchbacks, and the ball went to the defensive team on the 20. After 1938 (until 1941) a fourth down incompletion in the end zone was a touchback.

Only in the mid-thirties were these severe controls on passing relaxed, and probably the most notable instance was a change in the specifications of the football, reducing its circumference. Previously, few passers could actually grasp the ball. In 1945 the passer was no longer required to throw from 5 yards back of the scrimmage line; in 1952 the passer was allowed to use his hands in defending himself. Most of the rule changes affecting the forward pass since 1955 have been relatively minor, in general favoring the passer.

Slow as it was to develop, the forward pass advanced more rapidly than the other "reforms" precipitated by the Roosevelt White House conference. Mass plays lingered because many coaches adroitly devised circumventing maneuvers. In 1906, when the game's existence was in jeopardy, only two major changes alleviated football's savage aspect. One established a neutral zone the length of the football between the offensive and defensive lines. Heretofore the "zone" had been an imaginary line running through the center of the ball, requiring judgment calls by officials and perpetrating nose-to-nose combat that often resulted in mayhem. The other eliminated the effectiveness of the "guards back" and "tackles back" formations by requiring the additional "backs" to be at least 5 yards behind the scrimmage line. The sting had actually been taken out of mass formations in 1904 by requiring six players on the offensive line. The number was increased to seven in 1910, when still another important safety measure abolished interlocking interference and any aid to a runner by pulling or pushing. Further protective rules prohibited hurdling, added a second umpire, and limited each half to thirty minutes.

Most important of the other rule changes adopted between 1906 and 1917 included

1906: Distance required to gain for a first down increased from 5 yards to 10 yards (in three downs); all players except the kicker were onside automatically when punt hit the ground; substitutes required to report to referee before entering game.

1907: One of the two umpires established in 1906 changed to a field judge.

1908: Forfeited game scored 1–0 instead of 6–0.

1909: Field goal value reduced from 4 points to 3 points.

1910: Game divided into four 15-minute quarters; player withdrawn from game permitted to return at end of subsequent period; crawling prohibited.

1912: Teams allowed four downs instead of three to make 10 yards; length of playing field reduced from 110 yards to 100 yards, with 10-yard end zone behind each goal line; kickoff from 40-yard line instead of midfield; value of touchdown set at 6 points instead of 5.

The numerous rule changes in 1912 completed the evolution of American football from rugby. Allison Danzig, noted sportswriter and football historian, points out that a present-day football observer watching a game played in 1912 would see the game substantially as it is played today. The only major differences are the substitution rules that created the two-platoon system, the goal posts 10 yards behind the goal line, and the two-point conversion.

1914: Kickoff following touchback or safety abolished and ball put into play on 20-yard line. (Free kick from the 20 later awarded to team scoring a safety.)

1915: Players required to be numbered.

1917: Substitutes not allowed to communicate with players on the field until after one play.

Among the freshmen on the 1906 squad were two outstanding all-around athletes, both New York City boys who had attended the High School of Commerce. Larry Vorhis and Charles L. (Heff) Hershman were headed for Princeton, and their detour to Penn State has never been explained. Hershman immediately made the varsity at fullback, while Vorhis was the first substitute for Hi Henry, a senior quarterback. Vorhis, who proved that he had few equals as a drop kicker, replaced Andy Moscript, until then considered the best.

Vorhis also became the squad's first known forward passer—a talent especially needed in 1906. Carl Snavely, former Bellefonte Academy coach and later a Penn State nemesis at both Cornell and Bucknell, declared Vorhis the most successful of the early passers he knew anything about.[1] He recalled that the quarterback threw a spiral pass, and his chief target was end Harry E. (Bobby) Burns, captain in 1907.

[1] Allison Danzig, *The History of American Football* (Englewood Cliffs, N.J.: Prentice-Hall, 1956).

The 1906 team blanked every opponent but Yale. The Carlisle Indians, Navy, and Pittsburgh (still WUP) were its principal victims, and the only real blot on an almost impeccable season was an unaccountable scoreless tie with Gettysburg, the first game in which the home team had failed to score a touchdown on Old Beaver Field. Although the local papers did play up statistical superiority, credit deservedly was given to Gettysburg's "valiant defense."

Two weeks later came the annual meeting with Yale, final game in the series. Yale's 1906 team was considered slightly below the standard of its other great elevens of the decade. In the "off" year the Elis had only four All-Americas and were undefeated (but tied by Princeton). New Haven sources intimated that Tad Jones, invincible quarterback, had been injured and would not play, but even with this handicap it isn't likely that the home team took the Penn Staters very seriously, especially after the tie with Gettysburg. Yale still had available a number of all-stars, including Howard Roome, 1905 All-America halfback, and four of Camp's 1906 selections—halfback Knox, end Bob Forbes, fullback P. L. Veeder, and tackle Horatio Bigelow. At the other end was Howard Jones, Tad's brother, who would later win coaching fame at Southern California.

Yale won, 10–0, scoring the only points made all season against Captain Dunn and the tough defense. The record of the 1906 team, coached by the Fennell-Golden combination, was consequential in Penn State's drive for recognition out of the "small college" class. For almost the first time the eastern press, notably in New York and Philadelphia, commented favorably on the team's showing against one of the East's perennial powers. In fact, the slant of much of the coverage indicated that only a few bad breaks prevented a major upset.

A second significant result of the Yale meeting was Penn State's initial breakthrough on Walter Camp's first All-America, still dominated by Yale, Harvard, Princeton, and Penn. Camp, a spectator at the game, was so impressed with Mother Dunn's defensive play that the rangy center won his highest award on the spot, relegating the Yale center, Hockenberger, to the second team.

The Elis scored after about 5 minutes of play when Henry, starting quarterback, failed to cover a punt and Yale's Bigelow picked up the ball to run 35 yards for a touchdown. Knox kicked the goal, and a few minutes later added a field goal, at that time a 4-point play. Handicapped by rainy weather, neither side scored again, but Penn

State had most of the opportunities. Bull McCleary, freshman half-back, bested Yale's Roome in a punting duel. Before the first half ended, Henry and Yale's Arthur Erwin, right guard, were ejected from the game by Umpire Walter Okeson of Lehigh for some rough tactics. In those days the polite term "unsportsmanlike conduct" was not used to cover a multitude of football sins. When a player was tossed out of a game the penalty was generally called "slugging," and no effort was made to conceal the crime. The New York *Sun* described the Henry-Erwin fracas in this manner:

> Henry, quarterback for Penn State, and Erwin, right guard for Yale, were disqualified for slugging. The affair happened after a tackle of Henry. He contends that he was kneed and defended himself. Erwin was hit by two Penn State men and he hammered back most effectively. Morse and Forbes got in the game very briefly, although both wore openwork shoes because of sore feet.

Apparently sensitive about Yale's later accusation of "rough tactics," Penn State released a statement of its official position to eastern newspapers under a State College dateline:

> The recent rumors emanating from New Haven concerning State's rough play against Yale were not considered worthy of reply by State's football authorities. And the recent reports sent from Annapolis to the New York and Philadelphia papers demonstrates very clearly the worth of these New Haven rumors.

The following is clipped from the Philadelphia Press *account of the Annapolis game:*

> "The game was an exceptionally good one and the State College players did nothing to justify the reports of their rough playing sent out from Yale. In fact, the game with State is regarded as one of the most desirable on the Navy schedule on account of the sportsmanlike manner in which the members of the State team play the game."

Henry's exit gave Vorhis an unusual opportunity for a freshman: running the team against an opponent of Yale's reputation. With him as quarterback, the backfield was all-freshman (McCleary, Hershman, and Bob Coulson), and Larry Maxwell, a fifth freshman, played the entire game at right end. Behind a nearly veteran line these rampant yearlings kept Yale on the defensive most of the second half, and had some excellent opportunities to score. Four times, largely through the passing of Vorhis, the fine punting of McCleary, and some loose ball-handling by the Yale backs, Penn State came close enough for field goal attempts. Two were blocked, one went wide, and the fourth, from an almost impossible angle on Yale's 20, hit one of the uprights and bounced wide of the mark. Still another effort to score resulted in a fumble on the Yale 10.

Newspaper accounts noted the surprising performance of the underrated Penn State team and an odd event leading up to the victors' field goal. The Philadelphia *North American* story, headlined "Yale's Luck," said "Yale was outpunted and outpassed, but her teamwork and proverbial luck saved the day." "Luck" referred to one of the strangest and least publicized occurrences in Penn State football history—a "wrong way" incident predating Roy Riegels' famous run in the Rose Bowl by nearly twenty-four years.

Ellis R. (Cy) Cyphers, a strong sophomore guard, made the unfortunate blunder, all but forgotten in a few years. Most sportswriters reported that the visiting team lost the tying touchdown and Yale gained a field goal through Cyphers' confusion. One didn't bother to use the Penn Stater's name, and most of the others misspelled it.

With Yale on its 40-yard line and leading 6–0, Roome's punt was blocked by Captain Dunn, and the ball bounced high in the air. To everyone's amazement, Cyphers caught it, surrounded by teammates, and started for his own goal when the path to a touchdown seemed unimpeded. He said later that the blue jerseys all around him were confusing—he believed they belonged to Yale players and his only thought was to get away from them. Cyphers didn't realize his mistake until he had reached the Penn State 20, then turned around and headed back, but was tackled by Dines, the opposing quarterback. A few plays later Penn State lost the ball, and Yale's Knox kicked a field goal from the 25.

Yale spoiled an undefeated season, but the nine shutouts accomplished in 1906 established a record not yet equaled by a Penn State team. From the Geneva game in 1905 to the Penn game in 1907, its opponents were blanked 18 times in 21 games. Yeckley, Wray, Kunkle, Dunn, Gotwals, Henry, Burns, Cyphers, Maxwell, McCleary, Hershman, Weaver, Gray, and Dick Smith, leading players of this period, all were strong defensively.

Henny Weaver, an especially tough defensive player from Steelton, Pennsylvania, was a few years older than his teammates, to whom he seemed a mysterious stranger. He was said to have a silver plate in his head, the result of a machete wound suffered in the Spanish-

American War, and wore a very high headgear stuffed with anything he could find. Even then, if he'd get hit straight on—and he loved to hit—out he'd go. The trainer would revive him, pick him up, and put him back in position. He seldom would leave a game, and he won four letters from 1907 through 1910.

Before meeting Yale, Penn State had scored its one victory over the Indians in Williamsport, 4–0. The Carlisle team had previously overwhelmed Penn, 24–0. McCleary's field goal (placement) put the game's only points on the scoreboard, and the Indian stars—Mount Pleasant, Exendine, and Little Boy—were held at bay by the powerful defense. With the midseason arrival of Coach Fennell, the team became invincible in its last four games against Navy, Dickinson, West Virginia, and WUP.

Beneficial effects also may have emanated from the Canton Bulldogs, the pro team that came to the campus in early November for special coaching from the highly respected Fennell. This squad included Dave Cure '02 and Lynn Sweet, who attended Penn State briefly and played on the 1901 team. Quartered in Bellefonte, the Bulldogs left after a few days for a game in New York, then returned to prepare for their big rival, Massillon. They won in Canton, 10–5, came back again to get ready for a second date with Massillon, and gave Coach Fennell a gold watch for his assistance.

Fennell was the first Penn State coach to make effective use of the T formation, "old" variety, and his 1906 record reflects this. The line was balanced, the three backs shifting from their regular formation to a tandem, very much like a single wing with the quarterback over the center taking the snap for a handoff to one of the other backs.

The Navy and WUP victories were close but conclusive. The Middies lost only to Penn State and Princeton in 1906, both by 5–0 scores. McCleary's touchdown was set up by Hershman's relentless bombardment of Navy's line in a drive from midfield to the 2. Navy's acting captain, Jonas Ingram, was selected for the Football Hall of Fame in 1968. The season ended for Penn State at Pitt on Thanksgiving Day with another single-touchdown victory. A Pittsburgh paper's lead:

> Six to nothing against our own WUP, a coterie of gentlemanly football players from Bellefonte (sic), a village in the almost exact center of the Commonwealth, yesterday scored as above. The winning touchdown and goal were made by McCleary just 30 seconds before the game ended.

Dunn, center, emerged as the outstanding player on the 1906 team, and all Penn State was overwhelmed when he was named on Camp's All-America first team. The Pittsburgh *Press* All-Pennsylvania eleven included Dunn and John Gotwals, at right tackle. The Pittsburgh *Dispatch* picked Dunn, Burns, McCleary, and Bayard Kunkle, left guard, on its first All-State team.

To earn money for college, William T. Dunn worked for several years in the Youngstown steel mill and, at 22, was probably the heaviest, tallest, and oldest member of his class. Watching him head a group of his fellow freshmen across campus one day, an upperclassman remarked, "There goes Mother Dunn leading his chickens." The nickname stuck, and Penn Staters have never called their first All-America anything but "Mother" Dunn.

Dunn had saved $150 during the summer, but arrived with $75 in his pocket because he gave his mother half, thinking he wouldn't need that much. He did live in the Track House after his freshman year, but earned his other expenses despite winning four letters in football and taking a difficult course in mining engineering. He worked on campus in the McAllister Hall dining room, which he later managed with William H. (Babe) Wood '10. (The two saved enough money to invest in the first State College motion picture theater—the Pastime, on South Allen Street. Wood managed it while Dunn was a medical student at the University of Pennsylvania.)

Mother Dunn had never played football, but had read somewhere about a "flying tackle." On the first day of 1903 practice he tried it with such dexterity that he was made a regular immediately. Today he would be considered too small for a lineman at 190 pounds, but he was sinewy and solid. Because opposing quarterbacks avoided him and he hated not being in the midst of the action, he frequently left his center position to go where he thought the ball carrier would be. He was right so often that he became known as a "roving center" —possibly one of the first in the game.

Walter Camp seemed noticeably attracted by Dunn's personal qualities. Camp's inquiries after the 1906 Yale game revealed that the Penn Stater, who never drank or smoked, was of high moral character and also popular with his teammates, including those less exemplary. This was enough for Camp to know—Mother was "in."

Writing in *Collier's* magazine, Camp said:

> Dunn of Penn State was the best center of the season, and it
> was he who led his team to such a remarkable record, a good

deal of it depending on Dunn himself. He weighs just under 200, is something over six feet in height, and absolutely reliable in his passing, secure in blocking, active in breaking through, and in diagnosing plays. . . . He persistently broke through and blocked kicks. Able to run the 100 in under 11 seconds, he was down under his own side's kicks with the ends. Beyond all and giving him added worth was his earnestness of purpose and character.

Years later Dr. Dunn credited his reputation less to the impression he made on Camp in the Yale game than to being "promoted" by H. D. (Joe) Mason '07, a campus news correspondent. The backing by Mason, a varsity baseball player, who furnished the Tri-State News Bureau in Pittsburgh with Penn State news, unquestionably did build up Dunn's fame.

Instead of going into the steel business, Dunn coached for a year at Harrisburg Academy and then came under the influence of Frank Buchman, who became internationally known as the group leader of the Oxford and Moral Rearmament movements after a stint as general secretary of the YMCA at Penn State from 1909 to 1916. Buchman encouraged Dunn to become a medical missionary in China. The former football captain was admitted to the University of Pennsylvania Medical School and went to Hawaii for his internship. He never got to China, but spent nearly all of his life on the island of Maui as a physician and surgeon, returning to the mainland only once, for a three-year residence in San Diego.

In 1954 Dr. Dunn visited Honolulu to meet Coach Rip Engle and Adam (Bud) Smyser '41, editor of the Honolulu *Star-Bulletin*. They were the last Penn Staters known to have seen Mother Dunn, although he lived to the age of 81, and died at his home on Maui on November 17, 1962.

Exciting prospects for 1907 with the five tested freshmen as a nucleus and eight of the first team returning were unrealized, possibly because the loss of Dunn, Gotwals, and Henry had been underestimated. The 6–4 record was far from satisfying, even though the only drastic defeat (28–0), came from one of Penn's greatest teams, which lost only to the Indians.

The 1907 season brought one upset—victory over Cornell, 8–6, on Ithaca's Percy Field. Larry Vorhis made the difference with a 20-yard drop kick for an early 4–0 lead, and a 40-yard kick, which won the game after Cornell had scored the only touchdown. The *State Collegian* reported with some sarcasm that a "ten minute overtime" had been played "owing to an inexcusable error by Cornell's timekeeper."

The Navy game was lost in the final seconds (6–4) when Bill Dague picked up a fumbled punt and ran 50 yards to score the winning points. Dague, an end, was Navy's first All-America player. A field goal by Vorhis in the first half had put Penn State ahead. The season's dismal end was Pitt's 6–0 victory, which no one could explain. Vorhis had proved a worthy heir to Henry's quarterback job; McCleary scored 13 touchdowns, and Hershman, although out of the final two games through injuries, was reliable for crucial short yardage. Observing the need for a full-time coach, the Athletic Board offered Fennell fifteen hundred dollars if he could spend more time on the campus.

Coach Fennell arrived in 1908 much earlier than usual to supervise another veteran, hopeful squad, headed by Captain McCleary, Cy Cyphers, Alex Gray, Larry Vorhis, Dick Smith (Andy's brother), Heff Hershman, and Henny Weaver. Newcomers were Tom Piollet, a transfer from Cornell, and Vic Ballou, an excellent kicker. Bill Fuhs,[2] a senior previously on the squad, was expected to fill in for Maxwell, who had dropped out of college.

The season, again a disappointment (5–5) except for a 12–6 victory over Pitt, opened with a humiliating defeat by Bellefonte Academy, 6–5. It was a regularly scheduled game—not a practice scrimmage—although Gray at center was the only regular to start. Coach Fennell's subs were ahead 5–0 at half time, and the missed extra point seemed insignificant until the visitors from ten miles down the road scored after a Penn State fumble and kicked the point. The home forces rushed in the varsity, but the prep school team hung onto its lead.

The 1908 team went to Wilkes-Barre for the annual meeting with the Carlisle Indians, playing against the mighty Jim Thorpe for the first and only time. Thorpe was held to unusually low yardage, but accounted for all the Indians' points. Penn State scored first when Weaver converted a blocked kick into a touchdown, and had a 5–4 half-time lead after Thorpe kicked a field goal. Two more Thorpe field goals gave the Indians a 12–5 triumph. Listed in Carlisle's lineup were Little Old Man, Afraid-of-a-Bear, and Little Boy.

Games were lost by close margins to three "name" opponents—Cornell, Navy, and Penn. The Big Red won, 10–4, with a Vorhis

2 William Fuhs '09 of Pittsburgh is the oldest living varsity letterman.

field goal preventing a shutout. The *State Collegian* had a strange explanation for Tom Piollet's absence from the lineup: "Piollet was not in the best of condition, but he did not want to play against his alma mater."

Before the Navy game Coach Fennell switched Vorhis to halfback to replace the injured McCleary and started Burke M. (Dutch) Hermann at quarterback. Penn State made a good showing in its 5–0 loss to an exceptionally strong Navy team (9–2–1), whose stars were Ed Lange, quarterback, and Captain Percy Northcraft, tackle. Earlier in the season the Midshipmen had tied Harvard, 6–6, the only blemish on the Crimson record.

Coach Yost of Michigan with good reason rated Penn's 1908 eleven as the Number One team in the nation—the Red and Blue had swept through Michigan (29–0) and ten other opponents. The only black mark was gray, a 6–6 tie with the Indians. Never having beaten the Quakers and thought to be well out of its class against a team with two brilliant stars in Captain Bill Hollenback (fullback) and Hunter Scarlett (end), Penn State nearly came up with 1908's greatest upset, holding Penn scoreless in the first half. The roaring front line, led by Cyphers, broke through the surprised Penn defenders to block four of Hollenback's punts, all of which the kicking team unfortunately recovered. Ironically, although Ballou consistently outkicked Hollenback, a Ballou punt blocked in the second half allowed tackle Fred Gaston to score the game's only touchdown.

Following the season, Coach Fennell announced that his law practice in Elmira, New York, would not permit him to continue football coaching in 1909. The Athletic Board started its search for a full-time successor—a search that would usher in Penn State's most auspicious football epoch to date.

12

Big Bill Hollenback

One autumn afternoon on Franklin Field in the 1908 game between Penn and the Carlisle Indians, Big Bill fought to a draw with Jim Thorpe, and the 6–6 tie spoiled the Quakers' perfect season. Their sixty-minute rocking and tackling duel sent both fullbacks to the hospital for several days, but each earned the other's respect. Thorpe called Hollenback the "greatest and toughest opponent" he had ever faced.

William M. Hollenback and his brother Jack, predental students at Penn, appear in the Red and Blue squad picture of 1904. Four years later Bill captained a fine Penn team and was nearly everyone's choice for All-America, including Walter Camp's. He hoped to succeed Sol Metzger as Penn's coach, but youth and inexperience were against him, and the job went to Andy Smith, who had been on the coaching staff for three years. Bill accepted instead the Penn State coaching position, requiring him to spend a full three months on the campus. Although he was younger than some members of the Nittany Lion squad, the Athletic Board was delighted to sign Bill because of his reputation as a player, his vibrant personality, and his strong leadership qualities. Another asset, in the Board's opinion, was Hollenback's expressed desire to beat Pennsylvania. "Every coach," he said mildly, "wants to beat his alma mater."

The 1909 season had solid promise when Hollenback arrived to take charge. Bull McCleary, captain in 1908, had returned for another year, along with other veterans—Captain Larry Vorbis, Tom Piollet, Alex Gray, Henny Weaver, Heff Hershman, and Dutch Hermann. The only serious losses were Cy Cyphers, Vic Ballou, and Bill Fuhs. Pop Golden—director of physical training, fill-in coach, and unofficial recruiter—had harvested such future stars as Pete Mauthe, Dex Very, Dad Engle, Dick Harlow, Al Hansen, and Fritz Barrett, younger brother of Cornell's fine quarterback, Charlie Barrett. Fritz, who had played at University School in Cleveland and was considered a potential All-America, spent a year at Pittsburgh before Pop persuaded him to come a little farther East.

A less confident and buoyant young coach might have been disturbed to be named "advisory coach." True to its penchant for "alumni control" and a "wholly Penn State system," the Athletic Board gave the head coach title to Irish McIlveen,[1] a three-letter winner of average ability in football.

With Henny Scholl to complete the staff as an assistant, the setup didn't seem to bother Hollenback. Young as he was, self-assurance made him obviously the boss, and McIlveen's title was regarded as honorary. In 1909 more alumni than ever before responded to the Board's annual appeal for short-term help. On hand from time to time were George McGee '06, E. A. Whitcomb '04, Carl Forkum '05, W. T. Dunn '08, Ed Yeckley '06, and Earl Hewitt '02.

Big Bill had excellent rapport with the players despite having begun to coach when he was only 23 years old. He had played against most of his new charges the year before and may have assumed a sterner attitude to overcome this deficit, causing the players to consider him a "tough guy." A firm disciplinarian on the field, he was scrupulously fair in selecting a starting team—a varsity player had to beat a second-team opponent on the practice field to win his place each week. He insisted on immediate obedience and discipline at all times, allowed no swearing or use of tobacco during off-hours, and he controlled his own language—to some extent. When in-

---

[1] McIlveen, born in Belfast, Ireland, was a fine left-handed college pitcher, whose big-league hopes had been dashed by a short stint in 1906 with the Pirates during which he was knocked out of the box in two starts and made one relief appearance while the Pittsburgh fans chanted unhelpfully, "Get a football." He returned to Penn State to get his degree in mining (1907–08) and made one more try with the American League's New York team. He was listed as an outfielder and pinch-hitter in 1908 and 1909, appearing in 48 games.

furiated by an official, he might be heard muttering to himself, "Oh! you big bum. Oh! you *big bum.*"

Off the field, Hollenback could keep his relations with the players easy and informal, because he was admired as an almost legendary football hero and respected as a person. He lived with the players, socialized with them, and even submitted good-naturedly to their crude humor and sometimes elaborate pranks. During his regime, especially in the first three undefeated years of 1909, 1911, and 1912, the squad was nearly always relaxed, dissension was unheard of, and there were no cliques.

On road trips the players understood that Big Bill would go off with the cronies he seemed to have everywhere, but they knew he'd be on hand for the first practice of the week. If he disappeared, the team would roam the rival campus together. In 1911, up and down the hills of Ithaca they tirelessly sang a song someone had composed. With proper substitution this ditty later was inflicted on Penn, Pitt, and others:

> Goodbye old Cornell,
> Farewell to you,
> Penn State's team
> Is too much for you.
> Each man's a wonder,
> Tried and found true,
> Hang out your tail lights,
> It's all up for you.

Hollenback, six feet, three inches and weighing just over two hundred pounds, was handsome in a rough-cut way and casual about his deserved reputation as a ladies' man. He was said to be equally at home "in the locker room, drawing room, pool room, ballroom, or bar room," but his players always knew when he was "putting on the dog." They were amused when Bill invited Governor John K. Tener and State Senator Boies Penrose, the Pennsylvania political boss, to have dinner with him and the players in the Track House during a campus visit. The unimpressed athletes laughed outright when he said, "Have some of these delicious peas, Governor. They were especially prepared in our kitchen, just for you."

In September of 1909 a fair-haired young man with the face of a choir boy and the competitive instincts of a holy terror appeared for practice, destined to begin a college gridiron career unmatched in

some respects by that of any other Penn State player. Dexter W.
Very had learned the rudiments of the game at the Soldiers' Orphans
Industrial School in Scotland, Pennsylvania,[2] for which he had
qualified because his deceased father was a Civil War veteran. His
athletic ability gave him an opportunity in 1907 and 1908 to attend
Mercersburg Academy, where he was a teammate of the late Admiral John H. (Babe) Brown, Navy All-America in 1913. His coach
was Gus Ziegler, 1907 All-America at Penn and a teammate of
Hollenback's.

Dex was without means to enroll in college like his Mercersburg
classmates who were spreading out over most of the eastern schools,
but he was urged to try for a senatorial scholarship to Penn State—a
place he'd never heard of. Capt. George W. Skinner, the Scotland su-
perintendent and a former state senator, knew General James A.
Beaver, onetime Pennsylvania governor and then president of Penn
State's Board of Trustees. Letters exchanged by Captain Skinner,
General Beaver, College President Edwin Erle Sparks, and W. N.
(Pop) Golden were promising but noncommittal until General
Beaver wrote:

> It seems to me that a Trustee's or Athletic scholarship might be
> worked out for him, which is the most that is done for any-
> body. . . . Many young men in the condition of Very are able
> to help themselves through college by . . . canvassing or doing
> some sort of work in vacation. . . . If Very has the spirit
> which you think he has, I do not think there will be any trouble
> in his getting through.

Golden, director of physical training, investigated the case. The
President then found

> . . . his character is such that we can recommend him for a
> Trustee Scholarship at the opening of College in September.
> This means that he must satisfy the entrance requirements and
> will then be recommended to the Board of Awards who will ex-
> amine him with reference to his habits.

Dex was to report on September 13 for football practice, and also
write to Golden if he had any questions, but he arrived a week late
because he wanted to visit his mother after the year's absence.
Someone guided him to temporary quarters on the fourth floor of Old
Main. The next morning he found Pop Golden, who greeted him
with "You're not very big, are you?" and then turned him over to

[2] Now The Scotland School for Veterans' Children.

J. M. (Muckle) McKee '10, football manager that season. When he was finally introduced to Coach Hollenback, Very, never shy, told him they had met before. Looking hard at the freshman, the coach snorted—a habit of his—and Very explained that Gus Ziegler had been his Mercersburg coach and that his team had once practiced on Franklin Field. From then on Dex was Hollenback's "pet," or so the players thought, but none resented it because of the newcomer's complete dedication to the game. Very was quickly assigned to the Track House and remained there for four years.

Next afternoon Dex, uninformed about equipment procedure, reported to the practice field in his old Mercersburg uniform. Hollenback, McIlveen, and Scholl had already started heavy work with the squad, and no one noticed the blond youngster, who weighed only 150 pounds. The players were lined up to run down under punts. It was no dummy scrimmage—they were tackling. Watching from the sideline, Very was unimpressed and finally joined the line, uninvited. When his turn came, encouraged to note that the receiver was no larger than himself, he went full speed downfield and made a clean tackle before the receiver had taken a step. His adversary was Dutch Hermann, backup quarterback for Captain Larry Vorhis and later esteemed in Penn State athletic history. Repetitions of this performance convinced the observant Hollenback that he was watching something special. He had Very run along in back of the varsity to "learn the system," and in a few days the freshman was on the first team.

Dex established the remarkable four seasons record—still unequaled—of starting every game at his right-end position, except for a few times in the backfield. In major games with Navy, Penn, Pitt, Cornell, Ohio State, and the Indians, he played 60 minutes. In others he gave way reluctantly for a substitute a few times in the fourth quarter. He was never removed for injury or fatigue, and during his four-year career Penn State lost only 2 games in 32. His top weight was 162 pounds; he survived on speed, mobility, and fierce competitive instinct.

Another newcomer on the squad made a less propitious beginning. Al Hansen, from Central Manual Training School in Philadelphia, had a fine high school athletic record and the appearance of an athlete, but was an obviously cocky freshman. The incident that took him nearly three years to live down and almost ruined his career occurred when he was introduced to Alex Gray, who would be team captain the following year. Hansen spoke with a slight lisp, which made the following exchange even more difficult for his teammates to forget:

HANSEN: So your name is Gray, is it?
GRAY (courteously): Yes, that's my name.
HANSEN: You play center, don't you?
GRAY: Yes, I try to.
HANSEN: Well, you better go out for guard this year, because I'm going to play center.

Poor Hansen had a hard time with Hollenback, too. Bill was irritated most when anyone stood around while an opponent was still on his feet. He'd yell in practice: "Damn it, knock somebody down, knock anything down, knock Old Main down, for godsake." One afternoon early in Hansen's career, Bill went after him so relentlessly that Al set forth downfield almost in panic. Larry Vorhis, hit from behind, had to be taken to the bench. Bill was enraged. "Damn it, I didn't say cripple the best player I've got." Al was sent off the field, didn't make a letter until his junior year (1911), after Gray had graduated, but developed into an excellent lineman and one of the mainstays of the 1912 team.

In 1909, Very and another first-year student, halfback Pete Mauthe, played almost the entire opening game—the first on the recently constructed New Beaver Field—with Grove City losing, 31–0. The two freshmen shared financial problems. Very, living in the Track House with the varsity, hadn't heard a word about his "scholarship," while Mauthe was working as a janitor in the players' living quarters. On the train to the Indian game in Wilkes-Barre, Very revealed to another player that he'd have to drop out of school by Christmas. Overhearing the conversation, Assistant Coach Scholl must have reported to Hollenback, because both Very and Mauthe promptly received "class scholarships" from funds appropriated by the several classes.

The Indian game drew a large number of students and alumni from the area. George Ogilvie '10, head cheerleader, provided several hundred printed songbooks and wrote a special cheer for the occasion:

> We've come to beat the Indians
> Hoo Ray, Hoo Ray
> It seems a shame to take the game
> But this is Penn State's day.

See how they play around you
Hoo Ray, Hoo Ray
It's a joke, State's got your goat
Hip, Hip, Hoo Ray.

Penn State players had been cautioned to "tackle any Indian with a hump on his back" because Coach Hollenback hadn't forgotten the famous "hidden-ball play." When the two teams lined up for the first scrimmage, Very found himself opposite an old friend, Indian left end Newashe, who stood up and called to the Indian left tackle: "Hey, Wauseka, here's Dex." The three met first when Very had played for Scotland against the Carlisle juniors, and again when the Indian JVs played Mercersburg. It was a great reunion until Captain Vorhis yelled to Very, "Come on, freshman, let's get on with the game."

The Indians led 6–0 at half time on a 40-yard touchdown run by Hauser and Libby's goal, but Penn State scored early in the second half after two 15-yard runs by Dick Smith. A try for the extra point by Captain Vorhis hit an upright, but later he kicked a 20-yard field goal to give his team an 8–6 margin, good until near the end when he made one of the few mental errors of his career. Libby's field goal attempt was wide and the ball rolled into the end zone. Vorhis picked it up instead of downing it, running with it, or kicking it—the options available to him. He was tackled by Wauseka, and the Indians tied the game, 8–8, on a safety.

Rough play brought many penalties to both sides, three players were ejected for slugging, and the crowd of 10,000 was often unruly. At the finish, in an argument about who should have the football for a trophy, it was slapped out of the hands of an Indian player trying to take off with it. Wauseka, Dex's friend, jumped the would-be retriever and a free-for-all began, with spectators taking part. State troopers eventually restored order, but to this day no one knows who got away with the ball.

Coach Hollenback, in his first season, became a victim of his own strictly enforced discipline. A few days before the 1909 Penn game, fullback Heff Hershman, a senior, had the misfortune to meet Bill downtown. Heff had a sizable chaw in his mouth. Well aware of the tobacco taboo, he tried to conceal it while sputtering about having to go up to Ag Hill. Not fooled, Bill went along to plague Heff. About 100 yards up campus, Heff choked, "Damn it, Bill, I can't hold it any longer," and out came the whole mouthful at the foot of the Old Willow.

Much as he wanted to win the Penn game, Hollenback kept his star fullback out, moved Vorhis over to fullback, and started Dutch Hermann at quarterback. Bill relented only when Hermann was injured well into the second half. Hershman entered the fray and Vorhis moved back to quarterback, but some observers felt that Heff's presence throughout might have turned the 3–3 tie into a Penn State victory.

Bill didn't share the general satisfaction with the tie: "This is the last time Penn State will come to Franklin Field without a victory," he told reporters grimly. Most backers considered it a great achievement, remembering that fifteen previous trips to Philadelphia had ended in fifteen defeats, many by substantial margins. City papers had a different slant. Penn lost only one game that year (to Michigan, 12–6), and the Red and Blue was constantly trying to uphold its prestige as a member of the East's Big Four. The Philadelphia *Press* put it this way:

> Penn was battling against conditions such as a Red and Blue eleven had seldom faced. With a veteran team, coached to meet the Penn attack, State came down to Franklin Field determined to win. And that the Quakers, outweighed and handicapped by injuries, held Hollenback's charges at almost every point, is a tribute to the spirit which has carried the Red and Blue to victory in so many former gridiron warfares.

Reporters did give Coach Hollenback credit for putting "more dash and vim into the State College eleven than has been seen here in years." They praised Vorhis and Mauthe (for his punting and kick returns), and said Hermann, "the little quarterback who was carried from the field only after he had fallen in sheer exhaustion, gave an exhibition which could be inscribed upon the histories of gridiron conquests in State College." Hermann's "exhaustion" came about from a kick in the head, off the playing field. The guilty player was ejected from the game. His team was penalized 25 yards.

Penn's quarterback, Alex Thayer, tallied first after a scoreless half, drop-kicking 22 yards from a sharp angle when a short kick by Mauthe had gone out of bounds on the 25. Hermann's injury forced Hollenback to use Hershman, and Heff gained effectively against Penn's hitherto stingy defense, but the score wasn't tied until Gray

blocked a punt, allowing Captain Vorhis to drop-kick a field goal
from the 23.

Quick thinking by Very denied Penn an opportunity to win in the
closing minutes. Noticing that Thayer, about to try another field
goal, would be kicking from a sharp angle directly over his head,
Dex called to McCleary: "Hey, Bull, take my place in the line.
You're bigger, and I think you can block it." The skeptical McCleary
complied, warning, "You better be sure to cover the outside for an
end run." McCleary blocked the kick and saved the day. Coach
Hollenback's coaching philosophy showed after the game when he
heard some joshing about a "freshman shooting off his mouth."
"Look here," he said, "no freshman on this team has to keep his
mouth shut—except when I'm talking. If he has anything to say he
should say it, because he's on the team."

Fans at home listening to the telephone returns in the Old Chapel
were excited. More than one thousand snake-danced through campus
and town in a pouring rain. Prexy Sparks granted the recess they
demanded to greet the team on Monday, since the greeting was to
take place after compulsory chapel exercises. Then the entire student
body of 1,500 formed ranks in the auditorium and marched downtown to meet the returning heroes. One of the players, responding to
the cheering welcomers, noted that Penn State and Penn would get
"credit" for being the first colleges in the country to play a 3–3 tie.
The strange claim was probably valid, since this was the first season
for a new scoring rule giving the field goal a three-point value.

Penn State closed out its 1909 season with a victory over Pitt
(5–0) in the new Forbes Field, built by Barney Dreyfuss and
dedicated in June of that year. Previously the old Exposition Park
field had been the site of the Thanksgiving Day game. Penn Staters
little guessed how many dismal defeats would be suffered in Pittsburgh's Oakland section through 1924, with a few notable exceptions. In 1909 Pitt claimed a moral victory, since the predicted score
had been lopsided in favor of Penn State. The home team was held
without a first down in the opening half, but fought hard defensively,
twice holding the winners for downs a few yards from the goal line.

Conversion from a baseball diamond to a football gridiron wasn't
as skillful in those days as it is today, and the visitors' claim that they
seemed to be running uphill was partly justified. Hershman's fine
running on the mushy field late in the second quarter accounted for
the game's only score. He nearly broke away for a long gain, but

after 22 yards ran into the umpire and lost his footing. Short gains by Hershman and Mauthe enabled McCleary to score from the 2, but Mauthe missed the extra point. Near the end, reported the *State Collegian,* "Larry Vorhis's field goal attempt was a good one, but there was too much wind and the ball fell short."

Celebrating the victory that night in Pittsburgh, Dex Very and Pete Mauthe made a solemn pact to share the Penn State captaincy when the time came. Exactly as agreed, Very got it in his junior year, and Mauthe in 1912.

James Lester Mauthe, generally regarded as the best two-way full-back (or halfback) in Penn State's early football history, is one of its noteworthy figures. Tough physically, and tough-minded, a hard-hitting back of multiple abilities, Pete was a dependable ground-gainer in crises, outstanding defensively, and an excellent place-kicker, punter, and blocker, as well as one of the period's best passers. A graduate in metallurgy, Mauthe would reach the top in a competitive business not least because he was fearless and never dodged obstacles.

"Dex Very played football because he loved it," Mauthe said many years later. "I played because I had to." His immigrant parents of German origin were poor. They had a store in Turkey City, Clarion County, Pennsylvania, and later moved to Falls Creek in Clearfield County. Young Mauthe attended high school in DuBois where he met Ed Yeckley, once Penn State football captain, who persuaded him to enroll.

Rating Pete Mauthe against today's fullbacks would be difficult because he played 60 minutes, offense and defense. His one weakness might have been inconsistency as a punter, but he was among the few passers of his time who could get his fingers around the oversized football—most of the others palmed it. The Mauthe-to-Very passing combination, amazingly successful even with the restrictions placed on this weapon, predated Knute Rockne-Gus Dorais by a season, but never received the recognition of the Notre Dame pair, who gained fame with a dramatic victory over Army. Mauthe was most effective as a long passer, with the fleet Very as his chief target, but the long pass wasn't legalized until their final year, 1912.

Mauthe scored 119 points in 1912 and gained 710 yards by rushing. His 51-yard placement against Pitt in 1912 was a Penn State record until 1975, when Chris Bahr kicked three from the 55. Mauthe's record of eight field goals in one season (1912), equaled by Al Vitiello in 1970, also was broken by Bahr, but Mauthe is one of six Penn Staters to kick three or more in one game. His career total of 171 points and career extra points (56) were once records, and he was the first Penn State player to be elected to the Football Hall of Fame (1957).

Mauthe worked up through the ranks to become president of the Youngstown Sheet and Tube Company, and retired as chairman of its Board of Directors. He was named a Distinguished Alumnus of the University in 1969, and served on the Board of Trustees from 1938 until his death in January 1967, at the age of 76.

By defeating West Virginia and Pittsburgh in 1909, Penn State won the mythical title of an unofficial "Big Five" league concocted by Pittsburgh area newspapers, and also including W&J and Carnegie Tech. All members of the starting eleven were selected on one of the three All-Western Pennsylvania teams. First: McCleary, halfback; Very, end; Smith, tackle; Gray, guard; Vorhis, quarterback. Second: Piollet, end; Pete Johnson, guard; Watson (J. E. "Burley"), center; Mauthe, halfback; Hershman, fullback; Third: Weaver, tackle.

Late in November, in the overall eastern standings, which featured a "rating system" established by a columnist ("Linesman") on the Philadelphia *North American,* Yale was put in first place; Harvard, second; Lafayette, third; and Penn State, fourth. Centre County papers endorsed this initial breakthrough, but the next month, when the home team had slipped to fifth and Dartmouth moved up to fourth, the *Democratic Watchman* (Bellefonte) said:

> If State has any reason for being fifth she has just as good reason for being third in the standings. Neither Lafayette nor Dartmouth are any better on paper and we have felt all season that the former would not have been as good had she met State on the field.

From 1906 through 1909 Yale and Harvard upheld the Big Four's early prestige in the East, if not nationally, and Penn's fine 1908 team added to the "old line" domination. In 1906 Penn State almost broke the monopoly, but not quite. A new name briefly entered the national picture when St. Louis University won its eleven games and became the first team to use the forward pass with distinction.

Another "outsider," Auburn University, won all of its six games in 1908 and held opponents scoreless. On the West Coast the University of Washington under Gilmour Dobie started an unequaled string of unbeaten seasons extending from 1908 through 1916. Dobie, first coach to be called "Gloomy Gus," won 58 games in this span and tied 3 (Washington State, Oregon, and Oregon State). His 1916 record was marred by a scoreless tie with Oregon, where the coach was Hugo Bezdek. Coach Dobie brought Cornell to the top in the early 1920s.

13

Penn Syndrome Vanquished

Elated students and players were grateful to Bill Hollenback, who had accomplished a rarity in football—an undefeated season in his first year of coaching. They were keenly disappointed, therefore, by the news that he would not be around for the 1910 season because he had accepted an offer from the University of Missouri to replace Bill Roper, who was later to gain national fame as Princeton's coach. Hollenback may have felt that there was more future at Missouri, but perhaps there was more in the present, too: It was rumored that he would receive considerably more money than he did at Penn State.

The claim of Bill's friends that his Missouri contract was for only one year and that he fully intended to return gained credence when he convinced the Athletic Board to hire his brother Jack as the 1910 coach. Some interpreted bringing in Brother Jack as a "ploy" to facilitate a possible return.

John C. Hollenback, a year or so older than Bill, had played football briefly at Penn and received his degree in dentistry. He decided to give coaching a try and was hired by Franklin and Marshall. In those days youthful coaches, who had played under the revised rules of the increasingly complicated game, gained favor for this added competence.

Jack resembled Bill physically and had some identical mannerisms. He even talked like Bill. Despite these similarities and his experience at F&M, Penn State's players were uncomfortable with him. More hurt than anyone else by Bill's desertion, they considered Jack an interloper attempting to get by on his brother's reputation.

Jack Hollenback made the further mistake of trying to imitate Bill's "blackboard talk" before a game. Shorty Miller—a freshman in 1910—often mimicked him at the team's reunions. "Now you ends going down the field, clip your men hard—something which has not been done heretofore. Things are getting pretty serious, and from now on it's a proposition of dog eat dog and all friendship ceases."

Chances are some squad members played below their capacities in 1910, obviously not trying to help in an unhappy coaching situation. A good year had been anticipated with a strong group returning from 1909, but the loss of Vorhis, Hershman, McCleary, and Smith hurt more than had been expected. The initial impression that a newcomer—Eugene Ellsworth Miller—wasn't big enough to play on a college team was soon forgotten. Shorty held the varsity quarterback job for four years and earned lasting esteem as one of Penn State's first great running backs.

The "other" Hollenback had considerable help from "alumni assistants" who could almost form a team of their own at times. Henny Scholl was present for most of the season, and others drifted in and out for a week or more prior to the games with Bucknell, Penn, and Pitt—Fred Heckel '99, Eddie Wood '04, Bull McCleary '10, and Dutch Hermann '12, who had dropped out of college for a year. The team lost to Penn and Pitt, the only strong opponents on the schedule, and also was held to a scoreless tie by Villanova.

Penn State was expected to be without the manpower to handle Penn, which finished the season with a 9–1–1 record. After unbelievably dropping their opening game in 1910 to Ursinus (6–5), the Quakers were unscored on except by Cornell (defeated 12–6) and were held to a scoreless tie by Michigan. Adding to new Coach Hollenback's woes, Mauthe broke his ankle in the season's second game, with Carnegie Tech, and was out for the year. It wasn't known that Very had strained the ligaments in his ankle before the Penn game—the only injury of his career. He played the entire game, but without his usual dash. Under the circumstances, losing to Penn 10–0 was viewed as an achievement, even by the Philadelphia press.

Steady rain and a soggy field handicapped the speedy freshman quarterback, Shorty Miller, as much as anyone, but Penn thought the weather conditions were more to its disadvantage. The home team scored both its touchdowns in the first half—one after a fumbled punt—and the most exciting play was a 95-yard sprint by Miller on a punt return that was called back because an official ruled that Shorty had stepped out of bounds early in the run. Two other scoring opportunities misfired in the second half, once when Dad Engle, playing halfback for the disabled Mauthe, failed three times to make the distance from Penn's 2-yard line. The Penn State *Alumni Quarterly* reported that

> . . . Engle was undoubtedly over the line, but the swaying mass of players settled back with the ball just half a foot from the line.

Penn State stayed in Penn's territory 22 minutes of the second half (12½-minute quarters), but once had to hold the Red and Blue for downs on the three. Accounts of the game in Philadelphia were highly complimentary to Burley Watson, center; Tom Piollet, end; Captain Alex Gray, guard; and Miller. Pennsylvania fans apparently were more nonchalant about the game than the visitors from State College. At any rate, our band "beat" their band, it appears. The *Alumni Quarterly*'s added comment:

> The work of the band and the students who went down on the "special" gave Penn her first real insight with the State spirit. The cheering was more consistent and voluminous after we were 10 points behind than any time before, and our band had the Red and Blue musicians so frightened that they failed to report for duty at all.

The annual Thanksgiving Day Pitt game drew 18,000 to Forbes Field, the largest football crowd so far in Pittsburgh. Again the opposition was red hot—the 1910 Panthers were undefeated in nine games. The Nittany Lions held them closer than any other team, but even in those days only a victory could be an adequate finale. Over 300 yards in penalties were assessed by the officials, more than 200 against the visitors. Hube Wagner and Captain Tex Richards fought for the Panther touchdowns, and Penn State nearly scored after a 45-yard run by Very, but the home team held for downs on the 2 to protect its record of not giving up a point in the season.

A loss to Pittsburgh traditionally lengthens the cold winters around Mt. Nittany. The winter of 1910–11 became less grim when rumors circulated that Big Bill Hollenback would return in the fall of

1911. At Missouri, Bill had a tough act to follow in replacing Roper, who had led the Tigers to an undefeated conference championship season in his single year (1909). Although Hollenback lost only to Nebraska in a 5–1–2 year, he wanted to get back East where his friends were, and Penn State's Athletic Board eagerly made him an offer. The eagerness didn't extend to giving him the title of "head coach," yet he apparently was unconcerned about being "advisory coach" under Bull McCleary. Outwardly the two were good friends and roomed together in the Track House, but old-timers say that Bull, expecting to be more than a figurehead, was displeased when the Board gave Bill the head coach title in 1912.

Among the bevy of assistants in 1911 was the Reverend Robert R. (Bob) Reed, a former Princeton player who was college chaplain from 1910 to 1915. Alumni on hand for a week or more included Henny Weaver, E. K. Wood, Carl Forkum, and Mother Dunn.

The moment Bill Hollenback arrived, campus enthusiasm reached new heights, building a momentum for winning football that carried through two seasons. The experienced squad awaiting the prodigal coach was an important factor. For the first time Penn State was discovering what can happen when individuals merge into a team under a popular full-time leader. Personnel losses from 1910 had been light (Gray, Piollet, Watson, Johnson, and Weaver), and two outstanding veterans remained from Hollenback's undefeated 1909 team—Dex Very (captain in 1911) and Pete Mauthe, along with the capable Fritz Barrett, Dad Engle, Dick Harlow, and Al Hansen.

Dutch Hermann, who had understudied Larry Vorhis in 1909, returned for his final year, hoping that experience would give him an edge over other quarterback candidates. Sophomore Shorty Miller, however, wasn't to be dislodged, and Hermann had to continue as a backup, exceedingly valuable to the team as an excellent passer and kicker. Two sophomores who had lettered as freshmen—Al Wilson, end, and Red Bebout, guard—and John B. Clark, a substitute center on the 1910 team, were to develop rapidly into valuable regulars. R. N. (Punk) Berryman, a freshman, soon made the starting team at halfback and also became a replacement for Mauthe at fullback in midseason.

Attracting most attention that fall was another newcomer, Levi Lorenzo Lamb. Rumors of special inducements offered him to transfer from Grove City, where he had played for three years (after two seasons at California Normal), caused much interest, particularly among the veterans. He had an impressive physique, stood six feet, four inches in height, and weighed about 200 pounds—excellent statistics for a back of that day. At Grove City he had played guard, center, and fullback, participating also in track and basketball. Levi Lamb's nine-year athletic career at three institutions undoubtedly raised some eyebrows. He had four seasons of football, track, and wrestling at Penn State, where the single enforced eligibility rule, passed by the Athletic Board in May 1911, merely stated that a student must not represent the college for more than four years.

Bill Hollenback, impressed with Lamb at first practice, decided to make him a halfback. When contact work started, the newcomer displayed his ability as an open-field runner—he could run the 100 in 10 flat. He embellished punt receptions with extra-fancy stepping, cutting back and forth, and stiff-arming. The veterans put him down as a showoff, but he looked good to the two coaches, who watched every move. As they walked back to the Track House after practice, the following was heard

> HOLLENBACK: "Hey, Bullick, what do you think of that big steer out there?"
> McCLEARY: "He's big."
> HOLLENBACK: "Hell, he's not only big, he's good. All we've got to do is turn that big steer loose, pick up the water bucket, and go in and collect our paychecks."

The upperclassmen's reaction was "Show me." Newcomers—especially transfers—were job competitors for their bread and butter, and some of the varsity acted with cruelty more common in the pro ranks today. Dad Engle and Dick Harlow appointed themselves to give the big guy the business. As Lamb started his prance up the field, one of the big tackles hit him high and the other low with a ferocity not usually found in practice. In the crash, heard from one end of the field to the other, poor Levi's headgear flew off and the ball went the other way. The victim sat up, then tumbled over again—out cold. Engle and Harlow walked on, not bothering to look back. Lamb wasn't seriously hurt, but only gradually regained his broken spirit. Hollenback, sensing he'd be of little use as a running back, changed him to tackle and he developed into a good lineman, but he didn't letter in 1911.

Lamb actually achieved most of his athletic fame as a wrestler, losing only twice in 21 matches. He dropped the first to a Cornell man and the other in his senior year (1915) to Mike Dorizas, Penn's "mighty Greek," who had never been beaten. Ironically, Lamb's most publicized athletic achievement at Penn State was a losing one. Dorizas, shorter than Lamb, outweighed him by twenty pounds. Lamb appeared to carry the fight to his opponent and showed great courage, but could not overcome the weight and strength of Dorizas and was pinned in 3:30, after an early advantage. One of Penn State's first all-around athletes of his time, Lamb won over thirty first places in track meets from 1912 through 1915, competing in the dashes, hurdles, and nearly all the field events.

Serving as a lieutenant with Company K, 9th Infantry, 2nd Division in France during World War I, Levi Lamb was killed while leading his platoon during the Allied advance south of Soissons, on July 18, 1918. Penn State's athletic grant-in-aid fund was named in his honor many years later.

James D. (Red) Bebout, another lineman from 1910 through 1913, also lost his life in France. With the 318th Infantry Regiment, Lieutenant Bebout was killed on September 29, 1918, on the northern edge of the Bois de Brieulles. He was in charge of a platoon of volunteers on a dangerous mission and was shot down by German machine-gun fire.

The backgrounds of two "mystery men" on the 1911 squad—Philip Aloysius Barry and Francis Xavier King—weren't questioned until the Penn game, when Philadelphia newspapers claimed that Coach Hollenback had "stolen" them from Penn. It was revealed that both had played on Penn's 1910 freshman team and that King had previously attended Villanova. Matriculation complications prevented the two transfers from playing in the first two games in 1911 against Geneva and Gettysburg, but King started at Cornell, and both were in the lineup against Villanova and Penn, King having the experience of playing against his other two "alma maters." Both vanished after the Pitt game, but they are listed in the Penn State *Alumni Directory* (published in 1936) without addresses and also show up in the football brochures as varsity letter winners in 1911.

After their first two easy victories, the Nittany Lions traveled to Ithaca, bent on showing eastern football writers that they belonged in the company of the best. Their statistical margin over Cornell was wide, but frustration harassed Coach Bill's charges, who were referred to in the Philadelphia accounts as the "Little Quakers," much to their disgust.

Against Cornell, the usually sure-footed Mauthe missed four field goal placements. In the second quarter Harlow blocked a punt after the Big Red had held for downs on its own 15. Engle picked up the ball to score the only points of the game, won by Penn State, 5–0. Harlow blocked another punt, but this time the ball was recovered by Cornell. Hermann replaced Miller at quarterback in the last period, directing the team on a good drive, with Mauthe scoring an apparent touchdown. An official's decision that Hollenback had "coached from the sidelines" nullified the score. Big Bill, of course, was furious.

"The Penn game," for years something special to Penn State students and alumni, usually inspired the Nittany Lions to perform over their heads on Franklin Field. In 1911 the tradition of excellence at Philadelphia had yet to become firmly established, for in 17 previous games Penn State had salvaged only one tie (in 1909). But the background of failures didn't disturb Captain Very and his cohorts. Reminiscing, members of the 1911 and 1912 elevens invariably declared that the prospect of defeat never occurred to them—they expected to win every game. Faith in their ability was shared by Coach Hollenback, from whose own intrepid spirit much of it stemmed.

Bull McCleary, in his new capacity as "head coach," had to make a statement to the press after the squad arrived at its White Marsh Country Club headquarters. His remarks, quoted in the late-evening papers, combined some of the players' aplomb with the restraint typical of most coaches—then and now—before a big game:

> We think we have a strong team and the fact that the student body has come down 600 strong shows that we have confidence behind us. Even if we don't win, which we expect to do, Penn will not win by a big margin.

The traveling squad in 1911 was perhaps less than half the size of today's, while the "official party," almost negligible by comparison, consisted of two coaches, the graduate manager, one student manager, a team physician or trainer, and possibly an assistant manager if he could hide on the train beyond reach of the ticket taker. The party went to Lemont in horse-drawn hacks, then to Philadelphia on the old Pennsy railroad, and finally to within walking distance of the club by trolley. Players carried their own luggage and equipment.

Early arrivals from State College found the papers full of the game, making a big thing of the "family feud" involved because of Coach Hollenback's previous ties with Penn and his efforts to become head coach at his alma mater. Bill dismissed these allegations, admitted having been interested in the post, but noted that Bob Folwell, who had preceded him at Penn by a year and later did become coach (1916–19), was much more in the running.

The mysterious Barry and King got even more space. One paper, claiming both had "flunked out" of Penn, chided Penn State for accepting them and ignoring the one-year residence rule. The Philadelphia *Evening Bulletin* took to allegory:

> One morning those who sleep in West Philadelphia awoke and lo! When all the noses were counted, two young braves, Barry, one of the best line crackers and end runners, and King, a lad of great fleetness of foot, were missing. Then a strange thing came to pass. It was learned that mail addressed to them as halfbacks on the State team would find them in their afternoon residence. Penn was startled, also peeved, but true to the motto of Ben Franklin, she made no mention of the matter. King and Barry will be in the lineup against Penn.

There was little or no mention of the "Andy Smith story," which could have been a fascinating companion piece to the Barry-King features. Smith was then Penn's coach. In 1902 and 1903 the newspapers had been filled with explanations, accusations, justifications, and recriminations concerning the transfer of the great star from Penn State to Penn. The 1902 incident was reopened in 1903 when Harvard threatened to break off relations with Penn if Smith played against the Crimson. As a result, he was declared ineligible for the remainder of the season because it was alleged that he had played a few games for Penn State after officially enrolling at Penn. A statement that Smith had been in good standing when he left for Penn and that his transfer had been properly handled quelled the uproar temporarily. Nevertheless, *McClure's* magazine later published a grossly inaccurate "exposé," and Penn authorities, trying to get an extra year of eligibility out of Smith, further beclouded the issue by claiming that he could continue to play because "at State College, where Smith had prepared, four years is only equivalent to three at Penn." Penn State's student press denounced this heresy in a pointed, defensive editorial.

Estimates of student attendance at the 1911 Penn game ranged from 600 to 800. Several hundred who remained at home jammed Old Chapel on the first floor of Old Main to hear the "returns." According to the *State Collegian,* Penn State was the first college to get the results of a football game by wireless. The quarter scores were phoned from Franklin Field to the Marconi Station in Wanamaker's, and from the Philadelphia store the operator forwarded the report to the new college wireless station, to be relayed to the campus gathering. Professor N. M. Slaughter of the Electrical Engineering Department was in charge of the transmittal. Additional information came via a special telephone hookup to Philadelphia.

Before Old Chapel was completely filled, a wireless message reported a score of 6–0 in favor of Penn State. A tremendous roar went up, despite fear of some mistake—the game could hardly have begun. Next, an excited assistant manager ran out on the stage to pass the word, received by telephone, that Shorty Miller had scored on the opening kickoff—a 95-yard run. This time, the din was terrific.

Shorty had indeed stunned Penn partisans by catching the kickoff on his 15 (the field was still 110 yards long in 1911) and running through the startled Quakers. Many years later Bill Hollenback said Pop Warner had given him Miller's scoring kickoff play. All you had to do, Bill explained, was knock everybody down. Actually, the stocky Miller added his own touches to dazzle and befuddle his opponents, squirming through tacklers, twisting, and sidestepping. A number of Quakers had a shot at him—Dollin, Fisher, Jourdet, and Bell. The last man in his way, Captain Roy Mercer, was bowled over by Dex Very. Only one other player had previously scored against Penn on the opening kickoff—Ed (Kidney) Bray of Lafayette, in 1899. The irony from the Penn viewpoint was that the home team had won the toss and had chosen to kick off to Shorty Miller!

Curious about the commotion coming from Old Chapel, five coeds (not more than fifty were then enrolled) who were strolling past Old Main, timidly entered the nearly all-male sanctuary during a lull when another message was being read. Shorty had scored again! A few minutes after his first touchdown, the "Meteoric Midget" from Harrisburg broke loose for a 32-yard sprint and his second touchdown. The young ladies were almost blown from their seats by the greatest vocal explosion ever heard on the campus. They decided to stay, and never forgot the experience.[1]

Penn Staters—an estimated thousand of the 15,000 spectators—enjoyed the shocked dismay of Penn's supporters. The 1911 Quakers

[1] Two of the girls were Nan and Mary Bailey (Mrs. Henry O. Schultz), sisters from Titusville, Pennsylvania.

weren't outstanding (7–4), but they had won five of six games before the Penn State encounter. Their fans, accustomed to demolish-
ing their "country cousins," had taken another victory for granted.

Penn State's cadet band gave a fifteen-minute pregame show
headed by Andy Lytle, an elderly State College citizen popular for
his friendly generosity toward students. Penn Staters considered him
a good-luck omen, although he claimed to have attended every
Penn-Penn State game since 1892 without ever seeing his favorites
prevail. After marching around the field and playing Brooks' "Tri-
umphal March" in front of the Penn State cheering section, the
bandsmen formed a semicircle at the players' bench to further inspire
their warriors.

The two quick touchdowns against them aroused Penn's players,
who gradually penetrated deep into their opponents' territory.
Mauthe had to kick from the 1-yard line. His soaring punt to the
double safetymen—Captain Mercer and quarterback Marshall—
landed between them, and the ball took a high bounce on the State
40. On the spot to field it was the lightning-fast Very. Without missing a stride, he put the ball under his arm and covered the 70 yards,
so far in front of all pursuers that he circled around in the end zone
to plant the ball directly behind the goal posts. This move was then
strategic, allowing the kicker an unangled shot at the uprights.
Mauthe kicked it through, as he had after the first two scores, and
Penn State was ahead, 18–0, in the first eight minutes of play.

Before the period closed, the demoralized home team was pushed
back to its own goal. When Thayer missed Marshall's attempted lateral, there was a race for the ball in the end zone, but it was
recovered by Barr, Penn halfback, for a safety against Penn, and
"the greatest quarter in Penn State history" ended, 20–0.

Regaining its poise to some extent in the second quarter, Penn
scored the only points of the period when Jack Minds, son of a Penn
football hero of the 1890s, broke away for a 35-yard touchdown run.
Between halves Penn State players felt that they could almost name
the score—they were that jubilant and confident—but the anticipated rout was not forthcoming. The second half became a defensive
battle in which Penn gave no ground without a struggle. State wisely
decided to play it safe, taking no chances with a team that had found
its composure. In the final period Dick Harlow blocked a punt by
Mercer, who recovered the ball in the end zone after a struggle with

Harlow and Dad Engle. It meant another safety for Penn State, and the score remained 22–6 to the end.

Two wild celebrations ensued—one on the field and another in Old Chapel, where students were already planning an unparalleled reception for the team's return on Monday. Rival coaches Bill Hollenback and Andy Smith shook hands perfunctorily, and Big Bill disappeared into the crowd with an old crony, the famous Mike Murphy, Penn trainer and track coach. Bill's players didn't see him until they boarded the train early Monday morning.

With no scheduled connection from Philadelphia to Lemont on Sunday, Monday was the earliest possible departure time. This gave players a chance to gather up all the Philadelphia Sunday papers. One photograph in the pictorial supplement of the *Ledger* especially delighted them, because of the favorite Hollenback admonition: "Don't be a spectator. Do something. Hit somebody." Across the top of the section an action photo showed a huge pileup of players in the center, and at the far end stood Shorty Miller like a statue, without a care in the world. That clipped-out picture adorned the Track House bulletin board for some time. Above Shorty's figure someone lettered "The Spectator."

Many students had more than victory to celebrate. They returned with considerable cash from the Big City, since those who had money had no problem getting it covered at favorable odds. Betting, of course, was frowned on by both institutions, but it was impossible to control. Under the heading "S-S-H! THERE WAS GAMBLING," one Philadelphia paper reported:

> The odds were six to five on Penn, and the State students seemed to think that every bet made was just like combining Xmas and July 4. The Penn folk made the wagers with the air of persons who have taken the jump often and know the risk.

With no defeats and seven victories, including decisions over Cornell and Penn, Penn State and the local press took the upcoming Navy game as one that might decide "eastern supremacy." The undefeated Midshipmen had been held to scoreless ties by Western Reserve and Princeton, and the so-so seasons of Harvard and Yale also encouraged hope of a high ranking.

Navy coaches viewed Penn State's invasion of Annapolis with no alarm. Concerned about avoiding injuries before the Army game, a week away, they kept most of their regulars out of the game. Nittany Lion players were humiliated, especially since the game was scoreless, but the *State Collegian* and other local papers didn't mention that they had opposed, for the most part, a team of substitutes. According to Annapolis news stories, Navy's stars, Captain Jack Dalton and Babe Brown, didn't even suit up, to be sure coaches "would not yield to the temptation of using them." One who did play was Richard E. Byrd, later famed as the Arctic explorer.

This condescension infuriated Coach Hollenback, whose boiling point was low at best. He was further aggravated, recalls Dutch Hermann, because nothing seemed to go right on the rain-soaked field. Most of the backs couldn't hold onto the slippery ball during the steady rain, nor could Shorty Miller use his fancy footwork. Mauthe's kicking also was off—when he once kicked the ball almost straight up into the air, Big Bill blew his top. He looked right at Dutch:

"Hey, Heim, go in there. I want to get Mauthe out—you take Al Wilson's place at end and do the kicking."

"Take whose place?" Dutch asked incredulously.

He had never played on the line, but in he went for a good enough kick. He knew he'd be in trouble on defense—the right side of Navy's line towered above the 160-pound Hermann. Nearly killed on the first play, he unconsciously moved out a yard or so on the second, and on the third was five or six yards wide. For years he could hear Dick Harlow yelling at him, "Come on back, Heim, the game's in here." Dutch claimed he invented the split end on that series of plays. Hermann contended that "overcoaching" by Eddie Wood early in the season partially accounted for his missing an opportunity to score what would have been the winning touchdown—and the only touchdown of his career.

E. K. Wood, one of the short-time alumni coaches so plentiful in the era, relentlessly drilled the players to go after a loose ball. "Fall on the ball, fall on the ball," he'd scream in his high-pitched voice. He once observed Dutch pursuing a ball that had rolled out on the cinder running track. "Fall on the ball," was the falsetto command. Dutch dove at it and came up with his face and forearms badly scraped. Late in the game the Middies, backed up deep on their side of the field, had the ball. When it suddenly squirted from a pileup, right in front of Hermann, he could have picked it up and run a few yards to score. Dutch "fell on the ball," and a few plays later Navy had held for downs on the 2-yard line.

Penn State missed still another opportunity after Shorty Miller had put the ball near Navy's goal with a 25-yard run, the longest gain of the day in the quagmire. Fritz Barrett actually went over the goal line, but didn't have the ball—it had slithered out of his grasp. Coach Hollenback never forgave him. Big Bill's one glaring weakness as a coach was a tendency to hold grudges against certain players. Al Hansen and Levi Lamb couldn't live down their early mistakes, but Barrett was the most shocking example of Bill's unforgiving complex. Puzzled players thought Barrett was a great running back who didn't really have a chance. He left college, married a Lock Haven girl, and spent almost his entire life in that community, serving many years as postmaster.

Hollenback could be hard on players he liked, too. Part of his coaching philosophy was "Never bawl out a poor player—he'll get discouraged. Bawl out a star—he'll take it and then try to show you up by playing well." During the Cornell game in 1911 he gave Mauthe so much hell for a minor error that Pete wouldn't speak to him for three days. Very caught it in the Penn game for letting a runner get around him even though the Penn end was holding both his legs. Hermann recalled that many times he'd hate Bill's guts one day and the next outdo himself to please the coach.

Before retiring in 1956, Burke M. Hermann had had a close association with Penn State for fifty years. He enrolled in 1906, but a change in curriculum from chemistry to history, plus the necessity of leaving college in 1910–11, postponed his graduation until June 1912, with the result that Dutch Hermann is claimed by three classes (1910, 1911, and 1912) and celebrates class reunions with all of them.

Burke Hermann, whose father was a Snyder County school principal, had acquired his nickname "Dutch" when the family moved to the Wilkes-Barre anthracite coal regions where their Pennsylvania German dialect was noticeable. One day in class his teacher asked "Who discovered America?" He threw the class into an uproar with his prompt answer: "America by Christopher Columbus was discovered."

Following a promising athletic career at Wyoming Seminary, Hermann had offers of scholarship aid from Bucknell, Lafayette, and Penn, but was most interested in Wesleyan at Middletown, Connecticut, until his father decided he should enroll at Penn State.

While playing at Wyoming, Dutch suffered a mild concussion, which concerned his father enough to ask him not to play in college.

As a freshman he was sorely tempted and actually signed up officially to avoid the military drill he hated. His problem was settled during the winter when winning a letter in basketball automatically excused an athlete from military tactics.

By 1907, unable to resist the call of the gridiron, Dutch played a few games using the name "German." Instead of being upset, his father was proud of his son's perseverance, and young Hermann's football career was launched.

A reserve quarterback in the seasons of 1907, 1908, 1909, and 1911, Hermann also won four letters in basketball in spite of his short stature and 160-pound weight. He taught and coached for three years at Wilkes-Barre High School (now Coughlin) and Shadyside Academy in Pittsburgh, then returned to Penn State in 1915 as the first full-time freshman football coach. He later served on the football coaching staffs of Dick Harlow and Hugo Bezdek. When Bob Higgins took charge of football in 1930, Hermann was changed from freshman coach to varsity backfield coach. In 1916–17 he became the first full-time varsity basketball coach, holding this post until 1932 except for two years spent in the Army during World War I. He left coaching in 1932 to devote full time to teaching in the Department of History, specializing in political biography of the American colonial period. Fascination with history for many alumni began with his popular course in American political biography, History 35. In 1968 he was awarded the Lion's Paw Medal "for promoting the welfare and best interests of Penn State, and maintaining it's finest traditions."

Penn State's 1911 team approached the final game with Pittsburgh on Thanksgiving Day confident of an undefeated season. The Pitt "jinx," later to become almost a tradition, hadn't yet emerged, and Coach Hollenback tried to combat the dangerous overconfidence to no avail. His spirited charges wouldn't listen even though the Panthers, approaching their first "golden era," had lost, by reasonably close scores, only to the Carlisle Indians and Cornell, and had tied Notre Dame.

A 35-yard field goal early in the first quarter by Pete Mauthe was the only score of the game, because Shorty Miller's touchdown, pushed across in the final period, was denied by an official's ruling. After Dick Harlow blocked a punt—nearly an every-game occurrence for Dick—Miller carried the ball from the Pitt 6 and was piled up on the goal line. When the mass of players unpiled, the ball appeared to be over the line, but it was ruled that Shorty had pushed it across after he was downed. Dex Very and Hube Wagner, famous Pitt star of that period, both played end and were outstanding for their teams—great crowd favorites. The Pittsburgh *Gazette-Times* reported:

> Nearly half of the spectators were women. They came from all over western Pennsylvania to see their annual game of football and then go back home with memories of the black head of a Wagner or the flaxen top of a Very, their football idols.

Penn State's Pittsburgh alumni honored the team at a banquet that night in the Fort Pitt Hotel, State's headquarters for the game. Fifteen letters were awarded, and Pete Mauthe was elected captain for 1912.

While students talked about their team being the "champions of the East," newspapers generally called it even among Princeton, Navy, and Penn State, although the Midshipmen had played three scoreless ties—something of a record—and two of them were with the other challengers. Navy did gain some prestige for beating Army, 3–0.

Judge Fred G. White, former Illinois player who had officiated at one of the 1911 games, made this observation about Penn State:

> Never have I seen a team where there was so much harmony and good fellowship as characterized the Penn State team. Every man was always in a good humor and lost sight of himself in praising the other fellow. As long as a team has this spirit, it is bound to win.

Coach Bill Hollenback, who usually said good-bye to the squad when his contract expired at the end of the season, often made surprise visits to the Track House during the winter months to see how the boys were getting along. He never forgot one cold weekend of 1911–12. Competitive goldfish swallowing and the like were unheard of, but students vied with each other in conceiving diabolical pranks, and the "widow frame-up" was one making the rounds of eastern colleges.

Some of the players, who were generally on a relaxed "social" basis with their coach, contrived an escapade that many felt wouldn't work on sophisticated "man of the world" Hollenback. Others were just plain scared of Bill, but not Dex Very, Pete Mauthe, Shorty Miller, Dad Engle, Dick Harlow, and a few more. Dex, chosen to set the trap, told Bill he had a date that night whose friend was a widow —and dying to meet him. Was he interested? He was, and on a bitterly cold, snowy evening Dex led his coach to a house on West Beaver Avenue. Players in on the gag already were huddled about the house in the dark to see the fun.

As the two Romeos started up the porch steps, one conspirator, disguising his voice, hollered that now he knew who'd been after his wife. Hollenback, panicking, thought only of getting away, but the pair couldn't run very fast on the icy walks. They were just out of the yard when Shorty, as planned, fired a gun in the air. The script called for Dex to topple over, which he did, but poor Bill kept running, expecting another shot at any moment. Nearly exhausted, he finally reached the Track House and called out: "They've shot Dex. He's down in the alley." Practically carried in and stretched out on the round table in the Club Room, Bill was still trying to get his breath a few minutes later when the grinning culprits returned. Bill knew then he'd been had. He sat up, pointed his finger at Dex, and said: "Very, I hope God forgives you, because I never will."

Coach Hollenback did forgive, resuming his coaching in September with enthusiasm and the same insistence on strict training rules, discipline, and attention to fundamentals. He led his men to Penn State's greatest season in 1912, and no one ever dared mention "the widow" until many years after.

14

The Great Walkoff at Columbus

Early football games often ended in mutual huffiness, sometimes in violent disputes, and even fist fights, but none approached the brouhaha at Columbus, Ohio, on November 16, 1912. Penn State's records list the score as 37–0 in favor of the Lions. Officially the tally should be 1–0. With 9 minutes still to play, the Ohio State Buckeyes were led from the field by Coach John R. Richards, protesting emphatically that he would no longer subject his team to Penn State's "unnecessary roughness."

The astonishing exodus of the Ohio team was criticized by many Ohio fans, officials, and some newspapermen. A delegation went to the railroad station to convey the personal apologies of Ohio State's president, but the two institutions from neighboring states did not meet again on the gridiron for another forty-four years. No apology came from Richards, a Wisconsin graduate who had coached at his alma mater in 1911. This deed and an unexpected defeat by Michigan State after the Penn State affair may have caused his abbreviated, one-year regime at Columbus. He returned to Wisconsin in 1917 for a five-year term, compiling a commendable record of 24–8–3.

The Ohio State Athletic Board had initiated the agreement for a Penn State game, urging Athletic Director L. W. St. John to branch

out beyond traditional opponents in the Ohio Conference—Otter-
bein, Denison, Cincinnati, Oberlin, Ohio Wesleyan, and Case. Ohio
State easily won this conference title in 1912 and had not yet joined
the Big Ten (organized in 1896). Officials felt that defeating a
strong eastern team would bring deserved prestige.

The two land-grant institutions were in almost identical periods of
football development, both having outgrown the small colleges in
their respective areas and both ambitious to schedule stronger opponents. Unfortunately for Ohio State, the challenge came at a time
when Penn State boasted the strongest eleven in the first twenty-five
years of its football existence.

Graduate Manager Raymond H. Smith received a flat guarantee of
$1,200 for the Columbus venture, with the option of taking one half
of the net profits. If a division of the net receipts was accepted, $.25
for each student season ticket would be included, not to exceed 900
student tickets. This figure was later increased to 1,200 by mutual
agreement. Only 3,500 spectators attended the game, and Graduate
Manager Smith brought back a check for $1,300. By contrast, for
the 1964 meeting attended by 84,000 people, Penn State's share of
the receipts was $99,963.20.

The Columbus trip was a great adventure for the Penn Staters.
Only for the traditional encounters with Cornell and Navy had the
squad ventured beyond Pennsylvania to play a big game. With victories over Cornell, W&J, and Penn in their season's record of 6–0,
the players knew little about midwestern football, but they shared the
feeling of the 1911 squad that under Coach Bill Hollenback they
were unbeatable. Ohio State was known to have given Michigan a
tough battle (Michigan 14, OSU 0), but the cocky Nittany Lions
were unimpressed.

The Midwest scorned the eastern invasion. Ardent Columbus fans
and local newspapers—even in pre-World War I days—assumed
that Penn State couldn't possibly play the same game as the Ohio
Conference champions, an attitude persistent through all their subsequent meetings. This sectionalism was amusingly described by Joel
Sayre, author and magazine contributor,[1] who was a 12-year-old boy
in Columbus in 1912 and a red-hot worshiper of every Buckeye
player. Said Sayre:

[1] Joel Sayre, "Mayhem and Arson and Local Police," *Sports Illustrated* (September 24, 1956), p. N2.

Our wonderful line would make Penn State look sick. . . . We had arrived at this arrogant prediction by a process of simple deduction. All we knew or cared to know in advance about the Penn State team was that its right end was named Dexter Very. To every football fan in short pants in the Columbus of 1912, anybody with the name of Dexter Very could be only one thing—a dude. Dudes, as we know from the funny papers, were weedy, chinless, unmanly snobs. If the Penn State right end was a dude, we reasoned, no doubt dudes played all the other 10 positions. Just wait till that wonderful line of ours got at them!

Sayre reports his personal chagrin, that Very "didn't even faintly resemble the dudes of the funny papers . . . he had the invincible splendidly open face of a football player on the cover of *The Saturday Evening Post . . .* playing his position with an overwhelming dash and brilliance."

The author of "Rackety Rax" recalled that Shorty Miller was even more spectacular:

He ran like a hopped-up squirrel for what never seemed to be less than 25 yards. He had furiously pistoning legs and marvelous hip action; when our big linemen hit him he just bounced off and kept on pistoning—for a total of three touchdowns.

Penn State's squad and officials spent Friday night in the Southern Hotel, Columbus. Shortly before their departure for the field on Saturday, several players stopped in Coach Hollenback's room. He was in the bathtub, all his new-looking clothes neatly laid out on the bed. "Boy," he said, "I'll be a Beau Brummel today out on the sidelines." When he had dressed and was knotting his tie, Shorty spoke up: "Gosh, Bill, you'll bring us bad luck, wearing all that new stuff." Not replying, and glaring at them, superstitious Big Bill removed every stitch and put on the old, dirty suit he always wore at games.

At the Ohio field a vociferous little group of Penn State fans welcomed the arrival of their team, looking trim and businesslike but small beside their Ohio opponents. One spectator was President Edwin Erle Sparks, an Ohio State graduate, who assured a friend that his loyalty wasn't divided—he counted on Penn State to make a good showing and hoped for a victory.

Before going out on the field, Coach Hollenback illustrated his pep talk with Columbus newspaper clippings belittling the Lions, their record, and eastern football in general. The players were already upset by the condition of their practice field (used by the Columbus

Panhandlers, a local pro team), which was reported to have had trees growing on it and litter of all kinds spread around, including riveting hammers, rusted barrel hoops, and broken bottles. "We were mad at everything and everybody," grumbled Ollie Vogel, a substitute tackle. "We were ready to eat 'em up."

In a pregame interview, Coach Hollenback told newspapermen that he expected to win, though it would be a hard game. Coach Richards refused to give out his lineup, but Arthur (Bugs) Raymond, star Buckeye lineman, was not on the field, and it was rumored that he had been hurt the previous week against Oberlin and would be kept on the bench "unless he was needed."

The visitors made Raymond necessary very quickly. Said the *Ohio State Journal* the following day:

> The Penn State team is without a doubt the best drilled eleven that has shown in Columbus for years. It did not lack a single essential that goes to make a football team successful. There was a smashing line, a quartet of ripping backs, and last, but not least, a team with the proper spirit of going in and getting the yards regardless of the other fellow.
>
> Age and experience were also another noticeable feature. Team work was still more prominent. Every player knew what was expected of him and in nine cases out of ten performed his duties with exactness. This alone was enough to carry them through to victory, but other qualities came to the surface as the game progressed.

The *Journal* cited Miller—the "little, big-hearted, bow-legged, kidding quarterback"—as the best quarterback ever to appear on the Ohio field; praised Mauthe for his "remarkable ability on defense, having the intuition to be at the right place at the right time"; and called Very "great," but deplored his "roughness." "When it comes to getting down the field under punts, the rest of the team is too slow to keep his pace."

Pete Mauthe made the first score with a field goal from the Ohio 41, kicking the placement with an ease that astounded the home fans —he might have been practicing on a village green, someone remarked. Then Shorty Miller ran through the Buckeyes for 20 yards, passed to end Al Wilson for a first down on the 5, and scrambled through center for a score. Before the first period was over, Shorty tallied again on a 30-yard run, during which he seemed to be tackled by every member of the Ohio State team. Mauthe kicked one of his two extra-point tries, giving the Lions a 16–0 lead as the first quarter ended.

The game became a bit "physical" in the next period. Penn State participants later conceded that they might have seemed arrogant and cocky after the first period when they discovered how unprepared Ohio State was for the kind of football the Lions were accustomed to play. Dex Very, one of the principal "culprits," according to Ohio sources, described Lion play as "a little rough" but not "dirty." At any rate, in the scoreless second quarter both sides appeared to be more interested in personal vendettas than team play, with Coach Richards continuously berating the officials for not calling penalties on the visitors. A 40-yard touchdown pass from Mauthe to Very was denied because Penn State (Very) had been offside. "I was called for that a lot," Very reported. "I was pretty fast off the ball, and officials often thought I had to be offside to get down the field that fast."

With no dressing room to go to between halves, the Penn State squad assembled under a clump of big trees at one end of the field. Local bullies who had heard Richards' blast that the Lions "must have scoured the prize rings of the East to get that crowd" decided they would go after the Easterners as a matter of honor. Luckily, field policemen were present and the attackers withdrew. One was overheard remarking with some surprise: "Why, they're nothing but a bunch of kids."

The Penn Staters were administering to Red Bebout, bleeding from a bad head cut. "Look at him," Coach Hollenback told an onlooker. "They opened that gash over his eye on the first play of the game, but he wouldn't let me take him out. On the last play of the half they deliberately kicked him in the head. And they call us muckers."

In this atmosphere the second half started. Almost immediately Jim McClure, the Buckeye quarterback, fumbled one of Mauthe's great punts, which Very snatched up to run 35 yards for a score. A trick play with unexpected results produced the next touchdown when the Lions had the ball in Ohio State territory along the left sideline. The special "sideline" play had center John (Biggie) Clark on the end of the line next to the sideline and Shorty directly behind him, taking a direct pass. The play was to be a pass either to Clark or Very, but the center's pass to Miller bounced along the ground. Since he had no time to throw the ball, Shorty ran 40 yards for the touchdown. Mauthe's kicks for both points put Penn State ahead, 30–0, at the end of the third quarter.

Infuriating to Coach Richards as the "broken" play was, worse was yet to come. Six minutes into the last period Penn State was driving for another touchdown when the Ohio State coach dramatically tried to stop the advance by sending in his injured star, Bugs Raymond (nicknamed for the New York Giant pitcher of the era). What happened next is a legend with multiple versions.

As Raymond entered the game, the legend says Shorty announced: "Well, here we have the pride of Ohio, Mr. Raymond. Mr. Mauthe will take the ball on the next play, right through Mr. Raymond for a score." Shorty handed the ball to Mauthe, who went through Raymond for a long run and a touchdown. Actually, Very first spotted Raymond coming into the game and called out: "Why, here comes Frank Merriwell." Raymond heard the quip and answered: "Sure, bring it through here." And Shorty merely replied: "All right, cocky, here she comes." Mauthe went through Raymond for a single yard, but a touchdown. He then kicked the goal, and the score was 37–0.

The Great Walkoff occurred following the next kickoff. Apparently Very blocked reserve quarterback Carroll, knocking the Buckeye about ten feet backward—illegally, said Coach Richards, who immediately escorted his players to the sidelines. The referee, Dr. Jack Means (Pennsylvania), informed Captain Mauthe that the Penn State team must remain on the field 5 minutes, according to the rules, to claim a forfeit. Mauthe balked until reminded that unless Penn State followed the rules, Ohio State could win the game. Under police protection—which was needed—the squad assembled at the north end of the field surrounded by a ring of policemen with nightsticks.

Many years later, Coach Hollenback recalled his disbelief at the sudden developments:

I will always remember when Mr. Richards decided not to finish the game. He started to walk across the field with his team in back of him. In my wildest moments I had no conception of what he was doing. I thought it was some kind of a spread eagle formation they were using. I had no idea he was leaving the field. However, that was what happened. It might be interesting to you to know that Penn State had nothing to do with the selection of the officials. Ohio State chose them. I do recall that when the people filed out of the stands one fellow said, after seeing the Penn State team, "Why, these are only schoolboys." . . . We were playing modern football, and Mr. Richards did not seem to know what to do about it. Ohio State had beaten most of the teams in Ohio, and he didn't want any more points scored against his team. I think that was the real motive behind his action. The score could easily have been 60–0 or more.

Although Penn State had nothing to do with the selection of officials, it was ironic that Dr. Means, the referee, had been a half-back on the team Coach Hollenback captained at the University of Pennsylvania. Fortunately, the local newspapers didn't discover this coincidence. Means, a practicing physician in Columbus, and Umpire Clark P. Hinman, a graduate of West Virginia and also a Columbus resident, were subjected to considerable criticism in the local press for "letting the game get out of hand." Hinman bore the brunt of so much gaff that he issued a rebuttal. He denied a widely circulated claim that he had been warned to expect a rough game and in-structed to banish the first guilty player. Continuing his statement, he defended Penn State's conduct during the game:

I would say in this connection that I personally participated in three games against Penn State on their home grounds and was in a better position to judge the character of the athletic ethics of the teams of that institution than my advisor. Moreover, I will say that in all of these three contests, each of which was very much more closely contested than was Saturday's game, neither myself nor my teammates ever made any charges of lack of sportsmanship of Penn State players. Penn State always turns out teams that hold high rank among eastern colleges, and the players are coached to play the game with every ounce of nerve and muscle. Consequently, when a team like this year's, which is undoubtedly one of the very best in the coun-try, plays a team which is undeniably outclassed, the contest is bound to assume a strenuous aspect, especially to the weaker team and its coaches.

Hinman added that awarding him the entire blame was unfair be-cause the rules made all three officials (the third was Dr. John Eck-strom of Dartmouth) equally responsible for calling rough play. He pointed out that the only penalty inflicted for roughness was called by him because "it was the first deliberate infraction that I detected even though it was necessary for me to rule against the home team, which was being badly defeated." In 1950 Al Wilson (left end) recalled the slight penalty action without pleasure. "I took a hay-maker right in the mouth—that's when I lost all my front teeth."

Columbus press reaction to the Penn State team varied from admiration to scorn and sarcasm, the general conclusion being that the Lions were far too strong for the local favorites and that at least three Penn Staters—Miller, Very, and Mauthe—were sure All-Americas. One Ohio State player was quoted as saying that Penn State played "legitimate" football in the first quarter, but started "roughing" it when the officials were negligent. Divided opinion about Coach Richards' "walkoff" ranged from understanding and sympathy to derision. Probably the prevailing opinion in Columbus was that the Buckeye coach's action was justified—that in leaving the field he had protected his team against serious injury.

Coach Richards, in an official statement, declared that he had delayed drastic action thinking that with Penn State so far ahead there would be little reason for the continued rough play, and had hoped the officials would "tighten up."

> The rough play continued and I decided that the result of the game was in no way in doubt and the crowd seemed to have seen enough to understand what was going on. . . . I saw Very knock Carroll down in front of Dr. Means, and I ran out and asked him if he was going to eject Very. . . . He said no and I told him I was taking the players off the field to protect them. . . . As I was taking the players off, I stopped in front of the athletic board box and asked if I should order them back into the fray and was told to take them to the clubhouse.

The Columbus *Citizen* berated those who refused to pay off bets on the basis of the forfeited game:

> If a fellow who bet that Ohio State would not be beaten by at least 20 points has a drop of real sporting blood in his veins he will settle without a whimper. Penn State had run up 37 points when time was called, although technically the forfeited score is only 1–0. Anyone willing to take advantage of such a technical point is a pretty poor specimen of a sportsman.

Penn State officially reacted with amazement and indignation, although surprisingly little was written in student or alumni publications. Undergraduates were irate about an incident occurring while the Lions waited on the field for their victory to be made "official." A Buckeye freshman set a match to the blue-and-white bunting wrapped around a goal post and then disappeared into the crowd.

Ohio State students extinguished the fire and presented the charred colors to Penn State fans.

The *Citizen* claimed that this arson was "the act of an individual and not the student body, which stuck to the bleachers and behaved admirably. The freshman offender will probably be ostracized by the rest of the student body for his act." Only one other episode after the game was mentioned: An Ohio State fan who got a little too personal—and a little too close—to the Penn State players was firmly removed by the hot-tempered assistant coach, Dick Harlow.

President Sparks, who stayed overnight in Columbus for a dinner at which the Chi Phi fraternity honored him, received an official apology from a delegation of Ohio State officials when he went to the railroad station to say good-bye to the Penn State squad. Without mentioning the action of Coach Richards, the committee assured Prexy Sparks that disciplinary measures would be taken for the burning of the colors, which a newspaper likened to "the burning of the nation's colors in a foreign land." The hastily assembled dignitaries were H. E. Payne of New York, an officer of the Alumni Association; Professor George Rightmire, representing the faculty; Professor Alonzo Tuttle, the Athletic Board; W. J. Sears, the trustees; and Robert Stephan, the students.

The *Democratic Watchman* of Bellefonte, less partisan than State College newspapers, deplored the incident at Columbus, but not without a reminder that Penn State's freshman team had walked off the field several weeks before while playing Bellefonte Academy. This was a dispute over a ruling, not roughness.

Penn State's undefeated teams of 1911 and 1912 were generally classed among the East's strongest elevens, but not even the 1912 power house, which Coach Hollenback developed and later called "one of the best teams ever to play football on the Eastern Seaboard," could overcome the lingering prejudice among writers and athletic officials that only at Yale, Harvard, and Princeton could top football be found. Cornell, Pennsylvania, and Dartmouth were merely on the fringe of the élite group. Walter Camp continued to be the most respected and authoritative judge of football talent. Although his annual All-America team was primarily All-East, Camp gave reasonable consideration to the Midwest, but rarely to any other section of the country.

In 1912, for instance, nine players on the Camp team were from eastern schools, later dubbed the "Ivies." Only Bob Butler, Wisconsin tackle, and the great Jim Thorpe, halfback from Carlisle, broke through the monopoly. Despite strong support from some metropolitan sportswriters in the East, Penn State's trio of stars—Mauthe, Very, and Miller—were virtually ignored. More publicized during the 1910–14 period were such players as Thorpe; Charley Brickley, the renowned Harvard drop kicker; Eddie Mahan and Tack Hardwick, also of Harvard; Roy Mercer of Pennsylvania; Jack Dalton of Navy; and Army's stars, Lou Merellat, John McEwan, and Leland Devore.

Notre Dame, beginning to be recognized in the Midwest in 1911 and 1912, received little acclaim in the East until the Irish surprised the Cadets of Army with the forward pass in 1913. Illinois, Minnesota, Wisconsin, Chicago, and Nebraska were represented by strong elevens at this time, and now and then a few westerners would be included on the All-America team. The Far West and the South were outside the sphere of eastern recognition, although Auburn, Vanderbilt, Georgia, and Texas had gained some eminence south of the Mason-Dixon line.

Top billing in the East, hotly disputed by Penn State's supporters, went to Harvard, where the imaginative Percy Haughton started the Crimson's "golden era" in 1912 with an undefeated, untied eleven, undisputed leader in the Big Three. Dominant for 8 years (1908–16), Harvard won 64 games, lost 4, tied 5, and was undefeated in 33 successive games. More important to Cambridge alumni, Haughton was able to dispel the inferiority complex Harvard may have had during the years of adversity against Yale. Harvard won from its greatest rival three years running beginning in 1912, outscoring Yale 71–5.

In Penn State's triumphant 1912 season varsity letters were won by only thirteen players, eleven of whom probably were on the playing field over 80 per cent of the time during the eight games. Fortunately no serious injuries interfered with Coach Hollenback's plans. His veteran team started the opening game with Carnegie Tech and was together as a unit until the Thanksgiving Day finale with Pitt. Rugged but not big, the team had confidence in its superiority and was fiercely competitive. The charge by Ohio State and some other opponents (particularly Cornell) that it played "beyond the rules" was disavowed by its members and especially by Coach Hollenback, who pointed out that the Lions were greatly outweighed in nearly every contest.

Triple-threat Pete Mauthe, lean and unlike the classic fullback type, never weighed much over 165 pounds. Shorty Miller, the quarterback, was five feet, five and weighed 140—he scored the first touchdown of the season by returning a punt against Carnegie Tech for 78 yards. Dex Very, labeled a "rough player" largely because of the Ohio State accusations, never weighed more than 162 pounds.

The 1912 regulars were Al Wilson and Very, ends; Dad Engle and Red Bebout, tackles; Levi Lamb and Al Hansen, guards; John Clark, center; Miller, quarterback; Dan Welty and R. N. (Punk) Berryman, halfbacks; and Mauthe, fullback. Berryman and Mauthe often changed places in the backfield. The two other lettermen were Elgie (Yegg) Tobin, halfback, and Bob Whitney, a tackle. Substitutes who saw some action were Bert Barron, end; Ollie Vogel, tackle; Ralph Sayre, tackle; and Frank Keller, halfback. Mauthe and Very were playing their fourth year as regulars; Engle and Miller had been on the varsity three years; the other seven had been starters on the undefeated 1911 team. Coach Hollenback was blessed with experience, durability, and cohesiveness. What the squad lacked in size was made up in speed, unity, and competitive spirit.

Following the Carnegie Tech opener, Washington and Jefferson was faced on Beaver Field. This game was extremely important to Hollenback, as the western Pennsylvanians were coached by Bob Folwell, who had preceded Big Bill as captain of Pennsylvania's team (1907). The two were friends, but strong rivals. Folwell is credited with originating and perfecting the screen pass in 1912 at W&J. The innovation may not yet have been quite "perfected," because records indicate the visitors completed only one pass during the game.

Penn State expected a rugged contest from the Presidents, especially since W&J had played a scoreless tie with the Carlisle Indians, led by Thorpe. The Indians' record in 1912 was 12–1–1. Coached by Pop Warner, the Carlisle team's only loss was to Pennsylvania. W&J's leading players were Captain Stew Alexander, end, and Red Fleming, halfback, who made several All-America teams.

Mauthe kicked three field goals for the only points in the first half, but then the home team broke the game open. Thrilling the largest crowd yet to witness football in State College, Mauthe returned the second-half kickoff 95 yards to the 5. After the visitors had held for three downs, Miller finally passed into the end zone to Very for the first touchdown. Miller, again the running star, scored after a

W&J fumble, and Very caught another touchdown pass from him in the final period, the play covering 40 yards.

Keeping ahead of small regional rivals was gratifying, but only competition with the larger eastern colleges could bring real national standing, and the students eagerly anticipated coming games with Cornell and Pennsylvania. Athletic officials—also anxious for recognition among the East's top-flight elevens—were embarrassed whenever the press mentioned eligibility rules or the lack of them. No more lax than other colleges of the day, Penn State had never announced such regulations except in the most general terms. The Athletic Board's first specific eligibility requirement, proposed in 1912, was the "migration rule" (today's "transfer rule"), requiring a transfer student from another college to be in residence a full year before participating in intercollegiate athletics.

The Board also sought to eliminate freshmen from varsity play to encourage them to derive the benefits of coaching and preliminary training for the varsity. A limited freshman schedule was attempted in 1912, but a full-time freshman coach was not hired until 1915. Despite strong pressure from the Penn State *Collegian,* a student newspaper, the new eligibility rules were not officially adopted until the 1915 season. The *Alumni Quarterly* (October 1912) also joined the campaign for a new image by pointing out that in order to play, athletes at Penn State must have a 5 per cent higher standing than the ordinary students.

Sensing that a victory in the first away game with Cornell would bring metropolitan press attention, more than half the students saw the squad of 22 players off for Ithaca with Coach Hollenback and his line coach, Dick Harlow, a tackle on the 1911 team. A popular new staff member was Dr. Dan Luby, trainer and team physician, who had attended Exeter, Mercersburg, and Pennsylvania, and was a graduate of the Penn Medical School. He was an old friend of Hollenback's and had accompanied Bill to Missouri in the fall of 1910.

Cornell shocked the confident Lions by scoring early, after Shorty Miller touched a punt and let it roll until a Big Red player recovered it for a touchdown—a rare mistake by the little quarterback. As the team lined up under the goal posts for the extra point, the mild-mannered tackle, Dad Engle, angrily swore to his teammates: "I'll be damned if I'll ever stand under another goal like this." He never did

—the Cornell touchdown was the only score against Penn State that season. A Mauthe field goal and Punk Berryman's 75-yard return of the next kickoff gave the Lions their first lead, 10–6. In the second half, they routed the Big Red by a final score of 29–6, with Mauthe, Very, and Wilson scoring touchdowns, the last two on forward passes. The Lions were accused of being "overly rough."

Bill (William G.) Kerr, student manager in 1912, enhanced his popularity with players and fans by skillful schedule planning. Gettysburg separated formidable Cornell from the pivotal Penn game which had acquired that significance when the long string of Red and Blue successes was broken in 1911 by the "Bellefonte" school (a geographical error that was still being made by the Philadelphia newspapers). Actually, Coach Andy Smith's team was having a disappointing season. After easy warmup victories, Penn unexpectedly lost close games to Swarthmore and Lafayette, and then was soundly beaten by Brown.

Bent on defeating his alma mater, Coach Hollenback prepared meticulously and really worried over the game in Philadelphia, although sportswriters figured that Shorty Miller rather than Hollenback's superior coaching would bring about Penn's downfall. The Lion coach was concerned enough to take an unusual step: He "scouted" Penn against Lafayette, leaving his team in charge of Assistant Coach Harlow for the Gettysburg game. The term "scout" was not yet in the football vernacular, and the practice, not fully accepted as cricket, usually was handled discreetly. A newsman spotted Bill, and the conversation went like this:

"Hello, Bill, what are you doing down here?"

"Oh, I just came down to look things over. I brought my team with me."

"Where is it?"

"Here it is," said Bill, turning to Miller, his companion on the expedition. Sure enough, Shorty was missing the only game of his four-year varsity career because of a minor injury. Bill logically took him to Philadelphia for a look at Penn.

The reporter described Shorty's "peculiar conformation."

To start at the top, he has a very long head in more ways than one, a very short, powerful neck, and the body of a man of six feet. But the legs are very short. He is known in State College as "Shorty" Miller, but the "Shorty" only refers to his legs.

[Miller was only 5-5]. In short, this wonderful little quarterback looks as if he had once upon a time gazed into one of those trick mirrors and then grown that way.

"Watch Shorty Miller" was the Penn byword, and he got most of the advance press, based on his brilliant performance the year before. This attention tickled the Penn State junior, especially when he was greeted at Franklin Field with "Hello, Mr. Miller" by the same gatekeeper who had refused him admission the year before.

To bolster his own dressing-room histrionics, Coach Hollenback had his good friend Bob Folwell deliver a charge to his players. A Penn graduate and later coach (1916–19), Folwell was having one of his periodic feuds with the athletic authorities, and as "guest orator" his even gustier than usual language embarrassed the Penn State coach.

All this, and Folwell's close association with the squad prior to the 1912 Penn game, started a rumor that the two Penn alumni were trying to undermine the football situation at their alma mater. The conjecture was that they felt Coach Andy Smith needed more support from Penn authorities. Chandler Richter, *Evening Times* sportswriter, said these critics believed Penn's best talent was unresponsive because "there were too many men planning plays and running football who did not keep in close touch with the game." Folwell was quoted as saying: "It would be a good thing if Penn got trimmed every other game during the remainder of the season. It would wake them up to the fact that something must be done to save it."

Other newspapers used Penn's internecine squabble to build up the Penn State game, just as in 1909 and 1911 they had overplayed Coach Hollenback's alleged desire for revenge because he hadn't been given the head coaching job.

Enjoying the novelty of being favorites on Franklin Field, the official party, including 23 players and the college band, left from Lemont on two special trains Thursday night. Estimating that a thousand students would follow on Friday, the confident Penn State *Collegian* noted that Bill Hollenback, the miracle worker, had yet to lose a game as Penn State's coach.

Perhaps overconfident, the Lions were outplayed at the outset. Fearing Miller might repeat his demoralizing 1911 kickoff return, Coach Smith called for an onside kick when Captain Roy Mercer, two-time All America, won the toss. The home team skillfully negotiated the difficult maneuver it had practiced all week: Chester Minds drew back his foot as if to kick the ball, but Mercer ran up from the side and tapped a short kick, which was recovered in Penn State territory by Walter Craig, the new quarterback. The Quakers advanced to the 10-yard line before losing the ball on downs. This was the closest they came to scoring.

In the second quarter, Engle blocked a punt by Mercer and recovered on Penn's 15, but then the aroused eleven threw the invaders back until Miller's 16-yard run put the ball a yard from the goal. In that "fake shift, double pass" play the guards pulled out of the line and ran to the left, leading Berryman, who had taken the ball from quarterback Miller. Receiving a short lateral pass from Berryman, Miller then circled Penn's other end, fooling their left end, Young, who had been drawn inside by the fake. Mercer tackled Miller barely short of the goal line, and Mauthe made the final step in three tries.

The Lions dominated thereafter. Miller produced a total of 96 yards on runs from scrimmage and punt returns, but Very was acclaimed outstanding player of the day. Some professional observers rated it the finest performance of his career. The Philadelphia *North American* (November 2, 1912) called it the most notable exhibition of end play ever seen on Franklin Field.

> This giant was Dexter Very, playing his last game against Penn. The blonde right end did everything except fly. On defense he pushed Penn's ends and halfbacks out of the play as though they were so many stuffed dolls. No matter how intricate the formation, how clever the play he instantly divined its destination and was always where it reached the crux, there to do what was needful to foil it. He tackled hard enough to separate the various vertebrae in the spines of his opponents and he was glued to the ball any time it happened to get loose on a fumble.
>
> On offense his work was equally notable. He made the longest individual run of the game, a 30-yard gain. When for one period Mauthe was out, Very did the kicking and punted superbly either with or without the wind. Finally, he climaxed his work with a marvelous catch of a forward pass for a touchdown. In spite of all the work he did, Very never slowed up, and at the finish of the game was driving ahead just as hard as at the start.

Trailing by 7–0 as the second half started, Penn had boldly tried another onside kick, which Simpson, the center, recovered on the Lions' 45, but the home team was forced to punt when they held. A fumbled punt by Mercer, recovered by Levi Lamb on the Penn 12, led to the visitors' second touchdown early in the fourth period. Penn's line, difficult to penetrate throughout the game, was almost impregnable near the goal line. The Lions were 6 yards away from a score on fourth down when Miller looped a pass over the line to Very, who was covered by two men—one with his arms wrapped around him bodily. Very almost fell, struggling to get loose, but stretched for the ball and held onto it. Mauthe, injured in the first half, returned to kick his second extra point.

Besides his 30-yard run on a fake kick play, Very ran 57 yards after catching another pass from Miller for an apparent third touchdown. Referee Walter Okeson claimed, however, that he hadn't blown his whistle to start the play, because Head Linesman Weymouth had blown *his* whistle to signal the referee about the time remaining. The Lions, it seems, started on the wrong whistle and were deprived of a score on the technicality.

Penn's faithful claimed a moral victory, which so inspired the Quakers that they completed their season with three successive major upsets, over Michigan, the Carlisle Indians, and Cornell. Penn State was unconcerned—Lion teams from 1890 to 1911 had often won that kind of victory on Franklin Field.

At home prior to the Ohio State game, Penn State mercilessly ran up 71 points, largest total in 5 years, against Villanova's Wildcats in a game of interest only because it was the last home performance of the seniors—Captain Pete Mauthe, Dex Very, Al Wilson, Dad Engle, and Al Hansen. Mauthe, fully recovered from the severe bruises that had handicapped him for several weeks, scored two touchdowns, kicked a 46-yard field goal, and made 8 of 8 extra points—a total of 23 points.

Following the Columbus trip, Coach Hollenback tried hard to keep his men sharp for the finale on Thanksgiving Day with Pittsburgh, stifling all "eastern championship" talk and reminding them how the Panthers nearly embarrassed the undefeated 1911 team. With their 3–5 record, taking Pitt seriously was difficult, although the Panthers, still coached by Joe Thompson, had close games against Navy and Notre Dame. Hube Wagner, popular selection at end on the all-time Pitt team, played halfback against the Lions in 1912.

The 1911 Penn game has always been considered Miller's finest and the 1912 Penn game was Very's, but the Pitt game of 1912 belonged to Captain Pete Mauthe at fullback—he did everything.

His defensive play was superb, his kicking checked Pitt's scoring chances, and his long passes were eye-catching. During the seventh year of the forward pass few could equal him in hitting a receiver over 20 yards away. Local fans were stunned early in the game by his placement kick (with Miller holding) from a yard past midfield. This 51-yarder stood as a Penn State record until 1975, when it was broken by Chris Bahr. Mauthe scored two touchdowns on short runs and kicked both extra points, accounting for all of Penn State's 17 points in the first half.

Left-handed Miller often said: "I was a thrower, Pete Mauthe was a real passer." In the second half, three more touchdowns were made by Very (32-yard pass from Mauthe), Berryman (50-yard run on an interception), and Miller (16-yard run). The game's most spectacular play, however, led to the third touchdown—a 60-yard completion from Mauthe to Very, ending at the Pitt 20. The long pass (now called the "bomb") was almost a curiosity in 1912, the year the rulemakers had removed the 20-yard distance limit on a forward pass.

Very later wrote reminiscently about that pass from Mauthe:

I remember telling Pete to throw the ball as far as he could over the Pitt tackle because I thought the safetyman was coming up too far. "Don't even look for me—I'll be there," I told him. I ran right by the safety and was just about to give up when I saw the ball shoot out over a mass of players. Funny, but I can still remember what flashed through my mind. It was a game we used to play as kids called "Halley over the Schoolhouse." Never knew why at the time, but I suppose it was named for Halley's Comet. You'd choose sides and the best throwers would heave the ball over the schoolhouse—then the one who caught it could run to the other side and "burn" someone with the ball. If you hit him, he would be on your side.

Another player in State's backfield, overshadowed by the headliners but highly regarded by his teammates, was Dan Welty, a junior, who was an aggressive, skillful blocker and a steady defensive player. Especially anxious to perform well against Pittsburgh because he was a Greensburg boy, Welty turned out to be one of the offensive stars of the game.

Lion players might have savored the Pitt victory more had they known Penn State would defeat the Panthers only once during a long drought extending from 1913 through 1938.

While Mauthe, Miller, and Very were the most acclaimed members of the 1912 undefeated team, sportswriters and all-star selectors also honored others, notably Al Wilson, left end; Dad Engle, right tackle; and Red Bebout, who was named right guard on the Brooklyn *Citizen*'s All-East team.

Ernie Cozens, former Penn All-America, writing in a Pittsburgh newspaper, named Mauthe, Miller, Very, Bebout, Lamb, and Engle to the All-Western Pennsylvania eleven. Mauthe was selected by Louis Dougher (Washington *Times*) on the first All-America, and Miller was named All-America quarterback by the Philadelphia *Evening Bulletin*.

As a junior and captain of the 1911 undefeated eleven, Very had already been recognized by the Pittsburgh *Press* on its first team and by Walter Camp on his second-team All-America. In 1912 most metropolitan writers expected a Camp first-team citation for him. Said Cozens: "It will be hard to understand if Very is not placed on Walter Camp's All-America team." Richter of the Philadelphia *Evening Times* called Dex "the best end seen on Franklin Field. He possesses everything that goes to make a wonderful end. There does not seem to be anything he cannot do just a trifle better than anyone else." To Dick Guy of the Pittsburgh *Gazette-Times* he was "a second Hinkey; looks like the best wing on the eastern gridiron; Pittsburghers are practically unanimous in declaring that Very should make the All-America team."

Walter Camp didn't listen, and put Very on his second team again, but more generous experts selected him for the teams of Philadelphia's *Press, Bulletin,* and *Evening Times;* the Washington *Times;* the Scranton *Times;* the Pittsburgh *Leader;* and the New York *Sun.* He was named All-East by the Boston *Journal,* the New York *Sun,* and the Philadelphia *Public Ledger*.

Very's statistics during his senior year included 8 passes from Mauthe and Miller for 187 yards, 9 touchdowns, and 54 points scored from his end position. He was second only to Mauthe in scoring; led the team with 240 yards in kick returns; and was the fourth-leading ground-gainer, running the end-around 17 times for 234 yards.

One of the great all-around athletes of his era, Very played soccer as time permitted and was one of the team's stars in a scoreless tie against Penn on Franklin Field, where he had performed four times with the football team. When wrestling was organized in 1909 under Coach W. E. (Doc) Lewis, Dex was on the first team and won every bout but two during his undergraduate days in the 158-pound class.

After graduation Very joined the Pittsburgh Athletic Club and represented it as a wrestler in the Middle Atlantic and National AAU meets, winning regional titles at 158 and 175 pounds. In the national meet at Atlantic City, New Jersey, he scored a phenomenal double by winning national championships at both 175 pounds and heavyweight on the same day.

Thus ended the active athletic career of Dexter Very, who, at the age of 88 in 1977, was the only surviving member of the famous 1912 squad.[1] Never interested in playing professional football or serving as an official, he was completely dedicated to the amateur ideal and the fun of participation. He did officiate often at high school and college games, reaching the highest level as an official for Army-Navy classics, and the Rose Bowl game on January 1, 1933. Among his major eastern games was the 12–7 Yale victory over Navy in 1936 when Larry Kelley kicked a free ball that led to Yale's winning touchdown. Referee Very, backed up by the field judge (Shorty Miller), ruled that Kelley's kick was accidental. The incident brought about a rule change in 1937 making it illegal to kick a free ball on the ground regardless of intent. Following his Penn State days Very for many years was with Johns-Manville Company and later Sinclair Refining in a sales capacity. In 1975 he was still selling maintenance and building materials to major Pittsburgh customers of Republic Powdered Metals Company, Medina, Ohio.

Two of the 1912 players, James D. (Red) Bebout and Levi Lamb, lost their lives in World War I. A majority were successful in their fields, the most prominent being Captain J. Lester (Pete) Mauthe, who became president of the Youngstown Sheet and Tube Company and a member of the university Board of Trustees, 1938–67. Lloyd F. (Dad) Engle spent his life with the university as agricultural extension representative in Greene County. Albert S. Wilson was an executive of the Boone County (West Virginia) Coal Company; Daniel E. Welty, also an executive, was with the Blue Swan Mills, Sayre, Pennsylvania; R. N. (Punk) Berryman was a civil engineer in Cincinnati; and John Clark was an insurance broker in Staten Island.

[1] *Editor's footnote:* In 1976 Very was elected to the National Football Foundation's Hall of Fame when his qualifications were reviewed through the efforts of Ridge Riley and Coach Rip Engle.

Manager Bill Kerr owned his own company in Pittsburgh as a sales and service engineer representing power transmission machinery manufacturers. Albert A. Hansen was president of the Bear Film Company in San Francisco.

15

Some Little Sir

When the stocky man in white knickers unhesitatingly threw down his flag, the roar of delight from white-capped Midshipmen on one side of Philadelphia's huge Municipal Stadium was almost drowned out by the howl of anguish from the gray section of Cadets on the other.

Most of the 102,000 spectators at the Army-Navy game on November 28, 1936, had reconciled themselves to a scoreless tie—a rare outcome of the service classic—until late in the fourth period Navy drove to Army's 21, setting up the critical play. Bill Ingram II shot a pass right on target to end I. F. Fike, who had cut in front of the Army safety, Riggs Sullivan, on the Cadet 3. Desperately, Sullivan charged Fike from the rear, snatched at his elbows, and the ball slid off Fike's chest.

Field Judge E. E. (Shorty) Miller's courageous call of interference wasn't challenged, although the penalty unquestionably decided the outcome. Two plays later Sneed Schmidt, the Navy plunger, went over for the only touchdown of the game, and Ingram drop-kicked the goal.

The football fraternity accepted the judgment of one of its most respected officials, but what made the incident a *cause célèbre* was a follow-up column by General Hugh Johnson, an old West Pointer, who became a national figure during the early thirties as the crusty chief of President Roosevelt's National Recovery Administration. Having settled the nation's economic problems, the general turned to lesser affairs as a newspaper columnist for United Feature Syndicate. Not a sports commentator but an admittedly prejudiced spectator at the Army-Navy game, the general had been irritated that the decision of an official caused his alma mater's defeat. "When are these officials going to stop playing the game of football?" complained General Johnson. "There is such a thing as tact and judgment, even in a football official."

> When some little sir, who never in his life accomplished a deed of derring-do in the blood and sawdust of the arena, struts his "little hour or two" to blast a kid like Sullivan, this writer, for one, would like to have a moment alone with him.

Well! As one man, the eastern press came to the defense of Miller, led by John Kieran, erudite sportswriter of the New York *Times* and all-knowing star of a pioneer radio educational program, "Information Please." Kieran began his column[1] in this manner:

> ### Address to a General Officer
>
> Good General Hugh
> With the football you
> Have made a woeful fumble,
> And for the feat
> You now must eat
> The kind of pie called humble.

Kieran listed the "deeds of derring-do" accomplished by the "little sir" during his four years at Penn State and concluded this way:

> . . . The first fear in this corner was that the bitter blast would be the end of poor Shorty Miller. Yes, sir, if that came to his eye without warning he would be sure to laugh himself to death. . . . To show what it all amounts to in the end, apparently General Johnson had never heard of him. The only greater shock that could come would be to learn that E. E. (Shorty) Miller had never heard of General Hugh Johnson.

As an undergraduate the popular Miller received homage rare even at a time when most football players were revered as a special breed. This was not merely for his spectacular gridiron accom-

[1] New York *Times* (December 3, 1936).

plishments, but also for the constant friendliness of his shining personality. A classmate said of him: "When he spoke to you he made
you feel you were the only person he wanted to see—that he had just
been waiting to greet you."

Shorty handily won first prize, a motorcycle, as most popular undergraduate in a contest sponsored by a cigarette company, because
State College youngsters were solidly behind him, lining up at the
Athletic Store on Co-op Corner to vote with empty cigarette packages. An issue of *Froth,* the undergraduate humor magazine, was
dedicated to him, he made all the campus honoraries, and he was
selected as honor man of 1914 on Class Day.

At Harrisburg Central High School, where he starred in baseball
and football, his competitive career began in 1907 when Coach Bill
Shipp beckoned to his tiny 115-pound "bench warmer" to come in to
run the team against York. After Shorty quarterbacked Central's
rally to win, 11–5, he started every contest but one in both high
school and college. As a senior he captained the 1909 team that won
eight of ten games. One of the underclass cheerleaders, Ruth
Richards, later became Mrs. E. E. Miller. At Penn State he played
four years as a regular, and captained the team in 1913 and the baseball team in 1914.

Calling him the finest open-field runner Penn State ever had,
Dutch Hermann said he was like a waterbug

> . . . running all over the place—you couldn't see him. Actu-
> ally, he was too little to be lightning fast—legs too short—but
> he could start on a dime and go in any direction. Under punts a
> couple of guys would come at him—he'd take off and they'd
> knock heads together.

Shorty was one of the smallest players in professional football
(5-5, 140), when he quarterbacked the Massillon Tigers in 1916,
1917, and 1919, a teammate of such famous stars as Knute Rockne
and Gus Dorais of Notre Dame, Bob Peck of Pittsburgh, Tuss
McLaughry of Westminster, and Harvard's Charlie Brickley. Jim
Thorpe was still a terror on the gridiron with the Canton Bulldogs,
Massillon's great rival. The physically mismatched Miller and
Thorpe, never opponents at Penn State, met half a dozen times as
professionals. "In one game I was playing safety," Shorty recalled,
"and to my horror I saw Jim had eluded all our defenders. He was
twice my size, but I left my feet and brought him down. For that I

drew an extra ten dollars in my pay envelope." Later at a social function, Thorpe recognized him as "the little man who shook me up once."

Before he settled down as a Harrisburg schoolteacher, coach, school principal, and city official, Miller was athletic director and coach at Lebanon Valley College and managed the Steelton baseball team of the Bethlehem Steel League while employed in the Test Department of the steel mills. He had previously played semipro baseball at New Holland and Millersburg.

Harry Stuhldreher, one of Notre Dame's Four Horsemen, credited Miller with inspiring him to be a college football player. As a Massillon schoolboy, Stuhldreher followed Shorty's career with the town team. "I figured," said he, "if anyone that small could play against Thorpe and get away with it, I could."

Miller began his tenure as a coach and physical education teacher at Edison in Harrisburg when it was brand-new in 1919 and one of the first designated junior high schools in the East. He took a three-year leave of absence in 1936 to serve as city controller, returning to Edison in 1939 as principal. Although a firm disciplinarian, he was a beloved and respected principal during his eighteen years in this office. Always the school's Number One sports fan and cheerleader, he'd give rousing pep talks at school assemblies, and then, to show his still excellent physical condition because of participation in sports, he would walk across the stage on his hands—suit coat and tie dangling, coins dropping out of his pockets.

He stood no nonsense from school "toughies"—former students remember more than once seeing him hauling a "rowdy" twice his size down to the office. Also recalled is an important home basketball game with Lower Merion High School. A foul was called on the home crowd for unsportsmanlike conduct, and as a Lower Merion player went to the foul line, the Edison rooters began to boo. Suddenly Principal Miller was at the center of the floor, holding up his hands for silence. "I thought you were sportsmen," he said. "I still think so, but our visitors don't. I think in the excitement you merely forgot, but it's time you remember that Edison stands for fair play and good sportsmanship. Now a Lower Merion boy is going to try for a foul goal and I hope he makes it." In the silent gymnasium the goal was made. Lower Merion won the game, 15–13.

Shorty was in great demand as a speaker at sports banquets or whenever an inspirational talk was needed. He always prepared well, saved hundreds of clippings for references or ideas, and memorized innumerable poems and quotations. For one church father-son meeting he carefully memorized a poem which, to his dismay, was read by a young speaker who preceded him on the program. As Shorty concluded his talk, he turned to the former speaker: "And as this young man said earlier in the evening," he began, and then reeled off the whole poem, leading the spellbound audience to think he remembered the verse from having heard it once.

Miller's career as an official of high school, college, and pro football games spanned forty years. He was a charter member of the Eastern Intercollegiate Athletic Officials' Association, organized in 1921, and began his professional affiliation just before World War II as field judge and later back judge when a fifth official was added in 1945. Commissioner Bert Bell retained him for the National Football League in the mid-fifties as a rules interpreter on the technical adviser's staff, to lecture in training camps and elsewhere. Miller and Charlie Eckels of W&J were the oldest officials in point of continuous service. Aside from the famous Army-Navy game interference call, Shorty was involved in other controversial decisions. As field judge of the Yale-Navy game at New Haven, also in 1936, he ruled favorably for Yale when Larry Kelley kicked a loose ball, and his alleged failure to stop the clock to allow Penn a chance to defeat Michigan on Franklin Field in 1939 led to a scuffle in which his cap was swiped. Several months later, at a luncheon honoring him, he was given a helmet used by John Nicholson, Michigan lineman, and signed by Coach Fritz Crisler and members of the Michigan team.

For a number of years Miller was on the Harrisburg City Council, directing the City Parks Department. A newspaper columnist called him an honest, conscientious, hard-working, unspoiled politician—"one of the few who have gone through many years of life without becoming cynical, embittered, or distrustful of his fellowmen."

Shorty Miller is recognized as the first of Penn State's great running halfbacks in the tradition of Way, Killinger, Wilson, Haines, Moore, Campbell, Mitchell, Harris, and Cappelletti. He still holds Penn State's single-game rushing record (250) and for years held its individual records for most yards by returning punts in one season (35 punts for 596 yards); touchdowns in one game (5); yards rushing in one season (801); total offense in one season (1,031 yards); and most touchdown passes in one season (9). Yet Miller often said he was proudest of another record: He held the ball for

Pete Mauthe's 51-yard field goal against Pitt in 1912. "That record should have been 52 yards," he claimed. "I called the play and held the ball square on Penn State's 48-yard line." Mauthe, his teammate, wrote about him in 1952:

> Shorty was honest to a fault and a fair competitor in anybody's league . . . to me he is an example for any boy in sports. No finer character ever participated in football—and he carried more than his full share with never a complaint . . . he never called his own signal to add to his reputation . . . he was loved by every other member of the team and we all spent time in trying to help and protect him—and the Lord knows he didn't need it half as much as some of the rest of us.

On December 10, 1974, Eugene E. (Shorty) Miller was inducted into the National Football Foundation's Hall of Fame, a little more than eight years after his death on September 20, 1966.

Prophets of another successful season in 1913 were banking on the invincible Captain Miller and resourceful Coach Hollenback, but failed to evaluate the loss of Mauthe, Very, Hansen, Wilson, and Engle. A dearth of new material was attributed by some to the absence of Pop Golden, who was no longer around to "sell the college" to high school and prep school stars. Five newcomers made substantial contributions before graduation: Bill Wood, center; Cecil McDowell, tackle; Ran Miller, guard; George Morris, end; and Jeff Clark, fullback, one of the last four-letter winners of his era.

The season was a disaster to Coach Hollenback, a hard loser, who agonized over the string of six straight defeats. The opener, against Carnegie Tech, had been promising, largely due to the stupendous performance of Miller, who scored on runs of 23, 55, 47, 37, and 40 yards to amass his enduring single-game record. Penn State won the Tech game, 49–0, but the next week was held to the low score of 16–0 by Gettysburg, coached by Pete Mauthe.

In a following "breather" that turned out to be a shocker, the W&J eleven inflicted a shutout on the Lions, 17–0, the first defeat of Hollenback's coaching career at Penn State. They might have been able to recoup if the fourth game, against Villanova, had been retained, but a scheduling change occurred after the season started. Harvard athletic authorities approached Graduate Manager Ray Smith about a game at Cambridge because Norwich University canceled after its captain died of a football injury. The Crimson wanted a "hard" game to prepare for Yale and Princeton, and Penn State was eager for football relations with Harvard. Villanova "kindly consented" to the cancellation, according to the *Collegian.*

After meeting in New York with Harvard's Graduate Treasurer F. W. Moore to complete arrangements, Graduate Manager Smith reported that future games would depend on Penn State's showing in the coming encounter and "the conduct of its players." Harvard, at the peak of its power under Haughton, was to have its second successive undefeated, untied season in 1913. No one expected the Lions to handle Harvard's brilliant backfield, with the likes of Brickley, Mahan, and Hardwick. Extremely bad weather conditions at Cambridge prevented Miller from performing at his best in his anticipated duel with Mahan. Harvard won the game, 29–0, but the *Alumni Quarterly* pointed out that it really wasn't a one-sided contest. The Boston *Globe* praised Penn State's performance:

Shorty Miller lived up to his reputation—rain or shine. Penn State plays good, rough football with no "pardon me's."

The Boston *Herald* noted that the heavier Mahan could run under the trying conditions, where Miller played like "a man with his feet tied." Envisioning a "dream" backfield of Miller, Mahan, Hardwick, and Brickley, the *Herald* added:

Penn State, although badly beaten, presented a well-coached, well-conditioned team and (contrary to a local impression) did not rely upon roughness, but played hard, clean football all the way and never reached that groggy condition often noted in a badly beaten aggregation.

Coach Haughton expressed the hope that Penn State would appear on Harvard's schedule the following year. The *Collegian,* which usually put football on page 1, moved the Harvard defeat to page 3, but said that the team had been "honored in defeat, not disgraced." Shorty Miller, for one, was unmovable.

Some years later the Harvard All-America end, Tack Hardwick (who played as halfback against Penn State), wrote in a Boston *Daily Record* column:

. . . About as big as a pint of peanuts . . . it was impossible to see [Miller] behind State's large and powerful line, and when he ran with the ball, it was the devil and all where he was going to break out. As he ran his shoulders never seemed to vary in height, they just slid along on an even plane, but suddenly his neck would telescope a foot or so like a turtle's and Shorty's head would peek over the line, size up the field and then—plop! He'd pull in his periscope neck and again completely disappear. When you finally got a shot at him in the open field, he was next to impossible to smack cleanly. You'd drive for his knees and that very second he'd draw his knees into his body like a turtle's legs and you'd swish right under him. The legless body would travel a yard or so and then out would come his legs, churning away even before they hit the ground.

The loss to Harvard was Hollenback's second, but the worst was yet to come—a whitewash by Pennsylvania, 17–0, the first defeat experienced by Big Bill on Franklin Field. Sorely missing his great ends, Very and Wilson, Hollenback tried everything to bolster his flanks, first moving Berryman to one end and freshman Bill Wood, a center, to the other. Harry Weston, Gordon Voght, Harry Shupe, Bob Craig, and Elwood Cornog also had a shot at the position before George Morris and Bert Barron finally won. Barron had played in 1910, but dropped out of college and completed his career in 1914. He was head coach at Michigan State in 1921 and 1922 and for many years a coach and teacher in Philadelphia public schools.

The Notre Dame game was by far the most important yet scheduled at home. Despite its success under Hollenback, Penn State could not persuade "name" teams to visit isolated State College, nor could it afford to pay the required guarantees. Pennsylvania, Harvard, Yale, Princeton, and Cornell—frequent opponents in the early years—never once came to New Beaver Field. Navy, a regular opponent, didn't come until 1923. Army made its first trip to central Pennsylvania in 1957. Until well into the twenties, Dartmouth and Syracuse were the only major eastern teams seen on the home field.

The 1913 Irish were undefeated, but their schedule listed such modest opponents as Alma and the Christian Brothers. Coming East a week before the Penn State game, they slaughtered Army, 35–13, and thereafter no eastern opponent ever considered Notre Dame a minor foe. They defeated the Cadets and their great stars— Merellat, Prichard, and McEwan—by unprecedented use of the forward pass, with the formidable combination of Gus Dorais to Captain Knute Rockne. Army's only defeat in 1913 proved to eastern fans that a Midwest team could play good football, and introduced to the public the tremendous possibilities of an attack based primarily on the pass. On Pennsylvania Day (Friday, November 7), a record home crowd saw Notre Dame inflict the first defeat (14–7) on the Lions at New Beaver Field. The visitors, scoring late in the first half and early in the second, fought off a Penn State assault that nearly deadlocked the game. During a 70-yard drive for the first score, Rockne reportedly deceived Lion players by limping badly until he caught a pass from Dorais and then streaked past the last defender with no trace of an injury. Ray Eichenlaub's line-plunging led to Notre Dame's second touchdown, scored by the Irish fullback. Halfback Joe Pliska also helped in the victory, and Dorais kicked both goals.

A fumble recovered by tackle Cec McDowell set up Penn State's touchdown, made on a pass from Miller to Levi Lamb after the visitors had stopped a drive led by Miller, Berryman, and Tobin. Home fans suffered late in the game when an offside penalty nullified what they thought might be Tobin's tying touchdown.

After losing to Navy 10–0 at Annapolis, Penn State closed its dismal season in Pittsburgh on Thanksgiving Day, bowing to Pitt, 7–6. The Lions posted the first touchdown on a pass from Berryman to Clark, but Miller missed the extra point. Before the half ended, Guy Williamson tied the score on a 68-yard run and then kicked the winning goal.

Determined not to endure such a struggle again, Hollenback asked former players to contact high school and prep school talent. Names of the new "crop" listed by the *Collegian* in September 1914 as potential "All-Americas" now have an unfamiliar ring, but some made their mark in the prewar era, and a few who entered that fall were members of the mighty postwar eleven of 1919. The Number One acquisition, according to the *Collegian,* was Robert Arlington Higgins, who would captain the 1919 team after service in France.

Higgins established his precollege reputation as a great athlete at Peddie School, Hightstown, New Jersey. One of the most sought-after players in the country, he was supposed to be set for Princeton until Coach Hollenback sent his chief assistant, Dick Harlow, to divert him to central Pennsylvania's mountains. Harlow was rough on the football field but could turn on the charm. "Recruiter" was not yet in football's lexicon. The practice was, however, in full cry. "Bird-dogging," as it was also known, was at its cutthroat worst in 1914, with no limits, no regulations, and no holds barred. A story persists that Higgins went along on a weekend trip to the Poconos where Harlow kept him for a week, hidden away from his Princeton pursuers, until classes started at Penn State.

The persuasive personality of C. W. (Bill) Martin, a relative newcomer on Hollenback's staff, also helped attract young athletes. Bill, originally from Notre Dame, had come the year before to be track coach and general athletic trainer, and could do double duty on the road as a talent seeker. Lion runners and field men lost only five dual meets under his coaching from 1913 through 1922. (Martin's first salary was $1,500; it was raised to $1,600 in 1914–15.)

Dutch Hermann, who coached at Shadyside Academy in Pittsburgh that fall, was credited with lining up three good prospects from the Wilkes-Barre area: Earl Balbach, a 270-pound lineman, and a pair of tackles of lesser proportions. Balbach, listed as a substitute in 1914, never lettered, but Floyd Parrish and Rudy Kraft became valuable squad members from 1915 through 1917.

While Hollenback encouraged former players to help in the field, he was less enthusiastic about a lingering tradition that the "old boys" should come back for short periods to help coach on a non-paid basis. Bill preferred to rely on his permanent staff, small as it was. Nevertheless, John (Biggie) Clark, center, 1911–13, was a part-time freshman coach in 1914, along with Al Hansen, who was on the teaching staff as an instructor in botany. Hermann visited for a week or so in preseason, as did Ollie Vogel, new coach at Bellefonte Academy. The *Collegian* reported that "Hi Henry '07 will be here to assist. He is still full of State, and like Harlow, is married." The *Collegian* also solicited support from the administration: "It is hoped that Mr. Vorse [A. O. Vorse], the College News Editor, will find time to be present at a few practices."

Only a few of those who entered with Higgins achieved any measure of stardom. They were Ben Cubbage, a back from Central High, Philadelphia, who played with Higgins on the 1919 team; George Kratt, tackle; W. C. (Whitey) Thomas, end; and Stan Ewing, quarterback, who had been coached by Andy Kerr at Schenley High School in Pittsburgh.

Depletions from 1913 were not calamitous, except for the graduation of quarterback Shorty Miller, John Clark, and Red Bebout. An unexpected setback was the unforeseen academic ineligibility of Punk Berryman, halfback for the past three years. (He returned to win another letter in 1915.) Miller's place obviously would be difficult to fill, but the coaches had high hopes for Donald Ray

James. The rest of the backfield was set, with Jeff Clark at fullback and Captain Yegg Tobin and the veteran Dan Welty at the halves.

Westminster, Muhlenberg, Gettysburg, and Ursinus were held scoreless in the team's unimpressive early games. For the big test at Cambridge, students planned a mass meeting to rival the one before the 1912 Pitt game where Dr. Dan Luby made his stirring pep talk, and the memorable 1913 sendoff for Pitt when Shorty Miller delivered his famous last speech. The rally in the auditorium was organized by Neil M. Fleming, 1913 varsity manager and newly hired assistant to Graduate Manager Smith.

The 13–13 tie with Harvard in 1914 was a stunning upset, especially since it was unarguable that for over three quarters the Lions outplayed a Harvard team ranked by some experts as the greatest in its history.

This was one of Coach Percy Haughton's mighty Harvard machines, undefeated that season, later to shut out both Princeton and Yale, 20–0 and 36–0, respectively. The result could be rated as one of Coach Hollenback's greatest achievements. Much has been written about the 21–21 tie with the Crimson in 1921, but the 1914 deadlock was more significant because it surprised a Harvard eleven then at the very top of the football world.

So lightly did the home team take the visitors from State College, Pennsylvania, that Coach Haughton was absent on a scouting expedition with Assistant Coach Lothrop Withington and quarterback Mal Logan. Harvard also missed many of its great stars—Brickley had been stricken with appendicitis, and Mahan, Hardwick, Trumbull, and Pennock, all of whom appeared against State in 1913, were injured and unable to play. Assistant Coach Leary, left in charge of the Harvard team, did have available many excellent players, including Fred Bradlee, Camp's first-team All-America halfback in 1914; the Coolidge brothers, Jeff and Charles, at ends; Ted Withington, Bill Underwood, and Mel Weston, guards; Don Wallace, center; quarterback Ernie Swigert; and fullback Hugs Francke.

The game was a mere three minutes old when the visiting Lions advanced the kickoff into Harvard territory and Levi Lamb delighted the small band of Penn State fans in the crowd of 22,000 by kicking a field goal from the 33-yard line. The Penn State group included Dr. George Gilbert (Swampy) Pond, dean of the School of Natural Science, and Trustee Augustus C. Read. Before the first period ended, the Lions started another drive from midfield, with quarterback Don

James, running the team like a veteran, completing a pass to end Whitey Thomas, good for 27 yards. After Captain Tobin made 5 from the 18, fullback Clark crashed through for 13 yards and a touchdown. Lamb's goal gave Penn State a first-quarter lead of 10–0.

Less than a minute before half time, Jeff Coolidge caught a touchdown pass from Bradlee after the Crimson had recovered a fumble by Clark on the Penn State 8. Coolidge fell across the goal line just as he was tackled. Penn State dominated the play in the scoreless third period, and early in the final quarter Tobin intercepted a Harvard pass, giving Lamb an opportunity to kick his second field goal, from the 30.

Shortly over a minute from the end, the home team had to kick and seemed about to lose its first game since the Carlisle Indians won at Cambridge in 1911. (Harvard had a string of 22 games without a defeat or tie, finally broken by Cornell in 1915.) But the unfortunate Levi Lamb, so often the object of Coach Hollenback's ire, fumbled the punt, and it was recovered by Francke on the Lion 38.

Now the Crimson came through with characteristic resourcefulness. Assistant Coach Leary sent in a substitute named Westmore Wilcox, a track man who could run the quarter in less than 49 seconds. A "spot" player, Wilcox wasn't even in the official Cantab squad picture of 1914, but he was to be the hero of the Penn State game. The play used by Harvard, called "99," was selected because the strong Penn State ends—Higgins, Thomas, and Barron—repeatedly were crashing. Francke faked a buck at the line and, just as he was tackled by Barron, lateraled to Wilcox to the left side. The speedster was almost stopped by Bill Wood near the goal line, but momentum carried him over. Ted Withington tied the score, kicking from a difficult angle. (Newspaper accounts recorded Wilcox's run as anywhere from 38 to 60 yards.)

In 1914, possession of the game ball by the winning team was still a meaningful tradition, and the home team usually kept it after ties. In a fine gesture of sportsmanship, Wally Trumbull, the injured Harvard captain, gave the game ball to Captain Tobin, saying it was the first to leave the Harvard stadium since Jim Thorpe was presented one in 1911.

The only disgruntled fan was the manager of the Nittany Theatre in State College, who had planned to take movies at the game but was refused permission by the Harvard Athletic Association. He did secure several hundred feet at the team's training quarters in Auburndale, including shots of the squad leaving for the stadium.

New England alumni gave a dinner honoring the team at Young's Hotel, with speeches by Dr. Pond, Trustee Read, Captain Tobin, and Coach Hollenback, who said three things were responsible for Penn State's fine showing: student support, physical condition, and a team of fighters who did not know how to accept defeat. Jimmy Leyden '14 led the crowd in singing "Victory," the new fight song he had composed the year before and taught to students in the fall of 1913.

Fans listening to returns in Schwab Auditorium were uproarious. Cheering, singing, and high jinks lasted through Saturday night and began again when the players arrived Sunday night, but the climax was to come Monday evening because student leaders announced that Penn State would honor the Lion squad with the greatest bonfire ever witnessed on campus. All day Monday wagons hauled loads of scrap wood, gathered from miles around, to the drill field between the Armory and the old Beta house (between Willard and Deike buildings today). The order was to "get anything that isn't nailed down," but much of the "debris" included perfectly serviceable telephone poles, wooden sidewalks, fences, and outhouses. And many wagons, after their final runs, were thrown on, too. Woe to any freshman caught without a piece of wood in his hands—he was sent scurrying off for a contribution.

A crowd estimated at 3,500 assembled at 9 P.M. around the enormous woodpile, over fifty feet high, which had been saturated with five barrels of gasoline. With the football squad in the place of "honor" encircling the wood, Captain Tobin walked forward carrying the torch. He threw on the ignition and was instantly blown off his feet by the gigantic explosion that shook the whole valley, blowing out all the windows in the east side of the Beta house more than a hundred yards away, breaking some windows in Carnegie Library, and knocking down plaster in the president's house.

Tobin and Jack (George J.) Sauerhoff, sophomore class president, were hospitalized in Bellefonte with severe burns of face and hands. Other students received minor burns and bruises from flying firewood. It was reported that the football captain would probably be lost for the season. Those in charge of the historic conflagration excused themselves somewhat weakly in the *Collegian* by saying that previous bonfires had always been helped along by the application of kerosene, but the town dealer had kept this fact from the purchasers because he wanted to sell gasoline.

Without Tobin, Penn State had enough momentum to defeat a weak Lafayette team that Saturday, 17–0, but from then on the season deteriorated, with successive losses to Lehigh, Michigan State, and Pittsburgh. Fumbling, weak tackling, and general disorganization—completely uncharacteristic of Bill Hollenback teams—had much to do with the Lehigh defeat, 20–7. Michigan State aroused excitement among Penn State's followers on its first visit to the campus, and the "Aggies" made a most favorable impression, traveling with their fine band. They scored the only touchdown of the game when Captain George (Carp) Julian broke loose for a 65-yard run. One of the great midwestern players of his time, Julian was overlooked by Walter Camp on his All-America team. In a letter congratulating him on his career, Camp justified the omission because the "Aggies" permitted four years of competition, a policy he must have forgotten when he later named Bob Higgins, a four-year player. Lamb kicked a field goal, and in the waning game, Penn State was held twice for downs near the Spartan goal line, losing, 6–3. Coach Hollenback's use of Tobin caused considerable criticism. Tobin had been released from the hospital with his head and hands bandaged on Thursday before the game. The *Collegian* was rightfully indignant:

> The necessity of giving Captain Tobin a chance to star was ridiculous for he doesn't need such a chance. . . . Captain Tobin was not in condition. No man two days out of the hospital could have been. . . . Even more ludicrous was the sight of a pair of badly burned and bandaged hands trying to hold for a placement kick.

The defeat by Pitt (13–3) was set up by Penn State fumbles, one of them slipping through the still bandaged hands of Tobin. The worst moment came when the Lions tried to pass for a score after faking a field goal. Lamb threw the ball right into the hands of a Pitt player. It didn't help matters to be beaten by a Panther team beginning one of its finest eras. From its 1913 defeat by Penn State through the West Virginia conflict in 1919, Pitt lost only one game in forty-one (to W&J in 1914).

Not long after the 1914 season Hollenback accepted an offer from a Philadelphia coal company, realizing that it would prevent his association with intercollegiate athletics beyond the Philadelphia area.

While the business offer was probably the principal reason for his resignation, personal factors were involved. Defeat made him petulant, and he was embittered by criticism, especially over his premature use of the injured Tobin. Hollenback also felt that Penn State would have difficulty fielding good teams under eligibility rules, effective with the 1915 season, banning freshmen from the varsity and requiring transfers to have a year's residency to be eligible. These restrictions had been discussed and apparently favored since 1912–13, but a strong stand by the *Collegian* probably forced the committee's action. The student newspaper pointed out that most of the better eastern schools abided by such regulations, as did the Western Conference. The opposition claimed that Penn State wasn't ready for this stringency and that many institutions adopting such rules had failed to produce winning teams. The *Collegian* countered:

> Failures have only been at small institutions where the material is scarce. Penn State teams have consistently and repeatedly proven themselves on a par with the best in the country, but recognition is lacking and is given grudgingly . . . games with the big teams are hard to get. We are constantly forced to cater to their demands. Shall our Verys, Mauthes, Millers and Harlows of the future be placed on the honor roll with unstinted praise? . . . Do you believe in pulling against the current or floating with the stream? Are you progressive?

Eliminating freshmen from varsity competition was strongly supported with statistics in one *Collegian* editorial. During the preceding 17 years, of the 89 players awarded football letters, 30 did not graduate, and of those 30, 21 had won a letter their freshman year. This "wasn't a very strong advertisement for Penn State and her ideals," said the *Collegian*. Taking heed with the hope of bettering Penn State's image, the Athletic Committee then tried to concoct a new coaching system to keep the college among the football select.[2]

Hollenback did return to football briefly in 1916, taking on the head coaching job at Syracuse for one season (5–4–0), and then went back to his successful business career. Born in Pennsylvania's Philipsburg coal country, he once said, "I've always been a coal cracker, and I guess I'm always going to be one." He was long involved in the "politics" of football at the University of Pennsylvania.

[2] *Editor's footnote:* To this day, the controversy continues. Coach Joe Paterno plays freshmen, since the eligibility rule allows it, but has said that he would prefer a return to the old standard.

Following his undefeated season at Penn State in 1912, the Philadelphia *North American* led a strong movement to replace Coach Andy Smith with Hollenback, but when Smith lost his job, the post went to an older alumnus, George Brooks '89, who did little to improve Penn's football. In 1918, when Coach Folwell had influenza followed by pneumonia, Hollenback pinch-hit for his friend. Folwell returned in November, but Bill continued as field coach that season, with Folwell in an advisory capacity. The Hollenback Center is named in his honor, and he was the major contributor for this building, which contains locker and training rooms for athletic teams using Franklin and River fields. It also houses offices, classrooms, and other facilities of Penn's Army and Navy ROTC units.

Hollenback made infrequent trips to State College through the years, returning last for the fiftieth reunion of the 1912 team on October 20, 1962. He was elected to the Football Hall of Fame in 1953 and died on March 12, 1968.

16

The Harlow Years, 1915–17

Richard Cresson Harlow alone among Penn State's head football coaches gained greater professional fame after leaving the vale of old Mount Nittany. As a rugged, dedicated tackle in 1910 and 1911 he was considered by many of his contemporaries among the best linemen of his time.

For a big fellow Harlow moved fast, and in 1911 he blocked a record number of kicks. But he was slower than many other linemen in getting downfield. The riding he got for this sometimes goaded him to a super effort. During an early minor game on New Beaver Field in 1911, somebody yelled, "Tie a bell on Harlow this time," and Dick, with his dander up, tore after the opponent's kick-returning specialist, known to be fast and tricky. The visiting speedster began to run laterally, with Harlow after him. At the sideline, the pursued turned his back on the pursuer, heading for the goal line, then moved away from the charging Harlow toward the opposite sideline. Harlow had had enough. He halted and screamed: "For crimey sakes, lock the gate, he's stealing the ball!"

On the team Dick's weakness was losing his temper. Henny Scholl, an assistant coach who figured Dick played better when angered, would tell the player facing Harlow in a scrimmage to pick on him verbally. Coach Hollenback considered this strategy ineffective. When opponents worked on raising the big tackle's blood pressure, the job of cooling him down went to Dex Very, who played next to him in the line.

The hot-tempered Harlow also was extremely sensitive. After he became head coach in 1915, he was trying on one occasion to relax at the movies in the old Pastime Theatre, where the management was experimenting with a few acts of obviously seedy vaudeville. An old-time burlesque comedian appeared in outlandishly big, baggy pants, and the crowd hooted. "Don't laugh," said he. "I borrowed these from Dick Harlow." The audience roared, but Dick strode to the stage in a fury and threatened bodily harm unless the performer apologized.

Harlow stayed on after graduation for three seasons as Coach Hollenback's top assistant and line coach, beginning then to handle scouting assignments. Later, under Hugo Bezdek, he was regarded as one of the most astute scouts in the business. Soon after the 1914 campaign, Penn State's Athletic Committee (formerly Advisory Board) showed signs of moving toward a "graduate" policy with a full-time resident coach, and made no attempt to keep Hollenback when he indicated his intent to go into business. In December, Harlow was interviewed informally and was appointed head coach at an official meeting on January 2, 1915. His contract at $1,500 (later raised to $1,800) included the promise of at least two assistants— one for the varsity, the other to be freshman coach.

The committee, craving victories, seemed to favor a "Penn State system" but wanted a nonalumnus on the staff "in order to receive the best ideas from other coaching systems." In line with its desire to use one of the two assistants to coach another sport, Burke M. (Dutch) Hermann '12 was hired as freshman coach and varsity basketball coach. An unsuccessful effort was made to secure Charlie Brickley—the famous Harvard All-America would consider only a head coaching position at $3,000, which committee members thought excessive. Lawrence W. (Bud) Whitney was finally accepted as varsity assistant at $1,200 before his graduation from Dartmouth in June 1915, but signing of the formal contract was delayed to let him continue on the Dartmouth track team. On the 1912 American Olympic squad he had won a bronze medal at Stockholm. The former three-sport athlete at Worcester Academy had also been football captain at Dartmouth in 1914 and was selected fullback on Walter Camp's third All-America team.

Bill Hollenback, head coach 1909–14.

Action in the Penn–Penn State game of October 28, 1911: E. E. (Shorty) Miller (left, with hole in stocking) was the game's star (two sensational touchdown runs) in Penn State's 22–6 victory. Miller's teammates displayed the photo on a bulletin board in the Old Track House, captioning him ''The Spectator.''

Shorty Miller (right) races three Penn gridders for a loose ball in the 1912 game on Franklin Field, won by the Lions, 14–0.

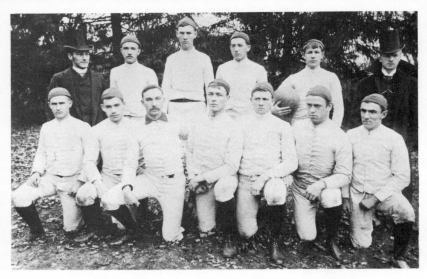

First Official Penn State Football Team, 1887
TOP ROW: Clarence G. Cleaver, coach; John Price Jackson; John S. Mitchell; James C. Mock; George H. Linsz, captain; John F. L. Morris, manager.
KNEELING: W. L. Barclay; H. B. McLean; John S. Weller; C. M. Kessler; Charles C. Hildebrand; J. R. Rose; Harry R. Leyden.

Undefeated, Untied Team of 1912
FRONT ROW: Bob Whitney, L. S. (Dad) Engle, Shorty Miller, Captain H. L. (Pete) Mauthe, Dex Very, Al Wilson, Al Hansen. MIDDLE ROW: R. N. (Punk) Berryman, Dan Welty, Levi Lamb, J. D. Clark, James D. (Red) Bebout, E. W. (Yegg) Tobin. BACK ROW: Coach Bill Hollenback, Assistant Coach Dick Harlow, Bert Barron, Manager Bill Kerr.

William T. (Mother) Dunn '07, Penn State's first All-America (center, 1906).

Three famous athletes (l. to r.): Earl E. Hewitt '02 captained the 1901 team. Andrew Latham Smith '04 transferred to Pennsylvania and was an All-America; in the early 1920s, he coached the California "wonder teams." Leroy Scholl is the only Penn State player to win six Varsity letters in football (1896–1901).

Eugene E. (Shorty) Miller '14, captain in 1913, was, like Very, later admitted to the College Football Hall of Fame.

Dexter W. Very '13, Varsity right end, 1909–12, captain of the undefeated 1911 team, never missed starting a game in four years.

Levi Lorenzo Lamb '15, a three-sport athlete, was one of the first Penn Staters killed in World War I. The athletic aid fund is named for him.

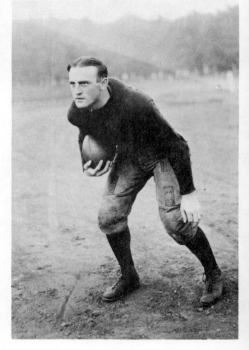

Halfback H. L. (Hinkey) Haines '21 was one of State's triple-threat athletes. He later played with the world champion New York Yankees baseball team and with the world champion New York Giants football team.

Hugo Bezdek, head coach 1918–29.

To stabilize football and assure successful teams on a long-term basis, the committee issued a public statement that it wanted Penn State graduates on the coaching staff without suffering the evils of the "graduate system," thus indicating its wariness of inbreeding. The new coaches were charged "to institute a comprehensive course of training for freshmen and other squad members not only during the fall season, but throughout the winter and spring."

Hermann's freshman program was an immediate success, due partially to Harlow's proficiency in recruiting, a phase of the game neglected during the last two seasons under Hollenback. The Lion Cubs, undefeated for three years, numbered the Penn and Pitt freshmen among their victims, with the Pitt victories especially pleasing because the Panthers were at the height of their power. In 1916 the young Lions defeated Pitt freshmen using Coach Pop Warner's own single- and double-wing plays, picked up while scouting the Panther varsity.

The earliest team coached by Hermann included Carl Beck, Harrisburg Tech; Larry Conover, Atlantic City, New Jersey; Harry Robb, Pittsburgh's Peabody; B. C. (Casey) Jones, Bellefonte Academy; Al Pond, State College High; Jim O'Donnell and Jim Thorpe, transfers from Notre Dame; Ed Ege, Wilkinsburg; and Al Krushank, Bethlehem Prep. While many of the 1915 "recruits" became well-known varsity players, at least one made his name in another field. Edward L. Bortz, a premedical student from Greensburg, won a minor award in football in 1916, but at the end of his sophomore year he transferred to Harvard Medical College, later becoming chief of medical surgery at Lankenau Hospital in Philadelphia and president of the American Medical Association.

Harlow enjoyed as healthy a climate as any coach could ask to start his first season. Not even the Athletic Committee expected him to field a big winner when only half a dozen regulars were returning from 1914 and he had to establish a new system with the handicap of new eligibility regulations. Pressure on Harlow was somewhat alleviated by Whitney's arrival in September and a short-term visit from Brickley, invited to work with the kickers. Commenting on Penn State's "very difficult" schedule, Brickley said in an interview that at Harvard "we wouldn't think of tackling such a schedule even with the championship team we had last year." Penn, Harvard, and Pitt were the only major games on the card, although Lehigh had been gaining prestige rapidly.

Dick Harlow's name is not attached to a football system, nor is he famed as an inventive coaching genius, but he became highly respected for meticulous attention to fundamentals. He got the most from available material by skillful handling of personnel and by emphasizing a variety of defensive maneuvers while keeping his offense relatively uncomplicated. Most of his strong qualities as a coach— later so apparent at Colgate, Western Maryland, and especially at Harvard in the middle and late 1930s—also were discernible during his first head coaching year at Penn State.

He topped his bachelor's degree in forestry with a master's in 1913, but his great lifelong love was ornithology—a passion he had acquired as a boy living in the Poconos. Any spare time he had away from Penn State football was spent on field trips to Bear Meadows and other places in the nearby mountains, where wildlife was abundant. Many of his players were persuaded or coerced into accompanying their coach on these weekend trips in pursuit of rare birds and plants.

Football practice under Harlow was noted for detailed organization, planned in advance like a laboratory experiment, with no time wasted on the field. The coaches worked in uniform until after 7 P.M. each day because classes were not over until five o'clock. Harlow fought this late-class obstacle and no doubt inspired a *Collegian* editorial urging authorities to excuse players from the four-to-five class, noting that Yale's practice started at two-thirty and Cornell's at three-thirty. Evidence exists of some concessions by the administration.

The new coach also succumbed to a bit of gadgetry at first, notably a wood-carved male figure. In 1915 during spring practice and into the fall, the backs threw passes at the mannikin from every conceivable angle—a drill that today would seem ludicrous. Another innovation, attributed to Coach Whitney, was the spiral pass from center, which Harlow insisted all centers should learn because it increased accuracy, reduced wind resistance, and enabled the kicker to receive the ball in the same position for every punt, thereby overcoming fumbling. Whitney also introduced "grass drills."

Initially Coach Harlow installed the Minnesota shift because of Whitney's familiarity with it, but he stayed with many of Hollenback's plays, and later applied his own variation to the single- and double-wing plays he got from Coach Warner at Pitt. He consistently adhered to a basic coaching concept that a team should perfect only a few plays for each game. Penn State was said to have used no more than seven plays in the 1915 Penn game, but "perfect execution made up for lack of variety."

Utilizing as many players as possible in early games was a Harlow gambit almost unique at a time when powerful teams liked to overwhelm their small-college opponents. He was among the first coaches who claimed to be satisfied with enough points to win. Of course, there were no weekly polls in those days.

Harlow was a master at dressing-room exhortation, a pioneer in employing sentiment, loyalty, and obligation to alma mater to spur the team to greater heights. P. W. (Red) Griffiths—former Ohio congressman and Marietta College coach who played under Harlow in 1917—writes that he has never forgotten Dick's inspirational talk on Penn State tradition delivered to freshman football candidates at the Track House.

In early-season victories over Westminster (26–0) and Lebanon Valley (13–0), the coaches were worried about weakness at tackles. Against Pennsylvania these positions were assigned to Captain Bill Wood, shifted from center, and Stanley John Czarnecki, a rugged sophomore called "Zarney" so frequently that the nickname appeared in most 1915 newspaper accounts. A fine heavyweight wrestler, he was a great asset to the team for three years and was a guard on Walter Camp's 1917 All-America second team.

Penn's 1915 team wasn't a powerhouse but won its first three games, later tied both Michigan and Navy, and lost to strong Pittsburgh by a single touchdown. Penn State's backers had become almost resigned to a mediocre season, believing that Coach Harlow needed more time to "perfect his system." Students and alumni in the Franklin Field stands were elated when their team trailed by only 3–0 in the first half, and ecstatic in the third quarter when the Lions scored two touchdowns, one on a 40-yard run by halfback Punk Berryman and another on a forward-pass play of 40 yards from quarterback Stan Ewing to end Bob Higgins. (Ewing was a replacement for Ray James, who had dropped out of college.) Penn State held its opponents scoreless in the second half, winning the game, 13–3. News accounts said the Lions' end play with Higgins and Thomas almost equaled that of the formidable Very and Wilson.

"Miracle maker" praise of Coach Harlow unfortunately ensued— and not only in the hometown press. A Sunday (October 17) Philadelphia *Public Ledger* feature, authored by "Touchdown," claimed that the "Penn State system" after only three weeks was completely successful. Headlined "Harlow Makes Good as Coach," the story extolled the Athletic Committee for wisely combining the graduate policy with a "corps" of associates from other colleges, "corps" presumably being Whitney from Dartmouth and Brickley from Harvard, but emphasized that in this "committee system" the head coach had the last word. "Touchdown" grandiosely described Harlow's plan to merge the best features of football at other colleges:

> Guards will play in the plunging Penn style; tackles follow the Princeton game, playing rather wide and fighting in; ends use a combination of the Harvard and Dartmouth systems, crossing the line of scrimmage and coming in fast from the rear. Such work, such ideas cannot fail. Dick Harlow has proved himself a first-class coach.

Defeat ironically first befell Harlow at Harvard. The *Collegian* listed impressive statistics indicating that the "heartbreaking" loss was all a mistake. The Lions had 19 first downs to Harvard's 11 and gained 393 yards from scrimmage to their opponents' 239. Berryman was credited with 177 yards by rushing compared to 97 by Eddie Mahan, the three-time All-America fullback. The potent Harvard team, last of the great Haughton elevens, would go on to defeat Yale, 41–0. Besides Mahan it had other All-Americas in King at halfback and Gilman at tackle. Excessive losses in penalties (100 yards) and fumbling led to Penn State's defeat, 13–0.

The Lions were within striking distance four times, and a touchdown by Berryman (on a pass from Ewing) was called back because of a holding penalty. Harvard scored in the second period when Mahan's punt was fumbled by Ewing. In pursuing the ball Ewing accidentally kicked it into the end zone where Ken Parsons, Harvard tackle, fell on it for a touchdown. Mahan scored from the 6-yard line following a drive from midfield in the third quarter. The Lions protested, claiming Mahan was a good foot from the goal line when the referee signaled the points.

Captain Wood, Berryman, Ewing, Jeff Clark, and Higgins were outstanding against the Cantabs. Walter Camp put Higgins and Berryman on the second and third All-America teams for their remarkable performances in the Harvard and Penn games.[1]

---

[1] The popular William Wallace Wood might have led the team for three years had it not been contrary to tradition. The Pottstown native remained after his graduation as an agronomist in 1916, helping with football and directing agri-

Victories over Lehigh (7–0) and Lafayette (33–3) encouraged Coach Harlow's team as the final game approached, despite Pitt's so far undefeated record in its first season under Pop Warner. "The battle for the Pennsylvania championship" aroused considerable interest throughout the East, and the *Collegian* solicited pregame comments from experts:

> GRANTLAND RICE: Pitt had better defeat Penn State before it claims a championship.

> WALTER CAMP: Really anybody's game. State has the stronger defense.

> BILL HOLLENBACK: Harlow's team is one of the best in the East. Few people know about the wonderful spirit at Penn State. Berryman, Mahan, and Barrett [Cornell] are the best backs of the year. Higgins, Clark, and Wood are great. I'd hate to face Bill Wood.

The *Collegian,* noting that the current season has been one of many upsets, prophesied victory:

> Yale has been Haughtonized, Princeton has been Shevlinized [Tom Shevlin, Yale coach of the period], why can't Pitt be Harlowized?

Realistically, Penn State wasn't in Pitt's class in 1915. Notwithstanding that the line had outplayed Harvard, Penn, Lehigh, and Lafayette, the Lions were no match for the Panther forwards, anchored by the illustrious Bob Peck, twice All-America. Andy Hastings scored 15 of Pitt's 20 points on 2 touchdowns and a field goal. With a big 20–0 victory, Pitt extended its Pennsylvania championship to encompass the entire East, and only one challenger

---

culture short courses. In 1918 he planned to farm near Seven Stars, outside of Gettysburg, but was persuaded to coach football at Gettysburg College for $300 a season. He also taught mathematics and headed the Christian Association before going to Middletown, Connecticut, in 1921 to coach Wesleyan and attend Yale Divinity School. That season Wesleyan won its first Little Three title in many years. Ordained a Presbyterian minister after receiving his B.D. degree from Yale, Bill served the New York Presbytery as Intercollegiate YMCA director of religious and social work and chaplain at several of the city's medical centers. From 1939 until 1957, he was chaplain at Sailor's Snug Harbor on Staten Island, while it grew to become the world's largest home for retired and disabled seamen. He then retired to his Seven Stars farm with his wife, the former Esther Chase '18, a Gettysburg professor of psychology and sociology, and died on August 20, 1966.

emerged: Cornell, the undefeated claimant, had ended Harvard's four-year unbeaten status, 10–0.

The Thanksgiving Day loss at Pittsburgh failed to shake faith in Harlow's ability to bring Penn State eventually to eastern leadership. The *Alumni News* of November 1915 fervently endorsed his

> high principles of sport and keen enthusiasm. . . . He proved himself a master of modern football techniques with the ability to easily impart his knowledge and efficiently organize the work of instruction. Harlow has given Penn State an all-around football system of which all alumni and undergraduates may well be proud.

The *Collegian* praised Harlow's moral influence on his players:

> Penn State men playing dirty football are removed not by officials, but by Harlow. Obscene language is absent. Many believe he is destined to rank with Haughton, Yost, and Warner. We at Penn State want him to continue along the Harlow line.

The Athletic Committee, meeting at the Fort Pitt Hotel in Pittsburgh on November 25, unanimously approved Coach Harlow's accomplishments with a two-year contract at $2,100 per year—an increase of $300. Harlow was present when its previously established policy of engaging an assistant coach from a different college each year was discussed. Granting that he had absorbed the best of the Dartmouth and Harvard systems from Whitney and Brickley, he preferred to delay making a recommendation for 1916, but later supported the rehiring of Whitney, who was very popular with the players. Harlow concurred in the committee's position on the importance of the Pitt game as the focal point of the season.

The 8–2 record the next year appeared satisfactory, but 1916 was perhaps the most frustrating season of Harlow's coaching career. The Lions eked out a 10–7 victory over Lehigh and swamped such teams as Susquehanna, Westminster, Bucknell, West Virginia Wesleyan, Gettysburg, Geneva, and Lafayette. Yet Penn State, topping no major opponent, was shut out by Penn (15–0) and Pittsburgh (31–0). The player losses from 1915 had not been severe, although Captain Bill Wood and Punk Berryman were among them. Whitey Thomas, end, transferred to Penn, and H. C. Painter, center, became ineligible. The upward swing was expected to continue with veterans Captain Jeff Clark, Bob Higgins, Stan Ewing, Stan Czarnecki, and

George Morris, bolstered by newcomers like Larry Conover, Ben Cubbage, Carl Beck, Bill Hess, Casey Jones, and Harry Robb.

The crushing Pittsburgh defeat solidified a growing trend among loyalists to measure the season by the outcome of the Pitt game. In 1916 the team entered the final contest with an 8–1 record and emerged from the defeat believing that nothing of importance had been accomplished during the year. Coach Harlow almost broke under the strain of the disappointment, and according to close friends, had to be talked out of resigning on the spot.

Signs that Harlow was feeling extreme pressure were apparent after the Penn defeat in midseason. He seemed totally out of character in a *Collegian* interview, berating some players by name, criticizing his quarterback's play-calling, and threatening a complete team "shake-up." His basic reasons for the Penn defeat were

> a green backfield and lack of judgment at critical moments. We took second to Penn in brains and brawn. Our secondary defense played back too far in spite of all instructions, and allowed Penn's runners to come to them instead of meeting the ball carriers.

Coach Harlow excused two members of the backfield, Harry Robb and Carl Beck, "who never played before more than 2,000 spectators and there were 20,000 at Franklin Field all yelling like demons." He was especially harsh about quarterback Ewing's pass call on first down at Penn's 13-yard line. In the next game, against Gettysburg, Casey Jones was the signal caller, but Ewing reappeared the following week and finished a good season.

A return to the football eminence of Hollenback's early years was doomed by the rise of Pittsburgh under Glenn Scobey Warner. Pitt was in the midst of a "golden era." When Pop Warner arrived from Carlisle, he had almost instantaneous success with undefeated teams from 1915 through 1918. The 1916 Panther eleven, often rated by Warner as the finest he had ever coached, included many names famous in Pitt grid history—George McLaren, Red Carlson (later the successful basketball coach), Pat Herron, Tiny Thornhill, Jock Sutherland (of coaching fame), Dale Seis, Pud Seidel, Jimmy DeHart, and Andy Hastings. With this kind of nucleus the Panthers under Warner won thirty-one straight games until defeated by Syracuse in 1919.

The futility Harlow faced in this predicament shattered his ego and led the Athletic Committee to an unwise decision that nearly undid the progress Harlow had made in two years. The committee at the time had a strong Pittsburgh orientation, although its chairman was George R. Meek '90 of Bellefonte. The influential C. W. Heppenstall, Sr. '93 and V. L. Henry '07 were Pittsburghers. J. L. (Pete) Mauthe '13 of Youngstown, Ohio, was a new member, and J. H. M. Andrews '96 of Philadelphia was the new trustee representative, replacing the late Augustus C. Read of Pittsburgh. Directly responsible to the committee was the graduate manager of athletics, Raymond H. Smith '03.

Neil M. Fleming, Smith's assistant, started a lifetime affiliation with Penn State following his graduation in 1914. A football substitute and varsity manager in 1913, Fleming later succeeded Smith and was additionally responsible for the management of all student activities, forecasting the present Student Union organization.

Since Ray Smith had dual responsibility for athletics and alumni affairs, Fleming was to be primarily concerned with the Alumni Association, but his involvement with athletics gradually broadened. His compensation came entirely from the Alumni Association until Graduate Manager Smith praised his services to athletics so highly that he was recommended for a "gift of $25 or $50 in appreciation for his work." (The committee generously voted Fleming $50 without a dissent.) The minutes of January 1917 note that he was actually an assistant in athletics, and he was granted a monthly salary of $20 from athletic funds, retroactive to September 1, 1916.

The state of football dominated the committee's meeting on January 13, 1917, at the Nittany Country Club in Hecla, near Bellefonte. To solve the continuing problem of late classes interfering with practice, Smith was instructed to try to have all varsity football men excused from Tuesday through Friday afternoons at 3:30 P.M. Measures also were taken to provide money for tutoring, but these matters were considered only minor parts of the trouble. Pittsburgh members especially persisted in equating the team's season success with recent performances against Pitt. The minutes state that "evidence the committee has been able to gather seems to point to the need of a more experienced assistant field coach, especially capable in the formulation of attack." Walter P. (Wally) Steffen, coach at Carnegie Tech, was proposed as a possibility.

Coach Harlow and Robert A. Higgins, captain-elect of the 1917 team, were present for the committee's next meeting (Duquesne Athletic Club, Pittsburgh, February 16, 1917). Apparently Steffen wasn't available, but Heppenstall had a candidate present. Xenophen C. Scott of Cleveland, Ohio, was interviewed, his credentials examined, and Heppenstall moved his election as field coach with "full responsibility for the development of the 1917 team." Since Harlow was still under contract as head coach and the motion created the possibility of a misunderstanding between the two men, Scott's appointment was announced merely as "field coach," with "Resident Coach" Harlow to decide his responsibility after a month of spring practice. Scott's contract for spring practice and the fall season at $1,750 contained an option on another year of his services, the committee "reserving the right after spring practice to ask Mr. Scott to assume full charge of the coaching of the team during the 1917 playing season."

This impractical administrative division of responsibility was grossly unfair to Harlow, who was never actually replaced as head coach but obviously had little authority on the field during a game. His sensitive nature rebelled against the arrangement, but he tried to live with it, and his restraint probably kept the bottom from falling out of Penn State football during the first war year of 1917.

Coach Harlow had other problems. The talented Bud Whitney was no longer on his staff, and Dutch Hermann, his freshman coach and close friend, had departed for the service. Bill Martin became acting freshman coach, assisted by Chuck Yerger '16, who also was named acting wrestling coach at $100 for the season. During the war emergency, as in the past, graduate players offered to help, and Bill Wood '16 and Pete Mauthe '13 were on hand.

Fullback Clark was the only varsity player lost by graduation from the 1916 team, but when the season started, the armed forces had taken all but three regulars—Czarnecki, Robb, and Conover, who was captain in place of the absent Higgins. Promoted to regulars from the 1916 reserves were W. S. (Red) Gross and Al Pond. Newcomers on the starting team for the opening game were Dick Rauch, Red Griffiths, Lee Hills, Bill Firsching, George Brown, and Rudy Kraft. A slightly built little player named Charlie Way, who was to become legendary after the war, broke into the starting lineup for the first time in midseason. Until then Coach Harlow apparently hadn't believed Charlie was real. Charlie came on his own from Downingtown, Pennsylvania, weighing then about 125 pounds, and didn't even make his numerals as a freshman in 1916. Way received scant attention until he entered the West Virginia Wesleyan game as quarterback and won it in the last 30 seconds with a sparkling performance.

Students were urged as a patriotic duty to come out for the depleted team. Several well-known athletes from other sports responded to the emergency—Olympic miler Larry Shields, baseball's George Wheeling, and basketball star Lloyd Wilson (brother of Light Horse Harry Wilson) were listed on the 1917 squad as substitutes, and all became captains in their respective sports after the war.

Although Washington exerted no pressure, Yale, Harvard, and Princeton eliminated football for the duration, but Penn State decided to retain it as far as possible. Justifying the policy, Graduate Manager Smith wrote at length in the *Alumni Quarterly* (October 1917) about its benefits to physical fitness and as a general morale booster. A strengthened physical education program emphasizing intramurals was promised, along with rigid economy in operating varsity sports. Smith also said Penn State would not abrogate the freshman rule and would maintain its high academic standards for varsity athletics. Acting on NCAA advice to cancel preseason practice in 1917, Penn State held its first session on the opening day of the fall semester.

Scheduling difficulties developed at once. Muhlenberg, forced to cancel, was replaced by the U. S. Army Ambulance Corps team for the opening game, played on Muhlenberg's field in Allentown, where the Army team was located. Three former Penn Staters performed against their alma mater—Clarence Beck, Ben Cubbage, and Jim O'Connell.

Cancellations by Penn and Lafayette caused vacancies more difficult to fill, but Graduate Manager Smith completed a nine-game schedule with the addition of Dartmouth at Hanover and W&J at Washington, Pennsylvania. Lafayette withdrew because the game was too near its annual contest with Lehigh. The complicated Penn disagreement had been brewing as early as 1915, when Penn State's Athletic Committee asked the graduate manager to arrange "more acceptable financial compensation for the game and assurance of a more permanent place on the Penn schedule." The teams met in 1915 and 1916, but not in the next two years. The *Alumni News* of December 1916 said the game was abandoned "owing to the development of circumstances which are unfavorable to Penn State."

Maryland State College (now the University of Maryland) became a new opponent. Maryland's president at the time was Dr. Harry J. Patterson, Penn State Class of 1886.

The 1917 season was considered unsuccessful, for again the Lions were unable to defeat a major opponent and lost to W&J and Lehigh as well as to Dartmouth and Pittsburgh. In the W&J defeat (7–0) Al Pond kept Penn State from more serious trouble by fine kicking, some sixteen times under pressure.

Charlie Way, whom Pittsburgh sportswriters nicknamed "Gang" Way, provided Penn Staters with their greatest moments. His sensational playing against West Virginia Wesleyan, coached by Earl (Greasy) Neale, was the talk of the campus. The Lions were behind, 7–0, with only a few minutes to play when Coach Neale directed his quarterback to give up an intentional safety. Rules in those days didn't require a free kick after a safety, and the visitors, ahead 7–2, tried to run out the clock but were forced to kick on fourth down. Way picked up the bouncing ball on a wet field and raced 40 yards for a touchdown, crossing the goal line just as time ran out. Penn State won, 8–7.

Because quarterback Frank Wolf was hurt in the W&J game, Way got his chance and stayed on the team as a starter following his West Virginia Wesleyan heroics. (Later, as head coach at Waynesburg College, Wolf had two victories over Penn State during the worst of the de-emphasis period of the early thirties.) Against Dartmouth, Charlie Way's runs of 35, 20, and 10 yards in the second quarter tied the score at half time, 7–7. He made the touchdown on a 1-yard plunge. Dartmouth won with a field goal in the last few minutes, but Penn State might have scored again except for four or five crucial offside penalties. Lion players claimed tackle Jim Black, the culprit, was "nearsighted."

In Penn State's fifth successive loss to Pittsburgh (28–6), Coach Pop Warner's stalwarts had a battle to the finish. Trailing 14–6 at half time, the Lions were very much in the game thanks to Way's brilliance on offense and superior defensive play by fullback Red Gross, who effectively stopped the Panther running star, George McLaren. Pitt pushed across two touchdowns in the final period after an injury sidelined Gross, later a successful coach at Schenley High School in Pittsburgh.

The victory completed Pitt's third successive unbeaten season, but the Panthers never received the recognition they deserved from eastern writers. Coach Warner's 1916 and 1917 teams could easily have qualified for the national title had football polls been used extensively. Eastern titles, too, might have come to Pitt all three seasons, 1915–17, with only Cornell's Big Red a challenger in 1915. That year Oklahoma had a 10–0 record, but its schedule included teams from schools the size of Kingfisher, Weathersford, Alma, and Kendall. Nebraska was forging toward a national reputation under Coach Jumbo Stiehm, who developed one of the early passing wizards in Guy Chamberlain.

In 1916 only Army could challenge Pitt in the East or nationally, although the Cadet schedule was less demanding. Yale, best of the Big Three, lost to Brown, which was beaten badly by Colgate. The Washington Huskies, completing a long undefeated skein under Gilmour Dobie, were tied by Oregon, where Hugo Bezdek was coach.

By today's ratings, Pitt's right to Number One in 1917 might have been lost to Georgia Tech or Texas A&M. Tech was 9–0, rolling up 491 points to 17 by opponents, including a 41–0 victory over Penn. The Aggies, 8–0, shut out all opponents while scoring 270 points.

Walter Camp, despite his standing as a national authority, continued to show partiality for eastern talent in selecting his All-America teams, and he ignored most of Pitt's greatest players. Exceptions were center Bob Peck in 1915 and 1916 and the Panther guards, Jock Sutherland and Dale Seis, in 1917.

For the 1917 Pitt-Penn State game Field Coach Zen Scott designed a surprise offense. After spotting Pitt two touchdowns in the first quarter, the Lions outplayed their favored rival in the second and third periods, using an unorthodox spread formation featuring a "triple pass." After a 35-yard run by Harry Robb, a pass from Gross to Robb to Way placed the ball on Pitt's 20. From there they passed the ball around as if they were playing basketball. Temporarily the home team seemed baffled by what Pittsburgh sportswriters called "this weird and uncanny offense." Center Red Griffiths passed the ball to Gross, who chucked it to Robb, then to Way, and finally to end Larry Conover, who scored.

Reviewing the game in the Philadelphia *Evening Ledger,* R. W. (Tiny) Maxwell, well-known former player and football official, declared that Penn State clearly outplayed its heavily favored foe in the second and third quarters with its new attack and "made Pitt look foolish." He described how the center, with the guards a yard or more away on each side, stood sideways to pass the ball to one of the wide backs, two of whom were lined up outside the ends, also spread wide. Maxwell gave Field Coach Scott full credit, but said he had seen similar formations at Tufts and Lawrenceville Academy. He faulted Penn State for springing its surprise in the first half, thereby giving wily Coach Warner time to devise a defense.

When the *Collegian* reprinted the Maxwell story crediting Scott with whatever success Penn State had achieved in 1917, the break between the coaches widened, and Harlow's situation became intolerable. The Athletic Committee, meeting on November 28, withdrew its impractical "dual system of coaching," did not renew Scott's contract, and also subscribed to a system that would have only Penn State men on the coaching staff. Heppenstall moved that "R. C. Harlow be retained as head coach for the season of 1918 upon a twelve-month basis with instructions to select his own coaches." Harlow felt vindicated—and with good reason—but was dissatisfied with the one-year contract. His request for a three-year contract at a salary of $2,100 per year was granted with the proviso that the committee could rescind the contract if war conditions made it impossible to continue football. There were rumors that Harlow wanted E. H. (Bull) McCleary '10 for his top assistant.

Early in July 1918, Harlow asked to be released for military service, soon followed by Bill Martin, last of the staff to join the armed forces. The committee accordingly had to find a complete staff to prepare for a difficult nine-game schedule including Dartmouth, Cornell, W&J, Lehigh, and Pittsburgh. Graduate Manager Smith resigned in July to become the college comptroller, and Neil M. Fleming was named to the vacant post.

Involved with the physical training program, Harlow coached an Army team based in Virginia during the fall of 1918 and returned to Penn State in time for the 1919 season. Meanwhile, Hugo Bezdek had been named director of physical education and head football coach with the privilege of selecting his own assistants. Surprisingly, he accepted the prewar staff intact—Harlow, Hermann, and Martin. Harlow appeared satisfied with the arrangement since the Athletic Committee granted him the same salary he had been promised as head coach, and close friends believed he realized he was better off without the responsibilities and pressures of the top job. He later magnified the negative side of the situation, perhaps because Bezdek had been hired during his absence.

Bezdek and Harlow both had short fuses. These temperamental, many-sided personalities had vastly different coaching philosophies. Bez was a driver, a hard taskmaster, and often embarrassed his players on the field with his harsh, sarcastic bellows. Harlow, a disciplinarian who could rough-talk with the best, generally had the gentler manner of an academician. But the rustic simplicity of his paternal approach wasn't perfected until the Harvard days.

At Penn State Harlow became a cushion between the players and their head coach, almost a father confessor. Many came to him for advice or simply solace when they had trouble with Hugo, which was often. Dick could quietly counsel them on regaining the good graces of the big boss. It's remarkable that open warfare was averted between Bezdek and Harlow for almost three years, although at one time Dick was rumored to have accepted the head coaching job at Lehigh. Some obvious friction developed during the winter of 1921–22, and Harlow finally resigned to become head coach at Colgate University.

Students, hating to see him leave, arranged a farewell mass meeting in the auditorium. He received a watch—apparently the only token of appreciation then within the imagination of undergraduates. Bezdek's sincerity in praising his departing assistant became questionable when he added an aside heard by everyone, including Harlow: "Of course, we'll have to be ready to stick the old stiletto in his back." Harlow was furious, but the incident causing a lifelong rift was yet to come.

When Harlow arrived at Colgate in the fall of 1922, six players from Bezdek's 1921 squad had enrolled on the Hamilton, New York, campus. The "disgruntled six" may have had various reasons for transferring, but it can be assumed that all disliked Bez, and five of the six were reported to be upset because they hadn't been awarded the varsity *S* during the previous season.

Harlow denied personal implication in this mass exodus of players, whom Bezdek called "the mainstay of my 1922 team." Both Dick's denial and Bez's wrath are understandable. Certainly the departing coach hadn't discouraged the transient players. They were S. E. (Buck) Runser, center and guard; R. O. (Pete) Redinger, halfback; E. (Eggs) Cornwall, halfback; C. F. (Frank) Hess, fullback; S. E. (Save) Crowther, tackle; and George Dewey Hynes, halfback. Only Redinger had lettered, with a minor award in 1920 and a varsity letter in 1921. After their year of ineligibility at Colgate in 1922, all were members of Harlow's 6–2–1 squad in 1923, and Crowther captained the Red Raiders in 1924. (As an alumnus, Dewey Hynes was on Colgate's Board of Trustees, 1963–66, president of the Colgate University Alumni Corporation, 1962–64, and a director until 1966, when he was elected to life membership.)

Without question, Harlow was a better coach after those three seasons with Bezdek, a man known as a superior strategist whose inventive genius added much to the game. At the same time, Harlow had contributed an ability to devise new defenses for special needs, the knack for scouting a team, discerning weaknesses in the team and in individuals, and judgment in using players where they could be most effective—a quality many thought Bezdek lacked. The record shows that with Harlow as his top aide from 1919 through 1921 Bezdek had his three greatest Lion teams; when Harlow departed, the road was all downhill in Bezdek's coaching career.

At Penn State in 1919 Dick Harlow introduced intercollegiate boxing, which flourished as probably its most popular indoor sport there for thirty years. He likewise started boxing at Colgate and later at Western Maryland. Colgate football had four successful years during his tenure, including the 1923 defeat of Syracuse, its greatest rival, at Archbold Stadium, 16–7. The Red Raiders spoiled an undefeated season for Coach Chick Meehan, scoring the only touchdowns made against the Orange that year.

In 1925, under Harlow, Colgate's first undefeated season in over thirty years (7–0–2) included victories over archrival Syracuse (19–6) and Princeton (9–0) when Coach Bill Roper had one of his best teams, notable for winning decisively from Yale and Harvard. Outstanding players during Harlow's regime were Tiny Welsh, a guard, and Eddie Tryon, probably the finest back in Colgate history. Harlow's four-year record was 24–9–3.

In 1926 Harlow was lured to Western Maryland College, Westminster, a small institution without a great football tradition until the Penn Stater came along. Colgate people reproached their departing coach for taking with him at least half a dozen huskies he had recruited for the New York school, including Charlie Havens of Rome, New York, who later succeeded him as coach and athletic director at Western Maryland. Dick's defection was ascribed to the persuasive powers and promised assistance of a successful Baltimore attorney and businessman, Robert Gill, an alumnus of Western Maryland.

Harlow soon gave real meaning to the Maryland school's nick-name—the Green Terrors—by coaching his teams to undefeated seasons in 1929, 1930, and 1934. The 1929 accomplishment was particularly satisfying since several important opponents, including Maryland, refused to allow the small school to use seven senior starters because they had played as freshmen in 1926, prior to the NCAA three-year-limit rule. Among these four-year men was Colo-nel Bill Pelton, who came to Penn State in 1957 on the ROTC staff and remained as head of the Department of Security after a distin-guished Army career. Another player on the 1929 team was Charles A. (Rip) Engle, who had played previously for Blue Ridge College of New Windsor, Maryland, and whose Uncle Lloyd (Dad) Engle had been Dick's teammate at Penn State. In 1934 Western Maryland had an outstanding back in Bill Shepherd, national scoring leader.

Coach Harlow in 1929 showed superstitious eccentricities, not un-common among coaches. Western Maryland played most of its schedule away from home, and the squad always traveled by bus. After winning the first road game, Dick ordered every player to retain the same seat going and coming—and for every subsequent game. Pete Gomsack, an injured player ruled out for the season with a broken shoulder, still had to comply with the order and was taken on every trip.

When Harlow replaced Eddie Casey at Harvard in 1936, neither Western Maryland nor Harvard alumni were happy, although there were no rumors of players jumping from Westminster to Cambridge. Bill Bingham, Harvard's athletic director, had broken tradition when he hired the first nonalumnus to lead the Crimson in sixty years. Boston newspapermen were skeptical and the *Harvard Crimson* was downright hostile, saying that Harlow had never been associated with any college not known for "proselyting"—a favorite word in those days. Dick eventually disarmed most critics and, more important, sold himself to Harvard players and the other students. He became a recognized ornithologist and oologist (birds' eggs), and was named curator of oology at the Harvard Museum of Comparative Zoology —something of a first for his coaching profession. His personal collection of birds' eggs numbered nearly a thousand species and was valued at $40,000.

As a coach Harlow practiced the creed he had always preached for winning football—sound fundamentals and common sense. He never claimed to be an originator and admittedly was greatly influenced by

Hollenback, Warner, Snavely, Sutherland, and Bezdek. Dick evolved a "looping" or "stunting" defensive tactic at Penn State in 1915 and used it against Bucknell successfully. After trying it against Penn in 1916 he described the experience ruefully:

> A fellow named Derr ran through us for about 70 yards, and Penn beat us. There was a bug in the defense at the time, and Penn discovered it. I lost my nerve and never used it again until after I went to Harvard, where we were so often out-manned we had to try something different. We beat Army, Yale, and Fritz Crisler's Princeton team with the looping defense. Greasy Neale at Yale picked it up and the next year gave us a lot of trouble, and then I knew we had something good.

Harlow had a five-, six-, and seven-man line with defensive players looping and slanting in from different angles, thoroughly befuddling their opponents. In 1941 he employed twenty-eight different defenses, using as many as seven variations in a single game.

To Harvard's power-based single-wing system Harlow soon added double-wing plays, thereby piling deception on brute strength, which was sadly lacking at Cambridge. With Bezdek, Snavely, and Steffen, he shares credit for the first use of fullback spinner plays. The deceptive spinners, mousetraps, and reverses of his 1937 Crimson attack enabled Harvard to shed the stigma of having been a victim of the Carlisle Indians' hidden-ball play. His modern version was based on real ball-handling deception, not hocus-pocus.

Without accomplishing miracles at Harvard, Harlow became recognized for strategic use of his material. He won over a somewhat fickle Boston press and satisfied most of the Crimson alumni constituency by defeating both Princeton and Yale in 1937, 1938, and 1941. Although he hadn't yet recorded a winning season at Harvard, at the end of the 1936 campaign (3–4–1) his peers named him "Coach of the Year," and in 1954 he was elected to Football's Hall of Fame. He was a lieutenant commander in the Navy's rehabilitation and physical fitness program during World War II, returned to Harvard for the 1945, 1946, and 1947 seasons, and then retired for health reasons, having suffered many years from hypertension. He left coaching with an overall record of 150–68–17 (.667). His home at Westminster became a mecca for coaches who came to him from all over the country with their problems. He enjoyed personal contact with dozens of his former players, and happily pursued his hobbies, both oological and botanical, until his death on February 19, 1962, at the age of 72.

At Penn State in the early 1950s Coach Rip Engle tried to revive Harlow's interest in his alma mater by utilizing his football expertise and his judgment in measuring opponents. He was placed on the Penn State staff as a nonresident superscout to make weekly recommendations to the head coach after reviewing the notes of the regular scouts. The plan proved impractical and was abandoned after a year's trial.

Harlow gave his affection to Harvard in his later years, directing his sentiment and nostalgia toward the institution where he had gained most of his national prestige and felt most appreciated. The unabated frictions of the "Bezdek Era" affected his relations with his alma mater despite enduring friendships, including those with Bob Higgins, Neil Fleming, Dutch Hermann, and Engle.

Penn State not only weathered the wartime upheaval general in the land but also made substantial progress during the presidential years of Edwin Erle Sparks, 1908–20.

President Sparks had ideal qualifications to continue generating public support, as Dr. Atherton had before him. Besides having an ambassadorial personality, he was familiar with Penn State. He had been head of the Preparatory Department from 1890 until he left in 1895 to complete his Ph.D. in history at the University of Chicago.

The goal of this magnetic executive was to "carry the college to the people," persuading them also to come to the campus despite its being "equally inaccessible from all parts of the state," as he is said to have remarked.

A tuition-free summer session for schoolteachers began in 1910 with 146 enrolled; ten years later it had 1,045 students. Extension and correspondence instruction expanded and the county agricultural agent program started when federal and state appropriations were acquired for these purposes. The Engineering Experiment Station was established in 1908, and the Mining Experiment Station in 1919.

Larger state appropriations were insufficient to meet admissions applications, especially as more women students were attracted by the home economics curriculum and broadened opportunities in liberal arts after that school was unified in 1910. Prelegal and premedical curricula, business and finance, and education and psychology shared popularity with the well-established programs in agriculture, chemistry, engineering, and mining.

To cope with the increase in resident enrollment from 1,199 in 1908 to 4,217 in 1920, additional administrative posts were authorized. Included were a registrar, public information officer, a dean of men and a dean of women heading a faculty advisory system, and directors of athletics and alumni affairs.

The genial and personable Dr. Sparks addressed meetings all over the state, cultivating friends further by extending the hospitality of the president's residence for special campus events to impress visitors with the extent of Pennsylvania's investment in its public state land-grant college. Stimulated by fifty-year reunions of early classes, beginning in 1911, the Alumni Association five years later led a "booster campaign," reminding the legislature of its duty to support and maintain public higher education for all qualified students seeking admission to the Pennsylvania state land-grant college.

The World War I emergency broke this momentum in 1917, diverting instructional and research capability to a defense effort that added to Penn State's stature in the state and the nation. Mobilized into the SATC (Students Army Training Corps), men students drilled and practiced trench warfare on athletic fields, lived in barracks on campus, and learned military discipline from Major James Baylies and his staff, who ruled the campus, sometimes to the discomfiture of President Sparks and *his* staff. An ambulance corps was formed, the Red Cross instructed women in nursing, and all hands cultivated victory gardens, promoted Liberty Bonds, and stopped studying German.

Student activities were curtailed and social affairs eliminated during the accelerated school year, and the football team in 1918 played an abbreviated schedule of four games. In November 1918, campus and community celebrated the signing of the Armistice with a victory parade to the music of Bandmaster "Tommy" Thompson's marching military band (alias the Penn State Blue Band) and blasts from the power plant's whistle beside the Old Engineering Building. The band was soon to put aside martial music for Jimmy Leyden's new "fight" song, "Hail to the Lion" (1919), and football was standing by, ready to resume its own march.

Part IV

THE MOUNTAIN AND THE VALLEY

Hugo Bezdek, 1918–29

17

The Arrival

Intercollegiate football could not resume its place in undergraduate life during the war summer of 1918. The call to colors had wiped out almost the entire squad and coaching staff. Under pressure from the War Department, all September and October games were canceled because it was believed that Student Army Training Corps (SATC) enrollees would benefit more from an intramural program. As a result, Penn State gave up its Dartmouth and Pennsylvania games, retaining only Rutgers, Lehigh, and Pitt. When the War Department rescinded its October ban, knowing that World War I was fast coming to an end, it was too late for Penn State to reschedule, but an extra game finally was arranged with the Wissahickon Army Barracks team for early November. The terrible flu epidemic eliminated the Cornell game as well as tentative agreements with Bucknell and Carnegie Tech.

Faced by the Army's widely publicized report that three hundred thousand young Americans had been found physically unfit for service, the Athletic Advisory Committee felt more obligation to find a director for an expanded physical education program than a coach for the football team. With this in mind, C. W. Heppenstall, Sr. '03, a Pittsburgh industrialist, presented the name of Hugo Bezdek at the August 25 meeting. The two men had become acquainted when Bezdek came to Pittsburgh during the summer of 1917 to take over the faltering Pittsburgh Pirates baseball team from Manager Jim Callahan and the interim manager, Honus Wagner.

The dynamic Bezdek, who had learned football under Alonzo Stagg at Chicago and successfully coached at Oregon and Arkansas, was leading the Pirates to a first-division finish in 1918. Another applicant for the Penn State position was Coach Fred Taylor of Williams, but the committee recommended Bezdek to the Board of Trustees as director of physical education with supervision over all intercollegiate sports. Football was not mentioned in the resolution.

The Pirate manager, meeting President Sparks in Pittsburgh, accepted the position of associate professor of physical education at a salary of $4,500 and agreed to investigate the Army physical fitness program, "put the best and most practical methods to work at Penn State," and report jointly to the trustees and the Athletic Committee his recommendations for the newly authorized Department of Physical Education. He was permitted to complete his contract through 1919 with the Pirates, then under the general managership of Barney Dreyfuss.

While Penn State officials emphasized expansion of the physical education program, Bezdek knew his star would rise or fall with the success of football. He immediately sought approval of freshman eligibility for the 1918 season, aware that he would be handicapped by thin material—no lettermen and only a handful of players remained from the previous season.

Mainstays of Bezdek's first team were Frank Unger (acting captain in place of the departed Harry Robb), Paul Grimes, George Brown, R. H. (Red) Henry, L. H. Logue, R. K. (Buck) Williams, Gene Farley, A. H. Knabb, and W. Glenn Killinger, an unheralded sophomore from Harrisburg. Joe Lightner, another future star from Harrisburg, went almost unnoticed in 1918 and didn't win even a minor letter. The only coaching assistant was H. C. (Chuck) Yerger '16.

Killinger, self-styled "worst player on the worst team Harrisburg Tech ever had," didn't turn out for football when he arrived at Penn State in the fall of 1917. He weighed 125 pounds. After watching him play basketball that winter, Dick Harlow persuaded him to report for spring practice, but Killinger quit in a hurry when baseball started. He came out in the fall at the suggestion of his friend Farley, a big tackle (later president of Wilkes College in Wilkes-

Barre). Killinger, who made the varsity without difficulty, suffered three broken ribs in the Wissahickon game (a 6–6 tie) when he had a collision with Duke Osborn, a sturdy Army lineman.[1] The injury kept him out of the next game, won by Rutgers (26–3) with a back named Paul Robeson. After defeating Lehigh 7–6, the Lions succumbed to Pitt in the final game, 28–6.

This mediocre first season didn't dim Bezdek's prestige and glamor. Pittsburgh papers praised Penn State's performance, pointing out that the Lions were spirited and "well drilled in fundamentals." Pitt had a better nucleus of players on hand and had swamped W&J, Penn, and Georgia Tech. In fact, the Lion touchdown was the only one scored against the Panthers that year.

Following the season, Bezdek surprised everyone in his important report to the trustees by recommending faculty organization and control of intercollegiates like an academic program, with time in the class schedule for physical education. The remarkable document, parts of which were published in the *Collegian,* bluntly demanded attention to the physical welfare of the students to equip them for maximum intellectual effort, and eventually led to the "athletics for all" slogan, known as Bezdek's byword.

Predicting that the department would become the School of Health and Physical Education, the new director explicitly listed its functions and requirements, making a strong plea for a physical education building with a swimming pool and an indoor dirt track. He projected outdoor athletic facilities on west campus, including a golf course and fields for various sports, and prepared an annual budget for the new department ($30,000). His detailed plans for the building stated exactly how the necessary $525,000 could be secured by a proposed fund-raising committee. Although Recreation Building ("Rec Hall") did not materialize until 1928–29, nearly all of his recommendations were implemented while he was the department head and later director of the school.

When Bezdek returned to the Pirates in the spring of 1919, a *Collegian* editorial (April 15) saluted him for changing dramatically the attitude of college officials toward physical and recreational needs of the students. The Pirates didn't better their 1918 record, but managed to finish the 1919 pennant race again in the first division.

---

[1] Osborn became a regular on the 1919 Penn State team, accompanied Bob Higgins to play with West Virginia in 1920, and was on the Canton Bulldogs' world championship eleven of 1922–23.

Coach Bezdek returned to campus for one weekend with his two assistants, Dick Harlow and Dutch Hermann, who were instructed "to get those fellows into shape—don't scrimmage them, but get 'em ready for me."

This wasn't an easy assignment for Harlow and Hermann, war veterans like 75 per cent of the 1919 squad, many of whom had seen active service in France. Bob Higgins was elected captain, and there were two other ex-captains in the group of returning lettermen—Larry Conover (1917) and Harry Robb (1918). The two assistants thought the squad was ready even for a most exacting head coach, but they didn't know Bezdek—not yet.

"The arrival" was memorable. The cadet band performed for a gala student welcome on New Beaver Field, and the ROTC regiment paraded to add a touch of color. Most of the waiting squad had never seen the coach, who sensed the need for an impressive entrance.

Bez, his cap on backward, raced out on the field in a Pirate uniform. "Run 'em up and down there," he ordered the other coaches. A first and a second team, tentatively picked by Dick and Dutch, dutifully started a signal drill, but after one trip up and down the field Bez stopped them with a single bellow: "LOUSY!" A lecture on conditioning ensued, stressing that every man had to come through with not just his best, but also with *more* than his best. He'd hardly begun when a "crackling birdie" resounded from within the assembled squad. Bez never learned who was guilty, but the players knew it was Dick Rauch, an outstanding lineman and from that moment a confirmed renegade.

The Bezdek debut, designed to establish him as boss, was poorly conceived for a squad dominated by older war veterans already well acquainted with martinet types. Some never got over their first unfavorable impression. They were antagonized by the toughness and sarcasm, boomed demands, and almost sadistic effort to scrimmage the squad into shape from Tuesday through Thursday. The first hard scrimmage of the week became known as "bloody Tuesday." Unfortunately, many who disliked his methods failed to appreciate their opportunity to be on a team as far advanced as any in the country under a superb coaching technician. Bez made stars of players like Killinger and Harry Wilson, who had minimum precollege experience, and Haines and Lightner, who had none.

Coach Bezdek rarely had a team without some dissension, and occasionally outright mutiny was threatened, yet his rapport with undergraduates as a whole almost always was excellent. The fearsome coach was far different from the director of physical education fighting for student recreational facilities. He was an exciting, inspiring campus personality who invariably had a good student press. *Collegian* writers, unlike student reporters today, sometimes were intimidated enough to call easy opponents "major threats" in advance stories, helping the coach make the team respect every foe. Not many coaches now would hold this tactic against Bez. Before the first game, with Gettysburg, the paper predicted an eastern championship and bestowed this accolade:

> Bez has no superior; he is a hard worker and drives his team hard, yet never demands the impossible. A real student of the game, and if there are any tricks of the trade Hugo doesn't know, they have yet to be discovered.

Optimism appeared to be justified.[2] The *Collegian*'s list of returning stars and near stars was lengthy. At the bottom of the squad list was "Haynes"—the Haines who was destined to be one of the most exciting Penn State athletes of all time, equally outstanding on the baseball diamond and the basketball court.

Robb won the starting quarterback job over the much smaller Ronald (Buck) Williams and over Glenn Killinger, who had yet to hit his stride. In 1917 Robb had scored thirteen touchdowns, six of them against Gettysburg—a single-game record still standing. At Columbia the next year, enrolled in the SATC program, he made Camp's second All-America team.

Restless and unhappy on the bench, Killy was stunned when he wasn't used in the Pitt game and missed his letter by a quarter. He kept his disappointment to himself, but some veterans thought Bez was playing favorites. Discontent over the coach's lineups plainly affected the squad's performance in the early games, despite victories over Gettysburg and Bucknell.

[2] Enthusiasm was further fueled when Jimmy Leyden '14 introduced a new "fight" song. In the summer of 1919 he wrote "Nittany Lion," now usually called "Hail to the Lion," and Bandmaster Tommy Thompson orchestrated it for the Blue Band. Students learned it quickly as Leyden, standing on the field, sang the words through a large megaphone, accompanied by a cornet soloist. The composer had used the same means in the summer of 1913 to launch his equally popular "Victory," which he had worked out while shaving in the Track House. The only Penn State football fight song approaching these two in popularity is "Fight On State" by Joseph Saunders '15.

The game at Hanover was another story. Part of Dartmouth's 150th anniversary celebration, it was played on "Alumni Oval," which seated only 2,500 spectators in stands very much like those at New Beaver. A Dartmouth graduate in the crowd was Fred Lewis Pattee, Penn State's professor of American literature and author of the *Alma Mater*. Professor Pattee said he was cheering for the Lions —"Dartmouth has enough rooters."

In a sensational first quarter Charlie Way, 145-pound halfback, took the opening kickoff 90 yards for a touchdown. Dartmouth went ahead 7–6, but near the end of the period Way picked up a fumble by the Dartmouth triple-threat star, Jim Robertson, and ran 85 yards for a 13–7 lead. Robertson got through the disorganized Penn State line to tie the score at half time, 13–13, and the Big Green won the game (19–13) in the third quarter by driving 60 yards, with the winning touchdown scored by Pat Holbrook, a back not much larger than Way. Dartmouth's defensive stars were its tackles, Gus Sonnenberg and Cuddy Murphy; guard Swede Youngstrom (Camp's All-America); and center Bill Cunningham.

The *Collegian* reported that the team was "defeated but not outfought, outplayed but not outgamed." Campus spirit was at its highest, and there was no hint of brewing trouble when the squad returned. A double line of greeters extended from East College Avenue all the way to the Track House. The sullen players had difficulty responding properly, and the squad leaders were furious with Coach Bezdek. A real mutiny was averted when Captain Higgins and Conover went to Bez to make certain demands. Higgins claimed he could pick a team from the squad that could beat the Dartmouth game starters. Bezdek made some concessions, and the future looked a little brighter.

Ursinus wasn't much of a test for a revamped lineup; the first trial was as underdog on Franklin Field against undefeated Pennsylvania. Bert Bell was Penn's captain, and its star was Heine Miller, an All-America end that year. Higgins was outstanding against the Quakers, and his punting was reported as the best seen on Franklin Field. Way, although handicapped by a wet field, was the game's top runner, and Hinkey Haines intercepted three passes. A fumbled punt led to a Penn State touchdown by Robb in the second quarter, and Conover gave the Lions a 10–0 victory by kicking a field goal from the 25 in the final period.

In the November Houseparty game on New Beaver Field, the

Lions coasted to a 20–7 victory over Lehigh. Larry Conover had regained his proper place at center, stabilizing the middle of the line —no team after the Dartmouth game found it as pliable as it had been against the Big Green. Conover was a spirited, vociferous competitor—a great goat-getter. Bob Higgins and Conover often chuckled over an incident that had taken place in the 1916 Lehigh game, played at Bethlehem. Conover was playing opposite Austin Tate. Tate, Conover, and Captain Higgins were all members of the Beta Theta Pi fraternity. Right before a play started there was a scream from Tate: "Conover, you're a dirty s. o. b." Apparently Larry had "accidentally" spit tobacco juice on Tate's hand. Higgins interceded: "Don't call him that, Austin, he's a brother." "Well," said Tate, "if he is, you fellows up there made a hell of a mistake."

The rejuvenated Lions took Cornell in stride, overwhelming the Big Red 20–0 with 11 first downs to 5 and a passing attack that gained more than 100 yards—considerable at a time when many pass restrictions were still in the rulebook. Higgins, Robb, and Brown excelled. One touchdown resulted from the quick thinking and chicanery of Red Griffiths, who was also never at a loss for words. After Higgins had kicked a high, short punt, Way led his teammates down the field, followed by Griffiths. The receiver was Fritz Shiverick, Cornell's quarterback, and Griffiths yelled at him: "Leav'er go, leav'er go!" Shiverick, confused, let the ball bounce— right into the arms of Way, who ran for a touchdown. "Not even the devil himself," someone remarked, "could catch Charlie Way in the open field."

The Harold Hess-to-Bob Higgins play that took the starch out of a good Pitt team in 1919 is down in the record book as the longest pass-and-run play in Penn State's football history. Hess, the fullback who had never thrown a pass in his life and never threw one again, and Higgins, the receiver who caught many during his career, are deservedly listed as the principals in the dramatic action, but the real hero was Assistant Coach Dick Harlow, one of the cagiest scouts the game has known. Harlow had noted that Pitt, under Pop Warner, continually rushed from eight to ten men whenever the Panthers had their opponents backed up near their own goal line.

All week the Lions practiced their surprise—a short pass from a fake kick. Hess, unenthusiastic over his role, each day became less confident, chiefly because few of his practice tosses reached the agile Higgins. Hess's attempt to switch places with a more experienced passer was futile since strategy depended on having the regular kicker go back to fake the punt. Bez, who hadn't been told about the play, was grumpy when he learned what was afoot. "It sounds okay," he growled, "but next time let me know what's going on around here."

The play couldn't have been set up better. In the first quarter, when Pitt was stopped inside Penn State's 10-yard line, quarterback Robb made the call, and Hess dropped back in kicking position. Pitt intended to apply a nine-man rush with center Herb Stein backing up the line and fullback Andy Hastings in the safety position, but Stein, eager to block the kick, edged up too close. Forbes Field, wet and muddy, was no place for a kicking fullback to throw a pass with a soggy ball. Hess ran a few steps to his right in the end zone and tossed the heavy ball, allowing Higgins to take it in stride. It was the best pass Hess had thrown all week. After George Brown, left end, took Hastings out of the play with a clean block (Duke Osborn had taken care of Stein), Higgins could have jogged to the Panther goal line, ninety yards away.

Game accounts written over fifty years ago vary in estimating the length of the pass and run, but the official *Spalding Guide* of 1920 credits Hess with a 15-yard pass and Higgins with a 90-yard run. Since the line of scrimmage was the 5-yard line, the ball must have been thrown from 5 yards back of the goal line and caught on the 10. Official statisticians today would list the distance of the pass-run play as 95 yards. Later in the second quarter Hess scored a touchdown after his steady line plunging. Way broke away in the mud for a thrilling third-quarter scoring dash of 53 yards to complete the 20–0 victory.

Coach Bezdek, popular in Pittsburgh for his moderately successful 2½-year stint with the Pirates, had become a miracle worker, "the only big-league baseball manager who successfully switched to college football." The writers seemed to forget that he had been an established football coach and that the switch to baseball was even more remarkable. Invited by Hugh S. Fullerton, noted sportswriter, to contribute to his series "Strategy of Great Football Games," Bez complied with an analysis of his victory over Pop Warner's team. In the article he gave credit to his assistants (without mentioning Harlow's name) for circumventing Pitt's nine-man rush, but also praised quarterback Robb for having the courage to call the play in the first four minutes of the game "when it would make or break the morale of the team." He also attached significance to his use of Way, a great open-field runner, as a line bucker on special plays.

Lionized at home, Bezdek learned what it meant for a Penn State coach to demolish the Panthers. Other Lion coaches had enjoyed this before and others would afterward, but such success failed to come again for another twenty years. Bez had been given a three-year contract in October 1919 at a salary of $7,500 for ten months, including $4,500 paid by the college for his services as director of physical education. In October 1920, the Athletic Committee awarded him a bonus of $500 for his work between July 15 and September 15 and then gave him a seven-year contract at $10,000, the Athletic Association to pay the increase. Deciding that the thirty-eight athletic scholarships currently in operation were inadequate, the committee authorized ten additional ones to be paid from alumni contributions. Committee chairman Heppenstall personally guaranteed two and William H. Teas '97, another committee member, guaranteed two more, with one to be used for track.

While there was no official method of selecting an eastern champion in 1919, Penn State had serious support for the claim. Robert W. (Tiny) Maxwell, sports editor of the Philadelphia *Evening Public Ledger,* ex-football player and official, rated eastern teams as follows:

1. Penn State
2. Syracuse
3. Colgate
4. Dartmouth
5. Pittsburgh
6. West Virginia
7. Pennsylvania
8. Harvard
9. Princeton
10. W&J

"Penn State deserves first place because it is the strongest, most versatile team in these parts," said Maxwell. He took into account the early-season Dartmouth defeat, but pointed out that the Lions proved themselves in November and "waded through everything with little difficulty." Harvard, undefeated (and subsequently victorious over Oregon in the Rose Bowl), was low-rated because of a weak schedule. The placing of Harvard and Princeton at eighth and ninth with Yale not even in the first ten was significant of the postwar period. In fact, the Big Three never again completely dominated the East as in the past, although the Ivies periodically showed spectacular strength. Coach Bob Fisher, who took over at Harvard after Haughton in 1919, didn't lose a game until little Centre College turned the trick in 1921. Yale, under Tad Jones, had big years in 1923 and 1927, losing only once to Georgia in the latter season. Princeton was undefeated in 1922 with Bill Roper at the helm, lost only once to Yale in those fine 1933–35 years under Fritz Crisler, and had two undefeated seasons in 1950 and 1951 when Charlie Caldwell was coach and Dick Kazmaier was in his prime.

Some of the other Ivies came to the top in the 1920s—Brown, 1920; Cornell with Gil Dobie's great elevens, 1921–23; Penn, 1924; and Dartmouth, 1925. The eastern "independents" were heard from more often in the next decade—Boston College, Carnegie Tech, Colgate, Lafayette, Navy, NYU, Pittsburgh, Rutgers, Syracuse, W&J, and Penn State.

Since 1936, when the Lambert Trophy was first placed in competition as a symbol of eastern leadership, Ivy League teams have won it only six times—Cornell, 1929; Princeton, 1950, 1951; Yale (tied with Navy), 1960; and Dartmouth, 1965, 1970. Pittsburgh, under Jock Sutherland and headed by the "dream backfield" team of 1938, was the outstanding power of that decade; the 1940s saw Colonel Red Blaik's legions supreme, inspired by Doc Blanchard and Glenn Davis; in the mid-fifties Navy came to the front with George Welsh breaking all Academy passing records. Syracuse gained national prominence from 1956 through 1960, first powered by Jim Brown and then Ernie Davis. The Orange were national champions in 1959. Navy came back into the picture, 1962–64, with Roger Staubach, but from 1961 on, Penn State under Coaches Rip Engle and Joe Paterno led the field most often and took possession of the Lambert Trophy ten times in fourteen years.

18

The Track House Gang

A memory or a legend to Penn Staters, depending on their generation, the Track House was home to varsity athletes from 1903 until 1924—a place rough and boisterous, but recalled with pleasure and nostalgia. Here they ate, slept, studied, pranked, and whiled away their few leisure hours. Nearly all major football men, a few track stars, and now and then a baseball or basketball player made up the roster of residents for twenty years.

Built in 1903 with alumni contributions, the large three-story frame house adjoined the west end of Old Beaver Field, its long, wide, rear porch close to the track surrounding the playing field. The name came from its location and also was a carry-over from the designation given to an earlier small building, which had been used principally to store track equipment and stood at the southeast corner of the football field.[1]

[1] Today Whitmore Lab occupies the approximate site of the Track House, but in 1903 the nearest buildings were Chemistry and Physics (later called Walker Lab but now replaced by Davey Building) and, toward the west, Ladies Cottage (later Woman's Building, where Chandlee Lab is now located). A square porch, topped by a railed balcony, was at the center front of the residence, which was a yellowish brown and usually in need of repainting. Double, half-glass doors opened from this entrance into a large clubroom with a fireplace,

Eight double rooms and a common bathroom on each of the two upper floors brought the top capacity of the Track House to about thirty-five athletes, and the "no vacancy" sign regularly was out. All rooms had double-decker beds and a study table shared by the occupants. The football captain and his roommate had the use of a larger, better-furnished room on the first sleeping floor.

Above the kitchen was the apartment of Mr. and Mrs. Frank Boyer Scott and their children—Otto, Frank, and Leota. Both boys grew up to be football players, Otto for Red Griffiths at Marietta College and Frank a local football hero at State College High School. "Scotty" was cook and major domo, ruling his kitchen with an iron hand, and so respected that even the toughest hesitated to trespass. "Icebox violations" were unheard of, though much contemplated.

The front porch balcony, accessible from the first sleeping floor, provided a "speakers' platform" when the Track House became the rallying point for students to greet returning players. The porch itself faced Ladies Cottage, only a short distance across the lawn, but proximity created no problem. The well-chaperoned girls were warned to keep their shades down. The Track House gang wasn't above muffled whistles and loud wisecracks if any of the bolder coeds strolled by, but Shorty Miller was one of the few who actually crossed into forbidden territory.

The end of the women's dormitory nearest the Track House was the "Domestic Science Lab," an experimental kitchen. One day when the coeds had placed two apple pies to cool on the windowsill, Shorty and a friend furtively transferred them to their room where they made short work of the pies. Shorty had almost forgotten his mild guilt feelings two days later when a coed stopped at the porch and asked for him. "Mr. Miller," she said, politely, "you were welcome to the pies, but could we have the plates back?"

Mother Dunn and William (Babe) Wood, among early dwellers in the Track House, carefully watched Scotty's food operation there and in McAllister Hall, the new men's dorm opened in 1905. Later they persuaded college officials to allow them to manage the Mac Hall dining commons, becoming thereby the first of the campus and town tycoons.

---

leather furniture, a piano, and a trophy case. Also on the first floor were the dining room, kitchen, a locker room with showers, and separate quarters to house visiting teams.

Dressing rooms were not among the facilities of New Beaver Field when it went into service for varsity competition in 1909, on the quadrangle close to the present Nittany Lion Inn. There were team rooms under the west stands for use between halves, but for many seasons the players as well as visiting teams dressed in the Track House before games and walked the uphill half mile to the playing field. Players not living in the Track House shared rooms with the regular tenants when they dressed for contests. This cumbersome handling of teams was partly responsible for the unenthusiastic response of larger colleges invited to play in State College. The problem was somewhat alleviated in 1924 with the building of Varsity Hall (now Irvin Hall) and vastly improved when the Recreation Building was completed in 1929.

"The Track House Gang" is depleted now, but at June class reunions there are always a few who reminisce about their old campus home, its feuds, scraps, and pranks. Players often fought among themselves, but were unified against outsiders. Heaven help the stranger who entered with the idea of starting something. Wrestling matches behind closed doors were favorite diversions, and it was a good day when a visitor could be enticed into a scuffle. While he was rolled around on the floor by one of the hosts, another deftly gathered up any loose change that might come out of his pockets.

Pranks inflicted on the regular inmates were routine, like the sprinkling of pebbles between bunk blankets. The sleeper usually pushed them down to the foot of the bed until the accumulated gravel resembled a pillow under the covers. Periodically authorities required that mattresses and springs be taken outside and searched for signs of life.

In early Track House days one or two of the "scholarship" athletes were employed as janitors (Pete Mauthe once held this job), which meant that the place was seldom ready for inspection. When this arrangement proved impractical, "Dean" Burrell was hired as full-time janitor and stock room attendant. He came by his title because of his authoritative supervision of the residents and as the dispenser of "Burrell's Secret Formula Rubbing Liniment" from the training quarters, adjacent to the team dressing rooms. Dutch Hermann, during his bachelor days, was a sort of counselor for a while, but actually more like a warden for Coach Bezdek. Dutch slept in the visiting team's dressing room to check on midnight revelers.

Football and baseball players would come into their rooms after practice and knock the mud off their shoes on the radiators. In time the mud and debris collected into impressive piles. One spring day Larry Vorhis shouted for his friends to come and see a most amazing spectacle. He proudly exhibited three healthy stalks of wheat, already over a foot high. This soon became a fad, and many players who never had the slightest prior interest in agriculture tried to cultivate wheat behind their radiators, with varying success.

In 1924, when the athletes moved up to Varsity Hall, temporary classrooms and chemistry labs were installed in the old building, although the Athletic Department kept part of the first floor for lockers, a shower room, and for storage purposes. The football team continued to use these facilities for the next five years. The end was in sight one day in the spring of 1929 when "Dean" Burrell sent two assistant managers down from the new Rec Hall with a pushcart to remove the last vestiges of a colorful compartment in Penn State's athletic history.

19

Bezdek's Roaring Twenties

Passing years and dwindling partisans have quieted a debate over the merits of Bezdek's 1920 and 1921 football teams, each undefeated and twice tied. Among great Nittany Lion elevens, few can match the Three Musketeers of 1920—Killinger, Haines, and Way—or the brilliance of Killinger and Light Horse Harry Wilson in 1921.

More talent was available in 1920, but the better-disciplined 1921 team made more effective use of what was on hand. Although the 1920 backfield of Haines, Way, Killinger, and Snell was noted for speed, the following year Killinger and Wilson could run behind the superb blocking of Lightner, Knabb, Bedenk, and Baer. Lightner, not a breakaway runner, was a dependable ground-gainer who produced short yardage in crucial situations.

Sensing a possible powerhouse, Coach Bezdek subjected his 1920 squad to merciless discipline in practice and training, enforcing a daily grind to perfect fundamentals and a few basic plays. The war veterans still around in 1920 submitted in smoldering rebellion. On Sundays after games he'd lead the squad in a long jogging hike, participating himself and keeping up with everyone. Monday, never an off day, meant hard drills against the plays of the next opponent, plus live scrimmage for all who hadn't played on Saturday. Long, tough scrimmages on Tuesday and Wednesday included defensive

work against the opponent's plays. Thursday's program was pass
scrimmage and defensive work, and Friday's, a long signal drill.
Daily practice began with a half hour of wind sprints. "Laps around
the track" were the penalties for inattention or serious mistakes.

Bez seemed to have trouble selecting a first team from his talented
veterans, and opening victories in 1920 over Muhlenberg (27–7)
and Gettysburg (13–0) were unimpressive. By the time of Dartmouth's first visit to New Beaver Field on October 9, Killinger had
taken over at quarterback from Williams to join Haines, Way, and
Snell in the backfield, with Lightner as a replacement for both Way
and Snell. Brown, McCollum, and Hufford were the three top ends.
A sophomore, Newsh Bentz, held down center most of the season
but the coach tried several combinations of guards and tackles.
Rauch, Hess, and Griffiths saw about equal service at guard, with
Beck, Baer, and Schuster at the tackles.

The Dartmouth game, undoubtedly the most important so far on
the home field, was a feature of the first official Alumni Homecoming. The *Collegian* called it the "greatest game in the East." The visitors scored first on a short pass from Captain Jim Robertson to the
"scatback," Pat Holbrook, who was about the same size as Way. At
half time the game was tied, 7–7, when Snell scored following a
40-yard drive featuring passes from Killinger to Brown. Later
Killinger intercepted a pass and ran 52 yards to Dartmouth's 2,
where he was pushed out of bounds. Penn State won, 14–7, with
Lightner, a substitute for the injured Way, going over for the touchdown. The Dartmouth student newspaper, claiming its team wasn't
ready for such a big game, criticized both schools for scheduling it so
early.

Dartmouth's giant tackle, Gus Sonnenberg, kept asking for Charlie
Way, who had run 90 and 85 yards against the Big Green at
Hanover the season before. When Killinger pointed at Charlie—all
145 pounds of him—Way whispered unhappily, "Come on, Killy, I
don't want to run into that fellow." Killy carefully ran Charlie very
wide, away from Sonnenberg, for most of the game. Way picked up
plenty of yardage, but not through the hungry Dartmouth tackle.

Walkovers against North Carolina State (41–0) and Lebanon
Valley followed the Dartmouth victory. Way tallied three times in
the first quarter after Lebanon Valley had scored first as a consequence of a fumble and pass that bounced off Killinger's fingers.

Ahead at half time, 48–7, Bezdek used three teams, but Penn State rolled up its highest score to defeat the Dutch visitors, 109–7.

At a spirited mass meeting before the Penn game, Bez was cheered roundly when he said: "I pick men who can always do a little better than their best. A player says to me, 'Coach, I'm doing my best.' I say, 'No good. It's absolutely no good. I want something better than your best.'"

Against Pennsylvania Coach Bezdek got all he could have wished from his fired-up players. Way's run of 25 yards put the Lions in scoring position for Killinger to make the first touchdown. Although Killy played with an injured shoulder until relieved by Williams in the second half, his handling of the team won compliments. Red Griffiths, Harold Hess (switched from the backfield to guard), and Bentz at center were outstanding on the line, but Hinkey Haines made it his game, distinguishing himself as one of the East's most exciting backs.

When the Quakers drove to the 1-yard line late in the second quarter, Penn State's 7–0 lead became precarious. Between halves Coach Bezdek announced that Way would not start the second half.

"Who gets the middle on the kickoff?" asked Hinkey, the rare player who spoke up freely to Bez.

"*You* do," blared Bez.

Haines recalled later that he felt something good was going to happen and went on the field hoping to get the kickoff.

> The ball came to me and I tore up the middle, then over to the right sideline, then back to the middle, just as we had rehearsed it. Our blockers had pushed their opponents toward the sideline, but some in the center left their feet to block for me. I can still see them flying at those Penn guys.

Hinkey's 85-yard return demoralized the Red and Blue, and enabled the Lions to push Lightner and Snell across for two more touchdowns in the third period to win, 28–7.

"State College has a new hero," said Ross Kauffman of Philadelphia's *North American*. James Isaminger wrote: "This Tris Speaker of halfbacks comes from Red Lion in York County, Pennsylvania, not from Muddy Creek Forks. In that part of the country a youth must run 100 yards in 10 seconds and be able to throw a grizzly bear to get along. Hinkey can do both."

Henry Luther Haines, one of the few Penn State athletes to star and win letters as a senior in three major sports, first saw a football game while visiting a cousin at Penn State. Red Lion High School had no football team, but he played baseball and basketball before enrolling at Lebanon Valley in the fall of 1916. His father, the Honorable Harry L. Haines, a congressman representing the Twenty-third District in Washington for six terms, wanted him to go to a small college. Hinkey played football at Lebanon Valley, sometimes looked upon as "fodder" for the larger colleges. Coach Rags Guyer gave Army a scare in 1916, although the West Pointers squeezed out a victory and had an undefeated season.

Hinkey, not on that 1916 team, had his first taste of college football in a junior varsity game with the Carlisle Indians, then attempting to revive the sport without Jim Thorpe. When the Indians led 21–0 at the half, Coach Guyer, thinking he had nothing to lose, inserted a fast but inexperienced halfback. On the first offensive play the center's pass was well over Hinkey's head and the ball rolled back to the 5-yard line with Haines chasing it. "A smart player would have fallen on that loose football," recalled Hinkey, "but I picked it up and started running with it." The 95-yard run won him a place on the second team.

This scrub game exploit, insignificant in itself, symbolizes Hinkey Haines. In his entire competitive sports career he was a self-assured athlete ready to try the unexpected and act on his own initiative, which probably explains why he was never on Bezdek's "right" list.

Haines enlisted in the Army for the summer of 1918 and entered Penn State that winter for the second semester. Ineligible for basketball and baseball in spring 1919, he occasionally made the fall football starting lineup—an achievement considering his inexperience and all the veteran power. He lost out to Charlie Way for 1920 All-America honors from Walter Camp, who put him on his third team in this season of such backs as Way, George Gipp of Notre Dame, Bo McMillin of Centre, Tom Davies of Pitt, Walter French of Army, and Benny Boynton of Williams. Haines was named on All-East teams and others.

Baseball came first, but Hinkey was equally impressive as a professional in football. He was a utility outfielder on the New York Yankees' 1923 world championship team, and in 1927 he played quarterback on the New York Giants' NFL and world championship eleven. This double distinction appears to be unique. While he was still in college, Coach Bezdek persuaded him to reject an offer from the New York Giants baseball club. He signed with the Yankees after his graduation in June 1921, and was farmed out to Hartford of the Eastern League. That fall he assisted football coach Bill Wood '16 at Gettysburg, then joined the Yankees in spring training, batting 1.000—that is, he came to bat one time and hit a home run in an exhibition game won by the Yankees, 8–7, against the New Orleans Pelicans, managed by Frankie Frisch. In 1923, when the Yankees moved into their new stadium, Haines was a utility outfielder in twenty-eight regular-season and two World Series games in which the Yanks defeated the Giants for the title.[1] Among his teammates were Babe Ruth, Waite Hoyt, Bob Shawkey, Wally Pipp, and Herb Pennock. He later played with Rochester, Montreal, and Scranton.

When Tim Mara spent $500 to buy a National League football franchise for the New York Giants, Hinkey and Century Milstead, the Yale All-America tackle, were top recruits at a $4,000 annual salary (most linemen received $75 a game). Jim Thorpe, just about washed up, signed for $200 a game to play not more than 30 minutes in any game. Mara hoped the great Indian athlete would be a big drawing card for his shaky financial venture, but Thorpe lasted only a short time, and Haines became the most publicized player on the squad.[2] Mara had picked him up after he had starred with the Philadelphia Quakers and the Frankford Yellowjackets, who were coached for a time by another Penn Stater, Punk Berryman '16. His backfield mates in the Giant lineup were Heine Benkert of Rutgers, Jack McBride of Syracuse, and Dutch Hendrian of Pittsburgh.

Hinkey quarterbacked under Coach Joe Alexander when the Gi-

[1] Haines and five of his 1923 teammates were guests in April 1976, for the rededication of Yankee Stadium II. It was the first baseball game he had attended in twenty years. Centre *Daily Times* interview, May 7, 1976.

[2] One stunt of the hard-working Mara publicity staff drew 4,000 spectators in midtown Manhattan for an attempt to break the football throwing distance record (72 yards) credited to California's famed Brick Muller. Haines, in Bryant Park, was to catch a pass thrown by a teammate, Lynn Bomar of Vanderbilt, from the 20th floor of the American Radiator Corp. Bldg. on West 40th St. (324 feet). Bomar was off target three times, and the fourth pass bounced off Hinkey's chest. Haines removed his suit jacket, signaled Bomar, took a deep breath, and neatly cradled the fifth throw. A record was claimed. Barry Gottehrer, *The Giants of New York* (New York: G. P. Putnam's Sons, 1963).

ants won the league championship in 1927, best of the early years, with an 11–1–1 record. In their crucial victory over the Chicago Bears (13–7) he saved the day by duplicating the daring Hess-to-Higgins play Penn State had used in 1919 against Pitt. Early in the game the Bears pushed to the Giant 5, on first down, but New York held. On first down Haines signaled for the expected punt from behind the goal line, and the Bears routinely prepared for a nine-man rush. Hinkey noisily alerted his kicker not to step out of the end zone, asked the referee for time to wipe off the ball, and then received the pass himself, throwing to Chuck Corgan of Oklahoma, who made it to the 36. They won their last two games against Red Grange and his Yankees, Haines having a 75-yard punt return in the first game.

Mara tried to talk Haines out of retiring in 1928. He played a short time and coached with the Stapleton, Long Island, team of the NFL, but continued as an official in the league (1933–53). He retired to his home in Penn Wynne, Pennsylvania, in 1968 after many years as Philadelphia district chief of the IRS field service and loan officer for the Small Business Administration.

After the 1920 season was well under way, Bez is said to have become convinced that Lion players weren't warmed up properly. Several opponents scored first against his team (including Lebanon Valley, beaten by more than one hundred points). Before the Nebraska game he sent them through a hard warmup practice on Old Beaver Field a half hour before the squad started its long hike up to New Beaver.

Penn State's third big intersectional game at home (Notre Dame in 1913 and Michigan State in 1914 had been the others) resulted in a 20–0 victory over Nebraska, a top team from the Missouri Valley Conference. The Cornhuskers had held all their 1920 opponents scoreless except Notre Dame, losing to the Irish 16–7, and en route to State College defeated Rutgers 28–0 on a Tuesday afternoon. The midwestern team outweighed the Lions up front and were anchored by two exceptional guards, the Munn brothers, Monte and Wade.

Nebraska's early drive almost to the goal line ended with a touchback when a fourth-down pass hit a goal post. The Lions scored shortly after on a 35-yard pass play from Killinger to Squeak Hufford. In the fourth period, with the score only 7–0, Bezdek sent

Way in to replace Lightner.[3] One of the garrulous Munn boys remarked to Red Griffiths, opposite him: "So this is the famous Way. He won't weigh much today." "Save your breath," retorted Griffiths, "you'll need it." On the first play, Killy called what the players referred to as "Old 42." Way, in the tailback spot, went right through the verbose Munn for 53 yards and the touchdown that broke up the game. Lining up, Munn was the last to arrive. "Come on," jeered Griffiths, "we can't wait all day for you."[4] There was no reply. Way had a 67-yard, nonscoring jaunt later in the quarter, but Killinger made the final touchdown on a 15-yard run.

After seven straight victories (twelve, counting 1919 games), the season closed on a subdued note with 7–7 and 0–0 ties at Lehigh and at Pitt. Penn State was heavily favored over the unbeaten Engineers at Bethlehem. Lehigh was out-first-downed, 10–4, and out-rushed, 167–66, but played a fine defensive game and took a 7–0 lead in the third quarter, scoring on a pass from Rote to Gulick. In the final 10 minutes, the Lions went 80 yards in a series of six first downs, Way then scoring from the 5.

One football axiom was proved: You have to be lucky to go undefeated. On a late drive the Engineers pushed close enough to try for a winning field goal. The kick barely missed, but under 1920 rules the kicking team could recover. As the ball bounced around in the end zone, a Lehigh player was in position to recover for a touchdown. Instead, a local fan ran onto the field, picked up the ball, and helpfully tossed it to the referee.

The Pitt-Penn State game on Thanksgiving Day was expected to have considerable bearing on "the eastern supremacy." Undefeated Pitt had victories over Geneva, West Virginia, Georgia Tech, Lafayette, Penn, and W&J, and a 7–7 tie with Syracuse. True to tradition, the game was played in the mud, which seriously checked the speed of Killinger, Haines, and Way. Way was a starter and led all backs with a net of 79 yards. Pitt had the better of the first half, once driving to the Lion 4 from where Tom Davies missed a field goal by

[3] Way thinks that Bez, usually cool to advice from outsiders, agreed with his Downingtown High School coach that the flashy little halfback was most effective as a "spot" player.

[4] Griffiths, touted for All-America by New York sportswriter Ray McCarthy, was passed over by Walter Camp. He chose Stanley Keck of Princeton for one of his tackles, with Tim Callahan, Yale's center, and Woods of Harvard as the All-America guards.

inches. Penn State evened the statistics in the second half, but couldn't come close to scoring.

Scouting Pop Warner's team, observant Assistant Coach Dick Harlow handicapped Panther star Davies. Harlow had noted that before a kick Davies always bent his elbows with the palms of his hands up. When his hands were out straight and relaxed he was going to run an end sweep. Pitt didn't make a yard on Warner's favorite fake kick play, nor on the quick opener up the middle with Davies as the ball carrier.

Penn State in 1920 was as good as any team in the East except undefeated Harvard, which was tied only by Princeton. The unfortunate upset tie by Lehigh and the scoreless deadlock with Pitt forestalled claims for national honors with California, Ohio State, Notre Dame, and Texas, all undefeated during the regular season. California walloped the Buckeyes in the 1921 Rose Bowl, 28–0.

Penn State's fans accepted the disappointing Pittsburgh tie with resignation and undampened respect for Coach Hugo Bezdek, who was still riding high, but the pending losses of such veterans as Captain Harold Hess, Hinkey Haines, Carl Beck, Dick Rauch, George Brown, Red Griffiths, Buck Williams, and Dick Schuster from the 1920 squad were ominous. The graduation of Charles Ash Way would leave a most unfortunate and special vacuum.

Nicknames bestowed by sportswriters—Gang Way, Pie Way, Rabbit Way, etc.—were ignored by friends and teammates, who generally called him Charlie. Scurrying rabbitlike in all directions, "to get out of the way of those big guys," he was seldom caught in a clear field. Bezdek's effective policy of using him as an exciting breakaway threat at big moments when the other team was tired heightened his dramatic aura and strong fan-appeal, though it irked Charlie. His reputation of being a "loner" off the field, a trait he vigorously denied, may be traceable to his reserve in comparison with the very outgoing personalities of other well-known running backs of his day, Killinger and Haines. Charlie enjoyed company, and he loved competition in any sport.

As a sophomore in 1914 at Downingtown High School in Pennsylvania, Charlie had participated and, in fact, was instrumental in starting football, baseball, basketball, and track under the leadership of the school's first athletic director, Bob Oberholtzer.

Charlie's high school coach tried to get a scholarship for his all-star athlete, but Harlow thought 115 pounds was too small for college football. Way came anyway and stayed at the Track House before he acquired a fraternity job washing dishes. He was unnoticed in the fall of 1916 until someone told Coach Dutch Hermann he had a freshman who could "run like a rabbit." Because Charlie split his hand playing baseball before the 1917 season, he had to switch to halfback from his usual quarterback position, but he started on the varsity frequently and was the signal caller in a few games when Frank Wolf was hurt.

The split hand was a fortunate accident—otherwise the by-now 145-pounder would have competed with Harry Robb and later Glenn Killinger. In the Army in 1918 Charlie "built himself up to his playing weight," had a chance to enter West Point, but came back to Penn State for his last two years and lettered in football in 1917, 1919, and 1920. Although he was kept out of the starting lineup for some important 1920 games, Walter Camp named him on his All-America first-team backfield in the company of Gipp of Notre Dame, Lourie of Princeton, and Stinchcomb of Ohio State. As a trackman he ran the 100 and broad-jumped, setting a Penn State record of 23 feet, 3½ inches (later broken by Al Bates, the Olympian, whose record still stands).

Way was successful in professional football with the Canton Bulldogs (1921), the Frankford Yellowjackets (1924), and the Philadelphia Quakers (1926). He also played some semipro baseball, once organized "Charlie Way's All-America Basketballers," with Killinger in the lineup, and taught and coached football at Allentown High School, Dayton University, and VPI. After twenty-seven years with the IRS in the Philadelphia district, he retired to his fourteen-acre farm in Thorndale, Chester County, Pennsylvania.

20

The 1921 Mystery Team

During a 1971 football weekend, many still hardy members of the 1921 squad had a fiftieth reunion. While students and younger alumni extolled the Lion eleven destined to win its first ten games and then demolish Texas in the Cotton Bowl, these proud veterans of the other "golden era" recalled with no less satisfaction their "mystery team" of 1921. It was said to be the finest product of Hugo Bezdek, under the All-America leadership of Killinger, Wilson, and Bedenk. Killinger unreservedly credits the coach, called by Cullen Cain of the Philadelphia *Public Ledger* "the game's greatest personification of genius in action."

The mystery tag may have derived from 1921's survival undefeated. Few teams had started out with such meager prospects for success. These were the first Lions to face such a thorny array as Harvard, Georgia Tech, Navy, Pittsburgh, and Washington—all to be played away during the season's last six weeks. Gone were the war veterans, including seven starters from 1920. Only eight lettermen were available. Captain George Snell, one of the four remaining varsity players, was lost early in the season because of serious illness, and injuries stripped the squad of other dependables. Most damaging was the loss of Snell, a fine leader and stunning defensive player, of whom a teammate observed, "When Snell tackles you he can hit you three times before you hit the ground."

Dismal early estimates of the 1921 potential didn't reckon on the All-America status that Killinger was to attain in his senior year; the developing stardom of two backs, Wilson and Lightner; and the emergence of newcomer F. Joseph Bedenk as perhaps the finest guard Penn State has had. Bedenk was named to Camp's second All-America team as a sophomore, an achievement without precedent in Penn State football.

As misfortune befell important players, previously unsung heroes were standing by. Frank (Guinea) Hess replaced Captain Snell; Al Knabb became a steady, reliable fullback substituting for the injured Hess; Lee Hills, relatively unknown, plugged the gap at tackle when Rags Madera was lost for the season; and Harry Wilson was a regular after Pete Redinger was hurt.

The easy handling of "warmups" surprised skeptics. The Lions rolled up a total of 112 points against Lebanon Valley, Gettysburg, and North Carolina State while holding these opponents scoreless; then they defeated slightly more troublesome Lehigh, 28–7. Coach Bezdek's team approached the Harvard showdown with high hopes but no overconfidence. Under Coach Bob Fisher, a Haughton disciple, the Crimson had early victories over Middlebury, Boston University, Holy Cross, Indiana, and Georgia. Generally considered the top eastern power, and undefeated in 1919 and 1920, Harvard lost to Centre College later in the 1921 season after twenty-eight games without defeat. Penn State, unbeaten since the Dartmouth game in 1919, had a non-losing streak of eighteen.

The 21–21 tie game at Cambridge was a classic. Bob Herron, a leading Boston football writer, said ten years later that it would "always remain in the minds of those who saw it as one of the greatest football games ever played." As in their 1914 tie, the Lions deserved a better fate.

Adversity struck even before the start, when Captain Snell, fullback, was sent to the infirmary with a throat infection. On the opening kickoff Rags Madera, sophomore tackle and one of the team's toughest competitors, suffered a badly broken thigh, which ended his football career (Madera, who later practiced medicine, was able to join the boxing team before graduation and won the intercollegiate heavyweight championship). Two other starters lost early by injuries were Hess and halfback Redinger.

Hurt and shocked, Penn State was powerless against Harvard's drive half the length of the field, giving George Owen the first touchdown. The cause seemed hopeless early in the second period after a short Lion punt enabled the Crimson to score again. Tiny McMahan, a six-foot, seven-inch tackle playing his first varsity season, recalls that Bez wasn't himself between halves.

> We were behind 14–7, and normally Bez would be raving. But he told us we were doing all right and to go out there in the second half and play just like we had been playing. He even patted me on the back. Actually, I think Bez was in shock—the injuries to Madera, Hess, and Redinger took a lot out of all of us in the first half.

The Lions tied the score at 14–14 in the third period following Wilson's exciting run of 56 yards, reported in the newspapers at anywhere between 55 and 65 yards.[1] Their three scoring plays, all made by Joe Lightner on short gains off tackle using the 41 play, are described by McMahan, who played opposite John Fisk Brown, reputed to be Harvard's toughest lineman.

> Lightner was to come right over me on "41." I should say, right under me, because I didn't have to move Brown much. Lightner kept telling me, "Just move him about a foot, Tiny." That I was able to do, and Joe went underneath me for three touchdowns.[2]

Seven minutes before the finish the Lions led 21–14, but a 15-yard pass from quarterback Charlie Buell to Winthrop Churchill and the vital point kicked by Buell tied the score again. With minutes to play, Penn State drove to the Harvard 14 where the Crimson held as the Lion backs ran into each other in the gathering darkness. Noting that they were fighting time and darkness, the Penn State *Alumni News* (November 1921) explained that Harvard's athletic management had a rule "that no football game can be played in the Stadium

---

[1] Wilson's record for the longest run yet made on the Harvard field lasted one week. Bo McMillin of Centre College broke it with a 68-yard gallop the next Saturday to win the game, 6–0, ending Harvard's non-losing streak. The Penn Staters claimed they had softened up the Crimson for McMillin and his Praying Colonels.

[2] Brown, selected on Walter Camp's first All-America team that year, again met McMahan during the winter when a Harvard wrestling team made one of its rare appearances on Penn State's campus. The two heavyweights faced each other in the old Armory, McMahan winning a decision.

earlier than three o'clock before November 1." The flashing of lighted cigarettes, like fireflies in the dusk, is a favorite recollection.

Penn Staters who played that day have other indelible memories. Glenn Killinger recalls Bezdek's pregame lecture warning them of Harvard's reputation for taking quick advantage of fumbles. "So don't fumble," roared Bez. "Killinger, you carry the ball on the first play. I know *you* won't lose it." Killy called his own signal for the first running play—and fumbled. Al Knabb fumbled on the first play after he replaced Hess at fullback. Knabb seems to have spent the season in disfavor as a ball carrier. Bez, it's said, ordered Killinger not to call Knabby's signal, but he's credited with the first touchdown against Washington and was an effective blocker as well as a defensive standout.

Joe Bedenk pictures Newsh Bentz, center, with a bad cut on his face and blood running down on his new bright yellow football pants. Told by a Harvard lineman that he shouldn't be playing, Newsh said, "You'll be out of the game before I am." Then there was Harvard's cross-eyed fullback—"It was hard to tell where he'd be running," says Joe.

Harry Wilson went up to Cambridge a sophomore substitute and returned a regular halfback, thereafter starting in every game of his prodigious career. He recalls his nervousness before going into his first big game more than the fact that he and Killinger were the ball carriers for 90 per cent of Penn State's running plays.

In the second quarter Bez said, "Wilson, warm up." I ran up and down for about 5 minutes, then got tired and sat down. Bez yelled at me again: "Wilson, I told you to warm up—go in for Redinger." I remembered that the Harvard boys were noted for stealing the ball, so when tackled I'd hold onto the ball for dear life and apparently would shut my eyes when I squeezed it. I can still feel those Harvard guys snatching at it. Once I was lying on the ground with a death grip on the ball and my eyes closed when Killy came up and I heard him say reprovingly, "Come on, Harry, give the referee the ball." And I remember getting kicked in the mouth and spitting out a tooth, leaving the nerve exposed. I called for time out and said someone had knocked out my front tooth. Killy didn't have much sympathy. He said, "What can we do about that?" That night in the Boston station the referee of the game came up and handed me my tooth.

Among other Lion headliners in the game were McCollum and Joe Lightner, who scored all three touchdowns and extra points besides plunging for any number of important short-yardage gains. But the unsung hero was Lee Hills, a senior who saw more action that afternoon than in his entire previous career. He substituted for Madera and remained a regular for the rest of the season. Although he was physically less rugged than the other linemen, Hills' courage and intelligence earned the respect of his teammates. The Blue and White had the better of the statistics, rushing for 294 yards to 105 and recording 19 first downs to 9. Both teams used the short pass with surprising dexterity, Penn State completing 6 of 8 for 69 yards and Harvard 7 of 10 for 62.

Gratified by the unexpected Harvard tie, Penn Staters were overjoyed when favored Georgia Tech was smothered 28–7 before 25,000 spectators at the Polo Grounds. The first New York appearance of the Lions launched a new four-game intersectional series with a team called the best in the South during the regime of John Heisman. Coach Bill Alexander, beginning his long, illustrious career as Heisman's successor, was without his Indian star, Joe Guyon, but had an equally glamorous back—Red Barron—whose stay at the Atlanta school seemed endless.

"The Heisman shift," still used by the Golden Tornadoes, baffled the Lions at first and enabled Tech to take an early 7–0 lead. The excited Georgia Tech fans and their colorful band are recalled by McMahan because this was his first sight of girl cheerleaders. He noticed them sitting atop low bleachers near the goal line. After the touchdown they had fallen over backward and only their legs were visible, flapping in the air.

Tech's lead was brief. Killinger, on his own 15, returned the kickoff 85 yards for the tying touchdown with the same spectacular play Haines used against Penn the year before. Again, newspapers reported the run as between 95 and 85 yards, but Killy thinks he started between the 10- and 15-yard lines.[3]

> I ran straight up the field as far as I could go, then broke at a 90-degree angle for the right sideline. Our blockers were supposed to cut back from the right to wall off tacklers and open up a lane for me along the side. . . . No one ever touched me.

[3] Years later, Frankie Frisch told Killinger he left his 50-yard-line seat to follow that run down the field. Rushing through the stands, he got caught up on a railing and ripped out the seat of his pants.

I was clear at the 50. Inside the 10 I could hear feet pounding behind me and it sounded like a lot of them were awfully close, so I dove for the goal line. As I rolled over I saw they were all Penn State players.

Killy's exceptional skill and generalship, rated his best, earned him a congratulatory visit from Walter Camp in the dressing room after the game.

The Lions overwhelmed Tech, scoring one touchdown per quarter and passing even more accurately than against Harvard, especially the reverse throw to end Stan McCollum. A worse rout was cut off when Lightner missed a field goal by inches and a fifth touchdown was erased by an offside penalty on a pass from Killinger to Lightner.

Their adherents claimed Penn State and Navy were playing for the eastern championship two weeks later on Franklin Field, Philadelphia. Under Bob Folwell, former Penn coach, the Middies had a string of nine victories after losing to Princeton in midseason of the previous year. Their stars were Steve Barchet, a stocky halfback with some speed; Captain Emery (Swede) Larson, center, who later coached them to three victories over Army (1939–41); and Clyde King, tackle, who had stroked the winning Navy crew in the 1920 Olympics. Killinger rated Larson the strongest player he had ever faced, tough and mean. "He kept taunting me, challenging us to run plays at him. I just laughed—and stayed away from him."

On the opening play Folwell successfully employed an old Bezdek trick for an onside kick, enabling the Midshipmen to go for an early touchdown by Barchet. Following a Penn State march in the same period, Killinger scored from 8 yards out, but Lightner's extra-point attempt failed for the first time in the season, and Navy held a 7–6 margin. The Lions won (13–7) in the second quarter when Lightner, the workhorse, scored after a 58-yard march. An offside penalty nullified still another second-quarter touchdown. Navy's bid for victory was thwarted on the Penn State 14 shortly before the end.

The two undefeated old rivals were so closely matched that the game was nearly a stalemate, lacking its usual color. It was won up front by the Lion tackles, guards, and center Newsh Bentz against a veteran Navy line comprised of Larson, King, Bolles, Frawley, and Art Carney, who later played with the New York Giants. Fine backs on both sides—Killinger, Wilson, and Lightner against Koehler, Barchet, and Conroy—had few chances to shine. Wilson recalls having a bit of trouble with Referee Tiny Maxwell involving a lineman who continually tackled around the neck and held on long enough to choke him:

> This guy went over to Maxwell and showed him where some-one had bitten him on the wrist, then pointing his finger at me. Maxwell came over and told me not to do it again. I felt ashamed until later Killy told me he was obliged to bite the same player.

The Lions had a promising newcomer in the starting lineup at left end—Hap Frank. No other defeat marred the Midshipmen's season, which included a cherished victory over Army.

Pittsburgh—losers to Lafayette, Nebraska, and W&J—owned impressive victories over Syracuse and Penn, and nearly spoiled the Lions' big year in the perennial mud of Forbes Field. For the second successive season, they fought to a scoreless tie, with Pitt having an edge in statistics. Wilson stopped the only serious Pitt drive with a pass interception, but Penn State couldn't get untracked in the rain and failed to capitalize on its single opportunity to score when Ray Baer recovered a fumble on the Panther 18.

The first Lion eleven to play on the West Coast, in 1921, broke the traditional Pitt game climax of every season since 1903. A game with the University of Washington on the first Saturday in December, not on the original schedule, was added early in October through Bezdek's contacts during his western coaching days. No longer the invincible power it had been under Gil Dobie, Washington was still considered important regionally and had tied a good Stanford eleven earlier in the year.

The Sun Dodgers, as the Huskies were then called, seemed aptly nicknamed to the Penn Staters, who saw little sun during the trip and could well understand why the playing field was mainly sand and sawdust. Coach Bezdek's fears that the strange playing surface would tire his players and prevent Killinger and Wilson from doing their stuff were groundless. The westerners were no match for the un-defeated Lions, who won easily, 21–7. Penn State reportedly had eight scoring opportunities, two of them lost through fumbles and excessive penalties (for 70 yards).

Some of the celebrating Lions found that a dive into frigid Lake Washington wasn't altogether enjoyable. The squad had sight-seeing stopovers in Portland, Salt Lake City, and Denver, traveling between the last two cities on the picturesque run of the Denver and Rio

Grande Railroad. It was an exhilarating experience for young men whose previous travel had been limited. They returned to the campus as heroes during the best time of the year, just before Christmas vacation.

The West Coast trip had unforeseen side effects in connection with the 1922 Rose Bowl. Penn State official records don't confirm it, but midseason newspaper stories reported that Lion athletic officials had refused an invitation because of the December 3 commitment. In the early 1920s, transcontinental trips twice in one season were utterly unfeasible.

Rose Bowl opponents on January 1, 1922, weren't finally settled until well into December. Starting its great years under Andy Smith, California had trampled its conference opponents and was proud of being undefeated in nine games, but withheld acceptance pending selection of an opponent. Washington and Jefferson, a likely eastern choice, mystified one West Coast sportswriter, who confessed he knew only that both were dead. When rumors of a postseason agreement to play Texas A&M in Dallas were cleared up, the Presidents accepted on December 2, with California signing about a week later.

W&J had sound credentials. Undefeated in ten games, the small-college team had beaten Pop Warner's Pitt eleven 7–0 and had won decisively from Syracuse and West Virginia. W&J was coached by Greasy Neale, a famous big-league baseball player, and captained by All-America Russ Stein, a tackle, whose brother Herb played center at Pitt. W&J represented the East with distinction, holding the great Brick Muller in check and outplaying the favored team from Berkeley. Statistics in the scoreless-tie game favored the easterners, who had an apparent winning touchdown nullified by an offside call. Coach Neale made no substitutions.

Nittany Lion fans believed Coach Bezdek's team, with its strong schedule, would have been equally tough for the Golden Bears, and eastern experts said the same of Cornell and Lafayette. Coached by Dr. Jock Sutherland, Lafayette had superperformers in Charley Berry (at end) and Dutch Schwab (a guard), who led the Leopards to an undefeated season, including victories over Pitt and Penn. Gil Dobie's Cornell team had the first of three undefeated seasons headlined by Eddie Kaw, fullback; George Pfann, quarterback; and Sunny Sundstrom, tackle. The East's Big Four (Cornell, W&J, Lafayette, and Penn State) ranked with the nation's finest teams—

California, Centre, Chicago, Iowa, and Vanderbilt. Chicago lost once to Ohio State, Centre dropped a postseason game to Texas A&M, and the others were unbeaten.

Bezdek's 1921 team, probably the strongest of his three greatest, had the weakest claim to sectional and national honors simply because there were more good teams than had been the case in the two prior seasons. Since good teams and much-publicized running backs were plentiful, it was an added fillip to a fine year when W. Glenn Killinger made halfback on Walter Camp's All-America, still the only all-star team of recognized prestige. Strong linemen received little attention in this period, and all Lion athletes had problems making names for themselves outside of isolated State College. Big-city newspapers used free-lance local journalists as "stringers" before Penn State's first sports information director was appointed several years later.

Killinger and Kaw of Cornell, the two top backs of the East's four undefeated teams, joined Mac Aldrich of Yale and Aubrey Devine of Iowa in the All-America backfield. Devine, whose 38-yard drop kick ended Notre Dame's twenty-game winning streak, was a surprise pick at quarterback since both Bo McMillin of Centre and Don Lourie of Princeton, selected in 1919 and 1920, also played in 1921. Other standout backs were George Owen, Harvard; Tom Davies, Pitt; Red Barron, Georgia Tech; Steve Barchet, Navy; Walter French, Army; and Johnny Mohardt, Notre Dame.

Killinger's rare versatility easily justified putting him at halfback instead of quarterback. In 1921 he had scored ten touchdowns, made his most dramatic run returning the Georgia Tech kickoff, and had a 70-yard run from scrimmage against North Carolina State. An excellent passer and above-average drop kicker, he could block sharply and play superb defense. He frequently was used as a punt-and kickoff-return specialist (in those days such terminology was nonexistent—a top player had to do it all). Killy's judgment as a quarterback and team leader seldom displeased his exacting coach.

Unsettled arguments invariably end comparisons of Killinger, Way, Haines, and Wilson—Penn State's best-known backs of the postwar era. All were superior athletes and each had a specialty as well as his own way of avoiding a tackler. But Killinger had the greatest array of talents. A "juke" runner, darting here and there to get away from defensive players, he could also hit the line with the slashing force of a good fullback. His 1919 statistics were five feet, ten inches and 156 pounds, but his 1920–21 playing weight was in the 165–70-pound range. The shorter Wilson and Haines (five feet, nine and five feet, eight inches) were a little heavier. Killy and Wilson appeared to be leaner and less rugged than the stocky Haines and yet were seldom injured. Way, the midget of the quartet (145), was well muscled and, like Haines, an exciting "breakaway" threat as a "spot" runner. Killinger and Wilson also excelled as pass defenders. Whatever their speed in the open field, few opponents ever caught any of them past the secondary. Killy may have had more good moves going through the line when the traffic was heavy, but Wilson also had fancy maneuvers to break away from a defensive halfback and was deft at following his interference. Joe Bedenk, who threw many blocks for both, kept track of Wilson by watching the defensive player's eyes. Harry seldom got hurt when a tackle was unavoidable because he could get his feet off the ground before being hit.

Contemporaries of Glenn Killinger class him as Penn State's finest all-around athlete—a regular in football, basketball, and baseball, he participated in probably a record number of intercollegiate contests. After his final football year the Lions owned a string of twenty-four games without defeat. During his 1920 and 1921 baseball seasons they won thirty consecutive victories, a record still unbroken. In his three years, the basketball team won thirty-seven games and lost only five.

A walk-on athlete with no scholarship offer, Killinger had arrived on campus in 1917 before the coming of Hugo Bezdek. As a freshman he gained 25 pounds over his weight of 125 when he was a Harrisburg Tech High School senior playing in three sports. He gives Bez credit for his development, but teammates maintain he made himself proficient by dogged perseverance, an intense desire to excel, and a fervent competitive spirit. A self-assured extrovert, he did his own thinking on the field, always put out 100 per cent, and expected the same of everyone. Off the field he was talkative and opinionated, justifiably sure of himself. Killinger and Wilson, almost exact opposites in personality, were good friends with genuine respect for each other. Dreamers hold that if they could have played two more years together, the Lions might have continued their close to all-winning ways through 1923 and 1924.

Killinger, a graduate in metallurgy, was Dickinson's head coach for a year, then returned to assist Bezdek for the 1923 and 1924 sea-

sons. Following five years as coach at Rensselaer (RPI), he worked
for a master's degree in physical education at Columbia. In off-
seasons he played some football with the New York Giants but more
baseball—with Jersey City (International League), Atlanta (Southern Association), and was a manager in Harrisburg, Williamsport,
and Allentown.

After a year (1932–33) as head coach at Moravian College in
Bethlehem, Pennsylvania, he finally settled at West Chester State
College, where he directed three sports for twenty-two years and in
football compiled a 146–31–6 record. A lieutenant commander in
the Navy during World War II, he coached the North Carolina
Preflight team at Chapel Hill. There he changed his celebrated pupil,
Otto Graham, from halfback to quarterback, a switch that may have
influenced the great player's career with the Cleveland Browns. Returning to West Chester as athletic director and dean of men,
Killinger received an honorary doctorate from Gettysburg, was
named to the Pennsylvania Sports Hall of Fame in 1964, and was
elected to the Coaches Hall of Fame (1970) by the American Association of Baseball Coaches and to the National Football Foundation's Hall of Fame (1971), the second Penn State player so
honored. In retirement at West Chester, he is a popular community
personality, esteemed for his contributions to scholastic and intercollegiate athletics.

Unbothered by football polls, Penn State fans and athletic officials
rejoiced in Bezdek's record of three seasons with one defeat against
strong intersectional competition, and with the profits therefrom. The
Athletic Association's annual report for 1921–22 showed a profit in
excess of $33,000 from the 1921 football season and a $23,000
deficit for all other sports. The Athletic Committee immediately used
part of the surplus for bleachers, increasing the capacity of New
Beaver Field to 12,000. Penn State's first press box, topping the west
stands, had been constructed before the 1921 season.

The trustees approved the committee's allocation of $20,000 for a
modern dormitory and dining facilities to replace the old Track
House. The long-dreamed-of Varsity Hall was to be included among
projects in the Emergency Building Fund campaign about to be
launched. The committee further enlisted the Varsity *S* Club and the
Athletic Association to aid the drive.

Bezdek's contract was extended for ten years beginning September

1, 1922, and his salary was increased to $14,000, but his $4,500 payment by the college as director of physical education was unchanged. Bonuses were awarded to the staff: Bezdek, $2,000; Assistant Coach Harlow, $500; Freshman Coach Hermann, $500; Trainer Martin, $500; Graduate Manager Fleming, $500; and Assistant Coach Rauch, $200. Scholarships for non-Pennsylvania athletes covered their out-of-state fees for the first time.

On another front, meeting on March 11, 1922, the committee registered unqualified opposition to professional football and decided to "discourage all former Penn State men from participating in professional contests, which would only bring discredit to the college."[4]

[4] The effect was negligible. Joining pro ranks in this period were Dick Rauch, Barney Wentz, Harry Robb, and two who played for the world's championship Canton Bulldogs in 1922–23—Duke Osborn and Larry Conover.

21

Backing into the Rose Bowl

Representing the East in the first Rose Bowl game to be played at the present Arroyo Seco site came as an incongruous finale to Penn State's 1922 season, which can be classified only as a disaster. More than a "feeler" seems to have been received that spring of 1922, indicating it was delayed recognition of the deserving 1921 team.

There was no newspaper announcement, but formal word must have precipitated unanimous action by the Athletic Advisory Committee on June 12 accepting "the Carnival of Roses Committee's offer of a New Year's football game at Pasadena next season, if satisfactory arrangements are made and providing a college or university team is selected as an opponent.[1] At the next meeting under "old business" (August 3), the situation was outlined and it was decided "to follow up the matter and secure a decision." Minutes of the October 21 meeting show continuing confusion:

> The status of the Pasadena game was discussed. As no formal invitation had been received, no action was taken.

Were Athletic Director Bezdek and Graduate Manager Fleming keeping it from the committee? Word reached the public when the

[1] The *Trojan Family,* published by the Southern California Alumni Association in 1973 on the fiftieth anniversary of the game, stated that Penn State had been invited and accepted the bowl invitation in April.

Collegian (October 27) announced that Penn State would play in the Rose Bowl on January 1, 1923. No opponent was named, but the invitation came from the Pacific Coast Intercollegiate Conference and was "a tribute to past achievements." The paper said that Penn State's net proceeds would go to the Emergency Building Fund campaign as "subscriptions from team members who played in the game." The next day (October 28) Penn State was tied by Syracuse, 0–0. Losses to Navy, Penn, and Pitt followed.

Coach Bezdek's excessive troubles began when his simmering feud with Assistant Coach Dick Harlow boiled over in the spring of 1922. Finding an adequate heavyweight was giving Harlow difficulty because of Madera's football injury in the 1921 Harvard game. When Harold Ave, a big, strapping young man with obvious experience, appeared in the Armory boxing ring as the second semester started, Director Bezdek was suspicious. Finding a past record of semipro fights and a somewhat dubious academic background, he refused to allow Ave to compete. The explosion was climaxed by Harlow's acceptance of the head coaching position at Colgate, an announcement followed by well-founded rumors that six varsity players would go with him, including letterman Pete Redinger. By the start of the season, one of the 1921 assistant coaches, Dick Rauch, had also decided to cast his lot with Harlow.[2]

The five regulars from 1921 on hand to begin the "Rose Bowl year" were Captain Bentz, Bedenk, Hufford, and McMahan, all linemen; and Harry Wilson, the lone backfield veteran. Other line possibilities included Hap Frank and Hal Logue, the remaining reserves; and newcomers Ted Artelt, Freddy Flock, Bill Hamilton, T. E. (Pop) Ellwood, Jules Prevost, Al McCoy, and H. R. (Horse) Johnson. Backfield material was less promising except for Mike Palm, a junior who had been groomed to take Killinger's place at quarterback. A protégé of State Senator Harry Scott (a Philipsburg, Pennsylvania, coal dealer), Palm gave the Lions two years of solid football as a better-than-average passer and a proficient place kicker.[3]

[2] Rauch coached the Pottsville Maroons to a 10–2–0 season (1925) in the National Football League, but their claim to the league title was disallowed because the Chicago Cardinals had hurriedly scheduled two soft games for a questionable 11–2–1 record. Former Penn Staters on his team were Duke Osborn and Barney Wentz.

[3] Palm '24 was an assistant coach under Steve Owen with the New York Giants, and coached at West Virginia, Harvard, and Georgetown. He owned and

This thin 1922 squad was further hampered by injuries. The backfield, except for Palm and Wilson, changed weekly, and even Wilson was shifted around. Johnny Patton was tried at quarterback for two games. Bez pulled one of his notorious switches before the Pitt game, moving Squeak Hufford from end to halfback. Earl (Kratter) Kratz and Earl Singer, relatively unknown players, started the Syracuse game; Hank Lafferty was a starter against Navy. The finishing touch came in the first practice at Pasadena when Captain-elect Joe Bedenk broke three ribs under a pileup of four players and had to be replaced by Pop Ellwood, a game but small junior. Bezdek's angry refusal to start center and Captain Newsh Bentz, who was accused of a pregame training violation, left the Lions without their two best interior linemen. Hamilton started at center, but Bentz later was substituted.

December's daily rain or snow made the practice field either muddy or frozen before the departure for the Rose Bowl on December 19. The party of twenty-five players, Coach Bezdek, Trainer Martin, Graduate Manager Fleming, and Student Manager C. W. (Chill) Parsons traveled via the Southern Pacific Railroad with a stopover to see the Grand Canyon and arrived at Pasadena on Christmas Day. Pop Ellwood was the only married player, but taking his wife wasn't even considered.[4]

In California Bez worked the squad hard and worried about the change in climate and environment. Strangers wandering in to his strictly secret practice were roared away. (Moon Mullins, Marquette's athletic director, claimed he was among those Bez personally threw off the field.) The coach insisted on a curfew, which wasn't entirely followed, but did allow some time for sight-seeing. Visiting the Hollywood studios, the boys were used as extras in a crowd viewing a boxing match. Bedenk and Bentz had their pictures taken with Mary Pickford, who was informed they were from Penn State. Her husband, Douglas Fairbanks, Sr., was acutely embarrassed when she asked why they were in California.

---

operated Mike Palm's Restaurant in Washington, D.C., until his death on April 8, 1974.

[4] Pop, a little older than the others but very popular, farmed near State College and was a varsity wrestler. He received a degree in animal husbandry (1924) and later was a successful coach and athletic director at Trinity High School, Washington, Pennsylvania. His son, Thomas E., Jr., played football under Bob Higgins.

This was Bezdek's third experience as a Rose Bowl coach. He is said to have criticized arrangements for the 1917 game, in which his Oregon eleven defeated Penn, 14–0, so bitterly that officials vowed never to invite him again. The very next year he coached the Mare Island Marines in the wartime game with an Army team from Camp Lewis. His Marines won, 19–7.

Stories about open hostility between Bezdek and Elmer (Gloomy Gus) Henderson, the Southern California coach, have mushroomed through the years. Henderson apparently assumed that Bez deliberately held up Penn State's arrival at the field for the psychological effect or to keep his team from playing during the hottest part of the afternoon. Their shouting match on the field before the game started was magnified in the press and has since grown into a "fist fight."

Actually, Bez was innocent. After watching the morning parade, the Lions had traffic trouble getting back to the Raymond Hotel for their pregame meal, but left again at 11 A.M. in a fleet of taxis in plenty of time for the 2:15 kickoff. There was no police escort through the much heavier traffic on this nightmarish trip to the new stadium. Graduate Manager Fleming, in the lead cab with Bez, Bentz, and Bedenk, performed the only miracle that would get them to the game on time. Thrusting a large bill at the driver, he asked him to go around the pileup by trespassing on the lawns of private homes. The other taxis followed, digging deep ruts in freshly seeded lawns while home-owners raged. At that, they had to walk the last mile down through the gorge to the stadium. Many of the 43,000 spectators weren't seated until the second quarter, even though the starting time was delayed until three o'clock. The game was completed in semidarkness.

For the first ten minutes, Penn State seemed to have control, allowing Mike Palm to dropkick a field goal from the Trojan 20-yard line. Wilson and Palm gained ground consistently in the opening quarter, but after the first long drive the Lions appeared to be exhausted in the balmy climate of Southern California.

Following the Penn State score, Leo Calland, the Trojan captain and guard who was also an assistant coach, called time out and went over to the bench to consult with another of Coach Henderson's assistants, Harold Hess, Lion captain in 1920. As USC's freshman coach in 1922, Hess used Penn State's offense and was kept on to help coach the varsity for the bowl game. In a letter of April 4, 1975, he says:

. . . the freshmen worked against the varsity, and we played a defense where the guards didn't charge, but floated. One always was responsible for Harry Wilson on the fake reverse. The other drifted back to break up the short pass play over the line that Bez used at that time.

For his inspired defensive play, Calland earned the honor of Outstanding Player of the Game.

In the second period Southern California got close to Penn State's goal line when quarterback Harold Baker, flat on his back, made a remarkable catch of a pass thrown by Roy Baker. Gordon Campbell scored two plays later from the 1-yard line. Baker, who gained 107 yards in 27 carries, accounted for the second Trojan touchdown in the third period. Southern California won, 14–3, auspiciously beginning its long string of eighteen Rose Bowl appearances. About a week after the team's return, Graduate Manager Fleming walked into Emergency Building Fund campaign headquarters with a check for $21,349.64, Penn State's share of the Rose Bowl profits.

The 1923 game had plunged the Tournament of Roses Association and the Pacific Coast Conference into an epic quarrel about jurisdiction over the game and selection of the teams. California, winner of the 1922 conference title and host team in the Rose Bowl the two previous years, apparently was disillusioned and refused to play. Eventually the NCAA settled the matter in favor of the Conference organization. Southern California, beaten by the Golden Bears, 12–0, thus became the second participant to enter the picture through the back door. Penn State's premature selection had caused some raised eyebrows, especially from adherents of Cornell, Iowa, Princeton, and Vanderbilt—all undefeated. Cornell was at the peak of its power under Dobie, and Iowa boasted one of its best elevens under Howard Jones. Princeton, coached by Bill Roper, often was referred to as "the team of destiny."

Such team labels ("the team called desire," etc.) are dear to coaches and the press. Bezdek's luckless 1922 eleven qualifies as "the team of destitution." Granted a minimum of prosperity, Penn State could have faced its Rose Bowl opponent with no more than one defeat, and even the Pasadena game might have gone the other way had the Lions been at full strength. A brief review of the season confirms this "might have been."

The Syracuse scoreless tie developed into a fierce line struggle in which Penn State lost the one chance either side had to score when

Roy Simmons fumbled a punt. Joe Bedenk recovered inside the 5-yard line, but the Lions couldn't put it over. (Joe believes that if he had known the game would depend on it, he might have picked up the ball and rolled over the line.) At Philadelphia, where Wilson gained 119 yards by running and by catching four passes of the eight Palm completed, Bezdek's team lost to Penn, 7–6 (the first time since 1916), when Palm missed an extra point. The Quakers, outrushed and outpassed, scored on a deflected pass. In the Pitt game a scoreless first half caused fans to wonder if the two rivals would play their third consecutive 0–0 game. The Panthers won, 14–0, largely on the fine running of Tiny Hewitt.

Some critics felt that the team had too many "warmups" in 1922, the Lions rolling up 166 points to 13 by opponents in the first five games. Middlebury College, defeated 33–0, had been added as the fifth to please President John M. Thomas, who had come to Penn State from the presidency of the Vermont college, his alma mater. For McMahan, the big Lion tackle, the season wasn't devoid of luck. He broke through to block a Middlebury punt, Bedenk grabbed it, ran fifteen yards, then fumbled the ball. McMahan scooped it up to score the only touchdown of his career, with Wilson blocking for him —a switch in roles that still amuses him.

Saddest of the 1922 defeats was the loss to Navy, 14–0, in Washington, D.C., on the first weekend in November. Originally scheduled for Saturday, the game had been moved up to Friday because another college had pre-empted the American League baseball field. Much interest developed in the match. Penn State had a thirty-game non-losing streak on the line, and the Midshipmen, with one loss (to Pennsylvania, in October), had been defeated only five times since 1918. Although the Lions hadn't been extended by five easy opponents, their poor physical condition forced Coach Bezdek to use three substitutes in the line and two in the backfield. At right half his "secret weapon," a scatback smaller even than Charlie Way, was Kratter Kratz from Toledo, Ohio. Poor Kratz fumbled in the third quarter, a misplay that led to Navy's clinching touchdown and his oblivion.

How they could have lost the Navy game puzzled the players, who outgained their opponents in yards gained on the ground, 213–100, and in first downs, 9–4. The Midshipmen won with an alert play called by Coach Bob Folwell in the second period—a successful fake field goal on fourth down from the Lion twenty-one, ending with Ira

(Pete) McKee passing to C. E. (Shaggy) Cullen for a touchdown. Navy's third-quarter score after the fumble was also scored by Cullen.

Several weeks before the season's end, encouraged by strong student support and his extended contract from the Athletic Committee, Coach Bezdek turned down a lucrative offer to manage the National League's Philadelphia baseball team. It wasn't a "million-dollar offer" from the Phillies, but it was rumored that Bez gave up a salary increase of several thousand dollars. "Ideals cost money, and I find that my ideals can best be accomplished in the college atmosphere," was his statement to the press.

Navy's playing on a Friday afternoon must have pleased Army—it freed West Point coaches to scout the enemy and led them to an invaluable recruit. Coming out of the Willard Hotel men's room Friday evening, McMahan was stopped by two Army officers—Major Charlie Daly, the West Point coach, and his assistant, Captain John McEwan, who moved into the head coaching job the following season. Daly asked Tiny if he'd be interested in attending West Point after his graduation from Penn State the coming June. The rigors of Army life and four more years of football didn't appeal to him, he told the two officers. Just then Harry Wilson passed by.

"Why don't you ask that guy? That's Harry Wilson."

"Is that Wilson? We'd like to have Wilson," said Daly.

Thus Army made its first contact with Wilson. Harry indicated interest in an Army career after graduating from Penn State and playing his final year of football in 1923. Daly and McEwan kept their promise to contact him later, and neither Wilson nor McMahan ever regretted their choices. Navy's victory celebrations in Washington and Annapolis might have been overcast with gloom and doom if the Midshipmen had known of Wilson's future. For the next five years Navy was unable to defeat a team with Light Horse Harry Wilson in the lineup. As for Tiny, sheer chance had brought Jay S. McMahan to Penn State in the fall of 1919. Born in Youngstown, Ohio, and orphaned early in life, he was reared on a farm, doing a "man's work" as a boy. Later, at Ravenna, Ohio, when he was a night clerk in the Western Reserve Hotel, he was "discovered" by Jimmy Hughes, famous headmaster of Bellefonte Academy, on a scouting expedition for athletes. Impressed by the towering McMahan (he was six feet, seven inches) who weighed close to 210 pounds, Hughes persuaded him to enter his preparatory school, at that time and in the 1920s a "football feeder" for many large eastern colleges.

McMahan tried to enlist in the Marine Corps in 1917, but was turned down because he was too tall. To help supplement his "scholarship," Hughes got him a job as chauffeur for the town's leading banker, Colonel Jack Spangler. One fall day in 1918 McMahan drove Spangler's Packard to State College to bring back President Edwin Erle Sparks for a parade celebrating the end of World War I. Dr. Sparks encouraged Tiny to enter Penn State.

A lifetime nickname was bestowed by Damon Runyon when he covered one of Penn State's home games and McMahan was his escort.

> I took him out to Phi Sigma Kappa where he met all the Houseparty girls, and returned him to his hotel room by 10:30 P.M. Cullen Cain, a Philadelphia newspaperman, had been calling me "Penn State's Big Indian." Runyon said, "I don't have time to write all that down. I need a short name, so how about Tiny?"

McMahan had reached his full height before maturity and he wasn't an especially well-co-ordinated athlete at first. He later developed into a three-sport performer—football, wrestling, and track—and was the heavyweight on Penn State's eastern intercollegiate championship wrestling team in 1921. A serious accident during practice before the 1922 season almost ended his athletic career.

One day in a wrestling match, a three-hundred-pound giant fell on his head, nearly forcing it into his chest. Teammates, fearing his neck was broken, carried him out of the Armory on a board, and Dr. J. P. Ritenour, college physician, had a leather collar made as a temporary measure. At Coach Bezdek's suggestion Tiny went to Youngstown, Ohio, traveling alone by bus and train, to see "Bonesetter" Reese, who had an impressive reputation for treating badly injured athletes. Reese snapped something in the back of his neck and fixed up a brace for him. McMahan never wrestled again, but he played football during the 1922 season, brace and all.

McMahan served on Bezdek's 1923 coaching staff before being graduated in commerce and finance at midterm, 1924. He started to work as a laborer almost immediately for Pete Mauthe at the National Tube blast furnaces in Lorain, Ohio. "I never wanted a whole lot of money," says McMahan, "I just wanted a steady income, and blast furnaces never shut down in those days." Gradually moving up in the industry, he became an executive with the Steel Company of Canada, in Hamilton, Ontario, and an internationally recognized expert on blast furnaces.

He retired to his home at Eagle Pass, Texas, but remains a consultant in this country and abroad, mainly in Canada, Great Britain, Japan, the Soviet Union, Greece, South Africa, Mexico, and Sweden. McMahan received the Judge Gary Award of the American Iron and Steel Institute for the greatest contribution to the steel industry in 1959 and was named a Distinguished Alumnus of the University in June 1975.

22

Light Horse Harry: Navy Nemesis

Penn State and Navy met for thirty years before Annapolis official-dom agreed to come to Penn State, and when the 1923 game on New Beaver Field had ended, the visiting delegation might well have hoped not to return for another three decades. (To be exact, it was thirty-two years.)

Off the field the college and community outdid themselves to make the visitors welcome. Storefronts on College Avenue and Allen Street were draped in blue-and-gold bunting. "Welcome Navy" (not "Beat Navy") signs were everywhere, and a Homecoming crowd of twenty thousand jammed all seats around the field, including the temporary bleachers. Standees surrounded the gridiron.

With the Lions leading 14–0 at half time, the unrestrained reception continued as Navy football players were named honorary members of Blue Key and given emblems of this undergraduate hat society. "Every effort was made," reported one account, "to make the Mid-shipmen feel at home."

One nonco-operator, halfback Harry Wilson, spoiled almost sin-gle-handedly what might have been an undefeated season for the Naval Academy. With typical freedom from vanity, he credits his teammates for the three spectacular plays that overcame the dismayed visitors (21–3). Except for Wilson's runs, however, the Lions were outplayed and had to fight to stay alive.

Flamboyant football leads were irresistible even to the best sportswriters of the 1920s, and Grantland Rice's famous Army-Notre Dame example—"Outlined against a blue-gray October sky, the Four Horsemen struck again. . . ."—was still a year away, but an unnamed *Collegian* reporter tried valiantly to say it all as he covered Harry Wilson's exploits:

> Twenty thousand people looked down upon New Beaver Field Saturday and marveled as they saw a new star flash across the firmament of the football heavens in a blaze of dazzling brilliance. Three times a cub of the Nittany Lion, reared in the shrewd strategy of Hugo Bezdek, plunged into the seething maelstrom of two teams locked in grim combat to burst forth a blue streak that put to rout the menace of an alien invasion. Each time the name of Harry Wilson was engraved more deeply on the roll of those football men whose feats are tradition in this peaceful Nittany Valley.

Only the home team's heroic line play kept Navy from a first-quarter score. Wilson reversed the game's direction, intercepting a pass by Shaggy Cullen (who had scored twice against the Lions in 1922) and returning 55 yards for the first score. Harry then electrified the crowd with his return of the next kickoff nearly the entire length of the field (95 yards) for his second touchdown. Finally, he broke Navy's back by running 72 yards from scrimmage on a fake reverse for a third score early in the second half. On this run, sharp blocking broke him loose, but he outmaneuvered the defensive backs, Alan Shapley and Pete McKee. The bewildered visitors, gaining 285 yards by rushing and making 16 first downs (to State's 5), scored only a single field goal, by Red Ballenger, late in the contest. The 1923 Navy team didn't lose again, going on to tie Army, 0–0, and playing a 14–14 tie with the University of Washington in the Rose Bowl.

Red Grange's five-touchdown splurge against Michigan the following season deservedly is recognized as the most spectacular individual achievement of any halfback of the 1920s, but Wilson's contribution to Penn State's 21–3 victory over Navy ranks close to the top. Harry's hot streak continued with both touchdowns against West Virginia in Yankee Stadium (13–13), the winning touchdown in the Georgia Tech game (7–0), and three touchdowns a week later for a

21–0 victory over Penn. From the Navy game to the end of the season, Wilson scored every touchdown made by the Nittany Lions in the final six games.

Light Horse Harry Wilson! It's assumed he acquired his nickname at West Point, since General Harry Lee, Revolutionary War officer and father of General Robert E. Lee, was known as Light Horse Harry Lee. Not so, says Colonel Harry E. Wilson.

> Grantland Rice used it in the poem he wrote about the Four Horsemen after our [Army's] game with Notre Dame in 1924. However, it was first used after our [Penn State's] Navy game in 1923. I first saw it in the Philadelphia *Inquirer,* and I think it was originated by George Trevor.[1]

The Navy game made Wilson a prime prospect for All-America, and his continued exploits seemed to assure that status. Lion fans were indignant when Walter Camp placed their hero on the second team, giving first-team honors in 1923 to Grange, Eddie Kaw of Cornell, Bill Mallory of Yale, and Earl Martireau of Minnesota. Camp's predilection for the 1923 Yale team further led him to name Mal Stevens as the second-team fullback. Ernie Nevers, the Stanford great, pulled up in third place.

The sting of the Wilson disappointment was softened somewhat when Camp selected Joe Bedenk as a guard on his first eleven—the first Penn State interior lineman so honored since Mother Dunn in 1906. Joe theorizes that he owes the citation to his interception of a pass in the first half of the Penn State-West Virginia game. Camp attended that game in Yankee Stadium, and used a photo of the play to illustrate a point he wanted to make in a magazine article. He hoped to convince rulemakers that the forward pass wasn't a dire threat to the game and that some of the restrictive rules against it should be repealed.

Camp's views on the forward pass had little effect on the Rules Committee, which curbed it further in 1926 by imposing a loss of five yards on all incompleted passes after the first one in the same series of downs. Perhaps the most interesting of the slight changes in the look of college football after the elimination in 1920 of the "punt-out" following a touchdown was the huddle, used in 1921 by its first advocate, Bob Zuppke of Illinois. Rushing or passing, in addition to the drop kick or placement, was allowed in 1922 for adding

[1] George Trevor was a well-known syndicated sportswriter of the New York *Sun.*

a single extra point after touchdowns, with the play starting from the 5-yard line. This was moved to the 3-yard line in 1923. In 1924 tees for kicking off were abolished and the kickoff spot was changed to midfield, but returned to the 40-yard line the next year. A severe penalty for clipping—25 yards—was established.

The moderate financial success of the New York games at the Polo Grounds against Georgia Tech in 1921 and Syracuse in 1922 impelled Penn State athletic officials to arrange a game at the new Yankee Stadium in 1923. When Vanderbilt couldn't accept, West Virginia was substituted, and the two undefeated teams drew an excellent crowd of 50,000. The papers played up the duel between Wilson and Nick Nardacci, an all-time West Virginia star. Wilson scored twice, and Nardacci scored once, on a 30-yard pass from Gus Ekberg, whose pass to Pete Barnum accounted for West Virginia's other touchdown in the 13–13 game. Defensive stars for Penn State were Bedenk, who made a key interception and blocked a kick; Hobie Light, whose punting was unerring; and tackle Jules Prevost. The Mountaineers went ahead in the final quarter, 13–7, but a 42-yard kickoff return by a substitute halfback, Ray Johnston, led to Penn State's tying score. West Virginia's fine season closed with one defeat, inflicted by W&J.

Georgia Tech's Yellowjackets (formerly the Golden Tornadoes) paid their only visit to Penn State's campus and went back to Atlanta outplayed, 7–0. The unspectacular game featured a single Wilson touchdown after 4 minutes of play. The Lions had many opportunities to score, amassing ten first downs to the visitors' two, but could not sustain an attack, partly because injuries to Palm and Bedenk, received against West Virginia, kept them out of most of the game. A new star emerged, August (Mike) Michalske, a sophomore guard who became one of Penn State's first stellar professionals.

If the *Collegian* report was accurate, Wilson carried the ball forty-five times against Penn, establishing a record never since equaled by a Penn State player. In this 21–0 victory the senior halfback repeated his Navy "triple" with three long touchdown runs of 30 (lateral from Light), 48, and 50 yards, the last score following an interception. Tension in the Pitt games had been increasing annually and wasn't helped by a Pitt protest the preceding year concerning the eligibility of Dick Schuster. On the eve of the 1922 Navy game, Pitt announced publicly that Schuster had played two games for Dayton University in 1921. Schuster, a regular tackle, was kept out of the Navy game, and a faculty committee found that the charge was true: Schuster had lettered in 1920 and dropped out of Penn State in 1921 to attend Dayton when Charlie Way went there to coach. Schuster was declared ineligible for the remainder of Penn State's 1922 season but played in 1923 and kicked the field goal in a 20–3 loss to the Panthers. Coach Warner's defensive strategy, plus the usual mud and rain, bottled up Wilson, who recalls only one detail from his final Penn State game:

> It seems to me I was chasing Karl Bohren [Pitt halfback] most of the afternoon. I recall running after him for about 50 yards, losing several yards in every 10 and praying for him to fall down on the wet field. He never did.

Harry Edgar Wilson was about to begin his last term at Penn State, but his football fame was far from over. Army, seeking college-tested material undeterred by the benevolent NCAA of the 1920s, remembered the promise made in the Willard Hotel. Approached at Christmastime by Ed Garbisch, the 1924 Army team captain, Wilson agreed to take the entrance examination at Carlisle Barracks, received a congressional appointment arranged by Academy authorities, and began his lifetime Army career on July 1, 1924.

> My first greeting at West Point after I had climbed that long, steep hill from the station was from a first classman at the induction table. He was a member of the Army football squad and he was very polite, saying, "So you are Harry Wilson. You must know a good friend of mine from Harrisburg, Hap Frank." I immediately stood at ease, smiled, and offered my hand. All hell broke loose, and I didn't get to relax until I got to my room.

Despite his four years at Penn State and his reputation, Wilson had a newcomer's typical insecurity in the world of West Point, and his momentary lapse into ordinary behavior was understandable at the mention of Hap Frank, his old friend and Track House roommate.[2] They shared unusual skill in competitive sports and probably

---

[2] J. Calvin (Hap) Frank coached football at Dickinson and Gettysburg after his graduation and in 1933 began a political career as a city councilman in Harrisburg, his hometown. He also conducted a successful insurance business and maintained a lifetime affiliation with the U. S. Army Reserve, rising from captain to major general. He commanded the 79th Infantry Division in World War II, serving in China, 1943–45. Hap Frank died suddenly at the age of 66 on August 17, 1967.

could have made any varsity team on campus. When Leo Houck, the popular boxing coach, needed a light-heavyweight for the intercollegiates, the relatively untrained Frank responded and won the 1924 intercollegiate title. The new lacrosse coach, R. H. Jardine, trying desperately to get the game established in 1923, asked Bezdek to excuse six of his football players from spring practice. Bez surprisingly let some of his regulars try the game, including Wilson and Frank. Hap made the team with only a week's practice and was the 1924 captain. It was three weeks before Jardine would trust the other gridders with sticks.

Wilson, trained under Bezdek's severe discipline, quickly adapted to the rigors of military life, but was slow to overcome his Penn State allegiance, even though he made both the West Point football and basketball teams as a plebe. When the Nittany Lion boxers visited the Point that winter he had a reunion with Coach Houck, Rags Madera, and other friends on the team and then found himself cheering loudly for Penn State, to the consternation of everyone around him.

Wilson wasn't the prolific scorer for Army that he had been for Penn State, where he made twenty-five touchdowns in 1922 and 1923, but in four seasons he never went stale while continuing to increase his competence and "savvy" on the field. On defense he'd be in the right place at the right time, loose and relaxed, but he was a constant threat against the pass and a dazzling runner in the open field. An action photograph of the Cadets defending near the goal line shows Harry leaning against an upright. Chances are he made the tackle. Penn State's record during his three seasons was 20–6–4 and Army's 28–5–3 during his four years in the lineup. He became more of a nemesis to Navy each year, as this comparison shows:

	Penn State	Navy
1921	13	7
1922	0	14
1923	21	3
	Army	
1924	12	0
1925	10	3
1926	21	21
1927	14	9

In the 1926 Army-Navy tie played at Chicago before 110,000 spectators—the first time college football attendance exceeded the 100,000 mark—Wilson, under extreme pressure, place-kicked the three extra points, scored one touchdown from 16 yards out, and ran for 148 yards in 14 carries. He captained the 1927 Army team (9–1–0), which defeated Notre Dame 18–0 and lost only to Yale. Against Navy Harry scored both touchdowns, outshining such stars as Red Cagle and John Murrell in that 14–9 victory. He was on Camp's 1923 All-America second team, but made several other first elevens that season (500 College Coaches, Percy Haughton, etc.) and was selected in 1926 by Knute Rockne, Tad Jones, and Pop Warner. The Veteran Athletes of Philadelphia elected him the most valuable eastern player in 1923, the National Football Foundation named him to the Hall of Fame in 1973, and he received unusual distinction when George Trevor, noted football historian, placed him on the all-time teams of both Penn State and Army.

Wilson distinguished himself in the Air Corps during World War II as commander of the 42nd Bomb Group in the South Pacific, recording 5,500 flight hours and flying forty-five missions as a command pilot. After the war he was assistant deputy chief for operations of the Continental Air Command. He retired in September 1956 with the rank of colonel, to New Smyrna Beach, Florida.

By 1927 Navy had had about enough of Wilson—and enough of Army. With bitter complaints about Army's lenient eligibility rules, Navy broke off football relations, having suffered in competition against the more mature Cadet players as far back as 1901, when Charlie Daly joined the Corps after playing three years at Harvard and twice making Camp's All-America. Wilson's presence for four years with Red Cagle, also a transfer, and following established migrating stars like Earl Blaik, Ollie Olyphant, Walter French, Ed Garbisch, Bill Wood, Tiny Hewitt, and many others, was too much. Congress finally intervened and the rivalry was resumed in 1930 after a two-year lapse, with Army conforming to the standard transfer and three-year rules.

Despite rumblings among western Pennsylvania alumni following the Pitt defeat of 1923, Hugo Bezdek was still riding high on the basis of his overall record and the three recent major triumphs over Navy, Georgia Tech, and Penn. Careful observers, however, might have noted that the material available for 1924, with some exceptions, could hardly replace such losses as Wilson, Bedenk, Palm,

Baer, Frank, and a few others. Exceptions were Captain Bas Gray at center; Jules Prevost, tackle; Ted Artelt, end; Mike Michalske, guard; and a local boy, Charles H. (Hobie) Light, who had developed into one of Penn State's best punters. (After graduation he entered the medical profession and practiced for many years in Centre Hall, a few miles from the campus.)

Injuries played havoc with the sparse backfield material, and once again Bez rarely had the same backs for any two games. G. H. Gier, M. E. Buckley, W. B. Helbig, and the Baker brothers from Johnstown, Bill and Gene, were heard from only briefly, but Bill Pritchard, Bud Bergman, and Ken Weston became valuable regulars of the future.

On September 15, 1924, the squad had the pleasure of moving into the new Varsity Hall (now Irvin), almost alongside New Beaver Field. This was little spiritual help when the team had the disheartening experience of losing the season's first road game, at Atlanta, to a Georgia Tech team unable to make a single first down. The Lions gave the game away during the first half on fumbles and interceptions, Tech taking a 15–0 lead. Penn State did fight back to score twice in the final period, but lost, 15–13. The next disaster was the Homecoming defeat by Syracuse, 10–6, the first loss on Beaver Field since 1918. Vic Hanson, a Syracuse all-time great, scored the only touchdown when he picked up quarterback Hank Lafferty's fumble and ran 21 yards. Prevost kicked two field goals for Penn State and Jack McBride one for the Orange.

The season's highlights were a victory over Navy at Annapolis (6–0) on the strength of Prevost's two field goals, and a scoreless tie on Franklin Field with Penn, which had won its first eight games. The Pitt defeat (24–3) ended the poorest season under Bezdek to date, and the Lions lost their position among the East's leaders, not to regain it for nearly three decades.

Yale and Cornell claimed top honors in the East in 1923 with identical 8–0 records, although Syracuse could have given either of them trouble. Dick Harlow's Colgate eleven thwarted Orange hopes for an undefeated season.[3] Some experts believed Yale's 1923 team

[3] In 1924 former Penn State players were college coaches possibly in greater numbers than before or since. They included Dick Harlow, Colgate; Bob Higgins, West Virginia Wesleyan; Andy Smith, California; Bill Wood, Gettysburg; Red Griffiths, Marietta; Ben Cubbage, VPI; Bert Barron, Temple; and Joe Lightner, Dickinson. Assistant coaches were Dutch Hermann, Glenn Killinger,

was its greatest, led by Captain Bill Mallory, Mal Stevens, and Century Milstead.

Illinois (8–0) and Michigan (8–0) were the best teams in the Midwest, Southern Methodist (9–0) in the South, and California (9–0–1) in the Far West. Illini and Wolverine backers disputed superiority long and loud, but the issue died the next year when Red Grange, the Galloping Ghost, exploded for five touchdowns, making four of these against the Michigan team in twelve minutes.

The East had no candidates for national honors in 1924. Pennsylvania (9–1–1) and Rutgers (7–1–1) shared regional acclaim, with Penn's Ed McGinley and Homer Hazel of Rutgers the best-known players on the Eastern Seaboard. All-America in 1923 as an end, Hazel was fullback on the last team named by Walter Camp before his death. The 1924 national championship was indisputable as Notre Dame (10–0–0), with its Four Horsemen, won the mythical honor hands down, defeating Stanford and Ernie Nevers in the Rose Bowl, 27–10.

A new president enjoyed Penn State's rising fortunes in the early 1920s. Pressures of the wartime break in academic routine had undermined the health of President Sparks, who resigned in 1920 but remained on the campus, with undiminished popularity as a lecturer in history. An executive committee of faculty and trustees took charge, with H. Walton Mitchell '90 as chairman in his capacity of president of the Board of Trustees, the first alumnus to hold that position.

In 1921 John Martin Thomas was induced to leave the presidency of Vermont's Middlebury College, apparently challenged by the problems of a growing land-grant institution. Miscalculating Pennsylvania's rigid political mores and rivalries, President Thomas in his inaugural address proposed that the growth and capability of Pennsylvania's only public state university, in fact if not in name, should be recognized by an official change of name to The Pennsylvania State University. He further appalled some of his hearers by proposing withdrawal of the state's generous aid to private institutions until public education received the support needed to fulfill the state's obligation to the people.

Ray Baer, and Dick Schuster, Penn State; Harold Hess, Southern California; Dick Rauch, Colgate; Mike Palm, Georgetown; and Hap Frank, Dickinson.

Setbacks came at once. Constitutional obstacles delayed a proposed bond issue referendum for four years, and Governor Gifford Pinchot, unsympathetic and economy-minded, rejected the legislature's increase in the appropriations. Pinchot supported a state education commission plan whereby the commonwealth's three largest universities—Pennsylvania and Pittsburgh, both private, with public land-grant Penn State—would have regional responsibility for public higher education, since all received appropriations. The private universities clung to their status, and Dr. Thomas issued masterful analyses defending Penn State's rights as Pennsylvania's one public college, his position confirmed by opinions of the attorney general of Pennsylvania. The plan withered away, not to make headway until the 1960s.

The drastic need of funds to cope with growth led Thomas to embark in 1922 on a $2 million Emergency Building Fund campaign involving alumni, staff, and students in an organized public solicitation. Net receipts of under $1.2 million paid in part for an infirmary, gymnasium (Recreation Building), and residence halls, one of which was Varsity Hall. The valiant effort publicized Penn State and clarified the need for income from other sources to support its statewide services.

The popularity of its winning football team strengthened the cause, especially among alumni. A Nittany Lion mascot cavorted for the first time at the Syracuse game played in New York in 1922, although his African mane was out of character.

Simultaneously there were impressive academic advances. A legislative council of faculty and administrative representatives was organized as the College Senate in 1921, followed by creation of the Graduate School in 1922 and the School of Education (1924), accompanied by an extension program of in-service training for schoolteachers who had to meet increased state requirements for certification.

When Dr. Thomas was offered the presidency of Rutgers University, he forsook the discouraging battle for state support and recognition, but left the campus community in 1925, better prepared to realize its potential if means should eventually materialize. Dr. Ralph Dorn Hetzel, becoming Penn State's tenth president the following year, had the advantage of experience in land-grant education and chose a more cautious approach to Pennsylvania's political and institutional sensitivities.

23

The Alumni Make Their Move

Compatability with the football coach was once essential to the well-being of an alumni secretary, especially in the rousing 1920s. Mike Sullivan, who became Penn State's first full-time secretary in 1919, accordingly realized he was off to a tremulous start when he heard the harsh voice of Hugo Bezdek on the phone one August afternoon.

"I'm on my way over there," growled Bezdek, "to bash your head in."

Bez never arrived, but he was wrathful because Sullivan had permitted local alumni to play on the college golf course—only four imperfect holes, but a domain Bez considered his own. Later clashes between the two strong-willed men were more consequential. Edward N. (Mike) Sullivan was dedicated to his alma mater, had a penchant for causes, and pursued some of them with more vigor than diplomacy. As early as 1924, he aligned himself with those who decried indiscriminate "athletic scholarships" and "overemphasis." Hugo Bezdek had reason to regard him with suspicion.

Sullivan set the tone when he reprinted in the *Alumni News* (November 1924) a New York *World* editorial on a series of articles in its sports section—"Confessions of a Football Scout." The editorial blamed alumni ("who really control football") for making the game "as thoroughly systematized as the bond business," with players "eagerly scouted down" and things "made easy for them financially and academically." The worst feature of such adult preoccupation with football, claimed the editorialist, was not professionalism but the sophomoric attitude of alumni who dictated appointment of coaches, found easy jobs for players, and paid their tuition. "Let the boys play their own game."

Pittsburgh, stronghold of Bezdek's support, gave indications that he was losing grace early in the fall of 1925, when George H. Johnston, the Alumni Club president, appointed a "College Relations Committee" to report on "the general athletic situation." Publicly Pittsburgh alumni said their motives were constructive, but there were undertones of discontent with Coach Bezdek and of a feeling that alumni should control intercollegiate athletics.

Meanwhile, back on the campus, the coach was preparing for an unusually tough schedule, including Georgia Tech, Michigan State, Syracuse, Notre Dame, West Virginia, and Pitt. Reasonably strong line material was anchored by Bas Gray, playing his second season as captain and center, and lettermen Ken Weston, Ernie McCann, Mike Michalske, and John Filak. Except for Bill Pritchard and Bill Helbig, holdovers with little varsity experience, Bezdek would have to rely mainly on sophomores for the backfield.

Few Lion stars of the middle and late 1920s came from western Pennsylvania. Because of alumni disaffection in the Pittsburgh area, the recruiting scene had shifted to the east, where Charlie Hildebrand '92 of Philadelphia was still doing his bit. Cy Lungren, Hal Hastings, Rog Mahoney, and Barney Slamp, all from eastern Pennsylvania, were among sophomores who won half the letters for the 1925 season. The leading "recruiter" in New Jersey for some years was Frank E. Enstice '16. In the fall of 1924, northern New Jersey alumni enticed Al Lesko of East Rutherford and Johnny Roepke of Jersey City to enroll. Roepke, 1927 captain, probably was the top running back of his era, a good passer and place kicker.

Alumni in the New Jersey-New York area hit the jackpot in 1925 with Steve Hamas and Allie Wolff, fine athletes who became, as it happened, best known for their boxing skills. Hamas, first Penn Stater to win letters in five sports (football, boxing, lacrosse, basketball, and track), was the only college boxer to reach the top bracket as a professional heavyweight, with notable victories over Tommy Loughran and Max Schmeling. Wolff was never defeated in the college ring and won three intercollegiate championships as a middle-weight.

To the west, the future seemed to depend on the activities of Ed Yeckley (1905 captain), who was avidly pursuing talent in Ohio, where he had settled in Lorain. His "boys" began arriving on campus in 1923 (Mal McPhie), but most came the next year. Without the Ohio contingent disaster might have befallen Bezdek sooner than it did. Cleveland, Lakewood, and Toledo appeared opposite many names on the roster from 1924 through 1927, but the majority came from Lorain and Elyria, close to the bailiwick of the energetic Yeckley. His support ended abruptly after 1927, and he became one of Bezdek's most belligerent foes, but he had brought such talented players as John Pincura, George Greene, Harold (Dinger) Danger-field, Joe Krall, Phil Houserman, and Donn Greenshields.

Major games at home against Michigan State and Notre Dame gave Lion fans their only satisfaction in 1925. After losing to Geor-gia Tech in New York, 16–7, Coach Bezdek indulged his recurring eccentricity—switching a big lineman to the backfield. Moving Mike Michalske, regular guard for the past two years, to fullback evidently paid off against the Spartans, because Mike scored both touchdowns on 10-yard runs in the 13–6 victory. The first followed a 35-yard run by the little sophomore halfback, Dinger Dangerfield, and the second came after tackle Ernie McCann blocked a punt. The prowess of Au-gust (Iron Mike) Michalske as a fullback qualifies this move as one of Bezdek's more successful team alterations, but he is rated along with Joe Bedenk as the best guard ever to play at Penn State.[1]

The Notre Dame 0–0 tie on New Beaver Field in 1925 is the source of a bit of lore in the Bezdek saga recounted by Don Kepler, a Centre Countian now retired from the Penn State physical educa-tion staff. At a postseason dinner honoring Altoona High School's team, Knute Rockne, the speaker, was asked to discuss his Novem-ber game with the Lions. He told how a manager had awakened him after midnight Friday, insisting that he come to the football field at once. He dressed and walked up to the site of the coming game. Said

[1] After graduation in 1926, Michalske spent many years coaching for Lafayette, St. Norbert, Iowa State, Baylor, Texas A&M, Texas, and the Baltimore Colts. His record as a player with the Green Bay Packers stamps him an all-time great in the professional sport. Mike started with Green Bay after Ernie Pyle's New York Yankees folded in 1929 and was selected all-NFL guard six times. He was named to the professional Football Hall of Fame in 1964, the first Penn Stater so honored. He resides in DePere, Wisconsin.

Rockne: "I watched a number of people engaged in hosing down the gridiron, and I was sure Bezdek had ordered this action to handicap our light, fast backs." He composed a scorching letter of complaint to the NCAA, but the next morning it was raining, and the downpour continued during the entire game. Mired in mud, neither team came any closer to scoring than one missed field goal apiece. Rockne, thoroughly disgusted, tore up his letter. The seriously told tale seems more likely to belong to the multitude of Bezdekian "tall stories." Before the game Rockne and his team stayed in Bellefonte, a good ten miles from the campus and hardly within predawn walking distance of the field.

In the final games of 1925 Penn State co-operated with two of its sectional rivals. This was the opening season for the $2 million Pitt Stadium in Oakland, and at Morgantown the Lions helped the home team dedicate Mountaineer Field. Coach Bezdek's men were also co-operative enough to lose both games, 23–7 and 14–0, scoring their only touchdown against the Pitt Panthers when Weston faked a field goal and Lungren, picking up the ball, passed to Roepke for the score. Amby Diehl, chairman of the Athletic Committee, termed the 4–4–1 season satisfactory, since the team "had pushed the Panthers to the limit and scored more first downs." This opinion was not shared by other alumni in the Pittsburgh area.

Portentous events in 1926 affected the quality of football at Penn State for the next twelve years. Issues were confused because motives became as varied as the alumni factions involved. Some simply wanted to get rid of Bezdek as football coach; others considered control of intercollegiate sports the key issue. A third group, which sincerely believed that all athletic financial aid should be eliminated on moral grounds, acquired leadership from the college administration. Since few scheduled opponents followed suit, Penn State embarked upon the most humiliating period in its football history.

A study by the Carnegie Foundation for the Advancement of Teaching to explore the role of athletics on college campuses was to have a far-reaching effect on Penn State's policies. The study by Howard J. Savage was authorized on January 8, 1926, but was not released until late in 1929 (published as Bulletin 23). Meanwhile, Alumni Secretary Sullivan had continued what his opponents interpreted as an antifootball position in the *Alumni News*. Recommendations of the Pittsburgh Alumni Club's College Relations Committee, endorsed by the Philadelphia Club, were reported in April

1926. At the association's annual meeting (June 14), President Harry W. Montz, urged by Sullivan, appointed the Beaver White Committee to consider the report.

The Pittsburgh committee, chaired by Clay Sprecher '98, recommended rewriting the Athletic Association constitution and bylaws. (Mike Sullivan was suggested as one of this committee's three members.) An "Athletic Council" of one trustee, one faculty member, one student, and four alumni (to be elected) was proposed to replace the existing Athletic Advisory Committee. A third major recommendation disqualified paid coaches as members of the council, which would employ a graduate manager to carry out its directions and policies.

Hugo Bezdek wasn't mentioned, but he was obviously removed from any position of leadership in the intercollegiate program. Alumni would have control, undergraduates would be without any real power, and the college administration would have only nominal influence.

A preliminary report of the Beaver White Committee (J. Beaver White '94, chairman) at the association's October Homecoming meeting asked for more time to complete its study of the Pittsburgh recommendations and listed alumni, students, faculty, staff, and townspeople who had been interviewed, including Sullivan and Hugo Bezdek. It was an unpleasant interview for the mighty coach. Stung by the desertion of his Pittsburgh backers, he masked his inner turmoil with a confident demeanor, but his harassed squad bore the brunt.

Enervated by September's unusual heat, the 1926 squad had lucky soft touches in its opening games, with Susquehanna (82–0) and Lebanon Valley (35–0). But Bez was dissatisfied and held two more hours of practice on the field immediately after the second game. It was six-thirty before the players dragged themselves down to the Track House for a shower and back up the hill to Varsity Hall, where most of them fell into bed. Beginning Monday, they scrimmaged nearly every afternoon, sometimes under the lights with the "ghost" ball. The next opponent, Marietta, wasn't strong enough to present much opposition, and the surly Lions ran up 48 points. No letup ensued in the practice schedule as Bez prepared his physically exhausted team for Notre Dame at South Bend, where misfortune of another kind was waiting.

Leaving by train Thursday for Culver Military Academy, the

squad practiced there on Friday afternoon. The mineral quality of Indiana water caused a steady parade from the dormitory to the end of the hall all night and most of Saturday morning. The weakened team lost to the Irish, 28–0. Again Bez was merciless, and practice sessions were not curtailed the next week. Experimenting with some things he had learned at South Bend, he installed a completely new offense for the Syracuse game, so confusing his quarterback that John Pincura recalls he nearly handed off the ball on a crossbuck to the Syracuse left end, Vic Hanson. The Orange won, 10–0, and over the weekend the breaking point was reached.

Roepke, Greenshields, and Lungren led the outraged delegation to Monday's skull session to inform Bez that practice would be omitted that day unless there were less scrimmaging, less time on the practice field, and a return to the offense used prior to the Syracuse game. Bezdek capitulated, as he had before when players threatened revolt. A written schedule of practice sessions was set up, and all the players pledged to keep the uprising secret.

Unfortunately, the season didn't improve, and no major games were won in 1926, a crucial year for Hugo Bezdek. The Lions lost to Penn, 3–0, on Paul Skull's 40-yard field goal, but gave Pitt a battle for the first two quarters before succumbing, 24–6. Pitt led by only 7–6 in the first half, Roepke scoring after a long pass had placed the ball on the 1-yard line. A Roepke pass to Pincura for 45 yards was unproductive, and in the fourth quarter Gibby Welch ran the Lions dizzy. It was the last game for Captain Ken Weston and Bill Pritchard.[2]

Dr. Hetzel, beginning his presidential duties on December 15, 1926, was no stranger to intercollegiate sports. While president of the University of New Hampshire and head of the New England Conference of Intercollegiate Athletics, he had led the way toward establishment of ethical standards, strict eligibility rules, and opposi-

_____

[2] Weston, long bothered by knee injuries, interestingly chose orthopedic surgery as a career and is now a prominent physician in Allentown, Pennsylvania, where for many years he worked with the Allentown High School football team. His advice has often been sought by Penn State coaches. William E. Pritchard, Weston's roommate, retired in 1967 after thirty-five years as a teacher and administrator in the Buffalo public school system. He had played professional football with the Providence Steam Rollers and the New York Yankees, officiated in the old All-America Conference and the NFL, coached high school football for six years, and at one time was head coach at the University of Buffalo.

tion to all athletic subsidies. As a Wisconsin undergraduate he had rowed on the crew, but had refused a football scholarship.

Aware of this background and misjudging his remarks about the value of college athletics, diehards supposed Dr. Hetzel was unfriendly toward athletics and football especially. This wasn't so, but he differed sharply with those who were sure the institution would collapse without a winning football team. Guided by his conviction that the administration must be wholly responsible for all activities affecting the reputation of the college, he skillfully influenced the various factions so that by the mid-thirties alumni involvement was purely advisory.

President Hetzel's commitment to improving the physical well-being of all students was far more popular than his stand on aid to athletics. He believed that "physical strength and competitive skills developed as natural and logical functions of the educational process of physical training, sane and sound, and available to every student of the institution" could win football games. This was impractical, because Penn State's traditional opponents were less idealistic.

The policy of eliminating all athletic aid was announced within a year of Dr. Hetzel's arrival and before the Carnegie Foundation study was completed, but Penn State was castigated, anyway, with a correction later hastily inserted in an obscure footnote generally unnoticed. Dr. Hetzel received congratulatory letters about the new policy from his presidential colleagues. All wished him luck without committing their own institutions to follow his lead.

Administrative decisions made in 1927 were to change the direction of Hugo Bezdek's life and adversely affect the development of Penn State as an eastern football leader. The Beaver White Committee submitted its final report on February 26 to Alumni Association president James Milholland '11. Major recommendations eliminated all athletic scholarships; abolished the Athletic Advisory Board and established a Board of Athletic Control with thirteen members (one trustee, four faculty members, three students, and five alumni); and separated the School of Physical Education and Athletics into two divisions, with intercollegiate athletics under the supervision of the Board of Athletic Control. The director of the Department of Physical Education could not be a coach of any sport.

Before action was taken, Sullivan and Milholland attended meetings called by association directors in Pittsburgh, Philadelphia, Wilkes-Barre, and State College to have alumni vote on the changes.

Results were reported in the *Alumni News* (May 1927): To eliminate athletic scholarships, 77 per cent favorable; to establish a Board
of Athletic Control, 93 per cent favorable; and to separate the Department of Physical Education from "athletic coaching," 91 per
cent favorable. These statistics seem overwhelming, but with Sullivan
and Milholland strongly advocating the changes, there was only cur-
sory opposition at the sparsely attended sessions.

The new board was established after necessary changes were made
in the constitutions of the Alumni Association and the Athletic Association. It soon became apparent that it was more "advisory" under
its new name and had had more "control" when it was advisory.

Separating intercollegiate athletics from the academic Department
of Physical Education was postponed because President Hetzel
believed the college administration should control the intercollegiate
program, which should be responsible to him and the trustees rather
than dominated by alumni.

The newly organized Board of Athletic Control at its first meeting
(August 10, 1927) officially ended all financial aid to athletes and
added (or took away) a further wrinkle:

> . . . an energetic effort shall be made to utilize and properly
> train all of the latent athletic ability in the general student
> body, and additions to the coaching staff and to the athletic
> equipment shall immediately be made to provide training and
> instruction for larger squads in the major sports. . . . The
> Board feels that ordinarily an adequate number of high school
> and preparatory school students can be drawn to Penn State by
> the attractiveness of the colorful student life and the unique en-
> vironment of the College. . . . Penn State will not scout oppo-
> nents' games regardless of the scouting policies of opponents.

The recommendation to abandon athletic scholarships surprised
alumni and undergraduates. The committee, defending Penn State's
past program, said there had been nothing sub rosa about it and athletic scholarships were a matter of public record, but the report
sharply criticized the system:

> Such scholarships, however, have not resulted in real benefit to
> the institution because many holding them have withdrawn
> from college before graduation and scholarships have tended to
> discourage the athletic development of students without them.

Commitments for scholarships to players entering in September 1927
were to be the last. No student at Penn State received an athletic

scholarship after the 1930 season until the grants-in-aid program was established in the late 1940s.

Over a period of thirty years, the Board of Athletic Control gradually lost effectiveness in policymaking, functioning only when the director of athletics infrequently requested advice. A Trustee Committee's recommendation (May 12, 1965) for its discontinuance was never officially endorsed, but on October 1 of that year the Executive Committee appointed an alumni trustee to serve as liaison with the Athletic Department.

In effect, the Athletic Board (as it came to be known) was never disbanded—it merely faded away. Procedure to elect alumni members disappeared from the Alumni Association constitution several years later with no argument from anyone. The cycle was complete: Control of intercollegiate athletics had passed from the students to the alumni to the administration, where most alumni now believe it belongs.

24

Bez Goes Down, Up—and Out

Beset as he was in 1927, Coach Hugo Bezdek came up with his best season since 1923. Former players agree that the minor revolt after a disheartening defeat by Bucknell (13–7) persuaded him to ease his brutal practice schedule and led to victories over Penn and Syracuse plus a tie with highly favored NYU.

Players complained about energy-consuming practice and overly conservative use of the forward pass—Bez forbade the team to throw inside its 40-yard line. Cy Lungren wrote from his home in San Rafael, California, on April 16, 1975:

> Life was anything but easy under Hugo and his snake whip, but I wouldn't take anything for the experience, nor would I want to go through with it again. . . . Our confrontation in 1927 occurred in the Varsity Hall dining room after the Bucknell game. We had walked from the Track House and bitched every step of the way about our practices. . . . Bez was over the barrel and had to come up with something to erase the Bucknell defeat. The players committed themselves to defeat Penn if he would lay off scrimmage. Hugo agreed, which put the burden on us. If we failed, Bez could say it was our fault.

The unexpected defeat began a string of six straight victories for the Bisons, who hadn't won from their central Pennsylvania rivals since 1899. In 1930 Coach Carl Snavely moved on to Cornell, where he continued to baffle Penn State teams year after year.

In the *Collegian,* a pre-Penn game story reported that "daily scrimmages had been cut to fifty minutes or less," and the workouts "are the shortest of the Bezdekian era," but gave no indication of difficulty between coach and team. Newspapermen liked Bez for his affable, courteous manner, though his answers were often uninformative and laden with platitudes. In Philadelphia the interview went like this:

"How do you expect to fare tomorrow?"
"Well, I do not say we will win. Yet, I won't say we will lose."
"Will it be a tie?"
"No, but you can say we will give them a fight. We are hoping for the best and the boys will do all they can to win. I expect a hard game and one that will be enjoyed by all."

Bezdek then mentioned injured players—Greenshields, Pincura, Krall, Hastings—and said his team hadn't been able to scrimmage much that week "because of heavy rains." Penn was favored, having won its first three games, including a victory over Brown. The Quakers later defeated Harvard, Columbia, and Cornell by wide margins.

Quarterback Lungren took things into his own hands against Penn. Without orders, he had Roepke throw passes from everywhere on the field to complete 10 for 184 yards. After a scoreless first half, the Lions caught fire early in the third period on runs of 28 yards by Roepke and 49 by Lungren, who was forced out of bounds on the 1 by Penn's Marty Brill. Steve Hamas made the first touchdown. In the final period a 50-yard pass from Roepke to Lesko, followed 2 minutes later by Roepke's 12-yard run, put the final tally at 20–0.

Next, the rejuvenated Lions surprised undefeated Syracuse in Archbold Stadium, winning 9–6 on Roepke's 21-yard field goal late in the last quarter. Lungren's 9-yard run had tied the score earlier in the period. It was the first touchdown and also the first victory for Penn State against the Orange since the start of the series in 1922. Against Gettysburg and Lafayette, both easier opponents, Roepke scored 28 and 27 points.

A tie (13–13) with NYU may have been the most important achievement of Bezdek's final coaching years. The "Violent Violets" lost only to Nebraska in 1926 and 1927, and had four nationally

known stars—Ken Strong, Len Grant, Al Lassman, and Frank
(Five-yard) Briante. Chick Meehan, midway in his three luminous
seasons, was a meticulous, hard-driving coach much like Bez. He
had gained sports headlines for the showmanship and awesome effect
of his "military huddle" and baffling attack, enabling the team to line
up in a balanced or unbalanced line without a shift because any of
three linemen could center the ball.

Ralph (Dutch) Ricker, sophomore tackle who developed into a
fine lineman, played one of his best games because he deciphered
NYU's starting signal and got a half-count jump on the ball. The
Lions led 13–7 at halftime with Roepke scoring the first touchdown
following a fumble recovery by Rog Mahoney, and Wolff making the
other.

A victory at Pittsburgh on Thanksgiving Day would have spelled
one of the best records of the decade. Only the Bucknell defeat had
marred the surprisingly good season, but the Lions lost by a wider
margin than usual, 30–0. Some thought the coach carried his new
"easy practice" schedule too far, with only a light workout Monday
and none Tuesday or Wednesday. The night before the game a few
players stayed up playing cards at the Chartiers Country Club (using
their $35 allowances provided by the Athletic Association). The
team's listless performance the next afternoon further angered
alumni in the Pittsburgh area—against Bezdek. The season ended on
its typical sour note, while Pitt went on to the Rose Bowl where Pop
Warner, then at Stanford, defeated Jock Sutherland's Panther eleven,
7–6.

Of nineteen players recruited in 1926, only four stood out—
Ricker, Turino (Toots) Panaccion, and Jack Martin, all linemen;
and Joe Miller, a back from Wilkinsburg. To toughen up the
linemen, especially the newcomers, Bez instigated winter practice in
1927. Assistant Coach Larry Conover, who had replaced Killinger,
put them through hours of two-on-one drills in the reeking old Stock
Judging Pavilion. "We smelled pretty bad after the workouts," recalls
Ricker, "but it made us better players."[1]

---

[1] Ricker '30, a Carlisle native recruited by Killinger, later was with him at
West Chester State College as a coach and history professor. After earning his
Ph.D. degree in history at Penn State, he taught history and political science
at Dickinson in 1946 and was head football coach there for four years. He
held similar positions at Lebanon Valley until 1952, when he joined Penn
State's staff. He retired in 1970.

John D. (Pin) Pincura '28 studied law at Maryland and Ohio State, and

Winning no major games in 1928 and ending the year with the Pitt debacle (26–0), Coach Bezdek experienced his first losing season (3–5–1) since the abbreviated war year of 1918, and was especially embarrassed because he was president of the National Association of College Football Coaches. The disastrous campaign could have been predicted, as only seven lettermen returned, and Captain Greenshields was lost through injury. Other veterans were Ricker, Panaccion, Martin, and George Delp, all linemen; and Wolff and Hamas, backs. The last group of scholarship holders, all sophomores, were linemen: Mike Kaplan, Earle Edwards, Mike Zorella, A. G. (Red) Duvall, and Cal Shawley; and backs, Cooper French, Frank (Yutz) Diedrich, Tommy Evans, and Jack Livezey.

Some help came from Marty McAndrews, Herb Eschbach, George (Spike) Collins, Joe Miller, and Neil (Skip) Stahley. McAndrews, later on the coaching staff under Bob Higgins, developed into one of the most popular athletes of his era and won the intercollegiate light-heavyweight boxing championship in 1930. Stahley became a fine end, playing in one of the early East-West Shrine games. He preceded Rip Engle as head coach at Brown University.

Realizing his material was scanty and mainly untried, Bezdek compulsively reverted to lengthy, intense scrimmages. Two days before the Lafayette game he picked two teams and told them the first to score a touchdown would be the starting eleven on Saturday. In the memorable two-hour fracas neither team scored, and the record also was kept clean at Easton, Lafayette winning, 7–0. Earlier in the season, Bucknell had protected a 6–0 lead until the final five minutes, when Steve Hamas and Joe Miller led a late rally, advancing the ball to a first down on the 3 with less than a minute to play. Hamas, the hard-driving fullback, plowed through center and over the line, but he didn't have the ball. Bucknell had stolen it and the victory.

A 6–6 tie with Syracuse relieved the pervading gloom, although the Orange owned a mediocre record. Coop French gained his first taste of stardom, making a touchdown in the first period on an

---

began practice in Lorain, Ohio, in 1932. After 8 successive terms as city solicitor, he was named (in 1950) Lorain County Common Pleas Court judge, a post he expects to hold until retirement (1977).

Hal Hastings and Cy Lungren have been successful businessmen. Hastings, a resident of Johannesburg, South Africa, for over thirty years, went there as a representative of Mine Safety Appliances of Pittsburgh. Lungren, on the West Coast with F. S. Webster Company of Philadelphia since 1944, has retired in San Rafael, California.

11-yard run. The Penn State-Syracuse series was notable for its low scoring, no team making more than 12 points in any game from the beginning in 1922 until 1934. Penn State won twice from 1927–1930, and there were two ties (9–6, 6–6, 6–4, and 0–0).

In the early fall of 1928 Coach Bezdek accepted an unexpected proposal from a psychology professor, Dr. George W. Hartman, to help the football situation with a study "to determine efficient learning methods and auxiliary problems." Dr. Hartman's premise was that the psychology of football lies as much with the coach as with the players. One of his first informal suggestions afforded much amusement when it "leaked" out to the players. Impressed with their "singing and general high spirits" while they showered following a game, the professor thought it would be advantageous if they'd shower *before* every game.

Dr. Hartman, who attended some practice sessions, came closer to the point in his first formal report (October 17, 1928):

> Men in general feel mildly resentful of criticism caused by their errors. This is not a serious disadvantage, but it seems to me should be balanced by an equally strong amount of praise and approval in the case of successful plays. My impression of the frequency of negative criticism to direct approval was that the former probably unduly exceeded the latter.

Before, during, and after the Pitt game, the psychologist observed that in the twenty-four pregame hours, based on behavior and speech, there was no "noteworthy evidence of poor morale or broken spirit . . . cheering, joking, and sprightliness of movement were dominant impressions." Gloomy resentment between halves (score, 14–0) caused no letdown in determination to win, he deduced, and the outcome was not affected detrimentally by such factors as temper, mood, or attitude.

Bezdek's reaction to Dr. Hartman's analysis of the causes of the Pitt defeat (26–0) and to his suggested remedy can be guessed.

> Defeat was due to lack of preparation in executing finer details of the plays. Remedy for such a situation lies in drilling the men to a maximum mastery of a limited number of promising plays. Errorless performance in scrimmage should be demanded.

The reports, received several times each month, covered a variety of subjects. The psychologist suggested awarding letters only at the beginning of the senior year, based on "supply and demand, and no more than 50 per cent of the squad should receive letters." To compensate for the eliminated scholarships, there was advice on getting material from the student body. "If 100 men do not report for practice, offer prizes for the best back who turns out, the best interference runner, etc."

Dr. Hartman was less than complimentary in appraising the academic caliber of the current freshman football candidates. Intimating that recruiting methods had been faulty, he said the "highest type of football demands a quick learner and a competent thinker." His modified "signaling system" proposed that every player have two numbers (to confuse opponents), such as 16, 61; 31, 13, and double numbers (44, 88) should mean "charge."

The report, completed on March 14, 1929, was of no avail to Bez. Three months later a trustee committee began action leading to his removal as football coach. The Athletic Association was billed $1,500 for the psychologist's professional services, plus $1,000 for equipment and incidentals.

Despite rumors of a new regime, the 1929 season produced some surprising successes. Fifteen lettermen were available for Bez's last squad, but of the new material only George (Judy) Lasich provided any real assistance. After struggling through early games with Niagara (16–0), Lebanon Valley (15–0), and Marshall (26–7), the team ran all over NYU in New York and yet lost, 7–0. The strain Coach Bezdek was under showed in his uncharacteristic bickering with the officials, which resulted in extra penalties.

The Homecoming game on New Beaver Field was humdrum until the storybook finish. Tedious and uneventful, it seemed to be a sure thing for Lafayette, with a single field goal kicked by Allan Cook four minutes after it began. When less than half a minute remained, the visiting team had the ball on its own 14-yard line, third down. Although another offensive play surely would have run out the clock, Ernie Woodfin, to everyone's astonishment, dropped back to punt. As his good kick soared into the air, a whistle was blown indicating that officially time had elapsed, but the play obviously had to be completed.

When Woodfin went back for the fateful kick, Penn State's Cooper French and Frank Diedrich scurried into double-safety positions. Diedrich, writing from his home in Sun City, Arizona (August 14,

1974), said the ensuing play wasn't really planned in advance, nor was it sent in from the bench.

> Coop and I played together at Staunton Military Academy for a year and we had roomed together for three years at State. We knew each other pretty well and tried all kinds of things in practice on the spur of the moment, such as reverse both on kickoffs and punt returns—sometimes handing off and sometimes not; also backward laterals. So the Lafayette play was really born on the practice field and matured when Woodfin decided to kick. From double-safety one of us may have yelled "Heads up" to the other—we both knew we would try something depending on the circumstances as they developed. When I saw the high kick go to Coop's side, I drifted to the sideline and hoped he would throw it to me. He caught the ball, waited until the tacklers were on him, and then threw it over to me.

French made the punt reception on his own 40, took one or two steps toward Diedrich on the left sideline, and timed his throw perfectly. Stunned by the unusual play, the Lafayette players offered the flying Diedrich little opposition as he sped down the sideline. To avoid one tackler (Woodfin) he cut to the center inside the 20 and crossed the goal line fully 30 seconds after the game-ending whistle. Fans immediately swarmed on the field to carry off both Diedrich and French—the first time this happened, said the *Collegian,* since Charlie Way won the West Virginia Wesleyan game in 1917. No effort was made to try for the unimportant extra point (score: 6–3). Coach Bezdek reported he had never before seen a lateral pass after a punt.

Herb McCracken, the Lafayette coach, years later claimed he had been an unwilling figure in two of Penn State's all-time spectacular plays. The first had been when he was Pitt's defensive halfback in 1919 and the famous pass Bill Hess threw to Bob Higgins sailed right over his head. To some extent, McCracken justified his quarterback's decision to kick on the last play. The Leopards had lost to Bucknell the previous week because the same quarterback waited until fourth down to punt and then fumbled the ball. All week Coach McCracken had warned his unfortunate signal caller not to repeat the mistake.

Joe Bedenk, who started as line coach in 1929, was scouting Penn on the Saturday the Lions played in Syracuse. Learning of the victory, with a score of 6–4, he immediately sent a telegram to Coach Bezdek: "Congratulations. Who pitched?"

Penn State had hung onto a precarious half-time lead for most of the typical contest after trailing early when French fumbled a poor pass from center in the end zone and recovered for an Orange safety. Late in the half Penn State had the ball on the Syracuse 40, very near the right sideline. In those days there were no inbound lines or hashmarks. French called the perfect play—a triple reverse—with Diedrich finally getting the ball, headed for the near sideline. Mike Kaplan, right end, ran straight down the field and took Diedrich's pass over his shoulder for the game's only touchdown.

The winning Diedrich-to-Kaplan razzle-dazzle play got less attention in the press than the last Syracuse points. Toward the end of the final period, when the home team seemed about to score, the Lions held fast and took the ball. In the closing minutes they had to kick from behind their own goal line against a strong wind, with a blocked kick distinctly possible. French, on his own initiative, gave up an intentional safety—a defensive maneuver not at all common in 1929.

Bezdek's teams generally played well on Franklin Field (5–3–1), and 1929 was no exception. Continuing his alert quarterbacking, French contributed two of six interceptions, resulting in a pair of touchdowns in the 19–7 victory over a Penn team that had beaten Navy the week before and would defeat both Columbia and Cornell. Alumni adjusted with difficulty to a defeat by Bucknell (27–6) the next week, but expected a poor showing in Pittsburgh. They were right and could rationalize the 20–7 loss because the Panthers had an undefeated regular season, although crushed by Southern California in the Rose Bowl.

The forward pass was at the height of its popularity in 1925 when Bezdek's star was beginning to fade, but Bez, after being an early proponent at Arkansas in 1908, had not remained one of its strong advocates. Three great passers of the mid-twenties were Swede Oberlander of Dartmouth, Grant Gillis of Alabama, and Benny Friedman of Michigan. Dartmouth had popular support for the 1925 national championship (8–0), although Alabama was also undefeated (10–0) and won from Washington in the Rose Bowl, 20–19. Michigan was unbeaten and unscored on, except for a 3–2 loss to Northwestern.

In 1926 Navy's partisans thought their team deserved the national title (9–0–1), but this was the year of many fine eastern teams— Brown's Iron Men (tied by Colgate, 10–10); Lafayette (9–0); Boston College (undefeated but tied twice); and NYU, with only one loss, to Nebraska. On the national scene, Alabama (9–0–1) and Stanford (10–0–1) played to a 7–7 tie in the Rose Bowl.

Pittsburgh, Yale, and Army were the East's best in 1927. Illinois had a perfect record until tied by Iowa State. In 1928 Boston College (9–0) was tops in the East; Southern California went undefeated on the Pacific Coast, but snubbed the Rose Bowl after a squabble with the Tournament of Roses Committee; and Georgia Tech beat California in the classic (8–7) with the help of Roy Riegels' wrong-way run.

The Panthers of Pittsburgh again led the East in 1929, and were again demolished by Southern Cal in the Pasadena Bowl, 47–14. Notre Dame (9–0), with the toughest schedule in the country and a victory against Southern California, probably deserved the national crown over Purdue, champion of the Big Ten (8–0).

Except for the rapidly developing forward pass, the game changed very little in the late 1920s. In 1927 the rulemakers moved the goal posts back 10 yards from the goal line and gave the offense a limit of 30 seconds to put the ball in play. To encourage laterals, a missed backward pass (other than the center pass) was declared a dead ball, but officials acquired an extra burden in 1928 when the defense was allowed to recover a backward lateral, although those thrown 2 yards or more could not be advanced.

Some critics chided the Rules Committee for legislating fun out of football in 1927 by prohibiting the kicking team from advancing a fumbled punt. This was extended to free kicks and kickoffs in 1929, when it was also ruled that the ball was dead after all fumbles and could not be advanced. In 1929, the yardmark for a try-for-point was moved from the 3- to the 2-yard line.

25

Hugo Bezdek: Martyr or Monster?

The Penn State coach of the early 1920s was in his prime, never again to reach the same heights. Alumni called him a miracle worker, students pleaded with him to turn down an offer from the Phillies ("Don't Hu-Go Bezdek"). Contracts were generous for the times. His posture as invincible king of the gridiron world is understandable, but he lived at Penn State amid controversy and strife—respected, revered, hated, feared.

Hugo Bezdek's parents emigrated from Prague, Bohemia (Czechoslovakia), to South Chicago when he was 5 years old. Built like a barrel, mobile and tough, the youngster was a dominating, aggressive athlete, playing baseball and football in high school and gaining a reputation as a semipro boxer. At the University of Chicago, Coach Amos Alonzo Stagg was concerned about the tackling ability of the freshman on his varsity football team.

"If you'd only cuss me out, I'd be better," young Bezdek said one afternoon. Stagg accordingly used some unaccustomed borderline language, and did notice improvement in the tackling technique of his promising battering-ram fullback. For two of his four years Bez was a teammate of famed Walter Eckersall, who made Camp's All-America first team as an end in 1904 and quarterback in 1905. The

selection of Bezdek as fullback on Camp's 1905 third team was a
real accomplishment for a midwesterner.

Bezdek always had wanted to be a football coach, and during his
career of twenty-four years he spent only one as an assistant—after
coaching Oregon to an undefeated season in 1906, he returned to
Chicago on Stagg's staff in 1907. His complete head-coaching record
at Arkansas (1908–12), Oregon (1906, 1913–17), and Penn State
(1918–29) was 123–53–16. Many fine coaches never experience
one undefeated season. Bez had five, at three institutions: two at Oregon, one at Arkansas, and two at Penn State. He is considered the
"father" of modern Arkansas teams and gave them their mascot
when he called his 1909 players (then the Cardinals) a "wild team
of Razorback hogs" because they had surrendered only twelve points
all season.

He considered his three greatest teams the undefeated Oregon
Rose Bowl champions of 1916, and the 1920 and 1921 Penn State
elevens. Late in life, persuaded to name his greatest players, he listed
Oregon tackle Johnny Beckett, and two quarterbacks, Glenn Killinger of Penn State and Steve Creekmore of Arkansas.

Bezdek's Oregon victory over Penn in the Rose Bowl on January 1,
1917 (14–0), was significant because the East then was ranked far
ahead of the West in football power. His severity as a coach already
begun, he drove the players to the limit of their endurance, working
them every day from Thanksgiving to New Year's. Fullback Hollis
Huntington claimed Bez "didn't believe in injuries. Only a broken
bone would get a man relieved."[1]

Oregon's practices before the big game were closed, while Penn's
Bob Folwell opened his to everyone, including Coach Bezdek. Penn's
quarterback, Bert Bell (later commissioner of the NFL), well
remembers that Bez had asked Folwell to show him Penn's reverse-
pass play. "Folwell told me to run it, and I did," said Bell. "Imagine
our chagrin when Oregon scored its first touchdown against us with
our very own play."

Hugo Bezdek's controversial reputation as a shrewd, self-seeking
curmudgeon began early and never died. A typical, partly exaggerated story details a "fist fight" he is supposed to have had with
Burleigh Grimes, a Pirate pitcher, in 1917. After they had hammered
out a settlement in a Pullman car between Pittsburgh and New York,

[1] Fred Russell and George Leonard, *Big Bowl Football* (New York: The
Ronald Press Company, 1963).

the story goes, the fiery Bez told the colorful spitball artist: "You
————, you'll still pitch tomorrow." Actually, for all his yelling, Bez
isn't known to have used bad language.

His personality was more coarse. Bezdek's rough, abrasive coaching and his harsh tactics did not inspire love or loyalty in most of his
players, but those most earnest in their lasting admiration were two
of the shining stars of his first years at Penn State, Killinger and Wilson. Colonel Harry E. Wilson wrote from his home in New Smyrna
Beach, Florida, on August 17, 1973:

> I think he was more sinned against than sinning. He never tried
> to run a love feast for anyone. His forte was his drive. . . .
> With his insistence on condition and the fundamentals, along
> with his basic system of reverses, fake reverses, and passes
> developing out of them, he should be given credit for develop-
> ing the game along with Warner, Rockne, Yost, and others of
> his time. After my last game at West Point I received a fine let-
> ter from him congratulating me on our victory over Navy and
> wishing me success in the Army. He was always demanding,
> but fair to me. . . . If he had a different personality he
> wouldn't have been the Bez we knew and no one knows what
> the results might have been. . . . The more you put out for
> something near to your heart the more you love and respect it,
> so I believe that as tough as Bez was he was responsible for a
> lot of our affection for Penn State.

Glenn Killinger wrote on September 4, 1973:

> . . . I was always a Bezdek man. . . . It has been a source of
> great satisfaction to me to have played at State under Hugo
> Bezdek. He was a great coach. Haines and Lightner did not
> even play in high school. Wilson came to Penn State to play
> basketball. I was a terrible high school player. We made All-
> America. . . . Bezdek was a great technician and our football
> was as advanced as that of any college in America.

One player, Al (Knabby) Knabb, recalls no practice sessions immediately before games during his four years. "Bez was never that
kind of coach," he said. Charlie Way faced the problem of Bezdek as
he faced other obstacles in life, with patience and stoicism. "Bez was
tough," he admitted, "but I never hated him. I decided to put up
with him and take things as they came."

Others less tolerantly describe him as heartless, unpredictable, and
even brutal. That he "played favorites" was a frequent complaint,
but players criticized him most for switching positions without regard

for their best talents, and for publicly embarrassing them. Ronald K. (Buck) Williams was a popular quarterback candidate in 1920, and sometimes a starter despite his small stature. During one rainy home game he dropped back to receive a kick, fumbled the punt, but recovered the ball and made about 5 yards. When he went to the bench for a towel, spectators in the stands could easily hear Bez blast him with "ALIBI, ALIBI!"

Because Bez got the idea that Jay S. (Tiny) McMahan, his six-foot, seven-inch tackle on the 1921–22 teams, couldn't take punishment, he had the second team run plays at him for an entire scrimmage. "I was really beat up," Tiny remembers, "but Bez said it would make me a better player. He saw me trying to limber my bruised shoulder and other aching arm, and assumed I was making the motions of playing a violin, something he'd caught others doing when they thought he wasn't looking. He just blew up—kicked me off the squad. I needed the football aid, and Coach Harlow advised me to apologize. I did, and Bez took me back."

In the 1921 North Carolina State game, Trainer Bill Martin asked Bez if sophomore Joe Bedenk should be taken out after receiving a cut on the jaw. "Is his jaw broken?" asked Bez. Told it wasn't, Bez replied, "Let him play." Killinger remembers the coach's insensitivity with more amusement than pain. He was walking on campus one day reading Bill Roper's book *How to Play Football* when Bez came alongside, eyed the book, snatched it away, and threw it twenty-five feet. "I never got the book back," Killy noted. "Bez said *he'd* teach me how to play football."

Often repeated is the fable that Coach Bezdek would run a hundred prospects on the field until all but eleven dropped out from exhaustion. The eleven still running would be his first team. Frank Diedrich, 1930 captain, tempers criticism with some admiration.

> Many times I cussed him under my breath during the vigorous and at times almost inhuman practice sessions and scrimmages, but if you got through it you were a better man. He was a great psychologist and treated everyone differently. If you were lazy you could expect the worst tongue lashing imaginable—and more sprints. I think Bez was a great coach and a great human being, but he was too tough on the practice field, resulting in too many injuries.

Although time has tempered hurtful memories, Bezdek's players from 1926 on remain the least forgiving of those who had strong opinions. His brusqueness and savagery, accentuated by the stress he was under, were felt by everyone. Judge John D. Pincura of Elyria, Ohio, quarterback from 1925 through 1927, wrote on March 20, 1975:

> He was honest, fair, and taught clean football. He placed what he believed to be varsity men on the varsity. Players on our squads had mixed feelings about him, but none of us would ever jump for joy when he came on the field. No one ever really got close to him. He rarely gave any credit, and this same shortsighted attitude was displayed toward his assistant coaches, former players, and other alumni. . . . Occasionally he may have acknowledged help and support from such alumni as Earl Hewitt '03 and Ed Yeckley '06, but even these men turned against him.

Bezdek's critics liked to say the game had passed him by in the late 1920s and that he barely held on because he was a good defensive coach. His reputation wasn't helped by the almost unblemished records against his teams of two great Pittsburgh coaches—first Pop Warner, then Jock Sutherland. Detractors forgot or ignored the notable contributions made to offensive football by Coach Bezdek, who is generally accepted as having originated or having much to do with the screen pass, fullback and halfback spinners, and the spread formation. His famous fake reverse, perfected from 1919 through 1921, was widely copied, and he was among the first coaches to use a "sleeper" play, having picked it up from Stagg. Bezdek is credited with perfecting the quick kick and the onside kick. Defensive contributions included use of a roving center and staggering the ends.

Without questioning his ability, "the actual absence of results and the general lack of confidence make it advisable to replace him." This was the message to the Board of Trustees from the Pittsburgh Alumni Club early in 1929. The trustee committee appointed then (Jesse B. Warriner '05, chairman) received the next letter, amplifying the charges and signed by C. W. Heppenstall '03 (who had recommended Bezdek in 1918), William Fuhs '09, James Milholland '11, and Ben C. Jones '19. Hugo Bezdek was cited for inability to inspire, failure to retain the confidence of students and his assistants, and, most damning of all, insufficient football sense or knowledge to occupy the position of head coach.

Actually, Bez had only two losing football seasons at Penn State—the war year of 1918 and 1928. His record with twelve Lion teams was 65–30–11, including a thirty-game non-losing streak, 1919–22. An equally impressive baseball coaching record (129–76) from 1920 through 1930 also included a thirty-game winning streak, 1920–21. He coached the basketball team in 1920, winning eleven of thirteen games.

The Warriner Committee, reporting to the trustees (June 13, 1929) that these views were based principally on the football team's poor record against Pitt, suggested referral to the Athletic Board of Control. Here President Hetzel showed his firm diplomacy by coming personally to persuade its members to revise their thinking about the organization of athletics. The Athletic Board recommended (January 9, 1930) making intercollegiate athletics part of a School of Physical Education in which all staff would have academic rank under a non-coaching director with the status of the deans of the other schools. Bezdek was to continue as director of the new school, which would replace his former department.[2] Wishes of the Pittsburgh alumni had been met only by removing Bezdek from his football coaching duties; in effect, Bez had been granted a reprieve that lasted six years.

President Hetzel's position was buttressed by the Carnegie Foundation's final report late in 1929 unfairly listing Penn State as an institution whose athletic standards were not consistent with its educational and ethical values in that it awarded seventy-five football scholarships, while "caring for" and providing special tutors for an indefinite number of athletes. The foundation had been notified promptly that all athletic subsidies were abolished after 1927, that initial steps were taken to remove athletic control from alumni, and that Varsity Hall administration was in the hands of the college. Dr. Hetzel succeeded in having the historic Bulletin 23 carry a footnote about Penn State's corrected policies, but in general this explanation has been overlooked.

Meeting in Governor John Fisher's Harrisburg mansion, the trustees took final action on January 17–18, 1930. The official news release stated, "Hugo Bezdek on Monday received trustee promotion to the directorship of the new School of Physical Education and Athletics, voluntarily stepping out of football and other active coaching duties."

Editor James H. Coogan of the *Collegian* scooped all area papers

---

[2] President Hetzel allayed misgivings of Amby Diehl, Athletic Board chairman, about elevating Coach Bezdek to the status of a dean by promising to follow recommendations of the board "whose members know him better than I."

by three days with a front-page byline story. Swearing a linotype operator to secrecy, Coogan banished all reporters from the printshop and put the type in form himself. His lead:

Hugo Bezdek stepped out of the football picture at Penn State with a reluctant stride. The Grand Old Man of football was wont to stay—but duty to a greater cause dragged him out of the picture that he has dominated during 12 years of unstinting service to Penn State.

In Jim's exclusive interview, Bez committed the cardinal sin of a retiring coach, saying he had intentionally quit at this time to give his successor the benefit of good material during his first year. Bez knew very well how Penn State football would fare with no athletic aid and with continuing contracts to play Pittsburgh, West Virginia, Colgate, Syracuse, and Bucknell—none of whom then subscribed to similar ideals. Opponents in the 1930s also would include Iowa, Temple, Harvard, Columbia, Pennsylvania, Cornell, Maryland, and Army.

The Athletic Board unanimously elected Robert A. Higgins '18 head coach on March 27, 1930, although a faculty representative, Dean of Engineering Robert L. Sackett, was concerned about his close association with Dick Harlow. Sackett also thought it inconsistent to bring in the former head coach of two institutions (West Virginia Wesleyan and Washington University of St. Louis) whose policies at that time were incompatible with Penn State's. Confidence was general, however, that Higgins could successfully instill "the old Penn State spirit" into the program. The need for more ingredients soon was painfully apparent.

Temporarily at least, Hugo Bezdek settled into his new life a happy man. He was "king" at Rec Hall in an office suite; coaching pressures were behind him; he seemed to adjust easily to academe, even if some cynics were amused by his weekly walk from the gymnasium down to Old Main for Council of Administration meetings. The deans, his counterparts, were friendly, and once in a while he'd be seen with President Hetzel on the golf course.

The cordial relations between Bez and the average student never diminished. To them he was a friendly, colorful, even glamorous personality. His administration of athletics and physical education made friends and enemies for Penn State, but a review of the record shows his ability to get things done.

The groundwork for the university's present broad athletic program had begun soon after Bezdek came to the campus. He started with new tennis courts, playing fields, and a nine-hole golf course, laid out in the spring of 1921 thanks to enforced labor from the football squad. A few years later nine more holes were added. He had the baseball field and track rebuilt, enlarged and improved facilities at New Beaver Field, and caused other play areas to materialize all over the campus. Penn State's extensive intramural program, equaled by few colleges, was initiated and administered by Bez in co-operation with the able Gene Bischoff, its first full-time director. Construction of Varsity Hall, into which athletes moved from the Track House in 1924, was pushed through his persistence, and Recreation Hall (now Recreation Building) was planned and completed under his direction in 1930.

Some of Penn State's most colorful coaches were Bezdek appointees: Bob Rutherford, Sr., golf (1922); Nate Cartmell, track (1923); Leo Houck, boxing (1923); Bill Jeffrey, soccer (1926); Charlie Speidel, wrestling (1927); Bob Higgins, football (1930); Joe Bedenk, baseball (1931); Chick Werner, track (1934); and Nick Thiel, lacrosse (1936). Intercollegiate sports he established were boxing (1919), golf (1922), gymnastics (1932), and fencing (1934). Swimming was recognized on an informal basis in 1935.

Bezdek generated unusual camaraderie within his athletic family, often fraternizing with them in raucous, off-hour handball sessions. Most of his coaches remained loyal throughout his trials as director. Charles M. Speidel wrote this tribute from his home in Gulfport, Florida, in June 1973:

> We would go all out for Bez. He did support his coaches, enlightened and encouraged them, and took them into the family. Many times we were in his home for our low-ante games, raiding his icebox at will. . . . He arrived at Penn State when the college was fighting for recognition, and he was always a headline copy figure. . . . As far as I was concerned, Bez was tops. You knew where you stood—he confided in you, and even when he gave you hell you'd like it because it was in the open without a whispering campaign against you. . . . There should be a building, a field, or some special plaque dedicated to Bez for what he accomplished in developing the sports program to a high level.

At least one staff dissenter would be Nathaniel J. Cartmell, the very successful track coach of the 1920s. Inevitably, something had to give in the violent clashes between these strong personalities. Bezdek's complaint of insubordination resulted in Nate's dismissal by the Athletic Board after the 1933 season. Winning this battle antagonized a strong group of former trackmen who idolized Cartmell. Dick Bartholomew, 1928 track captain, thinks the Bezdek-Cartmell feud may have started when he was a freshman on a track scholarship. Bez gave him and three other freshman sprinters permission to try out for football, but Nate refused to allow their participation in both. Nate blamed Bez and never forgave him.

Relations always were cool with Bob Higgins, who may have been nettled by Bezdek's ill-chosen remark about leaving him with plenty of football material. Coach Higgins absorbed some abuse for the mediocre seasons of the early 1930s, but Director Bezdek bore the brunt of alumni rancor—he was "interfering" with Higgins; he wasn't helping Higgins enough; he provided no leadership. Although his early antagonist, Alumni Secretary Mike Sullivan, had resigned in 1929, piqued because his efforts to establish an annual Alumni Fund had been thwarted, other quiescent "wolves" again were rampant. A succession of committees approached the problem beginning in June 1935, when Alumni Association President Miles Horst '14 appointed Eugene T. Gramley '19 chairman of a group to "investigate the athletic situation." Anticipating this report and using some of its findings, a trustee committee (chaired by Vance C. McCormick) went into action on February 14, 1936.

The Gramley Committee's final report (June 1936) recommended an expanding intramural program "to feed potential varsity material," reaffirmed the nonsubsidization policy while proposing a training table "for several varsity and freshman teams," and surprisingly encouraged alumni clubs and the Varsity S Club "to give aid to worthy athletes." Also suggested were a local committee to secure jobs for athletes and the scheduling of games with colleges having similar policies.

Referring to public criticism of "various coaches, especially the head football coach," the alumni committee recommended that coaches have more authority and more accountability for their teams, a clear implication of too much interference by the director. Then came the flat statement that new leadership was needed. "There exists," said the report, "within the School of Physical Education and Athletics, mistrust, fear for the future, and unrest."

Reporting to the Board of Trustees in September 1936, its McCor-

mick Committee supported a number of the alumni recommendations, but cautioned against utilizing alumni clubs and other agen-
cies "to give aid to worthy athletes" because this required careful
organization and supervision to avoid violating "the spirit of amateur
athletics."

The trustee committee approved reorganizing the Board of Athletic Control as the Athletic Advisory Board, with the director and
the graduate manager as ex officio members. Another proposal
changed the director's title to dean. Finally the issue of Director Bezdek's qualifications was faced. Noting that many specific complaints
could not be justified by the evidence, the report went on to say:

> . . . there has developed such a want of confidence in the lead-
> ership of the Director, particularly in his relations to the ad-
> ministration of intercollegiate athletics, as to qualify seriously
> the value of his service in that office. It is the judgment of your
> committee, therefore, that in the interest of the School and of
> the College, the present Director should be relieved of his re-
> sponsibilities as Director.

A year's leave of absence on salary, beginning October 1, 1936,
was recommended, with assurance that after one year Bezdek could
accept a position not connected with intercollegiate athletics, or an
honorable dismissal. After his leave of absence Bez wrote to President Hetzel asking for dismissal and requesting the "State involun-
tary retirement pension, as you promised and which I desire." His
request was granted as of September 30, 1937.

A bitter and disillusioned Bezdek went into retirement, but soon
signed a three-year contract as coach and general manager of the
newly organized NFL Cleveland Rams. His professional career
lasted less than two years and included only one victory—over the
Philadelphia Eagles. In 1949 he returned to coaching briefly at the
National Agricultural College in his hometown of Doylestown, Pennsylvania, but ended his life farming and operating White Eagle Farm,
a successful chicken business.

The late Steve Hamas, one of Bezdek's last great players, couldn't
resist an analogy when told about his former coach's activities as a
farmer. "Yeah," said Steve, "I can see Bez on that farm, visiting
those chickens in the morning and finding out his hens weren't laying
enough eggs. 'Okay, you loafers,' he'd yell, 'run three laps around
the farm!' "

Hugo Bezdek died in Atlantic City Hospital on September 19, 1952, at the age of 68, after suffering a stroke at his summer home in Ventnor, New Jersey. No official representative from Penn State attended his funeral. He was posthumously elected to Football's Hall of Fame in 1954.

Part V

FRUSTRATIONS OVERCOME

Bob Higgins, 1930–48

26

The Grim Seasons

Daily practice under Bob Higgins was almost a pleasure for veterans of Bezdek's squads. The 36-year-old Higgins, a close observer of their rugged workouts for two years, decided early to be himself as head coach. Easygoing, patient, tempering criticism with humor, he could be severe at times, but players familiar with Bez's withering thunder found it hard to quake when Coach Higgins sounded off in his high-pitched tones.

The problems of the early 1930s taxed the Hig's patience fully. He had ten scholarship holdovers, all seniors, but top-grade talent ended with this class. Eight juniors, persuaded to come to Penn State with no financial aid, were George (Judy) Lasich, Bill McMillen, Bob Snyder, Stan Stempeck, Ed DeCindis, Tom Curry, Bill Martz, and Chuck Gillard, the only one on the squad who weighed over 200 pounds. Martz transferred to West Point after the season. Recruiting for the past three years had been negligible, and not a single sophomore lettered in 1930.

The "new order" was to have enough coaches and equipment for all comers, but supplying "latent talent" fell lower in priority as the Depression came on. Higgins, Joe Bedenk, and Dutch Hermann represented the varsity staff, with Larry Conover replacing Hermann as freshman coach.

Another problem was the strict amateurism pursued by the still influential Athletic Board, which seemed determined to obstruct winning football. Its strange decisions included limiting varsity players to one training meal per day during season, and requiring that "coaches eating at the training table shall pay their own board beginning with the opening of college."

To combat the evils of recruiting, the board specifically prohibited any coach from attending an alumni meeting where a high school student might be present. Its stand on scouting sometimes unfairly handicapped Higgins against opponents known to have scouted his team.

Relations between the new coach and Director Bezdek, as rumored, were not cordial. One afternoon, when Bez impulsively appeared on the practice field and began to instruct a group of players, Higgins let his predecessor know he was displeased. Rumors of Bezdek's "interference" often were exaggerations, as one incident shows. The Lions, heavily favored against Lafayette at Easton, had to settle for a scoreless tie. Since the disappointed seniors thought they were being held back by undue conservatism, Captain Frank Diedrich called a meeting to clear the air, but the coaches interpreted suggestions drawn up by the players as "demands" inspired by Bezdek. Of this situation Diedrich wrote on May 5, 1975:

> Regarding Bezdek's interference with Bob Higgins, to my knowledge there was none. I talked often to Bez during that last season and he told me to keep plugging; that a new system always took a while to get in the groove and there was nothing we could do about the material we had to work with. Bez did not know about the meeting I called with the players. The previous Saturday Lafayette had held us to a scoreless tie because the coaches wouldn't let us run any weak-side plays or reverses and no passes. They wanted us to perfect strong-side power plays, and Lafayette soon caught on and overshifted to stop us cold. All the players were furious and dejected, so I called the seniors together to talk things over and try to smooth things out and buck up the morale. When the coaches heard about the meeting they blew their tops and an explosive situation developed. However, after I explained the situation they were satisfied, and Bob Higgins even apologized to me for suspecting that we were trying to undermine the staff. After that, the rapport between the coaches and players materially improved and they adjusted away from the power-play offense. I wish I could

say we went on to a successful season, but such was not the case. Too many bad knees and practically no reserves.

Another scoreless tie, with Syracuse, was as close as the 1930 team came to a major success, and against Colgate, Lion followers learned the fate of an undermanned squad facing a top eastern team. Coach Andy Kerr and his personnel—Captain Les Hart, Johnny Orsi, and Len Macaluso, national scoring leader that season—showed no mercy (40–0). On their first outing at Bucknell in over twenty years, the Lions again met one of the nation's top backs in Clark Hinkle, who led the Bisons to a 19–7 triumph. In November, student leaders organized a rally at Schwab Auditorium to get the Iowa game returns by telegraph, but they were disappointing—Coach Higgins' men wilted in the second half against their much heavier Big Ten opponent and lost, 19–0.

The Penn State team was at its best, playing a competitive, fairly close game, against a Pitt eleven defeated only by Notre Dame and Ohio State. Red Duvall blocked a kick, resulting in Earle Edwards' scoring a touchdown, but the Panthers won, 19–12. It was Edwards' last game after three years as varsity end.[1]

If 1930 was a grievous season, 1931 was horrendous. All scholarship men had departed, and the coaches in the Depression years could attract few players to the campus despite the Athletic Board's prediction and the administration's hopes. Waynesburg stunned home fans in the opening game, 7–0. Frank Wolf, a 1921 Penn State graduate whose promising football career was cut short by a knee injury, was coach and athletic director of the little college in Greene County.[2] To get his athletic program out of desperate financial straits, and against the advice of his friends, he scheduled two games with his alma mater—a power by comparison. Helped by a small scatback named Rab Currie, the Yellowjackets protected their first-quarter touchdown for the upset.

[1] He returned, on the coaching staff (1936–48) to begin a distinguished career, including service at Michigan State under Biggie Munn, and as head coach at North Carolina State, 1954–70. He was named Coach of the Year four times in the Atlantic Coast Conference and twice by the NCAA District Three coaches (1965, 1967). In 1971 he was president of the American Football Coaches Association.

[2] Wolf played varsity basketball at Penn State and still holds a scoring record set against Carnegie Tech in 1921—twenty successful foul goals. He spent most of his professional career coaching and teaching at Waynesburg, where he died in 1949.

Dickinson, the next Pennsylvania college to have its moment of glory on New Beaver, mortified the home team, 10–6, in the fourth game of the season. A full weekend of student celebration at Carlisle assumed proportions of a riot. The local constabulary put five in the pokey and had to restore order with tear gas. After the victory over Lebanon Valley (19–6) in the second game, a Penn State record of seven successive losses was set, and undergraduates were in a state of shock. The Lions fell to Temple (12–0), Dickinson, Syracuse (7–0), Pittsburgh (41–6), Colgate (32–7), Lafayette (33–0), and West Virginia (19–0), but Coach Jock Sutherland of the Pitt Panthers perpetrated the worst indignity. He mercifully started his second team and played most of the game with thirds and fourths, but after the final whistle signaling the 41–6 defeat, Jock's first eleven, fresh and full of pep, came on the field for a 15-minute warmup. To Coach Sutherland it was a logical preparation for important coming games with Carnegie Tech, Army, and Nebraska; to rankled home rooters it was a long-remembered insult.

A 1–8 season hardly qualified the team for a postseason outing, but Philadelphia community leaders wanting a Franklin Field benefit game for "unemployment relief" gave Penn State and Lehigh the honor of playing for expenses (which they barely made). The Engineers, after a goodly season, unexpectedly lost to the almost winless Lions, 31–0.

The dismal 1931 season had one good result: Alumnus Casey Jones began a personal crusade that eventually brought Penn State out of its self-imposed football shambles. He traveled thousands of miles to visit high school athletes, talk with coaches and parents, and attend hundreds of Friday night high school games. He bullied, cajoled, and argued with other alumni to help, gave cash when it was needed, or wheedled it out of others. On trips to the campus from his home in Pittsburgh, he filled his car with high school prospects, and got them job promises if they enrolled and summer jobs back home. Constantly prodding the coaches to further efforts, he encouraged, pleaded with, and raged at his good friend, Bob Higgins.

Ben C. (Casey) Jones, a solid and tough athlete but not big or fast, had lettered in football, track, and lacrosse in 1916 and left college for the armed forces. Higgins went into the infantry, but Jones preferred the excitement of becoming a pilot with Captain Eddie Rickenbacker's 9th Aero Pursuit Squadron in France. Soon after the two friends returned to Penn State in 1919, an injury ended Casey's football career.[3]

As undergraduates, Jones and Higgins had some memorable times together, once riding freight trains to join the track team in Charlottesville, Virginia, and Philadelphia because they hadn't made the official traveling squad. Coach Bill Martin was happy to have them. Higgins placed in the pole vault at Virginia, while at the Penn Relays Jones surprised the field by taking second place in the grueling pentathlon.

The war experience of Bob Higgins may have been less exciting than Casey's, but it was far from monotonous. Bob served in France with the 318th Infantry, 80th Division, and later became the division's national commander. Football was in the air after the Armistice, even in France, and when Captain Higgins was sent to the Army of Occupation, 89th Division, at Coblenz, he suspected the transfer had been arranged because of his background. The division's team was coached by Paul Withington, who had played at Harvard under Percy Haughton. The squad of ex-college stars, which included Lieutenant George (Potsy) Clark of Illinois, captured the Army championship, winning the title game in Paris from the 26th Division. Grantland Rice named Higgins on the All-AEF first eleven. After returning to captain Penn State's 1919 team and graduating in June 1920, Bob became, as noted, head coach at West Virginia Wesleyan (1920–24) and at Washington University of St. Louis (1925–27). He returned to Penn State as Bezdek's assistant in 1928.

Casey Jones was silent when Penn State gave up special inducements for athletes until he realized the dire trouble it was causing his old friend. Gradually he built up a cadre of equally dedicated "lieutenants," but fundamentally it was a one-man show. More than any other individual he paved the way toward a more realistic approach. Jones broke no NCAA rules that he knew about, but he did circumvent official policy before the Board of Trustees established grants-in-aid in the late 1940s.

A chance to work for their education and incidentally to play football was no way to get top-flight athletes even in the 1930s, and Penn State generally had to settle for "seconds," with now and then a

[3] Jones, a retired executive of West Penn Power Company, now resides in Punta Gorda, Florida. He served fourteen terms on the Executive Board of the Alumni Association, three years as president, and was on the Board of Trustees, 1951–69.

blue chip. One of the best was Dave Alston of Midland, Pennsylvania, selected after his freshman season in 1941 by a national magazine as "sophomore of the year." Shortly before the 1942 practice season he met tragic death following a tonsillectomy.[4]

Before Casey's efforts showed significant results, the grim Saturdays for Bob Higgins were acutely felt by the two dozen or so players of 1931 and 1932, who did their best with little of the glory they had dreamed about in high school. No plaques honor them; they won no big victories, but they never gave up when football was at its lowest ebb at Penn State.

Harold (Rosey) Rosenberg, an end, was a varsity wrestler at 135 pounds; Marty Hesch, a guard and not much bigger, helped organize the first gymnastics team. Clyde (King) Cole and Lou Kreizman were wrestlers who came out for football as linemen; C. Wilson (Andy) Anderson, now a professor in the College of Human Development, was a skinny center.[5]

Among the first "recruited" players who were promised nothing but mountain scenery and hard work were Frank and Jim O'Hora, only distantly related.[6] James R. Gilligan '12, the principal at Dunmore High School in the hard coal regions, thought they'd be happier at Penn State than at a city school. A third member of their team, Tommy Silvano, tried Notre Dame for a term and then transferred.

Jim O'Hora, a stable but undersized center for three years, has become an institution at Penn State. After ten years of high school coaching and service in the Navy as a lieutenant, 1942–45, he joined Bob Higgins' staff in 1946, and for thirty years under four head coaches has been an interior line coach and defensive co-ordinator.

[4] Robert T. (Red) Worrell, a promising 1957 freshman star, died of injuries in an accident during Christmas vacation, 1957.

[5] Also among these unsung were Parker Berry, Jesse Brewster, Johnny Grimshaw, Tom Slusser, Stan Zawacki, Bill (Whitey) Lohr, Tony Bedoski, Tom Harper, Leo Skemp, Harry Wattshouse, Harry Sigel, Merrill Morrison, Dick Woolbert, Bill Cooper, Ronald (Lefty) Knapp, Bob Weber, Frank Wismer, Phil Moonves, Ed (Killer) Kane, Johnny McAndrews, Rem Woolridge, Carl Wille, and Mahlon Heist.

[6] Frank (Red) O'Hora, quarterback for three seasons and shortstop on the baseball team, stayed out of college for a year in 1934 and graduated in 1937. He coached high school football in Pennsylvania and New Jersey, served in World War II, and then joined the athletic staff at Colgate University, where he spent most of his professional career as assistant football coach and varsity baseball coach.

To recognize his long service and special expertise, Coach Joe Paterno named him assistant head coach in 1974.

Al Michaels, well known in college football, also entered Penn State in 1932. Mike, from DuBois, Pennsylvania, shared quarterback duties with Red O'Hora and was the team's best punter. He led the Lions to a near upset over Columbia in 1934 and played a leading role in an unexpected tie (6–6) with Penn in 1933. Michaels was on the coaching staff from 1936 until 1954, when he became an assistant to Earle Edwards at North Carolina State, where he is still on the athletic staff.

That the 1932 season's highlight was a 13–12 loss to Temple in the final game shows the depth of Penn State's fall. The low point was another defeat by Waynesburg, 7–6, with Rab Currie again giving his team the edge. At Cambridge the Lions took a physical beating from Harvard in addition to losing the game, 46–13, and were smothered by Colgate at Hamilton, 31–0. This was Andy Kerr's undefeated, untied, unscored-on, and uninvited team that expected a Rose Bowl bid, which went to Pittsburgh. Coaches Higgins and Bedenk asked Coach Kerr to shorten the quarters to twelve minutes, but Andy refused because Homecoming alumni would be indignant. The Hig then tried a psychological ploy: His players walked on the field listlessly and their opponents fell into the same pattern, but only for the first half. What happened in the third quarter symbolized the nadir of Penn State football: The Lion punter kicked the ball right into the rear end of his halfback, who was therefore credited with blocking his own team's kick.

Signs of dawning sanity appeared in 1932 when athletic authorities broke off the Pitt series for three years, and the schedule was cut to seven games for the 1932 and 1933 seasons. Muhlenberg inflicted the final indignity by a small Pennsylvania college team, winning 3–0 in 1933 on a 38-yard place kick by Red Weiner midway in the last quarter.

Suffering Lion partisans had some chance to cheer in 1933 when halfback Jim Boring returned a punt for 100 yards against Johns Hopkins, which had replaced Pitt on the schedule and was beaten, 40–6. The first really bright sign came in the final game, at Philadelphia, where Captain Tom Slusser's touchdown enabled the team to score an upset tie, 6–6, against Penn.

Recruiting efforts instigated by Jones and Gilligan began to pay off in 1934 when a few sizable players joined the squad: Tommy Silvano, the fullback from Dunmore, became eligible after sitting out a year of penance because of his Notre Dame detour; Lou Barth, Roy Schuyler, Bob Morini, J. Franklin Smith, and Chuck Cherundolo added to the strength of the line material.[7]

The following year Casey Jones hit the jackpot by sending to the varsity squad three promising players from Greensburg—Danny DeMarino (later assistant dean of men), Paul (Dud) Enders, and Carl Waugaman. With the help of Red Gross, former Lion player who was coach at Schenley High School, John Economos (now Evans) started his three-year career as a small but active guard.

Concentrating his 1935 summer efforts in the western Pennsylvania town of Monongahela, Casey landed three high school all-stars —Sever Toretti, Alex Barantovich, and Joe Metro—along with John G. Patrick, another player from Schenley. Toretti, like Jim O'Hora, has spent most of his career at Penn State, but first was a successful high school coach at Steelton and Williamsport. He joined Joe Bedenk's staff in 1949 as a line coach, stayed on until 1963, and gave up coaching to become assistant athletic director. Tor primarily is concerned with recruiting, the Athletic Department's liaison with secondary schools, and counseling student athletes.

Penn State, lacking brawny backs during the dismal years, achieved some remarkable feats in 1936 and 1937 with a pint-sized backfield manned by Windy (Rabbit) Wear, Sammy Donato, Harry (High School Harry) Harrison, and Metro. Harrison and Metro were the "heavies," weighing between 155 and 160. Donato, the blocking back, was a welterweight (145) boxer. Wear was probably a little heavier than his program weight of 129. This diminutive quartet compensated for size with courage, determination, speed, and productive audacity in critical situations. In 1937 they were joined by another strong competitive athlete, Lloyd Ickes from Altoona.

At first, only promises of summer jobs were offered the incoming players, but Jim O'Hora recalls receiving $25 every few months from Jim Gilligan, who said it was from the "club," probably meaning he took it from his own pocket. Local restaurant owners were hiring football players by the time Toretti enrolled (1936), and he worked

[7] Cherundolo, from Old Forge, Pennsylvania, probably was the best football player at Penn State in the 1930s and later played with the Steelers. Schuyler, a tackle, is now general manager and vice president of DuPont's Chemical Division; and Smith, one of the last of Penn State's three-sport performers, is president of PenElec, a utility company based in Altoona.

in the Green Room (at College and Pugh) and later at Carey (Doggie) Alexander's Rathskeller. He also made beds and did other work in the residence halls for his room. Ed Brown, Athletic Store manager on Co-op Corner, provided books on a "loan" basis. By the mid-1940s, under pressure from the coaches, fraternities began to furnish board and room—O'Hora and Assistant Coach Al Michaels spent many nights convincing fraternity caterers that enough food was being thrown away to feed one football player. Funds raised locally eventually paid fraternities in part for support of players.

The largest source of income was Casey's "Scholar-Gram" program, a statewide raffle of an automobile displayed each fall outside Graham's Candy store on Allen Street. At pregame Pittsburgh headquarters in the William Penn Hotel, his "salesmen" reported from all over the state. Rolling the big raffle barrel Saturday night after the perennial Pitt defeat made at least one alumnus happy, but to alumni in general the Scholar-Gram idea was distasteful, and the college administration obviously frowned on it.

As a member of the Alumni Association Executive Board, and with the approval of S. K. Hostetter, college comptroller, Casey managed to have $5,500 added to the association's operating budget, to be dispensed to "worthy athletes." No one knew exactly how he arrived at this particular figure, but the "scholarships," duly distributed to football players and a few athletes from other sports, remained a budget item until the trustees, unquestionably influenced by Casey's persistence, officially established the grants-in-aid program in May 1949, within specifications of the tightened-up NCAA regulations.

During the 1930s, Penn Staters grasped at straws for signs of better days to come. In 1934 a Higgins team for the first time won a regular-season game away from home, defeating Lehigh 31–0 at Bethlehem. Losing to Penn (3–0) on a third-period field goal by Franny Murray was reckoned a moral victory of a sort, as was the Columbia game on Morningside Heights, where the slightly built Michaels (then Mikelonis) passed and kicked his team to a near triumph. The Columbia Lions, basking in their Rose Bowl victory over Stanford (January 1, 1934), still had fullback Bill Nevel, Ed Brominski, and Al Barabas, who scored the winning touchdown in the bowl. Michaels fairly upstaged them—his long pass to Frank Smith set up Silvano's touchdown; he kicked the goal, and his punting kept Penn State out of trouble most of the way, although Higgins' players were battered by superior manpower in the second half and lost, 14–7. The *Collegian* writeup extolled the Blue Band's performance on Baker Field.

Slightly brighter times came in 1935, when the team first won a game it was supposed to lose, beating Clipper Smith's Villanova eleven, 27–13. Oddly, too, the Lions defeated Western Maryland, 2–0, in an early game and lost the final one to Bucknell by the same score.

The first of the classic Syracuse series embroilments came in this 1935 season. At Archbold Stadium the Lions' Bill Cooper kicked a field goal for a lead lasting until the final quarter, when a long drive led by Vannie Albanese put the Orange ahead, 6–3, with a minute remaining. On the first play after Syracuse kicked off, Red O'Hora sent a high pass down the middle to midfield, where end Bob Morini had come to a full stop, surrounded by defenders. Morini leaped into the air, and so did the defenders, who appeared (to Lion observers) to knock the ball high and toward the Syracuse goal. Little Arthur Yett, a substitute halfback, was there and ready for his moment of glory. With the ball settled in his arms, he ran for the apparent winning score—a smash ending almost matching the 1929 Lafayette finish, except that the referee ruled the pass illegal. In those days, by college and pro rules alike, only one offensive player could touch a pass unless a defender touched it in between, which is what Coach Higgins claimed had happened. The play, well photographed in Syracuse Sunday papers, proved Higgins was right, in his opinion, and also proved Coach Vic Hanson was right, in his opinion.

Bob Morini commented on the incident in a letter written on June 26, 1975:

> In the midst of three Syracuse players, I leaped for the ball, caught it and was trying to bring it down to my chest when a Syracuse defender on my back leaped up at the same time and with an underhand motion batted the ball out of my hands into Art Yett's. A picture of the play was taken just before the Syracuse player made contact with the ball.

Pitt relations were resumed with better results, the Lions losing only 9–0, due to the defensive play of guard John Economos, a Pittsburgher. Pitt's first points were made on a field goal kicked by Frank Patrick, who eventually joined Penn State's coaching staff (1949–74).

Breaking even in 1933, 1934, and 1935 (3–3–1, 4–4, 4–4),

Coach Higgins had not succeeded in overcoming traditional rivals Syracuse, Penn, or Bucknell. He was victimized by alumni who had expected a miracle after Bezdek's expulsion, but the grizzled athletic director took most of the criticism on campus. In a front-page editorial of the *Collegian*'s Homecoming issue (October 18, 1935), Editor Harry B. Henderson wrote a "Wake Up Alumni" attack adjacent to a two-column-wide cartoon by James Dugan showing a gigantic Bezdek squeezing a midget Higgins between the palms of his huge hands.[8] The editorial said it was

> attempting to place clearly in the minds of the alumni of Penn State the true conditions of athletes here and the hypocrisy and rotten unfairness of Hugo Bezdek's plan for the non-subsidization of athletes. . . . What started out to be a system of decency and progress in all athletics has been converted into an intolerable and unjust exploitation of athletes, coaches, and alumni. . . . Candidly and frankly the football players here are being exploited by an Athletic Association that pays them nothing for four hard hours a day and yet takes in gates which approach former magnificence.

Accusing officials of "scheduling for box-office appeal" and failing to meet colleges with similar rules, Henderson absolved Higgins from blame because he had been forced to play "professional" opponents with a team subsidized on one meal a day. Coach Higgins saw the editorial as a boost to morale, and the players responded with a 26–0 victory over Lehigh, but two victory bonfires in downtown State College caused $1,000 in damages, and President Hetzel called the student reaction "silly."

Editor Henderson was on target in criticizing the administration for shortsightedness, but unfair in attributing the nonsubsidization policy to Bez, who had not originated it. The *Collegian*'s next issue announced that the Athletic Board had granted the squad "two meals daily on practice days and game days, as part of the conditioning process."

[8] Henderson, a former editor of *Argosy* magazine, lives in Croton-on-Hudson, New York, doing free-lance writing and co-ordinating research publications for a number of medical writers. James Dugan was a writer best known for his association with Jacques-Yves Cousteau in his undersea explorations, notably *The Silent World* and *Man Under the Sea*. He was doing *The World Beneath the Sea* for the National Geographic Society and Westinghouse when he died in Panama City, Florida, in June 1967. His earlier works included *Ploesti, The Great Mutiny,* and *The Great Iron Ship,* a 1953 Book-of-the-Month Club selection.

Penn State had its first all-graduate coaching staff in 1936. Higgins and Bedenk were joined by Al Michaels (a graduate assistant the year before), Earle Edwards, and Marty McAndrews (freshman coach). Captain Chuck Cherundolo deserved his popularity, especially with the team's many sophomores. Backing up the line invincibly, he'd call out to his young linemen: "You guys just take somebody out—anybody—I'll make the tackle." He'd get up from a pile, shaking his head to clear the stars away, while the hovering sophomores implored him, "Don't get hurt, team."

The 1936 losing season (3–5) had some bright Saturdays—the first victory over Syracuse (18–0) since 1929 and over Bucknell (14–0) since 1926. The Syracuse success, best of the Higgins years to date, featured outstanding play by Bill Denise, Metro, Cherundolo, and Economos. Albanese, an old nemesis, and Marty Glickman, Olympic sprinter, were completely throttled.

The team gave Cornell and Penn good battles before succumbing, 13–7 and 19–12. Harrison cockily wagered the sports information director two Pitt tickets that he'd return a kickoff for a touchdown against Penn—and won the bet. Philadelphia writers said the Quakers' "poor showing against the subpar Lions" was the reason they didn't get a Rose Bowl bid, hoped for because they had lost only to Yale.

Harrison almost repeated his Penn heroics against the Pitt Panthers, who had lost only to Duquesne and would defeat Washington in the Rose Bowl, 21–0. Taking a kickoff on the 2, Harry ran to the last Pitt man, lunged to get by, lost his footing—and his pants. Behind 14–0, the Lions moved the ball to Pitt's 13, with Windy Wear making 30 yards on a wide reverse. Near the sideline Harrison, unobserved by the Pitt players, initiated a "sleeper" play. He lay flat on his stomach and was noticed by Dan DeMarino, who told Wear in the huddle no one was within 25 yards of Harrison when he caught Wear's pass for a touchdown. It was a "high school" play in the newspapers, but Lion devotees hadn't had so much fun since 1919. Pitt won the game, 34–7.

The season's low point, an unaccountable 7–6 loss to Lehigh at Bethlehem, caused the *Collegian* to renew its attack, but this time sportswriter Charles M. Wheeler, Jr., criticized the players, accusing the seniors of letting down and provoking dissension, especially in the huddle:

Squabbling among themselves like babies, and playing listless and uninspired football, Penn State's 1936 excuse was thoroughly outplayed and beaten in Saturday's Lehigh game. . . . What fight there was in the team was displayed by the players mixing it up with their teammates rather than with the common foe. . . . When 1,600 students produce a simon-pure team [Lehigh] that can make a team of 5,000 students look bad, there is something wrong besides the breaks.

When the players' bus set out for Ithaca the following week, sportswriter Wheeler was missing. The angry seniors had ejected him.

Coach Bob Higgins enjoyed his first winning season (5–3) in 1937, losing by close margins to Cornell (26–19) and Syracuse (19–13). The Lions scored first on a good Cornell eleven led by the great Brud Holland. They tied 19–19 late in the game after Wear's 60-yard run, but the Ithacans won with a last-minute passing attack. Wear and Harrison teamed to beat Penn, 7–0, the first Lion victory over the Red and Blue since 1929. Wear threw a pass to Harrison for 21 yards to Penn's 17. The two then reversed roles, with Wear catching a Harrison pass for a touchdown.

For the 1938 season, Assistant Coach Joe Bedenk installed the "looping" line introduced by Dick Harlow as a defensive maneuver before World War I. Later Lions hadn't heard of it and assumed it was a Bedenk innovation, which in a way it was. Defensive players changed positions just before the snap of the ball, slanting through the line at a confusing angle to mystify the opposing blockers.

Coach Higgins was skeptical about this "looping." Since Maryland was outclassed, 33–0, the experiment was deferred until the second game, with Bucknell. Tor Toretti, the defensive signal caller, was told to wait for the right spot, and thought he had it early in the game when Craig White punted dead on the Bucknell 5-yard line. Sure that the Bisons would use only straight off-tackle plays, he looked over to the bench, got a nod from Higgins, and called for the line to loop toward the wingback. Bucknell ran a wide reverse the other way, and Frank (King) Funair went 94 yards for a touchdown. Later, when Bucknell was in a similar hole, Bob's near falsetto was loud and clear: "Hey, Tor, no more of that damn looping." The visitors pushed across again to win, 14–0.

The season's heights were a 33–6 trimming of Syracuse and a 7–7 tie with Penn. In a special sequence of plays to open the Syracuse game, Coach Higgins moved Harrison to wingback and used Chuck Peters, a high-stepping sophomore, at tailback. After a few routine off-tackle slants to confuse the Syracuse end, Harrison was to take the ball on a wide reverse. Peters didn't co-operate. On the first play he galloped 80 yards for a score. The Penn tie took quick thinking and an exciting extra-point attempt, under pressure. Both teams scored touchdowns after fumbles, but Penn State's came late in the game. When John R. Patrick's kick was blocked, the ball bounced back to the 20-yard line. Advancing a blocked try by running was unfamiliar in those days, but Lloyd Ickes remembered the rule. He ran through a surprised Penn team for the tying point.

The year 1938 is memorable for a variety of changes and innovations. Penn State's freshmen, including Bill Smaltz, Lenny Krouse, Pepper Petrella, and Leonard Frketich (a tackle who weighed 303 pounds), defeated the Pitt yearlings, 13–12. A radio network began, with Jack Barry from Rochester and Bill Sutherland of Pittsburgh's KDKA doing the announcing and also presiding in November when KDKA broadcast the Syracuse game pep rally from Rec Hall. For the first time Lion players donned their light-blue jerseys with silver pants and helmets.

Broadcasters and a public-address system, operated first by Dr. Elwood C. Davis of the Phys Ed faculty, joined occupants of the press box atop the new all-steel stands. An electric scoreboard and timer, run by Hal Byers of the Physical Plant staff, enhanced the setting, as did the colorful flags of all opponents spaced around the top of the stands. A steel fence enclosed the entire area, including the baseball diamond and football practice fields.

President Hetzel, a Wisconsin graduate who received a weekly account of Badger games written by Coach Harry Stuhldreher, suggested to Alumni Secretary Ed Hibshman that Penn Staters might enjoy a similar communication. Hibshman asked Ridge Riley of the Public Information staff to write a *Football Letter* as a service of the Alumni Association. A preview edition was mailed out on September 26, 1938. For thirty-eight years without interruption Riley wrote the *Letter* following all of Penn State's 372 games, and attended all but 5.

The well-known Little Lion cartoons reflecting reaction to games were first used in the *Football Letter* of October 2, 1950, when Penn State defeated Georgetown, 34–14, in Rip Engle's bow as coach. A set of four, drawn by noted illustrator Bob Bugg, was given to Ridge Riley by Robert L. Wilson '40. The collection was increased by three contributed in 1953 by Paul G. Kuhnle, a student architect. The collection shot up to twenty-seven two years later when R. H. Peach of Harrisburg volunteered twenty sample sketches after becoming acquainted with the *Letter* through Harold H. Doede '26. More recent additions were drawn by Jolanda Kauffman of State College and Donna Symmonds Clemson '55 of Bellefonte, editor of the Alumni Association's *Penn Stater* magazine.

The pennant-and-dink-equipped Lion traditionally adorning the Homecoming letter since 1953 is a Kuhnle creation. A lion tail disappearing off the side of the page was meant for defeat in Pitt games ending the season, and was one of the Peach group.

The 1938 team, with only 10 passes completed against it, set three NCAA pass-defense records, including fewest yards passing allowed per game (13.1 average), lowest average allowed per game (1.78), and lowest completion percentage (16.9 per cent). Among the defensive standouts were Captain Dean Hanley, Tor Toretti, Alex Barantovich, Grover Washabaugh, Walt Kniaz, Spike Alter, Tom Vargo, Leon Gajecki, Carl Stravinski, and Joe Peel.

Ending as a losing season (3–4–1), 1938 couldn't be called a banner year, but it proved to be the last one before a string of thirty-eight non-losing seasons (through 1976), a record unequaled by any major college football team. Penn State was at last headed in the right direction on the road to eastern and then national leadership, the goal of all Nittany Lions.

27

The Hig Fights Back

The fine season of 1939 had one strange interlude. Bucknell and Lehigh had been overcome (13–3; 49–7) and the team traveled to Ithaca, optimistic in spirit despite the known power of Cornell (which was to go undefeated with an all-major schedule).

Two unusual plays made the first quarter demoralizing. Five minutes had elapsed, halfback Steve Rollins was returning a punt, and when he was tackled, the ball shot straight into the arms of Hal McCullough, a Cornell back, who ran 30 yards for a touchdown. Thirty seconds later, on a scrimmage play, the identical calamity befell poor Rollins—this time Cornell's Ken Brown caught the fumbled ball and ran 45 yards, adding another score to the final tally of 47–0. The two freakish fumbles thirty seconds apart in a single game are unforgettably associated with Rollins, a good halfback who did some fine running in his three seasons of faithful service.

The *Collegian* sports editor, Robert L. Wilson, was bluntly uncomplimentary to coach and team. Now owner and general manager of radio station WKVA in Lewistown, Pennsylvania, Wilson claims his criticism was not only constructive and justified but also beneficial—the Lions lost no more games that year. His opinion wasn't shared by Mrs. Higgins, as Wilson discovered after the surprise victory over Pitt in the final game, when he encountered her in an officials' box next to the working press.

"Congratulations," said Bob Wilson politely. "I think it's wonderful, but I bet you'd like to kick me in the pants."

"I'd like to have done it a long time ago," replied Virginia Higgins.

"Maybe you'd like to do it now?" said Bob in fun.

And she did.

Heading North again after a week of morale rebuilding, the Lions got off to a disastrous start against Syracuse. On the first scrimmage play Leon Gajecki, the reliable center, sailed the ball over the snake-bitten Rollins' head, and Whitey Piro recovered for the Orange on the 5-yard line. Two plays later the home team led, 6–0. Somehow, the game was retrieved (6–6) with a 2-yard touchdown run by Pepper Petrella, who had been forced back to the 6 but who broke away from his tacklers. Petrella had an uncanny way of making a short run look exciting—churning along on his stocky legs, he was hard to tackle. He and Chuck Peters were the outstanding running backs during the 1939–41 period, with Bill Smaltz and Lenny Krouse the first of the fine passing combinations in Penn State's modern era. The Syracuse game appeared to be the season's turning point.

Two weeks later, led by Petrella, Ickes, Krouse, and Peters, the Lions dumped Penn 10–0. Petrella's first-quarter scoring run of 17 yards, Ben Pollock's extra point, and John R. Patrick's second-period 15-yard field goal from a difficult angle into the wind won for Penn State against 4–1 odds. It was a very special triumph for Coach Higgins, who had captained the team to a victory over the Quakers almost exactly twenty years before by the same score.

The Lions, continuing to surprise opponents, next tied Army 14–14 at West Point. Tackle Walt Kniaz ran 45 yards with an interception, and Ickes, running 55 yards on a fake reverse, put the Lions ahead 14–7 until Army tied it up after a long pass late in the final quarter. Ickes, fullback, and Gajecki, center, were considered the keys to Penn State's returning respectability in eastern football.

Alumni thought it would never happen, but on November 25, 1939, it was Penn State 10, Pittsburgh 0. Petrella and Krouse, two of the game's headliners, were unborn when the last Lion team had defeated Pitt twenty years before. Between a first-quarter score by Smaltz and a field goal by blocking back Patrick near the end, State's defense completely checked the Panther running stars, Edgar "Special Delivery" Jones and Dick Cassiano. A crowd exceeding 20,000 at New Beaver Field set a local record (disputed by old-timers who claimed attendance was equally high for the 1923 Navy game and Notre Dame's appearance in 1925).

Wildly storming onto the field, students captured their own goal posts and bore them triumphantly down campus to the main gate at Co-op Corner. Fearing more damage, their leaders successfully appealed for a Monday holiday to celebrate the end of the long victory-over-Pitt famine. Prexy Hetzel's request for no violence was respected.

The 62–17–7 record of Coach Bob Higgins in his final ten seasons (1939–48) compared favorably with that of any coach in the country and belies his unfortunate link with Penn State's darkest years. He should be credited with breaking the Pitt jinx by winning five of the ten games played in this period, although the Panthers spoiled State's otherwise undefeated seasons in 1940 and 1948. Defeats came from Navy (3), Michigan State (2), West Virginia (2), Cornell (2), Colgate, North Carolina, and Temple.

Higgins was handicapped at first by having little choice in his coaching staff. Director Bezdek needed physical education teachers in 1932 and gave responsibility for freshman football to three Phys Ed men—Nelson Walke, Mike Loebs, and Dr. Elwood C. Davis, with Walke in charge. Later, Dr. Arthur F. Davis assisted. When Dutch Hermann resigned in 1932, his place was filled by the new basketball coach, E. E. (Spike) Leslie, Oregon '22. Probably the first assistant Higgins had any part in hiring was Herman Everhardus, a former Michigan star who arrived in 1934. Walke, Leslie, and Everhardus resigned in 1936 to be replaced by Marty McAndrews, Earle Edwards, and Al Michaels. A fiery Irishman, McAndrews is remembered as a tough taskmaster given to penalizing lazy or otherwise rambunctious athletes with the loss of their training meal. His warning cry was famous: "I'll break your plate," or sometimes "I'll turn your plate." He meant it.

From 1936, when Bezdek was fired, until the appointment of Carl P. Schott in 1937 as dean rather than director of the School of Physical Education and Athletics, the intercollegiate program was supervised by a committee—Dr. E. C. Davis, Professor F. L. Bentley (chairman of the Senate Committee on Athletics), and Neil M. Fleming, graduate manager of athletics. Dr. Schott, formerly head of physical education at West Virginia University, had little experience with intercollegiate athletics. By the late thirties the football staff had reached full strength, with Jack Hulme as trainer (brought from Westminster by basketball coach John Lawther), boxing coach Leo Houck as freshman trainer, and three graduate assistants—Dan DeMarino, John Economos, and Wendell Wear.

Mentioned in 1940 preseason ratings as high as thirteenth nationally, the Lions responded by winning their first five games, unheard of since 1922. Good feeling pervaded the hard-working squad. During one long practice scrimmage a manager serving as a timer blew his whistle. "Quarter, Coach," he called. "All right," Bob said. "Everybody take a deep breath." He paused. "Now let's play."

The bubble nearly burst in Archbold Stadium at Syracuse, where the Lions have spent many a sad afternoon. Despite precision passing by fullback Bill Smaltz (14 in 21 for 193 yards and 12 completions in a row), with 4 minutes remaining Penn State trailed 13–6 and was in possession of the ball on its own 47. As Smaltz dropped back to his 40, Coach Ossie Solem and everyone else on the Syracuse bench expected a pass to Lenny Krouse, who had already caught 9. Bill wanted to cross up the defense by throwing to Chuck Peters because Syracuse had double coverage on Krouse. But when the moment came, Bill knew he *had* to go to the wingback. Well covered on the 3-yard line, Krouse leaped for a pass that traveled 57 yards in the air, caught it on his fingertips, and, with presence enough to circle around the Syracuse players, fought his way over the line. Syracuse fans claimed he hadn't made the last line when tackled, but the referee signaled a touchdown. The kick tying the score at 13–13 was made by Ben Pollock, one of the first of the modern extra-point specialists, who made 24 in 31 over 3 years.

Chuck Peters would do all right anyhow. In 1940, he established two Penn State records, returning the opening kickoff 101 yards against NYU in New York and achieving a season's average for kickoff returns of 52.2 yards.

Hearts were heavy after the Pitt game, and bowl hopes evaporated. The Panthers broke open a fairly even first half with two touchdowns in the final periods to win, 20–7. Twelve seniors had some solace because the season had been Penn State's best in nineteen years. Most were members of the forward wall called "The Seven Mountains"—a nickname suggested by Paul N. Hunsberger '25 and first used in the *Football Letter*. The "Seven Mountains" (a range southeast of the campus) were, from left end to right end: Lloyd Parsons, Carl Stravinski, Mike Garbinski, Leon Gajecki, Wade Mori, Frank Platt, and Tom Vargo. Walt Kniaz often substituted for Platt. Gajecki was named center on the NEA All-America, the first Penn Stater to be recognized on an All-America team since Joe Bedenk in 1924.

The 1940 team was cited for "poise and pride," and its backs had plenty of both. Patrick's capable understudy was Paul (Manny) Weaver of Harrisburg; Hank Day frequently relieved Petrella and Peters at tailback; Krouse and Craig White were almost equal as wingbacks; Smaltz got help from Ralph Ventresco and sophomore Earl (Sparky) Brown of Cazenovia, New York.

At this time President Hetzel had trouble over interpretations of his attitude toward football. Remarks he made at the 1939 football banquet were repeated before a group of alumni in Pittsburgh in 1940, where most of the aftergaff originated. Trying to position the game properly in the educational pattern, Dr. Hetzel said:

> In rejoicing with you because of the excellent performance of our football team this year, I want to go on record as saying that I hope we are not going to expect, or to have, teams that always win. Nothing so impairs the spirit of good sportsmanship as habitual victory. It is bound to bring in its wake the demoralizing influences which have done so much to injure this great sport on American college campuses.

After the Pittsburgh speech, the President was awakened by a late-night phone call. He was asked if he meant he didn't want the Lions to win any more. His reply was:

> I think college football represents a fairly competitive force in our academic life and it doesn't seem to me that universities of the same size with the same resources should ordinarily expect to win year after year.

Not bad for a pajama-clad president standing in a cold room in the middle of the night.

Nationally in the 1930s the big teams were Alabama, Notre Dame, Southern California, Michigan, Minnesota, Southern Methodist, Pittsburgh, TCU, and Texas A&M. The best were Wallace Wade's last Alabama team (1930); Howard Jones' elevens at Southern California in 1931 and 1932; Southern Methodist in 1935; and Pittsburgh in 1937. The Mustangs won all of their tough twelve-game schedule, then lost to Stanford in the Rose Bowl, 7–0. The air cleared a bit when the Associated Press began naming a national champion in 1936, but partisan buffs continued to argue through the winter. Minnesota, Pittsburgh, TCU, and Texas A&M were the first four AP champions.

Following an unusual number of casualties in 1931, significant rule changes began to make the game "safer." Equipment safeguards were addded in 1932 and flying tackles and flying blocks prohibited, along with slugging "about the head, neck, and face," for which the penalty was expulsion and loss of half the distance to the goal line. Clipping was broadened to include diving into a defensive player's back, with the penalty reduced from 25 to 15 yards "to encourage enforcement." On kickoffs and free kicks at least five men on the receiving team had to remain within 15 yards of the restraining line to prevent mass interference from forming. To discourage piling on, the ball was declared dead when any part of a player holding it touched the ground, except his hands and feet.

Endless, sometimes bizarre changes in substitution rules, culminating finally in the two-platoon system now in disfavor with some coaches, also began in 1932. A player removed in one quarter could re-enter the game in the next but only during an official's time-out. Since this rule didn't apply to an injured player, there were many "fake injuries," some notorious.

A defensive team's infraction on try-for-point plays in 1931 gave the kicking team the point even if it was missed, but later the penalty was made loss of half the distance to the goal line, and the kicker tried again.

Wearing numerals on both back and front of jerseys was adopted in 1937, but kicking technicalities predominated in the changes at that time. A second kickoff was not allowed if the kicked ball went out of bounds, the receiving team instead taking possession on its 35-yard line. A free ball kicked on the ground, regardless of intent, became a foul, and a kicked ball failing to cross the scrimmage line could be recovered or advanced by either side. Previously the kicking team could recover but not advance it.

Hashmarks, established ten yards from the sidelines in 1933, were moved to 15 yards in 1938. In a reversal of philosophy to encourage passing, a slightly smaller ball had been adopted in 1934, and in

1939 on forward-pass plays ineligible receivers could not advance beyond the line of scrimmage until the pass was thrown. Also in that year the ball had to be put in play in 25 seconds instead of 30.

Penn State's auspicious beginning of the 1940s seemed threatened by losses to Colgate and Temple in two of the first three 1941 outings, but the season was more than salvaged by six straight victories, something that hadn't happened since 1912.

Wrecking a good 1941 Syracuse team, the Lions throttled Ossie Solem's brand-new "system" designed to surprise Cornell earlier in the season. The key to Solem's scheme was a reverse center, who could pass accurately to flankers on either end of a Y formation by turning his back on the opposition and facing his own backs. After his shovel-like pass the center became a fifth back and an effective blocker.

The system bewildered Cornell at first, but Syracuse had trouble with the officials, who saw illegal maneuvers and ruled that part of center Ken Beehner's anatomy was offside. Losing 6–0 didn't discourage Coach Solem. He eliminated some questionable features but kept his reverse center and Y formation, to the consecutive confusion of Holy Cross, NYU, Rutgers, and Wisconsin. Running to the outside consistently, Syracuse backs had averaged more than 300 yards a game, and the Orange came to New Beaver Field having only the Cornell defeat to mar its record. With the Y approaching the rank of Clark Shaughnessy's Stanford T as part of American football lore, a large Syracuse contingent was confident of upsetting the Lions.

The antidote for the Y and reverse center is credited to Assistant Coach Earle Edwards, who had scouted Syracuse and noted that center Beehner generally beat a track to the ball carrier. At Edwards' suggestion, guard Johnny Jaffurs had orders to keep on top of the center's stern and trail him closely. Jaffurs—weighing only 180 pounds but fast, tough, and resourceful—had a field day in the first half and may have set nearly a world's record for solo tackles. When he tired, having become almost the sixth member of the Syracuse backfield, the harassment was continued by Lou Palazzi (now a leading NFL official). Guards Ken Kratske and Jim Bonham, center Bob Wear, tackles Ken Schoonover and Mike "Double Bubble" Kerns, ends Johnny Potsklan, Bucky Walters, and Wilbur Van Lenten all accomplished their assigned missions on a beautiful afternoon for

Lion defenders. Two Syracuse scores came late in the game when, much to the home crowd's amusement, Coach Solem reverted to the standard single wing. Before another year the vigilant Rules Committee made the reverse center illegal.

Scoring the highest point total by either team in the twenty-game series, Penn State's offense matched its classic defensive showing, gaining 300 yards by rushing and passing. "Dyna-mite" Petrella made two touchdowns in the first half, Bill Debler added another, and Krouse scored on a pass from Smaltz for a startling 27–0 margin after two quarters. The Lions went ahead 34–7 in the final period before the frustrated visitors narrowed the gap with a late passing attack. The final score was 34–19. The untraditional finale was the South Carolina game at Columbia, but the highlight and Number One objective was the fray in Pittsburgh, where the Lion coach, as Captain Bob Higgins, had led Penn State to its last previous triumph over Pitt twenty-two years before.

Pitt alumni were inclined to be hopeful because a mediocre Panther season had come to life by ending Fordham's Rose Bowl hopes (13–0) and surprising Nebraska, 14–7. Ten minutes after the game began, Pitt's Edgar "Special Delivery" Jones broke away for 43 yards to score on a weak-side reverse, getting the ball from Bill Dutton. The play had been expected, and Penn State had practiced against it daily.

Pitt's hope of redeeming its season was then dashed by a devastating attack featuring the running of Petrella and Captain Krouse, and the passing and kicking of Smaltz, who made the only field goal of his career. John "Pepper" Petrella of Downingtown, Pennsylvania—the leading ground-gainer and top star, playing his final season—scored three touchdowns, with the fourth made by Ralph Ventresco, a reserve fullback. Pepper's role in the 31–7 victory recalled the winning 1919 performance of another Downingtown player, Charlie Way.

A Penn State student from Pittsburgh, in the press box as a sports assistant for the Public Information Department, had trouble maintaining a professional demeanor when the Lions were piling up points in the second half. Finally his restraint gave way and he fervently remarked to the man beside him, "Boy, oh, boy! I've been waiting all my life for this!" Harold W. (Zez) Cohen '26, also a Pittsburgh Penn Stater but fifteen years his senior, surveyed him disdainfully. *"You've* been waiting! *You've* been waiting all your life!"

Cohen, now deceased, was the Pittsburgh *Post-Gazette*'s drama editor. The fledging, Robert H. Lane '41, is now Goodyear's vice president for public relations.

After Pitt, the Lions played South Carolina the Saturday after Thanksgiving before a cheering Carolina crowd constantly chanting "Awh team is red hot, awh team is red hot!" Hotter were the Lions. Petrella, Smaltz, and Krouse—the three seniors—were virtually unstoppable, with little Pepper netting 110 yards from scrimmage. The Smaltz-to-Krouse passing combination headlined the hard-fought 19–12 victory, Smaltz completing 10 of 15 passes, 8 to Krouse, who ended the season as the East's top receiver and third best nationally.

And on a younger level, things were looking up, too. With victories over Bucknell, Colgate, Syracuse, Cornell, and Army, Penn State's yearlings had their first undefeated season since 1916. Backfield stars Dave and Harry Alston of Midland High School (Ralph H. Jewell '29, principal) were Penn State's first black football players. Red Moore, Leo Nobile, and Steve Suhey, three who later played for the Pittsburgh Steelers, also showed varsity promise, along with Jeff Durkota, Cliff St. Clair, Ray Ulinski, Bob Weitzel, and John Wolosky. Dave Alston, the running leader, was the last of the drop kickers, demonstrating this "lost art" for an extra point against Colgate and another in the Cornell game. Following a touchdown against Colgate, Allen Davis, reserve halfback from Sharpsburg, went back in position to dropkick. The Colgate players yelled "It's a fake," not believing one team could have two drop kickers. Davis's kick was perfect.

The strong finish of the 1941 varsity and the exciting undefeated freshman squad loaded with potential stars stimulated local interest. Ready to promote practical support from the spontaneous enthusiasm were Assistant Coaches Edwards and Michaels, the crusading Casey Jones, and a number of State College citizens spearheaded by Howard L. "Pete" Stuart '22 and Robert Y. Edwards. The "Monday Morning Quarterbacks" evolved informally for a number of years but organized officially in 1941 and met regularly at Wednesday luncheons. With a membership now over three hundred, these town-and-gown boosters enjoy program co-operation from the football staff and maintain a State College Quarterback Club fund providing various forms of aid and recognition. An early treasurer of the fund was James H. Coogan '30, who became Penn State's sports information director in 1943.

The Nittany Lion mascot formally emerged at this time in a visible manifestation, endorsed by alumni and students. Accepting a gift of the Class of 1940, the Board of Trustees authorized adoption of the native mountain lion as Penn State's sports symbol and commissioned Heinz Warneke, noted sculptor, who was suggested by art professor Francis E. Hyslop. During the summer of 1942 Warneke carved the larger-than-life statue from a block of Indiana limestone at its campus site. Participants in dedicating the Nittany Lion Shrine on Homecoming Weekend included the one who had fathered the idea as an undergraduate.

The Nittany Lion was the flash inspiration of a born publicity man, H. D. "Joe" Mason '07, when he was a freshman on Penn State's 1904 baseball team playing at Princeton. He countered verbal threats of defeat by the Tigers with boasts about the king of beasts in the form of the mountain lions that once roamed Nittany Valley. Hunted by Indians and later settlers, the lions became extinct in the mid-1800s.

The Lions beat the Tigers that day, and Mason promoted the Nittany Lion in his sub rosa *Lemon* (issue of March 17, 1907). A period of confusion with the maned African species was climaxed in 1922 when Dick Hoffman '23 (now Dr. R. H. Hoffman of Corona Del Mar, California) became the first mascot on the field during the Syracuse game at the Polo Grounds, New York City. He put on the skin he had worn for a Penn State Players' production of Shaw's *Androcles and the Lion*. Lioning by his successor, Leon Skinner '27, was terminated by Coach Bezdek, who banished him as a bad omen. The native *felix concolor* (alias puma, panther, and cougar) prevailed when Penn State's sports mascot reappeared at games in the late 1930s, wearing the now familiar guise. The current mountain lion suit has evolved through various sartorial styles, and the antics of the Lion have changed through the years as interpreted by the many "occupants."

What World War II did to football showed immediately in the 1942 season. When the bombs dropped on Pearl Harbor eight days after the 1941 South Carolina game, elimination or curtailment of college football for the duration was predicted. Accelerated academic programs limited extracurricular activities not in tune with the war effort. Abbreviated athletic schedules were anticipated because gasoline and rubber shortages might cut attendance, but at Penn State, since enrollment was normal in 1942, a crippling loss of revenue at home games was not expected. Pittsburgh and Penn State scheduled an innovative doubleheader in Pittsburgh one week apart (November 21 and 28), the second game to be played for Army Relief, but for some reason the November 28 meeting was canceled.

The radio network organized by KDKA and Penn State in 1938 was dissolved prior to the 1942 season because the gasoline company sponsor had little gas to sell. A limited number of radio stations carried the Cornell, Syracuse, and Pitt games, and a strange situation developed at Ithaca. The game was played in rain, wind, and mud, resulting in little action and no scoring, but for "wartime security" a Washington edict made the mention of weather conditions unlawful on any radio broadcast. Mystified listeners and the play-by-play announcer were nervous wrecks by the end of the scoreless game.

The crippling blow dealt Coach Higgins was apparent when the players came on the field for the Bucknell opener. The armed forces had taken twenty, including six members of the 1941 varsity who had expected to return. Freshmen had been made eligible, but the squad totaled only thirty players, most of them in advanced ROTC or in some branch of the enlisted Reserves awaiting government call. Some were under the Selective Service age limit, and others were enrolled in courses considered "vital war production work."

The hard-fought Bucknell game was won (14–7) with an exciting 79-yard run by Sparky Brown (a short, stocky, prematurely bald junior), so nicknamed for his popular and valuable qualities. How he could run untackled for 79 yards, one yard short of the Penn State record, was unfathomable. His teammates kidded him about his lack of speed, pointing out that the referee followed the play down the field running almost sideways. Sparky was mortified until he learned that the ref was Ray Barbuti, Olymic 400-meter champion from Syracuse.

Most Penn State opponents had wartime problems, but nearly every game was highly competitive. The season's low at Morgantown, where the Mountaineers won 24–0, inspired the lead on the alumni *Football Letter:*

> Exactly seventeen years ago our Nittany Lions helped West Virginia dedicate its concrete stadium around Mountaineer Field. Saturday it fell in on them.

Excitement, drama, and a rags-to-riches angle regaled alumni Homecomers when Penn State won from Colgate 13–10 after the lead had changed four times. According to a story widely circulated the next week, Coach Higgins "dreamed" a play on Friday night to outdazzle the razzle-dazzle of Andy Kerr. Actually, the sleepless Hig planned the play in the early hours Saturday morning. Talking with Sunday visitors about the common view that a perfect play is one in which every player carries out his assignment unerringly, Bob explained that it works only "when the boys on the other team do what you plan for *them* to do."

The Higgins "dream play"—in his repertoire for several years but unused—was sent in after Colgate had gone ahead early, 3–0. Joe Colone, best known for his reliable punting, dropped back to his own 40, then threw a pass to left end Bucky Walters, who was facing his own goal line at a full stop on the Colgate 40 after cutting to the middle. Cliff St. Clair, right halfback, paced himself just right for Colone's perfectly timed pass. Walters drew the Colgate defenders to the middle, just as Coach Higgins had "dreamed," and when St. Clair took the handoff, running in front of Walters, St. Clair had a clear path to the goal line.

The hero of the final period was freshman Bobby Williams from Oliver High School in Pittsburgh. Small and unobtrusive, coming without fanfare, he had been promoted after a junior varsity game the week before in which he had completed twenty of thirty passes against Cornell. His first pass was intercepted, but he went in for another try when the Lions got behind, 10–6, with the ball on their 36. His pass traveled 45 yards in the air to St. Clair, who had outfaked the Colgate safety and cut to the right sideline. Taking it in full stride on the 20, St. Clair set out for the goal line with the explosive speed of the trackman he was.[1]

Although freshman Williams threw for the winning points against Colgate, and Harold Pratt, a tackle, entered the Bucknell game in the second period to become the first freshman on the Lion varsity since Bob Higgins in 1914, a youngster named Larry Joe (Lorenzo Giuseppe) took yearling honors in 1942. He scored a touchdown (9 yards) on his initial play against Bucknell; made the winning touchdown in the 13–7 defeat of Penn, covering 11, 14, and 9 yards in three consecutive runs from Penn's 34; and in the final victory over

[1] Williams, a valuable player on the 1947 team, is Greensburg High School's successful coach (his son Bob, Jr., entered Penn State on a grant-in-aid, but a severe shoulder injury ended his career). St. Clair is an attorney in Columbus, Ohio.

Pitt (14–6) broke a 0–0 tie by taking the second-half kickoff 90 yards for a score.

The fact that Penn officials had removed Penn State from future Red and Blue schedules was the theme of the stirring fight talk Coach Higgins gave his team in the dressing room before the game at Philadelphia. "Let's make them remember us," Bob pleaded. The Lions obeyed that impulse, upsetting the strongly favored conquerors of Harvard, Yale, Columbia, Army, and Cornell. The erudite Red Smith, then with the Philadelphia *Record,* was moved to write,

> In the face of appalling odds and bitter disappointment, these boisterous minors played with a sort of fierce gaiety that was like a violin bow across the heartstrings of the watchers.

While Larry Joe was the sentimental hero at Penn, it was lineman Ken Schoonover who made a key play in the first quarter to change the complexion of the game. He broke through to cleanly block LeRoy Pletz's punt on the Penn 39. Bob Davis picked up the rolling ball, nearly scored, but was tackled from behind by Bert Stiff. Sparky Brown's touchdown gave the Lions a lead, which was insured by Joe's heroics in the final period. The Higgins team had rebounded from the West Virginia disappointment to defeat its three keenest rivals—Syracuse (18–13), Penn, and Pitt—but for the first time in many years this Penn victory was sweeter than the season-ending triumph over Pittsburgh.

Despite losing a number of regulars to the service in 1942, football proceeded about as usual. Attendance at home and away games remained steady, and Coach Higgins effectively assimilated freshmen with his relatively few veterans. The 1943 season obviously held another challenge, with the campus dominated by over 2,500 servicemen in the Army, Navy, and Air Force programs. They filled many of the fraternity houses (leased to the government as barracks), marched "in singing cadence" along campus roads, and monopolized classrooms. At first, the administration questioned the idea of continuing football in wartime. Syracuse, Georgia, and Michigan State had discontinued it primarily because they lacked manpower. These scheduled opponents had been replaced by North Carolina, Cornell, and West Virginia. Coach Higgins wanted to field a team regardless of sparse material, arguing that the game would lift the morale of students, including servicemen on campus. Dozens of letters from Penn Staters, many of them overseas, urged him to keep on, and the cause received a boost when a number of former players who had been in advanced ROTC were permitted to return to campus (at their own expense) until the Army had space for them in Officer Candidate School. Back came Johnny Jaffurs, Red Moore, Aldo Cenci, and Sparky Brown. Probably the determining factor, however, was the Navy's strong feeling that its V-12 trainees would benefit from competitive sports *if* they could maintain satisfactory grades week by week. Conversely, the Army believed that the physical fitness of its trainees could be achieved more efficiently by its own typical mass-production methods.

Six hundred Navy V-12 servicemen were due, and the coaches had no idea what to expect. The all-Marine football group included one former Penn Stater, Bobby Williams, and other players of some experience from George Washington, Pittsburgh, Cincinnati, Dayton, Toledo, Western Reserve, and even out of Ohio State. Edward M. Czekaj of Mount Pleasant, Pennsylvania, an end from George Washington, returned to Penn State following the war and graduated in 1948, having played on the undefeated 1947 team.[2]

For Coach Higgins the year was rewarding and at times exasperating. He never knew who in his Marine contingent would be eligible, often not getting word until noon of a game day, nor did he know who suddenly might be transferred to another college. Tad Hapanowicz was lost to Pennsylvania and a week later faced a surprised Navy lineman.

"Where have I seen you before?" asked the Middie.

"I played against you two weeks ago in the Penn State game," replied Hapanowicz. He later attended the Naval Academy and the next season opposed his former Nittany Lion teammates. That was wartime football. Penn Staters were tickled when their squad was augmented by two former Pitt stars—Bill Abromitis (later an opponent at Navy) and Bill Kyle. With all the switches someone figured out that the government owed Penn State eight backs, nine linemen, a manager, and a scorecard.

Two of several civilian freshmen on the squad played regularly for the varsity—guard Bill Slobodnjak and tackle Marino Marchi. Charlie Stapel, a prize recruit from Avalon, Pennsylvania, was so badly injured that he saw service in only one game. Marine John Misie-

[2] After further service in Korea as a Marine Corps captain and three years on the Johns Hopkins athletic staff, he joined the business staff of Penn State's Athletic Department and advanced to athletic director in 1969.

wicz, like Czekaj, returned after the war and was on the 1949 team that played in the 1948 Cotton Bowl. Rowan (Tubby) Crawford, the best all-around athlete of the V-12 group, won letters in five sports, equaling a Penn State record set by Steve Hamas.

After the Pitt victory the Athletic Board commended Coach Higgins for the 5–3–1 season, continuing to attach major importance to the Pitt game. Higgins' three consecutive triumphs over the Panthers dimmed memories of Bob's early disastrous years.

28

Servicemen Depart; Veterans Return

Civilian freshmen outnumbered servicemen two to one on the 1944 squad in the third year of United States participation in World War II. Most of the Marines on hand when the season began were due to be shipped out on October 19, just before the fourth game (with Colgate). Whether the few V-5 Navy trainees could be retained for the full schedule was uncertain.

Over the next years the performance of these freshmen confirmed the judgment of Coach Higgins that they came better prepared than any he had ever seen. The newcomers included such future head-liners as Elwood Petchel, Bob Hicks, Negley Norton, John Simon, Johnny Chuckran, Larry Cooney, Al Bellas, Bronco Kosanovich, and Howard Caskey.

Chuckran, from Lansford, Pennsylvania, is now administrative assistant to Head Coach Paterno. A 1950 graduate with a Doctor of Education degree earned in 1969, he had been head coach at Allegheny College for twelve years before returning in 1970 as freshman coach and then offensive line coach. Larry Cooney was just 16 years old when he scored Penn State's first touchdown in the Cotton Bowl in 1948. John Simon was one of the "Brownsville Boys," of whom John Potsklan was the first, followed by John Wolosky. Later joined by Joe Drazenovich and then Chuck Drazenovich, they were prize acquisitions of Casey Jones, who had courted Earl Bruce, highly successful coach of Brownsville High School (Fayette County), with the help of Bruce's neighbor, Judge Vance Cottom '17. The five Brownsville players spent varying times in the service but became the nucleus of the undefeated Cotton Bowl eleven.

Recruiting in 1944, especially within the state, was easier than usual because many young men wanted to stay close to home until their draft numbers came up. Other colleges sought Pennsylvania talent, but not with the intensity of the present operation. Penn State coaches were hired on a nine-month basis, allowing them time for private ventures during the summer. Earle Edwards ran a camp in New Jersey and Al Michaels managed his fraternity house, rented out to summer students or conventioners. When Edwards returned to campus in late August a week before freshmen were to report, he found that no arrangements had been made to house the newly acquired talent. He quickly rented a fraternity house and, aided by Michaels, begged or borrowed furnishings. They persuaded one of the equipment men, Ralph Barnes, and his wife to live in the house as "overseers."

The unsettled year reached a low ebb when the Penn State Marines and freshmen were assaulted by Navy, 55–14, the highest score against a Penn State team in modern times. The starting center confronting the Midshipmen was a trainee, Chuck Klausing, now assistant coach at West Virginia. The first and second Lion teams had twelve freshmen and little else, but Navy Coach Oscar Hagberg poured in wave after wave of his four or five teams, all awash with an astonishing array of former college stars. Navy and Army had "honeymoon seasons" in 1944, 1945, and 1946, meeting college teams made up chiefly of 4-Fs (young men turned down by the military for physical reasons) and freshmen.

In 1944 the young Lions bravely fought a Navy team rebounding from a defeat the previous week by North Carolina Pre-Flight, coached by Glenn Killinger.[1]

---

[1] Navy's stars that season included Ralph Ellsworth of Texas; Fred Earley, Bob Hoernchemeyer, and Bob Kelly of Notre Dame; Clyde Scott of Arkansas; and Bill Abromitis of Pitt and Penn State. The Midshipmen also boasted three All-Americas in tackle Don Whitmire, guard Ben Chase, and halfback Bobby Jenkins, but Navy met its match against an Army team considered Colonel Red Blaik's greatest. Inspired by the sensational playing of two plebes—Doc Blanchard and Glenn Davis—Army spent a merry autumn trampling over its

Penn State's Marines left as expected before the Colgate trip, and seventeen of the twenty-one players were freshmen, eight of them starters. Johnny Chuckran, the first and only freshman accorded the honor of being elected captain, was the hero of the game, breaking a scoreless tie with 30 seconds to play by returning a punt 50 yards in the mud and rain. The 6–0 victory was a surprise. Colgate had beaten Cornell the previous week and outplayed Penn State until the sudden end. At the final whistle, the unseasoned freshmen momentarily stood in their places, unsure how to react; then they reached for Chuckran and carried him off the field.

Syracuse, having no service programs, was harder hit than most colleges during the war. After a year of no football at all (1943), the Orange resumed play in 1944 and probably wished it hadn't. Not until Coach Ben Schwartzwalder's third year (1951) did Syracuse come up with a winning season. To "outman" anyone was a novelty for the Lions in those days, but that's what happened when the two old rivals met in 1944. All Penn State's starters were freshmen, and on the second team (at blocking back) was ex-Sergeant Nick Ranieri, first war veteran to return. An unknown freshman tailback on the third team, Andy Pipa, became an effective passer, to the delight of poetry aficionados in the press corps. On this trip North when the team bus passed a burning barn in Homer, New York, Coach Higgins let the boys join a bucket brigade putting out the fire. The next afternoon the Lion brigade doused Syracuse at Archbold Stadium, 41–0.

Freshmen from West Virginia and Penn State played a dazzling varsity game, with the Mountaineers' ace passer, Jimmy Walthall, giving his team a 28–27 edge in the first home loss for the Lions since the Lafayette defeat in 1938. In addition to Syracuse and Colgate, victims of the Lions were Muhlenberg (58–0), Bucknell (28–6), Temple (7–6), and Maryland (34–19), but Pitt spoiled an otherwise respectable season by winning, 14–0. Injuries depleted Coach Higgins' team, leaving only four available running backs, all under 160 pounds: Petchel, Pipa, Cooney, and Harry Muckle.

Under the GI Bill a number of veterans appeared for the 1945 season, including some with unfamiliar names. Among the first was Joe Tepsic, an ex-Marine wounded at Guadalcanal, who made the

weakly manned traditional opponents: Notre Dame, 59–0; Pittsburgh, 69–7; and Pennsylvania, 62–7. The Coast Guard Academy was smacked down, 76–0, and Villanova battered, 83–0.

varsity immediately and was sought, according to rumors, by pro baseball scouts. Two new freshmen of promise were end Sam Tamburo and Wally Triplett, a halfback.

Penn State had the uneasy distinction of meeting Navy's star-laden team in a game at Annapolis celebrating the one-hundredth anniversary of the Academy's founding. Nothing happened to spoil the Middies' birthday party, the Lions giving up two touchdowns on blocked kicks and two on interceptions for a final score of 28–0. One Lion is said to have grumbled because he had expected to see Navy's players numbered from 1 to 99, but didn't like it when they came at him numbered 1a, 2a, etc. Between halves the small band of Penn State rooters in the end zone, led by Assistant Graduate Manager "Ike" Gilbert, cordially sang "Happy Birthday, Dear Navy, Happy Birthday to You."

It was a season for anniversaries—or near misses. To celebrate Bucknell's hundredth, Penn State had agreed to a game in Lewisburg, but learned between the halves that an embarrassing miscalculation had been made: It was only the ninety-ninth birthday. Except for the Navy defeat, the team sailed victoriously through games with Muhlenberg (47–7), Colgate (27–7), Bucknell (46–7), Syracuse (26–0), and Temple (27–0). Uncalled-for optimism was evident before the Michigan State game when alumni in Michigan held a pregame luncheon at the Student Union in East Lansing. Michigan State's dean of agriculture Ernest L. Anthony, formerly of Penn State's faculty, welcomed the visitors with the gracious remark that he wouldn't mind if the game ended in a tie. Assembled alumni never forgot the reply of Dean Carl Schott. Confidently stating that "our team is big, they are strong, they are fast," he turned to the previous speaker and said emphatically, "And let me tell you, Dean Anthony, Penn State will not settle for a tie." That afternoon the Spartans won, 33–0.

The next week at Pittsburgh the game followed a pattern prevalent in those years—the favored team seldom won. An 84-yard punt return by Jimmy Robinson in the first quarter was all the Panthers needed to win, 7–0. Alumni murmurs, dormant during the war years, caused Coach Higgins to observe that most people think they can do three things better than anyone else—"build a fire, run a hotel, and coach a football team."

After the Penn State game, Pitt's coach, Clark Shaughnessy, returned to Maryland, which he had left in 1942. During the T master's stormy Pittsburgh regime he had even antagonized Panther alumni in 1945 by dressing the team in scarlet. Having lost six successive games, he abruptly switched back to the traditional blue and gold just before the Lions came to town. Nittany Lion supporters claimed this gave their rivals an insurmountable psychological advantage. Anyhow, color was not the issue. Shaughnessy left Pitt because authorities there objected to his advisory connections with pro football.

To accommodate the number of war veterans returning to college campuses in 1946, Penn State worked out a novel co-operative arrangement with several state teachers' colleges, where the enrollment pressure was less acute. Coach Bob Higgins saw immediately that the plan to "farm out" freshmen for one year would be a serious obstacle to football. Receiving the news just before he left for an Army football clinic in Japan, he warned the other coaches of catastrophe.

Assistant Coach Edwards hit upon an idea that saved Penn State football. Working with his friend Ed Cubbon, athletic director at California Teachers, he secured an arrangement placing all Lion freshman football recruits at California, Pennsylvania. Higgins, enthusiastic about the plan, went with Casey Jones to visit Earl Bruce, the Brownsville High School coach, and convinced him (without too much trouble) to take the freshman coaching job. By agreement with Cubbon, Bruce was assigned to California, although Penn State paid his salary. Ted Nemeth, a Penn State graduate and former player, was hired by California as Bruce's assistant, and succeeded him as head coach when Earl came to the main campus in 1950. During the twenty years Bruce was freshman coach, his teams were undefeated seven times. His wide acquaintance in western Pennsylvania made him a valuable recruiter, and he is credited with attracting Richie Lucas from Glassport, All-America quarterback in 1959, and Steve Garban of Grindstone, captain and center in 1958. (Lucas is now business manager of athletics and Garban is the university controller.)

Previously a school without a team, California rose to become a small-college football power, won the state college 1946 championship with a 9–0–0 record, and even had a few bowl feelers, which wisely were ignored. This team produced such outstanding varsity players from 1947 through 1949 as Francis Rogel, Chuck Beatty, Fred Felbaum, Paul Kelly, Bob Ross, Clarence Hummel, John (Duck) Murray, and Clarence Gorinsky. The California co-operative plan continued through the 1949 season, although football recruits were not concentrated at a single school after 1946.

On the main campus, where most players had been living in rented fraternity houses for several years, it became increasingly difficult, as fraternities were reactivated, to find suitable quarters. Casey Jones and a few other Pittsburgh alumni solved the problem by raising $19,000 to purchase the Hamilton Avenue house of Theta Kappa Phi, which had merged with the Phi Kappa fraternity. Coach Jim O'Hora, in his first year on the staff, was installed as "counselor" and manager, since he had not yet moved his family to State College.

The players, most of them veterans, were expected to keep the house in reasonable order, but discipline was difficult. Discovering that simple housekeeping staples like cleaning supplies and toilet paper were always overlooked, Manager O'Hora negotiated with a friendly campus custodian to have a "package" of necessities delivered weekly. All survived. In 1949 this living arrangement was discontinued, players went to campus residence halls and fraternities, and the football house was sold to a fraternity.

Captain Red Moore led thirteen GIs back from the war to give the 1946 season a promising outlook, but optimistic observers failed to consider how long these young men had been away from football. For Larry Joe, John Potsklan, and Paul (Manny) Weaver it had been five years; four years for Joe Colone, Jeff Durkota, Leo Nobile, Steve Suhey, Bucky Walters, and Bob Weitzel; three for Ed Czekaj, Moore, and Bobby Williams; and two for Elwood Petchel. Still, Larry Joe substituted in the Bucknell opener, a 48–6 victory, as if he had never been away, carrying the ball on five plays for three touchdowns and 73 yards. Petchel netted 97 yards for three scores in 14 plays.

A game with the University of Miami (Florida) to be played at Miami on November 29 was on the schedule until midseason, when Penn State canceled. Miami officials had requested that black players not be included on the squad because "it would be difficult to carry out arrangements for the game." Penn State replied that policy permitted the team to compete only under circumstances where all members could play.

Penn State was surprised to win at Annapolis, 12–7, but Navy had lost most of its college transfers in 1946, and many games, too, under a new coach, Tom Hamilton. (The Middies, however, threw a

Dick Harlow '12, head coach 1915–17.

Undefeated Team of 1921

FRONT ROW: Stan McCollum, Harry (Light Horse) Wilson, R. A. (Squeak) Hufford, J. S. (Tiny) McMahan, Captain George Shell, Glenn Killinger, Joe Bedenk, Newsh Bentz, Joe Lightner. TOP ROW: Coach Hugo Bezdek, Pete Redlinger, Al Knabb, Ray Baer, Lee Hills, Ed Smozinsky, T. H. Ritner, Manager L. M. Forncrook.

Star-studded Bench in 1918

(Photograph taken during the first year of Coach Hugo Bezdek's regime, a home game with Rutgers.) Third from the left is Dr. Joe Ritenour, team physician; next, Neil M. Fleming, graduate manager of athletics; President Edwin Erle Sparks; Kenneth B. Kirk '20, football manager.

Charles A. Way '20, All-America halfback.

W. Glenn Killinger, in devil-may-care hairdo, was another All-America halfback (1921) and is in the College Football Hall of Fame.

Harry E. (Light Horse) Wilson '24, All-America halfback, 1923.

August (Iron Mike) Michalske '26 was a guard and fullback, 1923–25, and well named. He was the first Penn Stater elected to the Professional Football Hall of Fame.

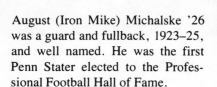

Robert A. (Bob) Higgins '18, head coach 1930–48.

Joe Bedenk '24, head coach 1949.

Charles A. (Rip) Engle, head coach 1950–65.

Steve Suhey's many contributions to Penn State football include his All-America honors in 1947 as a guard and his several sons, playing in this era.

Lenny Moore '56 was Varsity halfback (1953–55), went on to the pro ranks and into the Professional Football Hall of Fame (1975).

mighty scare into the final Blanchard-Davis Army team, succumbing 21–18 with the ball on Army's 5 in the final moments.)

Although most Penn Staters think Richard Nixon was the first
President to discriminate when he prematurely awarded the national
championship to Texas in 1969, Harry Truman preceded RMN as
an anti-Lion by twenty-three years. Before the Navy game, he told
the Brigade of Midshipmen,

> I think it will be a privilege for me to see Navy beat Penn State
> this afternoon. I am counting on you to do it.

Between halves (with Penn State leading 12–0) President Truman
not only missed a courtesy call from Penn State's President Hetzel,
but wasn't present to hear the Blue Band's rendition of "Missouri
Waltz." HST was in the Navy dressing room giving the players a pep
talk.

At midseason 1946, the Dunkel ratings had Penn State and Navy
tied at sixth place in the East, while the season ran its course true to
form with another massive rhubarb at Syracuse and a tantalizing
fizzle in Pitt Stadium. Coaches Higgins and Biggie Munn argued before the night game at Syracuse, Munn maintaining that Penn State's
white jerseys were unacceptable because the ball was white. Both
thought they had lost the argument: Higgins had his players wear
blue, and Munn had his manager darken the ball. When the game
started in the rain, everybody was furious all over again, and the
press had a fine time reporting it. The Lions won, 9–0, on Ed
Czekaj's field goal and a touchdown pass, Williams to Durkota.

Pitt, coached by Wesley Fesler, was the underdog against Penn
State, but Carl DePasqua and Bimbo Cecconi beat the Lions, 14–7,
something they couldn't do as Panther coaches some years later. The
attendance of 50,000 was a record for the series.

Justifiable confidence pervaded Nittany Valley in 1947. There
were fourteen holdover lettermen, a half dozen or more strong candidates from the California Teachers freshman group, nine returning
war veterans who had previously lettered, and such promising newcomers as Bill Luther and Dennie Hoggard. Selecting his first-team
backfield was pleasantly tough for Coach Higgins. He had four tailbacks (Petchel, Williams, Chuckran, and Luther), three fullbacks
(Colone, Weitzel, and Rogel), and three wingbacks (Triplett, Durkota, and Cooney).

At a time when opening the season with a major opponent wasn't customary, the cross-country visit of the Washington State Cougars aroused unusual excitement. Pressure from Harrisburg alumni and possibly some political persuasion caused a change in the game's locale from campus to Hershey Park Stadium, where it was played on Saturday night, September 20. The Lions lived up to their notices by winning handily, 27–6, with Larry Joe, Jeff Durkota, and Wally Triplett leading a 300-yard running attack.

The Lions next rolled up 169 points against Bucknell, Fordham, and Syracuse while holding their opponents scoreless. Placed second to Army in the East by the Lambert ratings, Penn State was ranked as high as ninth nationally. The experts began that familiar chorus about a "weak schedule" after marginal victories over West Virginia (21–14) and Temple (7–0).

If the 1947 team had a weak schedule, its quality in comparison with the nation's top teams was indisputable, as the Southern Methodist game in the Cotton Bowl later indicated. Defensively superb, the Lions set three NCAA records still in the books (as of 1976), allowing their opponents to average only .64 yards per rush and 17 yards per game by rushing. They set a third record in holding Syracuse to minus 47 yards by rushing and passing.

A fairly severe earthquake recorded on Fordham University's seismograph was reported in the New York *World* on Saturday afternoon, October 11. It could have been local. The Nittany Lions were whomping Fordham 75–0 at the Polo Grounds. A record forty points scored in the second quarter made the dismayed Ram fans yearn for Alex Wojciechowicz and the other "Six Blocks of Granite."

Undefeated before their game at Penn State, the West Virginia Mountaineers had accumulated 204 points against their first four opponents, and went ahead 14–0 in the first period with their ace passer, Jimmy Walthall, throwing from all over the field. Sophomore Rogel's 114 yards and Triplett's clutch running and pass receiving enabled the home team to go ahead, 21–14, in the final period after missing many other opportunities to score.

In a mud-mired game at Temple Stadium, the Lions were saved from a graceless defeat only by pounding out a 49-yard drive in the third quarter, a few yards at a time. For 16 straight plays Rogel and Williams alternated carrying the ball, with the latter finally scoring the game's only touchdown (score: 7–0). Penn State had been ranked first in the East and about fifth nationally before that troubled session. Temple came close to humiliating the undefeated Lions with a modern version of the old hidden-ball trick. Early in the game, end Joe Lee succeeded in getting loose for 46 yards on an end-around play before he was tackled from behind on the State 15 by John Potsklan. How did Lee get the ball? Coach Higgins and his players were mystified until several days later, when the movies revealed that Temple's quarterback took the ball fom the center and sat on it until Lee arrived. Temple called it the setting-hen play.

A 20–7 victory over Navy in Baltimore almost forced the critics— and the bowl pickers—to recognize Penn State, although the Cotton Bowl invitation didn't arrive until well after the Pitt game. Navy's record was spotty, but the Midshipmen had beaten Cornell, tied Duke, and lost to Georgia Tech by only two points. Having played an all-major schedule, they tried psychology against the Lions. The linemen taunted, "Penn State, you're not in the minor league now!" The chatter boomeranged, as did Coach Tom Hamilton's ill-advised five-man line, which allowed Penn State's reverses to function perfectly. Jeff Durkota scored twice on runs of 48 and 42 yards, the plays made possible by the ability of Sam Tamburo, offensive end, to block the opposing tackle, Navy's big Dick Shimshack. Excellent blocks also were made by Steve Suhey and John Nolan. The game's longest run—Larry Joe's 59 yards to Navy's thirteen—led to Penn State's third touchdown. Potsklan, right end, and Chuck Drazenovich, blocking back who played the full sixty minutes, were the top defensive players.

After the final 29–0 victory over Pitt, a long-time dream was fulfilled for Bob Higgins when he was carried from the field by players and fans. The 1947 team had the first undefeated, untied regular season in thirty-five years, and the best defensive record in the nation. Only Michigan scored more points. Steve Suhey, who later became Coach Higgins' son-in-law, made guard on *Collier's* All-America team.

President Hetzel did not live to see the upswing of Penn State football and the coming erosion of his espoused nonsubsidization policy. His death suddenly on October 3, 1947, shocked the campus community, which was adjusting that autumn to the double effects of the ex-GI Education Act and an above-normal volume of civilian students. Enrollment had reached 10,600, a figure he had not foreseen as likely in his time when he took office 21 years before with under 5,000 on the campus.

Within a framework of national and world crises—the 1929 crash, the Great Depression of the 1930s, and the World War II upheaval —Dr. Hetzel maneuvered physical plant expansion and some easing of faculty deprivation. Like all Penn State presidents, he was plagued by the commonwealth's disregard of its responsibility to provide adequate appropriations for its public state land-grant university, the first and foremost in the Northeast. Consequently, admission had to be selective, and tuition increases became as inevitable as they were unseemly.

Under Hetzel's steady guidance, Penn State specifically made undergraduate extension centers (now its Commonwealth Campuses) available when students couldn't afford college away from home and the state had ignored the junior college idea; had plans ready for overdue buildings when the federal Public Works Administration (PWA) and the Pennsylvania General State Authority (GSA) were set up to provide two-way relief; mobilized its extension services for a federal Engineering, Science, Management War Training program (ESMWT), among the nation's largest; adopted an emergency trimester academic year to accelerate and increase undergraduate instructional capability; and developed new fields of practical research aid for the state through institutes of local government, driver training, business research, labor education, and textile chemistry research. The U. S. Agriculture Department established a northeastern states Regional Pasture Research Laboratory on campus, and the Defense Department moved its Ordnance Research Laboratory from Harvard.

Accepting terms as president of the American Association of State and Land-Grant Universities and of Pennsylvania's Association of College and University Presidents, Dr. Hetzel projected Penn State's identity among the academics. Confusion became a little less persistent about its location (central Pennsylvania, rather than Philadelphia) and about the significance of land-grant education, the scope of which is less understood on the Atlantic Seaboard than in the rest of the country.

While the trustees sought a successor of similar quality, for 2½ years, Judge James Milholland '11 of Pittsburgh, then president of the board, served as acting president of the university.

29

Breakthrough Bowl

The 1947 Pitt victory climaxed a twenty-five-year climb back to national prominence, but an invitation from any bowls in the South seemed unlikely with two black players on the squad—Wally Triplett and Dennie Hoggard. Penn State's initiation into these rites began when Cotton Bowl officials called Coach Higgins direct. Was he interested? Of course, but what about the black players? Texas would be first to break this barrier in the South. Would Penn State accept if invited? Yes, was the answer after everyone was polled. Then came the official invitation and the announcement that Penn State would meet powerful Southern Methodist and the invincible Doak Walker on New Year's Day.

Hysteria gripped students and alumni. Tickets trapped athletic officials into the first mistake. Informed that Fordham, the last eastern team to play in the Cotton Bowl, had requested 800 tickets at that time, they felt sure 1,000 would take care of everyone and encouraged inquirers to order any number. Then came an avalanche of applications by wire, phone, mail, and walk-ins. Phone calls to Dallas for more and more halted at an absolute limit of 3,000 tickets, but handling applications for over 20,000 required decisions bound to foment ill will. Student leaders accepted a plan to allot 1,500 to undergraduates by lottery, with the remainder going to alumni, less those needed for official purposes and for the players. It was estimated that one alumnus in every ten had been disappointed, including many living in the Dallas area.

The players, hard at football since August 15, relaxed during the short Thanksgiving recess, but the glamor of the coming bowl trip began to wear off when practice resumed. The weather was miserable, there were no indoor facilities, no Astroturf, and few spectators. The saving thought was playing a bowl game, with all the trimmings to dream about—southern hospitality, lovely Texas girls, and gala receptions.

Cotton Bowl officials were handicapped by inexorable local laws and customs. Since Coach Higgins wanted all players together, and blacks could not even enter Dallas hotels, the squad had to stay at a naval air station fourteen miles from the city. Entertainment on the base couldn't compensate for the anticipated bowl frills so much a part of present postseason festivities. The players found themselves behind a guarded fence, eating service chow in a mess hall, and almost engulfed by hated military restrictions, which most of them thought were behind them forever. Sick of rigid discipline and regulations, the ex-GIs understandably allowed their perspective to become warped and didn't try to distinguish the important from the petty.

Sensing their discontent, Coach Higgins relaxed discipline slightly and made some concessions, but resentment and defiance didn't subside. Some broke training and some went "over the hill" by climbing the fence or finding other ways to get into Dallas. Typical of how the northern press magnified the situation was a Boston *Herald* column by Bill Cunningham, who unfairly placed all blame on the players. Actually, mistakes were made by administration, coaching staff, and players as the result of an unprecedented racial situation and inexperienced management.

No player *consciously* failed to give his best, but mental attitude had much to do with listless play in the first half. Except for one drive that ended on the Mustangs' 11, featuring line hitting by 180-pound sophomore Franny Rogel and Colone's superior punting, the Lions did nothing outstanding until late in the second quarter. SMU had elated its strong following in the opening period when the popular Doak Walker completed a touchdown pass to Paul Page, the play starting on the Mustangs' 43. After his second touchdown following a 19-yard run by Dick McKissack to Penn State's 3, Walker, who seldom made a mistake, missed the extra point when he was rushed hard by center John Wolosky. The miss seemed unimportant at the time—the only question was how high SMU would run up the count on the disorganized Lions.

The 13–0 score didn't bother Elwood Petchel. The smallest player on the field became a giant to Lion supporters on this cold and cloudy afternoon in front of the whooping Texans. With only two minutes of the half remaining, he passed successfully to end Bob Hicks on the SMU 47. Trapped trying to pass on the next play, he scooted 15 yards, then tossed a short pass to Triplett. Following a 5-yard penalty, Elwood threw a pass to Larry Cooney, who had outrun the defensive halfback on the Mustang 10. Ed Czekaj's placement for a 13–7 half-time score added sparkle to the game.

In the second half the Lions finally realized that the game could be won and that Doak Walker was mortal. Rogel carried three times in a row for a total gain of 26 yards and a first down on the 15. The Texans stopped this advance less than a yard from the goal, but Petchel returned Ed Green's punt 25 yards to the 9. Rogel plunged for 5, and on third down Petchel passed for a touchdown to Triplett in the left corner of the end zone. Missing the important extra point has exposed Penn State's athletic director, Ed Czekaj, to no end of latter-day ribbing. The players thought his kick was good, and when Ed left the game in misery, Coach Higgins asked him if it was. "I don't know, Coach, you always told me to keep my head down," replied Ed, whose consolation was that the great Doak Walker had also missed one.

Penn State outplayed Southern Methodist for the remainder of the game—statistics showed the Lions ahead in total yards, 273–215, while outrushing the Mustangs nearly 2–1. With seconds to play and time for one more pass, Petchel had both Triplett and Hoggard behind their defenders in the end zone. The line of scrimmage was the SMU 37, but his pass was thrown from the 45. The ball, obscured from the receivers and deflected by a defender, bounced off Hoggard's chest, giving him no chance to catch it. Twenty-four years later, Hoggard and his wife were guests of Czekaj at Penn State's Cotton Bowl headquarters in the Fairmont Hotel, Dallas. "I like having you around, Dennie," said Czekaj. "Maybe these people will forget that point I missed and remember the ball that bounced off your chest." No disaster—they had played to a 13–13 tie.

No "Outstanding Player" was selected in the 1948 Cotton Bowl, but the five players cited as the game stars were Doak Walker and two of the Mustang tricaptains, Sid Halliday and Earl Cooks, plus Petchel and Steve Suhey. Lion followers felt that Elwood Petchel deserved special honor. The 145-pounder (whose son Woody was on the 1975 varsity) passed for two touchdowns, returned kicks superbly, and was an inspirational leader in squelching the first-half doldrums. Coach Higgins used to say, "I never really know what Petchel is going to do. If I knew, it wouldn't make any difference." Wally Triplett, under considerable pressure, scored once and saved at least three touchdowns by flawless tackles.

Skeptical Texans became believers in Penn State's powerful defensive line when numerous offensive thrusts by Doak Walker and the other fine Mustang backs were checked by All-America guard Steve Suhey and Co-Captains John Nolan (tackle) and John Potsklan (end), backed up by Chuck Drazenovich.

Before a community banquet to honor the team, Coach Bob Higgins and Co-Captain John Nolan issued a joint statement in the *Collegian* to quiet rumors of dissension and the exaggerated newspaper criticism of the squad's conduct. Entitled "Let's All Shake Hands," the statement was addressed "To All Penn Staters":

> . . . Let's just say that both of us made mistakes—the coaches and the team members . . . but the important thing right now is not the past—it's the future. . . . Why can't we make the banquet a starting point for an era of co-operation and good fellowship? We've had a wonderful year, and have been talking about another fine year in 1948. So we're shaking hands all around.

Fans anticipating a strong team in 1948 weren't disappointed. Penn State came within a single yard of another undefeated season, another eastern championship (which went to Army), and probably another major bowl bid. Many Cotton Bowl stalwarts were on deck, although Potsklan, Nolan, Wolosky, Suhey, Williams, and Czekaj weren't easily replaced. Scantiness of new material caused few qualms. Sophomore John Smidansky developed into a fine end, and Czekaj's place as the extra-point specialist was ably filled by an unannounced walk-on, Carl Sturgis of Washington, D.C., who kicked 25 of 32 extra points during the season, usually under pressure.

The Michigan State game (14–14) drew a record Homecoming crowd of 24,000, although ticket prices soared to $3.00. For the second time in three years, the most dangerous back on the field was the

Spartans' stocky George Guerre—in 1946 he had gained 152 yards, scored, passed, intercepted, quick-kicked, and recovered a fumble. His team had won then, 19–16. In 1948 Guerre was held in check—with one exception.

After Penn State tied the game at 7–7 in the second quarter, an 80-yard drive seemed about to provide another score with only 10 seconds to go in the half. Petchel started a sweep to the right, spotted Tamburo in the end zone, and threw a low, hard pass. Out of nowhere came Guerre, snatching the ball on the goal line and setting out for the other end of the field, 100 yards away. He didn't seem to need blocking from his teammates, at least not the one Field Judge Karl Bohren called a clip as he dropped his flag and nullified the great run. In the third period the Spartans scored on a long pass, and the Lions climaxed an 83-yard drive with a Petchel pass lateraled by Tamburo to John Simon, who made the sole touchdown of his career.

Having to settle for a tie embittered the Spartans; they claimed their movies showed no infraction during Guerre's run. (John Finley, Penn State tackle, said he was the player clipped during the run.) George A. Alderton, a Lansing newspaperman, summed up instances of Penn State's discourtesy and "boorishness"—the visiting team's dressing room (Rec Hall) was too far from the field, lacked privacy, and was noisy (the Alumni Homecoming luncheon); Coach Biggie Munn had to go outside to inquire his way to the field; players had to walk over broken bottles through a parking lot jam-packed with mocking fans; the "spotter's" booth was poorly located; they received no courtesy call after the game; and the Blue Band didn't play Michigan State's "Alma Mater."

The home crowd may have seen a drop kicker for the last time in the victory over West Virginia (37–7) when Gene Simmons dropkicked the Mountaineers' extra point in the final period. Winning at Syracuse (34–14) convinced Penn Staters that they liked to watch their Lions after dark—they had won all games played under lights. The first was against NYU in 1941. Others in the period were at Syracuse (1946) and against Washington State (1947, at Hershey).

The Penn game buildup was intense because both teams had non-losing streaks to preserve. The Lions, with no losses since the final 1946 game, had won thirteen and tied two. Penn, tied only by Army in its past fourteen games, was among the leading eastern teams, having won twenty-six and tied one of thirty-one since 1945.

A consistently keen rivalry was aggravated by Philadelphia sports-writers inclined to accuse the Penn State team of "rough play" and their fans of "rowdyism" if a few hundred students went after the Franklin Field goal posts.

Expecting the 1948 game to be the last in the current series, Coach Higgins stressed its importance, but his players needed no extra incentive. Students practically deserted State College to jam every corner and all standing-room space. Game attendance was reported to be 71,180.

In the satisfying victory (13–0), top honors belonged to Franny Rogel. Ordinarily a short-gain runner, he broke loose for a 44-yard touchdown run in the second quarter on a fullback half spinner, faking a handoff to Petchel and then hitting off tackle. He found a big hole and had to shake free of only the mountainous All-America, Chuck Bednarik. Scoring again in the final period, Rogel took the pass from center, handed off to Chuck Drazenovich, and faked a buck up the middle. Drazenovich pitched out to Petchel, who faked an end sweep and then passed to Rogel in the end zone. The ball hit his chest, bouncing away, but he caught it close to the ground after a dive.

Triplett came through after Penn had nearly tied the score in the second period from a first down on the Lions' 4. Wally knocked down one pass and on fourth down tackled Penn's Carmen Falcone a few inches short of the goal line. The swift Bednarik denied Penn State another touchdown in the final period, catching Sam Tamburo from behind when he was in the clear with a pass from Petchel. Tamburo, from New Kensington, Pennsylvania, later was named end on *Collier's* All-America team.

The Lions prepared for the Panthers hoping to repeat their 1947 undefeated season in spite of the disasters known to lurk in Pittsburgh. Mauled by Southern Methodist, Notre Dame, and Ohio State in a mediocre season, Pitt had overcome Purdue and Indiana, but these ominous signs were overlooked by the Lions, still in the clouds after their own Penn conquest and resigned to the Michigan State tie.

Diehards considered the jinx still operative when Pitt won a hard-fought victory, 7–0. Lopsided statistics, showing Penn State with 14 first downs to Pitt's 4, and 242 yards by rushing and passing to 79 by the Panthers, became meaningless after Petchel tried to pass from his own 25 early in the last period. Guard Ralph Coleman broke through and tipped the ball into the arms of Nick Bolkovac, who ran 23 yards for the winning touchdown. Pitt stopped every drive of the desperate Lions, including one when 20 seconds remained. Petchel passed to Smidansky on the Panther 2, and at 12 seconds to go, the left side of Pitt's line converged to stop Rogel's diving plunge. The chunky fullback, who had made 116 yards that afternoon, would gladly have exchanged them for those last 2 yards.

The first Penn State squad to travel by air had a rough ride to Tacoma for its seven-point margin over Washington State. Sixty-five yards in penalties frustrated the easterners in their first-half drives, but late in the second quarter Larry Cooney broke away for 18 yards on a deep reverse to get the only touchdown of the game. Dr. Al Griess, team physician, swore he would never fly again.

Bob Higgins, concerned about his health, announced the following March that he would give up his twenty-nine-year coaching career and continue on the athletic administrative staff. He had discussed his replacement with Earle Edwards, and they talked over staff realignment the afternoon before the Athletic Board met.

Some board members, however, were reluctant to go along with Coach Higgins' recommendation of Edwards. Hap Frank, a teammate of Joe Bedenk in 1922 and 1923, convinced Chairman Jim Gilligan and others that Bedenk's experience and seniority on the staff entitled him to the position if he would accept it. At Gilligan's request, Dean Carl Schott sounded out Bedenk Thursday night before the Saturday board meeting. Joe at first was unresponsive because he felt the administration would make no important concessions to aid football. Through his close friend Judge James Milholland, acting president, he heard there might be some favorable action and, after another discussion with Dean Schott on Friday, Joe agreed to take the position of head coach, which was announced on Saturday, March 12, 1949.

Coach Higgins later told his family he had gone to bed Friday night sure that Earle Edwards would be his successor, but offered no explanation when he had to inform Earle of the board's decision. Crushed, Earle stayed on through spring practice and then resigned to become an assistant coach on Biggie Munn's staff at Michigan State. Writing on January 27, 1975, Edwards said,

It has all worked out well for Penn State and for me. . . . With family, friends, good health, and so much good luck I have had a wonderful life. The years at Penn State were enjoyable—I worked hard at my job and feel a very strong loyalty to my Alma Mater.

Bob Higgins, who retired in 1951, was elected to Football's Hall of Fame in 1954. In 1966 he received the Lion's Paw Medal "for his beneficial influence on countless young men; for his sense of humor in the face of adversity; for the great courage manifested throughout his life—a true embodiment of the Penn State spirit."

Recognition of Coach Higgins for his handling of wartime and postwar football was overdue. Dealing with freshmen and war veterans created unusual problems, and the Cotton Bowl setup was potentially explosive, yet Bob maintained control with tolerance, understanding, and a firm but light approach nearly always disarming to the mule breakers. As time went by, no one appreciated this more than his players. At reunions of the 1948 Cotton Bowl squad held every five years, he was the magnet drawing back as many as thirty-five members, and was loved and respected even by some of the most recalcitrant. Bob Higgins died at the age of 75 on June 6, 1969, a few years before the twenty-fifth reunion of the bowl team.

Coach Bedenk filled the two positions on his staff by adding Sever J. Toretti as a line coach and Frank Patrick, a 1938 graduate of the University of Pittsburgh, as defensive backfield coach. Patrick played on three great Panther elevens and scored two of Pitt's three touchdowns in defeating Washington in the Rose Bowl after the 1936 season. Pat had played professional football with the Chicago Cardinals.

The Board of Trustees in May 1949 approved a recommendation of the Athletic Board's Scholarship Policy Committee granting 100 tuition scholarships for all sports—the final step in abolishing the nonsubsidization policy established in January 1930. By previous action (July 1948) all funds for scholarships or other aid permitted by the NCAA had to be deposited with the college treasurer and dispensed by the Senate Committee on Scholarships and Awards, with recipients required to maintain a satisfactory average.

Coach Joe Bedenk's mainstays on the 1949 team were eight holdovers from the Cotton Bowl squad and half a dozen promising newcomers—Len Shepherd, Ken Bunn, Owen Daugherty, Chan Johnson, Tony Orsini, and Vince O'Bara. Reserve strength was lacking to compete successfully against such rugged teams as Army, Michigan State (24–0), Pitt (19–0), and Villanova (27–6), but the Lions achieved a winning season with victories over Boston College (32–14), Nebraska (22–7), Syracuse (33–21), West Virginia (34–14), and Temple (28–7). Army's onslaught was fought off in the first half, 7–0, on the fine running of Fran Rogel and Bill Luther, who threw the touchdown pass to Daugherty. After the intermission the all-star Cadet cast, led by Arnold Galiffa, Gil Stephenson, and Dan Foldberg, conquered the weakened Lions, 42–7.

At the close of the 1949 season, Coach Bedenk and Tor Toretti sought to supplement the aid program by allowing football players to serve as monitors in the new West Residence Halls, and Comptroller Samuel K. Hostetter submitted their plan to the Board of Trustees. The board turned it down in January, preferring to establish (March 31, 1950) 30 football scholarships for tuition, room, and board. Later called grants-in-aid, they were increased in value when the NCAA approved an additional $15 per month to cover "laundry." By an amendment in May, 5 out-of-state grants (additional tuition) were specified among the 30; in December, 45 full grants for football were authorized. A total of 150 tuition grants for all sports had been approved by the board in 1950, with 5 for out-of-state recipients and 50 including cost of room and board. In 1958 tuition grants for all sports went to 175 (75 also included room and board), and out-of-state grants were set at 10 per cent of the total. Penn State's football grants increased after 1958 to 100, but later were reduced to 95 to comply with new NCAA limits. In 1976 private gifts to the Levi Lamb Athletic Fund provided for the full athletic grant-in-aid program for men and women.

Despite the action of the trustees, Joe Bedenk was unhappy with the unalleviated pressures of the full-time head coaching job. He liked teaching (physical education) and enjoyed the line coaching and scouting duties for which he had a considerable reputation, but baseball was his love. When the snow cleared away each spring, he felt a strong call to the diamond, not the gridiron. Soon after the 1949 season began, he let close friends know that his tenure would be a one-year proposition. The announcement was made on March 4, 1950, but he remained on the football staff until his resignation as line coach in the summer of 1952.

Joe Bedenk's 25 years of college football coaching began at Rice under John Heisman in 1924 and continued at the University of Florida until he came to Penn State to be line coach for Bezdek in 1929. He succeeded Bez as baseball coach in 1931 and continued until his retirement before the 1963 season. Bedenk teams usually were among the best in the East, with a record for 32 seasons of 410 victories and 161 defeats. His 1957 team won 21 straight games, finally losing to California 1–0 in the last game of the College World Series. The Lions participated in 9 NCAA district playoffs, which they won 3 times. Bedenk had been among the earliest promoters of the baseball playoffs, was a founder of the Association of College Baseball Coaches, and was its president in 1949.

Nationally, five teams dominated, with some ups and downs, the World War II decade: Minnesota (1940, 1941), Ohio State (1942), Notre Dame (1943, 1946, 1947, 1949), Army (1944, 1945) and Michigan (1948). Minnesota, undefeated for two seasons, conquered Nebraska, 13–7, but the Cornhuskers received the 1941 Rose Bowl bid, losing to Stanford, 20–13. Oregon State defeated Duke, 20–16, in the 1942 Rose Bowl contest (played at Durham, North Carolina, because the military nixed a meeting on the West Coast so soon after Pearl Harbor). Ohio State in 1944 and Alabama in 1945 challenged Army's leadership with some justification. Notre Dame, victim of crushing defeats by Army those two years, avenged itself in 1946 by holding the last Blanchard-Davis edition to a scoreless tie. In 1946 the Pacific Coast Conference and the Big Ten (then the Big Nine) agreed to their Rose Bowl contract, causing a displeased segment of the West Coast press to howl "Bring On Army." Stung by being invited but unwanted, Illinois defeated UCLA, 45–14. Michigan's Wolverines defeated Southern Cal in the 1948 Rose Bowl, 49–0, but the Associated Press awarded the 1947 national title to Notre Dame. That was the first year Penn State broke into the AP's top ten, ranking fourth behind Notre Dame, Michigan, and Southern Methodist.

A notable eastern conflict was the 1940 defeat of Cornell, 7–3, by Dartmouth, which voluntarily surrendered the game to the Big Red when Referee Red Friesell was found to have given Dartmouth a fifth down prior to its winning touchdown. Boston College, Fordham, and Navy were Lambert Trophy winners in the East until Army began a monopoly extending from 1944 until 1949, with only one break when Penn State won it in 1947, the year Columbia stopped Army's thirty-two-game streak, largely through the magic catching of end Bill Swiacki.

The decade's most important rule change, put into effect in the early forties, permitted free substitutions, as many times as desired at any time. From this legislation the two-platoon system emerged, introduced by Michigan in 1945. Players entering the game could communicate with their teammates without waiting for completion of a play. A 1940 ruling repealed the granting of a touchback when a fourth-down pass was grounded in the end zone; now the defending team would place the ball where it had been put into play.

Other relatively minor changes included giving the receiving team the ball on its own 40 when a second kickoff went out of bounds (1945); increasing time-outs from three to four each half (1946); moving hashmarks 53⅓ feet from each sideline (1947); legalizing a kicking tee for all place kicks (1948); protecting a player below the waist only if a block is thrown from behind (1949); and requiring all blockers to keep fists against their chests (1949).

The search for a head football coach to replace Joe Bedenk was spurred by a *Collegian* campaign to secure "a big-time coach for a big-time college." With spring practice for 1950 approaching and the co-operative California State Teachers College program at an end, Earl Bruce was asked to take charge of the varsity for the spring drills.

Part VI

RISE TO EASTERN LEADERSHIP

Rip Engle, 1950–65

30

Not Happy Unless He's Sad

Charles A. (Rip) Engle was establishing himself during the late 1940s as a near miracle worker at Brown University. In 1948 and 1949 Rhode Island's Ivy League school won 15 of 18 games with Engle's original version of the "Wing-T" and a quarterback named Joe Paterno. Engle, 42 but prematurely white-topped when he came to Penn State in 1950, had surprised New England by winning eight of nine games in 1949, losing only to Princeton, 27–14. He was experiencing unusual success during his first tour of duty as a college head coach, his family enjoyed living in Providence, and everything pointed to a long tenure with the goal of keeping Brown among the Ivy leaders.

The first telephone call to jar the complacent satisfaction after the 1949 season was from Athletic Director Tom Hamilton of Pittsburgh. Engle was high on the list of prospects for a new Pitt head coach. He went for an interview, but decided to stay at Brown.

Next to call was Dr. Carl P. Schott, Penn State dean and athletic director. Engle had never thought seriously about coaching there, but indirect ties became an important factor. Rip's uncle, Lloyd F. (Dad) Engle '13, had been varsity tackle in 1910–12 and a long-time Penn State agricultural extension representative. Dick Harlow '12, his much-admired coach at Western Maryland, recommended him to

Dean Schott and Dutch Hermann, a member of the Athletic Board at the time.

Everything moved fast. Complying with Dean Schott's request to keep the call secret, Rip asked Brown's athletic director for permission to visit Penn State. Dr. Schott and Graduate Manager Ike Gilbert met him at the Lock Haven airport and his first appointment was an interview at the President's House on campus with acting president James Milholland. Rip decided almost at once to take the job—the academic rank with tenure was appealing, as was the straightforward explanation of immediate athletic aid and what could be expected. Already familiar with Penn State's football traditions, he could foresee a chance, if but a tantalizing one, to make it an eastern and possibly a national football power.

That night, when Rip called his wife in Providence, without waiting to hear what he had to say, Sunny told him that all hell had broken loose on the Brown campus. Because the athletic director had forgotten to inform the president of Rip's whereabouts and newspapermen had called the president's office with the news of his State College visit, it was assumed Rip had taken the Penn State job without telling anyone at Brown. Sunny's report removed any doubts in Rip's mind about leaving.

Acting president Milholland announced the Engle appointment on April 22, 1950, within months of having announced that Milton Stover Eisenhower would become Penn State's eleventh president on July 1. Judge Milholland, alumnus and trustee president whose aspirations had attracted little support, had become as involved in the search for a "big-time" president as he was in the concurrent process of re-establishing Penn State's prominence in "big-time" football. The coming of the two "Big E's" was celebrated in a special program at the all-class alumni luncheon in Recreation Building during June reunion weekend in 1951.

Rip made his first official visit as head coach at a practice scrimmage with Duquesne on the last day of spring drills (1950), which had been directed by Assistant Coach Bruce. Rip's arrival was accompanied by none of the "splash" that greeted the tumultuous coming of Hugo Bezdek in 1919. Remaining quietly on the sideline, he must have watched his first squad with some misgivings. Where would he get his T quarterback? Told that eight lettermen remained, he tried to identify them. After the scrimmage (won by Penn State), Coach Bruce agreed to his request for a talk with the players, most of whom hadn't met him and were a little excited—a new coach always creates this atmosphere. This one had a surprisingly soft voice, a mild-mannered, low-key approach. He spoke with earnest confidence about the future, not promising hope for instant success, and concluded by asking how many would stay out for two more weeks of practice to begin installation of his system. All were willing. The new coach had made his first strike.

Those who remember the early Engle days are amused at the way Rip inveigled his players and assistants into four spring practice periods. Penn State freshmen still assigned to California State were asked to come out for two weeks of special training under Bruce, who had absorbed the Engle system in three days. When they finished the California term, the freshmen came to the main campus for a final two weeks. Among them were interior linemen Joe Gratson and Don Barney, and end Joe Yukica, now the successful coach at Boston College. Gratson became co-captain of the 1952 team.

Coach Engle retained all the varsity staff on condition that he could name one assistant. Holdovers were Joe Bedenk, Al Michaels, Jim O'Hora, Tor Toretti, Frank Patrick, and Earl Bruce, continuing as freshman coach. Rip's assistants at Brown had been Bob Priestly, who had already decided to go to Norwich as coach and athletic director; Gus Zitrides; and Bill Doolittle, who had replaced Weeb Ewbank on Rip's staff. Rip asked each to join him at Penn State, but Zitrides decided to take the head coach opening at Brown, and Doolittle chose to remain with him.

Rip's third choice was his 1949 senior quarterback, who would receive a degree in English literature that June and planned to attend law school in the fall. Rip persuaded Joe Paterno to postpone the law degree, at least until Rip could get under way with some security in his changed environment. The closest Paterno has come to law is the honorary doctorate bestowed by his alma mater in June 1975.

Merely to discover a "potential" T quarterback became a major problem. Bruce groomed Gratson for a tryout, and Gratson passed his early test during the fourth spring practice on the main campus. A quartet of Gratson, Tony Orsini, Owen Daugherty (a farmout from Mansfield), and Ted Shattuck made up the first tentative backfield, but early in the fall, Vince O'Bara, a Johnstown senior, was shifted over to quarterback and Gratson to center. Dick Koerber was the only other player with any quarterback experience. Rip Engle always had a warm feeling about O'Bara, a 170-pound quarterback who worked hard to master the difficult assignment and became a steady, capable performer.

The team needed all its warmup practice games against Duquesne, Bucknell, Colgate, and Cornell to break in the new system and the fledgling quarterback. Georgetown, first regular opponent and, luckily, in its final season of intercollegiate football, was reasonably competitive, but not a good test. The enthusiastic home crowd, enjoying its fill of action and scoring, overlooked conspicuous flaws.

In their successful debuts, O'Bara and fullback Shattuck made good yardage on a quick trap play up the middle. Penn State's 34 points to Georgetown's 14 had alumni talking about "rapid movement of the ball" and how fine it was to have an "offense-minded" coach. Against Army the next week the harsh realities became more apparent. As was their custom, New York alumni held a Friday night "smoker" in New York and, of course, wanted to greet the new coach. As was *his* custom, Rip avoided a crowd on the eve of a game but sent his new assistant, Joe Paterno, for his initial confrontation with an alumni group. Joe listened unemotionally to the message of an Army public-relations major, who told the gathering that the Academy should have at least part of their allegiance as citizens and taxpayers. Mentally Joe said "the hell with that," but he was very politic in this first appearance and realistic in his estimate of the team's chances. He did make the mistake of telling a friend privately that he "had a feeling" about the game—a "good feeling."

Rip's neophytes couldn't combat Colonel Red Blaik's strong regular or reserve troops. Besides its great running backs—Al Pollard, Jim Cain, Gil Stephenson, and Gene Filipski—Army had two excellent quarterbacks in Gil Reich and Bob Blaik. The Cadets held back no weapons in rolling up the score (41–7) and went undefeated until submerged by Navy. The only casualty was Penn State's *Football Letter* editor, whose complaint about roughness, based on Army's 148 yards in penalties, was picked up the next week by the New York papers ("Alumni Editor Accuses Army of Dirty Football"). The outraged Colonel Blaik made an irate phone call to Penn State, which lost its punch because the recipient thought it was a gag, and so reacted. The week before Penn State's game, Army had been penalized 117 yards against Colgate, but Colonel Blaik said officials had not reported "undue roughness" to the ECAC and that most of Army's "roughness" penalties had been for "illegal use of hands." The conversation ended with the editor's wishing Colonel Blaik good luck against Harvard and New Mexico. (Army beat Harvard, 49–0, and New Mexico, 51–0.)

After the Army setback Penn State suffered successive losses to Syracuse and Nebraska. At Syracuse, the Orange had its first victory over Penn State since 1937, and Coach Ben Schwartzwalder triumphed over his great and "friendly" rival for the first time. When Temple tied the Lions 7–7 and the season's record was 1–3–1 past the halfway mark, the 13-year-old string of winning seasons was in jeopardy.

A diversion to enliven the scene was the modest beginning of Band Day, with eight Centre County high schools invited to attend and perform from their seats in the stands. Hummel Fishburn '22, Blue Band director and head of the Music Department, elaborated the second annual program on October 27, 1951, at the West Virginia game, inviting Pennsylvania high school bands whose directors were Penn State graduates. Approximately 1,599 musicians, majorettes, and baton twirlers participated from 24 high schools. The sight and sound of the colorfully uniformed groups unfailingly thrilled spectators as they assembled on the field at half time to play in unison with the Blue Band. Only the 1953 season was missed, canceled because of heavy snow, but Band Day was scratched in 1975 when the Temple game was moved to Philadelphia. In 1974, James W. Dunlop, late director of the Blue Band, conducted the concert by 58 high school bands with 6,424 participants.

Demonstrating its anticipated slow development, the team defeated Boston College, West Virginia, and Rutgers. This placed Coach Engle in uncomfortable need of a victory over Pitt to make his first year a success. Rip's team reached its peak against the Mountaineers, O'Bara gaining more poise as the season progressed. He inspired the squad with his courage and never had a defeatist attitude.

Recent rules opening up the two-platoon system definitely handicapped Coach Engle's undermanned squad, and often players more valuable where they were had to be shifted to other positions. A case in point was Paul Anders, a husky Monongahela boy who might have remained in the defensive lineup, but was moved over to offense in midseason and contributed a great deal to Lion success in the last four games. Rip opposed the two-platoon idea from the beginning, despite looking wistfully at some of his power-laden opponents. He figured, however, that fans would soon get used to the then ludicrous sight of teams running on and off the field, and was more concerned about the likelihood that the system eventually would divide college football elevens into the "haves" and the "have-nots."

In one of his first talks to alumni, Coach Engle brushed aside the existence of a Pittsburgh "jinx," but the young coach, whose "king of gloom" reputation came later, must have had some misgivings when a heavy snow began to fall Friday afternoon even before his squad left by bus for Pittsburgh. The snow fell all Friday night and most of Saturday, convincing the management that it would be impossible to play a football game. The squad and hundreds of Lion followers found themselves immobilized in a city brought to a standstill by the thick white blanket. Those who experienced being marooned in hotels call it the "Lost Weekend"—many could communicate with their families only through "ham" radio operators.

Pitt misfortune became personal for Coach Engle when he ventured out Saturday evening, fell into a snowdrift, and lost his wallet. Since this episode it's said Rip has always worn a money belt. The Pitt management had canceled the game outright; but, to retain a good part of the advance sales, rescheduled it the following Saturday (December 3) at Forbes Field, where snow-removal equipment was more easily available.

By Monday morning the Penn State staff secured open trucks to round up the squad, official party, and others who chose to leave their cars in Pittsburgh. They were hauled to the Pennsylvania Railroad Station for the train trip to Tyrone, where buses awaited them. Coach Engle and the squad promptly faced the obstacles normal to late November practice sessions in central Pennsylvania.

Only 7,000 spectators braved the grimy slush of Pittsburgh's streets on foot or by trolley to reach the Oakland site. They huddled in the lower decks on either side of the field, high enough to see over the mountainous snowdrifts surrounding the gridiron. Snow piles remained on the other seats, and the field surface, though cleared, was a morass.

Somehow, the visiting Lions had a 21–0 lead with the first half nearly over, and then almost blew it. Bill Leonard (later a successful coach at State College Area High School and now a local businessman) began the remarkably well-played game by intercepting Bill Bestwick's flat pass and slushing his way 65 yards down the sideline, ignoring the sticky mud and pools of water as he scored the points that gave his team the initial momentum. A fumble recovery and slashing runs by Paul Anders and Tony Orsini helped the Lions score twice more in the half, with Vince O'Bara kicking all three extra points. Penn State had designed a special kicking tee for the game—the holder inserted the ball into a scooplike funnel made of beaver board with shingle sides, and only a steady foot was needed for the point. A few years later the contraption was ruled illegal.

How these things happen mystifies alumni but not coaches. With a minute to play in the half, Bestwick passed the Pitt team to a touchdown, and suddenly the 21–7 half-time lead was less impressive. A radical change of momentum had Penn State fighting to hold on and its fans suffering anxiety pains. Led by the ferocious running of sophomore Joe Capp, Pitt scored on a ten-minute drive late in the third period, and with ten minutes to play, Bill Reynolds returned O'Bara's punt 49 yards to the Lion 14. Bestwick passed to Nick DeRossa for what Pitt fans rightly thought would lead to the tying points because their extra-point specialist, Nick Bolkovac, hadn't missed all year (13 for 13). He'd had a close call twice after Pitt's first touchdown when his kick was wide, but an offside penalty gave him another chance. Nick missed, but again the Lions were offside, and his third try was good.

Now, with the score 21–20 (two-point conversions were yet to come), the Pitt specialist sailed the ball clean through the uprights, but a flag was thrown. Pitt was discovered to have had 12 players on the field, predating the famous Kansas Orange Bowl *faux pas* by 19 years. Bolkovac missed his next attempt after the ball was set back for the penalty. How about that Pittsburgh jinx?

Alumni lionized the new coach for the triumph over Pitt, caring little whether it was by one point or 20. It didn't matter that statistics heavily favored the Panthers in 1950—the Lions had won that battle before! Pitt's new coach, Len Casanova, lasted just that one season.

Sunday morning after his first great Pitt victory, newsmen got their introductory inkling of Coach Engle's gloom-and-doom personality. Expecting to find him exultant, they heard instead how easily his team could have lost the game (the thought made him literally bite his nails). He also was filled with foreboding about the material Pitt would have *next* year, his own recruiting problems, and additions to the 1951 schedule—Purdue and Michigan State at the height of their power, and Nebraska's tough Cornhuskers under a *Pitt* coach. "Rip's not happy unless he's sad" was Ben Schwartzwalder's apt observation about his archrival.

On the alumni banquet circuit Rip was popular and well received on first impressions that wore well throughout his career. Unused to a coach who spoke softly and earnestly, and surprised to have one who never took a drink, alumni delighted in his homespun country humor and approved his avoidance of personally critical remarks about individual players. "The kind of coach Penn State should have," was a remark heard frequently, and "the kind you'd like to have your boy play under." He didn't tell them much, certainly no trade secrets, but his idiosyncrasies were amusing, and they thoroughly enjoyed his presence among them.

Rip occasionally treated his audience to one of his "Old Blue Ridge" stories—yarns, mostly fabricated, about a terrible team on which he said he had played. The team won no games, scored no points, and made all its yardage backward. Before enrolling at Western Maryland, Rip had in fact played for Blue Ridge College (in New Windsor, Maryland), which once lost to Temple by well over a hundred points. According to Rip, the school eventually had been converted into a bus company.

The mild and mellow Rip of off-season occasions was not the same as the fiery-tempered, harassed coach on the sidelines. His explosive field temper, sometimes directed at officials, probably reacted against him. Professionally ambitious, he brooded over losses, but the pleasure he should have had from victories generally was diluted by his immediate concern over the "next game" and the insurmountable difficulty of motivating his players to the same standard of excellence.

For Engle, as for all Penn State coaches, the Pitt game was the season's focal point, but Syracuse and Army soon became equal obsessions—Archbold Stadium and Michie Stadium were hated sites where incredible misfortunes beset Lion teams. Engle's violent and sometimes unpleasant rivalry with Ben Schwartzwalder, the Syracuse coach, was well known, although in retirement both say they've always been firm friends.

Syracuse was where Engle discovered the diabolical contrivances of home officials to keep his players from getting a good night's rest on Friday. Actually, it was Coach Engle, not the players, who couldn't sleep, either before or after a game. Sunny Engle used to say that Rip spent the first three days each week building himself up with vitamins, while she spent the last three days giving him sedatives. Rip ascribed the principal villainy at Syracuse to Schwartzwalder, who would turn in false fire alarms, said Rip, to have fire engines roar past the Hotel Syracuse at early hours. He also intimated that Ben hired professional door slammers to operate wherever the Lions stayed, and, most diabolically, incited fraternity men to stage special street celebrations after midnight.

The coach's persecution complex may have been fancied, but his insomnia was real, especially on Friday night. Early Saturday risers encountered him roaming the hotel lobby waiting for the coffee shop to open. He'd have coffee with the first person to appear, hopping from table to table as groups came and left, until ten o'clock, when he joined his squad for the team meal.

The custom of practicing on Friday at West Point's Michie Stadium was abandoned because Rip was sure the authorities would test the scoreboard horns just to annoy his players. Accordingly, he found a practice field adjacent to Bear Mountain Inn, where the squad stayed regularly until Rip changed to Newburgh because he found the crows kept the boys awake all night and raccoons would peer in their windows—a frightening experience for city boys.

At the Mark Hopkins in San Francisco, the seagulls perched on the window ledges—"the boys can never sleep," he groaned. The noisiest garbage collectors in the world were in Lincoln, Nebraska, where a notorious murderer had been one, Rip pointed out. A Lincoln newsman present when the team arrived for practice at the field remarked in Rip's hearing that the squad looked wonderful, like a pro squad. This was a terrible thought for Rip on the eve of a game. He started slapping at his legs, complaining about mosquitos in the long grass. "How can we play football under these conditions?" he wailed.

Like any coach, Rip expected meticulous handling of trip details and made no allowance for unpreventable mistakes. After a tiresome trip to play California at Berkeley in 1962 (the Lions won) he was edgy, worrying about the coming Maryland game. The plane arrived late in Harrisburg, and the regular buses to University Park failed to appear. After midnight another bus company finally agreed to take the Penn State party home. The drivers had never been over the mountains to Centre County, and the lead bus, with Engle navigating, missed a turn coming off the mountain at Potters Mills. As it sailed on toward Centre Hall, Rip shouted at the driver to stop and directed him to back into the parking lot of the Eutaw House, the well-known country inn. Gear trouble made it difficult for the driver to maneuver in the small parking lot, and the gears finally jammed, with the nose of the bus against owner Harrison Shawley's hedge.

"What's the matter now?" grumbled Rip.

"Can't get it into reverse."

"What the hell can you get it in?"

"Only forward."

"Well, put the damn thing in forward and let's get out of here." That's just what the driver did, cutting a neat swath through the green hedge—a disfiguration owners Harrison and Betty may find puzzling to this day.

31

Camp Hate-to-Leave-It

Recruiting remained Penn State's Number One problem when the twenty-year "purity" period ended, because young athletes and their coaches couldn't believe that real aid was available. The fifty full grants-in-aid offered by 1951 weren't easy to fill with the type of recruit required, although Coach Engle estimated he traveled nearly 30,000 miles that first year attending high school banquets and talking to prospects. His claim never to have missed a meeting because of bad weather—even driving the icy mountain roads of Pennsylvania—gained him statewide prestige, on which he capitalized by advertising on the visor of his car "Rip Engle, World-famous Snow, Ice, and Fog Driver." Uneasy companions couldn't dispute its validity.

Roosevelt Grier and Jesse Arnelle were prized recruits in 1951, when freshmen were eligible for the varsity. Grier later starred as a pro with the New York Giants and the Los Angeles Rams, and then became a folk musician and television performer whose avocation is needlepoint. Arnelle, a San Francisco attorney and now a university trustee, was outstanding in basketball and still holds most of Penn State's individual records. Others on the 1951 squad were Don Malinak, Pete Schoderbek, Buddy Rowell, Jim and Bob Pollard, and Jim Dooley, who later married Bob Higgins' youngest daughter,

Nancy. Tony Rados of Steelton, a quarterback of great promise, still holds (as of 1976) the career record for passes attempted (425). The skill of Rados added dimension to the offense, but Coach Engle's men kept looking for a blue-chip running back.

Opening the 1951 season at home, Penn State met Boston University in air warfare, the two teams scoring 11 touchdowns between them, with the Lions coming from behind four times to prevail over the brilliant passing of the "Golden Greek," Harry Agganis. Penn State's passer that afternoon was a sophomore surprise, unpronounceably named Robert Szajna (Shine-a). The new university president, Dr. Milton Eisenhower, came to the dressing room after the 40–34 victory to say it was the best game he'd ever seen. Al Michaels, scouting Michigan State at East Lansing, reacted differently. Mock-mindful of prosecutions for betting in sports in New York and elsewhere, he wired Engle: "Deeply concerned. Are you involved in basketball scandal?"

At the request of Lehigh Valley alumni, the Villanova game was played in Allentown, and Assistant Coach Toretti used the opportunity to have Rip lunch at the Hotel Traylor with a good prospect. Engle had agreed reluctantly because it was too close to the time of a tough game. The guest was late, and Tor brought him to the field instead. Fearing Rip's reaction to the splendor of the prospective recruit, who wore the latest in haberdashery, including a resplendent beaver hat, Tor tried to keep the lad at some distance on the sideline, but Rip called him over. "Who's *he?*" queried the head coach. "Don't worry about 'who's he,'" replied Tor. " 'Who's he' is going to win a lot of games for you know who." The prospect was named Lenny Moore.

Fortune helped the Lions defeat Nebraska 15–7 at Lincoln, thanks to a field goal by Bill Leonard—his first—and a game-saving tackle by Dave Simon, who caught Nebraska's freshman speedster, Bob Smith, when he had a clear field for what might have been the winning touchdown. Another break was the injury that sidelined All-America Bobby Reynolds, the one who slew the Lions in 1950. No luck intervened the next week at Michigan State, although the showing was surprisingly good against the powerful Spartans, rated Number Two in the nation. Engle learned from a Lansing newspaperman's quote that Biggie Munn was "afraid of those coal miners." "All the tough ones go West," was Engle's plaintive comment.

The 1951 season seemed a disaster, with losses to Villanova and

Michigan State, a near loss to West Virginia, and a game with Purdue played in miserable weather after an uncomfortable train ride to West Lafayette, Indiana. Despite the 28–0 humbling, the local press praised Coach Engle's team. Said Gordon Graham in the Lafayette *Journal and Courier:*

> What a dreary outlook Penn State had as it returned to the field in a near blizzard to start the second half 21–0 behind . . . with that gale blowing against the Lions for 15 minutes in the third quarter they didn't have one chance in a hundred. Why don't college football players give up? You rarely see one toss in the towel . . . they are a great breed . . . and Saturday Penn State belonged . . . the Lions battled even harder and more effectively in the last half than in the first . . . we must remember that when we invade Penn State next year.

For a 13–7 victory at Rutgers, the Lions did almost everything to lose the game—fumbling four times in Scarlet territory, nearly wasting over 500 yards gained on the ground and in the air. Bob Pollard's fine individual performance made the difference—he averaged 17.4 yards in 14 carries, scored both touchdowns (on runs of 75 and 71 yards), and played tirelessly on offense and defense, 52 minutes in all. The final game returned the Pitt series to its normal course. The best moment for Penn State came when the Blue Band spelled out "Pitt" on the Stadium turf in a bold, firm script—Palmer Method.

The Lions won their 1952 opener from Temple at Beaver Field, and Indiana newspapers were accurately predicting trouble for the Purdue Boilermakers in Nittany Valley. Purdue's ace passer, Dale Samuels, was outpitched by Tony Rados in the stunning 20–20 upset, but in a way the hero was the smallest back on the field, little Dick Jones. He made the key run leading to the tying score and topped all Lion runners with 74 yards. Game officials had an uneasy afternoon—ruling on extra points and conferring hotly with the coaches because they lost track of downs. Pollard's touchdown gave the Lions their first tie opportunity. Bill Leonard's extra-point try was wide. Purdue happened to be offside, but before his second kick the visitors were called for having twelve men on the field and penalized half the distance to the goal line. Bill's second kick made it 7–7. At 13–7 in the third quarter the Boilermakers lost a chance to go ahead when Samuels' extra point was cleanly blocked by Bob Smith, and again the officials saw twelve men in Purdue's lineup. The argument over whether the flag was dropped before or after Samuels' try was settled by allowing him to kick again after Purdue had taken a 15-yard penalty. Coach Engle fumed because Penn State had no opportunity to refuse the penalty. The tension eased when Samuels missed the kick. Two minutes later Phil Klezek raced 63 yards for a Purdue touchdown.

The officials were in a jam once more late in the game when a Penn State drive for an equalizing touchdown was stymied by a fourth down call. Captain Gratson's violent protest that it was only third down caused another conference, and Coach Engle was tearing his hair until it was announced that Gratson was right. The offensive unit came back and drove to a touchdown made by Rados on a third-down sneak. Leonard's placement tied the score at 20–20, but the officials delayed their call until they had counted the Purdue players.

In this dramatic aerial show, 15 different players caught passes from Rados and Samuels, who lived up to his high reputation among Big Ten passers. Completing 155 in 331 attempts for 2,023 yards in the past two seasons, he was said to have averaged a touchdown for every nine passes he threw, but Rados had the better of the duel, completing 17 of 29 for 197 yards—the best record for any Lion passer of that decade.

Satisfying victories were had over Nebraska (10–0) and Penn in a renewal of that series, won by the Lions 14–7 on two stirring drives of 5 and 8 yards. Rosey Grier's recovery of a fumble on the Penn 5 enabled the Lions to tie the score at 7–7, and four minutes before the finish Sam Green, the game's defensive star, blocked a forward pass by Glenn Adams. The ball, bouncing high, was caught by Stew Scheetz, who was downed on the Penn 8. The Quakers might have held, but Dick Jones, pint-sized piledriver, slithered through the heavy Penn forwards for the winning points.

Coach George Munger had done his best to avoid Penn's habitual blind spot and complacency about its meetings with Penn State. Said he:

> In preparation for this one each member of the coaching staff and every member of the squad gave every ounce of energy and football "know how." This was the one we wanted. Never did a Pennsylvania team play a better game and lose since I have been coach.

Losing to Syracuse (25–7) and barely beating Rutgers (7–6) made for an unimpressive season's record of 6–2–1 as compared with Pitt's victories over Notre Dame, Army, Ohio State, Iowa, and Indiana. Pitt seemed in line for an Orange Bowl bid, and wives of some officials were mentally packing for Florida. Panther coaches showed their jitters when they asked Skip Rowland to leave the stadium Friday afternoon, saying he was a Penn State spy whose notes on Pitt plays had been confiscated. An ardent Penn State fan, advocate, patron, promoter, defender, and apologist Skip was, but he wouldn't have known one Pitt play from another.

The surprising 17–0 victory of the Nittany Lions dislocated Pitt fans. Crateloads of oranges, on hand in the spirit of the expected outcome, were rudely thrown instead at Panther players. Penn State's leading ground-gainers were Keith Vesling and Buddy Rowell, the Erie boy who always did his best against the Panthers. Rowell scored one touchdown, Rados another, and Bill Leonard kicked a field goal. Al Michaels had done the scouting job on Pitt, considered remarkable by noted pro scout Jack Lavelle. Al suggested the switch from Engle's usual 5–3–3 to a 7–2–2, which confused the Panthers, shut off their running game, and enabled ends Dave Simon and Don Malinak to put a fierce rush on their passer, Rudy Mattioli. Sam Green, Danny DeFalco, and Pete Schoderbek were defensive stalwarts, and Ted Kemmerer's punting was another plus factor.

After the greatest victory of his three Penn State years, Rip was more worried than happy.

"It will be awful next year without Barney, Dooley, Leonard, Gratson, and Scheetz."

"But Rip," someone reminded him, "you've been calling this a young, inexperienced squad all along."

"Yes," he sighed, "I know. But those boys will be too old next year."

In 1953, when Dean Schott retired, Ernest B. McCoy, a Michigan graduate, was appointed director of athletics and dean of the college. Experienced in handling intercollegiate sports as Fritz Crisler's assistant at Michigan, McCoy brought about administrative changes that eliminated the position of graduate manager of athletics, traditionally held by alumni since the volunteer days when George R. Meek '90 was the first to have the title, 1907–8.

Harold R. (Ike) Gilbert '26, graduate manager since the retirement of Neil M. Fleming in 1947, became business manager of athletics. Fleming's assistant since his graduation, Ike is credited with perfecting the effective managerial system for Penn State's varied sports program, and was engineer-in-chief of many eastern and national tournaments from which Penn State earned its outstanding reputation for efficiency and hospitality. When he died on February 2, 1972, friends and classmates established the Harold R. (Ike) Gilbert Scholarship Fund to aid student managers planning graduate study.

Preceding the 1953 season, at a practice game with Cornell in Ithaca, Coach Engle met Lefty James, the Cornell coach, for the first time. "Say hello before you cry, Rip," was Lefty's greeting.

During this scrimmage Engle granted Rosey Grier's wish to become a kickoff artist. The giant tackle, when aroused, was a better lineman than any in the country; but, whimsical and easygoing by nature, he didn't enjoy undue exertion in practice. Sailing the first kickoff into the end zone, Rosey watched the ball's flight with such pride that he didn't notice a considerable Cornell blocker who came up and clobbered him from the side. Next time, Rosey was looking the wrong way again and his huge form went over like a giant oak. He got up shaking his head, and Rip heard him mutter, "Coach, I hereby resign from the kickoff team."

Rosey's whimsy continued into his professional career. "That mountain of amiability" (Arthur Daley, the New York *Times*) was with the New York Giants when Coach Jim Lee Howell feared an upset against the Eagles, although the Giants were heavily favored. "You fellows are going to lose this game," he cautioned. "Now, what are you going to do about it?" "Maybe we could write them a letter of apology," was Rosey's suggestion.

Excitement over the 1953 debut of Lenny Moore, the Reading Comet, was curbed by an untimely penalty in the opening game at Madison, Wisconsin. While the game was still scoreless, Moore slipped round right end for 65 yards and a touchdown, but Don Eyer, split wide on the left as a decoy, was called offside. The Badgers won, 20–0, and our spindle-legged sophomore had to give top billing to Alan (The Horse) Ameche, who broke the game wide open in the second quarter with his bull-like plunges. Moore's sophomore year, while not earth-shaking, was adequate and promising. He gained over 100 yards against TCU, Fordham, and Pittsburgh, averaging 5.4 yards per carry in nine games for 591 yards.

The Engle renaissance continued shakily in 1953 with a 20–14 triumph over Syracuse, success against Texas Christian (27–21), and the second straight 17–0 whitewashing of Pittsburgh. The Panthers, less potent and proud than in 1952, had tied Oklahoma and beaten Nebraska. Moore's 79½-yard run from scrimmage in this game was short of Chuck Peters' record set in 1938 against Syracuse by a half yard. Rados was the East's leading passer, completing 81 of 171 for 1,026 yards, and end Jim Garrity was among the top receivers with 30 catches.

The season also included a 20–19 loss on New Beaver Field to West Virginia and a surprise defeat (13–7) by Penn. A 92-yard Lion drive for the opening touchdown (Moore gained 56 yards) was checked by a Penn eleven working hard to "win this one for George." It was the final season for Coach Munger, who hadn't beaten Penn State during his sixteen-year stint. The Quakers presented the game ball to the happy Munger, reneging cheerfully on a half-time Franklin Field announcement that it would be given to President Dwight D. Eisenhower at his birthday party the next week. The popular and able coach was a great credit to the game, and Ike got enough presents.

Saturday night after the Syracuse game, Coach Rip Van Engle slept peacefully, untroubled by the recurrent dream of coaches about a blocked kick. As linemen crash in to save the game, the kick is blocked and the ball rolls invitingly toward the goal line. Is the ball scooped up for the winning touchdown? No, the player of the coach's dream falls on it. Against the Orange that afternoon, however, while the scoreboard clock on New Beaver Field was beginning its final revolution, Jim Garrity clutched at the ball without breaking stride and ran for the goal line 23 yards away. Dante DeFalco had blocked the punt in the tie-breaking play that gave the Lion coach a peaceful night.

Two weeks later, Penn Staters were incredulous when West Virginia's Bruce Bosley blocked a kick for a Mountaineer victory. On Sunday, Coach Engle praised his own team and the visitors, who led the nation in rushing. But hundreds of fans had yelled "offside!" just before the ball was snapped on the crucial play, and movies showed that a Mountaineer lineman had jumped the ball slightly. Sunday films educate quarterbacks, but Saturday scores stay the same.

Between the Syracuse and the West Virginia games, the Lions won a heart-stopper from Texas Christian, but the two schools almost missed their first meeting because the Texans thought Penn State was in (no, not Philadelphia) Harrisburg! Friendly Pennsylvanians at the airport told the startled Texans they had ninety miles to go. Expecting a larger than usual crowd, Penn State had erected temporary end-zone stands, which were empty—that is, until local small fry came over the fence while the cops were standing at attention for "The Star-Spangled Banner." The game itself was a contest between Lenny Moore and a highly publicized visitor, Ronald Clinkscale.

Snow beginning in Nittany Valley on Friday, November 6, 1953, made the Fordham game unforgettable. Ed Danowski, the personable young coach, was relieved to have his city-bred Rams safely bedded down that night before the wild wind piled snowdrifts on the highways to State College, considered inaccessible by New Yorkers even in summertime. The steadily falling snow made a game seem unlikely. But at 12:30 P.M. the next day, when Danowski peered through the team entrance to the field, he saw an incongruous bright green rectangle, neatly marked with white lines. Team benches were in place, the stands were cleared, and the crowd already was beginning to gather, marveling, and moving gingerly through piles of snow.

Penn State's Athletic Department, famed for its skillful handling of all kinds of tournaments, had recruited volunteer crews. Cheerleaders, members of the Blue Band, hat societies, and about 200 other students, including some from State College Area High, responded to radio and telephone appeals for the all-night emergency job. Anyone who could handle a shovel or plow came out in a clearcut example of togetherness, carrying on a tradition that football will be played come weal or snow.

"Better tell the boys to get ready," Danowski called to his manager. Seven years ago he had come here struggling for Fordham's football survival after the war, and the Lions had rained touchdowns on his outclassed team. The Rams were still struggling to survive.

"Don't get overanxious, Coach," he was told. "Penn State's still in seclusion. They're not even here."

As snowflakes had begun to fall the day before, the Lions had indeed set out for a mountain hunting camp owned by Titan Metal Company of Bellefonte. In the Clinton County hideaway, about twenty-five miles from campus, the players seemed to relax as Coach Engle had hoped when he decided they needed to get away to bounce back from the jolt with West Virginia and forget about Junior Prom weekend. Only the coach was nervous, watching the accumulating snow. He had Manager Dick Crafton check conditions, phoning Titan and Penn State officials and the bus company. By 6

A.M. Rip was pacing the cabin floor. At 8 A.M., when he dispatched Coaches Jim O'Hora and Joe Paterno to scout through the still falling snow for the expected bus, they couldn't even find the road. Volunteering at nine, Manager Crafton was ordered to blow the whistle sharp if he found the bus, but he returned in thirty minutes, mission unaccomplished.

Coach Engle was frantic: Who ever heard of the home team missing the game? Willie, the caretaker, offered to take his gun "and shoot once in the air if I find anything." "Better make it two shots," said the cautious Engle. "We might not hear one." Forty minutes later came the double bark of the rifle.

"There's our signal, boys," cried Engle, trying to be calm. "I'll go first. O'Hora and Paterno next. We're expendable." Rip cast a quick eye over the squad. "Third team next. You boys can help us beat a trail." As he called their names, the players filed one by one into the morning gloom. The varsity was last, with Tony Rados (852 yards passing) and Lenny Moore (429 yards rushing) in the comparative security of the rear. In thirty minutes they got through to the "rescue" party of three tractors, one bus, and three carloads of state police. At 1:30 P.M. (scheduled game time) the bus reached the dressing room under the stands. First to greet them was Coach Danowski.

Rip was apologetic, but Danowski replied politely, "Don't worry, Rip. It couldn't be helped. Too bad you had all that trouble. By the way, what was the name of that hunting camp?"

"Oh, that camp," said Rip, smiling sheepishly. "It was Camp Hate-to-Leave-It."

The hardy fans, 15,000 strong, and seven high school bands en route before word reached them that Band Day had been canceled, saw an exciting game that was unreal to Coach Engle—his team played well but mechanically, exerting itself only when necessary, winning, 28–21, because it happened to score first and barely had time to score last. Fordham seemed not to know when it was licked and very nearly wasn't, having a chance to match every touchdown and extra point except the final ones.

Expecting Rutgers to be a warmup for their Pitt finale, the Lions were trailing 14–6 midway in the second quarter at New Brunswick before Coach Engle sent in a wealth of running backs (seven had rushing yardage totals in double figures) to swamp the Scarlet, 54–26. Since Penn State legally had become The Pennsylvania State

University that week, alumni wags wanted notice sent to bowl selectors that Penn State was one of the few major undefeated *university* teams in the country.

At the close of the 1953 season the university established an official channel for athletic aid from alumni through the new Penn State Alumni Fund. The Levi Lamb Fund, named for a noted Lion athlete killed in World War I, was proposed by Dean Ernest B. McCoy, with Dr. Ralph (Dutch) Ricker as its director, to receive annual contributions of alumni and friends. An adjunct Nittany Lion Club, organized in 1966 for contributors of $50 or more, extends to members such privileges as preferential ticket consideration based on the amount given. Increasing each year in gifts and givers, the Levi Lamb Fund reached a record $584,143.25 from 8,100 contributors in fiscal 1975–76 under the supervision of Associate Athletic Director James I. (Jim) Tarman and Charles P. (Pete) Neidig '40.

A 1954 opening game with Illinois at Champaign posed hazards for the almost all-veteran Lions. Favored as one of the Big Ten's top teams, the Illini had "the nation's fastest backfield," with Abe Woodson, Mickey Bates, and the much-publicized J. C. Caroline. Midwestern and eastern newspapers as well succumbed to Coach Engle's especially disarming preseason lamentations, although the canny coach had an all-veteran team, with a nucleus of ten seniors and seven juniors. Senior ends were Jesse Arnelle, Jack Sherry, Bob Rohland, and Jim Garrity, co-captain with center Don Balthaser. Tackle Rosey Grier, like Arnelle, was playing his fourth season as a regular. Others were linemen Gene Danser and Earl Shumaker, Ron Younker (a fine running back), and the underrated Don Bailey, too often overlooked when Penn State's talented quarterbacks are enumerated. (Don played quarterback on the East team for most of the Shrine game and was named the Outstanding Player.)

The squad's juniors included Lenny Moore, Billy Kane, and Bill Straub, running backs; Bobby Hoffman, who backed up Bailey; Milt Plum, another quarterback; Charlie Blockson, all-purpose back; Otto Kneidinger, tackle; and Frank Reich, center. Sophomore material was light except for two linemen, Dick DeLuca and Sam Valentine.

Penn State's violent, gang-tackling defense, a surprise to Illinois, held Caroline to 116 yards and kept him from getting outside. Moore's total was 137, while Bailey gained twice as much as Woodson and Bates together. The confident Illini scored in four minutes, with Woodson running 28 yards on a screen pass from Em Lindbeck. Caroline missed an important extra point.

Bailey then replaced quarterback Hoffman and was also the kicker, with orders to kick away from just about everybody. A fumble recovery set up a scoring, 4-yard pass play, Bailey to Arnelle, and Garrity's kick gave Penn State a 7–6 lead, all before the crowd of 54,000 (a record for an opening game in Champaign) realized what was happening. The Lions' tackling was shattering, especially hits by Grier, Shumaker, and Sherry. Toward the end of the first half Bailey broke away on a keeper in the "belly" series, faking to Lenny Moore and gaining 50 yards to the Illini 24. Again on the keeper, Bailey faked to Moore, ran to the 12, then lateraled to Lenny, who ran past three befuddled defenders. The extra point was juggled, but Garrity got the kick away successfully for a 14–6 score at half time.

In a furious, second-half assault, Illinois scored on a 17-yard Woodson run, but the extra-point placement hit the crossbar (no 2-point conversions then). The game-winning play came when Illinois was 4th and 6 on Penn State's 16. The ball *had* to go to Caroline, who was knocked back 4 yards by Garrity and Reich (who played 60 minutes). At the finish Penn State was on the Illinois 5 after advancing toward another score against a beaten Illini eleven, having only to run out the clock and hold the ball. Defense had won for the Lions, and one of its leaders was senior guard Shumaker. "That Earl," marveled Rosey Grier. "He sure chased me out of a lot of tackles." The big victory for Rip Engle—his first in Big Ten country—was a shock to Illinois, which had a dismal season.

Weather at Syracuse can be a problem, but game time is when *real* trouble usually starts in Archbold Stadium. This was an ordinary game against a so-so Syracuse team (4–4–0), yet the 13–0 Lion victory was savored. Moore scored one touchdown on a 22-yard run, and the next was the work of great-hearted little Ron Younker, on a short gain after his 50-yard punt return had set up the score. Things were strangely tranquil between Rollicking Rip and Gentle Ben— Rip didn't know until afterward that the officials once had given his team only three downs.

Losing to West Virginia, 19–14, before a record Homecoming crowd of 32,221 at New Beaver Field was disconcerting, but Rip was more philosophical than usual, and even tried to show this Sunday visitor some slides he had taken in Japan. He said he had found the alumni saddened but not sadistic. The Mountaineers had a good team, with All-America tackles Sam Huff and Bruce Bosley; a fair-to-middling quarterback, Freddy Wyant; and even a little halfback named, nicely enough, Jack Rabbits.

Against Texas Christian when Lenny Moore gained 113 yards, Texas sportswriters conceded he'd "not been overrated." Before the game TCU Coach Abe Martin had said his team would be national leaders except for a blocked kick, an interception, and a fumble against Alabama and Arkansas. These three particular blunders cost Penn State a victory over the Horned Frogs. The Lions out-first-downed their opponents, 20–10, outrushed them, 191–172, and outpassed them (Bailey and Plum), 125–39. But they also lost to them, 20–7. Rip declared he'd never before had his offensive center called offside.

Travel by plane was still a novelty for the Lions in 1954, but a nine-game schedule called for trips to eight states, and they went to Fort Worth by air, staying Friday night at an abandoned ranch. Lenny Moore was the first black to play in Fort Worth, and—for the record—Penn State also played the first blacks in the Cotton Bowl (Triplett and Hoggard in 1948), the first in Miami (Dave Robinson against the University of Miami in September 1961), and in the Gator Bowl at Jacksonville (Dave Robinson against Georgia Tech in 1961).

The Penn, Holy Cross, and Rutgers games were easy preludes to Pitt. The Lions ran up their highest score in the Penn series and the widest margin of victory (35–13), effectively employing the scissors play (an inside reverse), which Coach Engle used long before it became famous at Syracuse and elsewhere. While the Quakers watched Lenny's 140 yards of a total 380 gained on the ground, Billy Kane (who had spent his freshman year at Penn) easily added 132, mostly on the scissors.

Having beaten Navy, Northwestern, West Virginia, and Nebraska, Pitt's Panthers were geared to stop Moore. Lenny, however, was used chiefly as a decoy, and Engle apologized for not giving him a chance at some eastern rushing records.

"Coach," said Lenny, "I had a wonderful time in there today. Faking is much easier on you."

Still, decoy Moore managed to set a single-season Penn State rushing mark of 1,082 yards, breaking Shorty Miller's record set in 1912.

Penn State's touchdowns were scored by Jack Sherry (on a pass from Bobby Hoffman) and by Bailey on a sneak from the 3. Mention of "serious dissension on the Penn State squad" in an unsigned letter printed in a Pittsburgh Sunday paper was puzzling—the only dissension noted was among the Lion regulars, most of them seniors, begging to get back in the game to keep Pitt from scoring. A more plaintive letter-writer asked the experts please, "Could Pitt and Penn State play for the eastern title, western division?" Dopesters, even before the game, were calling the Army-Navy classic a "Battle for the eastern championship," forgetting that Pitt had beaten Navy.

When Rip Engle escaped to the dressing room in the happy confusion after the 13–0 Pitt victory, his gaze fell on this blackboard message:

"Seniors 47; Pitt 0"

It was true. His seniors had played in three straight shutouts.

A major addition to the 1954 varsity coaching staff was John T. ("J.T.") White, who earned football letters at Ohio State and Michigan, playing center on the unbeaten, untied 1947 Wolverine team that won the national championship and defeated Southern California in the Rose Bowl. The 1976 season was his twenty-third on the staff as defensive end coach.

Most significant rule change in the early fifties was the elimination in 1952 of the free substitution rule, which temporarily broke the two-platoon system and even charged a time-out to insert a punting specialist. More than fifty colleges had abandoned the game because they were unable to compete with power-rich institutions.

The fair catch was another major concern. Eliminated in 1950, it was restored the next year, when a wave of the punt receiver's upraised hand was introduced as its signal. This practice was eliminated in 1955, although the raised-hand signal, minus the "wiggle," was retained. In 1952, a player so signaling could take two steps after catching the ball.

"Unsportsmanlike conduct" was closely scrutinized by coaches and the Rules Committee, but the "strong steps" taken were more in the nature of expressed disapproval than severe penalties. Faking injuries to avoid time-outs, and defensive signals designed to pull the offense offside were condemned. To discourage cases of sideline substitutes making spectacular tackles, the culprit was disqualified and a touchdown awarded (1954). Steps were taken to eliminate the "sucker shift," another method devised to get opponents offside, and an attempt also was made (1955) to abolish the "sleeper" or "hideout" play by requiring all offensive players to line up within 15 yards of the ball.

Notable safety measures in 1952 increased the defensive holding penalty from 5 to 15 yards, redefined clipping to include any block from behind against a player other than the ball carrier, and made suspension mandatory for unnecessary roughness, particularly striking with the forearm, clasped hands, or elbows. For some reason, flying blocks or tackles had been legalized the previous year.

Relaxation of substitution rules, beginning in 1955, allowed a player who started a quarter to re-enter the game in the same period, thus involving officials in complicated record-keeping. Minor changes allowed five time-outs per half instead of four (1950), and permitted a player holding the ball for a placement (with his knee on the ground) to get up and run, pass, or kick the ball (1955).

Compared with other sections of the country, eastern football was considered inferior in the early fifties, despite the acumen of strong coaches like Rip Engle, Charlie Caldwell of Princeton, Ben Schwartzwalder of Syracuse, Eddie Erdelatz of Navy, Earl Blaik of Army, and John Michelosen of Pitt. Furthermore, East was where it all began. Western and southern sportswriters were referring to the "effete East" nearly twenty years before Vice President Agnew made the term a weapon.

Caldwell's great 1950 and 1951 Princeton teams, with the storied Dick Kazmaier, were ranked only sixth nationally by the AP, probably because they played no intersectional opponents. Syracuse, awarded the Lambert Trophy in 1952, was humiliated by Alabama in the Orange Bowl, 61–6. Army's 1950 eleven, rated second nationally, lost to subpar Navy (3–6–0). Navy's 1954 "Team Called Desire," led by George Welsh and Ronnie Beagle, struck a blow for sectional prestige by defeating Mississippi in the Sugar Bowl (21–0), but the Middies' fine team had lost to Notre Dame and Pitt. Coach Erdelatz became a naval hero by defeating Colonel Red Blaik's Army elevens four out of five. The East reached possibly its saddest state when Pitt won the Lambert jewelry in 1953 with a 7–4 record and lost to Georgia Tech in the Sugar Bowl.

Naming a national champion became more prevalent in the fifties, with UPI joining the AP as an "unofficial" arbiter, awarding diadems before the bowls. In 1951 Tennessee won the national title, and Maryland's followers thought the Terps got a bad break in the AP's third place with a 10–0 record, including a victory over Tennessee in the Sugar Bowl. Michigan State's strong 9–0 claim was compensated the next year with the crown, and Maryland got its reward in 1953, although the Terps lost to Oklahoma in the Orange Bowl. In 1954 the press associations differed widely in their selection philosophy. UPI gave the title to UCLA, which had a perfect record (9–0) but was ineligible for the Rose Bowl, having played there the previous year. The AP awarded it to Ohio State, victorious over Southern California, 20–7, although the Trojans had been trounced, 34–0, by UCLA. Oklahoma (11–0), winner over Maryland (20–6) in the Orange Bowl, was the undisputed 1955 champion.

Athletic officials endeavored to arrange a 1955 calendar appropriate for Penn State's important Centennial year, scheduling the Pitt game as a home season climax, with Navy present for Homecoming —only the second New Beaver Field appearance of the Midshipmen. Syracuse, with Jimmy Brown, was another big home rival, and the major opponents to be played on the road were Army and Penn. Coach Engle disclaimed being a pessimist—"a pessimistic optimist," he called himself, "which means I'm a realist." His chief assets were Lenny Moore and junior quarterback Milt Plum, but realistically he thought his line strength and weight weren't equal to the schedule.

Rip's fears proved warranted when Army, in the second game, overpowered the Lions up front, although comparatively even statistics made the 35–6 score misleading. Moore, a marked man on every play, lost no stature, gaining most of his 76 yards through the tough Army forwards. Defeats by West Virginia (21–7) and Pitt (20–0) were bitter to take but not unexpected. The Mountaineers still had Huff, Bosley, Wyant, and two other senior backs—Bob Moss and Joe Marconi—as well as a tough sophomore fullback, Larry Krutko, and a mean guard, Chuck Howley. Pitt's tremendous size and strength, along with several inches of snow, which continued to fall throughout the game, didn't help the local situation. To have a senior of Moore's caliber end his college career on such a note was disappointing, but there was no way for Lenny to get outside the Pitt ends, Walton and Paluck. When he did, he wished he hadn't.

Navy's George Welsh had one of his greatest days playing against the Lions and spoiled the Centennial Homecoming. Welsh dominated the game, contributing to his side's victory almost as much as Light Horse Harry Wilson had against Navy on the same field thirty-two years before.

> When Penn State had Wilson
> Homecoming was fun.
> When Navy brought Welsh
> Alumni had none.

George completed 15 of 20 passes for 285 yards, establishing an all-time Navy record at the time and a New Beaver Field record seldom broken since. Rip Engle, sitting in the baseball bleachers the next spring, watched a Navy third baseman throw three times over his first baseman's head. "That guy," moaned Engle. "Not once did he throw over his receiver's head against us." "That guy" was the same George Welsh whose individual efforts had given his team a 34–14 victory the previous fall. He would be a valued assistant coach at State for many years, and then head coach at Navy.

Between routine wins over Penn (20–0) and Rutgers (34–13), the unexpected Syracuse victory almost made up for the disappointments of the hundredth anniversary season. It was an exciting personal duel, ending in a draw, between two of football's finest players—Lenny Moore and Jimmy Brown—with Moore's speed and deception matched by Brown's sheer power.

Penn State fought from behind, in the main, coming back from a 13–0 deficit after the first twenty minutes and from 20–7 after four minutes of the third quarter. Brown, later an all-time ground-gainer with the Cleveland Browns, did everything needed to win except that his second extra-point try was blocked by a sophomore end, Jack Farls. Besides his yardage on the ground, he scored all Syracuse points, caught two passes, intercepted a pass, and returned three kickoffs for 95 yards.

An interception by sophomore Joe Sabol late in the first half enabled Milt Plum to negotiate a touchdown pass to Billy Kane with 15 seconds remaining. The intercepted pass had been thrown by Ed Albright, Moore's teammate at Reading High School (a blocked Albright kick had given the Lions a last-minute victory in the 1953 game). The 13–7 half-time score supplied new vigor, but Brown took the second-half kickoff to near midfield, where a touchdown was saved by Moore's tackle. Brown immediately ran 26 yards from scrimmage to the 22, and on third down scored from the 6 to give the Orange a 20–7 lead. After a 59-yard Penn State drive in eleven plays, Moore went over from the two.

Plum, who saved a touchdown by tackling Brown on the Lion 13 after a 42-yard run (longest of the game), intercepted Albright's pass in the end zone, and the Lions drove 80 yards, with key gains by Moore and fullback Bill Straub. Plum made the tying points from the 1 and coolly place-kicked the winning point. After recovering a fumble in the last five seconds, with the home crowd roaring "More, More!," Penn State had a first down on the 2 as the game ended.

Coach Engle fervently praised offensive stars Moore, Plum, and Straub, but credited the defense for checking Brown in crisis situations, pointing out that Syracuse had scored seven touchdowns on previously undefeated Holy Cross. Lion defense leaders were Sam Valentine, Frank Reich, Otto Kneidinger, Earl Shumaker, Walt Mazur, Dan Radakovich, Jack Calderone, Dick DeLuca, and Willard (Bull) Smith.

Moore holds, as of 1976, three Penn State rushing records, averaging 19.8 yards per try against Rutgers in 1955; average yards per carry in one season, 8.0 in 1954; and 6.2 yards per carry for a career average, 1953–55. During the 1954 Holy Cross game he first broke the season's total yardage mark then held by Shorty Miller (set in 1912), who watched Moore's performance from the press box. (This record has since been exceeded by Lydell Mitchell and John Cappelletti.) Moore played his entire professional career with the Baltimore Colts and was named to the Professional Hall of Fame at Canton, Ohio, in July 1975.

32

Effete East Hits Ohio State

Interviewed about 1956 prospects early in balmy July, far enough from the season's opener with Penn to be lulled into uncoachlike security, Coach Engle said nothing to cause consternation in Columbus, Ohio, where the intense football atmosphere is well known and the critical, often provincial, press sees a non-Big Ten opponent as an unwelcome intruder (Columbus *Dispatch*), an interlude between "major" games. In fact, Columbus originated the "effete eastern football" notion with Penn State in mind. As one further hospitable gesture, the Nittany Lions also were called the "beasts from the East" by the Ohio State *Journal*.

How and why the game came about is cause for wonder. Captain of the 1912 Lion team in the unpleasant meeting between the two land-grant schools forty-four years before had been Pete Mauthe, president of the Youngstown (Ohio) Sheet and Tube Company. An advance story hinted that the renewal was pushed by Mauthe and his close friend John Galbraith, owner of the Pittsburgh Pirates and a Buckeye graduate. Charles T. Douds '22, a university trustee, suggests that his chance vacation meeting with Alfred B. Garrett of the OSU Athletic Board and their mutual desire to re-establish football relations also helped initiate the 1956 game and subsequent contests in 1963 and 1964.

However popular with Penn State fans, the move was an enigma to the Buckeyes and especially exasperating to wily Woody Hayes, who sensed the peril involved if his team, then undefeated, took the visiting Lions too lightly. He obviously couldn't convince his young men that the game would be anything but a warmup. Ohio State had smashed Nebraska (34–7), Stanford (32–20), and Illinois (26–6); boasted an eight-game winning streak; and was seeking its third straight undefeated Big Ten campaign. OSU deserved its rating as a three-touchdown favorite.

Penn State, suffering the throes of being an independent, opened its year by beating Penn 34–0 in a game lacking its past glamor.

The next week, at Michie Stadium, Army pulled away to a 14-point advantage in 12 minutes, and the Lions fought back courageously against a foe they hadn't defeated since 1899 and by whom they had been trampled mercilessly during post-World War II years. Like most opponents visiting West Point, Penn Staters resented the rude roaring chant of the Cadets, amplified by wired-in mikes, particularly because the noise seemed to peak when Army's adversaries were trying to get their offenses under way. Colonel Blaik used to say that nothing could be done to interfere with the "spirit of the Corps," but chances are that a wave of his hand from midfield would have quelled the din in a hurry. Quarterbacks could use their privilege to halt play and officials could assess penalties, but neither action had permanent results. A West Virginia team's sit-down strike was more effective on one occasion.

Milt Plum, coolest of many fine Penn State quarterbacks, seemed unbothered by the disagreeable sound. He had prevented two further Army touchdowns with great open-field tackles. Billy Kane and Bruce Gilmore led a drive enabling Maurice Schleicher to score early in the last period. Later, when Penn State was backed up on its own 6, Gilmore broke loose on a routine dive play and was in the clear on the right sideline, bound for the opposite end zone, where most of the Lion fans were sitting. Andy Moconyi was his bodyguard, but somehow Bob Kyasky, Army's quarterback, headed him off with a game-saving defensive play.

Holy Cross, another hapless independent, was a pushover as Penn State's third antagonist in a game of little value to either team.

And that's the way it was when the Lions went to Columbus. Coach Engle was blessed with Plum, a superb quarterback, and Sam Valentine, All-America guard (Football Writers, *Look* magazine) who weighed 194 pounds and backed up the line like a demon, especially in the game at hand, possibly because Ohio State had rejected him—too small. The Lions were well prepared, unawed by the largest crowd that had ever seen a Penn State team play (82,584), and convinced they could win. Furthermore, they had been stung by a quote in a Friday afternoon paper from Jim Parker, Ohio State's 254-pound All-America guard, who said: "We are looking forward to the game because we want to show an eastern team what Big Ten football looks like."

The 1956 Woody Hayes sample of Big Ten football didn't look like much for the first three quarters. A vicious Lion defense—Valentine, Radakovich, Mazur, Calderone, DeLuca, Rich McMillen, Charley Ruslavage, Les Walters, Doug Mechling, and Paul North—held on against Ohio State's typical grind-it-out offense while over 80,000 Ohio fans were expecting all hell to break loose any moment. In the second quarter the first of Milt Plum's exceptional kicks traveled 56 yards, rolling dead on the 1, to keep the Buckeyes in the hole until the first half ended scoreless.

A big move by the Buckeyes in the third period, also scoreless, reached the Lion 5, first down, before Gilmore pulled down an interception in the end zone and came upfield to the 21. Plum had punted 72 yards out of bounds on the Ohio 3, when Coach Hayes committed a crucial mistake. A mistimed substitution caused a 5-yard penalty. With field position inside the 50 and Gilmore, Kane, Babe Caprara, and Plum in the backfield, Penn State, when it got the ball, fought its way to a first down on the 14. A third-down pass, Plum to Kane, looked like a touchdown, but was called out of bounds one foot from the line. Caprara tried—no gain. The clock showed 3:35 to play when Gilmore finally went over and Plum kicked the goal.

Forced out of their hard-nosed game, the Buckeyes took to the air. Leo Brown, on a "transcontinental" pass play from Jim Roseboro at midfield, was run out of bounds on the 3 by Ray Alberigi, and Don Clark went off tackle for 6 points with 1:58 remaining. The entry of Frank Kremblas to kick the tying point caused a 5-yard illegal substitution penalty because this was the year specialists couldn't be used without a time-out. Kicking from the 7 instead of the 2 is more difficult psychologically than mechanically—Kremblas missed, and Clint Law recovered Ohio's onside kick. The game ended three plays later with Penn State holding the ball on the home team's 37. Rip Engle and Jim O'Hora, to their happy amazement, were carried from

Ohio Stadium on the shoulders of their tired, bruised players, who went around looking for other people to carry, too.

The letdown expected against West Virginia didn't materialize, and at Syracuse the following week, such a controversy flared that the atmosphere was charged for the rest of the season. With 1:49 to play, the Orange team was fourth down on its own 35 and a punt was inevitable. Fighting to overcome a 13–9 Syracuse margin, Coach Engle readied Plum, his ace quarterback, to replace Al Jacks. Immediately a howl went up from the Syracuse bench, activated by word sent down from Assistant Coach Roy Simmons that the substitution was illegal. The crux of the matter was a rule that a player could re-enter the game *once* if he had *started* the quarter and subsequently been removed. Plum insisted he was eligible, Coach Engle did everything in his power to convince the officials of their error, but Umpire Leonard Dobbins refused to allow Plum on the field, penalized Penn State 15 yards, and gave the Orange a first down at midfield. Perhaps the unkindest cut of all came when Rip arrived home to be greeted by his family with "Well, did you or didn't you?"

Whether Engle had made a mistake or not was argued until Monday morning, when Lion coaches viewed the films and the local press learned that Plum was legal. He had entered the game with several other Lion regulars shortly before the end of the third quarter, had remained to start the last period, and was removed for a rest approximately 5 minutes from the finish. The outcome of what would have been his passing attack is only conjectural, but Penn State was denied its rightful opportunity to take over the ball. The game films, escorted to Syracuse by Freshman Coach Earl Bruce, drew a sympathetic reaction from local newsmen who had been doubters, but the score nonetheless was 13–9. If future football writers face the dilemma of track writers today in having to wait for films to report meet results, such episodes may provide the motivation for changing the NCAA rule that a college football game is over after 60 minutes have been played.

Another kind of pressure was felt against North Carolina State. The rivalry was sharpened because the Wolfpack, full of former Pennsylvania high school stars, was coached by Earle Edwards, assisted by Al Michaels and Bill Smaltz—all Lion alumni. In the final 3 minutes, a scoreless battle became a 14–7 victory. Plum began the scoring action when he engineered a 57-yard drive that seemed likely to win the game. But with 1:30 to play the visitors made it a tie on a pass from Bill Franklin to Bob Pepe. Plum then led an almost perfect scoring drive, calculating every move to protect precious seconds. Getting the Lions to the Wolfpack 21 with 45 seconds to go, he threw a wrinkle pass to Kane, who stepped out of bounds on the 16, and then the same pass, good to the 9. Milt and Engle used the last time-out to plan one more pass play and, if it failed, to have the kicking tee ready for the last play. While North Carolina State watched the deep receivers, Plum spotted Les Walters on the 3, saw a little daylight, and threw the ball. Walters, making a stunning catch, struggled over with three defenders hanging on his back.

Plum's pro-like performance forecast his creditable career with the Cleveland Browns and later with the Detroit Lions. Senior Ray Alberigi's last appearance was one of his finest. In eight of the season's nine games, Ray either led all Lion ball carriers or was second.

Pitt had Cotton Bowl dreams and a 6–2 record before the Penn State game, with victories over West Virginia, Syracuse, Duke, Oregon, Notre Dame, and Army. Feeling letdown with the 7–7 tie, Pitt's Panthers went on to defeat Miami of Florida and then settled for the Gator Bowl, where they dropped a close decision to bowl-wise Georgia Tech. The tie also disappointed Penn State, especially because Plum missed a last-minute field goal which, had it been successful, might have kept Pitt bowl-less. A tie is supposed to be no more satisfying than the proverbial kissing-a-sister, but the Panthers almost kissed Milt for his miss.

Dr. Eisenhower had moved on to the presidency of Johns Hopkins University in July of 1956, and immediately was succeeded by his vice president and recent dean of engineering, Dr. Eric A. Walker, perhaps Penn State's first president with an all-around enthusiasm for athletics, a man concerned with the progress of all Penn State sports.

Milton Eisenhower's interest was apparent but muted, except his pleasure in being a fishing companion of his older brother, who enjoyed central Pennsylvania's streams as a guest at Penn State's President's House while he himself was occupying the White House.

Milton Stover Eisenhower was 51 when he came from the presidency of Kansas State, his alma mater and that state's land-grant university, and from previous service in governmental posts. His experience and national reputation answered Penn State's continuing need for stronger identification as the East's counterpart of the Midwest's large state universities.

Among dignitaries attending his inauguration in October 1950 on New Beaver Field, during Coach Rip Engle's inaugural season there, was General Dwight D. Eisenhower, then Columbia University's president and soon to become President of the United States. The close relationship of the brothers added public interest that Penn State hitherto had not experienced.

An eloquent and popular speaker, Dr. Eisenhower at once began tours of the commonwealth, from which his parents had migrated years before. Addressing alumni and other civic, educational, and business groups, he built up public and personal relations to match Penn State's academic and physical plant development, attracting increased legislative support and aid from gifts and grants.

On campus, his flair for involvement with students and faculty was conspicuous in a period of historic significance for the institution. Its long-deferred renaming as The Pennsylvania State University was authorized in November 1953, but the following year the community defeated a referendum to change the name of the borough that had been known successively as Farm School, Agricultural College, and finally State College.

Accordingly, when Penn State celebrated its Centennial in 1955, the opening of the University Park post office in the new Hetzel Union Building was a major event. The postal substation has its own zip code (16802) and is Penn State's official address and dateline for all press releases. Strangers once bewildered by a town without a name of its own now have a double identification problem, a problem not likely to go away, although the expanding, primarily residential area around Mt. Nittany (the defeated name) is also becoming known as the Centre (County) Region.

Centennial year milestones were many. Ground was broken for an all-faith chapel, provided from gifts, which was named for Helen Eakin Eisenhower, the president's late wife, who died after a short illness in July 1954. When Dwight Eisenhower delivered the Centennial commencement address in June (announcing his proposed peaceful uses of atomic energy), the United States President received from his brother one of the university's rarely bestowed honorary degrees and its first doctorate of laws.

Although the Milton Eisenhower family had come to Penn State with the thought of remaining, the deeply personal loss of his wife may have accentuated the president's reluctance to contend longer with mounting external and internal pressures of a state university hampered by insecurity over legislative support. His brother's coming campaign for a second term and the opportunity to be nearby in the Baltimore-Washington sector made the Johns Hopkins offer irresistible. He resigned his Penn State post in June 1956, but his close friendship continues, and he became an honorary alumnus in June 1975.

Rip was justifiably concerned about the 1957 season. In the opener Penn was troublesome, despite its weakness in the Ivy League, but the Lions succeeded in defeating Coach Steve Sebo's well-coached team, 19–14. Army's first visit to Penn State's campus proved the Cadets could play away from home, overcoming a 13–6 half-time lead by scoring 21 points in the third quarter. Pete Dawkins was Army's big gun. The Lions had another home disappointment against a very good Vanderbilt team, led by Phil King, a Cherokee Indian.

Frank Patrick, Penn State's perennial Syracuse scout, warned all week that center Mike Bill "could be annoyed." In the early moments at Archbold Stadium center Bill heaved the ball over the kicker's head with such "annoyance" that Syracuse never recovered from the resulting Lion touchdown. As the half ended, Penn State's Bucky Paolone caught a pass on the one-inch line and registered indignation when it was nullified, but it wasn't considered an incident, perhaps because the Lions were surprised to win, 20–12. The game marked the advent of Richie Lucas, who entered in the second quarter for the injured Al Jacks, the East's best passer at the moment. Richie pleased Rip with his strong running and defensive play against Syracuse and his showing the next week (8 for 14, 102 yards) when West Virginia was defeated at Morgantown, 27–6.

Notwithstanding victories over Syracuse and West Virginia, the 1957 season's highlight was, oddly enough, a triumph over Holy Cross at Worcester. An exciting game against a fine team was played in a refreshing collegiate environment, where a local boy proved that you *can* go home again, and as a hero.

After the sophisticated football climate of Columbus and Champaign, West Point's battlefield approach, and fan hostility in Morgantown and Syracuse, Penn Staters delighted in Worcester's old-fashioned pregame exhilaration. Nightly pep rallies had ended with a special one Saturday morning (after Mass). Students, many out-landishly dressed and sporting purple derbies, swarmed on the field to greet their team's arrival, the signal for din unabated throughout the game. In addition to good-natured spirit, Holy Cross had a squad inspired by the country's top offensive player, Tom Greene, whose passing and running made him almost a team by himself.

Fortunately, to counteract this force, Penn State had Worcester's own Dave Kasperian, abetted by other helpful Lions like workhorse Babe Caprara, Les Walters, Bill Wehmer and his memorable tackle, and the running wonders, Pat Botula and Eddie Caye.

The day belonged to Dave. He was carried off the field on the shoulders of the Armenian Club of Worcester, 200 strong, having re-alized his dream of coming home to play before family and friends.

The honors were earned. Kasperian, who came to Penn State after an Army stint, wasn't known to be football material until he came out for the team. Holy Cross people that afternoon wondered how he got away from Worcester. Between his one early mistake, a fumble after a 10-yard gain, and his leaping interception on the game's last play, he gained 97 yards in 16 carries, returned one kickoff for 66 yards, two punts for 33, caught one pass for 28 and defensively was at the right place at the right time.

The first half was an epic of frustration. There were other fumbles; Richie Lucas stepped out of bounds trying to pass on third down; the reliable Charley Ruslavage centered the ball high over Richie's head and sent it flying through the end zone for a safety; Skippy Stellfox, senior reserve guard, broke his leg. The home team led 2–0 at the half after Lucas missed Walters in the end zone.

The Crusaders' quarterback, Greene, top pitcher in the country, missed his first seven passes (he was fearfully rushed), but then hit end Charlie Pacunas for a 78-yard scoring play. Kasperian returned the kickoff to the Crusader 23, Moconyi added seven on a reverse, and a fake from Lucas to Caprara became a touchdown pass to Walters. Caprara kicked the extra point, but Holy Cross was ahead, 8–7. A fumble on the Crusader 17 recovered by Ruslavage got the Lions to the 1, and Lucas called a sure-fire dive play, only to have the dive man get by without the ball. Since no one tackled Richie, he stepped over the line for a touchdown, and the score was 14–8.

The rest of the game made up in thrills what it lacked in score, al-though Penn State seemed in control with the ball on the Holy Cross 20 seven minutes before the finish. Taking over on downs, the indomitable Crusaders began an unstoppable-looking advance as Greene completed a long pass to Dave Stecchi on the Lion 24. At four minutes to go, they had a first down on the 8. After three plays had been stopped, on fourth down and 5, Greene rolled out to the right with no intention of passing (the play that had beaten Syracuse). Wehmer raced Greene for the corner of the end zone and hit him back a few feet. Walters came up to help keep Greene from struggling forward for victory, and the official signaled that Penn State could take possession an inch from the goal.

In the two minutes remaining, Holy Cross was called once for offside, Penn State once for delay of game. Finally, on fourth down, Lucas dropped back to kick, turned his back on the rushing players, and coolly strolled out of the end zone, giving Holy Cross a safety. But the game wasn't really over until Kasperian's interception. Unimpeachable sources had it that Kasperian, Sr., a local barber, was moved up one chair in the shop.

Captain Joe Sabol played inspiring defensive football at guard against Syracuse and West Virginia, but was a loss at winning the toss. This caused the *Football Letter* to suggest replacing the traditional ritual—often an important factor in bad weather. Accepting football as a game of brains and brawn, why couldn't the two teams have their player with the highest IQ face each other in midfield (with the PA on) to answer a brain-teaser presented by the referee and furnished by the ECAC in a sealed envelope?

In 1958, before he left for a coaching clinic in Paris (of all places!), Rip Engle came up with one of the classic preseason interview lines: "If we are as good as every team we play, we should be expected to win only half our games." Captain Steve Garban, center, and his close friend, halfback Dave Kasperian (both selected All-East that year), were loath to differ substantially with their coach but felt that the Lions would be bigger and better than in 1957, with more determination and enthusiasm.

Sports information got a new director in 1958 when Jim Coogan moved up to head public information and hired Jim Tarman from Princeton to do the sports chores. Tarman began his indoctrination by establishing a close friendship with Al Clark, veteran sports editor of the Harrisburg *Patriot-News*. Al asked Jim, on his maiden voyage with the squad, to have Coach Engle, sometime on the trip out, diagram a "key play" he'd use against Nebraska. When the new publicity man returned from that disheartening defeat in Lincoln (14–7), Clark was at the airport with a bleak suggestion: "You guys go West, just keep going West." He told Tarman to put the "key play" in the mail. That was fine with Engle, who preferred to forget it. The play set up Nebraska's winning touchdown, made by Pat Fischer on a 92-yard kickoff return—the first time this had happened to Rip in his twenty-eight years of coaching.

Two weeks later Tarman endured induction into the humiliation of Michie Stadium. Coach Blaik was premiering his "lonesome end" act, starring Bill Carpenter, with immeasurable help from quarterback Joe Caldwell and two other tough backs, Bob Anderson and Pete Dawkins, both proficient passers. An awesome attack rolled up 26 points in the first half, and the second was scoreless, not because the colonel became charitable but because his first team fumbled unaccountably and Penn State's defense stiffened a bit.

The season's second game mercifully ended the Penn-Penn State series, the Lions winning 43–0 without really trying to run up the score. Coach Engle used thirty-five players, nearly all the traveling squad. The Lions had lost only nine of the thirty games played since Penn State's first victory (1911). The defeat may have hastened the departure of Coach Steve Sebo, although he wasn't fired until after the next year when, to Penn's embarrassment, Penn's Quakers won their first Ivy League title. This was when Cornell fired able Lefty James and Harvard bounced Lloyd Jordan. Those Ivies!

In the Penn game Captain Garban and Coach Engle won a long argument with the officials, indicating how silly and little understood the substitution rules had become. For years Rip's punter had two tackles and a fullback standing as a beefy barrier. Referee Brennan, informing Garban that it was illegal, started to step off a 5-yard penalty and told Coach Engle, who had rushed out on the field, that the blockers would be ruled illegal unless they were taken out and then returned as linemen. Rip argued that the rule didn't apply if the linemen were placed 5 yards or more in back of the scrimmage line, but Field Judge Montgomery sided with Brennan. They agreed to withhold judgment until they could study the rules at half time and then informed Engle that he was correct.

Penn State made its first television appearance against Boston University on October 18, 1958, in a regionally televised, one-sided game (34–0). More than a million people in New England saw Wayne Berfield, substituting for the injured Garban, intercept a pass and run 98 yards for a score, still a record. (Garban, who'd had a slight concussion, could remember his girl's name [Penny] but thought he was playing against Holy Cross.) The game's rushing leader was Sam Sobczak of DuBois with 74 yards. Wayne and Sam were unknowns who developed into valuable regulars along with Stew Barber, Norm Neff, Dick Hoak, Charlie Janarette, Don Jonas, Bill Popp, and Frank Korbini. On the freshman team that season were Pat Funair, Bob Mitinger, and Jim Schwab, all sons of superstars at Bucknell (Frank) and Lafayette (Bob, Sr., and Dutch).

Losing to Syracuse on New Beaver Field in 1958 (14–6) was unusual, but Saturday night talk was more about "that referee" than "that score." While Syracuse made its touchdowns on hard, crushing drives, Penn State could have won if an end, all alone in the end zone, hadn't dropped a Richie Lucas pass that had arrived in his hands. Coach and fans were outraged, however, because the Lions had been penalized eight times and the visitors not at all for more than 59 minutes. The referee, assigned by the ECAC, was Robert W. Van Lengen, a Syracuse law graduate. Six illegal shift calls, usually at crucial times, frustrated the Lions, who were confused by the Syracuse "jitterbug" defense that jumped on the word command "now." Captain Garban protested its continued use, and Coach Engle called the game the worst officiated he'd ever seen. Late in its course Syracuse gambled from its own 44, 4th and 1, with the marker exactly on the 45. Two officials (Ailinger and Tucker) marked the ball's progress inside the 45. Referee Van Lengen came running up and signaled a first down for the Orange.

Scheduling Furman exposed Lion officials to much ribbing: "Where is Furman?" they were asked repeatedly. A week before the game, Furman's publicity office called from Greenville, South Carolina, to ask where State College was. Theirs wasn't a gag—some of the official party had made hotel reservations in Philadelphia.

A 14–14 tie at Morgantown was the only near success of the Mountaineers against the Lions since 1955. Penn Staters thought they'd won when sophomore Dick Hoak took a pass in the flat from Richie Lucas and ran 80 yards for a score, but the play was nullified by a holding penalty.

Afterward Rip said he'd never give up on this team. "These kids deserve a break," he said. "Maybe we're like that guy who kept trying to get to the top of the hill and always slipped back. He finally made it, didn't he?" Sisyphus never made it, Rip was told, but was banished to Hades for saying mean things about officials.

The season was saved by an unexpected 25–21 triumph, after trailing 21–12 through three quarters, over Pitt, which had beaten UCLA, Notre Dame, Minnesota, and West Virginia, and tied Army. Captain Garban played his greatest game at center, and two sophomores teamed up to give the Lions their winning touchdown after Al Jacks had passed to Norm Neff for a score that made it 21–18. On the Panther 18 with half the final period gone, Dick Hoak (later a long-term Steeler utility back) took a pitchout from Jacks, ran to one sideline, reversed his field to the left, and was finally tackled on the 9. Don Jonas, an All-State quarterback at Scranton High (and later a standout in the Canadian Football League) then took a handoff from Jacks, who had faked to fullback Botula, slanted toward the left corner of the end zone, and made it.

The game was part of the city of Pittsburgh's 200th anniversary celebration, and Coach Engle lamented that his team couldn't play a bicentennial game honoring William Pitt annually. At that point, Pitt's alumni would willingly have postponed the next meeting for 500 years. Florida and Mississippi had both scouted Pitt as possible Cotton Bowl opponents.

The two-point conversion came into play in 1958 with many coaches dubious and some opposed to it. They said it would result in a "numbers guessing game" and add to the pressures; and they anticipated derision if they made the wrong choice. Fans loved the added element of excitement and the possibility of fewer tie games. The new rule had little effect on Penn State's season.

After scoring first against West Virginia, the Lions were successful with two points, but its use in that situation has been all but abandoned. When the Lions came within three points of the Panthers at 21–18, the crowd expected they'd try for a kick. That could have made a field goal the winning margin, but Jacks was instructed to try for a pass, which was grounded. Coach Engle explained later that if his kicker, Jonas, had gone in, he wouldn't have been "live" near the end of the game because of the current substitution rule. Jonas made the coach look good by running, not kicking, for the winning points.

33

Last of New Beaver Field

The summer of 1959 brought more furrows to the brow of white-haired Rip Engle. Scheduled for the historic fifty-first season were some real tartars—an opener with Missouri at Columbia; the ever-dreaded visit to West Point; the long-planned Illinois game, at Cleveland for no known reason; a bout with Syracuse, a preseason favorite for the national title; and then Pitt, waiting to spoil whatever success the Lions might have had. Ahead from 1960 through 1964 were schedules with such intersectional opponents as Missouri, Miami (Florida), California, Air Force, Rice, Oregon, UCLA, Ohio State, and Houston.

Furthermore, Penn State's admissions problems had implications for football recruitment. State land-grant universities bore the brunt of a great college enrollment crunch in this period, but the commonwealth's traditional broad distribution of its support for higher education kept Penn State's appropriations lower than was the case in other states. This had to be offset by raising tuition and admissions standards. Four out of five applicants were refused, 90 per cent of the new freshman class of 3,200 would be in the upper 20 per cent of their high school classes, and tuition had increased 30 per cent. Since the athletic budget paid the full cost of all aid to players, the staff had to think in terms of filling the new stadium, to be completed in 1960; scheduling good opponents to attract a hard core of season ticket buyers; winning games to hold them; and recruiting fast, brawny players—with brains.

For the present, the coach's blessings included Richie Lucas, potential All-America senior quarterback; at least nine other seniors, led by fullback Captain Pat Botula; and high-quality linemen like Andy Stynchula, Earl Kohlhaas, and Frank Korbini. Among capable juniors on hand were Dick Hoak, Jimmy Kerr, Sam Sobczak, and Dick Pae, all backs, with linemen Henry Oppermann, Bill Popp, and Stew Barber. Sophomore newcomers, traditionally ignored until fall practice, were rumored unusually promising—an end named Bob Mitinger, quarterback Galen Hall, centers Dick Wilson and Jay Huffman, tackle Chuck Siemenski, and backs Al Gursky and Roger Kochman.

Before the Missouri opener, a reporter asked Rip how long he had been at Penn State. "Ten years," he said, "but I have a feeling the next ten weeks will be longer." Alumni, however, congregated with undimmed enthusiasm in the lobby of Columbia's Hotel Daniel Boone, as they do in any hotel where the team stays. This kind of gathering was always a trial to the otherwise affable Engle. Such Saturday morning distractions made him prefer hell to hotel lobbies, where he had to talk with well-meaning but overly inquisitive and unduly optimistic alumni. He smiled while staring into space and, as usual, he didn't get much sleep on Friday. Those damn Columbia street cleaners had been working all night!

The game's proprietor was Richie Lucas, whose senior year buildup was unparalleled among Lion players. Hailed as "the best all-around quarterback in the nation," he was dubbed "Riverboat Richie" (by the Harrisburg *Patriot-News*) because he had the manner of a gambling signal caller. The somewhat farfetched nickname contributed effectively to the All-America campaign, but more valuable was his masterful quarterbacking against Missouri—he completed 10 of 11 passes for 154 yards, the miss being an accurate shot to Dick Hoak, who was just too well covered. Richie was Penn State's top ground-gainer and handled the team in its first game with cool, seasoned perfection. The double-wing attack Engle unveiled for Missouri and the deadly passing accuracy of Lucas were too much for Coach Dan Devine's Tigers. The Lions took a 13–0 lead very early in the third quarter, were never under serious pressure, and won, 19–8.

Against VMI the Lions started the third quarter ahead only 7–0, but some effective kick returns by Dick Hoak helped produce a 21–0 victory. Colgate, weaker than usual (58–20), was the third-game opponent.

The annual fruitless journey to the Military Academy had long been an irritant to Lion squads and coaches but had an opposite effect on students and alumni. They looked forward to their trek through the beautiful Catskills for a football game played in crisp, colorful autumn weather. They could rise above the traffic jams in Highland Falls, the uninformed and bored MPs, the Cadets' insidious chant drowning out visitors' cheers from the end-zone sections, and seemed not to care that Penn State hadn't won on the Hudson for sixty years. Facetious remedies were suggested by alumni, but this was the year Penn State would come to grips with Army's psychological warfare.

Sportswriters deservedly credited the monumental contributions of Richie Lucas. But they were unaware that an unsung hero in the stands had a hand in the *savoir faire* shown by the Lions. The team's twelfth man, never officially associated with Penn State football, was Hal Hein '45 of Thornwood, New York. Watching Penn State's 1958 defeat from his end-zone seat in the oppressive atmosphere of Michie Stadium, he concluded that the deflation he felt also afflicted the Lions. Putting his B.A. in psychology to work, he searched New York's broadcasting and recording studios for a West Point sound track—songs, cheers, and ordinary crowd noises. Two weeks before the game Coach Engle received the record and a letter pleading for its use to familiarize the players with the battle sounds ahead.

Something of a gadgeteer himself, Rip took to the idea, had the necessary amplifying equipment rigged up at the practice field, and prepared the squad the week before the game to the sound of music from Michie. By Thursday what had once been terrorizing was familiar and almost friendly. Hal must have been almost as pleased with another ploy devised to handle Army's neat trick of always asking the visiting team to come on the field first, before the home team, to the home crowd's barely polite applause, if that. The visitors then waited, cooling their heels nervously, until the Cadet legions surged out between two Long Gray Lines, while their guests stood by feeling like the Lost Battalion. Assistant Coach Jim O'Hora suggested deferring Penn State's entrance. "They can't make us come out first," said Jim bravely. "Let's get in there in the legal time, but not before Army. While West Point's players waited and their coaches fidgeted, nothing happened until the entrance had to be made. Out came the Lions with the Cadet players, both sharing the tumultuous applause. Score, first quarter: Penn State 7; Army 0. Score, first half: Penn State 17; Army 3.

The Cadets had a poor first half, made mistakes, incurred more penalties than usual, and had some bad breaks, but Lucas was sharp in everything he did—passing, scoring two touchdowns on rollouts, and playing well defensively. Kerr, having one of the best days of his career, was the leading ball carrier with 87 yards, nearly four times as many as the top Cadet, Roger Zaliskas. Sam Stellatella kicked a field goal and two extra points.

A bad break for Army occurred in the last moments of the first half. The Lions seemed set to score when a Lucas pass was batted into the air and intercepted by an Army guard, Mike Casp, who ran about 90 yards for a touchdown only to have an offside flag dropped against Army. The disgruntled noises from the Cadet cheering section were not among those on Hal Hein's record.

Correcting some mistakes in the second half, Army scored a touchdown in the third quarter, thanks chiefly to the passing of Joe Caldwell. The Lions had to fight off a final thrust of the Cadets that threatened to tie or win. With three minutes to play and West Point in possession on Penn State's 21, Richie gold-plated his gambler reputation. Sensing a pass up the middle, he left his man and played the ball. The pass hit smack in his arms. Penn State 17; Army 11.

Two octogenarians heard the news in their homes with great satisfaction. One was Earl Hewitt, Sr., of Indiana, Pennsylvania, who had scored the winning touchdown against Army in 1899. The other, a retired dentist in Tacoma, Washington, was Dr. W. B. Burns, who kicked the goal. An alumnus congratulating Lucas later said: "But, please, Richie, let's not wait until you're 81 before we have another hero."

Alumni at the game had a deliriously happy time. Phil Bell, Sr. '37 reported that his young son, noting the name of Michie Stadium, asked, "After this, will they call it Richie Stadium?" Over 400 alumni had come from New York, as usual, on a chartered boat of the Hudson River Day Line. One serenely tipsy alumnus leaned out the window of a bus and softly, politely sang to each passing Cadet, "We're sorry you lost." A small undergraduate combine, calling itself the Ying Yang Band, which made the trip at its own expense, eluded all MPs prior to the opening kickoff and paraded the length of the field playing "Anchors Aweigh."

An undefeated sweep toward the Syracuse showdown included easy victories over Boston University (21–12) and Illinois (20–9). Cleveland citizens made it plain that theirs is not a college football town, staying away in droves as two of the nation's better teams battled in the near emptiness of Municipal Stadium. The civic promotion planned for nearly three years drew only 15,045 fans, including Mayor Anthony J. Celebrezze, who called it "the most welcome event in Cleveland's gala Seaway Year calendar." Approximately 60,000 chose to wait for Sunday's Browns-Redskins game. Rip Engle's friends noticed his lack of tension Saturday morning—no one had told him that the Nickel Plate Railroad ran directly under the Hotel Cleveland, where the Penn Staters were quartered Friday night.

Roger Kochman, a much-publicized sophomore back who had appeared briefly as a pass receiver in a spot situation, made his formal debut against West Virginia with 111 yards rushing in 8 carries and a 52-yard gallop for his first Penn State touchdown. After Lucas suffered a concussion, his chores were capably handled by Galen (Butch) Hall. In fact, the Reddies, as the second team was being called (red practice jerseys to contrast with the varsity blue), played much of the game, quieting Coach Engle's fears, 28–10. The third team or Greenies, incidentally, preferred to be called the Gang Greens.

From the season's beginning it was obvious that Syracuse and Penn State would fight it out for the eastern championship, and excitement was rife with the Orange 6–0 and the Lions 7–0. Rather than wondering if there'd be a bowl bid, Syracuse was weighing which to accept, and it had the betting edge. Its victims, all defeated by generous margins, had been Kansas, Maryland, Navy, Holy Cross, West Virginia, and Pittsburgh. After going on to demolish Colgate, Boston University, and UCLA, Syracuse defeated Texas in the Cotton Bowl to be declared national champion.

Missing an early touchdown when Lucas' accurate 50-yard pass hit Hoak on the Syracuse 2 and bounced away, Penn State kept its early momentum going with Hoak's spectacular pickup catch on another Lucas pass. In six plays the Lions arrived at the 16 from the Orange 45. On fourth down Kerr was in the slot between end and tackle in a formation with an end split. Lucas faked neatly to full-back Botula, made an inside handoff to Roger Kochman, and continued to fake a rollout to the left. Kerr cut to the right, blocking the Syracuse left end, Fred Mautino. Kochman shot between right guard and tackle and ran headlong into Ernie Davis and Ger Schwedes on the 2, but pulled both Syracusans over the goal line with him. Sam Stellatella missed the extra point—only his second failure all year in this department but probably worth the national championship to Syracuse.

After the first quarter, reserve strength enabled the Orange to dominate their last game on New Beaver Field. In the second period Schwedes scored on a pitchout from Dave Sarette after a 43-yard drive and Bob Yates, a left-footed kicker, put Syracuse ahead 7–6 with his placement. Early in the second half a "big play" gave the Orange a 14–6 margin. Covering 46 yards in 8 tries, Syracuse reached the Lion 10. On third down, Lucas knocked down a Sarette pass in the end zone, but on fourth Sarette crossed up the Lions by throwing to fullback Art Baker—the first fullback pass he had used all year. The visitors scored again after 3:40 in the final period, going 41 yards in 9 plays, with Davis crashing over from the 1. Yates missed the point, but this seemed trivial because the score was 20–6. Then came the grand finale of one of college football's greatest games.

The kickoff by Yates, high and long, was caught by Kochman at the west side of the field's north end. Roger later described the play:

> I just ran where there wasn't anyone, but saw No. 39 (Baker) coming at me fast. Huffman [it was Kerr] took him out fast. I saw an opening to the right, and as I broke, Bud Kohlhaas made the big block that cut me free [the block was on Yates]. Out of the corner of my eye I could see someone coming up [Mautino at the Syracuse 35]. He missed me, just brushing an ankle. I made a quick decision not to cut to the center, but made up my mind I'd run as hard as I could along the sideline until I dropped. Someone was coming up [Ernie Davis]. I just wanted to get to the end zone as fast as I could.

Kochman pulled away from Davis in the last 20 yards, and Ernie slowed down as Kochman reached the 5. Coach Engle gave the unnecessary order to try for two points, but Lucas was rushed, and his pass to Hoak was short. The score was 20–12.

Again the momentum had changed, with excitement continuing at fever pitch. Penn State forced two kicks by Yates, and on the second,

Andy Stynchula made one of the year's best defensive plays. Running through Roger Davis (Orange All-America tackle), who was merely to brush-block him, Andy headed for the three Yates protectors—Sarette, Baker, and Maury Youmans. He lunged between Youmans and Baker, somehow getting his knee in the middle of Maury's back. Yates got off a perfectly timed kick, but Andy hit the ball with his right forearm and it bounced to the left corner of the field, chased by Mautino and Bob Mitinger. As Mautino was about to scoop it up, Sam Sobczak hit him like a steamroller and Mautino went over backward, the ball rolling to the 1-yard line, where it was pounced on by an unidentified Syracusan, with Mitinger on top of him. A single Sobczak lunge was enough for the touchdown. The two-point play attempted was the same as the one called successfully for Kochman's first-quarter touchdown. It was a good gamble for a tie game, but the play was jammed up by Gene Grabosky, a 250-pound guard who had spent his freshman year at Penn State.

The dauntless Lions still had plenty of fire, and Syracuse needed all the poise of the fine team it was. Proving great under extreme pressure, the Orange slowly and methodically advanced the ball after the kickoff, under which the Lions had come downfield as if possessed. Four consecutive first downs ran out the clock. The Lions—outweighed, outmuscled, and outplayed—had fought valiantly. Coaches Engle and Schwartzwalder, men of many differences, said sincere, gracious things about each other's team. The game itself was a great boost for eastern football.

Kochman's 100-yard return isn't listed as a Penn State record, because of what some believe is an unjust technicality of scoring statistics. Since the playing field is only 100 yards long, the maximum kickoff return should be 100 yards. Roger the Comet's run at least could be listed as the record for the field from the north going south.

One record established in the game can never be broken: The New Beaver Field attendance mark was set, at 32,800. Burke M. (Dutch) Hermann '12, retired professor of history and former coach, played in the first game on New Beaver Field when his team defeated Grove City 31–0 in 1909, and he watched the last—won over Holy Cross 46–0 on November 14, 1959—from the press box. Most opponents had found the Lions hard to beat on what would soon be "Old" Beaver Field, where, in 51 seasons, Penn State had won 184 games, lost 34, and tied 11.

The score was 39–0 against Holy Cross when the Lion second

team (Reddies) started a 50-yard drive with only a few minutes to play. From the 1 Sobczak was stopped dead. "What a hell of a time for a goal-line stand," lamented a Worcester newsman. Dick Pae tried next to make the last touchdown on the old field, but the ball squirted out of his hands, and Jim Smith, third-string 223-pound sophomore tackle from Latrobe (and the captain in 1961), fell on it. Sam Stellatella kicked the final point.

As Coach Engle left the dressing room he was accosted by Oscar Buchenhorst, "Executive Locker Room Doorwatcher."

"Rip," he said, "I can't do anything with those crazy kids on the field. Will you talk to them?"

The mellow Rip agreed. In the gloomy stadium with rain pouring down, he found eight students covered with mud, hard at work digging holes around the goal posts, two with shovels.

"Hey fellows," said Rip, "why don't you go home?"

"We can't, Coach," one replied. "Everybody would laugh at us. Besides, nobody needs 'em now."

"I need 'em. We have to practice on the field a few more years."

At that, the workers threw down their shovels and began to walk away. One looked back:

"If you need 'em, Coach, we'll leave 'em."

34

The Bowl Era Begins

The 1959 home schedule no sooner had been completed than athletic officials received a "feeler" from promoters of the first Liberty Bowl, tentatively set for Philadelphia's Municipal Stadium on Saturday, December 19. Coach Engle requested no consideration or mention of the proposition until after the Pitt game.

Each year the Pitt-Penn State situation defies analysis. Penn State had an 8–1 record and Pitt was 6–3 but had beaten UCLA, Duke, and Notre Dame. The Panthers lost to West Virginia, a victim of the Lions, and had been crushed by Syracuse 35–0, after which Coach Johnny Michelosen was hung in effigy. The Lions entered the game with their best record in ten years, an All-America quarterback, a bowl bid in their pockets, and spirits high. Pitt's C men (Cunningham, Clemens, and Cox) inflicted calamity, chaos, and catastrophe upon them (22–7) to turn one of their finest seasons flat.

The bowl invitation became a quandary, but Dean Ernie McCoy accepted it shortly after the Pitt game, and soon after that, Alabama was in prospect as an opponent. A variety of factors influenced the decision. It was twelve years since Penn State had participated in a bowl, and for Coach Engle it would be a new experience. Representing the commonwealth seemed appropriate despite unseasonable weather for football practice, playing, or game-watching, but the probable TV contract (which materialized) could be a mitigating circumstance.

The executive director heading the sponsoring committee of Philadelphians, former Villanova athletic director A. F. (Bud) Dudley, was capable, persuasive, enterprising, and at home with the ins and outs of politics. At Villanova the ingenious promoter once sold tickets to a college football game in a chain grocery store with every ten-dollar purchase, perhaps inspired by a gimmick reported about the first years of the Army-Navy game in Philadelphia's Municipal Stadium, when the promoters gave away a ticket with every ten pounds of hamburger—and it was cheap then.

While Philadelphia optimists envisioned a second Army-Navy crowd in the huge stadium, Dudley and George Kerrigan, copromoter, were having trouble getting a suitable opponent for the eastern team. "Suitable" meant one attractive enough to interest a major TV network. Georgia and Georgia Tech had been grabbed by "classics" of proven financial returns, and others considered were Southern Methodist and Navy, which had scored a smashing victory (42–12) over Army in Philadelphia just two weeks before. When Bear Bryant finally came through, as he so often has, the Penn State-Alabama game shaped up as a competitive scrap that could draw people in mid-December. Weather statistics were publicized to show that Philadelphia's third weekend in December almost always is clear.

THE LIBERTY BOWL,
DECEMBER 19, 1959

Philadelphia's new bowl began a long period of postseason games for the Nittany Lions with success almost unparalleled in bowl history. In thirteen appearances under Coaches Engle and Paterno, Penn State has an 8–4–1 record.

As a newcomer to the circuit, Coach Engle felt the responsibility of representing the East against long-time national power Alabama and bowlwise Bear Bryant, whose team was typically aggressive, though young, and not prone to mistakes. Rip wrote to Bobby Dodd, Georgia Tech's professional bowl-er, whose advice came back, "Keep 'em busy and interested—put in some new plays." Aware that mental stagnation was a hazard for a postseason game after the long regular schedule and under inclement weather conditions, he took Dodd's advice and installed a fake field goal play the Wednesday before the meeting.

Morale improved, despite the Pitt defeat, with the selection of Richie Lucas as All-America quarterback on ten first teams, including the U. S. Coaches' Association, American Football Writers' Association (*Look* magazine), and UPI. (He also won the Maxwell Award in Philadelphia and was runner-up to LSU's Billy Cannon for the Heisman Trophy. After two years with the Buffalo Bills of the AFL, Richie was employed by the university's Continuing Education Division and then joined the Athletic Department as ticket manager. He has since been promoted to assistant athletic director.)

Any advantage the Alabamans had because of balmy practice conditions was lost when their plane landed in Philadelphia, but the Crimson squad luckily had some Pennsylvania boys accustomed to wretched winter weather. The gaiety and excitement arranged by the entertainment committee couldn't conceal the dismal unreality of the situation, not improved on Saturday afternoon when 36,211 people (management's count) sat on icy, snow-covered seats in the vastness of the stadium.

The game became a standoff of sorts. In the first quarter, after Alabama's punter kicked the ball to a stop on Penn State's 1-yard line, the Lions fought a 30-mile wind (another uncomfortable feature) to get out of trouble, and probably won by maintaining ball control for nearly ten minutes. Lucas fumbled and was injured during a second-quarter 88-yard drive after completing a 24-yard keeper play, but Butch Hall, coming in to finish for him, thereby began his distinguished career as a regular. A few minutes before half time, Stellatella's field goal attempt was blocked by a hard rush from the right side of the Crimson line, which gave Rip an idea.

> I was mad at myself for not working the fake field goal we had practiced, ending up with Butch rolling out, but figured Alabama would be waiting for this if we had a chance to try again. Then, with less than a minute to go in the half, the opportunity came, and we decided to try a fake on a fake.

Captain Pat Botula went in to give Hall the message: Run a few plays and then try for the big one. Second down on the Tide 16 was almost too late, but Hall called a quick lineup for a fake field goal attempt. The kicking tee was missing, but the Alabama players didn't tumble even when a Lion player helpfully yelled, "Kick the damn thing without the tee." Center Dick Wilson snapped the ball with only one second left. The Lions had lined up on the left where the ball was placed, the right side of the 'Bama line crashed as expected, and Stellatella didn't bother to follow through with his fake kick. Hall, taking Wilson's perfect pass, rolled to his right, with most of the Alabama defense trailing him. Right end Norm Neff went straight down the field for a pass, covered by Alabama's safetyman, while Roger Kochman threw a phony block, then ran down the left sideline as Hall wheeled to his left, spotting Kochman at the right place—the beautiful screen in the diagram had been set up. Botula, in the line for Stellatella, held his block for an instant along with Henry Oppermann, Stew Barber, and Wilson to form the picture screen for Roger. Frank Korbini, Tom Mulroney, and Neff ran over to join the avalanche of white jerseys, and Barber cut down a lone Alabaman who sifted in. Roger, picking up momentum, was close to the end zone when Neff had to throw a block at Jim Blevens, Tide center, and halfback Duff Morrison. All three sprawled on the goal line in front of the Comet, who took off through the air. It was Roger and over. After Stellatella kicked the goal, nothing happened to equal that last minute of excitement, but the frozen players and a few spectators stuck out the uneventful second half.

Thanks to the TV contract, each team took away about $100,000 less expenses, but the promoters of the maiden Liberty Bowl, who obviously lost money, seemed irked about Penn State's ticket sales. Since more than a third of the tickets sold had been purchased by Lion fans (8,500) and Alabama (4,000), the promoters had fallen down in a city of two million people and the populous Delaware Valley.

The 1960 season had unusual interest as the first for Beaver Stadium, where June Commencement had been the initial event. Almost before the last spectator left old New Beaver Field in 1959, steelworkers began moving its stands one mile east in 700 pieces to be fitted under an upper perimeter, which had been completed before the season's close. The largest all-steel stadium in the country, and probably in the world, looking from a distance oddly like a wide-open book, was built by the Pittsburgh-Des Moines Company under the supervision of the Michael Baker, Jr., Company (Baker '36, president of the Beaver, Pennsylvania, consulting firm, was president of the Board of Trustees, 1973–76). The west side of the new shell is

80 rows high, and the east 90 between the goal lines. Closing the horseshoe at the north end is a section 40 rows high. Temporary bleachers could be placed at the opposite (scoreboard) end, which has a spectacular vista framed by Mount Nittany and the Tussey Mountains.

Beaver Stadium's capacity at first was 46,284, but sections added in 1969, 1972, and 1974 raised it to over 57,500. With portable temporary bleachers, total capacity is listed as 60,203 in the 1976 press brochure published by Penn State's Sports Information Department. An attendance record of 62,503 was set at the Ohio State game on September 18, 1976, when standees ranged the fenced-in track.

"Old" New Beaver Field's superb three-deck press box was moved and reassembled atop the stadium's west stands and refurbished with further amenities, the greatest being an elevator. Somewhat enlarged in 1969, it perches there like a giant chicken coop, perhaps spoiling the architectural symmetry of the stadium as a whole but so useful and oh! that blessed elevator. Waiting breathlessly in his New York office for such an event was Stanley Woodward, the incomparable sports editor of the *Herald Tribune*. He was the severest critic of the East's many ancient and inadequate press boxes, and he despised most the high ones without elevators. The lead of his syndicated column (September 20, 1960) following the opening game with Boston University was worth the price of the elevator's construction.

> Ringed by mountains, standing sheer and glorious as a beacon to the impious of Princeton, Pennsylvania and Harvard, behold her! . . . The first press box elevator ever built in the northeast section of our country! She is Pennsylvania State's new 102-foot beauty which Saturday lifted uncounted foot-pounds off the sagging frames of such curious antiques as Chester L. Smith of the Pittsburgh *Press,* Franklin Wetherell Sheppard Yeutter of the Philadelphia *Bulletin* and Rufus Stanley Woodward. . . . The Penn State press box has everything once you get to it. It is roomy, airy though enclosed, with adequate conveniences. When necessary there is heat. In other words, the "country cousin" makes the pompous and usurious city relatives look sick. "Thrombosis Towers," University of Pennsylvania's dreadful pigeon roost, has no one thing to recommend it. . . .

Penn State had good players to go with its splendid new facilities, as the preseason depth chart showed. Dave Robinson was a second-team guard, with Charlie Sieminski at left tackle—both played with the pros. The third team had center Bill Saul, later a Steeler, and tackle Hatch Rosdahl. Its quarterback, Pete Liske, was behind the second team's Butch Hall (now a backfield coach at Oklahoma), and the first string's Dick Hoak, later a Steeler. The varsity right end was Bob Mitinger, who was to be Penn State's next All-America.

The only sophomore on the first eleven was left guard Joe Blasenstein, a West Philadelphian, who received more preseason notices than Coach Engle usually allowed because he had fairly sparkled as a freshman in spring drills. The coach's eyes still light up when he thinks of this young man—a blood-and-thunder tackler, the kind of lineman true fans love to watch. With no regard for his own well-being and a startling ability to psych himself up for every game, Joe played three years of rock-steady, hard-nosed football, making his teammates glad he was on their side.

Bill Hollenback, Lion coach for the first game on the former field, attended the dedication of the new stadium along with eleven members of his first 1909 squad. They recalled that Larry Vorhis '10 scored the first touchdown against Grove City with no more than 500 spectators, some in an old wooden grandstand, but most pressed against a rope encircling the field. Dutch Hermann, also on the 1909 team, entered Penn State in 1906 and was one of the few living alumni who had played on both earlier fields—the first Old Beaver Field, located about where the Osmond Lab parking area is today, and "Old" New Beaver. Dutch, history prof emeritus, doubts that players in the Grove City game were aware of their historic deed.

Ed Caye probably remembers his touchdown, the first in Beaver Stadium, at 10:45 in the opening period, when it seemed he'd crossed over the goal line but dropped the ball. Only after Referee F. P. Brennan unscrambled the pileup did he signal that Ed had made history. The press called the Boston University game desultory and the Lion defense unimaginative as the home team ended all scoring with two more touchdowns in the first half. Hall and Hoak at quarterback were assets, but the team missed the fire and dash of Lucas, and lost Kochman for the season after a knee operation performed three days before the opener.

The record Homecoming crowd of 35,000 liked Beaver Stadium, but watched the Lions lose to a good Missouri team, 21–8. A truly tremendous roar went up from freshmen in the end zone when

Henry Oppermann scored Penn State's only touchdown (a pass from Hall) in the third period; later it was learned that the cheer followed an announcement ending frosh customs. Old-timers in the stands were shocked by the October 1 cutoff. "In our day they lasted a full year!"

Fans had little hope for the Army game: When had Army lost twice at Michie to the same team in consecutive years? Undefeated in three games, Army had beaten California at Berkeley the week before (28–10) and later downed Syracuse and tied Pittsburgh. Jimmy Kerr's fine afternoon (three touchdowns) no doubt had more to do with the 27–16 Lion victory than did the continuing use of pre-Army "noise" in practice, at which a sound truck daily blared "Brave Old Army Team."

The Cadets had some pregame fun with signs (*Lest We Forget, 1959*) but the Corps' manners hadn't changed much. Most Lions, getting the WP treatment for the first time, reacted like veterans. On Penn State's goal line, 4th and 3 with the score 14–13 against them, the Cadets went for a field goal. The kick was good but the choice wasn't. In the remaining 13 minutes, Kerr, Don Jonas, and Henry Oppermann led an attack putting Penn State in the lead once more, and the game was salted away when Buddy Torris, sophomore fullback, intercepted an Army pass and ran to the Cadet 18. A few minutes later Dave Hayes scored the clincher.

Coach Engle had unveiled his version of the "roving" defensive player against Army when Sam Sobczak's wild running covered dangerous receivers. The Lions dubbed it the "Hero Defense," but had Sam ever guessed wrong, it would have been the "Goat Defense."

College football rivalries commonly cause temper tantrums that are quick to evaporate and are of no lasting importance. But the Syracuse-Penn State rhubarbs invariably had a diabolic effect on the fortunes of each. The 1960 game, hard-fought and well-played, was 7–7 at half time, but in the third quarter the Orange went ahead 21–7 on a long interception by Mark Weber, and Penn State was held for downs inches from the goal. The home team scored again on a 66-yard drive, with runs by John Nichols and Don King. The hopeless situation improved for the Lions when Dick Pae caught a scoring pass from Hall, who then ran to the end zone for two points after faking a kick (21–15). Next came another classic donnybrook.

With 2:30 to go, Penn State began a drive from its own 11, 89

yards away from a touchdown. A halfback pass play, Jonas to Mitinger, was stopped on the Orange 40 with 1:12 left. Hall next threw
to Jonas on the 20 and Caye on the 12. He tossed what he thought
was a completion to Caye on the 3, but one official ruled a trapped
ball, and then there were 30 seconds. Hall ran to the right on an option play and lost his shoe when he was downed on the 4.

With no more official time-outs and the clock running ominously,
Hall's request for a halt to put his shoe on for the fourth-down play
was denied by Referee Francis Brennan. Although the rules require
proper equipment for safety, Brennan apparently thought a quarterback could play wearing one shoe. No claim was made that Hall had
kicked off his shoe to stop the clock. He said later: "I don't think it
bothered me too much, and I don't think I'd have called a running
play under the circumstances." The point was that Syracuse *knew* the
shoeless Hall was no running threat. He hobbled to his place, and
tried a pass to Mitinger, but Art Baker batted it down.

The Lion loss to Illinois at Champaign (10–8) was no cliff-hanger
because the Illini took advantage of a 20-mile wind to score early
and added a quick field goal that was partially blocked but sailed
over the bar like one of Early Wynn's knuckle balls. Chuck Raisig, a
good sophomore punter, kept the Lions in the game, but they
couldn't score until the last two minutes, when Al Gursky caught a
short pass from Dick Hoak.

A 6–3 record, even after beating Pitt, convinced Penn Staters that
their team was out of the running for the eastern title, but the controversy when Yale and Navy were cowinners of the Lambert Trophy
supplied some amusement. Larry Merchant in the Philadelphia *Daily
News* remarked that the committee was dewy-eyed about Yale,
which he rated good in a class with, say, West Chester, Wagner,
Humbolt State, etc. Navy (9–1–0) had beaten SMU, Air Force,
Washington, Notre Dame, and Army, losing only to Duke and to
Missouri in a close game at the Orange Bowl. Syracuse (7–2–0) had
beaten Kansas, Penn State, West Virginia, and Miami (Florida).
The writers faulted the Ivies for playing strictly in their own league
but wanting consideration when "championship" time came. To quell
such furor the sponsors of the trophy (not an official ECAC prize
but awarded with its blessing) announced that future selections
would not carry "championship" designation but would recognize the
team ending its season with the best "performance." Despite such

semantics, the public considers the Lambert symbolic of the East's best team.

THE LIBERTY BOWL,
DECEMBER 17, 1960

Promoters still dreaming of an eventual "eastern Rose Bowl" valiantly tried to win over fickle Philadelphians, pointing out that their 1959 crowd of 36,211 was the largest for a first bowl; they topped the Army-Navy game press coverage; outdrew the Orange Bowl on TV (Georgia-Missouri); and pleased the collegiate world by paying a record-breaking first-year sum of over $98,000 to each participant.

The selling job by Messrs. Dudley and Kerrigan moved a shall we say civic-minded New York group to start a rival Gotham Bowl to give the East not one but two "annual classics." Invitations to play the first game at the Polo Grounds in December were rejected by Oregon State and Colorado, among others, and no game was played.

The next year Robert Curran, Gotham Bowl committee director, gambled on the natural rivalry of Baylor and Utah State, but only 15,123 turned out for the game, although the Texas and Utah boys got to see New York. Undaunted, Curran succeeded in signing Nebraska and Miami (Florida) to play the 1962 game in Yankee Stadium (capacity: 67,000) after Mayor Wagner guaranteed each team $30,000 plus $35,000 expenses. Only 6,160 New Yorkers came, and the Gotham Bowl went into oblivion.

As defending champions, the Lions were a logical choice for the 1960 Liberty Bowl, since Yale and Navy were unavailable and Pittsburgh had lost to Penn State. Syracuse, which had a just claim although recently beaten by Army, preferred a game coming up with Miami in Florida. Penn State's players had divided opinions about the Philadelphia game, but voted to go when Oregon was named the visiting team, partly because they had something to prove to the Lambert selectors. Oregon's 7–2–1 record included victories over California and Stanford, with losses only to Michigan (21–0) and Washington (7–6).

Freezing sunshine for the game was an improvement over the 1959 weather, yet less than half as many spectators (16,624) appeared. A bad day for the Ducks of Oregon, it was a triumph for the

Reddie (second) team, led by Dick Hoak, which had developed such *esprit de corps* during the season that many didn't care whether they made the Blues, quarterbacked by Butch Hall. Hoak was named the game's Most Valuable Player. The one-two punch of the two almost-equal State elevens was too much for the Pacific Coast team after it scored first in the opening quarter. Oregon went behind 21–6 at half time and was smashed by three more touchdowns in the final period.

Red Smith, covering for the *Herald Tribune,* reacted this way about the game and the eastern championship:

> Altogether it was a spectacle to make the TV color cameras drool. The only thing lacking was an opponent worthy of Penn State, whose inalienable right to top eastern ranking was established today beyond cavil. Nobody watching the flashy Dick Hoak and his boisterous accomplices could conscientiously place them behind Yale or Navy in this region.

Once more television receipts saved the game (for the participants), but Dudley, announcing that the bowl would be a fixture, again criticized Penn State for poor support, causing Lion officials to retaliate with their figures. The "host team" disposed of 13,000 or 28 per cent of all tickets sold for the two games (47,000). Dudley persisted for three more years in the City of Brotherly Love. In 1961, although Penn State's record (7–3) obviously entitled it to bigger things, he smugly implied he'd settle for the Lions if he couldn't get any other eastern representative. He got Syracuse (7–3), beaten by Penn State 14–0, while the Lions went to the Gator Bowl.

Despite its doom in Philadelphia, the Dudley promotion can be credited with arranging competitive games. In 1961, Syracuse won from Miami (Florida) 15–14 in the final quarter on a two-pointer; the next opponents were Villanova and Oregon State; and in 1963 Mississippi State and North Carolina State played the final Philadelphia game. In 1964, Utah beat West Virginia at the bowl's new location in Convention Hall, Atlantic City. The eastern Rose Bowl has flourished since 1965 in that "cradle of liberty," Memphis, Tennessee, where its prestige is growing. And, if the promoters have participation problems, the Bear is just around the corner.

35

Coolie Hats and Hot Tempers

Maligning eastern football for inferiority was a practice steadily on the increase between 1956 and 1965, reflecting a popular notion that equated the East with the Ivy League. The small group of northeastern private colleges, which founded and at first controlled the game, gradually had come to schedule only other Ivy League opponents or those within the area conforming to their standards. These policies were inappropriate for public and large colleges seeking intersectional competition, national prestige, and the financial aid derived from consistently winning football.

As regional conferences developed in other parts of the country, only five eastern teams—Syracuse, Penn State, Pitt, Army, and Navy —attempted to be competitive. Their small number reinforced skepticism about the quality of the "Big Five" independents. Syracuse alone had been acclaimed a national champion (1959). In bowls, the Big Five won six and lost seven overall. Penn State and Syracuse are remarkably similar among top teams whose records substantiate claims of the East's defenders. The Lions won 17 and lost 9 of their 26 intersectional games between 1956 and 1965; the Syracuse record was 18–9–1. A few setup opponents pad the percentages—Penn State played Kent State and VMI; Syracuse had games with Richmond and Virginia Tech. But victims of the Orange included Notre

Dame, UCLA (4), Nebraska (3), Kansas (3), Oregon State (2), Miami (Florida) (2), and Texas. Among Penn State's defeated rivals were Ohio State (3), Oregon (2), California (2), Rice (2), UCLA, Illinois, Alabama, Georgia Tech, Air Force, and Houston.

Pittsburgh led eastern "independents" in scheduling intersectional opponents, and had a ten-year record of 29–25–3. Recent upward struggles of the Panthers obscure the murderous schedules Pitt once faced with laudable success. The Panthers won 5 of 10 games with Notre Dame, won 5 and tied 1 of 8 with Miami (Florida), 4 of 7 with UCLA, 2 of 4 with Southern California, 2 of 3 with Duke, 2 of 3 with California, 2 of 4 with Oregon, and had one triumph over Nebraska, Baylor, Oklahoma, and Washington, as well as ties with Michigan State and TCU. Surprisingly, they played in only one bowl game during the span, losing to Georgia Tech in the 1956 Gator Bowl, 21–14.

Intersectional opponents of Army and Navy have been numerous but generally of lesser quality. Navy meets William and Mary nearly every season, and Army has a host of minor conflicts. Against noneastern teams during the ten-year period Army had a 30–16–1 record, but played in no bowls. The Cadets defeated Navy only twice in the ten games (two ties), but won from Notre Dame (once), Nebraska, Tulane, Rice, Duke, California, and other such teams. Navy, intersectionally more impressive than its rival academy, won six of ten games with Notre Dame, and defeated Michigan (twice), California, Georgia, Washington, SMU, Duke, and Oklahoma. The Middies defeated Rice in the 1958 Cotton Bowl, lost to Texas in the 1963 Cotton Bowl, and lost to Missouri in the 1960 Orange Bowl.

Between 1956 and 1965 the only repeater in the consensus "national champion" picture was Alabama (1961, 1964). Other leaders, in order, were Oklahoma, Ohio State, LSU, Syracuse, Minnesota, Southern California, Texas, and Michigan State. Rip Engle's Lions won the Lambert Trophy three times in this decade (1961, 1962, 1964), when he was beginning Penn State's bowl era auspiciously, winning a majority of intersectional games and maintaining marked success with traditional eastern rivals. Only Syracuse (7–3–0) and Army (6–3) plagued him. Against other frequent sectional opponents, the Penn State record was Pitt, 5–4–1; West Virginia, 9–0–1; Maryland, 5–1; Navy, 3–1; Penn, 3–0; Holy Cross, 8–0; and Boston University, 5–0.

Something new made 1961 another unusual season. Heretofore, in the good old summertime, the players arrived for preseason practice during an August lull between post (summer) session and freshman orientation week, when the town seemed asleep. Old Main's quarter-hour chimes droned on, but at Graham's the pinball machine and AC bench outside were deserted, and the Corner Room closed at 9 P.M. The advent of the football huskies was welcomed by local small fry, girls, and area sportswriters starved for a change of pace.

The university changed its academic calendar to a year-round, four-term system with the 1961 summer term, ending that lazy, lengthy break. Taken with the NCAA's decree that practice will start no more than three weeks before the opening game, the changed atmosphere was noticeable to incoming players and the coaches as they buckled down.

Penn State's football public also was changing its ways. Highway improvements shortening driving time, and efficient handling of one-way traffic patterns, with wide-open spaces for parking, induced a trend away from football weekends to Saturday excursions (although a growing number of campers could be seen parked Friday evening). Beaver Stadium rates among the tailgating capitals of the college football world in convenience and for its setting on a rise at the northeastern edge of the beautifully landscaped campus, converging with the university's experimental farmlands and the town of State College. Convivial snacking lunches and stand-up gatherings save time for travelers and are popular with the sociable local gentry, all attracted by the panoramic beauty of the valley, with its distant bordering mountains and old Mount Nittany looming nearby.

In regional folklore Nittany (or Nita-nee) was a valorous Indian princess in whose honor the Great Spirit caused Mount Nittany to be formed. A later namesake, daughter of a chieftain, loved a white trader driven away by her seven brothers and left to die in Penn's Cave, another landmark and tourist attraction in the valley.

Beaver Stadium is named for a Pennsylvania governor and judge, General James A. Beaver, who lost a leg in the Civil War. A long-time president of the Board of Trustees and resident of Bellefonte (the adjacent "seat" of Centre County), Beaver concerned himself with the interests of the college and won the honor from the students for securing legislation that made Penn State's first athletic field a reality. In 1954, at its forty-fifth reunion, the Class of 1909, seniors when the original Beaver Field was moved to its second site, had placed a large boulder with a bronze plaque citation at the entrance to "New" Beaver Field, near the Nittany Lion Shrine. The "Beaver Rock" memorial was moved to the stadium entrance in 1960.

For Rip Engle, Penn State's selection as the 1961 eastern team to beat was a calumnious plot perpetrated by his rivals. "Oh, I know what they're saying," he wailed, "but it isn't fair. Just because we looked good in the Liberty Bowl and some of those big, slow guys are left over"—like Dave Robinson, Bob Mitinger, Chuck Sieminski, Joe Blasenstein, Jay Huffman, and Bob Smith. Newcomers included two of the country's top high school quarterbacks—Gary Wydman from Corning, New York, and Donny Caum, pride of Harrisburg—whose careers initially were frustrated by Pete Liske and Ron Coates. Injuries delayed Wydman's senior season until 1964, but eventually he had the satisfaction of quarterbacking the team brilliantly against Ohio State. He and Caum, who also had some great moments, had to struggle for attention on a squad loaded with specialists. Other newcomers were Junior Powell, loved by Penn State crowds for his superabundant spirit on the field; Bernie Sabol, Joe's brother; Joe Galardi, captain in 1962; center Ralph Baker, enduring linebacker for the New York Jets until 1975; and end Dick Anderson, now an assistant coach at his alma mater.

After a six-year lapse, Navy came to Beaver Stadium for the 1961 opener, with Wayne Hardin still its coach and the support of a howling cheering section of Middies 600 strong. The Lions broke a 10–10 tie in the final quarter on a 31-yard field goal by Don Jonas and a clincher touchdown sparked by Caum, who threw a 46-yard pass to Wydman and then scored from the 19 on some superior running.

The bubble burst when the Lions got to Miami for the second game, played in the Orange Bowl stadium. The sting might have been less if Penn Staters had known that six years later Coach Joe Paterno would win one of his first big games on this site as a warmup for three eventual Orange Bowl victories. The talented Hurricane quarterback, George Mira, was a Miami favorite. He excelled in football and histrionics. Capitalizing on a sore shoulder acquired against Kentucky, he groaned and rolled on the ground whenever he was tackled. End Bob Mitinger hit fairly, but to the Miami crowd he was a Goliath to boo and abuse. The notoriety probably helped him make All-America. Bob was selected by the Coaches' Association. He is now practicing law in State College. Unfortunately, Miami had better players than Mira—Bobby Weaver was his sub; end Bob Miller caught seven passes; and a fullback, Jim Vollenweider, gained 65 yards. Pete Liske completed 8 of 11 passes for the Lions and played fine defense when he replaced Hall, but the team lacked a consistent offense.

An easy time at Boston University helped the Lions recover from the humbling that goes with the first defeat in a promising season. No New England team ever defeated a Rip Engle aggregation after he left Brown. Losing to Army, 10–6, at Beaver Stadium was hard because the Cadets were mediocre during the last season of the unfortunate Dale Hall, who had a short term as successor to Colonel Red Blaik. Their victory, unexpected after a shellacking from Michigan, was largely a gift of the Lions, whose mistakes were more spectacular than those they made against Miami. The "Long Gray Line" of the 1,200 entering Cadets further clouded the spirits of Lion fans, unable to believe what they were seeing. The home team was 10–0 in arrears before Liske passed to Jonas for Penn State's only score.

The Syracuse game marked the 100th victory of Rip's coaching years at Brown and Penn State, although through mathematical miscalculations the occasion had been observed two years before, at the Liberty Bowl. Rip celebrated with a satisfying triumph over his old friend, Coach Ben Schwartzwalder, 14–0, and again in 1965, when the Boston College victory was his 100th with the Lions.

Pleased by the workmanlike defeat of the Orange, Rip was happy that quarterback Butch Hall and Roger Kochman (on his mended knee) were getting so many headlines, but pointed out that a team had to have defense to shut out a back like Ernie Davis—and the Lions had it with Jim Schwab, Mitinger, Rosdahl, Blasenstein, Huffman, and Saul. A bout with the officials at the end of the first half so upset Rip that he wandered by mistake into the Syracuse dressing room, where his spirits weren't helped by all those Orange jerseys. To prevent repetition of this error, Rip's players carried the coach to his own quarters after the game and presented him with the football. Spectators surprised at the sight of his uncovered snow-white hair even in bitter weather learned that Rip had to stop wearing a hat at games because he threw so many on the ground in excitement (not always at the officials). A suggestion that champagne was in order for his 100th victory was countered quickly. "After the California trip . . ." Rip started to say. "I mean the Pitt game, boys."

The year's silver lining didn't come until the visits to Pittsburgh and Jacksonville. Penn State lost to Maryland, the first time in history, on the type of "judgment call" by officials that never fully satisfies the losing team, even in this case when the fair-minded might feel that a Terp victory was overdue. Maryland, with players like quarterback Dick Shiner and Gary Collins, superlative receiver and punter, might have upset the Lions anyway, although Roger Kochman gained 100 yards and Junior Powell pulled down three dazzling passes for 74 yards in addition to making 24 on the ground. Junior also figured in the play that put the game in the "controversial" class, at least for Lion supporters.

Maryland, off to a 14–0 lead, stayed ahead by 21–6 into the third quarter when Penn State began to get the upper hand. Kochman had to leave the game limping, and Buddy Torris, after making 87 yards in 14 carries, retired from sheer exhaustion. But they had given the Lions a chance to win. Hall passed to Al Gursky for the points that cut the lead to 21–12, setting the stage for a gallant finish.

Needing 10 points or two scores to win, the Lions were at the Maryland 16 with 10 minutes to play when Coach Engle decided to go for a field goal. Jonas kicked his sixth of the year. An interception by Schwab ended Maryland's five long minutes of possession after the kickoff, and the Lions appeared set for a Hall victory pass. The place was in an uproar as Powell caught a pass on the Maryland 19. Then Butch, unable to find a receiver, picked his way for 10 yards. Roger made three for a first down on the 5; Maryland, blitzing to stop Hall, pushed the Lions back to the 9; Butch *had* to pass and did. Junior made a dive and claimed he caught the ball legally. Press observers couldn't tell what had happened—the ruling was slow— and Junior jumped around in high dudgeon. His belief is unshaken that the touchdown was legal, but officials on the spot ruled otherwise. One more pass was grounded before Maryland took over and Coach Tom Nugent, after running three plays, decided not to send in his great punter, Collins. Nugent sent in a messenger instead, to center Bob Hacker. Could he pass the ball through the end zone? Hacker replied he could put it through the goal posts to the tenth row of the bleachers if the coach desired, which the coach did. Collins was then allowed to punt after the safety, and he put the game away.

Beating Penn State seemed to clinch a Gator Bowl bid for the Terps, but Virginia dumped Maryland the next week and, as Coach

Nugent later remarked, "Something very funny happened to us on our way to the Gator Bowl." Maryland had the added discomfiture of seeing the Lions invited to their first major bowl in thirteen years. Having also beaten California, West Virginia, and Holy Cross, to take on Pitt with a 6–3 record and a tentative bowl invitation could have precipitated disaster, but Penn State reached its peak against Pitt. To have the Lions dashing all over the field for 437 yards and seven touchdowns made for a very unusual Pitt-Penn State meeting. The leading ground-gainer (64) again was Torris, who had given the offense unexpected punch with 145 yards against Holy Cross and 102 against West Virginia. Hall completed 11 of 14 passes for 256 yards. The total points were the most scored in any game of the Pitt series until 1968.

Jesse Abramson of the *Herald Tribune* hoped the Lambert committee would do the "honorable" thing and give Rutgers (9–0) the trophy, but it went to the Lions (7–3) on the basis of a tougher schedule. While bitter drums beat along the Raritan, John Bateman, the likable Rutgers coach, said with controlled fury, "The trophy was supposed to go to the team with the best record, wasn't it?" Actually, it had been decided on schedules and victories until the Yale precedent. In fairness, as a member of the award committee, Bateman had voted for his team and Penn State as co-champions. The Lions were expected to get their comeuppance in the Gator Bowl against Georgia Tech and Bobby Dodd, who had once given Coach Engle good advice about how to win postseason games.

THE GATOR BOWL,
DECEMBER 30, 1961

Coach Engle's entry into the rarefied atmosphere of the "major" bowls remains among the Lions' most satisfying moments. The southern press, especially in Atlanta, had the usual smug scorn for eastern football, but a record crowd of over 50,000 came to see the downfall of the Yankee intruders. The fans were skeptical about the talent, since the Lions had seemed to back into the meeting with Coach Dodd's bowl-seasoned Engineers.

Early in the game, Engineer backers whooped it up when an automatic safety was called, although few understood the official ruling. Quarterback Hall's rarely called infraction was "intentional grounding of a pass in the end zone," and the penalty was two points. To the astonishment of newsmen after the game, Hall settled the issue of whether he had purposely thrown wild:

> We called a screen play along the sideline but Bob [Mitinger] couldn't fool the Tech left end. We expected him to crash. I was afraid of an interception and didn't want to be tackled in the end zone. I knew what *that* was. So I threw over everyone's head. I didn't know anything about that safety rule.

The game had three distinct parts: the southerners' early 9–0 advantage, derived from the strange safety and a not-so-strange 68-yard touchdown run by Joe Auer; Penn State's courageous second-quarter rally, with drives covering 78 and 87 yards, ending in scoring passes from Hall to Al Gursky and Roger Kochman; and finally, Dave Robinson's game-clinching aerial tackle, a leaping dive over a blocker to nail passer Stan Gann, panicking him into a fumble recovered by the superactive Robinson on the Tech 35. Hall struck immediately, faking nearly everybody to get Junior Powell into the clear. Junior was so delighted he started his victory jig on the 10-yard line and joyously skipped into the end zone. The 20–9 margin seemed ample, but Georgia Tech fought into contention in the final period on a broken play when a pitchout by Bill Lothridge went astray. Auer chased it backward, picked up the ball, and ran 25 yards through the surprised Lion team for a touchdown.

Tech's passing backfired as the 20–15 score forced the Engineers into the Lions' pattern, and Penn State got position for a Don Jonas field goal from the 13. Jim Schwab's interception after the kickoff enabled Torris to score again with not much over a minute to play, but the game was not the rout it appeared to be. Galen Hall, nearsighted and on the stubby side, was by far the outstanding player, and ranks among Penn State's best quarterbacks for executing a game plan so effectively under relentless pressure. No one lately had scored 30 points on Georgia Tech, whose 1961 opponents had averaged 5 points per game. "We never did stop them," Dodd said. "It wasn't the plays they used, but the way they executed them." Hall, from Williamsburg, Pennsylvania, was the chief Lion executioner for three bowls in three years.

A usually refreshing month on Cape Cod was uncomfortable for Rip in the summer of 1962. Neighbors reminded him of his doleful 1961 predictions that ended as the "best in the East" and wondered about those 77 points in the last two games against hefty opposition. He mustered his compulsive alarmism by contemplating the loss of the matchless Hall, but this became a less critical problem when the availability of Caum, Coates, Liske, and Wydman was mentioned. Still, Caum was too small, Coates would be primarily a kicker, Liske was more valuable on defense, and Wydman was injury-prone (Gary did miss the season). How about Frank Potter? Inexperienced. Untried. Etc. Rip did concede that he had promising fullbacks in Dave Hayes, Buddy Torris, and Ed Stuckrath.

Lack of high-quality recruits seemed a valid point, although not from the perspective of later years. They included Frank Hershey, a fine punter; ends Bill Bowes (present coach at New Hampshire) and Bud Yost, both from Lock Haven; tackles Sandy Buchan and John Deibert; backs Tom Urbanik and Gary Klingensmith, who was the first totally deaf player on a Lion squad. Center Glenn Ressler, future All-America and Baltimore Colt regular for many years, wasn't even listed on the third team in the preseason depth chart.

Coach Engle was concerned, too, about the heavily headlined transfer of Paul Dietzel from LSU to Army. The master craftsman from the Southeast Conference had such a summer buildup that he was half expected to walk to his new job on the waters of the Hudson. Coach Dietzel's early statements indicated that he would trade on the vocal fervor of the Cadets, a possibility especially disconcerting to Rip.

A secret dream of "sneaking up on Navy" in the opening game was quashed, to Rip's dismay, when Penn State was listed as a possible national power in preseason estimates. The Middies must have been somewhat surprised, however, when they were trounced, 41–7, with Liske very ably handling the quarterback duties. Coach Engle couldn't sneak up on Rice, either, after blasting the Air Force Academy, 20–6, when Roger Kochman exhibited his old-time form; and he had to take the "favored team" role against Army after the Lions defeated Rice at Houston, 18–7.

Dave Hayes of Long Island scored all the points against Rice in a victory that was a trial of endurance played in the sunken Rice Bowl, an inferno in Houston's September humidity. An Austin resident, Karl Wagner '32, helpfully informed Dr. Bill Grasley that southwestern teams always use *coated* salt pills, with which northern teams seemed unfamiliar. Dr. Grasley, who had just replaced the popular Dr. Al Griess as team physician, accepted the medically

sound suggestion gratefully. The coated pills probably were beneficial, but more so was Coach Engle's use of the third team at the
start of the third quarter. The Greenies, whose existence he would
have denied in August, held their own long enough for the Blues and
the Reddies to push across the two winning second-half scores. Rice
had led at half time, 7–6.

Moving from Houston's humidity to the miasma of Michie Stadium was particularly hard on Rip because of all the premature talk
about Penn State's becoming the "first team to win from all three
service academies in one season." Besides reinstalling enthusiasm,
Coach Dietzel had turned his back on southeastern conservatism by
creating the granddaddy of unbalanced lines. The Cadet center and
quarterback seemed to be in a game apart, with the other linemen
and three backs 10–15 yards away. Fortunately, the Lion defense
adjusted well to the unorthodox formation—Hatch Rosdahl stayed
with the center, and the others drifted over to where the real action
was likely to be.

The innovative Dietzel also revived the Chinese Bandit theme for
a defensive unit, so successful at LSU. The Cadet sections donned
coolie hats whenever the defensive Bandits entered the game, but the
generals didn't allow the colorful shenanigans to go on very long.
The game was little affected and proved to be a defensive confrontation despite Dietzel's unique spread formation. The teams were tied
3–3 at the half on field goals by Coates and Cadet Dick Heydt in the
opening period. A second Coates field goal in the third quarter was
preceded by a play Coach Engle considers one of only two "bad
judgment" calls that brought defeat to his Penn State teams in sixteen years. (The other occurred in the 1965 California game.)

From the Army 12, Coates tried to pass to Bill Bowes, who caught
it in the end zone. No flag was thrown until after the score; then an
official claimed that Penn State's left tackle had "lined up offside." A
blocked field goal attempt and a dropped touchdown pass in the end
zone were among other baffling features of a frustrating afternoon
for the Lions. After Army went ahead 9–6, on a pass thrown from
the Lion 15-yard line on 4th and 7, nothing Penn State did was right.
Only a few seconds were left when Rosdahl, thinking the Army center had moved, jumped through the Army defense as linemen will.
Minor fisticuffs resulted, and efforts of officials to restore order were
impeded by hundreds of belligerent Cadets who dashed on the field
before the game was over. The costly loss for Penn State prevented

an undefeated season with a possible Cotton Bowl bid, and led to unpleasantness connected with the 1962 Gator Bowl.

West Point officials undoubtedly were sobered by strong press criticism of Army's "discourtesies" to visiting teams, especially in a nationally syndicated column by Oscar Fraley (UPI). It was accompanied in some papers by a photo of the Cadets swarming around Penn State players on the field. As much may have been accomplished in phone calls and letters initiated by Philip P. Mitchell '43, an Atlanta businessman who did not reveal his identity as a Penn State alumnus. Coach Dietzel's reply to his first letter seemed a bit pompous and unsatisfactory to Mitchell, whose next exchange was with Chaplain Theodore C. Speers. Finally, a phone call came from the superintendent himself, General William C. Westmoreland.

All parties were courteous. General Westmoreland felt the whole matter had been exaggerated and that the head of a military institution would have difficulty differentiating between exuberance and what might be considered poor sportsmanship in highly spirited young men. He assured Mitchell he would do what he could in the future to protect the image and reputation of the Military Academy, but said that frankly he believed absolute silence during a team's signal-calling would be more disconcerting than some noise. Mitchell disagreed, and read with some interest later that the general had officially reprimanded the Cadets for their conduct when VPI visited Michie Stadium and that the Cadets, probably behaving with more reserve, lost to their last three opponents—Oklahoma State, Pittsburgh, and Navy.

There was fine irony in the complaint of Coach Dietzel after his team lost the 1963 Army-Navy game in Philadelphia. "The Midshipmen were making a lot of racket and [our players] couldn't hear the quarterback." After one more season at West Point he "asked to be relieved of his contract" to take a job at South Carolina as coach and athletic director.

The loss to Army was the last setback for Penn State during the regular season, but the Lions had close calls against the Orange at Syracuse and California at Berkeley. They gained a 14-point first-quarter lead over the Orange too early, when Pete Liske caught a fumble in the air and sophomore Frank Hershey intercepted a wild pass by Walley Mahle two minutes later. Instead of being demoralized, the mishaps galvanized Syracuse into scoring two touchdowns. A tying opportunity was lost only because a lineman was called for holding on Tom Mingo's good extra-point try, and Mingo missed the longer effort. When Syracuse went ahead, 19–14, Mingo reasonably tried for two points. He faked the kick, tried to run, and was stopped by Liske, whose passes to Dave Robinson led to Penn State's winning touchdown by Hayes. The wild game wasn't really won until Lion fans heard that wonderful sound—the thud of a field goal attempt blocked by Rosdahl in the late moments.

The Lions almost lost a 7–0 lead over California, winning finally, 23–21. The Bears had scared the daylights out of the easterners midway in the second quarter by inserting sophomore quarterback Craig Morton. A prize high school star, Morton was returning after a knee injury operation and Coach Marv Levy hadn't expected to use him, but was glad he did, since Morton completed 20 of 30 passes for 273 yards and 3 touchdowns. The Lion victory was attributable to Liske's passing for 157 yards (8 completions were to Al Gursky) and Kochman's 130 yards on the ground. Coach Engle had made the "move of the year" before the California game by changing Gursky from a reserve position behind Kochman at left halfback to right halfback behind no one.

The Lions slaughtered West Virginia, 34–6, establishing a new record for first downs (thirty-eight). Chuck Raisig, leading punter in the nation prior to the Mountaineer game (by a tenth of a yard), didn't increase his average because he had no opportunity to punt against the visitors.

Penn Staters in Pittsburgh worried when their team came to town with an 8–1 record and a bowl bid in the offing, but for once the Lions were calm and unintimidated by Panther victories over California, Baylor, UCLA, Syracuse, and Army, or by the fine Pitt quarterback, Fred Mazurek, and such good runners as Paul Martha and Rick Leeson. They shut out the Panthers for the first time since 1954. Junior Powell intercepted his fifth pass of the year, ran nearly 100 yards back and forth across the field for a return of 47, and led the team in pass receptions for the season (32). Liske established 3 Penn State one-season passing records, which have since been broken: Most touchdown passes, 12; total offense, 1,312 yards; and yards passing, 1,047. The Pittsburgh Curbstone Coaches' Association named him the first recipient of its James H. Coogan Memorial Award to the game's outstanding player. Coogan, who died in the spring of 1962, was Penn State's sports information director from 1943 until he became head of public information in 1958. He was among the most popular and respected college public relations personalities of his time.

For the first time since 1923, two Penn Staters were named All-Americas. The Coaches' Association selected Roger Kochman, now with the Bell Telephone Company. End Dave Robinson, later with Green Bay and the Washington Redskins, made the first team of the American Football Writers' Association (*Look* magazine), AP, NEA, and *Time* magazine.

THE GATOR BOWL,
DECEMBER 29, 1962

Each major bowl management conducts the enterprise its own way, and the Gator Bowl at Jacksonville—opened January 1, 1946, with a game between Wake Forest and South Carolina—is outstanding for its entertainment of guests before, during, and after the game. Four times Penn State has enjoyed the warm hospitality of the Gator Bowl Committee, headed for many years by Executive Director George Olsen, but in 1962 much unfortunate publicity was generated by the Lions' alleged lack of enthusiasm for the game, the players supposedly "sulking" because they hadn't been bid by one of the older classics having more national prestige.

The distasteful situation began with the selection of an opponent. The University of Florida had accepted after unsuccessful efforts were made to get Georgia Tech, Miami, or Duke. The southern press elaborated on stories that Penn State players demanded Christmas at home while the Florida Gators had given up their holidays for extra practice. Believing the stories by the sportswriters that the Lions were downgrading them and the game, Florida's "angry young men" virtually mounted a crusade to prove themselves worthy of their selection.

Sensing how easily the Gator Bowl, such a glorious site for the Lions in 1961, could be a Snake Bowl in 1962, Penn State coaches and officials outdid themselves to prepare the team physically and mentally for an enjoyable experience. Since it was impossible to go south early and also return for Christmas, arrangements were made for nearly a week of practice at the Naval Academy, where the Field House was available for indoor work. Annapolis weather wasn't much better than the Nittany Valley's, but the team had a Washington excursion to present President John F. Kennedy with a Nittany Lion statuette.

Penn State's dismal performance, reflecting mental attitude, was reminiscent of the 1948 Cotton Bowl. There the Lions were the underdogs and recovered from their lethargy in time to salvage a tie, but the 1962 Lions did not. The situation convinced Penn State officials that bowl invitations should be accepted only when the players themselves are anxious to go—with subtle or not so subtle persuasion—and are prepared to make the necessary sacrifices. Commenting in the *Alumni News* on Penn State's new academic calendar, President Eric Walker made the point that football players are especially hard hit by the grueling, concentrated ten weeks of the fall term, almost simultaneous with the ten weeks of hard football. "Bowl games," he wrote, "are profitable to the university, extremely enjoyable to alumni and other friends, enhance the football reputation of the participating colleges, but they often mean great sacrifice and drudgery to the players who make them possible."

Because Jacksonville hotels did not accept blacks, Lion players, coaches, and officials stayed in St. Augustine at the old Ponce de Leon Hotel, then not open for regular customers until New Year's Eve. Older members of the party found it charming; to the players it was a bore, and St. Augustine was far from the "action," just as the naval air station had been at Dallas in 1948. Northern Florida in December was only slightly better than University Park or Annapolis. In fact, the plane carrying the official party, wives, and friends had to land at Tampa because of weather conditions at the Jacksonville airport.

Five pregnant wives of players or younger coaches were spared an uncomfortable bus trip across Florida at night in bad weather because Skip Rowland offered to take them to St. Augustine in a hired limousine. Having transported team equipment from University Park in the truck he owned, as he did for all bowl games until his untimely death in August 1974, Skip was expert in transporting this more valuable cargo. More than a football squad mascot, Skip was a Penn State tradition as a helper and generous friend to all. Those who knew this genial gentleman, physically massive and with a loud, gravelly voice, enjoy musing about the impression made during stops en route across Florida that night, especially in the motel dining room, when Skip entered escorting five lovely, very pregnant young ladies.

The pattern of the game itself developed early with Gator quarter-back Tom Shannon (voted the Outstanding Player) taking charge in the first quarter and moving his team into position for a 33-yard field goal by Bob Lyle (Florida's first for the season). Penn State had lost the ball three times all year on fumbles, and now they lost it three times to the Gators. A ball control team throughout its successful season, the Lions held possession for an improbable four plays in the first quarter and for only 19 minutes during the entire game.

Florida also added a touchdown in the second quarter, on a pass from Shannon to Larry Dupree to lead, 10–0. Somehow the Lions managed a 76-yard drive to score with 36 seconds left in the half. Passes from Liske to Bud Yost and Junior Powell had put the ball in scoring position, but Liske finally got the score himself on a rollout after the Lions had been held for three plays. Penn State hopes for a rejuvenated team in the second half were unrealized. Interior line-men Ralph Baker and Jim Williams, end Dave Robinson (voted Penn State's Outstanding Player), and kicker Chuck Raisig all helped avert a massacre as the Gators scored on another pass from Shannon to Hagood Clarke on the first play of the final period. Still, the last 14 minutes were strictly futile for Penn Staters.

36

Buckeyes Buckled Twice

When Coach Engle took his team to Oregon for the first game in 1963, his elaborate preparations for the Z-back and what he called a Swing-T formation were guarded secrets.

With Kochman, Robinson, and three agile quarterbacks, Engle and his backfield coach, Joe Paterno, weighed relegating quarterback Don Caum to a defensive halfback spot, but realized from spring drills that Caum was too good a runner for defensive duties. They had to capitalize on the passing skills of Pete Liske and Ron Coates to compensate for a lack of running backs. Furthermore, something new was needed psychologically to harass opponents, stimulate veteran players, and provide a relatively easy adjustment for the many newcomers. Thus the Swing-T was born, with high hopes that an opportunity to use it might come during the third Penn State trip to the West Coast since the Rose Bowl game of 1923.

The new formation—for "spot" use only—was called the Swing-T because a so-called Z-back played an open end position on either side, "swinging" from side to side. When a halfback on defense was open right, the line was unbalanced and the right end was ineligible as a receiver. When open left, the left end became a tackle and also an ineligible receiver. The key Z-back players were Caum, Dick Gingrich, and Tom Bedick.

Getting the first jump on Saturday night in Multnomah Stadium, Portland, was essential if the home team were to be shaken up with the new weapon. Oregon's Webfoots were equally anxious to unloose their "Fearsome Four," led by All-America halfback Mel Renfro.

Captain Ralph Baker did his part by winning the toss, but the team seemed nervous. On the first play Gary Klingensmith, usually unhampered by his deafness, shot through the center of the line before the ball was snapped and almost reached the Oregon safety before someone flagged him down. Bud Yost was tossed for a 6-yard loss trying to get around end, and the home crowd was delighted until Frank Hershey punted his team out of a jam. Klingensmith, Yost, and fullback Tom Urbanik were playing on the Blue team for the first time.

Klingensmith became a successful Juniata High School football coach in Mifflintown, Pennsylvania. Penn State coaches often recall his remark after the superoffside in the 1963 Oregon opener: "Well, everyone is always asking you about that deaf player, so I decided it was time to let them all know who he was." When Gary was a sophomore (1962), Coach Paterno asked his roommate to help him communicate. "Ask him," said Joe, "if he can play either right or left halfback." Klingensmith replied, through the "interpreter," "Tell Joe, 'not at the same time.'"

Back on the 20, the Lions tried again. Caum, primed to open up immediately, went wide to the right and, just as he was spotted by the surprised Oregon defensive backs, caught a book-pattern pass from Liske. Good only for 8 yards, it set up a 12-play, 80-yard scoring drive. On the Webfoots' 8, Junior Powell wandered into the area where the Z-back had been decoying, Caum became the blocker, and Liske's pass to Powell made the first six points. The Lions weren't expected to hold Oregon to a single touchdown with backs the caliber of Renfro and Larry Hill, and their only major defensive lapse produced the Webfoots' score. Penn State's right tackle was trapped. Hill got away for a long run, and Renfro scored after four plays from the 11. The 7–7 deadlock came five minutes before the end of the third period and lasted until the first play of the final quarter, when it was fourth and four on the Oregon 15. Ron Coates entered the game and angled a 32-yard field goal with Caum holding.

Behind 10–7 with less than a quarter to play, Oregon made its big move, advancing to the Lion 24. After Rosdahl tackled Renfro for a loss on third and two, the Webs set up for an obvious fake field goal attempt. Quarterback Bob Berry picked up the ball and tossed it to Renfro, who was hit by Yost for a 5-yard loss.

Newsmen in the press box, well briefed in advance, expected the "bomb." Z-back Caum was at left end, third and 11 on the Oregon 41. Until now the Z-backs had been decoys for short-yardage tosses. Caum's defender was the speedy Hill, but Don faked him with a hook and headed for the left goal post (the "post" pattern). Renfro, covering the middle, came over so fast he nearly gummed things up, but Liske rolled to the right for a perfect pass. Although Caum's view was obstructed by the Oregon defenders, he caught the ball blind on his chest and held it there for the last 10 yards.

Pete Liske, the game's top hero, engineered the new offense, completed 11 of 12 passes for 113 yards, including both touchdowns, and punted once for 54 yards. His percentage of completions, 91.7, is still a single-game record (as of 1976). The Swing-T was used in later games less than had been anticipated, but every future opponent had to worry about it.

Pregame publicity had emphasized an offensive battle. Coach Engle said afterward that defense won the game despite the fine playing of Caum, Liske, and Klingensmith (who gained twice Renfro's yardage). Most Lion defenders were two-way players—Terry Monaghan, Ressler, Sabol, Rosdahl, Baker, and the roving "hero," Stuckrath. Rip tried to give everyone credit, but headlines on Sunday, and later back East, went to the Swing-T and Z-back mystery and the carefully hidden trickery that actually produced the winning play.

The Lions won intersectional clashes with UCLA and Rice before losing to the supposedly weaker eastern teams, Army and Syracuse. Liske, Powell, Coates, and Caum were leaders of the fine victory over the Uclans, Liske establishing a second record in two weeks by completing 19 passes (in 27 attempts) for 176 yards (tied in 1971 by John Hufnagel in 29 attempts). Caum's contribution was largely on defense with two interceptions, and there was also spirited running by Yost, Klingensmith, and Urbanik. Powell made the most exciting run of the game less than two minutes before half time, catching Liske's pass on the sideline, seemingly covered by three defenders. Instead of stepping out of bounds to stop the clock, he eluded two tacklers, while an official neatly took out a third. Junior skirted the sidemark for a 52-yard touchdown run that put the Lions ahead at the half, 14–7. Recovering a fumble, then led by quarterback Larry Zeno, UCLA tied the score in the third period, setting up a great ending, the winning field goal by Coates. Powell caught nine passes, tying a record then held by Lenny Krouse (1940).

Homecomers were excited about the team when Rice was vanquished 28–7 with a second-half surge. The big guns in the attack were Urbanik, Klingensmith, and Stuckrath, the Baltimorean, who also excelled on defense. Playing Army at home before a record crowd of 48,850, the Lions were less unnerved than usual over a first-quarter field goal kicked by Cadet Dick Heydt of Palmerton, Pennsylvania. But it happened again—Penn State lost the game, 10–7. Cadet Heydt provided the victory margin for three successive years.

Refusing to alibi, Coach Engle said simply that Penn State was licked by a big, strong, typical Army team. In the 1950s and 1960s, on their infrequent sorties into Nittany Valley, the Cadets came with only a small detachment from the Corps, which could outshout Penn State students even though the noise at Beaver was much more diffused than at Michie. When the home crowd tried to give the West Pointers a taste of their own noisy medicine, Athletic Director Ernie McCoy made a little speech between halves about good manners. In this game Junior Powell caught three passes to establish a career receiving record. He didn't hold it for long. A certain Jack Curry was then a freshman.

The 9–0 loss to Syracuse was disappointing. The Orange had one of its better seasons (8–2), ending with a victory over Notre Dame. (Everything happens at Syracuse—even to the freshman team. A back named Floyd Little helped demolish the Lion Cubs, who had been harassed even before the game when someone let out all the air from the tires of their bus. Rip claimed Ben Schwartzwalder had confused it with the varsity's.)

West Virginia and Maryland were beaten, but not overwhelmingly. The Mountaineer victory was highlighted by the performance of a sophomore back from Reading, Pennsylvania, Chris Weber. The victory was Penn State's 400th, of which Coach Engle had been at the helm for 90. (These statistics had been ready for release prior to the Army and Syracuse defeats.)

Although Penn State went to Columbus with a respectable 5–2 record, the Bucks apparently would have been lulled to sleep by anything coming from the East, and the local papers, as usual, didn't help Coach Woody Hayes' cause. One (the *Citizen-Journal*) called the game "Non-League Nonsense." When it was over, the writers tended to be respectful of Penn State, but were almost venomous toward Hayes. To be embarrassed by the easterners again (even if the last time had been in 1956) was too much for the locals at a time when OSU was sharing the Big Ten lead with Illinois and Michigan. "Few women fans understand football strategy, or even Hayes," said Jack Clowser in the Cleveland *Press*. He quoted a lady spectator who said, "I don't understand why we wait until the end of the game before we start to pass." Clowser, indicating he didn't either, pointed out that Penn State, with "marvelous ball handling by quarterback Pete Liske and superb faking from other backs," passed seven times on first down, eleven on second, and six on third, while Ohio State threw only twice in the entire first half.

Another writer explained that Woody was experimenting for coming Big Ten games with Northwestern and Michigan on the assumption that what didn't work against Penn State certainly wouldn't against the Big Ten toughies. Football capital rumors hinted that Coach Hayes had a secret weapon in a versatile sophomore, Tom Barrington, who would start at quarterback. In fact, the Columbus papers had him starting at all four backfield positions. He played at right half, as Penn State scouts had predicted. Matt Snell, the current invincible 5-yard plunging fullback, and running back Paul Warfield had fair days, netting 147 yards between them, but Klingensmith and Stuckrath had 142, and the papers seemed to know nothing about them other than that one was deaf.

Three times Snell hit into the middle of the Lion line on fourth-down, short-yardage missions, and three times he was stopped by Ressler, Baker, and Sabol. Twice this confidence in power denied the Buckeyes possible field goals because actually their place kicker, Dick Van Raaphorst of Ligonier, Pennsylvania, was among the best in the country. Not until the closing minutes of the first half did they sustain a power drive. The Lions, behind 7–0 after two quarters, had a moral victory of sorts, but the sentiment of the press was that the dikes would soon be opened.

The second half was Liske's—he had a phenomenal game, faking with sheer artistry. Ohioans appeared never to have seen his bread-and-butter play, the scissor reverse. By moving right half Klingensmith about 3 yards away from the end, Coach Engle befuddled Ohio's defense, and Liske's adroit play pattern developed thereby led to Penn State's tying touchdown. The 18-yard scoring play began as a routine scissor reverse with Liske faking to Chris Weber, left half, then faking to Klingensmith, right half, hiding the ball, and ambling toward right end. His two possible receivers were fullback Stuckrath, who faked a block and then tried to get loose, and right end Captain Bill Bowes, who caught the ball. All the Buck defenders were pulled toward the center, and Bowes was at least 5 yards from Warfield, his defender.

A repetition of the touchdown play in the same quarter (the third), with Stuckrath the receiver, put the Lions in a threatening position. Liske completed passes to Dick Anderson and Klingensmith, was dropped for a 5-yard loss, and then ran Stuckrath up the middle on a draw to the 6. On fourth down Coates came in to kick a field goal from the 15. The 80,000 plus home crowd was roaring for the kind of action seen when the Buckeyes won the Iowa game in the final period. Pulled out of character, the home team was using Barrington, the mystery back, as a passer. He was intercepted by Junior Powell, who also picked off quarterback Don Unverferth's desperate heave a little later—and it was back to the Big Ten for the Bucks.

Critics of eastern football got something to think about from this strange season, when the Lions won from four mighty intersectional foes and lost to three traditional rivals—Army, Syracuse, and Pitt. Losing to the Panthers is never pleasant, but the 1963 game (22–21) was so well played and exciting that the pain was eased. No noneastern team beat either Penn State or Pitt (9–1), surely one of the nation's best unwanted bowl candidates. Its intersectional victims were Washington, California, Notre Dame, and Miami (Florida). Quarterback Freddy Mazurek was the difference for Pitt—he ran for 137 yards against the Lions, who had led 21–15 after three quarters, and engineered the winning touchdown on a 77-yard drive in 11 plays, scoring personally on a 17-yard rollout. Penn State had time to win, and Coates barely missed two field goals against a strong wind.

Penn State, Pitt, Syracuse, and West Virginia—sometimes called the East's Big Four—were completing the second year of a loosely organized "gentleman's agreement." In the spring of 1962, President Eric A. Walker of Penn State, Chancellor Edward H. Litchfield of Pitt, Chancellor William P. Tolley of Syracuse, and President Paul A. Miller of West Virginia approved a mutual pact that outlawed "red-shirting"—a practice of withholding an athlete from formal competition for a year to take advantage of "developing maturity"—

and also agreed to a "frank exchange of information" on student-athletes with regard to admission, eligibility, scholastic requirements, recruiting practices, scholarship aid, College Board scores, and rank in high school class, with the hope of eventually adopting uniform standards in these areas. The four institutions further agreed, in May of 1963, to honor a letter of intent that high school athletes being mutually recruited would be required to sign.

Hopes of some officials for the evolution of an eastern conference from these steps were unrealized. With the coming of Coach Johnny Majors, Panther officials announced that they would no longer be bound by the agreement. The pact was dissolved, although it might have succeeded if the presidents had continued to involve themselves beyond the organizational meeting.

When Penn State lost three of its first four games in 1964, Coach Engle began to receive daily calls from sportswriters asking him how he'd feel if his team's national record of twenty-four winning seasons was broken. Not once did he admit to callers that the possibility existed. Coaches reviewing their seasons have a variety of reasons for selecting those they consider most memorable. Sometimes it's achievement, sometimes sentiment. Rip Engle's favorite of his sixteen Penn State teams has never been in doubt:

> From midseason on we were a great football team, and I received my biggest thrill in football during those last five Saturdays of 1964. The team grew stronger day by day, game by game, and by the end of the season it ranked with any in the nation. When we upset Ohio State we thought it might be possible to avoid a losing season. We knew Houston would be tough in that 98° humidity, but after winning that one we couldn't breathe any easier, because Pitt was coming up. I have never seen a good college line manhandled the way Pitt's was in that game. It was a climax to five great weeks of football, and the 1964 eleven earned the gratitude of the coaches and fans alike. Even with a 6–4 record, it had to be our finest team and my most memorable one.

For a starter, the Lions were trampled by Navy, 21–8, although the defense held Roger Staubach (Heisman winner) to 29 yards passing and 14 rushing. Next came a West Coast trip to UCLA, where the team faced another superb quarterback in Larry Zeno, whose final quarter passing attack won the game, 21–14, because the Lions fumbled away a fine opportunity to tie or win. Coach Engle's first loss to a West Coast team was followed by another (22–14) when Oregon visited University Park. Bob Berry, the third excellent quarterback in a row, completed 17 of 32 for 209 yards, but the home team beat itself with 9 fumbles, losing the ball 6 times this way and twice on interceptions. Never before, it was announced, had Penn State dropped its three first games, and the next outing was to West Point.

Crowd conduct concerned leaders of both institutions, and *Pointers,* a West Point publication (edited by the son of a Penn State alumnus), carried an editorial, "The West Point Image." Michie Stadium was a little more sedate, possibly because the nature of the game wasn't conducive to cheering. Penn State's remarkable defense held Army scoreless (except for an intentional safety) and thwarted the efforts of Rollie Stichweh, another of the country's best quarterbacks. Coach Dietzel's gimmick this year was to alternate three teams—the Regulars, the Bandits (defense), and the Go team, a sort of superoffensive unit.

After a scoreless first half, the Lions took the second-half kickoff and acquired the game's only touchdown on a 62-yard drive supervised by Gary Wydman, with fine running by Dirk Nye, Bob Riggle, Ed Stuckrath, and a 36-yard pass from Wydman to Bill Huber. Faking to Stuckrath from the Army 5, third down, Wydman pitched out to Riggle, who outran an Army defender to the corner of the end zone. The missed placement haunted Lion fans until the end of the game.

"The fourth quarter is ours" chanted the Cadets, with good reason. Despite heroic defensive efforts by Ressler, John Runnells, and a senior nonletterman, Bob Kane, Army's attack was relentless. Two passes from Stichweh to Sam Champi put the ball on Penn State's 29 with 4 minutes to play. A first down on the 19 was made by inches, and Army next went to the 7. Don Parcells slashed up the middle for 5, then lost a yard—two downs for 3 yards. When Stichweh held up his hands for quiet, the Penn State crowd near the goal posts became silent immediately. (The Cadet sections had been scrupulously polite while the Lions had the ball.) Stichweh tried a pass to Champi that was knocked down by Huber. On his final pass, Stichweh overthrew his receiver.

Army was still fired up for the ensuing clock battle. Wydman took the snapback and fell on the ball; he took it again for a 1-yard gain, and then for another yard. Army had called two time-outs to stop the clock, but now it was fourth down. Frank Hershey dropped back in the end zone to punt, took the pass from center, and dashed for one side of the end zone, where he was finally swarmed over by four Army men after consuming 11 seconds and giving up a safety. Penn State's deliberate safety was "not the game's most sporting gesture," said J. W. L. (Rogers E. N. Whitaker), an Ivy-oriented columnist of long standing for *The New Yorker* magazine. "If Princeton had pulled this trick against Dartmouth it would have won the Ivy League championship," was his rebuke. Nonsense. The safety is intended to be a defensive play, and if the Princeton quarterback refrained from using it, he either didn't know the rule or should have had his head examined.

Penn State's Homecoming loss to Syracuse the following weekend occasioned dismay, but little criticism of the players or coaches was heard. The strong Syracuse eleven became the East's Sugar Bowl representative (and was beaten by the LSU Tigers, 13–10). The Lions led the Orange at half time, 14–7, finally succumbing to the power and speed of Jim Nance and Floyd Little, 21–14. Coach Ben Schwartzwalder rated his rivals the best 1–4 team in the country, saying they'd be "tough from here in. It wouldn't surprise me if they won the rest of their games."

Against West Virginia, Bob Riggle made Penn State's record long run from scrimmage on a scissor reverse (86 yards), good until 1968 (when Bob Campbell ran 87 yards against Syracuse). Don Kunit, a promising speed runner with a tendency to fumble, also had a good day against the Mountaineers, with total runs of 86 yards. The following week, the Lions easily defeated Maryland, 17–9, but fans could hear Ohio State players smacking their lips for anticipated revenge—playing an eastern team with a 3–4 record. Of the three Penn State teams visiting Columbus in the modern era, the 1964 eleven had the least chance to win against the Buckeyes, who were leading the Big Ten with an overall record of 6–0. Their victims had been SMU, Indiana, Illinois, South Carolina, Wisconsin, and Iowa. (Ohio State defeated Northwestern the following week, and lost the Big Ten title to Michigan, 10–0, in its final game.)

Past indications that Penn State didn't scare in Big Ten country prepared no one for the incredible performance of the Nittany Lions before 84,270 dazed spectators, the largest crowd to see a Penn State team play (except on TV) and the third largest in Ohio State history. The mimeographed statistical summaries dispensed in the press box at half time and at game's end should be museum pieces. Figures for the Big Ten leader: first downs, 0; net yards rushing, —14; passes completed, 0; total plays, 16. The second-half figures were almost as preposterous. The Buckeyes made their initial first down on a penalty midway in the third quarter and later added four others, while Penn State's total was 22. The Lion passing and rushing yardage was 341 to Ohio State's 103. Coach Engle's team scored in every quarter, playing almost flawlessly.

Coach Woody Hayes spoke ruefully after the game. "Penn State made only one mistake today, and recovered it in the end zone for a touchdown. Rip Engle may have a 4–4 team, but we didn't play that team today." Wydman made the second touchdown on a short rollout, and Don Kunit accounted for both second-half scores. Gerry Sanker kicked three of four extra points. With superb finesse, quarterback Gary Wydman put the team through maneuvers that kept the Buckeyes off balance. Defensive leaders Glenn Ressler, John Runnells, Jerry Sandusky, John Deibert, Bud Yost, and Bob Kane were particularly effective with their rush of quarterback Don Unverferth when he attempted to pass. Looking back, Rip Engle remembers

> being apprehensive when we missed the extra point after our third touchdown. But I finally realized that a great group of Penn State players was maturing into what I now believe to have been the finest team we have had.

Between Ohio State and Pitt, the Lions defeated a good Houston team in Rice's Humidity Bowl (24–7), where Tom Urbanik led all ball carriers with 122 yards. Anxiety over the final game with Pittsburgh lingered simply because the course of this rivalry was unpredictable. The Panthers had quarterback Mazurek, unstoppable in 1963, and a very fast sophomore halfback, Eric Crabtree, whom Penn State had wanted to recruit. Their record wasn't outstanding, but they had decisively defeated Army (24–8) the week before and had shaken Notre Dame's national championship hopes. The Panthers lost to the Irish 17–15 when they were fourth down on Notre Dame's 1-foot line, went for a field goal, and missed by a foot.

Dominating Pitt almost as they had Ohio State, the Lions tore the Panther forwards to pieces, with Urbanik and Kunit gaining at will. Mazurek was held to 28 yards on the ground and 36 in the air. On Sunday morning, Coach Engle repeated his favorite quote: "Success lies not in never failing, but in rising every time you fail." Most listeners thought it was an original. Actually he took that one from Woody Hayes, too. It applied aptly to Penn State's 1964 team.

When the Lambert Trophy was awarded to Penn State (6–4), there was a loud howl from Princeton (9–0), the Ivy League champion. The committee obviously named the team strongest at the season's end, and Penn State had conquered Ohio State when it was a very close second to Notre Dame, the nation's Number One eleven. Far more legitimate than the Tigers' claim was that of Syracuse— 7–3 during the regular season. The Orange had overcome Penn State, Pittsburgh, Army, and Holy Cross, and owned a one-sided victory over UCLA. Syracuse certainly would have won the trophy if it hadn't lost to West Virginia in the final game.

An opportunity to play in the Gator Bowl was declined by vote of the players, unquestionably influenced by the seniors who had been unhappy over the previous venture. Glenn (Zeke) Ressler was named on ten All-America teams, including the major selections by the Coaches' Association and the American Football Writers (*Look*). The first Penn State center so honored in twenty-four years and winner of the Maxwell Award, Ressler had a long career with the Baltimore Colts.

Recent rule changes had been relatively minor except for the committee's continued attempts to repair the substitution rule, apparently by compromising between the pro free substitution rule, which meant two-platooning, and restricted substitutions. As a result of the ludicrous 1964 changes, coaches and players devised ingenious means (like the old fake injury play) to stop the clock in order to substitute a full team. In 1964, when a coach wanted to substitute a defensive unit prior to an obvious kicking situation, the team would hold the ball long enough to incur a delay-of-game penalty, automatically stopping the clock. An official blew his whistle, the clock was stopped, and in came the defensive unit after the inoffensive 5-yard penalty was marked off against the kicking team. The asinine rule was soon changed, but the trend inevitably was back to two-platooning.

37

Rip Shares Last Game with Gemini 7

Envisioning his final season of football coaching with occasional optimism, Rip Engle sometimes dreamed of a mighty team, maybe even an undefeated one. How could he have foreseen that the season would be fraught with unimaginable calamity? A quarterback with a transistor in his helmet; a loss in his last stand at Archbold Stadium, Syracuse; two defeats, one hotly disputed, when the winners' points came almost at the final gun; and the ultimate—sharing his final game on national television with the launching of Gemini 7 on a split screen in the most bizarre electronic trickery of the day.

The coach couldn't have guessed that the first opponents would be the two Rose Bowl teams and that one, Michigan State, would become national champion. The Lions opened against the Spartans at home and lost, 23–0, put down by a fullback Coach Duffy Daugherty had recruited from Hawaii (Bob Apisa) and a barefoot kicker (Dick Kenney) from the same state.

Around midseason, Bud Wilkinson commented in a syndicated column on misleading football statistics, noting that Penn State had tied the Spartans in first downs, 15–15; lost to Syracuse, 28–21, though outscoring the Orange in first downs, 25–8; and been beaten by UCLA, 24–22, while ahead in first downs, 22–12. He quoted Rip Engle's remark that only the final score is meaningful:

Our problem in these games was that we failed too often to make the big play in crucial situations. That is what football is all about, and there is no way to indicate it statistically.

In an interview with Wilkinson Rip didn't mention a UCLA incident, feeling it had little bearing on the game's outcome. The Lions trailed, 24–7, in the final quarter, then rallied furiously, but too late. (To show what a zany season it was, that same afternoon West Virginia defeated Pittsburgh, 63–48. Penn State later defeated the Mountaineers, 44–6, and then lost to the Panthers.) Unbeknownst, UCLA used electronics against the Lions at Beaver Stadium. Coaches Tommy Prothro and Pepper Rodgers had an All-America halfback, Mel Farr, and a much-heralded sophomore quarterback, Gary Beban. To bolster his competence, Beban had a transistorized receiver inside his helmet, tuned in to Assistant Coach Rodgers in the seclusion of the visiting team's booth in the press box. This was the scenario:

(*UCLA in huddle. Play called from press box via radio*):
"Run 48 sweep to right. *Beban repeated this signal to his team and UCLA lined up, with Penn State shifting its defense to cover the right. Beban stepped back for another message in his earphone:*
"Check it. Run 48 sweep opposite." (*The quarterback then gave an audible checkout play to his teammates, and off they went.*)

Whether to pass or run on one rollout was decided by Rodgers, who said, "Run it, run it." The device also was used to steady the inexperienced quarterback in a critical situation—less than a minute before half time and ahead 17–7, UCLA was backed up on its own 2-yard line. "Calm down now," was the directive. "Take it easy. You just have to run out the clock. Use a sneak."

Penn State's discovery of these shenanigans (legal then but later outlawed) began with a tipoff from Ed Sarson, a Phys Ed staff member who helped with traffic control. Picking up the patter on his walkie-talkie, he knew it wasn't coming from *his* partner in the press box, and made for the Penn State bench to tell the coach what was going on. Unable to combat it at that point, Rip chose to ignore it, but Sarson sat on the bench (traffic no doubt became hopelessly snarled) to let the man next to him listen to Coach Rodgers' instructions. The man was an Engle house guest that weekend, Dr. George

Haller '27, then a vice president of General Electric (for advanced technology).

Since Coach Engle learned Sunday morning that Coach Prothro emphatically denied communicating with his quarterback via radio telephone, it was assumed that Assistant Coach Rodgers acted without the knowledge of his chief, who is well known, however, for his ingenious innovations. Rip pointed out that nothing illegal was involved in the coach-to-quarterback system. "I dunno, Rip," said Dr. Haller. "There might be a federal offense here. Better let the NCAA investigate with the FCC. Find out if UCLA has applied for a Citizens' Band. You know, it won't be long before we can do without coaches altogether. Just program your game into a computer and feed it back to the quarterback. No need for anyone on the sidelines." Rip dismissed Haller's needling, thus probably avoiding a college football Watergate, but another visitor remembered the pertinent cliché: "Give the game back to the boys."

Coach Engle's last pride of Lions, scrappy and deserving of a better fate, had a good leader in Captain and center Bob Andronici, of Plainfield, New Jersey. This happened to be when the two-platoon system was newly revived, divided for the first time in the official depth chart under offense and defense, with kicking specialists listed separately. Except for a junior tackle, Bryan Hondru, the offensive linemen all were seniors—ends Bill Huber and Jerry Sandusky, tackle Joe Bellas, guards Chuck Ehinger and Steve Schreckengaust, and center Andronici.

The backfield was less seasoned, with inexperience a problem for quarterback Jack White, a junior, and sophomore Tom Sherman, who was used mainly as a place-kicking specialist until his junior and senior years. Against UCLA, White set a Penn State record, taking part in 49 offensive plays—36 passes (also a record) and 13 rushing attempts. Dave McNaughton, a senior who had been Tom Urbanik's understudy, was the fullback, while running halfback duties were shared by seniors Dirk Nye, Don Kunit, and Bob Riggle, and junior Mike Irwin.

Defensively, the 1965 Lions had most trouble finding capable ends. Dave Rowe and Gary Eberle were the tackles, and Rich Buzin and Ed Stewart were the top guards; John Runnells, Ellery Seitz, Bob Kane, and Jim Litterelle were the linebackers; John Sladki and Tim Montgomery were the defensive halfbacks; and Dick Gingrich was the safety.

Winning from Boston College (17–0) at Boston was welcome, but the Lions were into the final quarter that day before their coach was guaranteed his 100th Penn State victory. It wasn't pointed out at the time that Rip was the first Penn State football coach with this distinction.

Archbold, that grim and ancient chamber of horrors for Rip Engle, was a stadium unchanged in impact during his last combat with Coach Schwartzwalder. Losing wasn't so bad as having a single man responsible. Floyd Little scored one touchdown on a 91-yard punt return, and two others on scrimmage runs of 69 and 25 yards, thereby overshadowing the unforeseen expertise of two inexperienced Penn Statesmen. Senior fullback Dave McNaughton gained 137 yards rushing, four more than Little. Sophomore Jack Curry, hurt in the opening game, caught 10 passes from Jack White, establishing a new Penn State record. The coaches had thought Jack was "too frail to play football," and the Danville, Pennsylvania, boy did look dwarfed beside the Orange defenders, but Curry had great hands, good moves, and seldom missed a ball thrown near him. The week before, Coach Schwartzwalder had unveiled his sophomore fullback, Larry Csonka, who gained 170 yards against UCLA. Csonka had less success against the Lions (29 yards), but they were to hear of him again, as was the general public.

West Virginia's offense, so potent against Pitt, collapsed in Beaver Stadium as the Lions amassed a total offense of 423 yards, and Tom Sherman set a modern record by scoring 14 points by kicking. His three field goals tied the record (since broken by Chris Bahr).

And now the Lions went west to absorb a defeat as fractious and "hard to explain" as any in years, certainly one of the few Coach Engle looks back upon with undiminished dismay, not so much because of a disappointing loss but because he genuinely believes that sloppy officiating brought it about. The Lions, admittedly uninspired for three quarters, were trailing California 14–7 in the final period when Sherman kicked a field goal with 12:30 to play. Six minutes later, on its own 32, Penn State lost the ball because of penalties, and when it was again retrieved on the 19, a touchdown was 81 yards away with 3:22 remaining. During the drive, Dirk Nye's request for a time-out to stop the clock was ignored until Captain Andronici came over, but 9 seconds were consumed in this little exchange. Upsetting as it was at the time, in retrospect Coach Engle wishes the delay had been one second longer. Finally, when 42 seconds were left, White's pass to Curry in the corner scored and, with Sherman's point, the Lions went ahead (17–14) for the first time. The game had been won—apparently.

A short kickoff started California's drive from the 37 as Penn State set up its standard "prevent" defense, to allow small gains and attempt to prevent long ones. This puts little pressure on a passer, and Coach Ray Willsey had inserted his second quarterback, Jim Hunt, because he was the longer thrower. Hunt, seemingly trapped, got off a shaky completion to Jerry Bradley, a 154-pound pass-receiving specialist. Only 20 seconds were left, with the Bears still not to midfield. Hunt looked for a long receiver, found none, and spotted Bradley again for 10 yards to the Penn State 43. Time was called with 10 seconds left. Coach Engle looked for a long pass because a short one would run out the clock. A few Lions tried to bottle up Hunt as the seconds ticked away. Two seconds flashed on the scoreboard. Rich Buzin finally nailed Hunt, and tense Lion fans figured that was the end, but the scoreboard still showed one second. How the referee was able to stop the play with his whistle, how the California captain was able to request a time-out and get the clock stopped all in one second is a mystery, but they did and it did.

That one second to play had to be a scoring pass, almost certainly to the end zone. John Sladki, Ellery Seitz, and Dick Gingrich lined up in front of the expected receiver, Bradley. The game-ending gun had exploded, almost unheard in the din. Penn State's movies show Sladki clearly interfered with in the end zone, nearly knocked off his feet, but he had his hands well on the ball. Seitz had a piece of it and may have knocked it away from Sladki. Lion fans watched in horrified disbelief as the ball took a crazy bounce into Bradley's arms. Nearly all of the 38,000 California fans were on the field, a situation in which most officials would have ignored the meaningless extra point. Yet long after Penn State's disconsolate players got to their dressing room, they were summoned for a command appearance on the field. Coach Engle halfheartedly asked them to heed the call of duty. One by one a white-jerseyed Lion threaded his way toward the scene of the atrocity—first McNaughton, then Seitz, next Nye, and a few others. When seven had arrived the officials apparently felt they had a quorum, and a most unusual goal-line defense for football

(7–0–0) went on record. Seitz made a good effort to block the kick. At least the Bears didn't go for two.

In the aftermath of groans and complaints, perhaps the wisest words were those of Bill Huber: "My father always told me no game was ever won or lost on one play." Jack White had his best passing record of the season (17 for 26, 227 yards), and Jack Curry tied his record for 10 completions in a single game, while his 148 yards continues a Penn State record for passing yardage in one game (as of 1976). Curry holds four others still on the books: 42 receptions (in 1965); 117 career catches (1965–67); receiving yardage in one season, 681 (41 catches in 1967); and career receiving yardage, 1,837.

Victories over Kent State and Navy gave the team a chance for a winning season. Coach Bill Elias titled his eleven the Team Called Tenacity, because the Midshipmen in their so-so season had held eight previous opponents to a rushing average of 84 yards per game, including Notre Dame, Georgia Tech, Stanford, and Syracuse. Fortunately, the service academies haven't a corner on courageous, competitive players—Dave McNaughton and Mike Irwin led the way to the 14–6 decision, compelling the Team Called Tenacity to give up 208 yards on the ground.

The Pitt game began and ended as a nightmare. Victory was a necessity for both teams and especially for Coach Johnny Michelosen, who was reported to be in a precarious position. The press had quoted Chancellor Litchfield two years before to the effect that Pitt played unexciting, unimaginative football, but its record in 1963 was 9–1, including victories over UCLA, Washington, California, Notre Dame, Miami (Florida), Penn State, and others; the loss was to Navy. The 1965 game somewhat duplicated the California affair except that the Lions outdid themselves to give it away in the first half, and the Panthers mounted an exciting last-minute winning drive led by Kenny Lucas (brother of the 1959 Lion All-America quarterback Richie).

Three devastating Penn State fumbles set up three touchdowns in the first half, which ended with Pitt ahead, 20–0, a lead that seemed to be for keeps when it went to 27–7 at the end of the third quarter. Then, in a span of 16 minutes, the Lions completed drives of 59, 68, and 88 yards, largely on the fine running of McNaughton and Kunit, who tried hard to make up for his first-half fumbles. He did score all three final period touchdowns, the last tying the score at 27–27. Sherman had already kicked three points under considerable pressure and missed only one all season, but was slightly wide with his attempt. In a way it was a blessing—a successful kick would have added to the bitterness of coming moments. After the kickoff, Pitt had 55 seconds on its own 40. Lucas passed to Crabtree and three times to sophomore Bob Longo, who made three difficult catches. Lion partisans in Pitt Stadium were pleading for an interception or anything to stop the inexorable drive as Lucas deftly used his few remaining seconds. On the 1-yard line Kenny called a time-out with 3 seconds to go. Coach Michelosen staked his professional reputation on a substitute whose two years on the squad had been spent mostly on the bench. Unlisted as a kicking specialist, Frank Clark took a half dozen practice swings with his leg and then kicked the ball between the goal posts. The clock was at one second when Pitt kicked off, and Bob Riggle made a valiant but futile effort to run it back, zigzagging all over the field as if trying to stave off the moment of truth. A statistician figured out that Penn State had lost two games in 1965 by a combined total of 9 seconds after the final gun. The California score was estimated to have come 10 seconds after the game officially should have ended.

Eastern football had a poor year generally, one of the worst in the decade, as was indicated when Dartmouth and Princeton were first and second in the Lambert rating. The vote revived the old argument that if the Ivy League wanted serious consideration for the trophy, its teams should meet some of the strong eastern independents, at least on the few dates available for nonleague games. Many writers in and beyond Syracuse thought the Orange (7–3) deserved the honor for victories over the traditionally strong sectional teams—Navy, Maryland, Penn State, Pittsburgh, West Virginia, and Boston College. Navy, too, had tied Stanford and beaten Oklahoma.

Coach Michelosen, hero for a day and among the best liked and most respected eastern coaches, was not rewarded for his spectacular victory over Penn State. Despite his eleven-year record of 5–5–1 in the series, he was fired to give the job to Dave Hart. Pitt has beaten the Lions once since Michelosen left.

A financially advantageous offer from NBC-TV had switched the Maryland game at College Park from September 19 to December 4. Coming two weeks after the Pitt misery made it an anticlimax, but the Lions had a chance to even their season at 5–5, and Rip closed his coaching career on a somewhat sentimental note. As a senior end on Western Maryland's undefeated 1929 team under Dick Harlow, he had played against Maryland in the final game, defeating the Terps, 12–0, for an 11–0 season. Not quite the same, striving for 5–5, but the parallel was significant to Rip, who was delighted to win, 19–7.

This late nationally televised game was meaningless except to decide which team would have a losing season (Maryland also was 4–5). NBC provided the pizzazz by contriving a novel stunt that allowed one of its weekly football spectaculars to be shared with the Gemini 7 takeoff, an arrangement unapplauded by millions of American sports fans. If Maryland and Penn State were unhappy to share their time with space history, it was a case of crying all the way to the bank.

As far back as 1962, Rip Engle had thought seriously about retiring at the age of 60. When the event was a month away he announced his decision quickly (February 18, 1966) at a fitting time, with dignity, and with sound personal reasons. His professional life at Penn State, dedicated to a game he loved, had been a typical mix of trials, triumphs, and tensions. Numbers of his friends, respected coaches for many years, had left the game under unnecessarily humiliating circumstances, and he wanted none of that. "I want to retire," he once said, "with my head high. I'd always like to be able to go out of my front door every morning." Robust in health most of his life, he feared the effect of heavy coaching pressures in advancing years. Conditions at Penn State, including the "single standard" principle imposed on athletes as an admissions policy, were satisfactory to Rip, but he was concerned that the football team might be handicapped with the pressure growing every season for high national ratings and bowl invitations.

Most announcements of Engle's retirement not quite accurately said he was a native of Salisbury, Pennsylvania (Somerset County). His birthplace was Elk Lick, which combined with Sand Patch and Pocahontas to form Salisbury some years later. As a boy of 14 he was a mule driver in a coal mine, became a mine supervisor at 19, and spent a year at Blue Ridge College (now defunct), where he played in the first football game he ever saw. From the Old Blue Ridge period he drew a series of droll stories his friends called "Rip's Humble Talks." Many audiences enjoyed the tall tales about his

hometown—"a single general store, one traffic light (now reduced to
a blinker), and a speed trap we were very proud of." He also described an authentic game that Blue Ridge lost to Temple, 110–0:

> We were behind 78–0 at halftime, so you can see we had a bet-
> ter second half. It was a tough-luck team. We couldn't pene-
> trate the 10-yard line to get in for a score (I mean our own
> 10-yard line). We had practiced a fumble play—fumble over
> the goal line and fall on the ball for a touchdown. But it was
> pretty hard to fumble 90 yards.

Dick Harlow heard about Rip, persuaded him to enter Western
Maryland, and there Rip met his wife, the former Mary Webber
Broughton. The two men—player and coach—formed a close relationship that lasted through Harlow's life. After graduation, Rip
taught and coached at Waynesboro, Pennsylvania, High School,
where he had a remarkable eleven-year record (86–17–5), with
three unbeaten, untied teams and eight conference titles. Concurrent
with graduate work at Western Maryland, he was freshman coach
and varsity basketball coach.

Rip's college coaching career started in 1942 at Brown University
as assistant to J. Neil (Skip) Stahley (Penn State '30), whom he succeeded as head coach in 1944. The record for his six years was
28–20–4, but this was among the most exciting periods in Brown's
football history. His 1944 team was Brown's first to beat Colgate
(32–26), coached by Andy Kerr, since Tuss McLaughry's team of
1928. The following year Brown upset Yale (20–7) using the fake
field goal play that was to beat Alabama for Penn State in 1959.
When Joe Paterno was quarterback in 1948, Brown won a thrilling
23–20 victory over Princeton, the Bruins scoring on a field goal with
9 seconds to play. That was their best season since 1928, but the
next year, with Paterno again at quarterback, Engle lost only one in
ten. Trailing 26–7 late in the third period, Brown rallied for a 41–26
victory over Colgate in the final game, on Thanksgiving Day.

Listed among the nation's winningest coaches, Engle never had a
losing season at Penn State (104–48–4), taking the Nittany Lions to
four consecutive bowl games, winning three, and also winning the
Lambert Trophy in 1961, 1962, and 1964. The Coach of the Year in
NCAA District 2 in 1962 also was elected president of the American
College Football Coaches' Association. Rip conducted five football
clinics for the Army and the Air Force—two in Europe, two in
Japan, and one in Vietnam—and was a favorite choice for coach of

all-star teams. He directed the North team in four Blue-Grey games at Montgomery, Alabama, the North team in the Hula Bowl of 1963, and the East in the first All-America Bowl, at Buffalo in 1961. He has maintained a close connection with the East-West Shrine game, which he coached in 1957 at San Francisco, as chairman of the East's selection committee, a post long held by the late Andy Kerr.

Rip's many honors include the annual award of the Touchdown Club of New York for his "contributions of permanent value to the sport of football." Among previous recipients were General Omar Bradley, General Douglas MacArthur, Admiral William F. Halsey, and Amos Alonzo Stagg. In 1970 he received the Amos Alonzo Stagg Award recognizing his outstanding services in the best interests of football, was elected to Brown University's Athletic Hall of Fame in 1972, and to the National Foundation Hall of Fame in 1973.

Penn State's "changing of the guard" was accomplished in 1966 without confusion because Coach Engle was determined that it should happen that way, and because of the dedication and solidarity of his staff. Joe Paterno, not one of the senior members, for some time had been the obvious heir apparent, and the succession was clear when Joe was named associate coach prior to the 1965 season after he had rejected an offer to succeed John Pont as coach at Yale.

Engle's strong feelings for his assistants, his attachment to Penn State, and his confidence that Paterno would carry on successfully are shown in his letter to all the new football recruits in the spring of 1966. He wrote, in part:

> Coaching football has been a great life . . . but I have decided to retire while it is still fun and there is time to explore some other areas that interest me. . . . I trust this will not alter your plans or your parents' interest in our University.
>
> Penn State football is on a sound basis. The objectives, the player-coach relationship, and the outlook for the program remain the same. The staff that has done such a wonderful job for me remains the same and Joe Paterno as head coach will establish himself as one of the fine young head coaches in the country. No one possesses more of the qualities for success.
>
> I will always retain a feeling of great satisfaction to have been a part of Penn State football. Nothing could make me prouder or happier than to see it continue to succeed and to excel under men I have learned to admire, respect, and love over the years.

The Engles, Rip and Sunny, indulge their enjoyment of travel frequently and their summer vacations at Cape Cod are now "extended," but they maintain their permanent home in State College only a few blocks from the university campus, where Rip is often seen. He can indeed "go out the front door" with his head high and with the assurance that his many friends—both town and gown—will be happy to see him.

Part VII

THE GRAND EXPERIMENT

Joe Paterno, 1966–

38

That Fourth Down Debate

When he was about to graduate from Brown University in June
1950, Joe Paterno had been helping out with the quarterbacks during spring practice at Coach Engle's request. Suddenly one day in the
locker room, the coach asked him, without preliminaries, if he'd be
interested in coming along to Lion Country.

Joe had never been in central Pennsylvania, and knew nothing
about Penn State except a little of its football reputation in the late
Higgins years. The offer was appealing because to get through law
school he needed a job (he had thought of prep school coaching in
the Boston area). That night at the Delta Kappa Epsilon fraternity
house he phoned his father, who was neutral about the project, except that he didn't want his son to give up law school. A fraternity
brother whose war training had been done at Penn State said it was
some place," but not one he could ever expect to get home from—
the old isolation theme. After a few thoughtful days, Joe accepted
the job, aware that Rip probably had offered it to two or three of his
more experienced assistants.

Meanwhile, Arthur Sampson, the well-known Boston *Herald*
sportswriter and close friend of Dick Harlow's, had "leaked" the
story as a rumor, headlined "Rip Engle Going to Penn State." The
news aroused the campus, but few knew that Paterno was involved.

After Rip's two weeks with the Lion squad, he returned to Providence and asked Joe to go back with him for two more weeks with the players who were coming in from the teachers' colleges. Of his first visit, Paterno says:

> On the way down . . . you know, I was just a kid and Rip and I didn't have much in common except football . . . we soon ran out of things to talk about. I remember Rip telling me how much he'd always wanted to coach there; what a lovely campus it was and how everything was so clean. "You'll really see how clean everything is, even the barns; you could even sleep in the barns." The only barn I'd ever been in was a trolley barn, but the first places Rip took me were the sheep and cow barns. They were clean all right, but they still smelled like barns and I was glad I didn't have to sleep there that first night.

Sunny Engle and their son, Chip, hadn't arrived at the house Rip had already bought on Woodland Drive, and there was no furniture, but Joe slept for two weeks on a cot until he moved in with Steve and Ginger Suhey for the first year, and then with the Jim O'Hora family. On the field, the adjustment was a little harder because the players were his own age, or older if they had been in the service longer than Joe. He was to work with four players, one of whom they hoped would develop into a T quarterback.

> We had Joe Gratson, Len Shepherd, Dick Koerber, and Vince O'Bara. I remember telling Rip there was one thing I was sure of—O'Bara was the one guy who couldn't do the job. As it turned out, Vince saved that first season for us, and I learned my first coaching lesson.

Most of the players were slow getting used to the young upstart, whose Brooklynese and direct approach contrasted sharply with Engle's fatherly, modulated tones. They quickly realized that Paterno was wrapped up in a job he considered temporary:

> I was involved in a challenge, really. Someone said, "Your job is to get a quarterback ready." I knew very little about coaching . . . spent hours in the office every night with a movie projector, looking at every Penn State film. . . . I knew more about the Cotton Bowl than a lot of the guys who played in it. I was trying to find out what kind of players Penn State had, what Pitt had, what kind of play would win, how good you had to be, trying to evaluate. Then, I had pads and pads of plays . . . every time I'd see something I'd draw it. I'd want the whole play right across the field—all 22 guys.

Joseph Vincent Paterno was the oldest son of Angelo Lafayette and Florence de Salle Paterno, both born in Brooklyn and living on Eighteenth Street when Joe arrived, some twenty months before his brother George. (George followed him to Brown and later became head football coach at Kings Point Merchant Marine Academy.) Paterno, Sr., had dropped out of high school to serve with the Army in World War I, returned to finish his education, including law school at night, and later was court clerk in the Appellate Division of the New York Supreme Court. He died in 1955, eleven years before his older son began his successful head coaching career. The boys attended St. Edmund's School and then Brooklyn Prep. Too skinny (125 pounds) for football at first, Joe soon made the New York City All-Met team. His contact with Brown was made through his coach, Zev Graham, whose friend Everett M. (Busy) Arnold, a New York businessman, recruited for his alma mater and offered to pay Joe's expenses. Coach Engle greeted Joe when he enrolled in the summer of 1945 a year after Rip had become head coach. Six weeks later the Army called Joe up, but he was able to return in the fall of 1946.

The smooth transition of Penn State's football regimes would be difficult to match. Joe was twitted, in fact, for deliberately accenting the harmony by compiling a first-season record identical with Coach Engle's last (5–5). Paterno wasn't born to be satisfied with modest success—new responsibilities added zest to tasks he had once considered routine. He learned to cool his outbursts of temper and tried to acquire patience with players, coaches, and problems in general. Veteran coaches sharing his responsibilities were O'Hora, Patrick, and White. Dan Radakovich was beginning his sixth season, Joe McMullen his fourth, George Welsh his third, and Earl Bruce would continue as freshman coach. Chuck Medlar was starting his twenty-first season as varsity trainer. Paterno hired Bob Phillips (Slippery Rock '50), who had completed a notable high school coaching record at Montour (92–12–4), and within a few years he was handling the offensive line, including ends, receivers, and place kickers. Bob's 1963 and 1964 teams had won Pennsylvania Class A WPIAL titles.

Joe wasn't happy with his first season. Self-critical by nature, he thought he had done a mediocre job, although he realized that Penn State was overmatched against Michigan State, UCLA, Georgia Tech, and possibly Syracuse. Michigan State (9–0–1) played its celebrated 10–10 tie with Notre Dame (9–0–1) and shared national honors with the Irish, a record that led experts to rate the 1966 Spartans one of the greatest college elevens of all time. Fear that he was "developing a dominating attitude toward the great guys on the staff I'd worked with so long" bothered Paterno:

> I wasn't sure then how good I could be as a head coach, but I was darn sure I'd find out pretty quick, not stagger around for four or five years. I'd make up my mind in a hurry about that.

In his first year as head coach, Paterno went against four other new coaches—Lou Saban at Maryland, Tom Cahill at Army, Jim Carlen at West Virginia, and Dave Hart at Pittsburgh—and won from all but Cahill. Saban, a seasoned coach who had won an AFL championship in the pros, gave the Lions a hard time in their opening game, which ended 15–7 largely on the strength of three safeties, two of them the work of sophomore Mike Reid. Happy to win his first game, Joe was eager for that first victory handshake, but couldn't find the losing coach. On Monday Saban called to apologize for not having a chance to congratulate him, and added, "But neither of us played very well." "Thanks anyway, Lou," was Joe's reply.

Scoring three safeties in one game was unusual and made the game a strong beginning for sophomore Reid. He got one by blocking a kick, another with an end-zone tackle, and should be credited with the third, said newsmen, for scaring the quarterback to death.

Jack White, first prospect for quarterback, was pushed hard by sophomore Frank Spaziani, but before long Tom Sherman had moved into first position, and Spaziani eventually became a defensive end. Senior backfield material was lean except for White and Mike Irwin. Hopes that junior Roger Grimes would provide some running strength were grounded when he was injured, leaving that department to Irwin, Bill Rettig, sophomore Bobby Campbell, and fullback Dan Lucyk. Along with Spaziani, Campbell, and Reid, the top sophomore prizes were end Ted Kwalick and lineman Dave Bradley. Paterno also had senior linemen Bryan Hondru, Jim Pollard, Dave Rowe, and John Runnells; juniors Rich Buzin, Jim Litterelle, Mike McBath, Bill Lenkaitis, Tim Montgomery, John Sladki, and Bob Capretto. Junior Jack Curry's proficiency as a receiver made it likely that Penn State would be a passing team, with Sherman as a field goal kicking threat.

Mayhem took place at East Lansing (42–8), where the Spartans yelled and howled their way down the field on kickoffs. Said one

Lion: "They came at you with everything but spears." Penn State started an advance that reached the 32, with 10 minutes to play and Michigan State ahead, 42–0, but Coach Daugherty put in his first defensive team to protect the six-touchdown margin. Later, when he was more merciful, he was roundly booed by the crowd as the Lions scored. Duffy could afford to let up now and then with such All-Americas as George Webster, Bubba Smith, Clint Jones, Gene Washington, and Charlie Thornhill.

Penn Staters scanning future schedules were relieved to find no game listed for the Lions in Michie Stadium until 1970, because in 1966 the rains on the Plains fell mainly on Penn State. Coach Paterno's eleven played its poorest game of the season under terrible weather conditions, and Army's victory (11–0) certainly helped earn the Coach of the Year award for its new leader, Tom Cahill, whose first season was 8–2. (Beating Penn State didn't help the able coach eight years later, when West Point officials fired him.) Boston College, not actually a breather (30–21), enabled the team to recoup before meeting UCLA on the West Coast. Tom Sherman came into his own as a passer, completing 13 of 26 for 220 yards and leading a second-half surge that brought his team back from a 15–8 halftime deficit. From BC on, Tom was the Number One quarterback.

UCLA won the 1966 Pac8 title by defeating USC, 14–7 (although the Trojans played in the Rose Bowl), but had slipped from Number Two nationally to Number Four because of a squeaker against Rice. Coach Prothro played his team against the Lions as if his job depended on it. Ahead 49–11 with 38 seconds to go, UCLA tried an onside kick. In the dawn of this Age of Football, it wasn't whether you won that counted, but by how much. The Lions played creditably in the first half, behind only 21–11, but couldn't defend against the speed of Mel Farr, Rick Purdy, Mike Bergdahl, and the general all-around ability of 1967 Heisman winner Gary Beban. UCLA also had a sophomore halfback, Harold Busby, who was a 9.4 hundred man.

Defeating West Virginia (38–6) and California at Homecoming (33–15) set the stage for the annual Syracuse fracas. Coach Paterno kept aloof from Penn State Dean Ernie McCoy's "electronic" battle with Syracuse authorities, who planned to install a closed circuit TV monitor in the Beaver Field press box as a coaching aid, a practice outlawed by the NCAA soon after. Adamant in his refusal, McCoy was reminded by the Syracuse press that the world was out of the "dark ages," and Coach Schwartzwalder said, "All we wanted to do was use a lousy little bit of electricity." Paterno offered to exchange two or three monitoring jobs for Floyd Little. Unfortunately, the Orange lost the battle of words but won the game, 12–10. Penn State, leading 10–6 after three quarters, found itself in a conservative pattern and was beaten on a pass from kick formation, an unexpected bit of trickery from Coach Ben. On the Lion 30 after the fake kick, the Orange merely gave the ball to Larry Csonka, who powered in. The big fullback gained 131 yards to Little's 110—quite a few yards for 12 points.

Georgia Tech dispelled any thought of an upset in about five minutes, winning 21–0 on a poor passing day for Tom Sherman (2 for 12). The expected Pitt Stadium brawl materialized with both regimes trying to save mediocre seasons by winning (said Chet Smith of the Pittsburgh *Press*) the "championship of Route 22." The Lions were accused of running up the score when they won 48–24, but Paterno's charges, after a baffling season, were reacting to the guideline of their new coach, "We will play every play as if we were behind," the first of many Paterno aphorisms that spice his coaching credo. Old Ironsides, trophy for the winner of a tri-state Pitt-West Virginia-Penn State round robin, again remained in Rec Hall, where it had worn an indentation on the floor of the trophy case. Syracuse (8–2) won the Lambert Trophy, after an unsettling period for the committee when three Ivy teams were tied for the league's first place. At that point, the Lambert people put Harvard first and Penn State eighth behind Massachusetts (seventh).

Paterno's Crisis Number One followed the Navy defeat in the first 1967 game, at Annapolis, 23–22. Asked later about Crises Numbers Two and Three, he denied their existence, but he has never minimized what happened the week after the opening loss of his second year. It was earth-shaking because the season had held such promise. The Lions had Bobby Campbell, among the East's finest running backs; Tom Sherman, veteran quarterback; Jack Curry, the best pass-catching end Penn State had ever had; Ted Kwalick, a receiver of no mean talent; Don Abbey, a sophomore place-kicking specialist; and a highly-publicized junior tackle, Mike Reid, who was hurt after a few plays and was lost for the year.

Navy, ahead 10–3 in the first half, lost its lead to the Lions after three quarters (14–10), but went ahead again, 17–14, with 8 minutes to play. Campbell's remarkable catch of Sherman's pass was good for a third touchdown and, faking a placement on the extra point for the second time, the Lions ran for a two-pointer (Campbell). The game seemed iced at 22–17 with less than 2 minutes to play, but John Cartwright needed only a minute to pass his team to victory.

Coach Paterno, who had tried his now famous 4-4-3 defense—a long winter's work with the other coaches—worried and wondered if he had the material to make it work. He had, but it had been dormant, a situation that would change. Paterno looks back:

> Here we were, 5 and 6 in my first 11 games. Our staff was confused and needed strong leadership. I had to either prove myself or, well, there was no use prolonging it. We were being second-guessed by a lot of people, but that didn't bother me—that's part of coaching . . . after that trip I made up my mind if we were going to lose, we'd lose with the best material we had, regardless of seniority. . . . We started to play more sophomores.

Coach Paterno's innovation for the Miami game, played on a Friday night in the Orange Bowl, was an unorthodox experiment. Instead of flying down a day in advance, as most teams did, the squad bused to Pittsburgh and spent Thursday night at the Airport Motel, left by jet in the morning, stayed at the air-conditioned Miami Airport Hotel until game time, and went to the Orange Bowl site by air-conditioned bus. The boys were kept off their feet and had no problem with the heat. Sophomores were injected into the game one or two at a time, and by the fourth quarter more than a dozen were playing varsity before they knew what was happening. This was a baptism at the glamorous bowl site for defensive players like Jim Kates, Denny Onkotz, Pete Johnson, Steve Smear, and Neal Smith; and offensive players Paul Johnson, Tom Jackson, Wally Cirafesi, George Kulka, Charlie Pittman, and Don Abbey. Defensive sophomores John Ebersole and Ed Stofko might have made it except for injuries at Navy. Miami was beaten 17–8 in its own backyard by psychology and coaches who believed in and weren't afraid to experiment with a dozen eager and talented sophomores. A single mistake in the final minute kept the Lions from a shutout.

The lively Lions were in fine fettle during the first half, surprising Miami with their vigor, unusual for a northern team in the tropical nighttime humidity. The Miami *Herald* said, "Nothing like this should have happened from a team out of the unproductive East," forgetting that nine or ten of the Miami players were easterners, including three Pennsylvanians in the starting backfield. Penn State's first scoring sequence came when Bobby Campbell, trapped at one end, reversed his field for an exciting 50-yard run. Sherman faked to two backs and passed to Kwalick in the end zone for the touchdown, but the extra point was missed. From then on it was all simple sailing for the young Lions, core of a squad that would return the next two years to win Orange Bowl games.

UCLA and Beban again nosed out Penn State, 17–15, with a blocked kick in the third period and Beban's last-quarter touchdown. The UCLA quarterback apparently was minus his electronic helmet, but probably had more effective Prothro resources. Beban regularly stepped up to center, surveyed the Lion defense, and if he found it changed or unusually complex, he held up his hands for crowd silence (and there *was* noise), went back in a huddle to check out the play, and off UCLA would go. Officials *can* have their problems!

Moving upward, the Lions won their seven remaining regular-season games, beginning a record of thirty-one consecutive contests without defeat; received a Gator Bowl bid; and won the Lambert Trophy over the wails of Navy and the Baltimore press. The Midshipmen (5–4–1) had beaten Penn State, hadn't they? The Lambert committee at last was assigning the award to the team with the best record and strongest at the season's end, although officially holding "best performance" as the criterion.

There were stumbling blocks en route. West Virginia, coached by Jim Carlen in his second year, had the surprised Homecoming fans in Beaver Stadium on edge. Sophomore Charlie Pittman of Baltimore accounted for 264 yards by running, receiving, and returning kicks to certify the Lion victory, 21–14. They escaped the usual misery at Syracuse (29–20), although the matter wasn't clinched until Denny Onkotz intercepted quarterback Jim Cassata's pass and ran 47 yards for a late touchdown. Beginning with this game, the defensive unit became a key to the offense for the next two years. Penn State generously awarded Syracuse statistical honors, compiled largely on the power running of Larry Csonka (112 yards).

Some of the Syracuse public had solved the parking problem prevalent at most large universities (but not Penn State—yet). They bought lots in a cemetery reasonably near Archbold to park in and tailgate, too.

Maryland succumbed at College Park with Confederate flags flying all over the stadium, causing Penn Staters to wonder if the sixteen Pennsylvanians, eleven New Jerseyites, and ten New York boys on the Terp squad knew what they were. North Carolina State, coached by Earle Edwards '31, was Coach Paterno's first exposure to a nationally-ranked team. The Wolfpack, undefeated and untied, was third behind Southern California and Tennessee, whereas Penn State didn't appear in the top ten named by one press association, and wasn't even listed alphabetically "among those receiving votes" in another. One release ineptly called this the worst match since Jack Dempsey mauled Jess Willard. Dennis Onkotz won the game in the opening quarter. Penn State's first touchdown was scored when Ted Kwalick made a fingertip catch of a Sherman pass. A few minutes later, Denny intercepted a pass by quarterback Jim Donnan and returned it 47 yards for the clincher score. The Wolfpack, down 13–0 and not previously scored on in a first quarter, refused to be demoralized and nearly pulled the game out in the final minutes. NCS had made six points in the third period on two field goals by Gerald Warren, highest-scoring kicking specialist in the country.

The visitors, following a holding penalty, had first down on the Lion 20 with 2:51 to play. Their next first down, inside the 10 with 1:41 remaining, allowed time for four plays. Fullback Bobby Hall picked up six because Penn State had expected a pass, but Tony Barchuk was held to a yard. It was now third and three. When the Lion goal-line defense halted Hall a little more than a yard from victory, the Wolfpack called time-out with 40 seconds left. The Lions were looking for Barchuk, who was battered safely away from the line by Kates and Onkotz. Wolfpack time-outs thwarted Sherman's attempts to run out the clock on three plays, and on fourth down Coach Paterno decided to give up a safety. There was nothing cute about it—one Lion even addressed his opponent: "Hey, man, we're going to give you two."

Coach Edwards' comment to the press afterward was frank and unusual:

I blame myself entirely. I've been coaching for many years. With fourth and one on the goal line, if I couldn't give my quarterback a scoring play, who else can I blame?

Earle's old coach, Bob Higgins, often used to say that a perfect play usually depends on what the other fellow does.

Ohio University (not Ohio State), the Pitt warmup, was Paterno's first experience as a head coach in handling his team when a bowl bid was likely to follow a victory. To forestall fatal daydreaming, he promulgated some rules for bowl preparation that he has scrupulously followed ever since. There can be no talk about a bowl until the final regular-season game is over, no interviews, no mention of a bowl at any time in his presence or that of his players. Concentration must be on the job at hand—winning the next game.

The Pitt clash was another old-fashioned grudge battle. Coach Dave Hart, also in his second year, had been recruiting heavily and with fanfare, in contrast to Paterno's policy of silence. The two coaching staffs had often crossed paths, and the comparative merits of each freshman squad were newsworthy. The Lion freshmen under Earl Bruce in 1966 had little trouble with the Panther Cubs, but in 1967 Hart was reported to have the "cream." The Lion frosh, nevertheless, surprised the Pitt Cubs, 16–9. Penn State overwhelmed the Panthers at Beaver Stadium, 42–6. Junior Ted Kwalick made the Coaches' and the NEA All-America tight end positions. Tom Sherman threw four touchdown passes for a school record, and Jack Curry ended his three-year career with six Penn State game, season, and career all-time receiving records.

THE GATOR BOWL,
DECEMBER 30, 1967

Having already dealt with the effect of an early bowl invitation, or even the rumor of one, Coach Paterno turned to the more serious problem of preparing for the game itself. First, he ascertained that his players were anxious to go and realized he would expect them to make sacrifices. Next, he insisted that athletic officials be ready to reward players within NCAA regulations. Paterno believed that Penn State would be investing wisely for the future by making the bowl trip a reward, not merely for the playing members of the squad, but also for everyone who contributed to the season's success—substitutes, managers, cheerleaders, and the Blue Band. He wanted everyone to enjoy the reward without detracting from the importance of winning. The administration concurred, and the squad practiced at Daytona Beach, ninety miles south of Jacksonville, moving to the bowl city three days before the game. Paterno held closed practices to prepare for Florida State's renowned passing team, but was persuaded to take the media into his confidence at a press conference after a day or two.

The coaches made drastic defensive changes, increasing the speed of the Lions' secondary to neutralize the effectiveness of the Seminoles' combination—Kim Hammond, the nation's Number Two passer, and All-America flanker back Ron Sellers, a receiving giant. This was risky, because players had to learn new assignments in a short period. Sophomore Jim Kates switched to middle guard; Paul Johnson moved from offense to defense; sophomore Neal Smith moved to rover back; and sophomore Wally Cirafesi joined Tim Montgomery and Bob Capretto in the deep secondary.

Even more radical offensive changes were designed to get the ball to Ted Kwalick freely and to confuse defenders as to the eventual whereabouts of the big All-America tight end (now a halfback). Moved into the backfield on the wing, Ted was replaced in the line by sophomore Gary Williams. Lion fans wondered why the backs went into a sort of tight Y formation before shifting to the right or left, with Kwalick nearly always on the same side as split end Jack Curry, but Paterno cited psychological reasons:

> If you don't try something new in the two weeks of practice before a bowl game, the team gets bored and then goes stale. If you stay with the old, the players say, "We know these things, so why do we practice so long." This way you give them something to learn . . . make them want to practice . . . and you just can't play a good game without it. And then, of course, anything new will temporarily upset the other team—at least at first—and that's what happened in the Gator Bowl . . . in the first half, anyway.

A 17–0 lead at half time, surprising Penn Staters and astonishing the Seminoles, was the handiwork largely of the secondary, especially Capretto. Receivers were dropping some of Hammond's accurate throws, but he wasn't exactly chained down at all during the game, completing 37 passes in 55 attempts for 361 yards—all record figures against the Lions.

Penn State obtained its first good field position when Montgomery intercepted a pass, and Kwalick and Dan Lucyk caught passes from Sherman. Charlie Pittman's running gave the Lions a first down on the 6, but they had to settle for a field goal by Sherman. A daring interception by Neal Smith, the new "hero" back, led to a touchdown pass at the Seminole 10 from Sherman to Curry. At 4½ minutes before half time, Pittman's fine running again set up a touchdown, with Sherman passing this time to Kwalick from the 12. End of half: Penn State 17; Florida State 0. Crowd reaction: amazement.

Early in the second half the undaunted Seminoles advanced to the Lion 3 only to be turned back again in four attempts to score from close in. On fourth down, Jim Litterelle brought Hammond to the ground at the 5. Pittman, the game's leading ground-gainer with 128 yards, made 8 yards in three attempts and appeared to reach the first-down stakes on third down, but the ball was placed inches short. This set up the most controversial call of Joe Paterno's first decade as a head coach and caused all kinds of speculation.

Sports publicist Jim Tarman, standing with President Eric Walker and Dean Ernie McCoy, must have been guided by intuition.

"Joe's going to go for it," he predicted.

"He'd never," said McCoy.

"He'd better not," added Walker.

During a time-out, Sherman and other players said they wanted to go for it, and Joe agreed. Taking the snap from center Bill Lenkaitis, Tom tried to sneak behind him for the few inches, and was absolutely certain he had made the sticks.

> We had 6 inches to go, just a little past the 15. The play piled up, I looked down, and the ball was more than a foot past the line. Someone caught the seat of my pants and pulled me back. Then the official came in, grabbed the ball, and spotted it where I was after being pulled. We *made* that first down.

Officially, Florida State had possession and two plays later Hammond passed to Sellers for a score against the weary Penn State defenders. When the ball was jarred loose from Pittman after the kickoff, the Seminoles scored again, in three plays from the 23. Coach Bill Peterson might have won by going for two points after either touchdown, but in the last quarter his problem was time. His team reached the Lion 14 with less than a minute on the clock, and was fourth and four on the 8 after Capretto knocked down a third-down pass meant for Sellers. (Who else?) Following the game Coach Peterson defended his decision to go for a tie, with 15 seconds to play, instead of trying another pass.

> There was no question in my mind. Our boys had made a tremendous comeback. Penn State had showed how tough it could be in there. I think we did the right thing.

Grant Guthrie's field goal tying the score at 17–17 teed off the controversy Coach Paterno will hear about to the end of his coaching days. Sportswriters defending his "fourth down decision" were hard to find. In a roundup of bowl games, one Florida paper called it "the most stupid play of the weekend." Northern papers, more reasonable, at least let Paterno have his full say—and that's saying a lot. Technically he knew it was a wrong call and not in anyone's coaching book.

> Sometimes you've got to do the things you feel. Otherwise you do things in a tiny corner. If you worry about how it's going to go over with fans or alumni, you'll never do anything worthwhile. I'd do the same thing again.

Penn State couldn't control the passing of the Seminoles, one of the nation's most explosive teams. The Lions might still have been in trouble if they had punted from back near the goal line, but a first down at this point, Paterno felt, could have sent them home free. He recalled his cautioning words between halves:

> "Don't feel you're afraid to lose it—play all the time as if you're going to win. Play as if we're behind and have to make good on every down." Then when this thing came up and the players said, "Let's go for it!" I wanted to go for it—I couldn't reverse my philosophy then. And I still think it was the play to make at that time.

At winter banquets he told of Jack Curry, his great little receiver who, as a senior, still looked angelically unaggressive:

> On the plane coming home Jack told me he knew how I was feeling about the game, so he wanted me to know how the players felt. I thought it would be something consoling, but he said, "We'd like you to know we all agree. You blew it!"
>
> Then he added: "At least something good came of it. Until now a lot of us were concerned because no one really knew who was coaching Penn State. They thought it was Rip Engle. But when you went for that first down we figured 30 million people sat up asking, *"Who the hell* is coaching Penn State?"

This story was a fabrication of Paterno's inventive after-dinner-speaking brain, but he used it to make some serious points. He believes the decision was consistent with the team and coaching image he wants to project for Penn State football. The public soon came to understand Paterno's interpretation of the true value of football.

Those sophomores out there—they understood what I meant when I said, "If you're sure you know what you want to do, don't be afraid to take a chance. Don't just stand back and play the way you're coached. A great player must rise to the occasion and turn the game around on his own." I may be rationalizing, but in the long run that fourth down call may have been the best thing I ever did for Penn State football.

39

All He Did Was Win

The first rumor circulating that Joe Paterno was being sought by the professionals followed the 1967 season. In fact, he had never talked to anyone from the New York Jets, the most frequently mentioned, and disregarded calls and letters of acquaintances assuring him he could "have the Jet job any time you want it." Joe was preoccupied with convincing his local public that it was too early to expect this talented 1968 squad to reach the top. He was being a realist as he approached the third season of his now carefully designed plan to bring "greatness" to Nittany Lion football fortunes.

No one had appeared to replace Tom Sherman at quarterback. Graduation had taken such quality players as Jack Curry, Rich Buzin, Bill Lenkaitis, Bob Capretto, and Tim Montgomery. Questionable material was available for the defensive ends, and the interior offensive line was a problem. Then there were the Three Knees —operations had been performed on the most vital joints of Mike Reid, Bobby Campbell, and Don Abbey, the loss of any of whom loomed as a possible disaster.

On the bright side were the sophomore defensive stalwarts, now juniors, who had turned the 1967 season around, together with an extra-fine sophomore group including Greg Edmonds, Fran Ganter, Jack Ham, Bob Holuba, Vic Surma, Gary Hull, George Landis,

Warren Koegel, Joel Ramich, Mike Smith, and Charlie Zapiec. The Lions had their first All-America who made it as a junior, tight end Ted Kwalick, and for the first time in memory, two of the team's captains would be juniors, defensive tackles Mike Reid and Steve Smear, along with senior lineman John Kulka. Coach Paterno was helpless to keep his team from being considered a shoo-in to hold the Lambert Trophy and being ranked as high as sixth nationally.

When Joe was the Brown quarterback, Stanley Woodward wrote, "He can't run and can't pass. All he can do is think—and win." Some curbstone critics thought Chuck Burkhart, the 1968 junior quarterback, had fewer virtues than Woodward allowed Paterno and were inclined to believe that Penn State won in 1968 and 1969 "in spite of Burkhart." From the opening game with Navy, Paterno stoutly defended his quarterback, who had been coached, like Kwalick, by Assistant Coach Bob Phillips at Montour High School in McKees Rocks. Burkhart was the apple of Joe's eye because he was a clutch player and never rattled when things were tough. A quarter-back who led his team to twenty-two straight victories, including two triumphs in the Orange Bowl, can hardly be faulted.

A buoyant team greeted a matching crowd for the Navy opener in Beaver Stadium on one of Nittany Valley's brightest September days. (The 49,273 attendance was the third largest in history but now doesn't rank in the first ten.) Student representation was an issue because for the first time since what alumni call the "good old days" undergraduates had to buy tickets. The Student Government president had warned of apathy toward football caused by this requirement as well as the scheduling of the first game before the beginning of the fall term and the finale with Syracuse between terms.

The big year had started off as "the season of discontent." In the spring it was announced that the Syracuse Homecoming encounter, listed for October 19, had been moved to a December date to catch the ABC national TV network schedule. The university's frank explanation that it couldn't afford to turn down the estimated $185,000 then received by each participating institution did not appease the *Collegian* and some graduates who already had made Homecoming room reservations, which were hard to obtain.

Athletic and alumni officials stressed the advantages of TV funding beyond the building of a better football team to attract bigger crowds to build a better stadium, etc. Football, the only paying sport at Penn State, supports all other athletic teams (men's and women's) and pays for facilities used by all students—playing fields, tennis courts, ice rink, outdoor swimming pool, and other recreational areas. TV exposure provides wide publicity and prestige for the sports program and the university and enables many more alumni, fans, and prospective students to watch the games.

Far from being apathetic, students filled their sections to see Navy overwhelmed, 31–6, and their enthusiasm helped compensate for a lack of the usual between-halves fanfare. The shirt-sleeved Blue Band, not yet organized, sat in the stands to play "The Star-Spangled Banner" and some traditional numbers. The effect of starting to sing the "Alma Mater" between the third and fourth quarters when the crowd was intact instead of while it was leaving might have fascinated its author, Fred Lewis Pattee. Before it was over, the game resumed, and Paul Johnson was returning a punt over half the length of the field for a touchdown as the crowd sang "To one heart that loves thy name." He crossed the goal line perfectly timed to "May our lives but swell thy fame, dear old State, dear old State."

Discussion centered that night on the rambunctious defensive unit, which gave a third dimension to the offense, and the obvious continuation of Coach Paterno's fourth-and-one philosophy to let the players do it their way, forgetting the book and sometimes the "musts," ready to do and dare—an effective philosophy if the team is winning.

Coach Vince Gibson had begun the previous year to change Kansas State from a doormat to a power in the strong Big Eight. Penn State felt the first effects of the renaissance in the person of Mack Herron, a Gibson find in Chicago. Californians, Texans, Alabamans, Georgians, Arizonans, Pennsylvanians, New Yorkers, New Jerseyites, Ohioans, and one from the District of Columbia also were on the Kansas State squad. But Herron, particularly, took the joy out of every Penn State score because the ball then had to be kicked, and Mack usually was there to get it, a constantly dangerous 9.5 sprinter. The Lions, who had read their ratings (fourth, behind Purdue, Notre Dame, and Southern California), found themselves trailing at half time, 9–7, then managed to pull ahead and pull it out, 25–9.

Newspapermen, generally satisfied with one good quote after a so-so game, were rewarded with two from Mike Reid and Joe Paterno. The sporting world knows now that Mike is (1) a concert pianist who escaped from Paul Brown and (2) never at a loss for words. Early in 1968 these facts had not been established. Asked if any of his old injuries bothered him, he replied: "I may not be able to play the organ next week. My index finger was rendered concave." Mike's reaction to a question about the 23-point odds Penn State had been given over Kansas State: "My goodness, their offensive line averaged 225 pounds. I think the point spread was highly unrealistic."

Nervous over being rated fourth in the nation after two games, Coach Paterno made the first of his many comments on football polls:

> A political poll represents a reflection of public sentiment, but football polls are little more than calculated guesses. Very seldom do they end the way they started. They do create interest, but serve no purpose as far as the outcome of the season is concerned.

Mountaineer Stadium at Morgantown, West Virginia, generally is hard to find and a relief to escape from. Coach Jim Carlen in three years had accomplished wonders with his typically beefy, not too mobile squad, which, by 1968, was a sleek, well-disciplined, aggressive outfit. This discipline was notable following a 31–20 defeat after an even first half. The heartbroken Mountaineer squad ran from the field, not mingling with friends and foes, with heads high, helmets on, and chin straps buckled—an impressive exit for a defeated team.

The crude West Virginia crowd was unaffected by their fine example. Students carried signs ranging from funny to foul, booed every entrance of the Penn State squad, and roughly attacked cheerleaders trying to protect the Nittany Lion. Campbell and Abbey missed the game because of prior injuries, but Charlie Pittman had a fine running day (127 yards), and the defense again was superb, holding Mountaineer running stars Jim Braxton and Bob Gresham to a total of 36 of the 56 yards West Virginia made on the ground. Dave Bradley, an offensive tackle from Burnham (just over the mountains, near Lewistown), did the best job of clearing a path for Pittman. The Lion defensive charge was so vigorous and erupted in so many parts of the field that the players were christened "The Rover Boys" in the *Football Letter*. The name stuck until the graduation of the Onkotz-Kates-Smear-Reid-Johnson (Paul and Peter)-Neal Smith crew.

Syracuse defeated UCLA the week before Penn State played the Uclans on the Coast, and Los Angeles papers said there was no way a Prothro team could lose to eastern teams two weeks in a row. Nevertheless, the Lions won rather easily, 21–6, with a blocked kick by

Jack Ham contributing to the margin. Responding to radio alerts, 2,000 students were waiting to welcome the Lions when their buses arrived at Rec Hall Sunday morning at five o'clock. That "We're Number One" chant was heard for the first time. Officially, Penn State had moved up to Number Three, making the final game with Syracuse in December a battle for eastern supremacy.

Joe Yukica '53 was beginning his first season as head coach at Boston College, and moving fast toward changing the East's Big Five to the Big Six (Temple's resurgence hadn't begun). Joe Paterno, a sound sleeper compared with his predecessor, had a dream the night before the game in Boston. He was trailing the Eagles by five points with a few seconds to play, his team on the 8-yard line, and he called the wrong play. Told of Paterno's dream, Yukica revealed he'd had a different dream: He was ahead by five points, but his rival coach sent in a field goal kicker just to cut down the lead. In actuality, the Lions won, 29–0, but didn't score for the first 25 minutes. Knowing that Penn State would gear its defense to stop his fine passer, Frank Harris, Yukica had conceived a daring offensive plan: He didn't start Harris, but stayed on the ground almost entirely, keeping the ball long enough to hold down the score until the half.

Coach Tom Cahill's Army team had beaten California, Rutgers, and Duke in the three weeks before the Penn State game, and the Cadets prepared for the Lions with the intensity of a Navy buildup. Word from West Point was that "Beat Penn State" signs were plastered all over the reservation. A Penn State alumnus in Washington, D.C., entering the Army-Navy Town Club for lunch during the week of the game, noticed a high-ranking general emerge from a big black limousine. The general handed his hat to an enlisted man to be checked, and the observant alum was amused to note on the inside of the hat a sticker inscribed "Beat Penn State." He then recognized General William C. Westmoreland, Academy superintendent.

The general and 1,200 Cadets came to the Homecoming game armed with shrieking air horns. Penn State had never defeated Army on New Beaver Field or in the Stadium, and this time Joe had an accurate "feeling" about the game. He said he could hardly wait, and hoped his team would be equal to the challenge. The Brown '50 English lit major remembered a line from Shakespeare's *Henry V*—"Can this cockpit [playhouse] hold the vasty field of France?" His Lions proved equal to the battle on the "vasty field" of Beaver despite the onslaught of Army's Steve Lindell, a sure passer, brilliant receiver Gary Steele, and its strong runner, Charlie Jarvis. Bobby Campbell and Charlie Pittman, gaining 195 yards on the ground between them, made the difference, but Ted Kwalick's unusual run was the talk of town and campus Saturday night.

Army had pulled within five points (22–17) after a 60-yard pass play from Lindell to Steele. With 2:29 to go, an onside kick was expected, but what followed wasn't. The short, well-placed kick traveled the necessary 10 yards, Dave Bradley apparently fell on it with three Cadets diving in seconds later, and then half the Army team seemed to be on his back. As the ball suddenly squirted from the pileup, Kwalick was there to snatch it, and he ran all the way for a touchdown, followed by only a scattering of surprised players. About two minutes were left when Lindell closed the gap by completing four successive passes, one to Joe Albano and three to Steele, including another touchdown throw. Charlie Zapiec clutched the ensuing onside kick, which didn't squirt out.

Miami came north as a bowl contender and top ten candidate. Feeling sorry for the Hurricanes in the cold Pennsylvania weather was unseemly, since again most of their stars were Pennsylvanians except for Ted "The Mad Stork" Hendricks. They were ahead 7–0 at half time, but Mike Reid led a charged-up second-half parade. When Tony Cline, Miami's other fine end, was injured in the first half, Hendricks was moved from one side to the other to stop Pittman and Campbell, but proved only that a football game can't be won with one end. The Lion halfbacks made over 200 yards between them, mostly on end sweeps. At the next Quarterback Club meeting in State College, Coach Paterno read a letter addressed to the Alumni Fund from an alumnus so impressed by Paterno's knowledge of philosophy (as revealed in a *Sports Illustrated* feature) and of Shakespeare (as revealed in the *Football Letter*) that he doubled his contribution—to Pattee Library.

After smashing Maryland, the Lions received a bid to the Orange Bowl, plunging their young third-year coach into a frenzy about the mental state of his charges. His concerns were Pitt and Syracuse, still to be played; defense of the eastern championship (Lambert Trophy); prospects for the first undefeated, untied season since 1912; and the possibility of a Number Three national rating. Pitt's lone victory, over William and Mary in a murderous schedule, didn't obliterate memories of humiliating experiences the Lions had suffered in the Panther den. The Lions went almost too far, winning

65–9, but at least a Pitt coed was named ECAC Queen, and Pittsburgh sportswriters chose a Pitt pass receiver as the game's "Outstanding Player."

The Syracuse game on national TV from Beaver Stadium was no longer billed as the one for the eastern title—the Orange had stumbled over West Virginia. The Lions amassed over 200 yards in the first quarter, and Bobby Campbell, in his last home game, made a mighty effort to break Shorty Miller's 1912 single-game rushing record of 250 yards. Toward the end of the last quarter, press box statisticians had noted that Campbell had 243 yards but wasn't in the game. Publicity Director Jim Tarman, uncertain of coach reaction, phoned the sidelines with the information. The coach reacted by sending Campbell back into the game, but Bobby fumbled on the first play. Penn State unexpectedly regained possession and in went Campbell, to be thrown for a 4-yard loss. By this time, Paterno decided somebody didn't want Shorty's record broken, and out came Campbell.

No matter. He had his record. His 87-yard run was the longest from scrimmage ever made by a Lion player. Tight end Ted Kwalick became the first two-time All-America in Penn State history, and Dennis Onkotz, a junior, joined him on six of the team selections as a linebacker.

The progress of his defensive ends had concerned Coach Paterno at the beginning of the season, but this was settled by the rapid development of a senior with an Ivy name, Lincoln Lippincott III. On the other side of the line he had switched Frank Spaziani from quarterback to end because of Burkhart's quick progress. Accused of playing favorites with Spaziani, Joe once replied, "I don't like Spaz because *he's* Italian. I like him because *I'm* Italian."

THE ORANGE BOWL,
JANUARY 1, 1969

In the closing two minutes of a game 77,719 spectators will not forget, Penn State showed that a good eastern team could match the Big Eight, probably the strongest conference in the country; that Coach Paterno's unwavering confidence in quarterback Burkhart was fully justified; and finally, that the Lions had learned how to follow their instinctive judgment and win.

Ignoring the book and even explicit instructions to pursue procedures constantly urged upon them, the Lions brought coaching philosophy into focus as seldom before. Burkhart, who never started in a losing game in high school or college, frequently was called erratic, incapable of leading his team to greatness. He had quietly accepted a lesser role on a team of publicized stars—Kwalick, Reid, Onkotz, Campbell, and Pittman among them.

The situation in those two minutes indicated that only a major break could win for the desperate Lions. The two teams were fairly even in quality, but the Kansas Jayhawks had the upper hand because they were leading 14–7 and had possession on their own 38, first down. On the field, Kansas was directly in front of its demonstrative band and wild fans, whose noise and waving banners dominated the huge stadium. With the Jays set to hold onto the ball for the one series of downs they needed, Coach Paterno's first move was to use two of his remaining time-outs to get ready for whatever last resort the team could undertake.

Kansas quarterback Bobby Douglass first elected to try a keeper around Lippincott's end—no gain. What Douglass or Coach Pepper Rodgers had in mind for the next two plays is unknown, because Mike Reid came in so fast that no play developed, and there was a loss of 13 yards to the 25. Penn State stampeded the kicker with ten men, while Neal Smith got one hand on the ball and partially blocked it. The kicked ball bounced strangely along the sideline, not out of bounds until it was about half a yard from midfield. During a TV time-out, as the teams inserted new units with 1:28 remaining, Coach Paterno had a chance for a word with Burkhart and Campbell.

We had two time-outs left and really plenty of time to win the ball game—I mean if we have any kind of outfit. Kansas is the one under the gun. We had Campbell and Kwalick, two great receivers. Kansas would be looking for a short pass—this I knew, right? They thought we'd be playing it safe and careful and that's what I wanted them to think. But I said to Bobby, "You run a deep post pattern, run for the goal post. Chuck, you go back and just throw the ball out of the end zone. I'm not interested in completing a pass here. They'll think we're desperate or stupid, but then we'll throw a short one to Kwalick. Next play, delay Kwalick, let everybody clear out and dump him a short one." I knew if he got the ball in an open field he could run over everybody and at least get it in there deep. So that was *my* plan. Even if Ted made only 15 or 20 yards we'd be down in there and then they'd have a lot to worry about. I said, "If that happens, call time out, right?" I thought this was pretty good strategy, but I'm not sure Chuck and Bobby were even listening to me. I heard Bobby say to Chuck, "I'm going to be at the left goal post, the ball better be there." And Chuck answered, "Don't worry, it'll be there." I yelled at them, "Don't even try to complete it. Get it out of bounds—no interception."

The Big Play was coming up. Burkhart raced backward, wound up, and released the ball an instant before he was knocked flat. Two Jayhawks trying to cover Campbell were a step too late. Sailing through their waving arms, the ball was caught by Bobby, who was in the clear until defender Tom Anderson made a successful lunge for him on the three. Even fans who were screaming in the stands could hear Captain John Kulka yell for a time-out. Burkhart trotted to the bench to get Coach Paterno's next order: a three-play sequence, no huddle, with fullback Tom Cherry hitting the line twice. "I'll send in the third play if we need it," said Joe. The Lions needed it—Cherry didn't make an inch, and Greg Edmonds brought in a "scissor" play, with Pittman running a slant inside the quarterback.

In position again, Burkhart's football instinct told him the play wouldn't work, and with no time for an audible play change, he bravely took responsibility on his own 20-year-old shoulders. Sensing the defenders were keyed on Pittman, he kept the ball and rolled around left end to score the only touchdown he ever made for Penn State. The "fake" was a surprise to his coach, the opposition, his teammates, and especially to Pittman:

For an awful moment I thought I had missed the handoff; then I was piled up—I looked over, and Chuck was scoring.

The final action in the tense drama was yet to come. With the score 14–13, no one doubted that Paterno would send in a two-point play —win or nothing. Kwalick and Campbell, prospective receivers, were well covered. Chuck threw high, hoping Ted could jump for it, but the pass was batted away. Kansas fans enveloped the entire end of the field in ecstatic celebration although 15 seconds remained, and the flag Umpire Foster Grose had dropped was unnoticed. Coach Paterno didn't learn until sometime after the game that Grose, in counting the players, noticed that Kansas had sent in a linebacker (Rick Abernethy) and no one had come out. The field was cleared as Referee Earl Jansen stepped off a 1-yard penalty, and Kansas obligingly called time-out to set its new defensive alignment, giving Paterno and

Burkhart time for another sideline exchange. Campbell was to take a quick pitch to the right. From center, Burkhart raised his hands to quiet the crowd and was allowed to bring his team back in a huddle. Coach Paterno seized this moment to change his mind about the two-point play. Suddenly realizing that his team was having more trouble with left end Vernon Vanoy than with All-America right end John Zook, he sent in another play, calling for a handoff to Campbell and a sweep to the left. Guard Charlie Zapiec blocked Zook just enough, and fullback Cherry took the outside linebacker. Both defenders moved in on Campbell, but too late—he dove between them and his own blockers for the winning two points. After the kickoff, Douglass had one chance for a pass, but he was surrounded by Reid, Smear, and Spaziani. Douglass turned and wearily threw the ball toward the sideline, to no one. A red flag was thrown, but the game was over.

The defeat was tough for the spirited Kansans and produced countless interesting interviews. Three days later, stories were still coming out of Lawrence, Kansas. A linebacker was quoted to the effect that the Jayhawks couldn't have had 12 men on the field—it was either 11 or 13. Umpire Grose, asked how he happened to notice the twelfth man, sidestepped by saying it was his job to count the players and he always did. A Kansas defensive coach, however, admitted that his team had inadvertently used 12 players not only on the extra point, but also for the entire series of plays when the Jayhawks almost stopped the Lions with their defense on the goal line. Movies confirmed this. The incident wasn't soon forgotten in Lawrence. At an important basketball game, Kansas students came in with a sign reading, "Coach, Use Only Five Players." Coach Paterno didn't allow his assistants to forget it, either. Four Lion coaches had been observers high in the press box with telephone communications to the field. "What were *you guys* doing when Kansas stayed in that 6-6?"

"Cheering," was George Welsh's answer.

Pepper Rodgers, the loquacious Kansas coach (now at Georgia Tech), said he should at least have credit for turning a dull victory into an exciting defeat. A Rodgers decision probably lost the game: Leading 14–7, fourth and one on Penn State's 5-yard line with 10 minutes to play, Kansas disregarded an almost sure field goal and sent John Riggins off tackle, where Pete and Paul Johnson converged on him for no gain.

Kansas scored first in the game on three plays up the middle while Penn State's defense concentrated on protecting against the outside sweeps by Douglass or Donnie Shanklin. After fumbling once within the 5-yard line, the Lions tied it up at 7–7 and drove 47 yards with Pittman's 13-yard burst up the middle climaxing the advance. On the last play of the half, they missed an easy field goal, and in the third period were held for downs on the 1 after moving the ball 60 yards in 12 plays. Shanklin's 40-yard punt return led to the Kansas go-ahead touchdown early in the fourth quarter, with Riggins next getting two cracks up the middle to score. An open field clip on Leon Angevine was obvious during Shanklin's return, but the field judge was in no position to drop a friendly flag. He was hopelessly tangled in a television cable.

Quarterback Burkhart played an average game—gaining 5 yards on the ground, completing less than half his passes, and giving up two interceptions until the last fateful seconds that counted. Running the team with steady confidence, he then proved, as he consistently did, that he was, indeed, a clutch player. All he did was win.

Conscious of their coach's ancestry, students popularized the slogan "Numero Uno," which lasted all through the 1969 season and after the 1970 Orange Bowl. The Lions retained the Lambert Trophy, but were voted Number Two by the UPI and Number Three by the AP in the final polls. Coach Paterno was named Coach of the Year by the American College Football Coaches' Association, and since then has been eastern Coach of the Year four times.

Persistent rumors that Joe would leave the Lions for the pros disturbed his many Penn State admirers, because he had been approached before the game by the Pittsburgh Steelers and had spent some time with Dan Rooney. He was fond of the Rooneys, liked Pittsburgh (the city), and was tempted by the challenging opportunity to revitalize the Steelers. After the Orange Bowl, he returned to Pittsburgh for another talk and decided not to accept the offer. A jubilant community honored the team and its coaches at a memorable rally in Rec Hall, conspicuously bedecked with "Numero Uno" signs.

40

Joe and the Presidential Plaque

As any season approaches, coaches habitually talk about the unusual pressures ahead, and Joe Paterno had as much justification in 1969 as at any time in his experience. His team faced prodigious stress in maintaining a string of seventeen consecutive regular-season victories, which brought the 1968 Lions to the Orange Bowl championship and Penn State to its highest national ranking—Number Two. In 1967 and 1968 the Lions had won the Lambert Trophy, and Paterno himself was recovering from a postseason banquet circuit befitting one whose peers had named him Coach of the Year.

In the summer of 1969 the coach and his team confronted a difficult schedule. Ready to strike down the gradually building national prestige of Penn State were six of the country's finest quarterbacks, and two top teams in the Big Eight Conference (Colorado and Kansas State). With every opponent keying on the Lions, Paterno summed up the challenge: "We'll need momentum sustained week after week, preparation styled for each opponent, and toughness to take each game as it comes."

Coach Paterno allowed that a few opponents might be concerned about his team. Mike Reid and Steve Smear, the defensive co-captains, gave the Lions perhaps the best one-two punch in college football. The original Rover Boys were seniors—Dennis Onkotz, Jim

Kates, Neal Smith, Paul and Pete Johnson, with ends John Ebersole and Dave Rakiecki valued additions to the group. Jack Ham and Gary Hull, outstanding junior linebackers, and Mike Smith, a remarkably versatile halfback, bolstered the team defensively. Offensive senior linemen were Captain Tom Jackson (tackle) and Wally Cirafesi (switched to split end); juniors were Bob Holuba, Greg Edmonds, Warren Koegel, Charlie Zapiec, Vic Surma, and Jim McCord. The predicted starting backfield included Chuck Burkhart, senior quarterback (backup: Mike Cooper '71); halfbacks Charlie Pittman '70 and Gary Deuel '71 (backup: Joel Ramich '71); fullback Don Abbey '70 (backup: Fran Ganter '71). Kicking specialist Rusty Garthwaite of Montclair, New Jersey, a junior, was to get help from Mike Reitz '72. Lean sophomore material had high quality individually, but the coaches foresaw some switches. Gregg Ducatte, formerly a backfield star from Plattsburgh, New York, would be tried as a linebacker, and Bob Parsons, considered most likely to succeed Burkhart, would be changed over to tight end. Gary Gray was a well-thought-of linebacking prospect from Levittown, Pennsylvania; Dave Joyner, Frank Ahrenhold, and Craig Lyle had the makings of strong linemen. Preseason anticipation for Penn Staters centered around two New Jersey boys—Lydell Mitchell of Salem and Franco Harris of Mount Holly, destined for important careers with the Baltimore Colts and the Pittsburgh Steelers, respectively.

Joe Paterno prefaced the season this way:

> We've developed our football to the place where pride is the ingredient working for us—the pride of our alumni and students, the pride we have in ourselves. A lot of people have worked hard to build our program from the dismal '30s when we were losing to small college teams in Pennsylvania, to a place where playing on a Penn State team means something great . . . we're close to No. 1 and our incentive is to stay there.

A valuable addition to the coaching staff, Jerry Sandusky '66, had played both offense and defense as a sophomore, and defensive end in 1964 and 1965. Originally from Washington, Pennsylvania, he had gained coaching experience at Juniata College and Boston University. Jerry was assigned to coach Penn State's linebackers, and helped develop seven All-Americas in eight seasons.

The Penn State public politely ignored Coach Paterno's anxieties, and astute athletic officials were ready for the record high season ticket sales with an enlarged stadium and press box. The team was likely to dominate most opponents—and if the offense faltered, there was that group likely to be remembered as one of the great college defensive teams of all time.

The squad arrived late for its first game in the Navy-Marine Corps Memorial Stadium at West Annapolis. Traffic is stopped on roads leading to the stadium when the Midshipmen march over College Creek bridge to the field, and the approach streets are narrow. Coach Paterno fumed as his squad, despite a motorcycle escort, almost missed the kickoff, but the Middies soon may have wished that their "Long Blue Line" could have gone on indefinitely. Rolling up a total offense of 513 yards, with Charlie Pittman gaining 177 yards on the ground, the Lions simply overwhelmed and outmanned Navy. Penn State's non-losing streak (counting bowls) had reached 20 and its consecutive victories 12.

Colorado, a Big Eight leader, was surprised in the next game. The Rover Boys swarmed all over Bobby Anderson, playing his last game as one of the best quarterbacks in the conference. A running quarterback generally, he was sacked for 28 yards, with a net of 5 yards, and connected on only 8 of 26 passes. Penn State scored 17 points in the second quarter, and Paul Johnson returned a kickoff all the way after Colorado got its only points with a field goal in the third. (Visiting newsmen, accommodated in the expanded press box for the first time, called it the Tarman Hilton.)

Coach Vince Gibson had accomplished some remarkable changes at Kansas State, and Manhattan was aglow with Purple Pride when the Lions arrived. The manager of the motel where the team stayed refused to put up the usual "Welcome Penn State" sign. "No, sir," he said. "They'd tear it to pieces and maybe the building." The Penn State Alumni Association had arranged an Alumni Holiday tour with some qualms, but the travelers found everything up to date in Kansas City, stayed in the new section of the old Muehlbach Hotel, and frolicked Friday night in the old section (Playboy Club) of the new Hotel Continental. The club called it "Penn State Night," making amends for the motel's lack of hospitality. Everything in town was splendidly purple, even the carpet in the Wildcat dressing room. The home team, without a winning season for 15 years, had local fans agog over the first two victories, against Baylor and Arizona. They were dying to see Coach Gibson's whiz, Mack Herron, and the other under 9.8 sprinters awaiting the eastern champions.

A record home opening crowd of 57,000, however, was disappointed soon after the start. The well-prepared Lions withstood all Purple pressure with poise, patience, and pride. Mitchell ran for 120 yards, and Burkhart passed not spectacularly but well for 101 yards. The easterners held a 17–0 margin until midway in the last quarter, when substitutes carelessly gave up two touchdowns. The deceptively close 17–14 final score gave critics an opportunity to belittle the Lion record by referring to the game as a "squeaker," yet Kansas State, with all its fine runners, was held to —7 yards on the ground in the second half. Paterno quote after the game: "Football games are won or lost on five or six plays—the trouble is you never know when they're coming."

"How do you get ready for a Reid or a Smear?" fretted Coach Jim Carlen before the West Virginia game. Coming to University Park with a 4–0 record and the two top ground-gainers in the nation (Braxton and Gresham), the Mountaineers were shut out (20–0) for the first time in forty years. Lenny Moore, visiting on the sidelines, inevitably was asked how he compared himself with Charlie Pittman. "I can't," he replied. "Charlie has his thing, and I had mine." This was the most impressive Lion victory of the season.

At Syracuse, the team was less welcome than at Manhattan, Kansas. Here the motel sign read, "Welcome NE HS Wrestling Coaches Clinic." The 1969 Penn State-Syracuse game was doubly distinctive: Its pattern was uncommonly similar to that of the 1969 Orange Bowl game with Kansas, and the encounter generated even more controversy and bitterness than usual. Syracuse was striving to end Penn State's dominance in the East, and almost succeeded. Coach Schwartzwalder's team led 14–0 going into the last quarter, while nearly everything went wrong for the Lions, who seemed jittery and unpoised. Normally able to come up with the big play, they turned over the ball three times by interceptions and once on a fumble, almost insurmountable obstacles against a team as fired up as the Orange.

Coach Ben's boys had the Syracuse Homecomers enthralled. A back named Gregory Allen, poor-mouthed by the coach prior to the game as "too small for college football" and "out of gas after 15 plays," had gas enough in the first half to run back three punts for 170 yards. The luck of the Lions seemed to hinge on a single play late in the second quarter. Already ahead 14–0, the Orange arrived at the Penn State three following the third of Allen's runbacks. On fourth down and a yard and a half to go, the obvious play to put the game out of reach was a field goal, but coaches sometimes get greedy. Instead of three points, Coach Schwartzwalder wanted it all. Young Allen tried to circle end and finally did run out of gas. He fell down. That missed field goal opportunity was the first of the striking similarities to the Orange Bowl, where Coach Pepper Rodgers had made the same mistake.

Tempted to indulge in some half-time oratory, Coach Paterno settled for a subdued reminder that his players could lose this game and still maintain their pride if they tried hard until the end—he spoke of how many past Penn State teams had kept trying "until something good happened." His attentive young men did keep trying, and the first break came when the Orangemen, who had virtually blown their rivals off the field for three periods, seemed to lose their spark in the last quarter.

When the unfortunate Allen fumbled on Penn State's 32, Coach Paterno, who had replaced Burkhart with Mike Cooper, sent Chuck back in because he'd been a winner for two years and was entitled to this chance now. An interference penalty helped put the ball on the Syracuse 4, but the Lions were fighting and clawing for yardage. Lydell Mitchell finally went in for Penn State's first points with a little over 10 minutes remaining. Everyone knew Paterno would try for 2, thus putting the pressure on Syracuse.

Watching Burkhart go to the sideline for a conference, as he had on January 1, a newsman in the press box asked if the umpire was counting the Syracuse defenders. The conferees decided on a fake to Pittman up the middle, with a pass to fullback Franco Harris. Harris was open and caught the ball on the 2, but an unyielding defensive play by linebacker Don Dorr kept him away from the goal line. A flag was down! Syracuse had been detected holding, giving Penn State a second try. Having seen the Orange defense against the two-point play, Burkhart knew what to call. Harris swept around the Orange left end, and the score was 14–8.

A partially blocked kick by Jack Ham, still holding to the old Orange Bowl script, gave Penn State its chance from the Syracuse 36. Faking to Pittman, Burkhart handed the ball to Harris, who ran through the frayed and worn defense, easily outpacing the safetyman. With the score tied at 14–14, sophomore Mike Reitz came in and coolly kicked the winning point. There were seven minutes left to play, but the final score was 15–14.

Coach Schwartzwalder issued loud complaints about the officiating, but his protest to the ECAC was not upheld by Commissioner Asa Bushnell. At the weekly New York Sportswriters' Association luncheon, under the guise of only repeating what "his boys had told him," Coach Ben reported that the "Pennsylvania officials" who imposed the interference and holding penalties on "his boys" had deliberately overlooked Penn State's many infractions. A Syracuse writer called the officials inept and dishonest, saying that one dropped his flag before Reitz kicked the winning point, in case he'd miss the kick.

The able Ohio University coach, Bill Hess, thoroughly prepared his capable team for the Lions and tried to lull the opposition with a rumor that Cleve Bryant, his Mid-American Conference passing ace and record-holder, couldn't play because of a damaged knee. Bryant, making the most impressive recovery since Lazarus, was in there pitching from the beginning, but was unable to prevent a 42–3 Lion rout. An alumnus, Matt Matthews '59, suggested the Rovers should be renamed the ROKS (Reid, Onkotz, Kates, and Smear).

Boston College, coached by Lion alumni Joe Yukica '53 and Bill Bowes '65, caused a mild scare by going ahead 13–10 at half time, using the Penn State fake field goal play that beat Alabama in the Liberty Bowl. The Eagles succumbed in the second half, 38–16.

Reviewing the 1969 season, writers in Big Eight country bragged about the 6–0 record of their teams against Big Ten elevens, but didn't mention the Nittany Lions' 3–0 record against Big Eight teams since January 1. This was the beginning of the hottest seasonal controversy about ratings, polls, and "Number One," in which the principals were Darrell Royal, Bud Wilkinson, Joe Paterno, the entire Texas football fraternity, press, and fans, and President Nixon. Dartmouth was still getting one vote for the Lambert Trophy, probably from Coach Bob Blackman.

Ohio State appeared to have a clear road to Number One until detoured at Ann Arbor. *Sports Illustrated*'s Dan Jenkins prematurely wrote that the title game could be played between Woody Hayes' first offensive and first defensive outfits (later Jenkins joined the Texas bandwagon). At this point Penn State was getting strong Orange Bowl feelers and seemed under serious consideration for other bowls. The players, informally polled, strongly favored playing the Big Eight champions in Miami, but this was before Ohio State lost to Michigan and before Texas Coach Darrell Royal urged Paterno to "hold out" for the Cotton Bowl (prior to his Arkansas game). Paterno deferred to the preference of his players, admitting later that if they could have known it would have a bearing on Number One, he was sure the vote would have been different. Royal pointed out that in meeting Missouri the Lions might face the top team, certainly the greatest offensive power in the country. The Missouri offense had smashed Michigan's vaunted defense, and the Wolverines went to the Rose Bowl. Nebraska, another Tiger victim, went to the Sun Bowl. Missouri had lost only to Colorado (which went to the Liberty Bowl).

Long before the bowl pairings, ABC's Bud Wilkinson was touting the Texas-Arkansas game as the national championship match. Wilkinson, who had been Oklahoma's successful coach and was a presidential adviser on physical fitness in addition to his network role, was being a good promoter when he helped persuade President Nixon, then in need of headlines, to present the Number One "trophy" to the winner of the ABC-televised Texas-Arkansas game. At ceremonies in the dressing room of the winning Texans, the smiling President unilaterally dubbed Texas Number One. Trying to placate the commonwealth of Pennsylvania and Republican Governor Raymond Shafer, he announced that he would later present a plaque to Penn State for having the longest winning streak in college football. Coach Paterno rejected the gesture promptly, with tactful finality:

> Although I have heard nothing about a President's plaque, it would be a disservice to our squad, to Pennsylvania, and to the East to accept such an award, and, perhaps, to Missouri, which just might be the nation's best team. Because I had to baby-sit during the Texas-Arkansas game, I missed the President's final remarks, but it would seem to me to be a waste of his very valuable time to present Penn State with a plaque for something it already indisputably owns—the nation's longest winning and unbeaten records.

Coach Paterno's pique had disposed of the President's plaque, but Joe had to prepare his team for Maryland, Pitt, and North Carolina State, while keeping the squad from thinking about fun and sun in Miami. Meanwhile, there were plenty of honors for the Lions. For the first time, four Penn Staters were selected on All-America teams —Denny Onkotz (second year), linebacker; Mike Reid, tackle; Charlie Pittman, halfback; and Neal Smith, safety. Reid placed fifth for the Heisman Trophy, highest standing of any lineman. He won the Maxwell and Knute Rockne awards, and the Outland Trophy as the nation's best interior lineman. Steve Smear, the popular and underrated "other" tackle, received the Swede Nelson Award for Sportsmanship. Neal Smith, a "walk-on" (non-scholarship) player, established a Penn State season's record with 10 interceptions and a career record of 19 in 1967–69.

Mike Reid, who pounded quarterbacks and a piano with equal zest, scored the only touchdown of his college career in the Maryland game when he intercepted a pass and ran to the goal line 25 yards away. Fond of ham on likely occasions, Mike held the ball high in the air as he crossed the line. That night he played Liszt for Heywood Hale Broun on CBS in the course of a chat about the compatibility of football and music.

Coach Ray Lester of Maryland, after losing 48–0, joined Burkhart detractors by remarking that his own sophomore quarterback was ten times a better passer than "what's his name," whereupon a reporter noted that the Maryland quarterback could watch "what's his name" in a bowl game on TV New Year's Day. The Pitt Panthers, with an improving program and a capable, physically strong team, held the Lions to a 7–7 tie in the first half, but were overcome in the second. Penn State officials completed their Orange Bowl plans.

"Teams in high places have been known to lose faces," a saying goes, but the 1969 Lions polished off the regular season and North Carolina State on national TV with no apparent tension. The Lions went berserk after the game in Raleigh, tossing everyone within reach into the shower to celebrate a second consecutive 10–0 regular season. One other record was broken: Chuck Burkhart threw his first touchdown pass of the year with help from Pittman, who stole the ball from under the nose of the Wolfpack's Gary Yount in the end zone.

The 100th year of collegiate football was one of exceptional achievement for Penn State—more national prestige and recognition, more individual honors, and a third straight Lambert Trophy. Yet the year of unreserved alumni pride had an element of dissatisfaction. Joe Paterno's claim that the Number One team should be decided on the field of play and not by presidential decree or network prestige was not sufficiently debated or upheld. He made enemies in Texas by insisting that Penn State, with the longest non-losing and winning streaks in college football, had as much right as any team to Number One recognition. The Lions ranked Number Two in both the AP and UPI polls.

THE ORANGE BOWL,
JANUARY 1, 1970

Safely through the season of discontent, Coach Paterno concentrated on the game ahead, diverting his team from brooding about being the Avis of college football to preparing for Missouri, the best offensive team in the country and at that point probably the real Number One eleven, and possessor of the Big Eight's greatest passer, Terry McMillan. A cardinal Paterno principle for bowls is emphasis on defense:

> I don't think you can be a consistent winner in the bowl games without great defense, and it is easier to keep your defense sharp during the long pull from the last game in November until January 1.

Some coaches might have envied Paterno's worries over his offense, especially in a Power-I with Mitchell, Harris, and Pittman in the backfield, and a defense that had held five of the nation's top quarterbacks to minus yardage and all ten to an aggregate of minus eleven during the regular season.

The Miami media expected no repetition of the 1969 dramatics or a replay of the Joe Paterno-Pepper Rodgers show. Coach Dan Devine (now at Notre Dame), cautioned about Paterno's penchant for clever repartee during pregame socials and press conferences, had a droll reply: "I'd better start practicing." A TV reporter made a helpful suggestion: "How about saying, 'We want to be a ferocious Tiger, not a paper Tiger'?" "That's pretty good," replied Devine, writing it down in his notebook.

Another Paterno characteristic is his co-operation with pre-bowl alumni affairs. Rather than secluding his team on bowl day, he draws on the moral support of students and alumni, and has his entire aggregation appear at a traditional rally the morning of the game. On New Year's morning, with the Blue Band, cheerleaders, and the Nittany Lion on hand, alumni and students packing into the ballroom of a large Miami hotel met a special guest when Coach Paterno introduced Dr. John W. Oswald, the university's newly elected president, who would take office July 1.

Alerted that this would be Dr. Oswald's first Penn State appearance, Joe alluded to his academic reputation as a plant pathologist.

Noting that Dr. Oswald's specialized research in diseases affecting the artichoke had stamped out one disease threatening the very life of the plant, Paterno said with feeling: "As an Italian, that's enough recommendation for me—any man who could save the artichoke is good enough to be president of our university."

Dr. Oswald confirmed Joe's artichoke information and added that his thesis had been translated into Italian. In closing, he said: "I, Giovanni Oswaldo, wish you, Giuseppe Paterno, and your team the greatest of luck tonight. I know you will win. Numero Uno!" Ray Shafer, then governor of Pennsylvania and often called Penn State's Number One fan, addressed himself to the players: "I don't want you to prove anything to anybody tonight. You don't have to prove you're Number One to the newspapers, the fans, or even to the President [of the United States]. Just go out there, play this game, and win it for yourselves."

What Penn State did that night proved the football application of the adage about irresistible forces and immovable objects: One of the greatest defenses in the college game prevailed against one of the finest offenses. Missouri, playing in the nation's reputed superconference and averaging 450 yards in its 10 games, was held to 175 yards on the ground and 117 in the air. McMillan, pride of Missouri but a native of Coral Gables, Florida, spent the evening on his back, completing ten passes, of which seven went to Lion defenders. The seven steals, an Orange Bowl record, made Mike Smith (2), Denny Onkotz (2), George Landis (2), and Gary Hull his chief receivers (one of the interceptions was thrown by McMillan's understudy, Chuck Roper). Not only was this an Orange Bowl record, but only once before in the history of bowl games has a team intercepted seven passes. (Alabama did it in the 1952 Cotton Bowl against Texas A&M.) Joe Moore, who had rushed for 1,300 yards in 10 games, was held to 36; Mel Gray, who had caught 26 passes for 705 yards, caught none. Said McMillan the next day:

> I've never seen a defense like Penn State's . . . they always rushed four men and forced me to throw before I was ready. Seven men were in their pass coverage . . . they covered my men like blankets. . . . I threw a few passes away to avoid interceptions at first, but when we got behind I had to try to hit, but heck, the receivers were always covered. I never even saw Mel Gray once.

Coach Devine, viewing films of the game, called Penn State "the best defensive team I've seen in twenty years of college football. It may not have been obvious at times, but our staff put more time and effort into this bowl game than in any of our five previous bowl trips."

Penn State played football Paterno's way for bowl games, making its points in the first quarter, then keeping to a safe, controlled pattern. He's sometimes criticized for such conservatism, but it's hard to argue with his record. Mike Reitz opened the scoring with a field goal from the 19, following a 68-yard advance covered by Chuck Burkhart's completions to Greg Edmonds (2) and Lydell Mitchell, Charlie Pittman's clutch third-down gains, and Franco Harris's 16-yard run up the middle on a trap. A few minutes later, after a fumble recovery on the Tiger 28, Burkhart struck quickly, passing to Mitchell on the sideline. Lydell faked his defender and then ran over him for the touchdown. Missouri's field goal by Henry Brown in the second quarter was the result of the Tigers' best drive, from their own 8 to Penn State's 7, where Mike Reid came through with one of his "spectaculars" and tossed Moore for a 10-yard loss.

Missouri threatened once again in the game's last few minutes as Penn Staters stopped breathing at the thought of an 11–10 score in retribution for the 1969 game. With 1:42 to go, Coach Paterno recalls that he was planning his defense for a two-point conversion play, because Missouri had a first down on the Lion 14. Roper grounded two passes; his third was nabbed on the goal line by Landis, whose run up the sidelines to the Tiger 42 was the game's most thrilling for Lion fans, because the clock had run out during his dash. Since the referee said that 55 seconds remained, Burkhart wasted three plays and then had Bob Parsons kick. At that, the skies over Miami let loose the rain clouds, but all the Lions were oblivious. The game was over.

In the dressing room the exultant players joined in the general Numero Uno chorus and tossed Governor Shafer into the showers. Coach Paterno, asked by reporters what he thought of the national ratings, replied that he didn't know if Penn State was the best team in the country, nor did he know of any team that had a better right to that honor.

Number Two was Penn State's reward for its perfect season and great bowl victory, the championship having been decided long before. Joining President Nixon's bandwagon in his *Sports Illustrated* wrapup of the bowl binge, Dan Jenkins devoted four pages to the Cotton Bowl victory of Texas over Notre Dame and voted Texas Number One because the Longhorns "won under more pressure in their big games. . . ." The "big games" apparently were with Arkansas, loser to thrice-beaten Mississippi in the Sugar Bowl, and Notre Dame, unable to win any of *its* "big games." The Irish, ahead in the Cotton Bowl, couldn't stop two long Texas drives because they wouldn't chance crashing their linebackers. To match the Texas "big ones," Penn State held Colorado (which trampled Alabama), West Virginia (10–1, and the Peach Bowl winner), and Missouri (the Big Eight winner) to no touchdowns. *Sports Illustrated* lumped Rose Bowl, Sugar Bowl, and Orange Bowl coverage into slightly more than two inches of small type toward the back of the magazine.

41

A Crisis That Wasn't

Coach Paterno once admitted that the first major crisis in his coaching career followed the 1967 opening game, a loss to Navy. He denies that Crisis II took place in 1970, when his Lions lost three of their first five games. "Why is losing three games a crisis?" was his logical question.

Nowadays, if Penn State loses three games in five weeks, most of its partisans are perplexed, if not critical. Crisis or not, halfway into the 1970 season, Coach Paterno switched quarterbacks, a rare gambit for him. Since his team then finished with five straight victories, the coach had "averted a crisis" by his unorthodox move, or so his following reasoned.

Who was worried about the 22-game winning streak? Who brooded over consecutive seasons without a losing record dating back to 1939? Not Coach Paterno. This was his view of the 1970 squad's burden in upholding records:

> We have enough problems with things we can do something about. If you get worked up over a winning streak, all of a sudden you don't have one. We don't want to manufacture problems—it doesn't make sense. I expect the 1970 team to have the same major quality others have had in the past—pride in themselves, pride in winning. You have to develop poise—that comes with experience.

The "problems" were the graduation of Chuck Burkhart (the "winner") and most of the great 1968 and 1969 defensive unit players. The dear departed included John Ebersole, Dave Rakiecki, Mike Reid, and Steve Smear—the front four; Charlie Pittman, the great running halfback; and linebackers and defensive backs like Denny Onkotz, Jim Kates, Wally Cirafesi, Neal Smith, and the Johnsons, Pete and Paul.

Only Penn Staters who had majored in pessimism could brood long over the offensive team's potential, with Lydell Mitchell and Franco Harris on board; Bob Holuba, Vic Surma, and Dave Joyner as part of the front line; and split end Greg Edmonds, a skilled pass receiver, threatening some of Jack Curry's records. Defensively, the lost front four had adequate, if inexperienced, replacements in Bruce Bannon and Jim Heller (both sophomores), Steve Prue, and Frank Ahrenhold. Among linebackers and defensive halfbacks were Jack Ham, Jim Laslavic, Gary Gray, John Skorupan, Charlie Zapiec, Gary Hull, George Landis, Mike Smith, Terry Stump, and Charlie Wilson—most of unknown quality in 1970, but later to develop into defensive greats and some into All-Americas.

The Lions showed no strain in overcoming Navy, 55–7, establishing a Penn State all-time non-losing streak of 31. It was a coincidence that in 1922 Navy had broken the previous record of 30. Mitchell and Harris ran wild for 220 yards between them, while Mike Cooper, apparent Number One quarterback with Bob Parsons as backup, passed his first test, completing 6 of 10 passes for 108 yards and two touchdowns. John Hufnagel, third in line and considered a strong runner but not much of a passer, was later to garner nearly all of Penn State's passing records. At the start of 1970, few fans could spell his name.

At a postseason coaching clinic, Coach Paterno had met a Colorado coach who told him their players had watched the Orange Bowl game on TV, rooting for Penn State because they wanted to smash the Lions' winning streak. The game became a nightmare for Penn Staters when Cliff Branch (with 9.3 hundred speed) returned the second-half kickoff the length of the field. Until then the Lions appeared to have a chance; but Mike Cooper's passes, sometimes with open receivers, sailed over their heads in the thin Colorado air.

The dreadful day began early. Linebacker Charlie Zapiec, stricken with appendicitis Friday night, was operated on at 2 A.M. Saturday. Gary Gray (at 205 pounds) took on Zapiec's inside linebacker position, where he spent a long afternoon trying to handle the Big Eight's toughest center, 237-pound Dan Popplewell. A cheerful alumni holiday group from back East and the new president, Jack Oswald, attending his first away game, were unaware of the Zapiec catastrophe, which was first revealed to the millions who viewed the national television broadcast of the Lions' humiliation.

Jack Ham, outside linebacker, was the hero for the losers, getting 15 unassisted tackles. Offensively, Penn State was almost throttled, with Mitchell and Harris held to 60 yards apiece. Cooper and Parsons completed 14 of 27 passes for 147 yards, but were stung by two damaging interceptions, and the Lions had three other turnovers on fumbles.

Joe Paterno met newsmen outside the dressing room as relaxed and smiling as if he'd had a winner. When the team arrived in front of Rec Hall at 3:30 A.M. on Sunday, over 2,000 students, who had stood in the rain for an hour, were chanting, "You're still Number One with us." Coach Paterno addressed them:

> We've come home from many trips during the last three years when it's been easy for us to come back and easy for you to come out here and meet us. We appreciate it deeply. We've won a lot of games during the past few seasons and we've always tried to be gracious winners. Now I hope we can be gracious losers. We've shared many moments of glory, and I'm sure we'll share more such moments in the future. But right now we must regenerate ourselves—and we'll need your support—the kind of support you've shown us this morning.

The Wisconsin defeat at Madison baffled Lion partisans, but the coach had an explanation, not an excuse. He felt that some of the players were embarrassed about losing to Colorado, a better team, on national TV, and knew they hadn't been at their best.

> We went to Wisconsin determined to prove the Colorado thing was a fluke—and we played like maniacs. We even coached like maniacs. Everything was "Go right after them." We played without poise and got licked. It was as simple as that. We should have gone out there with the attitude, "Okay, Colorado beat us, but we'll still stay with our game."

The "maniacal" Lions threw Neil Graff, an excellent quarterback, and his replacement, Tim Healy, for an unheard-of loss of 111 yards on 16 "sacks." Rushing sometimes seven and eight men, the crashers had a field day until the inevitable happened. With the score 16–16 in the final quarter, Graff threw two touchdown passes, of 27 and 52 yards—he had previously thrown one for 68 yards. The Lions led in rushing, 184 yards to −22 yards, in first downs 23–12, and were only a few yards behind the Badgers in passing, but four interceptions, two fumbles, and inability to defend against deep passes did them in.

When Gary Gray blocked a kick, the tide turned slightly in the Boston College game, which the Lions led only 7–3 at half time. Many on the squad had a chance to play, including halfback Joel Ramich, who made 60 yards on the ground, 2 yards more than fullback Franco Harris. Gary Deuel, another halfback, gained 51 yards to Lydell Mitchell's 40. All three quarterbacks were used. Cooper and Parsons together completed 11 for 17, and John Hufnagel had a perfect score—1 for 1 for 2 yards, his first pass of the season.

Racist trouble afflicted Syracuse at the season's start. Nine outstanding black players, most of them regulars, left the squad as a protest and did not return, although Coach Schwartzwalder, who consulted with the administration, invited them back under certain conditions. After losses to Houston, Kansas, and Illinois, Syracuse defeated Maryland a week before meeting Penn State at University Park. The momentum of the elated Orangemen continued and the Lions were never in the game, trailing 17–0 at half time. Ramich had another fine day with 96 yards. Marty "Jan the Man" Januszkiewicz, a typical Syracuse steamroller fullback, rushed the middle for 152 yards, carrying the ball on 36 of the Orange's 60 running plays.

While the Syracuse game was in progress, Coach Paterno already was thinking about changes, sensing that the two preceding defeats had weakened morale and showed a need for leadership. Huffy was allowed to throw three passes, but he didn't complete any, and one was intercepted. Opposing Army at West Point, however, Hufnagel came into his own as a starter and his very presence seemed to restore confidence. His passing was only average (3 of 10 for 22 yards), but he gained 66 yards and scored two touchdowns on runs. Winning at Michie was a relief, even though the Cadets were having a doleful season. Deuel, Hufnagel, Ramich, and Ganter all were used in the three complete backfields, Coach Paterno surprising Army with two formations—the Power-I and a double Wing-T giving the flanker back (Deuel) more chance to run with the ball.

The victory generated strength for the final games with West Virginia, Maryland, Ohio University, and Pittsburgh. Starting their season in fine style, the Mountaineers won four in a row, including a victory over Indiana, and then lost to Pitt, 36–35, surrendering a huge first-half lead. At Beaver Stadium they were victims once more (42–8) of their strange perennial jinx. Maryland's students fired their abominable cannon only once during the game at College Park, when the Terps first came out on the field. Thereafter it was silent, the Lions winning, 34–0. Attendance was only 23,400, with Penn State selling 3,500 of the tickets.

Penn State's freshman team provided late season action at Pittsburgh under new coach Johnny Chuckran, who had succeeded Pappy Bruce when he retired. The Cubs were behind 20–13 with less than 30 seconds to play. Pitt, on the Lion 26-yard line, fourth and five, took a time-out to set up for a field goal, which Joe Carlozo blocked. Linebacker Gary Hager picked up the ball and ran 64 yards for a touchdown, whereupon Steve Joachim passed to tight end Randy Crowder for the two points that gave the Lions a 21–20 victory. Joachim became Temple's quarterback in 1973 and 1974; Crowder made All-America defensive tackle at Penn State in 1973.

Although Pitt's varsity had its best season since 1963 (5–5) under Coach Carl DePasqua, the Lions toyed with their rivals and rolled up a 35–9 first-half lead. The typical strong November finish completed a 7–3 season that had started so disastrously, and produced Liberty and Peach Bowl bids, which the players voted not to accept. The team and Penn State fans would watch all the bowl games on TV for the first time in four years.

Jack Ham, now premier linebacker for the Pittsburgh Steelers, won individual honors and was named to every All-America team. Greg Edmonds, split end, set a Penn State season record by catching six touchdown passes, and defensive halfback Mike Smith, with four interceptions against Ohio University, set a single-game record. The team's 26 interceptions tied a Penn State record made in 1952 (broken in 1971 with 28).

For several seasons the *Football Letter* had run weekly standings of the East's "Big Seven"—Penn State, Syracuse, Pittsburgh, Boston College, West Virginia, Army, and Navy. In 1970, Penn State and Syracuse led with 5–1 and 4–1 records (7–3 and 6–4 overall). The same group was called "The East Indies" in the Boston College weekly football report of 1970 and 1971 by Tim Cohane, former *Look* magazine sports editor now on the Boston University teaching staff and a free-lance writer. By midseason the Lambert Committee was expecting to award the trophy to Dartmouth if the Indians won the Ivy League and remained undefeated.

Since the Lamberts finally had made it clear that this trophy was no longer awarded for the "eastern championship" but for "outstanding performance by an eastern team," no one could quarrel with the selection of the Big Green. After the *Football Letter* unsuccessfully urged the ECAC to recognize an official eastern champion based on competition with each other, allowing the Ivies to fight it out for their own championship (and the Lambert, too, if it would continue), at Cohane's instigation the Cool-Ray Cup was put into competition in 1974 for the first time to symbolize the eastern championship. It was won by the Nittany Lions.

Penn State made no claim to the 1970 Lambert Trophy, but many believed that Syracuse deserved it by virtue of defeating such strong eastern teams as Pittsburgh, Penn State, Navy, and Army. The Orange had also beaten Miami (Florida) and Maryland in intersectional games.

Coach Paterno's liveliest press conference of the season followed the Pitt game. After telling newsmen that Penn State would not accept any bowl invitation, he issued a startling challenge to Dartmouth for a regularly scheduled game, which required no NCAA approval, on December 5 at Shea Stadium in New York. Reporters called it the "Lambert Bowl," but not Coach Paterno. He suggested later that it might be played to aid the families of the Marshall and Wichita State players and coaches who had been killed in tragic plane crashes.

Dartmouth's athletic director, Seaver Peters, told the New York *Times* that Ivy League rules would prevent such a meeting, adding that he thought Coach Paterno was "just trying to salvage the Lambert Trophy." No such thing, replied Paterno. He was merely trying to make it something more than a reward for the Ivy League champions. Coach Bob Blackman (now at Illinois) angrily accused Paterno of "grandstanding" and likened it to challenging a man with "one hand tied behind his back" (the Ivy League rules). Some of the people close to Paterno felt his gesture might have been a mistake and that he had been slightly less than serious in talking to reporters. While he now admits it was for fun, Joe claims he was surprised it was taken so seriously, especially by Dartmouth's Coach Blackman.

It was all kind of tongue-in-cheek, but I thought it might do some good. The Ivy League coaches were always complaining about their rules and the fact that their presidents wouldn't let them do anything. I thought this might help them break down some resistance, at least for a charity game.

Selection of the All-America teams by the College Football Coaches' Association in the 10-year period between 1961 and 1970 illustrates the sad plight of eastern football. Only 16 players from the East were chosen in the list of 176, made up of only one team, 1961–64, but of offensive and defensive teams, 1965–70. Eight of the easterners were from Penn State: Bob Mitinger, 1961; Roger Kochman, 1962; Glenn Ressler, 1964; Ted Kwalick, 1967, 1968; Charlie Pittman and Mike Reid, 1969; and Jack Ham, 1970. The list did not include Dave Robinson, Neal Smith, and Denny Onkotz, who were selected for other official All-Americas. The only other colleges in the East represented on the coaches' teams were Syracuse (3), and Maryland, Rutgers, Navy, Army, and Dartmouth (1 each). Of 176 players!

The summer of 1970 was a time for changing leadership of the university and of the individual college within which Penn State football functions. Dean Ernest B. McCoy, who came from Michigan in 1952 as athletic director and dean of the School of Physical Education and Athletics, initiated academic developments that led to its redesignation in 1963 as the College of Health and Physical Education and six years later as the College of Health, Physical Education and Recreation. Ed Czekaj took over the duties of athletic director in 1969. Retiring as dean emeritus on July 1, 1970, McCoy could claim credit for broad expansion of the academic and intercollegiate programs and of recreational facilities available to students, faculty, the entire university "family," and, to some extent, the general public.

Additions to the physical plant, made possible, as noted, partly by the financial success of football (legislative appropriations apply only for instructional purposes), included the ice rink, stadium, indoor and outdoor swimming pools, and tennis courts, a second 18-hole golf course, playing fields for intramurals and practice (one surfaced with Astroturf and available for university-wide use, such as for the band, military drill, etc.), and enlarged gymnasium units, with areas for bowling alleys, court games, and dressing rooms. Development of Stone Valley Lake in the nearby mountains permitted expansion of recreational facilities for Penn State's important parks and recreation curriculum, public school outdoor education programs, and general recreational usage. To further the study of athletic capabilities in relation to environmental conditions, the biomechanics and human performance laboratories were developed into the Sports Research Institute, of which McCoy was the first director.

A past president of the ECAC and Eastern Intercollegiate Football Association, McCoy was secretary-treasurer and vice president of the NCAA and on its Executive Committee before leaving Penn State to become athletic director at the University of Miami (Florida). He has since retired, and the McCoys have returned to their home in State College.

Dr. Robert J. Scannell, who had been associate dean for academic programs and undergraduate resident instruction, succeeded McCoy as dean of the college on July 1, 1970. A Notre Dame graduate and former football player, he came to Penn State in 1961, obtaining his M.S. and Ph.D. degrees, and was in charge of the college program in the university's Commonwealth Campus system before becoming associate dean. Dr. Scannell has been a University Senate officer and its president (1968–69), and chairman of the Council of Academic Deans.

President Eric A. Walker retired at 60, as he had planned and announced in 1968, and Dr. John W. Oswald took over on July 1, 1970. The Walkers, last presidential family to live in the campus residence built in 1864 for the first president (Evan Pugh), moved to their Rock Springs farmstead near the university's agronomy experimental tracts. The Oswalds became the first occupants of an off-campus president's residence near Boalsburg, retaining the historic dwelling for official entertaining as University House.

A dramatically changed university environment dictated this migration from the campus. Dr. Walker took office as the twelfth president in 1956 at the onset of Penn State's second century, when it was hurtling along like the rest of the academic world at a pace unprecedented in American higher education. Then and later, it was propelled by the post-World War II population explosion, the development of electronic automation in technologies, and a related new respect and new need for education and research.

Walker was well equipped to quarterback Penn State to a high position in the academic "ratings," although obstacles to recognition of an eastern state university lingered in some circles other than football. He earned his three degrees from Harvard and was on the engineering faculties at Tufts, the University of Connecticut, and Harvard before coming to Penn State as head of the Electrical Engineering Department and director of the Ordnance Research

Laboratory when part of this underwater sound research facility was moved here from Harvard in 1946. He became dean of the College of Engineering and Architecture in 1951 and had been appointed the university's first vice president in nearly fifty years before succeeding President Milton S. Eisenhower.

A research-oriented engineer, Dr. Walker resembled his one scientist predecessor (Dr. Pugh, an agricultural chemist) in having the aggressive energy to adapt the Morrill Land-Grant Act to the kind of higher education most needed in his time. "To promote liberal and practical education of the industrial classes in all the pursuits and professions of life" during the act's centennial years had multiple challenges impossible even to outline here, despite their implications for Penn State's broad athletic program, in which football plays the key role.

While realigning the academic structure to equalize the arts and humanities with Penn State's vigorous scientific and technological resources, the university also faced demands that compelled expansion of faculty, staff, and physical plant. Enrollment more than tripled (to 40,000), faculty more than doubled (to 3,200), and the annual operating budget went to $165 million during the crunch and crises of the Walker years. The University Park campus became the hub of a statewide system of Commonwealth Campuses, ranging in character from two- to four-year undergraduate curricula, graduate and research centers, and later the College of Medicine at Hershey, Pennsylvania, with its Medical Center and animal research unit.

As President, Dr. Walker extended his two-year engineering technology associate degree program to other fields, and utilized his involvement in professional and governmental activities to promote faculty participation in research grants. More faculty and students at all levels benefited from federal, state, and private funds made available for scholarships, professorships, international study, and awards, and had the advantage of expanded library facilities, a university press, experimental theaters, an educational TV channel, and other varied instructional services.

The activism of the late 1960s interrupted this constructive pattern of change, although violence was less publicized and consequently more subdued than at campuses like Berkeley and Columbia. Vocal and visible minorities, not always campus-related, disrupted the university's way of life, forced it into the courts, and liberated students and young faculty from disciplines once considered integral to learning. The despised administrative establishment operated amid special tensions of demands and demonstrations. Football, fraternities, and other collegiate manifestations persisted, though sometimes scorned, in an unacademic atmosphere that reached its height in 1970, when Dr. Walker adjourned to the more congenial and respected position of vice president for science and technology with Alcoa in Pittsburgh.

President Walker's interest in competitive athletics as a participant and as a spectator had exceeded that of most of his predecessors, and Penn State's excellent facilities for squash and tennis (including indoor courts) are attributable partly to his preference for them. He seldom allowed his busy schedule to omit daily recreation even at odd hours, for which his regular tennis and squash partner, Larry Perez, professor emeritus of civil engineering, was on call—and still is. As president in office and emeritus, Dr. Walker has enjoyed attending home and away football games whenever possible, and frequently has come to Rec Hall for wrestling, gymnastics, and basketball contests.

42

Texas Changes Its Mind

The Nittany Lions of 1971 were the first in three years to start a season without having to defend a long winning streak or the Lambert Trophy. Free to build their own image without surveillance from multiple summer previews, they were completely written out of the national scene by one periodical, which claimed to have "computerized" predictions and named Syracuse first in the East. The computer failed to place a single Penn Stater on the ninety-man All-America squad, which included players from Syracuse, Brown, Villanova, and Lehigh. As oblivious to the computer as it was to them, Penn State ended the season 11–1, won the Lambert Trophy, and defeated Texas in the Cotton Bowl.

Lacking much media support except locally, Lion enthusiasts generated their own heat, fanned by news of a four-game series scheduled with Stanford in the seventies and hints that Notre Dame and Alabama would be played in the early eighties. Optimism centered around Lydell Mitchell and Franco Harris, the two great running backs, while promising sophomores waiting in the wings were John Cappelletti, Tom Donchez, and Ed O'Neil, a defensive back who developed into one of the great All-America linebackers.

Coach Paterno was unworried about pressure on junior quarterback John Hufnagel. Other upperclassmen whose value was unquestioned included Dave Joyner, offensive tackle; Mike Botts, center; Bob Parsons, tight end; Bruce Bannon, defensive end; Frank Ahrenhold, defensive tackle; Bob Knechtel, offensive guard; and linebackers Charlie Zapiec, Jim Laslavic, Doug Allen, Gary Gray, and John Skorupan. The defensive secondary, where O'Neil was first placed, caused most concern, but the return of Gregg Ducatte (safety) added some strength to the corps of deep defenders.

The eastern service academies, entering a period of decline, turned to sideline shenanigans to entertain their spectators. During Penn State's opening game at Annapolis, the Middies "shot" Superman from the cannon employed to salute touchdowns. (It had become somewhat rusty of late.) A go-go-girl, barely in a bikini with *Go Navy* and the name of a State College bistro printed on the back, dashed out for a brief confrontation. Other and perhaps more suitable entertainment was provided by Mitchell's five touchdowns (102 yards) and by Hufnagel, who completed 7 of 7 passes and ran the ball once for 58 yards. Scoring 42 points in the second and third quarters, the Lions erased Navy, 56–3, which pleased Coach Paterno but did not erase memories of what had followed 1970's easy Navy victory. Iowa wasn't Colorado, yet there was something ominous about the next trip West.

Although Iowa had lost only eighteen home openers and only four of its previously televised games, the imperturbable Lions posted 23 points in the second quarter and won the game handily, 44–14. This time Harris was the big charger, scoring four touchdowns to tie the Iowa Stadium record. Charlie Zapiec, formerly a guard, played his third game as a linebacker and won the ABC Network "Best Defensive Player" award, with Mitchell getting the same honor (209 yards) for the offense. Their two $1,000 prizes, according to custom, were added to the university's general academic scholarship funds. Penn State's first visit to Iowa City in forty-one years (since 1930) proved satisfying.

Ranked ninth nationally after the Iowa game, the Lions came back to earth in their home opener against the Air Force Academy, an alert, aggressive team smartly coached by a veteran Navy man, Ben Martin. With only four minutes to play, Penn State trailed, 14–13, and Alberto Vitiello's missed placement after the second Lion touchdown was the difference. The dejected Alberto brooded on the Lion bench, hoping his team's late drive would produce a touchdown. When the fighting Falcons stopped the advance at 4th and 1 on the 5, Coach Paterno didn't think twice about putting his new place-kicker under pressure again after his earlier failure. "I've got to have faith in him," said Joe. "You never know what you can do until you try it." Al's perfect kick made the victory.

Paterno doesn't consider deciding on a field goal a weighty part of coaching. He applies his personal formula unless very special circumstances are involved. With *less* than 2 yards to go, if a field goal will win, go for it. If a field goal merely ties, try for a touchdown or first down. With more than 2 yards to go, try for a field goal if it will help. A good kicker simplifies the choice.

Early-season Lambert ratings presented an almost ludicrous picture of eastern football. Army, victors over Georgia Tech at Atlanta (a feat few northern teams had accomplished), just made the first ten behind Villanova and such Ivies as Dartmouth, Cornell, and Yale, all scarcely into their schedules. Pitt had beaten UCLA and scored 29 points on Oklahoma in a losing cause, only to be forgotten entirely. Other sections of the country couldn't be expected to take eastern football seriously with this kind of raffle, apparently blessed by the ECAC.

The Lions reached their playing peak against eastern rivals Army (42–0) and Syracuse (31–0) and also savored an intersectional victory over TCU. Their first taste of a Wishbone offense was licking good—the 66–14 TCU score was the highest in twenty-four years for a Lion team, which set an all-time game record of 632 yards total offense (485 rushing, 147 passing). Army had held Penn State scoreless until a few seconds before half time, then collapsed and gave up 28 points in the third period.

Lion coaches got fine results from hard work designed to stop the powerful inside running of Syracuse. The year before, the Lions had been humiliated in their own stadium, with fullback Marty Januszkiewicz gaining 152 yards in 36 attempts. The Paterno-O'Hora defense, with extra power in the middle, held Jan to 17 yards through center and 18 more on his one attempt to get outside. The Orange passed more than Coach Ben liked, but the 13 completions were unproductive. The 1971 Syracusans did have victories over Indiana, Maryland, West Virginia, and Miami (Florida), and a tie with Wisconsin.

Nothing they had experienced before, anywhere, could compare with the cyclone awaiting the Lions this year at Morgantown. Since West Virginia had upset the Penn State soccer and freshman football teams that week, talk of a "clean sweep" was in the air. Only Charlie Zapiec had previously endured the menace of Mountaineer Field, but Coach Paterno, mindful of the undisciplined undergraduate cheering section at the 1968 game, had the right words for his squad: "Keep your cool no matter what happens. The crowd can beat you only if you let 'em."

The West Virginians came out to play so hopped up they knocked each other down along with everything in their path, including an official who fell flat on his back. When West Virginia lost the toss, Lion fans almost expected the West Virginia co-captains to take a poke at Zapiec and Dave Joyner. Checked in time, such fury tends to have a reverse effect if the psyched-up team gets behind. Early in the second half, with the score 7–7, a Mountaineer fumbled a punt, two Penn Staters made a dive for the ball, it rolled out of bounds, and the official (the one knocked over?) ruled that the Lions had possession in-bounds. West Virginia sports journalists almost unanimously decided the controversial play was a bad call, the "turning point" of the game against the Mountaineers. Coach Bobby Bowden said he couldn't see the play; Coach Paterno thought his team might have gotten a break. Bowden referred to all this in a 1972 preseason statement: "I'm through trying to psych Penn State out of a game. We'll beat them when we have better players than theirs."

Defeating two Atlantic Coast Conference teams, Maryland and North Carolina State, and having a 9–0 record made the Lions prime candidates for the big bowls, all of which had representatives watching the team overpower most of its opponents. Asked at the local Quarterback Club about the problem of getting "up" for the final pre-bowl games with Pitt and Tennessee, Paterno harked back to the previous year's Wisconsin defeat, when the Lions had destroyed the Badger quarterback and most of the opposition, won the statistics, and lost the game:

> I decided never to work on emotion again. We'll play our own game, the best we can, and if we practice well, we'll play well . . . sometimes we'll get licked, but it will be because the other team is better, not because they're "up."

Pitt Coach Carl DePasqua told the press that his team would be loose and "up"—it had nothing to lose. The Panthers, who won the toss, obeyed instructions to kick off, and the Lions started poorly on a miserable, drizzly, windy afternoon that reminded old-timers in the stadium of the doleful thirties. Ed O'Neil juggled the kick and had to scramble to recover on the 16. Tom Donchez, in for the injured Franco Harris, bobbled Huffy's first pitchout and lost 5 yards. Lydell Mitchell was pushed back to the 10. The Cotton Bowl's Wilbur Evans, lone representative on hand in the press box, must have shuddered: Was he to observe the dreaded jittery collapse of one of the "chosen"?

The indomitable Lion quarterback, John Hufnagel, followed *his* instructions to keep cool. He knew he must pass, and Pitt knew it. The Panthers covered his receivers as two husky linemen crashed in toward Huffy. Avoiding them, he shook loose and fought his way to the 29 and a first down. The danger of collapse was over, the Cotton Bowl observer relaxed, and Lion fans smiled again as their team won a convincing 55–18 victory, with Mitchell running for 180 yards and Huffy completing 7 of 11 for 163 yards. The Lions' total offense was 530 yards.

Penn State officially accepted the Cotton Bowl bid—twenty-four years after the last invitation to this classic—to meet the Southwest Conference champions, not yet named. National polls placed the Lions sixth, to the indignation of Penn State patrons. The "questionable schedule" canard, prevalent in 1968 and 1969 but laid to rest by Orange Bowl victories over the Big Eight champions, was loud again. Habitual belittling of mainly sectional schedules overlooks the fierce efforts of all eastern opponents to defeat Penn State. This, plus regular success in bowl games, makes Coach Paterno's three undefeated, untied teams in ten years (1968, 1969, 1973) a significant achievement. In 1971, one major obstacle remained in the way of a fourth: Tennessee. Northern teams don't defeat the Vols in Neyland Stadium, Knoxville, said the southern press, especially when televised nationally. No one was more conscious than Paterno that his northern team, picked for a bowl and undefeated, was playing in Tennessee. When he saw the papers, he regretted his remarks about having as much right to Number One as anyone if the Lions beat the Vols, because he felt the players weren't ready mentally for this trial.

Emotional factors once were analyzed in this comment by Colonel Earl H. (Red) Blaik, coach of some great Army teams:

> Successful football depends on sharp blocking and tackling, which are impossible without quick movement. Quickness, in turn, is conditioned by attitude, dedication, and desire. No group of humans can achieve a peak of dedication every week.

Emotional graphs vary, and, with them, proficiency in the execution of fundamentals. The results are some seemingly strange, yet quite logical scoreboard stories.

The Lions were put down by a keyed-up southern team. Ranked sixth to Tennessee's twelfth, with the nation's highest-scoring offense, they moved the Vols' "immovable defense" 368 yards, but there were serious flaws: six turnovers and weak kicking coverage. This enabled the home team to roll up a massive total of 361 yards on returns, including 76 acquired by cornerback Conrad Graham when a fumbled handoff popped right into his hands as the Lions were 24 yards from a score.

After that play, return artist Bobby Majors carved at the Lion return defense like a skillful surgeon, and the patient never recovered. The younger brother of Pitt's former coach, Johnny Majors, Bobby made 195 of the return yards with punts and kickoffs. Shaky kick coverage, always dangerous, was fatal against Tennessee, even though it was almost the only statistic in favor of the home team. Penn State's ground and air statistics were deceiving because drives often began deep on its own side of the field, only to be stopped in Vol territory by mechanical blunders or by the heroic Tennessee defensive unit, with linebackers Jackie Walker, Ray Nettles, and Jamie Rotella in the lead.

Ecstatic Tennessee officials enshrined Bobby's Number 44 jersey in the Volunteer Athletic Museum. A disappointed Penn State administrator returning to the team bus was passed by a pickup truck loaded with Tennessee football gear on which a student manager was sitting. With a broad, friendly smile, the student called out sympathetically, "Hey, we were all hell in there, weren't we?" The southern airline stewardess who had kidded the team on the way down, wisely refrained on the return trip, reading the disappointment on all the faces. The appearance and manner of players returning from a defeat may be one distinction between collegians and professionals. After a perfect season, this rude jolt to pride was a dismal prelude to final examinations and practices in freezing weather with the cold night wind swirling snow over the Astroturf.

Lydell Mitchell, the game's leading ground-gainer, arrived back on campus at nine o'clock Saturday night, weary and dispirited. He slipped into Rec Hall to see the tail end of the Cornell basketball game, walked under the stands, and found an inconspicuous seat at one end of the bleachers. During a time-out, a few students spotted the great Lion halfback, and several spontaneously stood to applaud. Suddenly all 6,000 in the building, including basketball coach John Bach and his players, joined in the tribute for his three years of fine contribution to Penn State football.

At about the same time, Coach Paterno reached a home oddly quiet for a Saturday night. The children were in bed, and there were none of the usual drop-in callers. Sitting there not wanting to talk about the game, Joe and Sue were soon joined by Betts and defensive coach Jim O'Hora—misery loves company. Before long, Sue heard sounds outside and opened the door. A group of fifty or sixty students began singing "Hail to the Lion" and the alma mater, "For the Glory of Old State." Kappa Sigs and their dates had come from the other side of town to show the coach how they appreciated what he had done for Penn State football and the university, said their spokesman, and to wish him good luck in the Cotton Bowl.

These incidents contravene the belief of many observers that students have no sentiment, no feeling for what used to be called "college spirit." The fact is that the majority of undergraduates today probably keep intercollegiate sports in better perspective than do alumni, who are likely to believe that winning or losing a game is all-important.

The 1971 Lions rank with the teams of 1968, 1969, and 1973 despite the Tennessee loss—how many elevens go through a season without one? Penn State advocates campaigned, perhaps too quietly, to promote Lydell Mitchell for the Heisman Trophy, but the East was divided between the Lion and Ed Marinaro, the fine Cornell halfback who had almost unanimous backing from the New York press and newscasters. While Marinaro set Cornell and Ivy League records, Mitchell set three NCAA records (without bowl games): touchdowns (28); touchdowns by rushing (26); and most points per season (174), still standing in 1976. An outstanding blocker, runner (inside and outside), and pass receiver, he holds ten Penn State season and career rushing and scoring records (as of 1976). Both easterners were beaten out by Pat Sullivan, the Auburn quarterback. Mitchell has since been making records as a Baltimore Colt and Marinaro has been a back with the Minnesota Vikings and the New York Jets.

John Hufnagel established most of his passing records in 1972, but his 19 completions (in 29 attempts) at Tennessee tied Pete Liske's 1963 record (in 27 attempts against UCLA). Alberto Vitiello was

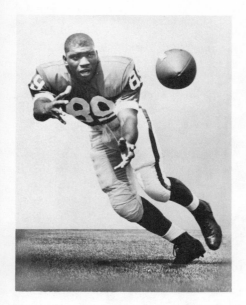

All-America end honors in 1962 went to Dave Robinson.

The Old Track House: Home of Varsity athletes, 1903–24, when it was replaced by Varsity (now Irvin) Hall.

Coach Joe Paterno makes a rare pep talk to his squad between halves of the Maryland game at College Park in 1973. The two teams were tied at half time, 22–22. The Lions won, 42–22.

Heinz Warneke, sculptor of the Nittany Lion Shrine (1942), visited Penn State thirty-three years after he created the renowned work of art. He was made an honorary alumnus, attended his first football game, and was greeted by the Lion mascot on November 8, 1975.

State's first Heisman Trophy winner was All-America offensive halfback John Cappelletti '74. (Photograph by Dick Brown.)

Lydell Mitchell '72 went to the pros, like his teammate Franco Harris, and was an All-America defensive halfback in 1971.

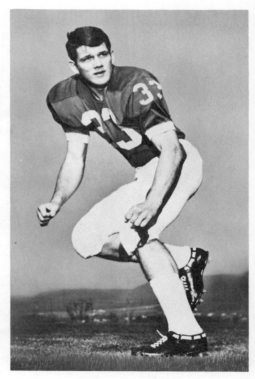

This young stalwart, currently busting things up as a pro, is Jack Ham '71, an All-America linebacker in 1970.

The Paterno family, 1973, near their home. Coach Joe (carrying George Scott), Diana, Jay, Sue Paterno, David, and Mary Kay. (Photograph by Bill Coleman.)

Study in concentration: Coach Joe Paterno instructs his quarterback, Chuck Burkhart, just before sending him into a contest at Beaver Stadium, 1968. Burkhart started every game for two years (1968 and 1969) and acquired a record of 22–0 and two Orange Bowl victories.

Mount Nittany.

The author, Ridge Riley, often called "Mr. Penn State," sits beside the Lion (the Warneke statue) in a pose appropriate to the teamwork of the two—a man and a symbol, part of the Penn State effort to be "Number One" as a university, in athletics, and as a community.

another record-breaker. His most important new mark was "most points by kicking in one season"—74 (59 points after touchdowns, 5 field goals). His three field goals and 12 points by kicking were both Cotton Bowl records. The 1971 team (11 games) produced the all-time Penn State scoring record with 454 points and 5 others still standing in 1976: most interceptions in one season, 28; most rushing yardage in one season, 3,347; total offense in one season (11 games), 4,995; pass completion percentage in one season, 57.5 (103 of 179); and most first downs during season (11 games), 249. Rushing average per play in one season (5.2 yards); and total offense in one game (632 yards, against TCU) were others since eclipsed.

Mitchell and Co-Captains Dave Joyner and Charlie Zapiec were All-America selections. Both the coaches and the football writers picked Joyner as an offensive tackle. No rumors of professional coaching offers were circulated about Coach Paterno, but at the beginning of the year, while he was at Hawaii's Hula Bowl with Jack Ham and Warren Koegel, he accepted an invitation from the Green Bay Packers to stop by in Wisconsin. He left Green Bay officials with written conditions under which he would consider an offer, but was not contacted again.

THE COTTON BOWL, JANUARY 1, 1972

Comments after the Tennessee defeat weren't totally unkind. F. M. Williams of the Nashville *Tennessean* wrote to John Morris, sports information director:

> It is always a pleasure for those of us even remotely connected with Tennessee, to play games against first class opponents, and Penn State certainly was that in every respect. I know most people say there is no virtue in defeat, but you never really know people until you see them react to adversity, and I know that no team ever was frustrated more than yours was down here. So it is most complimentary to Coach Paterno and your players when I tell you they were first class all the way. I hope the series continues for years to come.

Coach Paterno and company had more than Texas jibes over the Tennessee defeat to overcome in Dallas, where their selection was far from popular. Ridicule and complacency were general. "Penn

State is only the best of the crop of the East's weak sisters, a team 'made' by a weak schedule," etc. The Longhorns, as dear to Texas sports lovers as the young Arnie Palmer was to nearly everyone, represented "class," and only their equals were worthy to meet them in combat. Penn State couldn't be taken seriously, nor was Paterno a match for the admirable Darrell Royal. All that about being Number One, after having turned down a chance to play the Longhorns in the 1969 Cotton Bowl, didn't endear Joe to the local populace. In Texas, Penn State suffers, too, from being confused with Ivy League Pennsylvania, while also having to explain, "What is a Nittany Lion?"

The good-looking, mannerly Paterno squad revised the image of the underrated Penn State team, champions of a faraway territory where citizens scarcely had heard of the Wishbone. The Lions received a high compliment from the newspaper columnist who ended, "Why, their haircuts were even shorter than the Longhorns'!" Coach Paterno has always insisted on good appearance—long hair and mustaches were never an issue if neatly trimmed, and in hotel lobbies coats and ties were required. Texans noticed this, especially in the elegant Fairmont Hotel. The media observed in television interviews that the Lions could talk spontaneously and sometimes disagree with each other, whereas other players relied heavily on PR-prepared remarks. This is the fruit of another Paterno policy that permits players to be interviewed individually after each game as part of their training. (Ill-considered quotes don't go unnoticed.) About Penn State's "new image" in Texas, Paterno has his own ideas:

> . . . we weren't very popular when we went down there . . . but that was a psychological carry-over from the ratings of 1969—and I think it helped that we didn't say a lot of stupid things after we'd won . . . no one tried to make the game a national crusade.

Paterno was low-key, never exactly "poor-mouthed" his squad, and yet gave the modest impression that the Lions didn't belong on the same field as the Longhorns. Coach Royal obviously wouldn't buy this, but the ploy affected many Texans—it was what they wanted to hear, and repetition of such a theme makes for overconfidence. Joe's frankness, quick wit, and easy repartee with newsmen provided great copy before and after the game, and he quickly became one of the most popular luncheon and dinner speakers the Cotton Bowl had ever had.

For Penn State, the game was soul-satisfying beyond measure, a convincing performance, run off in the presence of former President Lyndon B. Johnson, who spent an unhappy afternoon repeating the symbolic Longhorn victory gesture with his fingers for cameramen. The proud Texans suffered their worst bowl beating since Coach Royal's first year of 1957, when Ole Miss had defeated his team, 39–7, in the 1958 Sugar Bowl.

The first half was unspectacular, but had a surprise for Texans who hadn't dreamed the Lions could handle the Royal Wishbone with such dexterity. This wasn't accidental. Although they had fun in Dallas during off-hours, in keeping with the Paterno code that bowl games are a reward for hard work and success in the regular season, the Lions on the field had prepared for the main event. Fran Ganter '71, now freshman coach, visited the squad's practice and was recruited to play the role of Jim Bertelsen on the "foreign" team. In consequence, he watched the Cotton Bowl with his leg in a cast, but had the satisfaction of seeing Lydell Mitchell outgain Bertelsen, now with the Los Angeles Rams, 146–59. But the beginning was rocky.

Eddie Phillips, W.M. (Wishbone Master), who had been named the "Outstanding Player" in the 1971 Cotton Bowl, was in rare form at the start, and Penn State was slow to cover Bertelsen, his pitch man and the second leading rusher in Longhorn history. A half-time deadlock seemed inevitable, with the teams in an unexpected 3–3 tie on field goals by Steve Valek and then Vitiello, until Texas had the ball on its own 40 with 19 seconds to play in the half. Phillips completed his only passes of the first half, two for 19 yards each to Pat Kelly, and on the last play Valek neatly kicked a 40-yarder to set a Cotton Bowl record. The Texas crowd relaxed, sure everything would go well from then on.

What went well wasn't for the home team, which collapsed as the Lions had in their first half at Nashville. Penn State capitalized fully on jittery Longhorn mistakes in the second half, crossing up the Wishbone offense by stunting and switching defensive alignments. Playing almost perfect football, especially the defensive unit, they did everything right to achieve a memorable victory, scoring 17 points in the third quarter and 10 in the fourth. Vitiello made two more field goals, and Hufnagel threw two key passes—a brilliant one to Bob Parsons on the goal line (Mitchell took it over), and another to Scotty Skarzynski, good for a touchdown. On a rollout play with Paterno yelling for him to run, Huffy had spotted Scotty 15 yards ahead of his defender and let him have it instead. (Coach Royal later explained that the defender had been "stunned" on the previous play.) Near the end, Hufnagel did score, skirting right end and barely making the flag at the corner of the field.

Among standouts in the stalwart defensive unit were Charlie Zapiec, Frank Ahrenhold, and end Bruce Bannon, who was named the outstanding player. Gary Gray (linebacker) was credited with 14 tackles, 9 unassisted; end Jim Laslavic with 12; and Gregg Ducatte, playing the best game of his career, had 11.

Penn Staters probably relished most on Dallas sports pages the following morning this review by Blackie Sherrod in the *Times-Herald:*

> Cotton Bowl old-timers vow Penn State visitors, coaches, players, administrators, alumni . . . made the best impression of any game bunch in the 36-year history [of the Cotton Bowl]. Locals were flabbergasted when Penn State folk entertained *them* at a party. . . . The vaunted Wishbone-T offense of Darrell Royal's crowd was most ineffective. This was due partly to poor execution on the part of the Steer offensive unit and partly to a rather savage Penn State defense. In essence, such line defenders as Gray, Laslavic, Bannon, Zapiec and other unspellables [Note to Mr. Sherrod: You spell it G-R-A-Y.], were the heroes of the day. These bruisers held the Texas offense without a touchdown for the first time in 80 games.

And there was this one by Sam Blair in the Dallas *Morning News:*

> Penn State stormed through, over, and around the Longhorns for a resounding 30–6 victory. When it was over not a soul was making jokes about the so-called eastern style football which the Lions supposedly play. . . . Rarely, if ever, has a good Royal team, supposedly operating under normal strength, been subjected to such a licking.

43

One and a Million

Heartaches and satisfying triumphs marked the 1972 season, which saw the team start slowly and gather momentum halfway along. The coaches at first were most concerned because the offense missed the Mitchell-Harris punch, running behind such strong offensive linemen as Dave Joyner, Bob Knechtel, Mike Botts, and Bob Parsons. Assets were the encouraging development of John Hufnagel, whom Coach Paterno was to call "the best college quarterback in America"; the running of John Cappelletti, moved from the defensive unit; and exciting receivers like Jimmy Scott and Chuck Herd. Sophomores Dan Natale, Jeff Bleamer, and Jack Baiorunos were among those expected to bolster the offensive line.

Defensively, the team seemed solid, with a front four anchored by ends Gary Hager and Bruce Bannon, and tackles Randy Crowder and Jim Heller. Hager later joined the usual corps of tough linebackers and was replaced at end by sophomore Dave Graf. The uncertain offense developed rapidly, while the defense surrendered more points (175) than any Paterno team since 1966. But, looking back, doubts about the 1972 team hardly seem justified.

Injuries were troublesome in the spring, when nine regulars missed the warmup Blue-White game. The unflinching Paterno was concerned about meeting Tennessee in the opening game, and shared the irritation of local fans over the refusal of the Volunteers to make the short series a home-and-home arrangement. He prepared with his usual thoroughness but no hysteria, and attempted to subordinate a "revenge" element connected with the game.

A first game against a strong opponent that had won its opener from Georgia Tech would be no tea party. Lion scouts felt the game at Knoxville was not beyond the capabilities of the team, and recommended keeping the offense simple to avoid turnovers, especially in the early periods, when it would be deadly to give the hyped-up Vols an advantage. The win-win atmosphere at Knoxville beats anything most northern fans have experienced. Not all fanatics live in Columbus, and Orange country no longer means just Syracuse.

Knoxville visitors see orange ties, blazers, and pants on every other male; orange miniskirts on the girls; orange shoes on the waitresses; and orange vests on the bartenders. Orange football helmets are mixed in with fashion displays in shop windows, orange ironing boards are sold in department stores, and orange bowling balls are used in the alleys. The 100-page stadium program has black type in orange blocks on nearly every page. Description of the visiting team begins on page 77, following an account of Vol basketball prospects. Spectators file into the stands two and a half hours before the kickoff to yell and scream and chant and stomp their feet. Northern visitors are inclined to envy such togetherness and wonder if strong eastern teams might benefit and become more numerous through such support. In Knoxville, Birmingham, and Baton Rouge, football isn't just an undergraduate activity—it's also a way of life for the entire community or state.

This was the hot (75°), humid, embattled atmosphere of the first night game in Neyland Stadium, attended by the largest crowd (71,647) to witness a sporting event in Tennessee.

The jittery Lions seemed destined to repeat the previous season's failure on the same gridiron, giving the home team the advantage of interceptions and fumbles, helping them to roll up 21 points in the first half. The easterners, courageous and resourceful in a second-half comeback, finally earned the respect of Tennessee fans, but it took six quarters in the two games at Neyland Stadium. Coach Paterno, true to form, refrained from ranting between halves and emphasized instead that the waiting game was over, the foe had to be pursued to stave off disaster: "Play as if you were ahead."

Huffy came back brilliantly (12 of 25 for 190 yards, and two touchdowns), first contributing a "bomb" to Jimmy Scott, the IC4-A sprint champion, who outdashed everyone on the field for 79 yards. Doug Allen, before the third period was over, blasted fullback Dave Chancey hard enough to shake the ball loose, to be recovered by Graf on the Vol 22. At this juncture, John Cappelletti began his career of power running, taking the ball six times in a row. On the seventh ground play of the series, Bob Nagle vaulted over a pileup for Penn State's second touchdown, closing the gap to 21–14 at the beginning of the final period.

The Vols showed their class before the thunderstruck home crowd. Unaided now by any Lion mistakes, they were led on an 80-yard drive by their intrepid quarterback, Condredge Holloway, then a sophomore, who sparkled in 13 plays consuming seven minutes and then scored the winning touchdown himself. The Lions pushed on for a 79-yard drive powered by Cappelletti and Nagle and ending with a 14-yard scoring pass from Hufnagel to Dan Natale. Penn State fought to go ahead, getting the ball to midfield with 40 seconds left, but on the last play, Hufnagel completed a pass to Gary Hayman, who made a futile effort to get out of bounds on the 26. The game ended with the score 28–21. Al Vitiello, placement specialist, was asked how he felt sitting on the bench waiting to kick the tying point if Penn State had scored. "I wasn't nervous a bit," he replied. "Coach Paterno would never let us go for one point."

The first game of the 1972 season at Knoxville and the home opener with Navy were played before the fall term began, without benefit of organized spectator support. A change was in the making, brought about by the Age of TV and bowl games. During the collegiate Roaring Twenties, showmanship was conservative; there was the popular Penn State Blue Band, supported by energetic cheerleaders. The marching military band, distinctive for its musicianship and quick-step precision, had evolved from the Cadet Corps unit and the College Band under the command of Colonel Wilfred O. (Tommy) Thompson, the first full-time director (1913–39). Bandmaster Tommy's successor was his assistant, Dr. Hummel Fishburn '22, who also headed the School of Music after the retirement of Richard W. Grant in 1941. After turning over active direction of the band to his assistant, Dr. James W. Dunlop, in 1947, Hum continued to develop intricate formations for half-time concerts and was a consultant as well as the home field public address announcer until his death on April 19, 1976. When Jim Dunlop died suddenly on August 7, 1975, Dr. Ned C. Diehl, his assistant, was named director.

The authentic look of Penn State's mascot was firmly established in 1940 when Gene Wettstone, gymnastics coach, supervised the designing of a lion costume and cavorted in it himself at early games until a student, Tom Kelly '42, was selected and began his chores at the Temple game in Philadelphia. Simultaneously, the Class of 1940 designated its gift. The money would be used to commission a statue. The so-called Nittany Lion Shrine was carved on its site near Recreation Building by Heinz Warneke, the distinguished sculptor, and dedicated in 1942. Crouching larger than life, the lithe and powerful lion is Penn State's most photographed subject, alone or with visitors and Penn Staters of all ages.

A repertoire of stunts soon enlivened the lion mascot's role, performing with the cheerleaders and the Blue Band's drum major, usually a skilled baton twirler and contortionist. In 1948 Bill Bonsall '49, head cheerleader and a gymnastics champion, was particularly resourceful in planning the lion's maneuvers. These include, since the mid-sixties, doing obligatory push-ups and being tossed high and caught in a blanket to mark each of Penn State's scoring points.

The advent of female cheerleaders during World War II preceded by 20 years the band's permanent admission of women musicians, but resistance to "frills" may have been eroded by the popularity of the spectacular Band Day, inaugurated in 1950 for Pennsylvania high schools, which had dancing majorettes, baton twirlers, and flag corps accompanying their instrumentalists. Capitulation came about when the Blue Band, still recognized for its superb traditional musicianly quality, had to compete for TV attention in half-time shows and colorful bowl game parades and festivities.

A desire to rekindle that old-time "college spirit" scorned by the activists of the 1960s caused Jon Fox '68 to lead a group in organizing "Students for State." They worked on pep rallies, wore bright buttons, and formed a flashcard Block S display section in the student stands, beginning in 1967. The first group of Penn State majorettes appeared at the 1972 Iowa game, with Judy Shearer '74 as the baton-twirling soloist. Among its first members was Leann Czekaj, daughter of Athletic Director Ed Czekaj and Virginia Gallup Czekaj '48, who had been a cheerleader.

An aggressive town, gown, and alumni movement to articulate enthusiasm for all of Penn State's varsity sports teams began after the

1972 opening game at Knoxville, where the Lions were defeated in the stands as well as on the gridiron. The initiators were Betsy Kepler (Mrs. G. Don) of Pine Grove Mills and Carol Lingle (Mrs. Walter T.) of Centre Hall, nearby communities. They were aided by the State College dailies, radio stations, and a local advertising firm, together with university staff members Richie Lucas (then athletic business manager), A. Mac Saddoris (religious affairs associate and adviser-manager of the cheerleading troupe), and Bob Goerder '39 (Alumni Association field director), who handled operations for away games, bowl games, and alumni affairs. Their "Back the Lions" campaign raised funds for skimmers and blue-and-white shakers, which perked up a rousing Sugar Bowl sendoff rally at Recreation Building and were supplied to Penn Staters at New Orleans. From then on, Lion fans have effectively made their presence known in the stands, joining with the Blue Band, cheerleaders, majorettes, the flag drill team, the drum major, the baton twirler, and particularly the tireless Nittany Lion. Bob Welsh '75 brought the mascot to new heights as a frolicking, captivating creature of wide renown, a welcome presence at many social, sports, and charitable functions of the campus and the community. Andy Bailey, his successor and Beta Theta Pi roommate, continued in the same spirit.

Among important supportive staff members, the earliest were the trainers, first mentioned in the 1890s through 1902, when they also coached and were "directors of physical training" for all students. Of the first three (Hoskins, Newton, and Golden), Dr. S. B. Newton, head coach (1896–8), was an M.D. graduate of the University of Pennsylvania, but Hoskins and Golden had longer service. The first full-time trainer, appointed in 1912 at the insistence of Coach Bill Hollenback, was Dr. Dan Luby, who left after one year to practice dentistry. Coaches of other sports then served as football trainers for many years. C. W. (Bill) Martin, who came from Notre Dame in 1913 to coach track and cross country, was both trainer and assistant football coach under Hollenback, Harlow, and Bezdek, until Martin resigned in 1923 to coach track at Harvard. Track coach Nate Cartmell, football trainer until his falling-out with Bezdek, was succeeded by Leo Houck, the boxing coach, and later for a few years by Charlie Speidel, best known as Penn State's successful wrestling coach.

Jack Hulme, the first full-time trainer for all athletic teams, held the post from 1937 until his death in 1946. Charles E. (Chuck) Medlar '46 advanced immediately from assistant to head trainer, was appointed to the physical education staff in 1948, and has been head trainer for athletic teams ever since. An outstanding Penn State pitcher, who succeeded Joe Bedenk as varsity baseball coach in 1963, Chuck is recognized in both capacities. As one of the nation's foremost athletic trainers, he was on the U. S. Olympic team's staff at Tokyo (1964) and was head trainer for the U.S. team at the 1968 Olympic Games in Mexico City. Medlar's assistants for all sports are Penn State graduates W. James (Jim) Hochberg, Edward A. (Eddie) Sulkowski, Gerald W. (Jerry) Slagle, and Ray V. Ulinski. Two are varsity football letter-winners—Ulinski in 1947, and Hochberg, a therapy specialist, in 1955. Sulkowski succeeded Leo Houck as varsity boxing coach in 1950.

Until the Bezdek era, the graduate manager's office was responsible for football equipment and other athletic paraphernalia, cared for by undergraduate managers. Ollie DeVictor, the first equipment manager hired by Bezdek in the early 1920s, soon left to take the same job at Pittsburgh. A. P. (Dean) Burrell, his successor, cared for the equipment and bossed the student managers for many years until he retired in 1941. Ralph Wert, Oscar Buchenhorst, Mel Franks, Bud Thompson, John Tomco, and Ed O'Hara had held the post before John J. Nolan '48 was appointed in 1971. Over a number of years the position acquired broad responsibility involving the purchase, care, distribution, and repair of all equipment for the varsity teams, and transportation for away games. Nolan, who was co-captain in 1947 of the Cotton Bowl team, also works with the university's Sports Research Institute in testing and developing new and safer equipment.

Major staff appointees in 1972 were Booker Brooks, full-time coach of wide receivers, and Dr. Sam Fleagle, team physician. Booker, from Akron, Ohio, and a 1959 graduate of Wilmington (Ohio) College, had been a graduate assistant for three years, with five years of high school coaching experience in his home state. His wife, the former Chris Baster of Auckland, New Zealand, coaches the Lady Lions' varsity track and cross country teams.

University Health Service physicians have cared for athletes as needed since the formal organization of the department in January 1915, when Dr. W. S. Forsythe of Michigan was appointed its first full-time director. Dr. Joseph P. Ritenour '01, well known to all

Penn Staters for his freshman hygiene course, followed as Health Service director (1917–46), but the Athletic Department acquired its first full-time team physician in 1939 with the appointment of Dr. Alfred H. Griess. A Nebraskan who attended the University of Pennsylvania Medical School and retired in 1966, Doc Griess had Dr. William Grasley as an assistant for four years before Bill took over. When Bill left in 1972 after 10 years' service to join Centre Community Hospital's Mountainview unit adjacent to the campus, Dr. Samuel Fleagle became team physician with two assistants, Dr. James Whiteside and Dr. Alexander Kalenak, who is an orthopedic specialist on Penn State's Hershey Medical School staff. Sam Fleagle played high school football at Waynesboro (Pennsylvania) under Rip Engle and, like Engle, was on the varsity at Western Maryland. The team dentist is Dr. Martin McFeatters, successor to the late Dr. Dan Lonberger '27, first in that position. All have been associated with the university's Ritenour Health Center, so named in 1958.

The Tennessee setback—Joe Paterno's only opening game defeat in his 11 years as head coach—dissipated some of the confident hope for the 1972 season. The second-half resurgence at Knoxville helped restore it somewhat, but the letdown lingered until half time of the home opener, when Navy held a 3–0 lead. In a down-to-the-wire struggle, the Lions finally won, 21–10, on John Skorupan's interception and 32-yard touchdown scamper less than two minutes from the end.

The tendency of even the most loyal followers to be morose unless the team overwhelms an opponent they consider inferior provokes Coach Paterno perhaps more than being asked to explain or justify a defeat. Paterno lamented this attitude after the Navy victory:

> Why can't we go to a football game and sit there enjoying an exciting and successful afternoon without having anxiety pains and being dissatisfied if the team doesn't win by four touchdowns or more?—some mythical oddsmaker's prediction. Because our fans think we'll lose our standing in the polls, that's why. You can't just win any more. You have to win big. Those polls have taken a lot of fun out of Saturdays.

Paterno's forecast was accurate. Winning from a talented, well-coached, fighting Navy team sent the Lions deeper into the second ten, while Nebraska moved into the top ten for mercilessly humiliating Army. Coach Bob Devaney said he was "sorry," but he wasn't sorry enough to take out his regulars until they had run up 56 points.

Beaver Stadium, enlarged to 57,538 capacity, enjoyed its first sell-out for the second game, when the crowd may have been attracted partly by the well-publicized debut of the majorettes with the Blue Band. Like Navy, Iowa led 3–0 in the first half, and the Lions again kept their friends in suspense until their 14–10 victory was assured in the final 30 seconds. Eleven turnovers by fumbles in the first three games had unnerved home fans, and some took it as a bad omen that a majorette lost her hairpiece during the half-time performance. (True to showmanship tradition, she didn't pick it up.) Surviving their four fumbles against the Hawkeyes after being behind 10–7 with three minutes remaining, the Lions marched 80 yards, led by John Hufnagel. The pass-action plays were thrown mostly to Gary Hayman, a new junior running star; John Cappelletti; and finally to Dan Natale for the touchdown.

Five of the last six opponents in 1971 and 1972 had been from the Southeast (two), Big Ten (two), and Southwest (one) conferences, with the Lions winning from three. Meeting Illinois next at Champaign, they scored a gratifying 21 points in the first quarter, although six turnovers showed continuing erratic play. Owning a 28–10 half-time lead, they coasted to a 35–17 victory over Coach Bob Blackman's second Illinois team, but injuries to Tom Donchez, Carl Cayette (who had played well against Tennessee), and Cappelletti had hurt Coach Paterno's offensive plans. Before Hayman was injured, he had played three different positions.

Michie Stadium no longer seemed so ominous in 1972. "You don't hear the Cadets when you're winning," was Coach Paterno's observation. Unlike the old days, when they were quartered at picturesque Bear Mountain Inn, the official party went by plane for an overnight stay at a Newburgh motel and had a quick bus trip to West Point Saturday morning just in time for the game. Nostalgic Penn Staters may have missed their leisurely Hudson River boat trip or the drive through the beautiful Catskills, yet they probably preferred having their fun at the game, which they did, 45–0. Huffy had one of his greatest days, running the option for 71 yards and throwing 12 completions in 18 attempts for 152 yards. For the second time in two years, Penn State shut out consecutively its two rivals, Army and Syracuse.

When the Lion margin over the Orange was 17–0, the home

crowd began to realize how good it was to have both Hufnagel and Cappelletti in the backfield at the same time. Syracuse sacked Huffy efficiently, holding him to five completions, but Cappy gained 163 yards, enough to win by his own power. Coach Ben Schwartzwalder, paying his final official visit to University Park, refrained from complaints about the officials. He saved his "last hurrah" for later in the season at Pittsburgh, where he implied to reporters, who made the most of the interview, that Penn State and West Virginia were "cheating on the Big Four agreement with respect to recruiting." He didn't indict the Panthers, having beaten them, 10–6. Ben did admit that Penn State recruiters had outdone Syracuse in every case but one on players both teams had sought, but didn't allow that better recruiting methods had anything to do with it.

The West Virginia visit was traumatic, as always. One Lion player commented after the game: "We were given a ten-minute standing boo when we came on the field before we did anything." Both teams as a rule exhibit mutual courtesy, but publicity in and out of Morgantown with a "This Is The Year" theme generally pollutes the atmosphere. This time newspapers statewide played up West Virginia's desire to avenge Penn State's "controversial" victory the previous year, when the Lions had won, 35–7. The coaches parried pregame quotes along these lines:

BOWDEN: Penn State is our team's Number One mission in 1972. The percentage just has to run out on them sometime.
PATERNO: If the percentages are with West Virginia it will be because they have better players this week.
BOWDEN: It will be West Virginia emotion vs. Penn State poise. I'd kind of like more of the poise myself.
PATERNO: Maybe it's poise, but it may be just common sense. Football is a game of concentration. I just don't see how you can concentrate on what you're supposed to do with all that jumping around and yelling.

Penn State's vaunted poise was essential because West Virginian Kerry Marbury returned John Reihner's opening kickoff 101 yards. The frenzied crowd was almost out of hand, and the Mountaineer squad jumping around Marbury (already well spent) almost pounded him into the turf. Penn Staters, who should have built up more confidence by this time (West Virginia hadn't bested the Lions in Morgantown since 1955), were almost afraid to see what might follow.

Coach Paterno's team caught up methodically. Cappelletti

pounded out 158 yards on 34 carries (a record he later broke), while Hufnagel got 64 on the ground and 165 in the air with seven completions, including two touchdowns. Early Lion retaliation was helped by two interceptions and an unusual safety—a typical "mysterious" play in the rivalry—on a punt blocked by John Skorupan. When Ed O'Neil missed the first chance to pick up the ball around the Mountaineer 25, the home team's Danny Buggs, who rarely lost one in the air, accidentally booted it downfield, like a soccer play. As the ball bounded through the end zone, the officials unhesitatingly gave Penn State a safety.

After Cappy's 68-yard punt return to the 2, Bob Nagle slammed into the line and fumbled, setting up another controversial Lion touchdown on Mountaineer Field. The referee awarded West Virginia the ball on the 1, but two other officials ruled that Nagle had crossed the goal line before losing the ball. To the accompaniment of boos, they went on to win the dogfight, 28–19, rescued once more, said the local legions, by luck and the officials.

Staying in high gear for the four final regular-season games, Penn State received its first word of a Sugar Bowl invitation—ten straight victories had dimmed the impact of the Tennessee defeat. The Lions scored early and easily against Maryland after Jimmy Scott's exciting catch on a pass play from Hufnagel that gained 47 yards. Settling down comfortably in Beaver Stadium with the promise of an early lead, veteran fans were startled when Maryland's inventive new coach, Jerry Claiborne, resurrected a play Temple used to advantage against Bob Higgins' Cotton Bowl eleven of the 1947 season. Temple's "setting hen," which Claiborne called "the bumarooski," came about shortly after the kickoff, on third down. The Terps put the ball into play on a short count, and in no time Jamie Franklin streaked down the sideline all by himself. Somehow he was headed off by Gregg Ducatte and Jack Koniszewski, but Maryland had a first down on the 12 and scored from there, setting up a 10–10 half-time tie. Besieged by the press later, Maryland's publicity man said the play was "the Deacon," but wouldn't reveal how Franklin got the ball. Coach Claiborne spoke of "the bumarooski" as a little "ripple" he had devised for a quarterback "slide" to one side and a pitch to the ball carrier. The mystery of the hidden ball was never revealed, and the big lift Claiborne said his team got from it lasted only through the half, for the Lions went on to win, 46–16.

North Carolina State's new coach, Lou Holtz, experienced the effect of having his star freshmen passing combination on the cover of *Sports Illustrated* the week before playing Penn State. The Lions ignored the prestigious pair and won the game, 37–22, with Cappy getting his routine 125 yards and Huffy hitting 10 of 19 for 213 yards.

A few hours after the 45–26 victory over Boston College in Boston, the 26th consecutive triumph for the Lions over the three New England independents (Holy Cross, Boston University, and Boston College), Penn State officials formally accepted the Sugar Bowl invitation for New Year's Eve. The Panthers, still to be played, held no terror for these 1972 Lions, who scored 28 points in the second quarter and enjoyed a comfortable 49–27 victory.

Smarting from a 1–10 season, Pitt announced "unilaterally" before the game its intention to break away from the "mutual agreement" pact with Penn State, West Virginia, and Syracuse. The four institutions in 1962 had arranged not a miniconference but merely to abide by certain standards of recruiting, admissions, and rules limiting grants-in-aid, with a later ban on "red-shirting." Pitt's surprise decision was interpreted to mean that it would not limit grants-in-aid to 25 per season and would resume red-shirting. Rumors also circulated that this would be the last year as coach for alumnus Carl DePasqua. Although never entirely pleased with the pact's results, Penn State declared it would continue to adhere to Big Four standards.

Freshman eligibility for varsity teams was approved by most major college NCAA members, and some Penn State opponents used their freshmen in 1972. Penn State voted against the move, and Coach Paterno continued his opposition until 1974, when Jimmy Cefalo played briefly against Stanford in the opening game and made the varsity toward the end of the season. Paterno continues to work freshmen into the lineup because their widespread use by opponents makes it necessary, particularly as a recruiting asset. In principle, his policy is unchanged, but he no longer contends that too few qualify to make their participation worthwhile. He now believes that his estimate of their potential value was wrong and feels that able Penn State recruits should not be deprived of opportunities available elsewhere.

Three Lions made All-America teams in 1972—John Hufnagel, quarterback; Bruce Bannon, defensive end; and John Skorupan, linebacker. Bannon was picked by the Coaches' Association, UPI, NEA, and three other recognized selectors. The Football Writers'

Association, AP, and NEA named Skorupan, and Hufnagel was a choice of the AP and the Walter Camp Football Foundation. Huffy, recognized by most opponents as the moving force behind Penn State's offense in 1971 and 1972, was also a Heisman candidate. Identified primarily as a strong runner among quarterbacks, he is entered in the Penn State record book for 10 varied passing marks, along with several game, season, and career records for total offense yardage and total number of offensive plays. His contributions account largely for three Penn State team passing records in 1972— most passing yardage in a single game (Pitt, 329) and season (2,195 in 11 games); and most passes completed in a season, 123.

THE SUGAR BOWL,
DECEMBER 31, 1972

The Southern press, and Oklahoma's, did not take kindly to the selection of Penn State. Most felt the Sooners deserved a "higher ranked" opponent. Despite Penn State's success in three major bowl games during the past four years, they continued to consider the Lions unworthy.

A crowd of more than 80,000 attended the New Orleans game, which wasn't the spectacular offensive show it might have been because the heralded confrontation between Greg Pruitt, Oklahoma's All-America, and John Cappelletti didn't come to pass. Cappy, downed by flu and a high temperature the morning of the game, watched the defensive battle on a TV screen. Oklahoma's awesome array of runners—Pruitt, Joe Wright, Leon Crosswhite, and Joe Washington—had Penn State's defense sagging at times, but none broke loose for more than 9 yards, and Pruitt was held to 83 yards in 20 carries, far below his standard.

Penn State was shut out (14–0) for the first time in 68 games by Oklahoma's impressive defense, but the persistent and well-balanced offense of the Sooners was halted within a yard of the Penn State goal line three times on jarring tackles by Gregg Ducatte, Ed O'Neil, and Doug Allen, once so forcibly that the ball shot out of the runner's hands and catapulted all the way through the end zone. Coach Paterno commended his team's performance in a brief analysis of the action:

> Most people didn't understand the character of that game. We were in it until the fumbled punt in the last quarter. All we

needed was one break before that fumble—but they got it and knocked it in for a score. We were never out of the game until then.

The Big Eight champions, ranked second nationally, scored in the second quarter on a 77-yard, 11-play drive culminating from the 27 with a well-executed pass play from quarterback Dave Robertson to freshman Tinker Owens, who was named the game's Most Valuable Player. The second touchdown followed a fumbled punt in the last quarter when Wylie, on the Lion 18, rolled to his right and passed to Owens. He dove for the ball on the 1 and Crosswhite plunged over, but the pass was controversial. The press box PA announcer said the TV replay indicated Owens had caught the pass on a bounce, and it was so reported in the two New Orleans papers. The official who called it ignored the protest of Gregg Ducatte, nearest to the play.

In postgame interviews, Coach Paterno wouldn't discuss the protested play, merely saying he couldn't see what happened, and mentioned Cappelletti's illness reluctantly, not as an excuse for defeat. Cappy, who had gained 1,117 yards during the regular season, was sorely missed, and his replacement, Walt Addie, reinjured his ankle after a few plays. Having to move Gary Hayman to tailback upset another part of the game plan. Fearing the strength of the Sooners' line, Paterno planned to open it up by passing to Hayman as the flanker back. The unexpected move also negated use of a planned option series, which hadn't been timed out with Hayman at tailback. Dejected Penn Staters saw the New Year in, returning to their hotels by bus. Singing "Auld Lang Syne" and "Hail to the Lion," they managed to temper disappointment with pride in the Nittany Lions who had battled doggedly in spite of a jarring, unforeseen handicap.

Oklahoma athletic authorities announced not long after the game that two ineligible players (freshmen) had been used, and complied with the subsequent NCAA ruling on the case. Oklahoma was placed on two-year probation, charged with illegal recruiting, and was required to forfeit all games in which the players were used, including the Sugar Bowl. Coach Paterno was asked for his comment.

It's a shame a great effort by an Oklahoma football team has to be marred by an inexcusable recruitment violation such as this incident. However, our players and the Oklahoma players know who won the game. Perhaps the irony is that if freshmen were not allowed to participate, recruiting irregularities would have come to light before their participation caused another embarrassing situation for intercollegiate athletics.

The Sugar Bowl Committee officially lists Penn State as the winner in its annual brochures. Penn State's official records and media press guides show Oklahoma as the winner.

Few coaches in these days of tough 10- or 11-game schedules, transcontinental rivalries, and bowl battles, could match Joe Paterno's record at the end of the 1972 season. His team had lost only six times in the past five years and won three of four major bowl games (50–6–0).

Paterno's career, starting in 1950 as a preliminary to law school, had stretched to 23 years, seven as head coach. The tireless drive and ingenuity of the still-young coach, whose personality almost demanded attention from the news media, had been noticed by several professional teams, but only one offer had tempted him. Following his team's defeat by Oklahoma, he faced, however, the most important decision of his professional life.

The New England Patriots launched an all-out effort to lure Paterno away from college football. William H. Sullivan, Jr., then Patriot president and a founder of the American Football League, met the Lion coach "secretly" in New Orleans at the Royal Sonesta Hotel, which happened to be Penn State alumni headquarters for the Sugar Bowl weekend. Many alumni spoke of seeing Paterno with a "stranger," but a few recognized Sullivan, and before the curious Penn Staters arrived back home, rumors had become news stories. The Patriot president had indeed made Coach Paterno an offer that "exceeded a million dollars."

Boston newspapers, TV, and radio gave in-depth coverage to New England's hottest sports story. A Penn State alumna from State College, teaching high school history in suburban Boston, realized that her class was talking about the reported offer and made it a current-events discussion ending in a vote: Would Joe Paterno accept? The class agreed unanimously that no man could refuse such money to coach football, but the teacher voted that he would stay.

After a week of agonizing, the Lion football coach announced at a press conference in Recreation Building on Saturday morning, January 6, 1973, with university president John Oswald present, that he would remain at Penn State. He had turned down, said newspaper accounts, the most lucrative financial inducement ever made by a professional team for a head coach—a six-year contract worth 1¼ million dollars, plus an unspecified amount of stock in the club, an offer that would have meant lifetime financial security for the Paternos and their five children.

The high school teacher read her Boston Saturday afternoon paper with a glow of satisfaction. She could hardly wait to meet her class Monday, knowing her students would ask what there was about the man and this university, which had little identity for them, that had made her so sure he would reach this improbable choice.

Coach Paterno's announcement answered some of the questions besides giving the teacher and thousands of other alumni added pride in their alma mater and respect for the character of Joe Paterno. In the media, sated with reports of warped values in government and business, it touched off a spark of approbation for one man's decision to place financial opportunity beneath benefits more consequential to himself and his growing family. Joe said:

> I've always hoped to be able to work in an atmosphere where the approach by the administration toward athletics was such that I can be more than a coach. That's what Penn State has allowed me to be. The overriding factor in my decision was my realization that I enjoy working with young people and having an influence over their lives. I also feel there is still a challenge here for me. When I walked off the Sugar Bowl field after getting a good licking, I felt as if we still had a lot to accomplish.

Dr. Oswald expressed his delight, calling Joe an "acknowledged outstanding coach" and pointing out that football was very much a part of the educational thrust of the university. "There is no doubt," Dr. Oswald said, "about Coach Paterno's ability to coach and to exert a wholesome influence on young people. We are delighted that the Paterno family has decided to remain in our community."

During his struggle to resolve the question and the days of relief after he had, Joe often thought of a favorite poem by Robert Frost, *The Road Not Taken:*

> . . . I shall be telling this with a sigh
> Somewhere ages and ages hence:
> Two roads diverged in a wood, and I—
> I took the one less traveled by,
> And that has made all the difference.

Five months later, in the Commencement address June graduates had asked him to deliver, Coach Paterno was even more explicit about his feelings:

> I accepted [the invitation to speak] because of the realization that in a day when materialism is rampant many of you felt that my interest in doing other things besides making money has in some way helped you to reaffirm your ideal of a life of service, of dignity, and a life of meaning, which goes beyond financial success.

When he mentioned the term "Grand Experiment" in a newspaper interview, he wasn't thinking of a crusade, nor did he realize how constantly it would be used to describe his personal philosophy in coaching intercollegiate football and his ambition to reach definite goals at Penn State under *certain conditions*. Never among those who think "winning is everything," he has wanted success because he believes the drive toward winning is important. His obsession is that success ultimately must come within a framework of honesty and respectability without concessions in academic quality. And that's the pattern for Penn State recruiting.

> We want our players to enjoy football. We want them to enjoy college. We want them to learn about art and literature and music and all the other things college has to offer. College should be the greatest time in life; it is the only time a person is really free. We don't want our players just tied to a football program.

Long before freshmen became eligible for varsity football, Penn State subordinated its freshman program; at one time in the early sixties a yearling game had to be canceled because there weren't enough players to field a full team. Coach Paterno is utterly opposed to a "football dormitory," preferring to have his players in campus residence halls and fraternities, participating in campus life as much as time permits. This is the Grand Experiment.

The appeal of such an approach to the kind of player Penn State coaches seek is evident from their academic progress in varied curricula. The 47 football letter-winners in 1974 were distributed in nearly all colleges of the university, and only three had a cumulative average below the 2.00 required for graduation. More than 90 per cent of all football lettermen graduate—a record surpassed by few universities with major football programs.

Since 1966, seven Penn State varsity players have received NCAA postgraduate scholarship awards, requiring at least a "B" average (3.00 in Penn State's grade system). They were Joe Bellas '66, CPA with Price Waterhouse & Company; John Runnells '67, an attorney in New York City; Bob Holuba '71, graduate of the University of Virginia Law School; Dave Joyner '72, a graduate of Penn State's Hershey Medical School; Bruce Bannon '72, pursuing his career in geological science; Mark Markovich '74, who attended graduate school at San Diego State while playing for the Chargers; and Jack Baiorunos '75, studying in the Boston University Dental School. Both Bannon (whose Penn State cumulative average was 3.91) and Baiorunos were selected by the NCAA among the nation's top five student-athletes. In the past five years Joyner, Bannon, Markovich, and Baiorunos have been recipients of $1,000 graduate fellowships awarded annually on a nationwide basis to a dozen players by the National Football Foundation.

Coach Paterno has faith that this program can keep Penn State among the nation's best in football year after year and eventually take it to the very top. He is acutely sensitive to his place in Penn State's football history. "We are all part of a great tradition. We have a responsibility to carry on that tradition."

Sometimes Paterno's candor and vigorous actions are questioned by his peers, who may be less committed to the kind of reforms the Penn State coach advocates for football survival. He clings to the belief, for instance, that varsity football for most freshmen could be harmful to their overall best interests and would prefer limiting a varsity career to three years. He thinks the NCAA is remiss in enforcing recruiting regulations; and he believes that drastic reduction of grants-in-aid is the one way to the economy everyone agrees is overdue.

44

12–0 and the Paterno Poll

Turning down the Patriot offer increased speaking demands on Joe Paterno far beyond those every important coach expects from high school banquets, service clubs, and booster organizations. The Lion coach also accepted invitations from national management and professional groups, seeking him for his combination of career success and inspirational sense of values.

Editorial writers and sports columnists from all directions checked out the much-publicized Paterno philosophy by phone or in person, sometimes with irritating questions. The wary avoided those that could backfire, because Paterno is quick and sometimes stings with the answering quip. One writer of some renown asked:

"Is it true, Mr. Paterno, that you said no man is worth a million dollars?"

"No, I didn't say that. I said no football coach is worth a million dollars. Of course, some sportswriters are."

Given the right place, Paterno had the light touch. He liked to come to the podium after the introduction, slowly turn in a full circle, and say, "Just wanted everybody to see what that jackass who turned down a million looks like." At an alumni meeting not long after the Sugar Bowl downfall, he was asked if plans for enlarging Beaver Stadium included an upper deck. "Well," he replied, "I'm opposed to it. Coaches who lose games often get hung from high places."

An inevitable event following such nationwide attention was an all-Pennsylvania "Joe Paterno Day" held in centrally located Camp Hill, near Harrisburg. It was masterminded by the Reverend Elton P. Richards, Jr., of Reading, a nonalumnus but long-time Paterno admirer, with the co-operation of Penn State alumni in the area. The congregation of the Reverend Mr. Richards discovered his allegiance when he lettered on the church bulletin board, before the Cotton Bowl in 1972, "God Is Impartial. But some Ministers Are Not. Go Penn State!" And before the Sugar Bowl: "Now Is the Time for All Christians to Root for the Lions. Go Penn State!" Nearly everyone who had touched the life of Joe Paterno attended the dinner, including his Brooklyn high school coach and friends, Brown University teammates and fraternity brothers, President Oswald and others from Penn State, former Lion players, state officials, and garden-variety fans. As a climax, the Paternos were given a check for a vacation trip to Italy "whenever they could go." They got off more than a year later.

Joe Paterno's rapport with the average student has always been good and his *Daily Collegian* "press" far better, in general, than that accorded university administrators. Students at a midwinter basketball game gave him a round of applause when they spotted him in the balcony at half-time intermission as he stood to go out. Joe turned, waved, and departed down a ramp, but said to friends that he was a little embarrassed since he was only going to the men's room. He never had reports that any football players participated in the student uprisings of the late sixties—they were more likely to have been among the disinterested majority or the opposition "squares."

The head football coach was Phi Beta Kappa's guest speaker for its spring 1973 initiation banquet, but he was even more surprised when Dr. Oswald informed him that a senior class committee had voted unanimously to invite him to be the June Commencement speaker. The largest of Penn State's four annual commencements, with an audience in the neighborhood of 30,000, is held in Beaver Stadium, weather permitting. For Joe, the setting was familiar, but not the costume of academic cap and gown. On the sideline at games, he goes hatless and wears white athletic socks with flashy slacks. In mild weather, sports jacket or sweater, if worn, is removed early in the first quarter.

Surely among the few football coaches to speak at a major university commencement, he was guiltless of the clichés usually addressed to graduates and their families. His view of the nation's troubles and need for unity was frank and uninhibited, and he didn't hesitate to cite football as a unifying influence, saying the nation and football can survive with honor and success if individual ambitions are joined for action together. He spoke with some emotion about how grown men, huddled in a locker room before a game, reach out and become part of each other as a team. "They lose themselves in something bigger than they are," said Paterno.

> I cannot describe to you the love that permeates a good football team—a love of one another. Perhaps, as one of my players said, "We grow together in love—hating the coach."

Promising he'd be the year's only commencement speaker who wouldn't expound on the nation's painful scandal, he couldn't resist wondering how the President who knew so much about college football in 1969 could have known so little about Watergate in 1973. The coach noted that our forefathers could have blind faith in America because they had no obligations to the world and had only to do what was best for the new nation. Cautioning the graduates not to have a "blind spot" about our government and institutions, he stressed viewing them with patience and understanding, the signs of maturity.

> In my game people talk about offensive formations as the cure-all. Believe me, it isn't the plays or the offensive formations that do the job. It's the quality of the players. . . . [The players] make the organization work or become its victims. . . . Don't look for touchdowns all the time; think about hitting in there tough, play after play, and then the big play will present itself.
>   . . . Now we cannot morally escape our responsibility to the rest of the world, can never do what is right only for America. . . . We must be mature enough to admit that we didn't win in Vietnam, that we really didn't have peace with honor, that we can't force all citizens to love each other—only then can we stop tearing each other apart. Our country, right or wrong. Yes, but love her enough, respect her enough that when she is wrong, we stand bigger for admitting it.

Commencement mornings are traumatic for university officials who have to know about the weather, minute by minute. Elaborate planning the week before permits moving the ceremonies indoors to several locations via closed circuit TV, but with 4,650 degree recipients and their families and friends to consider, officials took a chance —a Paterno-like chance—in spite of uncertain reports from the university weather station.

The warm rains came while the speaker was in full cry. Paterno stoically clutched his damp manuscript and didn't miss a line. He holds that when games have to be played under adverse conditions, the good team adjusts and survives; he was accustomed to ignoring the elements on this very field. President Oswald and the university marshal curtailed the formal ceremonies, and if the new graduates were too drenched to catch the meaning of all the speaker's words, what they missed could be absorbed from its wide coverage in newspapers and periodicals. *Sports Illustrated* used more than a column.

Joe Paterno's coaching methods—the sharp criticism, relentless absorption in preparing for *Saturday's* game, the way he drives himself and all around him—preclude his becoming the type of coach who is "loved by his boys," nor does he work to that end. Players respect him as a coach they can depend on to make sound decisions in their best interests, keeps cool under pressure, and who is always fair. Penn Staters now in the pros know they were well coached by Paterno and his able staff. His "itch to switch," as one magazine writer called it, his constant shifts to strengthen the team, which could cause contention, are among his coaching assets. Quarterbacks, often the best and most versatile recruits, are likely to wind up as cornerbacks, linebackers, or safeties. The "switched" players eventually realize they are well adapted and can see more action on Saturdays.

Coach Paterno's decision to stay in college football had an indirect impact on his players. Charlie Getty, offensive tackle (now with the Kansas City Chiefs), turned down a $1,500 Senior Bowl offer after the 1973 season because he felt an obligation to the wrestling team that winter. (He won the eastern intercollegiate heavyweight title.) John Cappelletti, the 1973 Heisman winner, rejected one pro offer and accepted less money to be with the Los Angeles Rams because he felt their environment was more congenial, "like a family."

The winter excitement of '73 didn't divert Coach Paterno from his pursuit of Penn State's recognition as the Number One team in the nation. In five of his seven years as coach, the Lions were "eastern champions" (Lambert Trophy winners). Syracuse and Dartmouth took the trophy in 1966 and 1970, the only years Paterno's teams failed to make the national "Top Ten." Penn State ranked as high as second in 1968 and 1969 and fifth in 1971. National honors had gone to Ohio State in 1968 after the Buckeyes' victory over Southern California, 28–16, and to Texas in 1969 when the Longhorns won from Arkansas in December and defeated Notre Dame in the anti-climax Cotton Bowl. National champions crowned by the Associated Press, *after* bowl games, had been Notre Dame (1966), Southern California (1967), Nebraska (1970, 1971), and Southern California (1972). Notre Dame, feeling the economic pinch, became a prime bowl contender each year after 1968. Heisman winners of 1966 through 1972 were Steve Spurrier, Florida; Gary Beban, UCLA; O. J. Simpson, Southern California; Steve Owens, Oklahoma; Jim Plunkett, Stanford; Pat Sullivan, Auburn; and Johnny Rodgers, Nebraska.

Coach Paterno made no rating claims in 1972, but he was building for the next season without launching an open crusade. An undercurrent of optimism pervaded his guarded preseason remarks to the press, and one encouraging aspect was the probability of less "soft schedule" flak in the media. Penn State would open at Stanford (on national TV), later meeting the Air Force Academy in Colorado (regionally televised). Maryland and North Carolina State were expected to be bowl contenders (and were) in the Atlantic Coast Conference, and Pitt was due for a resurgence under its new coach, Johnny Majors.

A hindsight look at the 1973 preseason depth chart shows a team with the potential of a winner, the kind able to avoid the big mistakes that lose games, gifted with a fine kicking and passing game, good receivers, a stalwart defense, and powerful, consistent running featuring John Cappelletti as the "iron man." After spring practice, fans wondered if Tom Shuman could adequately replace John Hufnagel at quarterback, but Coach Paterno had full confidence in him. The only significant worry was the availability of senior tackle Randy Crowder, who had a doubtful knee. Randy's aggressive stability put him in the Reid-Smear class, and junior tackle Mike Hartenstine wasn't far behind.

On the offense list Cappelletti, Natale, Getty, Markovich, Hayman, LaPorta, Baiorunos, Nessel, Shuman, Nagle, and Scott led the way;

with Donchez, Petchel, Herd, Addie, Eaise, Barvinchak, Rafferty, Masella, and Bland in the wings. On defense, the first team had Hager, Graf, Hartenstine, Murphy, Devlin, Tom Hull, O'Neil, Allen, Ellis, Koniszewski, and Bradley, with backups like Quinn, Tesner, Rosecrans, Johnson, Buttle, Orsini, Kriston, Odell, Hite, and Mitchell. Bahr, Reihner, and Masella were there to do the kicking. Crowder, who had a great junior season, wasn't even listed as a "possible" in the early lineups because of his knee. In this group were eight All-Americas (1973, 1974 and 1975), and many who were drafted and are playing for the pros.

A summer disappointment was the departure of George Welsh, former Navy quarterback who had been an assistant coach for ten years, to become head coach at the Naval Academy. Two former Lion players, Dick Anderson '63 and Fran Ganter '71, joined the staff. Anderson, who had coached with Harry Gamble at Lafayette and later at Pennsylvania, coaches the offensive line. Ganter, fullback on the squad three years, was a graduate assistant until he replaced John Chuckran as junior varsity coach in 1973.

An estimated 3,000 alumni, more than had ever assembled on the West Coast, were on hand to see Penn State defeat Stanford, 20–6, in the nationally-televised opener at Palo Alto. The Californians' Mike Boryla, among the nation's best passers in 1972, gave the defense some trouble, completing 17 of 29, but most of his passes were harmless. After a shaky start, Tom Shuman made a heartening debut with 11 completions in 18 attempts for 117 yards and a touchdown. On the same afternoon Pitt's young team, recruited nationally for the Panther revival, tied Georgia 7–7 at Athens, and West Virginia overcame Maryland in the last 9 seconds, setting the stage for the three-cornered rivalry billed as the championship of Routes 22 and 19. The mythical Coal Bucket trophy, a fixture at Penn State for years, at last seemed in line to travel.

After the Lions defeated the Middies 39–0 without trying too hard, Penn Staters at Annapolis observed the meeting of the coaches at center field with keen interest, knowing of the strong friendship existing betwen Joe Paterno and George Welsh. Before the two men could get together, their squads surrounded them—Welsh had been exceedingly popular with Penn State's players. Photographers were trying to extricate the two coaches when Navy's Band struck up "The Navy Blue and Gold." As the Academy players came to attention, Penn State gridders stood beside them, helmets in hand, not moving a muscle. The sight made even doubters in the crowd feel good about young people and especially college football players. When Sandra Welsh greeted her friend Sue Paterno on the sideline, Sue burst into tears.

A Skylab I astronaut, Captain Paul J. Weitz '54 (on campus as an Alumni Fellow), and 60,000 other alumni Homecomers saw Penn State take all the real competition out of the Iowa game by scoring 21 points in the first quarter The weather was miserable at Beaver Stadium, which ordinarily affords all the fringe benefits of autumnal football rites in beautiful mountainous country with plenty of tailgating room, but most of the crowd, with polite respect for the players, remained to the close of the one-sided game. (Two Penn Staters at other places had impressive opening games as coaches that afternoon —Bill Bowes '68, coach at New Hampshire, won from Dartmouth; and Joe Yukica '53, of Boston College, upset Texas A&M in Texas.)

Remembering the 1970 Colorado disaster 50 miles away at Boulder, Lion partisans were gratified to have a weapon like John Cappelletti against the Air Force Academy, juiced up for its Homecoming game. Cappy's 188 yards were nearly three times as much as the whole Falcon force made on the ground. The Cadets were expected to excel in the air with Rich Haynie, their star passer, but Tom Shuman outshot him, 12 of 20 to 12 of 28.

The Lions won a good game, 19–9, although they had to come back from a 3–0 deficit in the first quarter—a slight touch of the adversity Coach Paterno says is necessary to prove a team's greatness. The Air Force Cadets displayed all the pomp and ceremony of the West Pointers or Midshipmen, except that the government has to *bus* them to the stadium for their pregame show, so broad is the plateau near Colorado Springs where the Academy grounds are surrounded by the majestic Rockies.

In spite of the earlier Colorado experience, Coach Paterno is unconvinced that the "thin air" in high altitudes is hard on visiting teams—on a distance runner, maybe, but not on a football player. Contending it's largely a psychological hangup, he refused to take his squad to Colorado a day in advance. He had reluctantly scheduled a Friday afternoon practice at the stadium to get accustomed to the tricky air currents and wind, but canceled it at the last minute in favor of a scenic tour.

Why college football scheduling must be done at least ten years in advance is a mystery to the layman. This game was the third in a series of three that were played over a twelve-year period (1962, 1971, 1973). Each was closely competitive, the players seemed to share mutual respect, official relations were friendly, and Coaches Martin and Paterno regard each other as worthy adversaries, yet no future games are scheduled (as of 1976). Since University Park airport facilities have been improved, perhaps the generals won't mind flying in here.

From Addie to Zur, Coach Paterno used everyone on the squad to score a second "triple" over the three service academies in what might appear to have been a ruthless attack on Army (54–3). John Cappelletti, who averaged 25 carries and 121 yards per contest in his first five games, continued to lead the ground attack, with 151 yards. Rumors abounded that he'd be a Heisman candidate, but Lionites were dubious about an eastern player's chances.

Coach Paterno had difficulty making anyone understand that injuries might cause problems at Syracuse. Cappy had hurt his shoulder in practice, and Walt Addie, his Number One replacement, had come down with suspected mononucleosis. The team fortunately was well stocked with tailbacks. Sophomore Woody Petchel, leading high school scorer in Pennsylvania two years back, started and was about to score a touchdown when his knee was badly damaged. He was later operated on for torn ligaments and was out for the season. In came sophomore Rusty Boyle, promoted suddenly from Number Four to Number One, to play most of the game, with some help from Duane Taylor, a freshman and tailback Number Five. Taylor's touchdown was the first made by a freshman since Jesse Arnelle's against Pitt in 1951. He also contributed to another when he gained 12 yards, fumbled on the 20, and Dan Natale picked up the loose ball for an 80-yard scoring dash.

Holding to Syracuse tradition, the incident caused some press box discussion after newsmen heard that the Syracuse Radio Network announcer said, "Anybody knows you can't run with a fumble." Apparently he didn't know that "anyone" on the offensive team can run with a teammate's fumble. Still, the uprising was minimal at Coach Ben Schwartzwalder's last Penn State game, which his hated adversaries won, 49–6. The game at Syracuse, poorly attended for a Penn State visit, was Homecoming for alumni, whose reaction to the rain of touchdowns can be guessed. Their criticism was unfair if it was directed against Coach Ben. Outspoken, cantankerous at times, and often undiplomatic, his contributions to football, nevertheless, had been significant. Only critics with short memories forget his rugged and well-coached teams and some of his brilliant stars. He didn't believe in fancy football—plain power was his forte. The last years before his retirement were darkened by inadequate administrative support, but he ended his coaching career with personal dignity, no complaints, and the respect of his peers.

The Syracuse Marching Band tried to save the day for the Orange by outdoing the famous Blue Band during their half-time encounter. At the Orange Band practice Friday afternoon, its director was heard delivering this pep talk: "Look, gang, they have a hell of a band, 200 strong, with a lot of brass, but from the horns down, we got 'em licked." The game had special meaning for one Lion coach—it was Penn State's 200th victory since defensive coach Jim O'Hora was appointed by Bob Higgins in 1946.

Against West Virginia, Cappy was back with a vengeance. The key to his effectiveness was great balance and a kind of "quiet power." Not the explosive type, and without blinding speed, he could run in a formidable fashion, and he could cut, always for vital yards. As Mark Markovich remarked, "We knock people down, and when they get up, Cappy comes by and knocks them down again." Penn State next faced a real challenge at Maryland. The Lions took charge when Gary Hayman scored on the opening kickoff (98 yards), and a minute later Bob Nagle tallied a second touchdown, three plays after Greg Buttle recovered Chris Bahr's kickoff which Maryland fumbled. Apparently the scores came too easily. Trailing 14–0, the Marylanders fought back and tied the score 22–22 at half time to the huge delight of a near-record crowd in Byrd Stadium.

Coach Jerry Claiborne yearned to defeat Penn State, something the Terps hadn't accomplished in twelve years. He resisted trying the "bumarooski" again, but he had tailbacks and wingbacks throwing passes, installed a shotgun offense for one series, used the flea flicker, and once had a kickoff receiver flip the ball backward to a receiver who lateraled across the field to a teammate. The play backfired, and Penn State scored 20 points in the third period to win, 42–22.

The North Carolina State game has been called one of the greatest ever seen in Beaver Stadium, packed to a 59,424 capacity. Behind at the half 14–9, the Lions had to overcome the adversity Coach Paterno so frequently said they needed. The Wolfpack made the mistake Maryland had the week before when Cappy carried the ball. Instead of going after the solid-legged halfback, they pursued the ball. His total yardage in the two games was 422 (202 and 220) against defenses that were keyed on him. He set a Penn State record of 41 carries against the Wolfpack and averaged 26 carries in each of 11 games of the 1973 season. Actually, his average was 28.6 in 10 games—he had played only the first three downs against Syracuse, where he was used as a decoy. Cappy also holds the career record for carries with 519.

At the end of the third quarter, the two teams were locked at 22–22, but the Wolfpack wasn't about to fold, as Maryland had. Hayman's 83-yard punt return had put the Lions ahead, 22–14, until Stan Fritts evened the score again. Nagle's burst up the middle for 10 yards gave the Lions another lead, 29–22, when Bahr kicked the extra point. The game was tied once more, 29–29, in 2 minutes when Charlie Young ran 69 yards and Ron Sewell place-kicked the goal.

Six plays and 2 minutes later, almost entirely due to Cappy's power running, the home team went ahead to stay. John made his winning touchdown from the 27, but the excitement wasn't over, and every play was crucial. The Wolfpack had reached the Lion 40 with 54 seconds left, when Don Buckey raced for a goal-post position and his twin brother, Dave, let a desperation pass fly through the air. The ball was nearly caught but had been thrown against the wind. To the relief of Jim Bradley, the Lion defender slightly in front of the receiver, it fell short and rolled across the field.

Bowl commotion accompanied the two final games. The Ohio University meeting was a background for Penn State's acceptance of its third Orange Bowl bid in six years and also a warmup for the Pitt game, yet to come at University Park, which had the committee in a dither because the Lions were facing a dangerous opponent. Likewise, LSU, chosen to represent the strong Southeastern Conference, still had to play Alabama and Tulane, while the Sugar Bowl and the ABC-TV network were openly angling for a Notre Dame-Alabama meeting to determine the "national championship." With no one willing or able to do anything about early "informal" invitations, the NCAA edict that none could be issued before November 17 at 6 P.M. was laughable, and the situation was out of control. Bowl committees had too much at stake, and there were "leaks" at least two weeks before the legal date—as soon, in fact, as Coach Bear Bryant of Alabama decided where he wanted to play.

Confidence, mingled with bitterness and jealousy in the Pitt camp over Penn State's 10–0 record and Orange Bowl bid, made this a tricky assignment for the Lions. Panther followers had justifiable pride in Coach Johnny Majors' first-year mark of 6–3–1 up to the Lion engagement, a record earning a date against Arizona State in the Fiesta Bowl (where Pitt lost, 28–7).

Tony Dorsett—the first Pitt freshman to make All-America and the greatest freshman ground-gainer (1,596 yards) in major college history—was checked by the staunch Lion defense. Held to twenty running plays (5 in each quarter), Dorsett gained a net of 77 yards, lost yardage on five of his plays, and actually had only two of any consequence—his early touchdown run of 14 yards, and a late gain of 17 while Penn State was in a prevent defense and had the game well in hand. The Lions also had to contend with a dangerous option quarterback in Bill Daniels.

Sparks flew when the Panthers took a 13–3 half-time lead on Dorsett's touchdown and two field goals by Carson Long. The freshman kicking specialist, after booting a 50-yarder on the last play of the half, turned toward the Penn State bench and raised his arm, fist clenched in triumph. As if this were a signal, the entire Pitt squad poured onto the field, surrounding the 18-year-old Long, one of the prizes Majors had acquired for his first Pitt team. Penn State fans expected the Panthers to carry Coach Majors off the field, and the Lion players contemplated the premature celebration soberly as they ran to their dressing room.

Pitt had indeed celebrated too quickly. The Panthers bravely struggled in the third quarter and still led going into the fourth, 13–11, but Cappy more than doubled Dorsett's output, and Penn State scored three touchdowns and a field goal in the final period for a 35–13 victory and another undefeated season.

"Is this 1973 team your best at Penn State?" was the first question asked Coach Paterno after the game. "It's as good as any," was the reply, "but we'll have to prove it in Florida."

Records, honors, and awards made news from the season's close until bowl time. In 1973 Penn State outdid itself. Individual records were set by wide receivers Chuck Herd and Gary Hayman as well as by flanker back Jimmy Scott. Hayman's 442 yards for punt returns and his 19.2 average were national highs and are still Penn State rec-

ords (as of 1976). Herd's distinction was his total career touchdowns (10) by pass receiving; Scott's was a 30.7-yard average per
reception for every pass caught during his 1971–73 career. In addition to these 1973 receiving marks, Penn State established an all-
time team record of 643 rushing plays for one season, largely because of the endurance and dependability of John Cappelletti. These
still stand.

The big halfback, only Penn Stater to go over 1,000 yards by
rushing in two consecutive seasons, had a two-year career mark of
2,639 yards, which has been exceeded only by Lydell Mitchell's
three-year output of 2,934 yards.

All-America laurels went to Cappelletti, offensive halfback on
eight major teams; Ed O'Neil, linebacker choice of three; and Randy
Crowder, defensive tackle on two. Cappy, who played only two seasons as an offensive back, was the first Heisman Trophy winner from
a Pennsylvania college. He also earned the Maxwell Award as the
best college player in America, thus topping all Lion players by winning both honors. In some quarters, the esteemed Heisman award,
established in 1935, was played down for lack of real competition.
Cappy had 229 first-place votes and 1,057 points; runner-up John
Hicks, Ohio State offensive tackle, had 114 votes and 524 points;
and Roosevelt Leeks of Texas was third, with 74 and 482. Coach
Joe Paterno turned to an essay by Cardinal Newman to describe his
distinguished player:

> You look up that essay and I think you'll find all the charac-
> teristics of John Cappelletti—consideration, humility, placing
> God before himself. . . . We've gotten away in this country
> from the idea of respect for authority, but John got that respect
> from his family and his schools and he brought it with him to
> Penn State. He's quiet . . . not a loudmouth . . . he has lead-
> ership built into him. He has commitment to principles . . . he
> won't submit to peer influence. Kids like Cappy uplift your
> whole program.

The prestigious 39th annual Heisman Award Dinner, a function of
the Downtown Athletic Club of New York, brought 4,000 persons
(at $50 a plate) to the New York Hilton's Grand Ballroom on De-
cember 13. Socialites, the sports crowd, 21 former Heisman winners,
Penn State President Jack Oswald and other university representatives, state and national political leaders, and sportswriters set-

tled down for the usual long program and principal address by the newly appointed Vice President of the United States, former House Minority Leader Gerald R. Ford. But John Cappelletti and his Upper Darby family—parents, three brothers, and a sister—made the 1973 Heisman Dinner an occasion to remember.

Cappy began his acceptance remarks with personal tributes to those who had helped him along the way. Then he said that someone present deserved the award more than he did—his 11-year-old-brother, Joey:

> I'd like to dedicate this trophy to the many who have touched my life and helped me, but especially to the youngest member of my family, Joseph, who is very ill. He has leukemia. If I could dedicate it to him tonight and give him a couple of days of happiness, it would mean everything to him. For me, it's a battle on the field and only in the fall. For Joseph, it's all year round. I think this trophy is more his than it is mine, because of the inspiration he has been to me.[1]

When he finished, he and his hearers were in tears, and unashamed. The master of ceremonies acknowledged his words with an accolade in the vernacular: "John Cappelletti, you're something else!" Archbishop Fulton J. Sheen, who was to give the benediction, deftly put the situation in perspective:

> Maybe for the first time in your lives you have heard a speech from the heart and not from the lips. Part of John's triumph was made by Joseph's sorrow. You don't need a blessing. God has already blessed you in John Cappelletti.

THE ORANGE BOWL, JANUARY 1, 1974

Louisiana State's upset by Tulane lessened the glamor of the New Year's night bowl, and the media concentrated instead on the Rose Bowl meeting of Ohio State and Southern California along with the Alabama-Notre Dame battle in the Sugar Bowl. ABC's broadcasting twosome, Chris Schenkel and Bud Wilkinson, ignored Penn State's 11–0 record at the National Foundation's Hall of Fame Dinner in December, boosting instead their network's Sugar Bowl "national championship" game. Cappelletti received a perfunctory introduction.

---

[1] Joey died April 8, 1976. The Cappelletti story was done on television in 1977.

Penn State and Orange Bowl officials met in Recreation Building's football lounge the night of November 16 for the formalities. Coach Paterno chatted on a conference phone call with LSU's Charlie McClendon in New Orleans and newspapermen in Miami, during which one writer wondered what Joe thought of Bear Bryant's statement that he disliked the Orange Bowl because Miami had too many distractions. Joe said he'd liked those distractions when he was young, and he wanted his players to enjoy themselves because they had enough character to do their job on the field. The 1968 and 1969 squads, he recalled, had a good time in Miami and played "pretty well."

Displaying their "Back the Lions" regalia, the 14,000 Penn State devotees added welcome color to the Orange Bowl pageantry, which acquired little luster from the game itself. Cappelletti's bowl bad luck continued—kept out of the Sugar Bowl the year before by the flu, now he had injured his ankle prior to the game and could muster little power on the slippery turf. The injury was a well-kept secret and was not used to explain his low yardage (50). Paterno said, "Cappy was great—he made some fine plays for us when they counted," and gave LSU full credit for placing its linebackers up so tight that Penn State's greatest weapon was neutralized.

Shocked Lion fans watched LSU take the opening kickoff and boom-boom-boom down the field on sheer power with no spectacular plays. Later Coach Paterno explained that his defense had been slow to adjust to the quick-starting LSU backs. When the moment of truth arrived, they were able to hit their own pace and the kind of super-defense performance they had produced all season. Brad Davis, a hero against Alabama with 143 yards, accounted for 39 of his team's 51 yards in the early drive, but was held to 33 yards for the remainder of the game.

Chris Bahr's 44-yard field goal (an Orange Bowl record) in the opening quarter encouraged Lionites, who were even happier with the sudden go-ahead big play in the second. Chuck Herd, denied a touchdown a short time before on a controversial play, made the most remarkable catch of his career. Eluding his defender, Dale Congelose, by a few yards, he caught Tom Shuman's pass on the fingertips of one hand before somehow getting his other hand on the ball at the Tiger 35. It was a touchdown pass covering 72 yards.

Miami writers in general were slow to appreciate the classic defensive battle that followed—some even found the game less interesting than the half-time show celebrating Mickey Mouse's birthday. Others thought if two official "calls" against Penn State had been favorable, the game might have been a great "spectacular" in Orange Bowl history. Coach Paterno didn't apologize for his "play safe" tactics after pulling ahead of an explosive team in a bowl game:

> As long as we are playing well defensively—and we were—I saw no reason to try a lot of fancy things. We waited for a break and finally got one. That's the way we always play. We were ahead and could have done other things, but it seemed best to let them take the chances—if they were able to get the ball.

Following the "bomb" to Herd came the "break"—a 35-yard punt return by Gary Hayman to the Tiger 35 and then the bruising drive by Cappy, Bob Nagle, and Shuman, with Cappy finally going over a goal-line pileup for a score to post a 16–7 half-time lead. In the second half, Penn State gave up a safety on a bad center pass that missed Brian Masella, but the ball was recovered in the end zone. The Tiger offense, which had outrushed Alabama (212–191) and out-first-downed the Crimson Tide (21–12), was unable to score another point.

TV replays seemed to confirm claims of Penn State players to two other touchdowns that were disallowed in the first half. A 35-yard pass from Shuman to Herd deep in the end zone was called out of bounds, but he appeared to have one foot in when he caught the ball. The other frustration occurred when Hayman caught an LSU punt, slipped on the tricky Polyturf, regained his footing, and ran 72 yards for a score. The play was recalled. "My elbow was on the ground," Gary insisted, "but I remember pressing up so my knees wouldn't touch, and they didn't." Defense won the game, stopping the Bengal Tigers on the Lion 5 at the end of the first half, and never letting them get any closer to score. Quarterback Tom Shuman was named the outstanding offensive player, and tackle Randy Crowder won the honor for defense.

Elated by their 12–0 season and bowl victory over a respected opponent (LSU had played in nineteen bowl games since 1937), some Lion players were annoyed by their "also-ran" treatment in official national polls, which generally harked back to the argument that

Penn State's schedule was "suspect." Again not out of line with most
of the top ten contenders, State's 1973 list of 11 opponents included
three bowl teams and Stanford, a 1-point loser to Southern California.
Ed O'Neil, one of the defensive co-captains and a typically articulate
player, had this view:

> I don't care what other people say about us. There can't be an-
> other team in the country as close as this one. Mark [Mark-
> ovich] stood up a few minutes ago [after the Bowl victory] and
> gave the game ball to the defense, and I thanked the offense for
> putting enough points on the board. Everyone took a hand in
> winning this one, and that's the way it's been all along. Each
> guy in this room would do anything for the others. We're all to-
> gether and we're all part of a very great experience. To me,
> that's more important than anything else. I'll carry all this with
> me throughout my life, and there won't be one bad memory
> from it all.

To Coach Paterno the 1973 team was the best since his first days
as Penn State's head coach, which equates with being about the best
in Penn State's history. Reporters interviewing him New Year's night
were startled when he stated seriously that Penn State had just been
named Number One.

> I had my own poll—the Paterno Poll—and the vote was unani-
> mous. Penn State is No. 1. I just took the vote a few minutes
> ago.

Aware that they took it in fun, he explained that he really didn't
know who was Number One or if Penn State could win from teams
rated above it (the Lions were fifth, behind Notre Dame, Ohio State,
Oklahoma, and Alabama), but he believed his team had as much
right to claim top place as anyone. The undefeated Lions had attained every goal they set for themselves and could rightly consider
themselves as good as anyone unless proven otherwise.

Frank Roessner of the Clearfield (Pennsylvania) *Progress* wrote
that Penn State had pulled itself out of the Number One controversy
by its emphasis on more important ideals and achievements:

> The Lion coach and his players are above all of that. They're
> living in a world of higher ideals and more meaningful rela-
> tionships. They're number one in the Team Poll, where friend-
> ship, dedication, class, poise, intelligence, and humanity are the
> only things that count.

The polls notwithstanding, the Nittany Lions of 1973 had accomplished some notable feats:

The only major team in the country with a 12–0 record.

John Cappelletti won the Heisman Trophy, Maxwell Award, and other honors, as the best college player in America.

Cappelletti, Crowder, and O'Neil were on first teams of several All-Americas, and other players won various distinctions.

Ten Lions from the 1973 squad were drafted by National Football League teams, five going in the first two rounds (Cappelletti, O'Neil, Allen, Getty, and Markovich).

Markovich, offensive co-captain, won a Scholar-Athlete Award from the National Football Foundation and an NCAA postgraduate scholarship.

Coach Paterno was named the Coach of the Year by the Washington Touchdown Club and the eastern Coach of the Year by the New York Football Writers' Association.

Paterno partisans regretted that the American Football Coaches' Association had not designated him Coach of the Year (he had been so named in 1968). Bear Bryant of Alabama was the 1973 winner. Their award generally honors the leader of a top-ranked undefeated team, but at one time it was bestowed for significant professional contributions beyond winning games. Dick Harlow was named in 1936, when Harvard couldn't be ranked (3–4–1), and in 1966 it went to Tom Cahill, after his first year as Army's head coach, although Notre Dame and unranked Tennessee had beaten the Cadets. In 1973 Coach Paterno had a superlative coaching record and brought unusual credit to the profession through his widely admired personal sense of values.

45

Lions Meet Cinderella in Dallas

Preseason events in 1974 thoroughly agitated most Lion watchers and confused even experienced newswriters into believing that another great crisis would menace the ninth year in the head coaching career of Joe Paterno. The first indications were the words of the coach himself:

> You're going to find a football team that will have to scrap and scratch and scrape, get a break here and there, have tremendous enthusiasm, hustle all the time. With all these things working for us, we'll survive, but our people must look at the situation realistically. There is no way this team can dominate its opponents as we did last year. You just can't all of a sudden turn good athletes into great ones. This doesn't mean we're not going to win some games. And because we'll be in a weekly struggle it's going to be a fun season and I hope the fans will look at it that way.

Key people were lost by graduation in every area—wide receivers, return artists, defensive secondary, linebackers, offensive linemen, and running backs (including Cappy). A reporter who timidly suggested the kicking game might be good received a Paterno glare: "What you people don't know is that half the kicking game is dependent on the center (Markovich) who passes back to the kicker, and he's gone. We had two bad passes this spring."

As the coach had predicted, the Lions started slowly, almost putting their followers to sleep in the game closing spring practice (White Squad 7; Blue 3). Senior quarterback Tom Shuman improved rapidly; the defensive line developed, led by Mike Hartenstine, Greg Murphy, Dave Graf, and Dennis Zmudzin, a real comer in late season; the anticipated great linebacking from junior Greg Buttle materialized; and, after a somewhat shaky start, fullback Tom Donchez did a super job. Little by little, they "scratched and scraped" all the way to the Cotton Bowl.

Lack of attention in the preseason magazine ramblings once more helped Penn State. One writer did note the cheerleaders: "Penn State has never made the top ten in this department because a lot of the better-looking girls have a tendency to look like Joe Paterno." (Penn State's cheerleading squad was ranked the nation's best in 1976).

Among the few personnel changes, an important one was the retirement of defensive (and kicking) coach Frank Patrick from active coaching after twenty-five years on the staff, although he remained as an academic counselor and associate professor of physical education. Pat's departure left only two coaches whose services extended through all the Engle and Paterno years, Jim O'Hora and J. T. White. The newcomer replacing Patrick was Gregg Ducatte '72, first Penn State player who had participated in three major bowls—the Orange, Cotton, and Sugar, in which his defensive play was praised by Chuck Fairbanks, Oklahoma's coach in 1972, who said he'd never seen a more aggressive player against the run from the safety position.

Opening at home with Stanford on national television, Penn Staters were sobered by advance publicity from Palo Alto about the Cardinals' new sophomore quarterback, Mike Cordova, a "dead-ringer" for the fabled Jim Plunkett, and two All-America defensive ends returning from 1973—Pat Donovan and Roger Stillwell, both six feet, five inches and in the 235–50 range. What Cordova *looked* like didn't matter, but he passed like a demon, setting a new Beaver Stadium record, with 23 completions in 51 attempts. Al Neville of Maryland had completed 23 in 1971, but no one had thrown 51 before. Still underrated, the Lions scratched out a victory (24–20) with 2:09 to play, when Tom Shuman courageously brought his team from behind and Woody Petchel finally crashed over the goal line behind Tom Donchez. Cordova ended his active afternoon by throwing 60 yards in the air, right to the arms of Tom Giotto, junior Lion safetyman.

TV watchers marveled that a national production at last had shown the expanse of the campus and its beautiful setting in the heartland of Penn's Woods, with Mount Nittany standing guard over Beaver Stadium. The scene was enlivened by the serene presence of the Goodyear blimp, which hovered over Nittany Valley through the following week, until the Navy game.

The Midshipmen came to University Park with some trepidation and left for Annapolis Saturday night victors by 7–6. Coach George Welsh, in his second year as Navy's head man, was as surprised as the eastern football public, which considered it the "year's greatest upset." Saturday's rain and wind resulted in 8,000 "no-shows" (ticket purchasers who stayed home), phenomenal for Beaver Stadium, but difficult playing conditions were not used as an excuse by Coach Paterno:

> Navy adapted to weather conditions better than we did and deserved its victory. George did a good job; his team was well prepared and he has more good athletes than most people think. Our only consolation is that we still feel he's one of the family (an assistant coach at Penn State for ten years).

One of Navy's "good athletes" was fullback Bob Jackson, a former quarterback who nearly came to Penn State. He threw the winning pass in the second quarter to wingback Robin Ameen. And Navy had indeed adjusted better to the nautical conditions—Penn State lost the ball five times on fumbles, most of them well into soggy Navy territory, and the reliable Chris Bahr missed four field goal attempts. The Lions finally scored in the last period, going 58 yards in 9 plays, aided by an interference call, in a drive Shuman climaxed with a 5-yard touchdown pass to Jerry Jeram, a newly used flankerback.

Coach Paterno couldn't fathom the "surprise" caused by his immediate decision to try for two points. Only a few minutes' playing time remained, and his team seemed unlikely to get into scoring position again under the conditions. The one tie on Paterno's coaching record didn't come about through his choice. His determination to go for a possible victory was praised as far away as California ("A Worthy Gamble" in the Los Angeles *Times*):

> While there may be room for risk in such a decision, many would recoil from the opportunity. But Paterno rolled the dice, giving an otherwise forgettable game something to be remembered for.

The wives of the two coaches greeted each other demonstratively. This time Sandra Welsh burst into tears. "I don't want to lose," she wailed to Sue Paterno, "but, darn it, I don't want to beat you guys." The *Football Letter* editor received sympathy calls, albeit mystified, from points between Tucumcari, New Mexico, and Pensacola, Florida. Tom Slusser '34, former football captain now living in the heart of Navyland, described the exultation of his neighbors. "Penn State must be really great," he told the needlers, "to make you this happy."

The Iowa Hawkeyes, victors over UCLA (21–10) the previous week, had Iowa City and even Grand Rapids all agog, but local enthusiasm was dampened quickly by Penn State's best performance to date. Few teams in the country played a tougher schedule, and the Hawks never recovered from the 27–0 loss, posting a 3–8 record for the season. Shuman, not yet a consistent performer, hit 5 of 17, but five Lion runners were in double figures, paced by a surprising leader, junior Rusty Boyle. Freshman Jimmy Cefalo was used sparingly as a flanker and gained 32 yards in only 3 carries.

Although hard hitting predominated, there were relatively few penalties. A damaging one assessed against Penn State for tackling a punt receiver before he had the ball was offset by a clipping against Iowa. The near-penalty pinpointed a tricky "judgment call" rule revived in 1974 after some years in the discard. As it now stands, the fair-catch rule requires the receiver to *wiggle* his upraised arm, making him fair game for the tackler if he gives the signal erroneously, thus raising an issue that could involve "unsportsmanlike conduct."

Another 1974 judgment call problem for harried officials concerned the locale for a successful field goal or extra point. Formerly, if any portion of the ball went over one upright, the goal was good. It could hit an upright, bounce over the crossbar, and be declared a successful kick. Under the 1974 rule the ball must go "between" both uprights—the kicker has less margin and sometimes an official has trouble with the call. Many observers questioned field goal decisions in both the Stanford and Navy games.

Possibly the most important change since the two-point conversion was adopted as an extra-point option, was the elimination of below-the-waist blocking on kick returns. A good rule for preventing injuries, it also curtailed the exciting kick return, because blocking is less effective.

The busy committee must also be alert to prevent coaches from taking advantage of loopholes. For instance, at one time a player, or even a manager or player without full equipment, legally could come into the huddle to bring in a play and then leave the game before play proceeded. Joe Paterno is said to have commented: "We could send in a coach if he could remember the play that long." The rule now states that a substitute must remain in the game for at least one play.

What constitutes an "intentionally grounded pass" is commonly misunderstood. The Panthers complained after Penn State's 1973 victory that an official had denied them their rights (and probably the game) by failing to call Tom Shuman for "intentional grounding" at a critical point. The rule (No. 7, Sec. 3) states that "if *any* player occupies the area into which a pass is thrown it is not to be considered as intentional grounding." As Coach Paterno pointed out at the time, a quarterback has enough to do without trying to identify a number on a jersey. In fact, if he wants to take a chance, he can throw to an opponent without violating the rule.

The trip to West Point shouldn't have caused concern, but after the first quarter the Cadets held a 14–0 lead over the Lions, who seemed unable to solve the Wishbone offense installed by Army's new coach, Homer Smith, and executed proficiently by quarterback Scott Gillogly. Although the "favored" team's offense was guilty of three lost fumbles, the Lions managed to "scratch" out another one, 21–14.

The team and a Homecoming crowd of 56,500 showed signs of vigor in the Wake Forest game. An illustrious Wake Forest alumnus, Arnie Palmer, saw the Deacons put up a plucky fight, but it was Penn State in a 55–0 runaway. Tommy Shuman passed accurately, with 12 of 14 for 183 yards, and sophomore Duane Taylor led the ball carriers with 88 yards. Jerry Jeram was the top receiver, catching four passes for 64 yards.

Starting his first season at Syracuse, Coach Frank Maloney injudiciously said he saw no reason why the Orange couldn't be a bowl contender in 1974. He hadn't yet experienced the central Pennsylvania hex—since 1934 the Syracusans have won only five times on Penn State's field and only nine times since the series began in 1922. Maloney's first team battled to a first-half lead (14–10), but succumbed to the bull-like rushing of Tom Donchez (119 yards), reminiscent of the fullback pummeling the Lions usually got from the

Orange. Shuman's passing tally was satisfying (13 of 20), with Jeram again his main target.

The West Virginia Mountaineers, also luckless at University Park and with no victories at either place since 1955, seemed to accept their annual tribulation as inevitable. In 1974, even the booing of the abusive Morgantown populace was less enthusiastic. Danny Buggs, West Virginia's brilliant pass receiver, wasn't in the best physical condition, and Artie Owens, most prolific ground-gainer in its history, never did have good fortune against Coach Paterno's defense. Typically for the series, Penn State scored its usual unusual touchdown in the 21–12 victory. John Reihner attempted what looked like an easy field goal when the Lions were ahead 14–6 early in the second half, but his team was set back to the 17 on a delay-of-game penalty. Middle guard Jeff Merrow, the best Mountaineer defensive player, blocked the kick cleanly, and the ball was knocked toward the West Virginia goal by a Mountaineer. Ordinarily, a team blocking a kick stands to gain from it, but State's Ron Coder, who happened to be nearest, fell on the ball for a touchdown, he hoped. Ron had seen a red flag fall and was in doubt until he learned that West Virginia had been offside.

The top-flight attraction of the Maryland contest carried on regional TV was the defensive unit's Jeff Hite, who was substituting for the injured Jim Bradley. Hite, the opportunist, was the difference between the two teams, causing two defensive lapses that brought about the downfall of the Terrapins, 24–17. Terp passer Bob Avellini had his team at the Lion 19 in the scoreless first quarter, and, on second down, he tried a flat pass to running back Lou Carter. Timing his move perfectly, Hite picked off the ball and had nothing but daylight ahead, a 79-yard Beaver Stadium interception record (as of 1976). Act Two in the Hite drama came after Penn State had taken a 14–7 lead in the second period and Reihner had kicked off following the go-ahead touchdown. Recalling a warning that Maryland sometimes used a lateral play after a kickoff, Hite was watching closely when Dick Jennings reached the 21 on his return. Across the field he observed that a possible receiver was covered, and then noticed Carter running a few steps behind Jennings. The Marylander tried to flip the ball back to the speedy Carter, but Hite was in position and quick enough to snatch the ball to score his second touchdown before the crowd knew what was happening. A new sophomore halfback, Neil Hutton, had his day, too, leading all ball carriers, but Hite's two steals, covering exactly 100 yards, stole the show.

Historically, this Maryland game was Penn State's 500th victory since the first official game with Bucknell in 1887, but records certify the victory against Ohio University two weeks later. (The Penn State brochure doesn't report the 1893 game with the Columbia Athletic Club of Washington, which ended in a dispute, although it was completed. Playing on a Monday following the conquest of Virginia at Charlottesville, the pioneer Lions were "robbed" when the officials allowed the game to continue after its technical ending, and even spectators took part in the "winning" touchdown claimed by the CAC team.) Only eight other universities had attained the magic 500th—Yale, Princeton, Harvard, Pennsylvania, Michigan, Notre Dame, Texas, and Alabama.

After the Maryland victory, with three games remaining on its regular-season schedule, Penn State received an "unofficial" Cotton Bowl bid and indicated acceptance of the invitation "if offered." Coach Paterno had misgivings about it because of two dangerous opponents ahead, including the Pitt game, which had been moved to Thanksgiving night in Three Rivers Stadium for national TV exposure. The Cotton Bowl committee was taking a big chance, caught in the bowl uproar with sportwriters lining up unofficial matchings long before the legal announcing date set up by the NCAA (November 9). Since the Southwest Conference race was far from settled and every other major bowl appeared to be jumping the gun, the committee felt reasonably safe with the 7–1 Lions, whose 1972 visit had been mutually satisfactory.

The three gentlemen from Dallas in their sharp green Cotton Bowl blazers, hopeful but unrelaxed in the press box November 9 at Raleigh, North Carolina, witnessed the defeat of the Lions, 12–7, by a strong Wolfpack team. Playing an almost perfect game, North Carolina State deserved its victory. The northern visitors had a meaningless statistical edge. Key to the Wolfpack's first success in the seven-game series during the Engle-Paterno era was Penn State's inability to stop Stan Fritts when it counted. The senior fullback made 111 tough yards, and the home team was ahead 12–0 until the final period, when the Lions averted their first regular-season shutout since 1966. Moving the ball 80 yards in 10 plays, they scored their lone touchdown on a pass in the flat at the 13 from Tom Shuman to Jim Eaise. Fritts spearheaded both Wolfpack thrusts for touchdowns in the second and third quarters. He threw to tight end Pat Hovance for the winning score on a fullback pass, the play that had caused Penn State's other downfall, against Navy.

North Carolina State has all the fierce pride of other southern schools but shows more respect and friendship for a visiting team. Emotion filled the Wolfpack dressing room for hours, and the game ball was presented to Al Michaels, defensive co-ordinator, a Penn State alumnus and former coach under Bob Higgins, Joe Bedenk, and Rip Engle.

Coach Paterno, in his dressing-room interview, scoffed at the idea of a letdown after the hard Maryland game and premature thoughts of the Cotton Bowl:

> That's an alibi I won't buy. Anyone would have to be stupid not to be ready for a team as good as North Carolina State. Before the game I told everyone Fritts would be the best fullback we would face all season, and I still think so.

Always quicker to shake off defeat than most of his associates, he introduced his glum and slightly embarrassed players to the three Cotton Bowl officials—Wilbur Evans, executive director; Starke Taylor, president; and Field Scovell, past president. Scovell made a graceful presentation of the invitation to meet the still undecided Southwest Conference champions:

> We wanted Penn State before the game and we want you now. We know today has been a big disappointment to you and Coach Paterno—more than it has been to us.

They personally transferred three sealed packages to Dean Bob Scannell, Athletic Director Ed Czekaj, and Assistant Athletic Director Jim Tarman. Entering the Raleigh-Durham Airport later, the three Penn Staters saw the Texas executives heading for them. "You can't have the tickets back," quipped Tarman, but the unsmiling trio walked by in a daze. "Southern Methodist 18; Texas A&M 14," said Scovell. "Baylor 34; Texas 24, " murmured Taylor. The Southwest Conference might very well end in a four-way tie, but at least they had one contestant for their game.

Ohio University provided little opposition in the last of an inconsequential five-game series that had merely given the Ohioans from Athens five nice purses instead of victories, but it was the background for some unrevealed, behind-the-scenes action. The Cotton Bowl announcement didn't sit well in some eastern spots. Temple

Coach Wayne Hardin declared that Pitt was easily the best team in the East after the Owls (8–2) lost to Pitt, and the Panthers (7–2) grumbled because bowl selectors had ignored them. Coach Paterno was undisturbed, but had an idea. A strong advocate of some kind of playoff for the national championship, he made a statement at the Friday night press party and asked the writers to keep it off the record until after Saturday's games. A victory against Notre Dame would give Pitt the same record as Penn State (8–2), assuming the Lions would win from Ohio University. If the Panthers beat the Irish, Paterno said, he would let the Pitt-Penn State game decide the East's representative in the Cotton Bowl, adding that he was sure Penn State and Cotton Bowl officials would consent.

The unprecedented statement caused one reporter to comment: "Do you mean to say you'd take the chance of giving up a Cotton Bowl net of over $400,000?" Paterno fixed his questioner with another: "What makes you think I expect to lose to Pitt?" His one request was that they wouldn't mention his intention if Pitt lost to Notre Dame, knowing he'd be accused of a "grandstand" act. During the Ohio game a press box messenger brought him the Pitt-Notre Dame score after every quarter, so that he'd have his statement ready. The Irish won a close game, 14–10, there would be no playoff, and the writers kept the faith with old-fashioned journalistic ethics.

Three Rivers Stadium, home of the Pittsburgh Pirates and Steelers, had much of a bowl's glamor, excitement, and tension. Pride was the compelling emotion, even though no bowl bid was at stake. Pitt's coach, Johnny Majors, had made giant strides in two years and was confident that his All-America halfback, Tony Dorsett, could run with brilliance against Penn State, as he had against nearly every other opponent, notwithstanding his mediocre performance at Beaver Stadium the previous season. Dorsett's freshman running mate, Elliott Walker of Miami, Florida, was said to be even more swift in the open field, and the Panthers thought that Carson Long, their kicker, was superior to Chris Bahr. The taunted victim of the "East's greatest upset" (Navy) was said to deserve no better than meeting Pitt in the "Turkey Bowl." Traveling to Pittsburgh by bus Wednesday afternoon, the squad worked out briefly at Three Rivers Stadium to test the lights (they were excellent).

After Thursday night's warmup, the team returned to its dressing room for a private meeting, a Paterno custom, where the seniors speak their minds before the coaches, doctors, and trainers join them for the pregame prayer. Mike Hartenstine, usually the least verbose Lion, surprised his teammates with an opening inspirational talk. Tom Donchez, more vehement, reminded everyone how devastating a defeat would be, and was so carried away that he closed by heaving his helmet against the side of a locker. It bounced off, hit starting linebacker Greg Buttle right between the eyes, and knocked him cold.

At that moment Assistant Head Coach Jim O'Hora came in with the others for the prayer. He noticed, but paid no attention to, some commotion at one end of the locker room, and left for the field. When players and coaches ran out, Buddy Tesner, another starting linebacker, asked Jim to go over the defensive signals with him because Buttle, who usually called the defensive plays, was hurt and couldn't play. Coach Paterno, overhearing as he ran by, muttered "Oh, God, can't we even get through the team prayer without an injury?"

The mystified O'Hora obliged Tesner, and Coach Paterno told sophomore Ron Crosby to replace Buttle. Just after Pitt won the toss, O'Hora saw Buttle running slowly toward the Lion squad, patched up like a prizefighter, revived and taped by Trainer Eddie Sulkowski, wobbly and a trifle pale, but ready to take his place in the starting lineup. Buttle reported later that the first quarter seemed to be in slow motion, like a bad dream, and between halves six stitches were put in a gash over his eye. "But he never missed a signal," O'Hora announced proudly.

After trailing 7–6 at half time, Penn State repeated its 1973 domination of the Panthers, wearing them down to win the "eastern title," 31–10. Bahr's four field goals set a Penn State record, and Jim Eaise scored two touchdowns on passes in the second half from his new position at split end, a switch that the baffled Panther defense was unable to cover as he ran free into the end zone. Freshman Jimmy Cefalo quietly moved to a starting position at wingback in the Ohio game and gained 73 yards against Pittsburgh, nine more than Dorsett's 64. Chief offensive assets were the running of Donchez, who led the ground-gainers of both sides with 87 yards, and the passes of quarterback Tom Shuman, who tossed for 166 yards, with 9 of 17.

Pitt's offensive line couldn't cope with Hartenstine, Greg Murphy, and John Quinn, the leaders up front. Despite his injury, Buttle was king of the linebackers, although exceptional performances were turned in by smallish Rich Kriston, linebacker, and Dennis Zmudzin, defensive end, both starting their first games. Pitt was overwhelmed for the ninth season in a row, but this victory was especially sweet.

Penn State won its fourth consecutive Lambert Trophy and the first Cool-Ray Cup, awarded to the top "independent" team in the East. Pittsburgh, Syracuse, Boston College, Army, Navy, and West Virginia were the teams eligible for the new cup, with Temple added in 1975. Fullback Tom Donchez won the $2,000 scholarship for postgraduate work accompanying this cup.

Mike Hartenstine, defensive tackle, made four of the major All-America teams, while John Nessel, offensive tackle, was selected on the Walter Camp Football Foundation first eleven. Tom Shuman, in Penn State's record book as the top career touchdown passer (28 in 1972–74), was to be named the Most Valuable Player in the 1975 Cotton Bowl. Five Lions of 1974 drafted by professional teams were kept on their 1975 regular squad rosters. In the National Conference, Hartenstine and Donchez played with the Chicago Bears, and Jeff Bleamer, offensive tackle with the Philadelphia Eagles. In the American Conference, Dave Graf was retained as a Cleveland Browns linebacker and Chris Devlin as a linebacker for the Cincinnati Bengals. Nine Penn Staters (through 1974) received $1,000 Chevrolet scholarships as "outstanding players" in games televised by the ABC network since the program began (Hartenstine and Donchez won in the 1974 Pitt game). Together with John Cappelletti's $5,000 scholarship grand prize for the 1973 Player of the Year, these TV awards added $14,000 to the university's general academic scholarship funds.

Both press association polls (AP and UPI) ranked the Lions seventh nationally in 1974, but the East otherwise received scant attention. Temple advanced (8–2), although Pittsburgh and Boston College were generally considered the top teams after Penn State (Temple defeated Boston College). Oklahoma won the national championship in the AP sportswriters' poll, but Southern California was given the UPI title. The coaches eliminated Oklahoma because of its probationary status.

President and Mrs. John W. Oswald were as delighted as any Penn Staters to celebrate the New Year of 1975 at another major bowl, their third as the university's hosts in the South (Sugar) and West (Cotton), regions of the country familiar to both.

Dr. Oswald had come East from the embattled Berkeley campus, where he had been executive vice president of the University of California's entire system after five years as president of the University of Kentucky. Eager to apply his energy to the cause of the East's foremost land-grant state university, he courageously met the barrage of issues generated by student activism, and paid with a heart attack a year later (June 1971). He recuperated with the resilience of an athlete—Jack Oswald, a Phi Beta Kappa at DePauw, had been football captain. He was named to *Sports Illustrated*'s Silver Anniversary Football Team (1962) honoring excellence in the sport and in subsequent life work. He studied plant pathology for his M.A. and Ph.D. degrees from California, was a World War II PT boat captain in the Navy, and held a Fulbright research grant in the Netherlands during the course of his teaching and administrative years at California.

In the years of his presidency at Penn State—also embattled with problems of faculty unionism, civil liberties lawsuits, incessant budget constraints, et al.—Dr. Oswald stressed alumni participation in the university's life, in line with a national trend toward increased support from alumni and friends. The annual Penn State Fund of gifts and endowments enabled Penn State to proceed with its Museum of Art, large concert auditorium, Faculty Club, campus beautification, and a variety of academic benefits, especially student aid. An Alumni Fellow seminar program for students and faculty and the Summer Alumni College for continuing education and recreation were additions to the activities of the Penn State Alumni Association, of which Ross B. Lehman '42 became executive director when Ridge Riley '32 retired in April 1970.

Within the university Dr. Oswald emphasized further integration of the statewide Commonwealth Campus system, enrollment stabilization, participation of students and faculty in advisory governance capacities, and continuing development of faculty access to instructional and research grants from federal and state sources. Through his official service in national higher education organizations, the president and other university representatives accepted opportunities to visit China (1974) and the Soviet Union (1975). Dr. Oswald was president (1975–76) of both the Association of American Universities and the Pennsylvania Association of Colleges and Universities.

THE COTTON BOWL,
JANUARY 1, 1975

The Baylor Bears were a Cinderella team for sophisticated Dallas. Their rise to the top of the tough Southwest Conference was phenomenal. They had beaten the Texas Longhorns coached by Darrell Royal, who probably could be elected mayor of Big D if he visited oftener than once every January 1. After losing its first two games, to Oklahoma and Missouri of the Big Eight, Baylor swept through its own conference like a tornado and gained a reputation for exciting second-half comebacks.

Penn State's fine showing and genuine cordiality during the 1972 bowl season won Texas hearts, but "the little Baylor boys" had come from rags to riches almost overnight; they were from rural Waco, and they even had an outstanding player named Thomas Turnipseede. Their pregame crusade reached religious fervor when Evangelist Billy Graham came to town, planning, it was said, to wear Baylor's Green and Gold and the Bear button inscribed simply "I Believe." Penn State's Back the Lions badge crassly said "Skin the Bears."

Having the Reverend Dr. Graham sign with Baptist Baylor bothered Joe Paterno, busy as he was dazzling the Dallas crowd all week at luncheons and press conferences with wit and serious football talk. At Tuesday afternoon's pep rally, he discounted the psychological advantage of the Baptist opposition, said to be 4,000 strong. "In all that crowd, I'll bet you won't find a single set of rosary beads. I'll stake my mother's prayers and her beads against them all." Joe had used his devout mother once before, publicly crediting her for the astounding last-minute Lion victory over Kansas in the 1969 Orange Bowl. This brought a note from his friend Art Rooney, owner of the Pittsburgh Steelers, whose team was having a struggle in 1968–69. Rooney's two sisters are nuns, his brother is a priest, and his letter was an offer. "I'll trade my brother and two sisters plus one linebacker, even up, for your mother."

Coach Paterno recalled that two United States Presidents had worked against him in Texas before, and now an internationally famous religious leader, Billy Graham, was coming forward. The Cotton Bowl committee agreed to see that the Lions were favored with a pregame visit in their dressing room from the distinguished evangelist, who was pleased with the spontaneous welcome and interested attention he received from the Penn State squad.

Spartanlike training regulations enforced by Grant Teaff, Baylor's popular coach and a lay Baptist preacher, were favorably reviewed in the press, which reported that the Lions were enjoying Dallas nightlife. At a players' news conference Greg Murphy was questioned about how his teammates would react to Coach Teaff's reported 11 P.M. curfew. "It would never go over," Murph replied breezily. Asked what curfew Penn State had, Greg answered: "Eleven-fifteen."

Baylor's aces were a stubby (five feet, seven inches) 196-pound halfback, Steve Beaird, who had gained over 1,100 yards, and quarterback Neal Jeffrey, who passed for more than 1,300 yards with 100 completions in 181 attempts. No Lion coach had seen Baylor play, but Coach J. T. White co-ordinated the final scouting report from films. His thorough analysis included a prediction that Beaird would take a handoff up the middle on the first play of the game. When he did, Mike Hartenstine, shaking off a double block, was in front of him like a wall.

Holding a half-time 7–3 lead, like Texas in 1972 (6–3), the Bears had crossed midfield only once for any real advance, but the Lions couldn't seem to stop Beaird's worrisome five-yard gains. On first down at the four, when he cracked off right guard for the game's first points, the jubilant halfback carried the football all the way back to his bench before remembering to surrender it to the referee. Lion players were confident by half time that Baylor was vulnerable to passing and Beaird could be stopped. His second-half statistics were 13 yards in 7 attempts, and his game output was 85 yards in 21 carries.

For State, Tom Shuman completed 9 of 19 passes for 226 yards, and galloping Tom Donchez ran 118 yards in 25 attempts. Two secret weapons were freshman Jimmy Cefalo, who caught three passes for 103 yards and one touchdown, starting at flanker, and ran for 56 more and another touchdown; and sophomore Neil Hutton, whose runs for 79 yards seemed to give the offense swift outside speed previously lacking. (As the nation's most sought-after recruit, Cefalo had been invited by the New York *Times* to write an article for the sports pages explaining his choice, and wrote a follow-up in 1975 confirming his favorable reaction to the Penn State program.) The Lions made a final touchdown unintentionally in the 41–20 victory with less than 30 seconds to play. Baylor had scored on an 11-yard pass. An onside kick was obvious, and Coach Paterno, always prepared for anything, turned to his onside kickoff return team, the last word in specialty units, with the agile Dan Natale, Chris Devlin, Tom Giotto, and Joe Jackson in the front line. A senior art student from Brimfield, Massachusetts, Joe had had a discouraging career, marked by damaging injuries and position switches that held up his progress, and the onside kick couldn't have bounced into more deserving hands. Getting the jump on most of Baylor's defenders, whose momentum was in the opposite direction, he saw nothing but open space in front, and pranced into the end zone after a happy run of about 52 yards. His score enabled Penn State to set a Cotton Bowl record for points and also made for spectacular TV.

Notoriety followed Penn State's announcement that an estimated $1,173,000 would accrue in the 1974 season from televised games, including the Cotton Bowl. Typical was a Philadelphia columnist's comment about the "rich getting richer" and "commercialized college football." University authorities were quick to point out that any danger comes not from receiving a large amount of money for football, but from its disposal. At Penn State, as noted, football receipts offset deficits in other intercollegiate sports, including the women's teams, and are utilized even more importantly for the general welfare of all students. In spite of the apparent healthy state of Penn State's football finances, Athletic Director Ed Czekaj warned in the summer of 1975 that the intercollegiate program might be in the red in 1975–76 unless bailed out by TV. Penn State had not been listed on 1975 television network schedules. This economic outlook and the feeling that Penn State's interests would be served better as an eastern independent, scheduling as many intersectional games as possible, induced the university to withdraw from the Eastern College Athletic Conference, a loosely organized body with 214 members. Paying an estimated $50,000–$60,000 annually into the ECAC treasury from bowl and television receipts (10 per cent), and prorated dues, seemed unjustifiably expensive in relation to benefits received from membership.

The carefully studied decision was reached unanimously by Czekaj, Dean Robert Scannell, Coach Paterno, and all other varsity coaches. A year before taking final action the university notified ECAC Commissioner Robert M. (Scotty) Whitelaw that it would withdraw unless the organization made some substantial policy changes. Some were promised, but major objections were not satisfied, and the decision became effective July 1, 1974. Athletic officials were in close communication throughout with President Oswald, who met personally with Commissioner Whitelaw and consulted trustees and other administrators before putting the decision in the hands of Dean Scannell and Athletic Director Czekaj.

The immediate problem of securing home game officials, formerly assigned by the ECAC, was solved for 1974 by obtaining them from the Big Ten. In 1975 a satisfactory arrangement was made with the Tri-State Intercollegiate Association of officials, a Pittsburgh-based organization not affiliated with the ECAC.

Unfortunately, the ECAC used its influence to discontinue Penn State's membership in various eastern athletic associations connected with it, many of which were founded long before the ECAC itself, in spite of the fact that several of the constituent groups literally had been financed by the success of tournaments conducted at Penn State, especially in gymnastics and wrestling. This "blanket dismissal" from associations in cross country and track (IC4-A); wrestling (EIWA); gymnastics (EIGA); and golf (EIGA) meant that Penn State can qualify its athletes for NCAA tournaments only through special regional tournaments. In 1975 the NCAA approved a new Eastern Wrestling League tournament as a qualifying event, and Penn State also was instrumental in the formation of the Eastern Collegiate Basketball League for the same purpose. In cross country and track, Penn State now belongs to the Central Collegiate Conference.

Separation from the ECAC in no way affects the university's academic requirements for athletes, which are higher than standards required by the NCAA. That body "enforces" a minimum "C" average for a high school athlete's eligibility for aid, almost making poor scholarship "respectable." Penn State requires all applicants for admission to take College Board examinations and uses these scores combined with high school marks as testing measures. Tests and records of applicants must predict a 2.00 average (minimum for graduation).

With Coach Paterno's full blessing, Penn State committed itself to establishing a national football image as the East's top university independent. Paterno had long felt such action would, in the long run, help eastern football, and that other large universities would follow this lead. At this time, only Pittsburgh has made the move. Traditional football relations continue with Pittsburgh, Syracuse, West Virginia, Maryland, and Temple, and the Boston College series resumes in 1981, but Penn State's future schedules, virtually completed through 1990, are intersectional in character. Upcoming intersectional opponents highly rated at present are Ohio State, Iowa, Kentucky, North Carolina State, Miami (Florida), Duke, Houston, Southern Methodist, Texas Christian, Texas A&M, and Nebraska. Some of these games continue into the 1980s when Notre Dame, Alabama, Tulane, Tennessee, Minnesota, Auburn, and Florida are added. New football kinships have been formed with two teams *now* considered top quality—Alabama and Notre Dame have signed for ten games beginning in 1981 on a home-and-home basis.

46

Year of the Big E

(John Black '62, who wrote this 1975 résumé based on Ridge Riley's observations, is assistant executive director and executive editor for the Penn State Alumni Association. As successor to Ridge in writing the *Football Letter,* John has the perspective of a player and a journalist. At Lancaster's McCaskey High School he was the backup (mainly benchwarmer) for an all-star quarterback; during a two-year stint with the U. S. Marines he made first string for the First Pioneers Battalion at Camp Pendleton; and at Penn State he served a year of benchwarming behind All-Americas Richie Lucas and Galen Hall. He switched to journalism as a sportswriter for the *Daily Collegian* and was its editor for two years. His B.A. degree in political science and journalism led to work with the U. S. Information Office before he joined the Alumni Association staff in 1970. [Excerpted from July–August *Penn Stater* magazine.])

If it were ever to be called the Big E, to coexist appropriately with the Big Eight and the Big Ten, eastern football took a great stride forward in 1975. Pitt beat Big Eight representative Kansas in the Sun Bowl, 33–19. Maryland beat Southeastern Conference runner-up Florida in the Gator Bowl, 13–0. West Virginia beat North Carolina State in the Peach Bowl, 13–0. And Penn State gave

Southeast champion Alabama a tense time in the Superdome's first Sugar Bowl.

One southern writer was man enough to admit the phenomenon. Will Penegay of the New Orleans *Times-Picayune* put it this way:

Let's open the new year [1976] by trying to purge an archaic prejudice from our football minds. After all, it's going to be awfully difficult to maintain any doubts about eastern football if you've been watching Penn State, Pittsburgh, Maryland, and West Virginia do their thing during the past six days.

Penn State broke its own record as the top collegiate attraction in the East, drawing an average of 60,085 for five home games. All were sellouts, as were road contests against Ohio State, Syracuse, Maryland, and Pitt. At Maryland nearly 20,000 temporary seats were needed for "the largest football gathering in Washington area history." (And that includes the Washington Redskins.) The nationally televised game with Pitt captured the highest viewer rating of a regular-season college game all year.

Whether conclusions are based on the opposition's won-lost record, the number of winning teams played, or the number of bowl teams played, Penn State had the toughest schedule of the nation's top-ranked teams. Eight of eleven opponents had winning records, five went to bowl games, and three won their bowl games (losers were Ohio State and North Carolina State). The won-lost record of opponents was 66–51–4 for a .562 percentage. Subtracting nine inflicted by the Lions themselves, the opposition had a 64–42–4 mark or a 60 per cent winning average. No longer is the schedule being called "soft." "Patsies" couldn't do what West Virginia did, upsetting Pacific Eight contender California, 28–10. Pitt knocked Notre Dame out of the postseason bowl picture and gave Cotton Bowl-bound Georgia one of its two defeats. Future schedules, Paterno says,

. . . will certainly be an asset toward reaching top ranking in the country. The question is no longer whether our schedule is good enough, but whether we're good enough—whether our personnel and our facilities can keep up with the competition.

Paterno called the 1975 eleven a "coach's team." It had character and no prima donnas, meeting a hard schedule without flinching. He tried to make an objective evaluation:

It wasn't a great team. There were limitations in personnel and in some early coaching decisions that didn't work out the way we had hoped. We had an outstanding defense . . . the best kicking game in Penn State history, and one of the greatest college kicking games of all time. This team played closer to its potential than any I've been around.

Chris Bahr was "worth at least a touchdown a game." The son of Lion soccer coach Walter Bahr, Chris was a soccer All-America for three years and played professionally in the summer of 1975, leading the Philadelphia Atoms in scoring and earning Rookie of the Year honors in the North American Soccer League. A 1974 NCAA rule permitting an athlete to be a professional in one sport while retaining his amateur status in others enabled Chris to return for the fall term, complete a bachelor's degree in biology, break almost every Penn State kicking record, and become in turn a football All-America.

In 1973 and 1974 he had sandwiched football place kicking between soccer games. After his soccer eligibility was over, his became the finest foot in football. In the regular season, he made 18 of 33 field goal attempts, including 3 from 55 yards and another from 52. On attempts up to 40 yards he converted an amazing 11 of 14. In the Sugar Bowl against Alabama, he scored all six of the Lions' points, splitting the uprights with field goals of 42 and 37 yards. Early in the first quarter, he attempted a 62-yard field goal that was straight enough, but dropped just a few yards short. Booting 19 of 20 extra-point attempts made him the team's leading scorer with 73 points—all off his talented right foot. Bahr set Penn State records for most field goals in one game, 4 (Pitt, 1974); season, 18 (1975); career, 35 (1973–75); longest field goal, 55 yards (Temple, Ohio State, Syracuse, 1975); and most points kicking in a career, 168, 105 by field goals, and 63 extra points (1973–75).

Another Bahr contribution to the team was his handling of punting and kickoffs. Most of his kickoffs went so deep into the end zone that only 28 were returned—and those for an average of only 18.4 yards. He boomed one kickoff 70 yards through the middle of the uprights. Unfortunately, kickoffs don't score. His fantastic punting averaged 38.6 yards, and he lofted a kick so high that by the time the ball finally descended, the receiver was usually surrounded by the coverage team, daring him to run with it. Only 24 times out of 56 did the receiver decide to do so, and then for an average of only 5.3

yards. Bahr, the first collegiate kicker selected in the pro football draft, was grabbed by the Cincinnati Bengals in the second round.

Middle linebacker Greg Buttle and offensive guard Tom Rafferty, team co-captains, also earned All-America titles, bringing to thirty-five the number of Lions selected as first-team All-Americas. Buttle, a Linwood, New Jersey, beach boy who patrolled the Margate City shoreline each summer and Beaver Stadium each fall, was picked by the New York Jets in the third round, the latest of Penn State's great linebackers. Buttle blitzed opposing quarterbacks before they could even cock their passing arms. He also had the lateral speed to angle across the line of scrimmage, nailing tailbacks as they tried to turn the corner. And how many fullbacks burst through a gap in the line only to be stopped dead in their tracks as Buttle plugged the dike? Rafferty, picked by the Dallas Cowboys, was only the third Penn State offensive lineman to gain All-America honors in the era of two-platoon football (Dave Joyner in 1971 and John Nessel in 1974 were the others.) As a pulling guard, Tom had a special talent for crushing blocks delivered at the corner, allowing backs to turn upfield for long gainers.

Ron Coder, drafted by those sly Pittsburgh Steelers, played defensive tackle only one year and didn't have the preseason publicity buildup so necessary for a shot at the All-America laurels he deserved. A selfless player, he moved from offensive guard to fill a hole on the defensive line left by departed All-America Mike Hartenstine. Son of Air Force Colonel Ron Coder '51, former Penn State soccer great, young Ron switched at Paterno's behest for the good of the team and justified his coach's confidence by participating in 93 tackles. He led in quarterback sacks, passes batted down, and stopping ball carriers for losses.

Coder and his younger brother Craig, a freshman linebacker, were one of *five* brother combinations on the 1975 squad. Larry Suhey, junior fullback, and Paul Suhey, freshman fullback and tight end, are sons of Steve Suhey '48,[1] All-America guard on the 1948 Cotton Bowl team, and grandsons of the late Bob Higgins, All-America guard in 1919 and Penn State coach, 1930–48. Matt, the youngest brother, enrolled as a freshman in 1976 after earning All-State and All-America honors in high school. Dave Shukri, a 265-pound center, and his "little" brother Rob, a mere 215-pound linebacker, mi-

---

[1] He died January 8, 1977.

The Grand Experiment

grated to Nittany Valley from Lindenhurst, Long Island. The tiny town of Holsopple, Pennsylvania, contributed Ron Hostetler, a starting outside linebacker as a junior, and his brother Doug, a quarterback and one of the few freshmen to make the varsity squad. Another of those freshmen is Scott Fitzkee, a lightning-fast split end, whose elder brother Ron, a defensive end, transferred after a year at Virginia and wasn't eligible to play in 1975.

Together with John Quinn, the third co-captain and a lineman, were tailback Woody Petchel, fullback Duane Taylor, split end Dick Barvinchak, tight ends Dave Stutts and Mickey Shuler, linemen Brad Benson, Mark Thomas and George Reihner, linebacker Jim Rosecrans, and that stingy secondary of Tom Odell, Mike Johnson, and Gary Petercuskie.

The announcement in July 1975 that Penn State would open the season on September 6 in Franklin Field against Temple had alumni reminiscing about the classic Penn State-Penn battles on that same field before the Ivies de-emphasized football. The 600 lucky enough to revel at a pregame buffet and pep rally in the nearby Hilton Hotel fully expected a nice warmup for the Lions before taking on nationally ranked Stanford and Ohio State. Coach Wayne Hardin's Owls co-operated with Philadelphia's Bicentennial program by displaying some fireworks of their own. On the first play from scrimmage, Temple halfback Bob Harris burst through the line and outran everyone to the goal line 76 yards away before half of the 57,112 paying customers could squeeze into their seats.

Before the largest crowd to see a Temple game (as well as the largest for a collegiate game in Franklin Field in many a year), the delirious, delighted Owls played above their heads for almost four full quarters. The Lions sealed a one-point victory with one of the oldest and least used plays in the book—a deliberate safety. Assistant Coach John Rosenberg is credited with suggesting it to Paterno to get out of a hole deep in their own territory with just 15 seconds remaining. The safety gave Temple two points, but allowed Chris Bahr to get off a free kick from the 20 and drove the Owls out of scoring territory before the clock ran out. (Intentional safeties figured prominently in winning games with Syracuse [1929], Holy Cross [1957], Army [1964], and North Carolina State [1967].)

Though Penn Staters, jaded by prosperity, hadn't expected such a close game from upstart Temple, football buffs couldn't have asked for a more exciting contest: a 76-yard touchdown run on the first scrimmage play by a three-touchdown underdog; a heart-stopping 100-yard kickoff return by a young player more at home with a lacrosse stick; a twisting, turning 66-yard punt return by a player who wasn't even supposed to catch the ball; a 55-yard field goal by a professional soccer player who had just been named Rookie of the Year; a game in which the lead changed hands five times after the first quarter; and two teams scoring by every means in the rulebook —touchdowns, field goals, one- and two-point conversions, and a safety. It was only the second Penn State game in twenty years in which both teams scored in each quarter.

Chris Bahr, whose 55-yard field goal set a school record, and Don Bitterlich, Temple's soccer-style kicker who holds the NCAA record for consecutive extra-point conversions, hooked up in a kicking duel for which Bahr's father, in a way, was responsible. Before Walter Bahr came to Penn State in 1974, he had been soccer coach at Temple for three years. While there he tipped off football coach Wayne Hardin to a player he had who, like Chris, had a "pure" kicking style. Bitterlich became the best place-kicker in Temple's history.

Two runbacks by Rich Mauti and Woody Petchel spelled the 26–25 victory for the Lions. Mauti, an All-America lacrosse player whose varsity football playing time had been limited to a few brief appearances late in the 1974 season, was the deep middleman on kick returns. Near the end of the first quarter, after the Owls had taken a 10–3 lead, Mauti wrapped his arms around the ensuing kickoff on the goal line and started full-speed-ahead straight up the middle behind a perfect wedge, which broke a hole for him at the 25. Surging through, he juked the last Temple defender off his feet and sailed untouched to paydirt to put the Lions right back in the ball game.

Woody Petchel's runback was the gamebreaker, with less than four minutes remaining. Hopes were fading for the Lions, behind 23–18, when Woody caught a Temple punt in full stride, cutting in front of Mauti. Sidestepping and weaving his way down the right sideline, shaking tacklers off his back, Woody was tripped by Brian Eckhart in a desperation dive on the 3-yard line just as he cut to avoid running over a fallen referee. Duane Taylor hurdled in for the face-saving touchdown.

The sky-high Owls, one of the better teams in the East, grounded their whole season on Franklin Field that night. They were shot down the next week by West Virginia, 55–7, and weren't on the wing again until the second half of their schedule.

One week later, a very different ball club easily handled a Stanford team (one that moved on to Ann Arbor the following Saturday and held mighty Michigan to a 19–19 draw). The aerial-minded Cardinals would go on to average 29 points a game. But against the tough secondary of Petercuskie, Odell, and Johnson, ably assisted by linebackers Buttle, Hostetler, and Kriston, they could muster only two touchdowns while giving up four interceptions. Meanwhile, the Lions amassed 34 points, unleashing a devastating running attack sparked by freshman Tom Donovan, who wasn't listed in pregame depth charts. Paterno keeps such close wraps on his freshmen that not even the press box staff knew anything about the first Penn State freshman to gain more than 100 yards in a game. Picked to fill in for the injured Jimmy Cefalo just a day before the game, Donovan soon made 61,325 fans (a Beaver Stadium record) stand up and take notice. Sweeping around right end in the second quarter, he cut behind three crisp blocks by Rich Mauti, Tom Rafferty, and George Reihner, angled across field against the grain, and dashed 61 yards for the Lions' touchdown run of the year.

The largest crowd ever to watch a Penn State team play (88,093) gathered in Ohio Stadium on a glorious autumn afternoon to see whether the highly ranked Buckeyes could break the jinx this eastern squad had held over them since 1912. In four games, Penn State had beaten the Bucks by a combined score of 81–13—the last (1964) a 27–0 humiliation later voted by sportswriters as the biggest upset of the decade.

The Lions won the second and third quarters, but the Buckeyes won the first and fourth quarters by wider margins. Ohio State scored first after Brian Baschnagel, a Pittsburgh lad, took a wingback reverse around right end for 49 yards to set up the touchdown just four minutes into the game. Unprepared for such a radical play from a Woody Hayes-coached team, the Lions were caught with their defenses down and had to start in a 7-point hole. When their first drive stalled at the Ohio State 38-yard line, Chris Bahr walked in and, while Buckeye fans wiped their sunglasses in disbelief, calmly accomplished his second 55-yard field goal of the young season—the longest kick in the 44-year history of Ohio Stadium.

Penn State dominated the middle quarters against the 17-point favorites but couldn't break through the Ohio defense for a 6-pointer.

Duane Taylor, leading Lion rusher for the day, came closest on a breakaway run along the left sideline before he was stopped by safetyman Tim Fox. In the end Ohio State's patented, methodical, relentless marches beat the Lions, 17–9. Two-time Heisman Trophy winner Archie Griffin made a spectacular diving catch of a Cornelius Greene pass and from there Peter Johnson, a 245-pound battering ram disguised in a helmet and pads, carried on seven of nine plays to the clinching score.

The jinx was broken, but the Lions lost little face despite the disappointment of their coach, who said, prophetically, "We're a young team and will get a lot better."

New respect in Big Ten country was evident the following week when they met Iowa. One local paper dubbed them "Penn State's mean machine from the East," and after a sluggish first quarter, they lived up to the billing, coming home with a 30–10 victory. No Paterno-coached eleven before had held an opponent without a single pass completion! Penn State's aerial game, on the other hand, reached its apex, and two uncharacteristic bombs put the game out of reach for the Hawks. Split end Dick Barvinchak caught the first one for 75 yards.

Barvinchak, disappointed on the freshman team, had switched to basketball—where he was second string, too. Back to football. In 1973 he was backup quarterback to Tom Shuman. In 1974, with Shuman at the helm again, Dick decided to try catching rather than throwing the ball, and he broke into the lineup at split end. After an operation kept him out of spring practice, his football career seemed over. Giving it one more shot, he became the Lions' leading receiver for the year with 17 receptions for 327 yards. Rich Mauti caught the second bomb thrown by junior quarterback John Andress, who had perhaps his best performances of the year in the two Big Ten games. (Against Ohio State he completed 11 of 17 for 135 yards, and against Iowa, 8 of 14 for 196 yards.) Mauti took the picture-perfect pass on his fingertips, in full stride and two steps behind the defensive halfback for a 70-yard touchdown.

Beaver Stadium was the setting when Penn State underwhelmed Kentucky in a 10–3 game that left a capacity Homecoming crowd talking more about the spectacular autumn scenery than the unspectacular play on the gridiron. Nonetheless, to the discerning fan it was a classic defensive battle that the victors could be proud to win and the vanquished unashamed to lose.

Durable halfback Sonny Collins, the Southeast Conference's all-time leading ground-gainer, could not cross the Lions' goal line. He battered the line for only a few yards on each of his thirty-two tries —a Kentucky record. Collins was tackled hard even when he was only a decoy, but he had respectful words for the Lions after the game: "Penn State deserved everything they got—they are a well-developed team and they should be higher in the ratings than Number Ten. They'd pick me up after many tackles, and I respect that very much. That's what really makes the game."

John Andress drove the Lions 80 yards for the only touchdown, tossing three perfect strikes to Barvinchak for 15, 13, and 28 yards. Strangely and suddenly, John's passing turned cold in the second half. He did not learn until after the game that his father, John, Sr., had suffered a heart attack in the stands at half time.

After mounting the 10–0 half-time lead, Penn State had to rely on its impregnable defense to save the day. Coach Paterno offered an interesting insight into crowd psychology to counter disparagement of the offensive unit: "If the first and second halves had been reversed, the fans would have thought it was a terrific game."

West Virginia media and fans haven't learned the dangers of the excessive buildup. As they had so many times in the past, the exuberant folk flowed into Beaver Stadium, set to watch their tenth-ranked team end the two-decade victory drought against the Lions. They had upset California in Berkeley and SMU in Dallas as well as thumping Temple and Boston College. They were fourth in the nation in scoring (141 points) and were averaging 411 yards per game, including 329 on the ground. Who could blame Coach Bobby Bowden for instructing his captains to receive the kickoff, if they won the coin toss? In the postgame interview, he admitted that that was his first mistake.

A tenacious defense pushed West Virginia runners backward for 66 yards, more than half as many as they made forward (115), and shook loose five fumbles with vicious tackles. Meanwhile, the Lions gained 376 yards on the ground—more than half the total compiled by the Mountaineers' four other opponents combined. Senior Woody Petchel went over 100 yards for the first time in his career; Artie Owens, Petchel's biggest high school rival in the Poconos four years ago, gained exactly 11 yards for West Virginia. The man destined to become the leading ball carrier in West Virginia history with 2,562 yards thus closed out a four-year career against Penn State with a total of 87 yards. The 39–0 final score was almost merciful. With no interceptions or fumbles, the Lion offense played easily its best game of the year, and could seemingly do no wrong on this beautiful Saturday afternoon in Nittany Valley.

A razzle-dazzle play gave the Lions a 19–7 victory over Syracuse, their reviving eastern rival. Dick Barvinchak, who held the ball for Chris Bahr's placements all season, was in position to put it down for a 47-yard field goal attempt in the third quarter. Instead, while Bahr swung his foot at thin air, Dick took the snap from center and rolled right with enough running room to make the first down. Spotting tight end Dave Stutts all alone at the goal line, Barvinchak threw his only pass of the season for a touchdown. No wonder the Orangemen were caught flat-footed. Earlier in the game Bahr had successfully kicked his third 55-yard field goal of the season, against the wind.

In a 31–0 win over Army, the defensive secondary of seniors Mike Johnson and Tom Odell and sophomore Gary Petercuskie showed how well they could play Penn State's intricate shifting zone. Cadet Leamon Hall, who had a 56 per cent pass-completion average, connected on only 7 of 27 attempts. The following week Maryland quarterbacks Larry Dick and Mark Manges were limited to 4 out of 14, but the game itself was a different story.

In Byrd Stadium the Lions needed all the stability under pressure, equanimity, calmness, coolness under fire, self-reliance, aplomb, and assurance they had exhibited. Feeling the Marylanders would be keyed up and tense for their biggest game, Paterno wanted them to start out with the ball. He instructed his captains to take the wind if they won the toss. The coach's hunch was correct: The Terps were jittery, the Lion defenders applied some hard tackles to cause two fumbles, and within six minutes Penn State had a 12–0 lead. Linebacker Jim Rosecrans, playing his finest game, was responsible for the first break, rushing the quarterback and knocking the ball loose. Ron Coder recovered the fumble, and four plays later Chris Bahr kicked his first field goal, from the 27. Linebacker Kurt Allerman knocked the next one loose from Terp fullback Tim Wilson, leading to Bahr's second successful kick, from the 34. Then the Lions began their own offensive drive, ending with Woody Petchel's 36-yard touchdown run. Woody swept left end with a pitchout from John Andress, cut behind blocks by Mark Thomas and Tom Rafferty, and ran back against the grain to the end zone.

The Terrapins settled down for 10 points in the second quarter and went ahead on a third-period field goal by Mike Sochko. It took Bahr three tries to put the Lions back in front, but he did it with a 40-yard field goal midway through the final frame. Maryland had one last shot at the upset. In the waning minutes they drove from their 19 to the Penn State 32 with less than 30 seconds to go. The crowd fell silent as Sochko lined up for a 42-yard field goal attempt with the wind. The kick sailed wide to the right, and the Lions sailed toward a major bowl bid.

One week later Chris Bahr missed a 46-yard attempt with 13 seconds left. Thus North Carolina State for the second year in a row threw a wet blanket on the Lions' bowl hopes. In nearly ten years, Paterno's teams had lost only four times at home—to Syracuse (twice), Navy, and UCLA. And only five times at home or away had the Lions allowed an opponent to come from behind to win. Lou Holtz's Wolfpack added another marker in both those categories by turning a 14–0 deficit into a 15–14 win.

The Lions made it look easy at first, scoring two touchdowns by the middle of the second quarter, and their followers began daydreaming about a repeat of the West Virginia rout. But Wolfpack quarterback Dave Buckey took to the air, connecting with twin brother Don Buckey and Elijah Marshall for a score just 20 seconds before half time.

During intermission, spectators observed a ceremony honoring 80-year-old artist Heinz Warneke, sculptor of the Nittany Lion shrine in 1942.

The break in the action didn't dull Dave Buckey's passing talents, and he quickly led his team to another touchdown and field goal for the one-point margin. With just 2½ minutes left in the game, Johnny Evans got off a 78-yard quick-kick that put the Lions on their own 13-yard line. They struggled back as far as the Wolfpack 29 to set the stage for Bahr's unsuccessful field goal try.

Ironically, while the Lions took a Saturday off, they were put right back in the bowl picture by their biggest rival, the season's final opponent. The resurgent Pitt Panthers destroyed Notre Dame, 34–20, eliminating the Irish from bowl consideration and opening the door again for Penn State.

Bowl pairings proved to be the oddest in memory. The Sugar Bowl was maligned as a putup job allowing Bear Bryant to hand-pick an opponent against whom he could end his eight-year losing streak in postseason encounters. But look at the others: The Rose Bowl rematched the nation's clear-cut Number One eleven, Ohio State, and a UCLA team that had been drubbed by the Buckeyes, 41–20, in the regular season; the Orange Bowl, looking for an undefeated Nebraska, got instead Oklahoma (defeated by Kansas) against Michigan (beaten by Ohio State and tied by Stanford and Baylor); the Cotton Bowl stabbed in the dark and came up with Georgia (an early-season loser to Pitt) to meet Arkansas, a last-minute dark-horse titlist in the Southwest Conference. Mighty Southern California was relegated to the Liberty Bowl against Texas A&M, which had climbed to Number Two before it got dizzy from the height and fell before Arkansas; Nebraska and the pride of the Big Eight suffered a severe blow when the Cornhuskers were humbled by Arizona State in the Fiesta Bowl.

Why did Bear Bryant recommend Penn State for the Sugar Bowl? Joe Paterno saw it this way:

> I think Alabama felt its only shot at the national championship would come if it could play the Big Eight champion in the Orange Bowl and hope that the Big Ten champ lost in the Rose Bowl. Alabama really wanted the Orange Bowl, but was turned down in favor of the Big Ten runner-up. They felt that the Big Eight could have persuaded the Orange Bowl people to invite them if they had wanted to play Alabama. Alabama didn't want to meet the Big Eight runner-up in the Sugar Bowl. On the other hand, a game with Penn State could start to build the rivalry for the series between the two scheduled in the 1980s. From our point of view, our squad wanted to play in the Sugar Bowl. It was the only major bowl in which our seniors had not played. And we wanted to play Alabama.

Again the question arose of a logical playoff system, long advocated by Coach Paterno as a foundation for a "World Bank" type of financing to aid threatened collegiate athletic programs.

> I would like to see a two-game playoff evolving after the bowls. The money from these games, after deduction of costs and an appropriate remuneration to the participating teams, could go into a development bank for investment. After four or five years there should be a sizable accumulation of capital from which to provide loans at low interest or grants to schools having difficulty maintaining athletic programs. This could be particularly helpful in helping finance the growth of women's athletic programs. . . . It was a real shame when the University of Vermont had to give up football, and other schools face similar problems.

Going into their nationally televised encounter with Pitt at Three Rivers Stadium, the Lions had to maintain their pride as well as prove that they deserved to be in the Sugar Bowl. A stout defense and the foot of Chris Bahr once again brought them through. This time Bahr's foot was important not for kicking three-pointers, but for booming those high, deep, unreturnable punts and kickoffs. Pitt's freshman Gordon Jones, one of the most electrifying kick returners in the country, returned Bahr's nine punts a total of two yards, and two kickoffs three yards.

The key defensive play that won the game for the Lions in more ways than one, was a blocked extra-point attempt. Pitt scored first, in the second quarter, on a 37-yard run by Elliott Walker. But as the Panthers' center snapped the ball for the conversion, Tom Odell came flying over the middle and smothered the pigskin just as it came off the foot of kicker Carson Long. Long, one of the nation's finest placekickers, finishing his third year of service for the Panthers, was stunned and appeared to be gun-shy the rest of the game. Though Odell never got a hand on another placement, he was always coming, and the normally sure-footed Long missed three fourth-quarter field goal attempts, any one of which could have won the game for the Panthers.

The blocked placement was not a fluke, but a carefully planned and well-executed play specifically developed as a result of a scouting report by assistant coaches J. T. White and Gregg Ducatte. They observed that the Pitt center lifted his shoulders an instant before passing the ball. Odell was trained to take advantage of the giveaway by getting a running start and hurdling over the center before that player could come up to a blocking position.

While the Lion defense held Dorsett, Walker, and company in check better than any other team except Navy, the Lion offense sputtered for three periods. Finally, in the fourth quarter, freshman quarterback Chuck Fusina drove State 69 yards, handing off to sophomore tailback Steve Geise for the last 28. Geise popped through the left side of the line, slanted to the outside, and outran the defensive secondary to the goal line. Bahr's extra point proved to be the margin of victory.

For the second time in four years, Penn State celebrated New Year's Eve in New Orleans, playing this time in the Superdome. If Alabama's cogent Coach Bryant truly had wanted easy pickings, he had a tough bird to chew on that night.

The Bear, smarting from media and fan taunts about his snake-bitten record in bowl games, had his club superbly prepared for this one. Playing a near-perfect game—not one turnover against the vicious-hitting, keyed-up Lions—the Crimson Tide fought with tenacity to earn its seven-point victory. The Lion defense effectively shut down Alabama's vaunted running attack, limiting Willie Shelby, Johnny Davis, Mike Stock, Calvin Culliver, and Richard Todd to just 100 net yards. Coder led all defenders with eight solo tackles and six assists. Buttle was next, with six and seven. Alabama unleashed a passing attack that surprised most of the 75,000 fans. After dropping their season opener to Missouri (20–7) on national television, the Tide rolled over all its opponents without the need for a passing game. Todd had thrown for 661 yards and seven TDs during the season, only 60 yards per game. Inside the Superdome, he displayed pinpoint accuracy in completing 10 of 12 passes for 210 yards. Todd and split end Ozzie Newsome victimized a freshman defensive halfback on a 55-yard bomb that set up the only touchdown in the game. Tom Odell, the Lions' All-East halfback, who led the team in interceptions and fumble recoveries, pulled a rib cartilage on the last play of the first quarter and was out for the game. Freshman Bill Crummy played well in a tough situation until he fell for a fake and let Newsome get behind him to catch the third-quarter bomb.

Penn State, playing almost as well as Alabama, had only one turnover, but it was enough to change the flow of the game. Late in the first half, John Andress threw to Dick Barvinchak at the Alabama 6-yard line. Barvinchak, going high to make the catch, might have been able to stagger in for the score, but on the way down, Alabama defender Mark Prudhomme wrestled the ball away from him in a neat exhibition of grand larceny, and the Tide went to the locker room with a 3–0 lead instead of a 7–3 deficit. Bahr tied the contest with a 42-yard kick before the Todd-to-Newsome bomb set up Mike Stock's 14-yard run for the go-ahead touchdown. After a Bahr 37-yarder in the fourth quarter, the Alabama defense refused to let the Lions get into the end zone and thus ended an eight-year drought in bowl games.

Ecstatic, the Alabama players and coach had only good things to say about their foe. "I think we beat a great football team," the Bear said. "I told Coach Paterno after it was over he's got the kind of team I'd hate to prepare for every week. They did so many things we prepared for, but many things we didn't." Said Todd: "They had the best defense we've played against in at least a couple of years." "Penn State is the best team we played this year," added Mark Prudhomme.

The losing coach—gracious in defeat as he is magnanimous in victory—spent fifteen minutes after the final whistle seeking out Alabama players and shaking their hands. "It was a great college football game," Paterno said. "Both teams played well. I thought Alabama played an outstanding game. Todd threw the ball very well, and they caught it well. They did everything a good football team should do, and they didn't turn the ball over to us."

A fine season in the well-established tradition won no Number One votes from the pollsters but continued the quality performance that has kept Penn State in the Top Ten eight of the past ten years, with the best record in the nation for the past decade.

Suppose Penn State ever is voted that mythical crown, that Numero Uno. Would that be the end of the road? Not according to Joe Paterno. It would merely be a new beginning, because the end accomplishment isn't what counts. It's the anticipation, dedication, and striving to get there that really matters.

"The quest is the thing," says Joe. "And once you reach your goal, you set new goals. When you reach the top, the quest then becomes staying on top with new kids. We owe it to our people and our fans to become the best and stay the best."

Conclusion

Subscribing to Coach Paterno's philosophy, as John Black quotes it, the author called his book *Road to Number One* to underscore the continuity of that quest. If he had written the last chapter, certainly he'd have touched down again, as John has, on the full meaning of Numero Uno, the Grand Experiment, and the merit in a national championship playoff. He had been seeking a realistic system for playoffs, including the probability of a shortened regular season, acceptance by players of added contractual obligations, and other adjustments by colleges and the NCAA.

The prime 1976 news for him, however, would have been the election of Dexter Very '13 to the College Football Hall of Fame by the National Football Foundation. That this surviving player of the illustrious 1912 team should at last receive such high distinction, symbolic of eastern excellence formerly overlooked, is the outcome of a determined, informative assault on the foundation's nominating committee by Ridge, Coach Rip Engle (a member), and the Penn State Athletic Department. Dedication to Dex of the 1976 Ohio State game at Beaver Stadium made this an exceptionally happy Penn State family occasion.

Like Coach Paterno, Ridge scorned visionary, blanket condemnation of "football schools" and their susceptibility to "big money" from TV and the like. Neither would condone warped values in using these resources, but both believe they can serve constructively in the best interest of the university community and the public when they are perceived from all angles and allowance is made for the human behavior factor. Adapting to TV's vagaries may be irritating, yet benefits can accrue on all sides by letting this limelight also illuminate more significant but less newsworthy facets of the academic scene.

As long as football remains the national favorite intercollegiate spectator sport, it should be encouraged to stay that way, at least in colleges and universities obligated to maintain large enrollments, minimal tuitions, and broad education opportunities.

Football is a good provider, contributing to the extensive athletic programs found at most state universities and especially at those like Penn State, which are members of the national system created by the 1862 Morrill Land-Grant Act of Congress—the first legislation uniting the states and the federal government in sharing the "endowment and maintenance of colleges combining liberal and practical education in all the pursuits and professions of life."

The act, always wrongly interpreted to limit "pursuits" to agriculture and the "mechanic arts," today is further misconstrued when the stipulation "for the industrial classes" is assumed to mean the laboring class and educationally disadvantaged, instead of being given its intended application to all who work for a living and pay taxes to support their state land-grant universities (among others!). Actually the language of the act's Section 4 makes it equally pertinent for urban and rural society at all levels and in all times.

Appropriations and gifts that may seem to be generous at present are inadequate to support most public and private collegiate institutions, considering what's expected of them. (Yesterday's teachers wouldn't believe how enmeshed a university now becomes in legal proceedings, reports, government hearings and investigations, student confrontations, and faculty unionization.) Inflation and, to some extent, vandalism offset costs that might have gone down with temporarily declining full-time enrollment at many schools, but physical plants built to handle the post-World War II crunch have to be kept at the ready for new emphasis on adult education and for changing economic, industrial, and social patterns.

Chronicler Riley would have supported Coach Paterno in his bid for gifts to help Penn State continue to acquire amenities already enjoyed by some of its competition—lights for night games, for instance, and a field house to ameliorate practice conditions and amplify facilities for other sports. Also in sympathy with separation from the Eastern College Athletic Conference (ECAC) in 1974, he would have felt that the first problems stemming from that much-criticized action were cancelled by the advantages of independence to participate in NCAA affairs on a more representative basis. Realignment in four divisions and study of a superconference were among NCAA trends he expected in which Penn State now has its rightful opportunity to speak up for the major eastern independents.

Scholarship figures interestingly in charges and rebuttals arising from recurring arguments about big-time football. Players recruited for the Nittany Lions have to measure up to university-imposed standards higher than the NCAA minimum, and maintain "normal progress" to keep their eligibility. Of 250 student athletes on grants-in-aid during Paterno's ten years, 235 have earned their degrees in all of Penn State's undergraduate colleges, and a number have gone on to graduate studies. Some have had NCAA scholarships, while two were among the twenty recipients of the "top five student-athletes" honors awarded annually by the NCAA from 1973 through 1975.

An architectural engineering freshman was enrolled in 1976 on Penn State's first merit scholarship endowed by prizes earned for most valuable players' performances since Chevrolet began its program as a sponsor of ABC televised games. Anne Hubbell, honors graduate of Wheaton (Maryland) High School, owes her "grant-in-aid" to the prowess of Chuck Zapiec, Tom Shuman, Lydell Mitchell, Jeff Hite, Mike Hartenstine, Tom Donchez, John Cappelletti, Greg Buttle, and Bruce Bannon.

Penn State's good fortune in recent years, as Ridge pointed out in his closing chapter (45), kept its broad athletic program solvent and progressing, despite precarious financial conditions all around. Women's athletic activities, for one instance, got a healthy head start in meeting Title IX requirements through these resources, and all-student recreational areas also were increased. A sanguine outlook influenced university trustees to authorize expansion and improvements at Beaver Stadium.

Ridge would be asking wryly how the Lions' Beaver Stadium can still be described as equally inaccessible from all points when close to 70,000 people can manage to be at University Park regularly to enjoy competitive games and tailgating in this scenic setting, already called the football capital of the Big E. Aware that some big intersectional opponents meet their ticket demands by exacting gifts, athletic officers set a similar policy in 1971, which wasn't resorted to until the 1976 deluge of season-ticket orders. The air turned blue, but sellouts for all games assuaged the pain of alienating disenchanted fans and reaping diatribes from the *Daily Collegian* for "exploiting student athletes."

In the long run, it's evident that colleges and universities benefit the many the most by making use of whatever respectable resources they can attract without sacrificing their academic function for any reason, athletic or socio-economic. That's inherent in the Grand Experiment and in the Penn State Alumni Association's publication of the *Football Letter,* which continues in its fashion to keep football-oriented alumni in touch with their university as a totality. Their generosity toward the Ridge Riley fund for academic alumni scholarships, established in his memory in 1976, clearly identifies the Road to Number One as a worthwhile path for all seasons.

—M.T.R.

Editor's Note

The 1975 season was the last Ridge Riley was to observe. The next season began uneasily, as the Lions won the opener and then proceeded to drop the next three games in succession. Coach Paterno moved with characteristic skill, cool, and daring, moved younger players into key situations, and made the kind of changes, and took the kind of chances for which he has become renowned. Penn State went on to win the next six games. Ultimately, they faced Pitt, ranked—yes—Number One in the nation, and Pitt and Johnny Majors and Tony Dorsett had their day. Score: Pittsburgh 24; Penn State 7. The Lions had another winning season. They won seven and lost four, then went on to the Gator Bowl, with a Notre Dame 20, Penn State 9 result.

But such statistics are out of order. This is Ridge's book, a "personal chronicle," and what he would have made of the season can never be known. What he made of the seasons and years, the characters and the decades preceding has just been told. The book ends where his life did.

We are grateful—and thankful—that Peg Riley and Joe Paterno and Anne Riley, John Black, and John Morris and other true blue-and-white people were around to help finish the book. But it remains, as it began, his book. Ridge wanted it to be more than just a history of Penn State football, and it is—just as he was more than one of its former students. He, too, was a Number One guy.

That road to Number One-ness was well described by Joe Paterno. It is, he observed, a perennial goal, "not a journey with a destination. Its ninety-year path at Penn State has proved that football can be played at its peak by people who belong in a university. Such young people, in fact, give more than their football abilities and gain more than football experience. They run the road toward Number One striving to be as good as they can be without sacrificing ideas, ideals, or principles. It is their pursuit of excellence that makes them excellent."

Acknowledgments

With special regard for his weekly-in-season *Football Letter* reader-ship, Ridge wanted this book to be as reliable, orderly, literate, and readable as he could make it. "Personal chronicle" is a disclaimer of completeness, certainly not of accuracy. Painstaking research proved necessary to repair omissions and discrepancies found in books no less than in newspapers, periodicals, and reminiscences, and the bulky manuscript delivered in October 1975 covered the story with more amplitude than publishability. He knew there'd have to be substantial cutting and some fine-print footnotes, but he was compulsive about putting it all together for the sake of future histo-rians.

The Penn Sate collection of university and regional history in Pat-tee Library at University Park was a headquarters where Ridge's welcome never wore out from the time he began the big push in 1973 until the afternoon of the day he died in January 1976. Through him at least one university trustee learned firsthand that li-brary workers are indispensable to amateurs delving into these manifold, unsuspected resources. Archivist Leon Stout, Louise Kelly (Lee's predecessor as curator), Betty Welch, Mary Louise King, Kitty Morris, and this writer guided him also to the helpful people in reference, microfilm, and manuscript collections.

Access to the university administration's documentary central files, with "instant" assistance from supervisor Evelyn Evangelista and from Eleanor Ferguson, then assistant secretary to the Board of Trustees, typified the courtesies extended by university officers in Old Main, and especially in the offices of his long-time former haunt, the Penn State Alumni Association. Executive Director Ross Lehman, John Black, Robert Goerder, Donna Clemson, and Ruth Patterson were hosts-in-chief of a uniformly resourceful staff.

At the citadel of the Athletic and Sports Information departments and the College of Health, Physical Education, and Recreation in Recreation Building, hard by the Nittany Lion Shrine, cordiality and aid were unfailing. Dean Robert Scannell, James Tarman, John Morris, Edward Czekaj, Richard (Richie) Lucas, David Baker, Glenn (Nick) Thiel, Ronald Smith, and their cohorts met all challenges. Sever Toretti interpreted the play diagrams drawn by Dick Rosenfeld of the Graphic Arts staff in the university's Division of Instructional Services, and Jean McManis, director of publications, gave valuable assistance.

Prints Ridge selected for illustrations, mainly from the Penn State collection, Sports Information, and the Centre *Daily Times,* had professional attention from *Times* photographers Dick Brown and Thelma Robinson, and from John Mertz and the university's Still Photographic Service staff. Others he credited were Dave Hamilton and the Pennsylvania *Mirror;* Bill Coleman, State College photographer, and Tom Leask of the Harrisburg *Patriot-News.*

Master key to the entire enterprise was head football coach Joseph V. Paterno, whose affectionate deference to his older friend did not deter him from appropriate professional judgments. Ridge approached Joe about writing a Foreword and offered helpful notes. "Yes, of course," but "No, thank you" was his firm answer. It's printed as received on the date promised.

Before his last football trip, to the Sugar Bowl in December 1975, Ridge jotted down his sources and acknowledgments, singling out for special thanks Sam Akers of the public relations staff for the Tournament of Roses Association; James Campbell, librarian-researcher for the Professional Football Hall of Fame at Canton, Ohio; and, collectively, the obliging Sports Information directors of the institutions with which Penn State has been associated through the years. Among personal friends, not mentioned elsewhere, whose interest, needling, and encouragement kept him on course were Jerome Weinstein '38, John Branigan '47, Robert L. Wilson '40, Steve A. Garban '59, and Woodrow Bierly '38. Contacts with alumni were sheer delight and invariably productive. Those he interviewed, or with whom he exchanged letters, or who gave him access to scrapbooks are noted among sources in these listings he had prepared.

Offices of the Alumni Association and Athletic Department yielded important minute books, miscellaneous documents, and memorabilia, including scrapbooks of the one-time Athletic Association. Personal scrapbooks Ridge borrowed, or found in the Penn State collection, he listed as follows: William G. Binder '14, Alex R. Chambers '17, Henry L. (Hinkey) Haines '21, Charles H. (Hobey) Light '26 (loaned by his brother, Dr. Jack Light of State College), Harrison D. (Joe) Mason '07 (given to the Penn State collection by his son, Captain John D. Mason of State College), Eugene E. (Shorty) Miller '14 (given for the collection by Mrs. Miller), Sever J. Toretti '38, Dexter W. Very '13, and Charles A. Way '20.

The final typing of the manuscript was the work of Ridge's former secretary and our good friend, Betty Jean Korman (Mrs. Jack). Only an oral history editor like another friend, Mae Smith (Mrs. Warren), could have transcribed his tape-recorded sessions with Coach Paterno.

This section presents what I could glean from Ridge's folder of "Credits." Bulging files, orderly after his fashion, are voluminous beyond my capacity to check for possible unintentional oversights. I apologize for both of us, hoping the circumstances will be accepted as the sole cause of such delinquency. Although I considered myself a partner in this work from its inception, my role became more important when Ridge's sight began to deteriorate rapidly in the summer of 1975. My own special guardian angels have been daughter Anne Riley, brother Robert Tschan, John Morris, and Doubleday's Betty Heller. It is gratifying to have been able to assist our publisher-editor, Sam Vaughan, in the realization of this long-dreamed-of "labor of love."

M.T.R.

Bibliography

BOOKS (GENERAL)

Baker, L. H. *Football Facts and Figures.* New York: Farrar & Rinehart, 1945.

Blaik, Earl H., and Cohane, Tim. *The Red Blaik Story.* New Rochelle, N.Y.: Arlington House, 1974 (includes *You Have to Pay the Price* by Blaik and Cohane, 1960; and *As I Knew Them* by Blaik, 1974).

Camp, Walter. *Walter Camp's Book of Football.* New York: The Century Company, 1919.

Classen, Harold. *Football's Unforgettable Games.* New York: The Ronald Press, 1963.

Cohane, Tim. *Great Football Coaches of the Twenties and Thirties.* New Rochelle, N.Y.: Arlington House, 1974.

Danzig, Allison. *The History of American Football: Its Great Teams, Players, and Coaches.* Englewood Cliffs, N.J.: Prentice-Hall, 1956.

Davis, Parke H. *Football: The American Intercollegiate Game.* New York: Charles Scribner's Sons, 1911.

Gobrecht, Wilbur J. *The History of Football at Dickinson College.* Chambersburg, Pa.: Kerr Printing Company, 1971.

Gottehrer, Barry. *The Giants of New York.* New York: J. P. Putnam's Sons, 1963.

Green, Lawrence J. "A Chronicle of Changes in Collegiate Football Rules, 1873–1954." Ph.D. dissertation, University of Iowa, 1955.

Hyman, Mervin D., and White, Gordon S., Jr. *Joe Paterno: Football My Way.* New York: Macmillan Company, 1971.

March, Francis A., Jr. *Athletics at Lafayette.* Easton, Pa.: Lafayette College, 1926.

McCollum, John D., and Pearson, Charles H. *College Football, U.S.A., 1869–1971.* Official Book of the National Football Foundation. Greenwich, Conn.: Hall of Fame Publishing Company.

Maule, Tex. *The Game,* rev. ed. Official Pictorial History of NFL and AFL. New York: Random House, 1967.

Russell, Fred, and Leonard, George. *Big Bowl Football.* New York: The Ronald Press, 1963.

Townsend, Doris (ed.). *The College Game.* Indianapolis, Ind.: The Bobbs-Merrill Company (Rutledge Book), 1974.

Walsh, Christy. *Intercollegiate Football.* Garden City, N.Y.: Doubleday, Doran & Company, 1934.

Weyand, A. M. *American Football: Its History and Development.* New York: D. Appleton Company, 1926.

PENN STATE SOURCES

Ackerman, William, and Coogan, James (eds.). *Penn State All Sports Record Book.* University Park, Pa.: Public Information Department, 1955.

Dunaway, Wayland F. *History of The Pennsylvania State College.* Lancaster, Pa.: Lancaster Press, 1946.

Edwards, Earle L. "A History of a College Program of Football: An Historical Analysis of Intercollegiate Football at The Pennsylvania State College." Unpublished M.S. thesis, The Pennsylvania State College, 1939.

Stark, Lois. "The Role of the University Administration in the Development of Physical Education at The Pennsylvania State University." Unpublished M.S. thesis, The Pennsylvania State University, 1969.

ALUMNI ASSOCIATION PUBLICATIONS

Magazine: *Alumni Quarterly* (1910–18); *Alumni News* (1914–71); *Penn Stater* (1971–   ).

Football Letter: published annually in season (since 1938) after each game.

SPORTS INFORMATION DEPARTMENT PUBLICATIONS

Football Press Guide. Paperback printed annually since 1963.
Programs: *Beaver Field Pictorial* (1920–59); *Beaver Stadium Pictorial* (1960–).

STUDENT PUBLICATIONS

Lemon. Anonymous student journal. March 17, 1907 issue.
Newspaper: *Free Lance* (1887–1904); *State Collegian* (1904–10); *Penn State Collegian* (1911–40); *Daily Collegian* (1940–).
Yearbook: *LaVie.* Junior, senior class annual (1890–).

INTERVIEWS

F. Joseph Bedenk '24
George W. Brown '21
Earl J. Bruce
Charles A. (Rip) Engle
William Fuhs '09
Helen Atherton Govier '99
   (Mrs. C. E.)
Walter (Red) Gross '18
Henry L. (Hinkey) Haines '20
Burke M. (Dutch) Hermann '12
Kenneth L. Holderman '31
Ben J. (Casey) Jones '19
Rilla Keller
W. Glenn Killinger '21

Jay S. MacMahan '24
William Meredith, Sr.
Mrs. Ruth Miller
   (widow of Eugene E. [Shorty] '14)
James J. O'Hora '36
Joseph V. Paterno
Ralph R. Ricker '29
Howard L. (Pete) Stuart '21
Steve and Virginia Higgins Suhey
   ('50 and '48)
Sever J. Toretti '38
Dexter W. Very '13
Charles A. Way '20

CORRESPONDENCE

Richard H. Bartholomew '28
George Buckhout '31
Alexander R. Chambers '17
Frank Diedrich '31
Charles T. Douds '22
Earle L. Edwards '31
Sally Rolston Goas '58
   (Mrs. Thomas S., Jr.)
P. W. (Red) Griffiths '20
William H. Hess '19

Dr. Richards S. Hoffman '23
Albert H. Knabb '22
James A. Leyden '14
Jeanne Barwis Lopez '33
   (Mrs. Aaron)
John G. (Cy) Lungren '29
Peter G. Meek '32
Philip P. Mitchell '43
Robert E. Morini '37
George C. Morris '17

Robert D. (Duke) Osborn '20
Edward L. Pierce '33
Judge John D. Pincura, Jr. '28
Charles M. Speidel '39
Edward N. (Mike) Sullivan '14

Grover Washabaugh '40
Mrs. Frank N. Wolf '20
Esther Chase Wood '18
   (widow of Wiliam W. '16)

Appendix A

Scores by Season

GAME BY GAME, 1887 through 1976

(No formal coaches until 1892)

1887—(2–0)

54	at Bucknell	0
24	Bucknell	0

1888—(0–2–1)

6	Dickinson	6
0	at Dickinson	16
0	Lehigh	30

1889—(2–2)

20	Swarthmore	6
0	at Lafayette	26
0	at Lehigh	106
12	Bucknell	0

1890—(2–2)

0	at Penn	20
0	at Franklin and Marshall	10
68	Altoona	0
23	at Bellefonte	0

1891—(6–2)

14	at Lafayette	4
2	at Lehigh	24
44	at Swarthmore	0
26	at Franklin and Marshall	6
18	at Gettysburg	0
10	at Bucknell	12
2	Dickinson (forfeit)	0
58	at Haverford	0

Coach: G. W. Hoskins

1892—(5–1)

0	at Penn	20
44	Wyoming Seminary at Kingston	0
16	at Pittsburgh AC	0
18	Bucknell	0
18	Lafayette at Wilkes-Barre	0
16	Dickinson at Harrisburg	0

1893—(4–1)

6	at Virginia	0
6	at Penn	18
32	Pitt	0
36	at Bucknell	18
12	at Pittsburgh AC	0

1894—(6–0–1)

60	Gettysburg	0
72	Lafayette	0
6	at Navy	6
12	Bucknell at Williamsport	6
6	at W&J	0
9	at Oberlin	6
14	at Pittsburgh AC	0

1895—(2–2–3)

48	Gettysburg	0
0	at Cornell	0
16	Bucknell at Williamsport	0
4	at Penn	35
10	at Pittsburgh AC	11

6	at W&J	6
8	at Western Reserve	8

Coach: Dr. S. B. Newton

1896—(3–4)

40	Gettysburg	0
10	Pitt	4
8	Dickinson	0
0	at Princeton	39
0	Bucknell at Williamsport	10
0	at Penn	27
5	Carlisle Indians at Harrisburg	48

1897—(3–6)

32	Gettysburg	0
0	at Lafayette	24
0	at Princeton	34
0	at Penn	24
0	at Navy	4
0	at Cornell	45
27	Bucknell at Williamsport	4
10	Bloomsburg Normal	0
0	Dickinson at Sunbury	6

1898—(6–4)

47	Gettysburg	0
0	at Penn	40
5	at Lafayette	0
45	Susquehanna	6
11	at Navy	16
0	at Princeton	5
5	Duquesne AC at Pittsburgh	18
16	Bucknell at Williamsport	0
11	at W&J	6
34	Dickinson at Williamsport	0

Coach: Sam Boyle

1899—(4–6)

38	Mansfield	0
40	Gettysburg	0

6	at Army	0
0	at Princeton	12
0	at Navy	6
15	Dickinson	0
0	Bucknell at Williamsport	5
0	at Yale	42
0	at Penn	47
5	Duquesne AC at Pittsburgh	64

Coach: W. N. Golden

1900—(4–6–1)

17	Susquehanna	0
12	Pitt at Bellefonte	0
0	at Army	0
0	at Princeton	26
5	at Penn	17
0	at Dickinson	18
0	Duquesne AC at Pittsburgh	29
6	Bucknell at Williamsport	0
0	at Navy	44
44	Gettysburg	0
0	at Buffalo	10

1901—(5–3)

17	Susquehanna	0
27	Pitt at Bellefonte	0
6	at Penn	23
0	at Yale	22
11	at Navy	6
0	Homestead AC at Pittsburgh	39
39	Lehigh at Williamsport	0
12	Dickinson	0

1902—(7–3)

28	Dickinson Seminary	0
27	Pitt	0
0	at Penn	17
32	Villanova	0
0	at Yale	11
55	Susquehanna	0
6	at Navy	0
39	Gettysburg	0

23	at Dickinson	0
5	at Steelton YMCA	6

Coach: Dan Reed

1903—(5–3)

60	Dickinson Seminary	0
24	Allegheny	5
0	at Penn	39
0	at Yale	27
59	at Pitt	0
17	at Navy	0
0	Dickinson at Williamsport	6
22	W&J at Pittsburgh	0

Coach: Tom Fennell

1904—(6–4)

0	at Penn	6
50	Allegheny	0
0	at Yale	24
34	West Virginia	0
12	W&J at Pittsburgh	0
30	Jersey Shore	0
9	at Navy	20
11	Dickinson at Williamsport	0
44	Geneva	0
5	at Pitt	22

1905—(8–3)

23	Lebanon Valley	0
29	California State	0
0	Carlisle Indians at Harrisburg	11
18	Gettysburg	0
0	at Yale	12
29	Villanova	0
5	at Navy	11
73	Geneva	0
6	Dickinson at Williamsport	0
6	West Virginia	0
6	at Pitt	0

1906—(8–1–1)

24	Lebanon Valley	0
26	Allegheny	0
4	Carlisle Indians at Williamsport	0
0	Gettysburg	0
12	Bellefonte Academy	0
0	at Yale	10
5	at Navy	0
6	Dickinson at Williamsport	0
10	West Virginia	0
6	at Pitt	0

1907—(6–4)

27	Altoona AA	0
34	Geneva	0
5	Carlisle Indians at Williamsport	18
46	Grove City	0
8	at Cornell	6
75	Lebanon Valley	0
52	Dickinson at Williamsport	0
0	at Penn	28
4	at Navy	6
0	at Pitt	6

1908—(5–5)

5	Bellefonte Academy	6
31	Grove City	0
5	Carlisle Indians at Wilkes-Barre	12
0	at Penn	6
51	Geneva	0
12	West Virginia	0
4	at Cornell	10
33	Bucknell	6
0	at Navy	5
12	at Pitt	6

Coach: Bill Hollenback

1909—(5–0–2)

31	Grove City	0
8	Carlisle Indians at Wilkes-Barre	8
46	Geneva	0

3	at Penn	3
33	at Bucknell	0
40	West Virginia	0
5	at Pitt	0

Coach: Jack Hollenback

1910—(5–2–1)

58	Harrisburg AC	0
61	Carnegie Tech	0
45	Sterling AC	0
0	at Penn	10
0	Villanova	0
34	St. Bonaventure	0
45	Bucknell	3
0	at Pitt	11

Coach: Bill Hollenback

1911—(8–0–1)

57	Geneva	0
31	Gettysburg	0
5	at Cornell	0
18	Villanova	0
22	at Penn	6
46	St. Bonaventure	0
17	Colgate	9
0	at Navy	0
3	at Pitt	0

1912—(8–0)

41	Carnegie Tech	0
30	W&J	0
29	at Cornell	6
25	Gettysburg	0
14	at Penn	0
71	Villanova	0
37	at Ohio State	0
38	at Pitt	0

1913—(2–6)

49	Carnegie Tech	0
16	Gettysburg	0
0	at W&J	17

0	at Harvard	29
0	at Penn	17
7	Notre Dame	14
0	at Navy	10
6	at Pitt	7

1914—(5–3–1)

13	Westminster	0
22	Muhlenberg	0
13	Gettysburg	0
30	Ursinus	0
13	at Harvard	13
17	at Lafayette	0
7	at Lehigh	20
3	Michigan State	6
3	at Pitt	13

Coach: Dick Harlow

1915—(7–2)

26	Westminster	0
13	Lebanon Valley	0
13	at Penn	3
27	Gettysburg	12
28	West Virginia Wesleyan	0
0	at Harvard	13
7	Lehigh	0
33	at Lafayette	3
0	at Pitt	20

1916—(8–2)

27	Susquehanna	0
55	Westminster	0
50	Bucknell	7
39	West Virginia Wesleyan	0
0	at Penn	15
48	Gettysburg	2
79	Geneva	0
10	at Lehigh	7
40	Lafayette	0
0	at Pitt	31

1917—(5–4)

10	U. S. Army Amb. Cp. at Allentown	0
80	Gettysburg	0
99	St. Bonaventure	0
0	at W&J	7
8	West Virginia Wesleyan	7
7	at Dartmouth	10
0	Lehigh	9
57	Maryland	0
6	at Pitt	28

Coach: Hugo Bezdek

1918—(1–2–1)

6	Wissahickon Barracks	6
3	Rutgers	26
7	at Lehigh	6
6	at Pitt	28

1919—(7–1)

33	Gettysburg	0
9	Bucknell	0
13	at Dartmouth	19
48	Ursinus	7
10	at Penn	0
20	Lehigh	7
20	at Cornell	0
20	at Pitt	0

1920—(7–0–2)

27	Muhlenberg	7
13	Gettysburg	0
14	Dartmouth	7
41	North Carolina State	0
109	Lebanon Valley	7
28	at Penn	7
20	Nebraska	0
7	at Lehigh	7
0	at Pitt	0

1921—(8–0–2)

53	Lebanon Valley	0
24	Gettysburg	0
35	North Carolina State	0
28	Lehigh	7
21	at Harvard	21
28	Georgia Tech at New York	7
28	Carnegie Tech	7
13	Navy at Philadelphia	7
0	at Pitt	0
21	at Washington	7

1922—(6–4–1)

54	St. Bonaventure	0
27	William and Mary	7
20	Gettysburg	0
32	Lebanon Valley	6
33	Middlebury	0
0	Syracuse at New York	0
0	Navy at Washington, D.C.	14
10	Carnegie Tech	0
6	at Penn	7
0	at Pitt	14

1923 Rose Bowl

| 3 | USC at Pasadena, Calif. | 14 |

1923—(6–2–1)

58	Lebanon Valley	0
16	North Carolina State	0
20	Gettysburg	0
21	Navy	3
13	West Virginia at New York	13
0	at Syracuse	10
7	Georgia Tech	0
21	at Penn	0
3	at Pitt	20

1924—(6–3–1)

| 47 | Lebanon Valley | 3 |
| 51 | North Carolina State | 6 |

26	Gettysburg	0
13	at Georgia Tech	15
6	Syracuse	10
6	at Navy	0
22	Carnegie Tech	7
0	at Penn	0
28	Marietta	0
3	at Pitt	24

1925—(4–4–1)

14	Lebanon Valley	0
13	Franklin and Marshall	0
7	Georgia Tech at New York	16
13	Marietta	0
13	Michigan State	6
0	at Syracuse	7
0	Notre Dame	0
0	at West Virginia	14
7	at Pitt	23

1926—(5–4)

82	Susquehanna	0
35	Lebanon Valley	0
48	Marietta	6
0	at Notre Dame	28
0	Syracuse	10
20	George Washington	12
0	at Penn	3
9	Bucknell	0
6	at Pitt	24

1927—(6–2–1)

27	Lebanon Valley	0
34	Gettysburg	13
7	Bucknell	13
20	at Penn	0
9	at Syracuse	6
40	Lafayette	6
13	George Washington	0
13	New York University	13
0	at Pitt	30

1928—(3–5–1)

25	Lebanon Valley	0
12	Gettysburg	0
0	Bucknell	6
0	at Penn	14
6	Syracuse	6
0	Notre Dame at Philadelphia	9
50	George Washington	0
0	at Lafayette	7
0	at Pitt	26

(1929—(6–3)

16	Niagara	0
15	Lebanon Valley	0
26	Marshall	7
0	at New York University	7
6	Lafayette	3
6	at Syracuse	4
19	at Penn	7
6	Bucknell	27
7	at Pitt	20

Coach: Bob Higgins

1930—(3–4–2)

31	Niagara	14
27	Lebanon Valley	0
65	Marshall	0
0	at Lafayette	0
0	Colgate	40
7	at Bucknell	19
0	Syracuse	0
0	at Iowa	19
12	at Pitt	19

1931—(2–8)

0	Waynesburg	7
19	Lebanon Valley	6
0	at Temple	12
6	Dickinson	10
0	at Syracuse	7

6	Pitt	41
7	Colgate	32
0	at Lafayette	33
0	at West Virginia	19
31	Lehigh at Philadelphia	0

1932—(2–5)

27	Lebanon Valley	0
6	Waynesburg	7
13	at Harvard	46
6	Syracuse	12
0	at Colgate	31
18	Sewanee (U. of South)	6
12	at Temple	13

1933—(3–3–1)

32	Lebanon Valley	6
0	Muhlenberg	3
33	Lehigh	0
0	at Columbia	33
6	at Syracuse	12
40	Johns Hopkins	6
6	at Penn	6

1934—(4–4)

13	Lebanon Valley	0
32	Gettysburg	6
31	at Lehigh	0
7	at Columbia	14
0	Syracuse	16
0	at Penn	3
25	Lafayette	6
7	Bucknell	13

1935—(4–4)

12	Lebanon Valley	6
2	Western Maryland	0
26	Lehigh	0
0	at Pitt	9
3	at Syracuse	7
27	Villanova	13
6	at Penn	33
0	at Bucknell	2

1936—(3–5)

45	Muhlenberg	0
0	Villanova	13
6	at Lehigh	7
7	at Cornell	13
18	Syracuse	0
7	at Pitt	34
12	at Penn	19
14	Bucknell	0

1937—(5–3)

19	at Cornell	26
32	Gettysburg	6
30	Bucknell	14
14	Lehigh	7
13	at Syracuse	19
7	at Penn	0
21	Maryland	14
7	at Pitt	28

1938—(3–4–1)

33	Maryland	0
0	Bucknell	14
59	at Lehigh	6
6	at Cornell	21
33	Syracuse	6
0	Lafayette	7
7	at Penn	7
0	at Pitt	26

1939—(5–1–2)

13	Bucknell	3
49	Lehigh	7
0	at Cornell	47
6	at Syracuse	6
12	Maryland	0
10	at Penn	0
14	at Army	14
10	Pitt	0

1940—(6–1–1)

9	Bucknell	0
17	West Virginia	13

34	at Lehigh	0
18	at Temple	0
12	South Carolina	0
13	at Syracuse	13
25	New York University	0
7	at Pitt	20

1941—(7–2)

0	Colgate at Buffalo, N.Y.	7
27	Bucknell	13
0	at Temple	14
40	Lehigh	6
42	at New York University	0
34	Syracuse	19
7	West Virginia	0
31	at Pitt	7
19	at South Carolina	12

1942—(6–1–1)

14	Bucknell	7
19	at Lehigh	3
0	at Cornell	0
13	Colgate	10
0	at West Virginia	24
18	Syracuse	13
13	at Penn	7
14	Pitt	6

1943—(5–3–1)

14	Bucknell	0
0	at North Carolina	19
0	Colgate	0
6	at Navy	14
45	at Maryland	0
32	West Virginia	7
0	at Cornell	13
13	Temple	0
14	at Pitt	0

1944—(6–3)

58	Muhlenberg	13
14	at Navy	55
20	Bucknell	6

6	at Colgate	0
27	West Virginia	28
41	at Syracuse	0
7	at Temple	6
34	Maryland	19
0	at Pitt	14

1945—(5–3)

47	Muhlenberg	7
27	Colgate	7
0	at Navy	28
46	at Bucknell	7
26	Syracuse	0
27	Temple	0
0	at Michigan State	33
0	at Pitt	7

1946—(6–2)

48	Bucknell	6
9	at Syracuse	0
16	Michigan State	19
6	at Colgate	2
68	Fordham	0
26	Temple	0
12	at Navy	7
7	at Pitt	14

1947—(9–0–1)

27	Washington State at Hershey	6
54	Bucknell	0
75	at Fordham	0
40	Syracuse	0
21	West Virginia	14
46	Colgate	0
7	at Temple	0
20	Navy at Baltimore	7
29	at Pitt	0

1948 Cotton Bowl

13	Southern Methodist at Dallas, Tex.	13

1948—(7–1–1)

35	Bucknell	0
34	at Syracuse	14
37	West Virginia	7
14	Michigan State	14
32	at Colgate	13
13	at Penn	0
47	Temple	0
0	at Pitt	7
7	at Washington State	0

Coach: Joe Bedenk

1949—(5–4)

6	Villanova	27
7	at Army	42
32	Boston College	14
22	Nebraska	7
0	at Michigan State	24
33	Syracuse	21
34	at West Virginia	14
28	at Temple	7
0	at Pitt	19

Coach: Rip Engle

1950—(5–3–1)

34	Georgetown	14
7	at Army	41
7	at Syracuse	27
0	at Nebraska	19
7	Temple	7
20	at Boston College	13
27	West Virginia	0
18	Rutgers	14
21	at Pitt	20

1951—(5–4)

40	Boston University	34
14	Villanova at Allentown	20
15	at Nebraska	7
21	Michigan State	32

13	West Virginia	7
0	at Purdue	28
32	Syracuse	13
13	at Rutgers	7
7	at Pitt	13

1952—(7–2–1)

20	Temple	13
20	Purdue	20
35	William and Mary	23
35	at West Virginia	21
10	Nebraska	0
7	at Michigan State	34
14	at Penn	7
7	at Syracuse	25
7	Rutgers	6
17	at Pitt	0

1953–(6–3)

0	at Wisconsin	20
7	at Penn	13
35	at Boston University	13
20	Syracuse	14
27	Texas Christian	21
19	West Virginia	20
28	Fordham	21
54	at Rutgers	26
17	at Pitt	0

1954—(7–2)

14	at Illinois	12
13	at Syracuse	0
34	Virginia	7
14	West Virginia	19
7	at Texas Christian	20
35	at Penn	13
39	Holy Cross	7
37	Rutgers	14
13	at Pitt	0

1955—(5–4)

35	Boston University	0
6	at Army	35

26	Virginia at Richmond	7
14	Navy	34
7	at West Virginia	21
20	at Penn	0
21	Syracuse	20
34	at Rutgers	13
0	Pitt	20

1956—(6–2–1)

34	at Penn	0
7	at Army	14
43	Holy Cross	0
7	at Ohio State	6
16	West Virginia	6
9	at Syracuse	13
40	Boston University	7
14	North Carolina State	7
7	at Pitt	7

1957—(6–3)

19	at Penn	14
13	Army	27
21	William and Mary	13
20	Vanderbilt	32
20	at Syracuse	12
27	West Virginia	6
20	at Marquette	7
14	at Holy Cross	10
13	at Pitt	14

1958—(6–3–1)

7	at Nebraska	14
43	at Penn	0
0	at Army	26
40	Marquette	8
34	at Boston University	0
6	Syracuse	14
36	Furman	0
14	at West Virginia	14
32	Holy Cross	0
25	at Pitt	21

1959—(9–2)

19	at Missouri	8
21	VMI	0
58	Colgate	20
17	at Army	11
21	Boston University	12
20	Illinois at Cleveland	9
28	at West Virginia	10
18	Syracuse	20
46	Holy Cross	0
7	at Pitt	22

1959 Liberty Bowl

7   Alabama at Philadelphia, Pa.   0

1960—(7–3)

20	Boston University	0
8	Missouri	21
27	at Army	16
15	at Syracuse	21
8	at Illinois	10
34	West Virginia	13
28	Maryland	9
33	at Holy Cross	8
14	at Pitt	3

1960 Liberty Bowl

41   Oregon at Philadelphia, Pa.   12

1961—(8–3)

20	Navy	10
8	at Miami	25
32	at Boston University	0
6	Army	10
14	Syracuse	0
33	California	16
17	at Maryland	21
20	at West Virginia	6
34	Holy Cross	14
47	at Pitt	26

1961 Gator Bowl

| 30 | Georgia Tech at Jacksonville, Fla. | 15 |

1962—(9–2)

41	Navy	7
20	Air Force	6
18	at Rice	7
6	at Army	9
20	Syracuse	19
23	at California	21
23	Maryland	7
34	West Virginia	6
48	at Holy Cross	20
16	at Pitt	0

1962 Gator Bowl

| 7 | Florida at Jacksonville, Fla. | 17 |

1963—(7–3)

17	at Oregon	7
17	UCLA	14
28	Rice	7
7	Army	10
0	at Syracuse	9
20	West Virginia	9
17	at Maryland	15
10	at Ohio State	7
28	Holy Cross	14
21	at Pitt	22

1964—(6–4)

8	Navy	21
14	at UCLA	21
14	Oregon	22
6	at Army	2
14	Syracuse	21
37	at West Virginia	8
17	Maryland	9
27	at Ohio State	0
24	at Houston	7
28	Pitt	0

1965—(5–5)

0	Michigan State	23
22	UCLA	24
17	at Boston College	0
21	at Syracuse	28
44	West Virginia	6
17	at California	21
21	Kent State	6
14	Navy	6
27	at Pitt	30
19	at Maryland	7

Coach: Joe Paterno

1966—(5–5)

15	Maryland	7
8	at Michigan State	42
0	at Army	11
30	Boston College	21
11	at UCLA	49
38	at West Virginia	6
33	California	15
10	Syracuse	12
0	at Georgia Tech	21
48	at Pitt	24

1967—(8–2–1)

22	at Navy	23
17	at Miami	8
15	UCLA	17
50	at Boston College	28
21	West Virginia	14
29	at Syracuse	20
38	at Maryland	3
13	North Carolina State	8
35	Ohio University	14
42	Pitt	6

1967 Gator Bowl

17	Florida State at Jacksonville, Fla.	17

1968—(11–0)

31	Navy	6
25	Kansas State	9
31	at West Virginia	20
21	at UCLA	6
29	at Boston College	0
28	Army	24
22	Miami	7
57	at Maryland	13
65	at Pitt	9
30	Syracuse	12

1969 Orange Bowl

15   Kansas at Miami, Fla.   14

1969—(11–0)

45	at Navy	22
27	Colorado	3
17	at Kansas State	14
20	West Virginia	0
15	at Syracuse	14
42	Ohio University	3
38	Boston College	16
48	Maryland	0
27	at Pitt	7
33	at North Carolina State	8

1970 Orange Bowl

10   Missouri at Miami, Fla.   3

1970—(7–3)

55	Navy	7
13	at Colorado	41
16	at Wisconsin	29
28	at Boston College	3
7	Syracuse	24
38	at Army	14
42	West Virginia	8
34	at Maryland	0

32	Ohio University	22
35	Pitt	15

1971—(11–1)

56	at Navy	3
44	at Iowa	14
16	Air Force	14
42	Army	0
31	at Syracuse	0
66	Texas Christian	14
35	at West Virginia	7
63	Maryland	27
35	North Carolina State	3
55	at Pitt	18
11	at Tennessee	31

1972 Cotton Bowl

30   Texas at Dallas, Tex.   6

1972—(10–2)

21	at Tennessee	28
21	Navy	10
14	Iowa	10
35	at Illinois	17
45	at Army	0
17	Syracuse	0
28	at West Virginia	19
46	Maryland	16
37	North Carolina State	22
45	at Boston College	26
49	Pitt	27

1972 Sugar Bowl

0   Oklahoma at New Orleans, La.   14

1973—(12–0)

20	at Stanford	6
39	at Navy	0
27	Iowa	8
19	at Air Force	9

54	Army	3
49	at Syracuse	6
62	West Virginia	14
42	at Maryland	22
35	North Carolina State	29
49	Ohio University	10
35	Pitt	13

1974 Orange Bowl

16	Louisiana State at Miami, Fla.	9

1974—(10–2)

24	Stanford	20
6	Navy	7
27	at Iowa	0
21	at Army	14
55	Wake Forest	0
30	Syracuse	14
21	at West Virginia	12
24	Maryland	17
7	at North Carolina State	12
35	Ohio University	16
31	at Pitt	10

1975 Cotton Bowl

41	Baylor at Dallas, Tex.	20

1975—(9–3)

26	Temple at Philadelphia	25
34	Stanford	14
9	at Ohio State	17
30	at Iowa	10
10	Kentucky	3
39	West Virginia	0
19	at Syracuse	7
31	Army	0
15	at Maryland	13
14	North Carolina State	15
7	at Pitt	6

1975 Sugar Bowl

6   Alabama at New Orleans, La.   13

1976—(7–5)

15	Stanford	12
7	Ohio State	12
6	Iowa	7
6	Kentucky	22
38	Army	16
27	Syracuse	3
33	West Virginia	0
31	Temple	30
41	North Carolina State	20
21	Miami	7
7	at Pitt	24

1976 Gator Bowl

9   Notre Dame at Jacksonville, Fla.   20

Appendix B

Play Diagrams

CODE

· · · · · · · · FLIGHT OF BALL

——— RUNNING PLAYER

∿∿∿∿∿ PLAYER WITH BALL

(⊙) BALL CARRIER

‖ FAKE

THE PLAYS OF BILL HOLLENBACK

Hollenback was twenty-three when he arrived at Penn State in 1909, three months after his graduation from Pennsylvania, where he had played under Dr. Carl S. Williams (1904–7) and Sol Metzger, who coached only one year (1908). Hollenback adapted parts of the Penn offense and added new wrinkles while gaining experience. According to Ray Smith '05, graduate manager of athletics and a good friend of his, Bill received a weekly letter from Pop Warner, Carlisle's coach, presumably with suggestions for an offense against the next opponent.

These Hollenback plays and formations, selected from a playbook carefully preserved by Dexter Very for more than sixty years, are in partial use to some degree today. For instance, Hollenback's regular or basic formation is nothing but the "Power I" currently in vogue at many colleges, including Penn State.

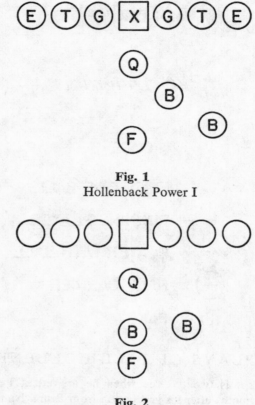

Fig. 1
Hollenback Power I

Fig. 2
Modern Power I

(Can be used right or left)

From this formation (Fig. 1), Hollenback's teams ran the ends with quarterback or fullback (guard pulling), executing fullback bucks, end around, or cross buck. An interesting series called "tackle-back" plays worked as follows:

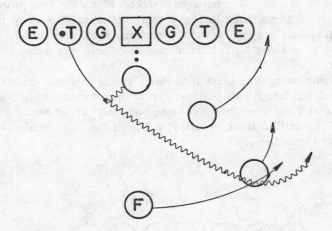

Fig. 3
Tackle-around

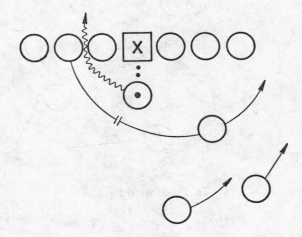

Fig. 4
Fake Tackle-around
Quarterback Keep

In Fig. 3, left tackle pulled out, was handed the ball by quarterback, and circled wide around right end with three other backs as interference. In Fig. 4, quarterback faked to tackle and proceeded through the tackle hole. In Fig. 5, quarterback handed off to tackle, who faked an end run to right, then pitched back to fullback, who passed to left end. Quarterback ran downfield as a secondary receiver.

Legislation against mass formations swung coaches gradually to forward and lateral pass plays as well as open formations or spreads. Note that Hollenback had the "lonesome end" about fifty years before Colonel Red Blaik at Army, although the Army variation was executed from the T.

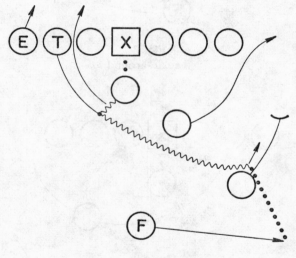

Fig. 5
Tackle-around Pass

In Fig. 6, fullback took a direct pass from center for a quick forward pass. Many plays, both running and passing, were run from formation in Fig. 7, with one end very wide and fullback getting direct pass from center. Note that tackle on left is also an eligible pass

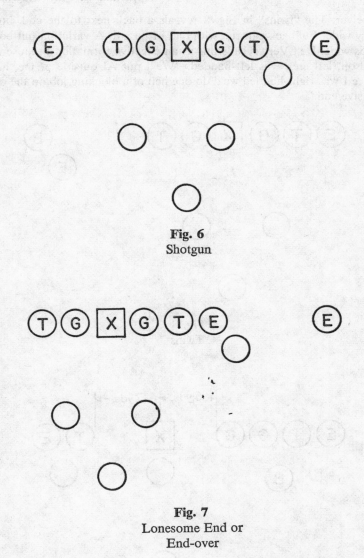

Fig. 6
Shotgun

Fig. 7
Lonesome End or
End-over

receiver. The "twins" in Fig. 8 reveals a back next to the end, both very wide. Fullback can run with ball or pass it. A variation put both ends wide. Dex Very recalls this as an effective formation because Al Wilson, left end, was left-handed. "We'd put Al outside of me, and since I was right-handed we'd do one hell of a blocking job on the defensive end."

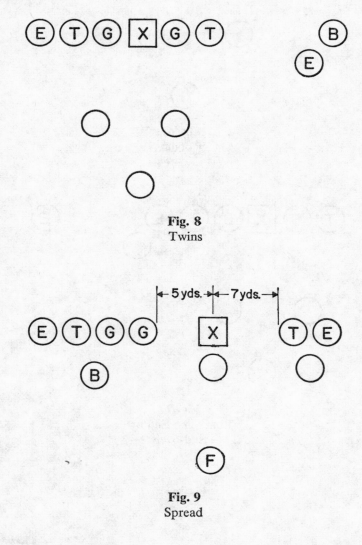

Fig. 8
Twins

Fig. 9
Spread

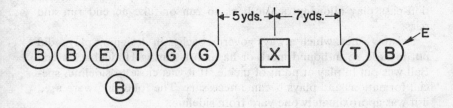

Fig. 10
Spread

In Fig. 9 spread, ball is lateraled to either halfback after handoff for a straight-ahead run, or thrown to fullback for a forward pass to the ends or any of the three backs. In another spread (Fig. 10), tackle and end on right might drop back, making center eligible for a pass, or two halfbacks on left could drop back to make left end eligible.

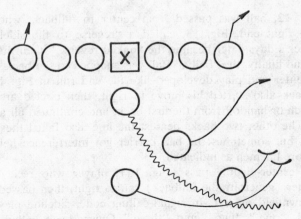

Fig. 11
Rollout Option-pass

Fig. 11 shows Coach Hollenback's version of popular rollout option-pass play allowing quarterback to run or fake an end run and pass.

Existing rules, which always govern coaches in designing plays, did not include an in-bound mark or hashmark during Hollenback's era. Ball was put in play at point of tackle. If it was close to sideline, special formations and plays became necessary. The following were used if it was approximately one yard from sideline.

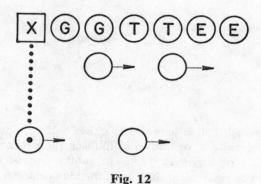

Fig. 12
End Run

In Fig. 12, ball was passed from center to fullback, who ran a sweep to right end. Fig. 13, called a "reverse to the sideline" in Hollenback's days, later became the "naked reverse," then the "Sally Rand," and finally, the "Sally." Ball was snapped to the back directly behind center and play developed like the end run in Fig. 12. The middle back also started his move to right, then circled around to take a pitch or handoff from the first back, and continued all alone to the left. The other two backs nearest the line also faked the play to the right, but sometimes the ball carrier got interference help from one or more linemen as indicated.

In the center-eligible pass (Fig. 14), player who received ball from center (generally the fullback) ran to right, then passed to the center downfield on left. In signal-calling code, sideline plays were numbered, "one," "two," and "three." Quarterback called proper play after a time-out by asking referee, "Is this the *first* time-out?," or "Is this the *second* time-out?" etc.

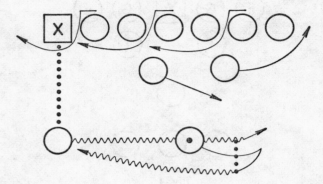

Fig. 13
Fake End Run
Reverse or "Sally"

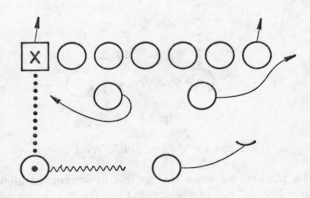

Fig. 14
Center-eligible Pass

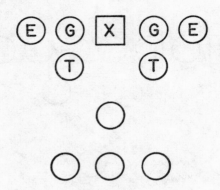

Fig. 15
Preshift, Tackles-back

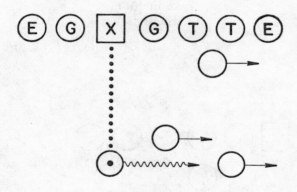

Fig. 16
After Shift
Unbalanced Line, Single Wing

Since six players had to be on the line of scrimmage after 1903 (seven after 1909), Hollenback couldn't use the famous guards-back formation originated at Penn, or the tackles-back executed so effectively by Yale. In his own variation, he placed his tackles in the backfield (Fig. 15) and, on a count, shifted them to the line on right or left side (Fig. 16), an efficient formation for end sweeps since players were not required to come to a one-second stop after the shift.

THE PLAYS OF HUGO BEZDEK, 1918–21

At Penn State Coach Bezdek installed what was then known as the Notre Dame shift, with his own variations. Actually, both Knute Rockne and Bezdek developed their systems from the same source. Rockne inherited his from Jesse Harper, his predecessor; Harper and Bezdek both played under Amos Alonzo Stagg at Chicago. Bezdek used an unbalanced line with the two guards side by side for either

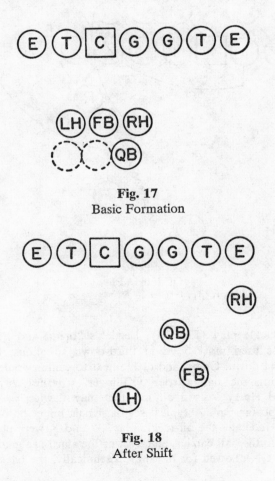

Fig. 17
Basic Formation

Fig. 18
After Shift

right or left formations. Fig. 17 is the basic formation right, indicating that the quarterback could take one of three positions. Penn State often caught its opponents off guard by quick-bucking or throwing a screen pass before the shift. Fig. 18 shows position of backs after the shift. Any one of three backs (LH, FB, QB) might shift to tailback position. The author is indebted to W. Glenn Killinger for his recall of these Bezdek plays and formations.

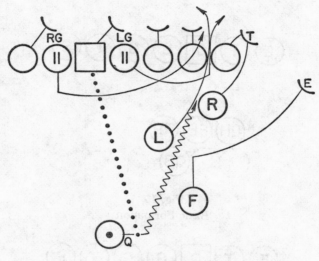

Fig. 19
Off-tackle Play

The off-tackle play (Fig. 19), Bezdek's "bread and butter" operation, was used most often in third-down situations, but many times on first down. Guard and tackle next to center would pull, the guard leading the ball carrier (Killinger, Charlie Way, Hinkey Haines, and Harry Wilson all ran this play flawlessly). Fullback blocked opposing end. A typical set of signals might be 41-37-QX-97—the 41 indicates the off-tackle play, 37 and X were phony calls, Q referred to the ball carrier, and 97 was the starting signal. A slight pause after QX allowed for the shift. Technically, the backs were to come to a complete halt for one second after shifting. Bezdek worked his players so long and hard that a perfect rhythm was developed, but it's questionable if they ever halted for a complete second. The off-tackle play could become a wide end run, using the same line blocking except that an effort was made to block the end in. Says Killinger:

> During my experience as a player, coach, and spectator, I've never seen any team run this play more precisely or more compactly. The 1921 team executed it best because Joe Lightner, George Snell, Al Knabb, and Harry Wilson were beautiful blockers. Joe Bedenk (guard) was our very best running blocker, with Ray Baer a close second. Joe did more blocking for me than any other player. I often hung on Joe's belt, and he would actually pull me through holes.

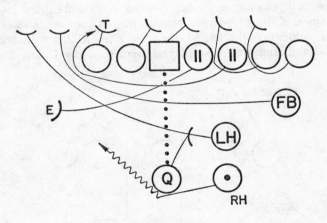

Fig. 20
Reverse Play

Fig. 20 is a powerful reverse complementing Bezdek's off-tackle play, sometimes run wide, outside the defensive end. Killinger often shifted from quarterback to tailback to hand off the ball. Signal call could be 42-63-QM-11-99—the first number indicated a reverse, 63 was a dummy number, Q called for a quarterback shift to tailback position, and M was the right halfback or ball carrier.

On the fake reverse or half spinner (Fig. 21), ball was passed to tailback (H), who faked handing off to Q, who faked wide to draw the defense out of position. FB and RH faked one step to the weak side and then both went through the first available hole to block linebackers. H would make a half turn to fake handling the ball to Q, then followed FB or RH through the line. H bucked through any available hole between the two defensive tackles. Signals could be 22 (play)-79-HQ (backs)-63 (starting signal)-65.

Killinger thinks Penn State's 1920 team ran this play for the first time in the history of football. "In the first quarter of the Penn game we used the half spinner for Haines and Way to make successive gains of forty and thirty yards, to enable me to score from close in."

Bezdek had used a variation as early as 1909 at Arkansas, when his star was Steve Creekmore. It's supposed to have originated when signals were mixed up as the quarterback spun around, leaving him with the ball. Bezdek and other coaches refined the play into the full spinner. Killinger believes present play-action passes developed from the spinner. In the 1920 Penn game when Killinger did the faking, Red and Blue defensive players were so badly fooled that the

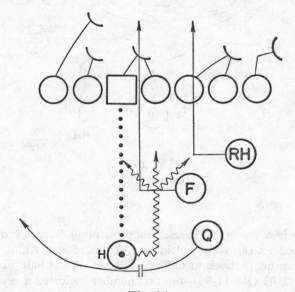

Fig. 21
Fake Reverse or Half Spinner

Lion quarterback was tackled about five yards from the sideline each time.

Penn State completed the reverse pass (Fig. 22) three times against Nebraska in 1920 for 105 yards, and also used it effectively in 1921 against Georgia Tech at the Polo Grounds. Most often thrown to the deep end, it could become a pass to the shallow end for long yardage—in third-down situations. Left guard blocked end, and right guard took the tackle. LH and FB went wide and formed a blocking screen for passer (QB). RH protected rear of QB.

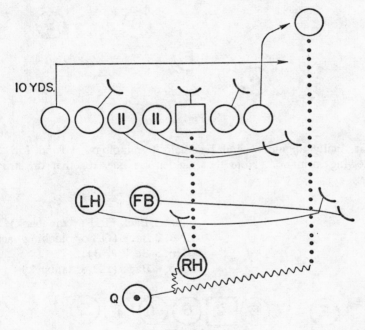

Fig. 22
Reverse Pass

THE PLAYS OF BOB HIGGINS

Higgins was among the last of the unbalanced-line, single-wing coaches, using both tackles on the strong side, right or left. In the late forties he did experiment with an unbalanced line, T formation, but never tried it in a game. In goal-line scrimmages the off-tackle play invariably would be called, the offense wouldn't huddle, and the defense braced for "63 (or "33") on 3," an off-tackle play on the count of "3." This was the basic formation of the early thirties (left or right). Note that strong-side guard is between the two tackles.

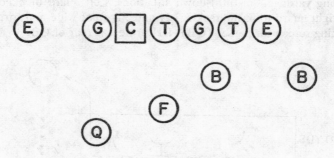

Fig. 23

Gradually alignment and backfield terminology evolved for the following formation. Note that tackles are now together on strong side.

No. 1 Back (RH or wingback)
No. 2 Back (QB or blocking back)
No. 3 Back (FB)
No. 4 Back (LH or tailback)

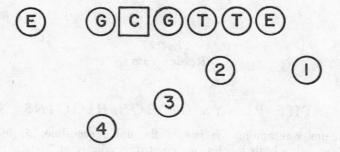

Fig. 24

Higgins astutely altered his approach to fit his material, using a tailback offense if he had an exceptional tailback (Petchel, Petrella, Peters) or a "spinning" series if he had a good fullback (Ickes, Smaltz, Rogel). When he had both—sometimes with a great passing combination like Smaltz and Krouse—his offense was well conceived and precision timed, the line featuring double teams (two men on one) with traps or sucker blocking (allowing defense to penetrate so as to block from side). Shown here are selected plays from fullback spin, tailback, and buck-lateral series.

FULLBACK SPIN SERIES (FROM RIGHT TO LEFT FORMATION)

Using fake spinner (Fig. 26), Rogel spun, faked a pass-off to Petchel, and went off tackle for forty-four yards for the first touchdown against Penn in 1948.

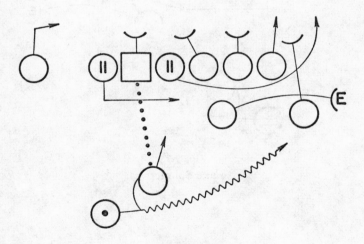

Fig. 25
Off-tackle
(FB to LH)

In Fig. 27 fullback spins, fakes to left half, and then hands off to wingback coming from right to left. Fig. 28 shows fullback faking handoff to left halfback for an off-tackle play. Fullback keeps ball and can pass either to wingback or end, whose patterns cross. This was one of the most effective passes used by fullback Smaltz to wingback Krouse. Fullback can also hand off to tailback, who can

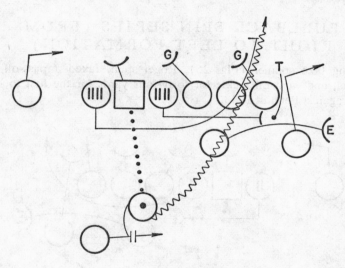

Fig. 26
Fake Spinner

pass to wingback. This version (Petchel to Cooney) produced Penn State's first touchdown in the 1948 Cotton Bowl. In Fig. 29 the hand-off pass (flea flicker) won the Colgate game in 1942. Fullback spins, fakes to tailback, then passes to left end, who hands off to wingback.

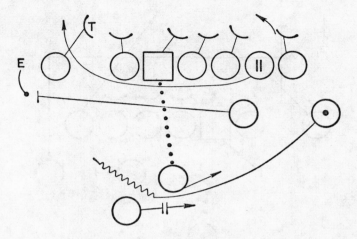

Fig. 27
Reverse to Wingback

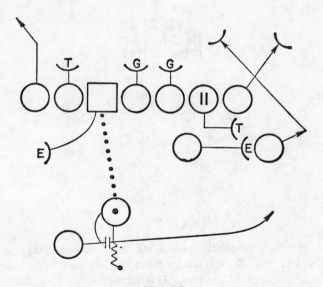

Fig. 28
Pass After Fake Off-tackle

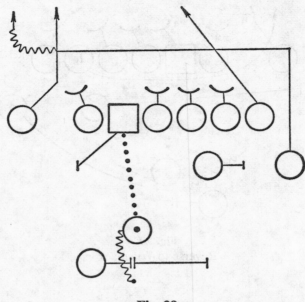

Fig. 29
Hand-off Pass
(Flea Flicker)

TAILBACK SERIES

The tailback-to-wingback reverse was used to beat Navy in 1947 (Fig. 31), but Penn State lined up strong to left (not as in diagram), Durkota taking ball inside from Petchel twice for long touchdown runs off right tackle, who was blocked in by Lion end.

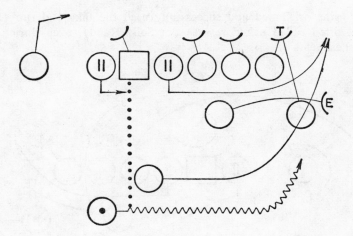

Fig. 30
Off-tackle
(Direct to Tailback)

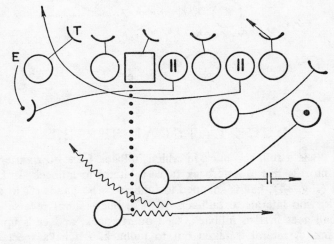

Fig. 31
Reverse
(Tailback to Wingback)

Higgins originated and successfully used the fake end run (Fig. 32), often called naked reverse (or Sally Rand), even during his toughest years.

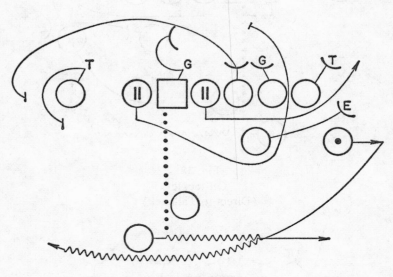

Fig. 32
Naked Reverse

BUCK-LATERAL SERIES

Fig. 33 is a fullback buck in which fullback fakes to quarterback going into the line, quarterback fakes a lateral to tailback. In buck-lateral (Fig. 34), ball is snapped to fullback, who hands off to quarterback, who laterals to tailback. In fake buck-lateral reverse (Fig. 35), ball goes first to fullback, then quarterback, and ends up with wingback. A lateral is faked out to tailback. Petchel's spectacular pass to Rogel in the 1948 Penn game was the buck-lateral pass (Fig. 36) in which fullback hands off to quarterback, bucks into line, and goes down for pass. Quarterback laterals back to tailback, who passes to fullback.

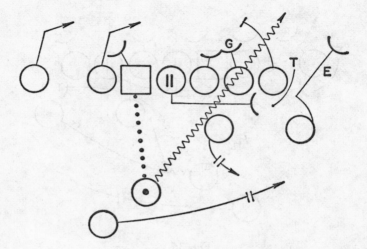

Fig. 33
Fullback Buck—Fake Lateral

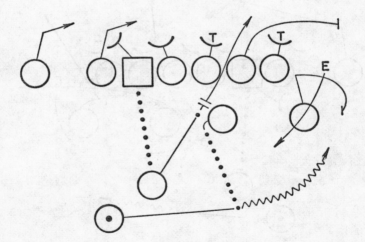

Fig. 34
Buck-lateral

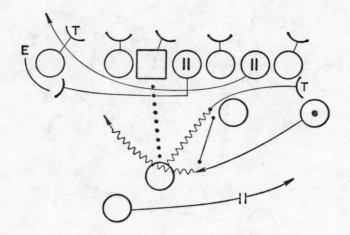

Fig. 35
Fake Buck-lateral Reverse

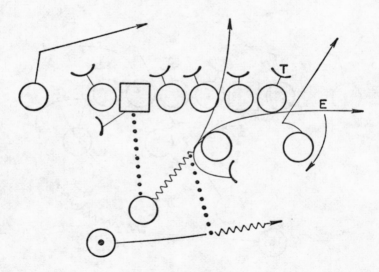

Fig. 36
Buck-lateral Pass

THE PLAYS OF RIP ENGLE

The Wing T system Rip Engle brought to Penn State in 1950 evolved from his successful short punt formation at Waynesboro, Pennsylvania, High School, as freshman coach at Western Maryland, and at Brown as head coach. Penn Staters had to learn a brand-new lexicon—the meaning and execution of (1) trap blocking vs. an "even" defense, and the automatic change vs. the "odd" defense; (2) rule blocking on numbered plays; (3) call blocking (by the tackles) on words such as "dive," "slant," and "power," and (4) drop-back and run-action pass blocking. In the early fifties Coach Engle's basic formation was the Wing T. The X-Back went in motion quite often to influence the defense.

A-Back (left half or tailback)
X-Back (right half or wingback)
C-Back (quarterback)
B-Back (fullback)

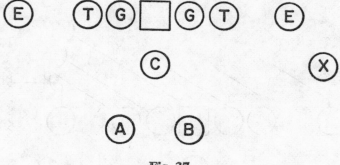

Fig. 37

Engle's earliest successful plays included the quick trap to the A-Back (Fig. 38), the end sweep (Fig. 39), and the scissor or dive to the X-Back (Fig. 40). The quick trap, often checked out by the quarterback at the line of scrimmage, accounted for Ted Shattuck's good yardage gains and touchdown in Engle's first game against Georgetown, and was one of Lenny Moore's favorite gainers. Another Moore favorite was the end sweep, similar to a punt return, requiring the A-Back to take a pitchout and run laterally. He would turn upfield outside the block of the X-Back and inside the end's block, with the line going through to set up a "picket fence," as in

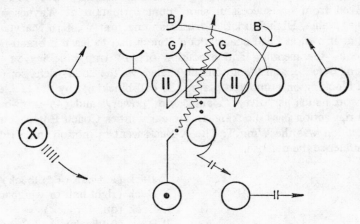

Fig. 38
Quick Trap

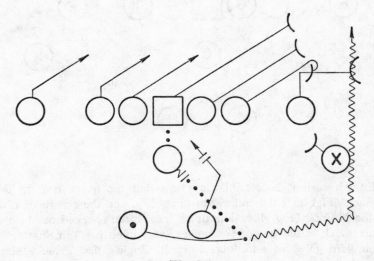

Fig. 39
End Sweep

punt returns. Fig. 40 was really the pioneer scissor play. The quarterback faked the sweep and gave the ball to the X-Back on an inside handoff. The X-Back "ran to daylight." Ron Younker and Bob Pollard used this with special effect against Virginia, Rutgers, and Pittsburgh.

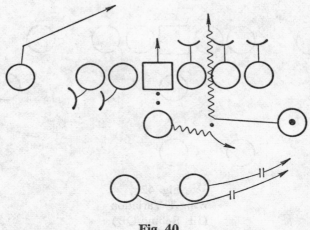

Fig. 40
Scissor

In 1956 Coach Engle retained his basic Wing T, but added the Full-house T (Fig. 41), and the Wing T variation (Fig. 42), with the fullback behind the quarterback. The Full-house T was impor-

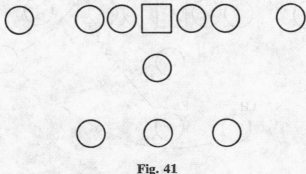

Fig. 41
Full-house T

tant in the victory over Ohio State in 1956. Ray Alberigi and Billy Kane were effective with dive plays. The fullback-behind-the-quarterback T became Coach Engle's basic formation and from it evolved the famous "40 series" (inside belly).

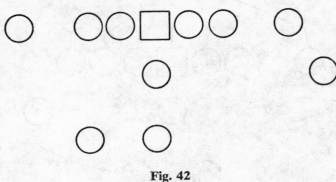

Fig. 42
Wing T Variation
(FB Behind QB)

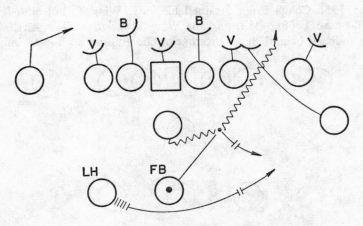

Fig. 43
Inside Belly to Fullback

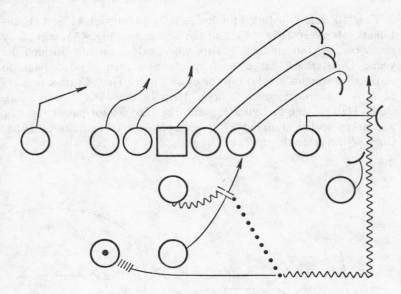

Fig. 44
Automatic 40 Sweep

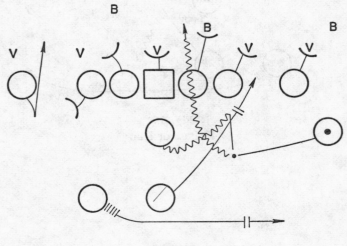

Fig. 45
42 Scissor

The "40 series" included the inside belly to fullback (Fig. 43), automatic 40 sweep (Fig. 44), and the 42 scissor (Fig. 45), copied by many coaches but credited to Rip, who made it famous through the years. Quarterback faked to fullback, and then handed back to X-Back or wingback, who ran for closest hole. The "42 pass or run" (Fig. 46) scored against Georgia Tech in the 1961 Gator Bowl, Butch Hall passing to Junior Powell. The fake scissor pass (Fig. 47) was a key to the stunning 27–0 triumph over Ohio State in 1964, Gary Wydman passing to Tom Urbanik.

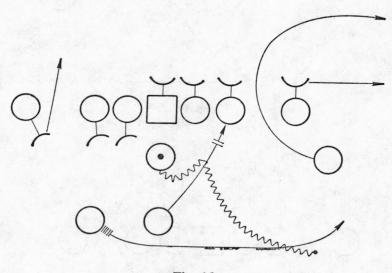

Fig. 46
42 Pass or Run

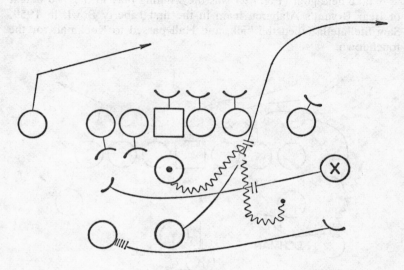

Fig. 47
Fake Scissor Pass

The double-wing slot T (Fig. 48), allowing Richie Lucas to utilize his run-pass ability, shocked Missouri at Columbia in the 1959 opener. Lucas completed ten of eleven passes. From this formation the inside belly (40) series was effective, since Lucas could roll out to either side and pass or run.

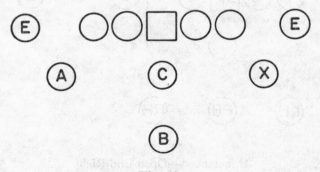

Fig. 48
Double-wing Slot T

A fake field goal (Fig. 49) was the winning play in the 7–0 defeat of Bear Bryant's Alabama team in the first Liberty Bowl, in 1959. Sam Stellatella faked the kick, and Hall passed to Kochman for the touchdown.

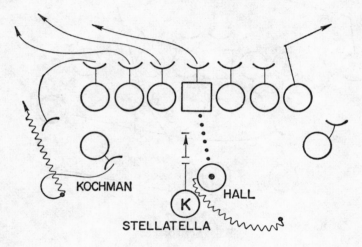

Fig. 49
Fake Field Goal

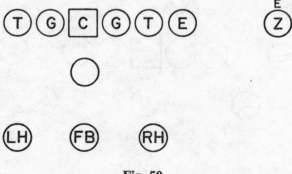

Fig. 50
Unbalanced—Open End Right

Coach Engle surprised Oregon in the 1963 opening game at Portland with his final innovation. The "Swing T" was so called because one player, the Z-Back, could play an open position on either side, thereby "swinging" from side to side. Pete Liske threw a vital touchdown pass to Donny Caum in the second half, but this formation, operable from two possible alignments, was seldom used in later games.

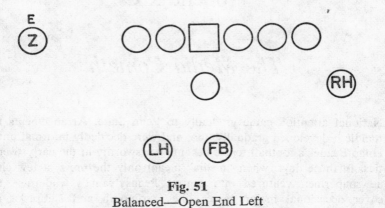

Fig. 51
Balanced—Open End Left

Appendix C

The Media Cometh

National attention came gradually to Penn State. Arrangements to handle it developed gradually, too, and were decidedly informal until Hugo Bezdek's football teams became newsworthy in the early twenties. In those days, when "media" meant only the press, a few city newspapermen ventured into central Pennsylvania's wilderness to cover occasional major games like Dartmouth and Nebraska in 1920, Navy and Georgia Tech in 1923, Syracuse in 1924, and Michigan State and Notre Dame in 1925.

Visitors then were protected from the elements in a primitive press box—a wooden shacklike enclosure on top of the wooden west stands, with a single long board to hold typewriters. The newsmen were ranged along a stationary bench with so little leg room that few could stand for the national anthem.

Both facilities and staff had modest beginnings, although publicity-minded alumni repeatedly had suggested the importance of news coverage in general. George Meek '90, who succeeded his father as editor and publisher of Bellefonte's weekly *Democratic Watchman* and was the first part-time graduate manager of athletics, probably influenced the setting up of a Department of Publicity in 1914 with Albert O. (Barney) Vorse in charge as college news editor, doubling as an instructor in journalism.

Sports news had begun to emanate from the campus when H. D. (Joe) Mason '07 (of Nittany Lion fame) became the first of a series of regular "stringers" retained by several eastern metropolitan newspapers. To receive payment from the accounting departments of the papers, these local representatives mailed in clippings of their monthly output of stories, pasted in a strip or "string," and were paid by the newspaper column inch. Mason and his brothers—Dale R. '11 and Charles R. '15—cornered the business as free-lance writers and correspondents for the Tri-State News Bureau of Pittsburgh, with Alex R. Chambers '17 succeeding them during the Hollenback and Harlow coaching days. In 1919 Donald M. Cresswell '18 became the full-time head of publicity, which was enlarged in scope and renamed the Department of Public Information in 1922.

With the heavier demands for sports coverage accompanying Bezdek's success, Cresswell hired a full-time sports publicity director, George W. (Pat) Sullivan '19, whose brother Mike was then alumni secretary. When Pat left to manage the town's new Cathaum Theatre in 1926, he was replaced by Wes W. Dunlap, a Wisconsin graduate. "Stringers" continued to operate even after the college started furnishing a free news service. Julius S. (Jules) Schwartz '29 represented a number of the large dailies as student correspondent until 1928, when he turned his business over to Hugh R. (Ridge) Riley '32. Riley followed Dunlap as head of sports publicity, working under Walter F. Dantzscher, successor to Cresswell as director of public information. After Dantzscher resigned in 1943 and Riley joined the Alumni Association staff, Louis H. Bell '29 became Public Information director, with James H. Coogan '30 in charge of sports publicity.

The need for better press facilities at New Beaver Field was acutely felt during the 1923 visit of Navy's Rose Bowl team, but only minor improvements were made until suitable space had to be provided for regular radio broadcasting in the late thirties. At this time a few small sections also were reserved for college officials and special guests who previously had been content with seats in the stands. When the field's permanent capacity went up to twenty-eight thousand in 1948–49, the first "three level" press box was constructed, planned and supervised by Coogan and Walter Trainer, head of the Physical Plant Department, who visited many other colleges to gain ideas. At this time the electric scoreboard and timer were moved to the south end of the field. "Coogan's press box" was cited in 1954 as one of the four best in the nation by the Football Writers' Association of America "for convenience, comfort, operational efficiency, and hospitable atmosphere." The other three honored were at LSU, Texas A&M, and Notre Dame.

After Lou Bell's death on October 25, 1958, Coogan advanced to director of the department and was succeeded by James I. Tarman, a Gettysburg graduate who had held a similar position at Princeton. General expansion of the intercollegiate sports program, the football team's recognition as a national power, need for supervision of more extensive radio and television programming, and a desire to increase aid for student-athletes so enlarged sports publicity responsibilities that transfer from Public Information offices in Old Main to the Athletic Department in Recreation Building seemed logical. This move materialized in 1970 when Tarman became assistant to the athletic director and director of athletic public relations. In 1973 he was named associate director of athletics and assistant to the dean.

John M. Morris '63, present Sports Information director (1977), joined the staff in 1970 after six years as SID at the University of Delaware. He is a former president of the ECAC-SID's Association, and has won six national awards for his sports publications at Delaware and Penn State. David L. Baker '73, assistant SID since 1974, had an impressive series of predecessors, including Bob Lane '41, now public relations vice president for Goodyear Tire and Rubber; Dick Peters '41, managing editor and columnist for the Reading *Times;* Ernie Accorsi, assistant general manager of the Baltimore Colts of the NFL; and Barry Jones '70, now in the athletic business office.

The structure atop the towering west stands of Beaver Stadium bustles with activity on Saturday afternoons of home games. Outwardly a "three deck" press box, it has a lower level for concessions, where media personnel and other visitors can get snacks before the game and between halves. On the second level are separate private sections in which the president, dean of the college, and athletic director entertain the university's special guests; smaller "phone" booths for home and visiting coaches who communicate with the sidelines; and another for the field public address announcer and electric scoreboard operator.

The third "main floor" level is reserved for the working press *only,* a regulation assiduously enforced through the years. Guests are barred—*all* persons admitted must have news coverage jobs, and the onetime "no women allowed" rule has been revised. Scouts from other colleges may sit in the rear row by reciprocal arrangement. This section houses members of the SID's staff, including a PA announcer for the working press and a crew to furnish newsmen with lineups, play-by-play accounts of each quarter, and final game statistics. Near the center is a statistical staff of four headed by J. William (Bill) Wilson, the university's assistant to the vice president for business. His long-time associates, all from the university Personnel Division, are Ray Fortunato (assistant vice president of that division), John Pezzoni, and Allan A. (Al) Derzak. Outside telephones also are on this level. Nick DeLallo types the play-by-play.

The fourth level, top stop for the elevator, provides six radio booths, facilities for television coverage and motion picture operators, and separate sections for home and visiting team cameramen who film scouting and teaching movies. Ray Conger has headed Penn State's camera crew for many years, with Glenn (Nick) Thiel as his Number One helper, until John Palmgren took over after Thiel retired.

In the twenties, when city reporters began to cover Penn State's games from the original press box, the transmitting of their copy by telegraph was the responsibility of Lloyd Wilson, manager of the State College Western Union office. Ordinarily an easygoing and pleasant man, Lloyd was irascibility incarnate the moment things went wrong with his old Morse code ticker. If his signals weren't answered on the other end while he was being harassed by anxious and impatient reporters with deadlines, he'd pound his fist on the sending key in rage. Wilson retired in 1936 and was replaced for a year by John Fisher, who then exchanged jobs with mild-mannered and efficient William S. Meredith, who held the job from 1937 until he retired in June 1970. He brought up his family in the community, and William S. III is now the university's business manager of athletics. Bill began as a Morse operator and took over the new teleprinters in 1939, but for several years after they were installed he was obliged to maintain one old ticker exclusively for the Philadelphia *Bulletin*'s Frank Yeutter, who is said to have demanded it solely to hold a job for an old friend in his paper's newsroom.

The switch to Western Union Telex equipment in 1967 involved transmitting copy on tape—the days of the Morse code were long gone. Meredith's successor was Dick Webster. In 1974 the more sophisticated Telecopier machines were acquired, and for the first time in nearly forty-five years Western Union had no part in operations from the field, although the WU ticker service from Chicago was still used to get scores of other games across the country. Telecopiers swallow a reporter's copy in no time and reproduce it on a counterpart machine in the newsrooms of papers and press associations.

Penn State's radio network was set up for the Maryland game on October 1, 1938, originating at Pittsburgh's KDKA with its senior announcer, the late W. C. (Bill) Sutherland, doing the color and Jack Barry, then of Rochester, New York, handling the play-by-play. Almost ten years before, however, the first Penn State game was on the air. Gilbert S. Crossley '22, an electrical engineering instructor who developed the first Penn State radio station (WPSC), asked a sophomore if he'd like to try broadcasting a football game. Kenneth L. Holderman '31, who retired in 1975 as vice president for Commonwealth Campuses and is now a university trustee, did a play-by-play of the Lebanon Valley game opening the 1928 season. Ken did his own "color," too, and continued with the home game broadcasts from the press box until he graduated. At the request of Graduate Manager Neil Fleming, he also took on some road work, making his longest trip to Iowa City to send Iowa game returns in 1930 by telegraph (sometimes by telephone) to students assembled in Schwab Auditorium.

The Penn State Radio Network grew from a relatively few stations in 1938 to one of the largest college football networks in the country. In 1976 three states were covered by sixty stations, with color by Jim Tarman and play-by-play the assignment of Francis E. (Fran) Fisher, a professional announcer who joined the university's Division of Broadcasting ten years ago and is now co-ordinator of radio and TV services for the Athletic Department (1976). Other play-by-play announcers through the years have been Tom McMahon, Claude Haring, Bob Prince, Gene Kelley, Bill Campbell, Milton J. (Mickey) Bergstein '43 (former manager of WMAJ in State College), and Tom Bender.

The Nittany Lions have shared in national and regional television through the NCAA program since 1958, when the Boston University game was regionally televised from Boston, and all thirteen bowl games since 1959 have been carried on national networks. In 1961 the university attempted closed circuit television broadcasts of the Miami and Boston University games, which were financial disasters, and a similar program in 1975 in Recreation Building for the Ohio State and Iowa games was not much more successful. The Athletic Department began delayed TV broadcasts of all games in 1970 with Dick Schorr doing the play-by-play and Dick Richards providing background and color. The 1975 team probably had more coverage than any of its predecessors through the expanded radio network, the closed circuit attractions, and delayed TV broadcasts of all games in whole or in part over eleven channels in four states. Ray Scott and Max McGee were the regular announcers, with Coach Paterno and some past and present players occasionally working on the sidelines.[1] Scott is one of the nation's most prominent sports announcers. McGee is a former split end with the Green Bay Packers. Penn State's popular "TV Quarterbacks" show, originating at WPSX-TV on campus each Wednesday during the season, is widely viewed on Pennsylvania's educational channels. Fisher and Tarman are co-hosts, Coach Paterno is the weekly star, and guests are his assistants and players.

The coming of Coaches Engle and Paterno was simultaneous with more regular and representative coverage by metropolitan papers and the press associations, although the old days brought some famous sportswriters to the campus now and then, among them Damon Runyon, George Trevor, Allison Danzig, Stanley Woodward, Red Smith, and Davis Walsh. The late Chet Smith, sports editor of the Pittsburgh *Press* for many years, was a great friend of Coach Bob Higgins and a frequent visitor.

Perhaps the most unusual writer to work in Penn State's press box was Homer Bigart, who was famed as a war correspondent but covered his first football game at New Beaver Field. In 1947, the New York *Herald Tribune* sports editor, Stanley Woodward, hearing that his paper's Pulitzer Prize winner was visiting at his home in Hawley, Pennsylvania, called him to suggest that he cover the West Virginia game. The assignment startled Bigart, but he came and saw an exciting game, won by Penn State, 21–14. A painstaking writer, he kept the lights on in the press box until 7 P.M., and became such a Nittany Lion fan that he attended the Navy game in Baltimore and the Pitt game in Pittsburgh that year on his own. He was planning to go to the Cotton Bowl when his paper sent him off to cover some trouble in Greece.

City paper "regulars" attending nearly every home and away game at present include Ronnie Christ, Harrisburg *Patriot-News;* Bill Heufelder, Pittsburgh *Press;* Bill Lyon, Philadelphia *Inquirer;* Frank Bilovsky, Philadelphia *Bulletin;* Gordon White, New York *Times;* Bill Conlin, Philadelphia *Daily News* (when the baseball season is

[1] In 1976, Scott's partner was Coach Paterno's brother George.

over); Bill Carroll, Lancaster *New Era;* Bill Fisher, Lancaster *Sunday News;* Al Benshoff, Lancaster *Intelligencer-Journal;* David Fink, Pittsburgh *Post-Gazette;* Jack Lapos and John Kunda, Allentown *Call-Chronicle.* Regulars on hand for the press associations are Ralph Bernstein of the AP and Joe Juliano, UPI.

Among those covering regularly for other Pennsylvania dailies are Doug McDonald and Ron Bracken, Centre *Daily Times;* Terry Nau and Dave Bloss, Pennsylvania *Mirror;* and Herb Werner, Altoona *Mirror.* Of course, the *Daily Collegian* is always well represented. The talented local photographers are Dick Brown, Centre *Daily Times,* and Dave Hamilton, Pennsylvania *Mirror.* Regular photographers from out of town are Tommy Leask, Harrisburg *Patriot-News,* Pat Cahill for UPI, and Paul Vathis for the AP.

Aside from the local papers, Harrisburg's *Patriot-News* gives more weekly in-depth coverage than any other paper in the state. Al Clark, its former sports editor, was a frequent visitor for many years before turning the assignment over to Rusty Cowan and present sports editor John Travers. Other newsmen who formerly came often were Jesse Abramson, New York *Herald Tribune;* Jack Hand, AP; Russ Green, UPI; Len Elliott, Newark *Evening News;* Bill Livingston, John Dell, Sandy Padwe, Frank O'Gara, and Frank Dolson, the Philadelphia *Inquirer;* Frank Yeutter, Philadelphia *Bulletin;* Joe Sheehan, New York *Times;* Myron Cope and Al Abrams, Pittsburgh *Post-Gazette;* Phil Musick and Roy McHugh, Pittsburgh *Press;* and George Kiseda, Pittsburgh *Sun-Telegraph.*

Index

S